7th Edition
ADULT DEVELOPMENT AND AGING

John C. Cavanaugh
Consortium of Universities of the Washington Metropolitan Area

Fredda Blanchard-Fields

Australia • Brazil • Mexico • Singapore • United Kingdom • United States

CENGAGE
Learning®

Adult Development and Aging, 7th Edition

John C. Cavanaugh and
Fredda Blanchard-Fields

Product Director: Jon-David Hague

Product Manager: Clayton Austin

Content Developer: Nicole Bridge

Content Coordinator: Jessica Alderman

Product Assistant/Associate Media
   Developer: Audrey Espey

Content Project Manager:
   Charlene Carpentier

Art Director: Jennifer Wahi

Manufacturing Planner: Karen Hunt

Rights Acquisitions Specialist:
   Roberta Broyer

Production Service: Integra

Photo/Text Researcher: PreMedia Global

Copy Editor: Hyde Park Publishing Services

Illustrator: Integra

Text/Cover Designer: Jeff Bane

Cover Image:
   All Photos: ThinkStock
   Shelves: 75626928—Photographer:
      ULTRA F/Photodisc/Thinkstock
   People in frame: 126534041—
      Photographer: Top Photo
      Corporation/Top Photo Group/
      Thinkstock
   People in frame: 81177503—
      Photographer: Valueline/Thinkstock
   People in frame: 86518704—
      Photographer: Jupiterimages/
      Stockbyte/Getty Images

Compositor: Integra

Library of Congress Control Number: 2013956199

ISBN-13: 978-1-285-44491-8

ISBN-10: 1-285-44491-4

Cengage Learning
200 First Stamford Place, 4th Floor
Stamford, CT 06902
USA

Cengage Learning is a leading provider of customized learning solutions with office locations around the globe, including Singapore, the United Kingdom, Australia, Mexico, Brazil and Japan. Locate your local office at **www.cengage.com/global**

Cengage Learning products are represented in Canada by Nelson Education, Ltd.

To learn more about Cengage Learning Solutions, visit **www.cengage.com**.

Purchase any of our products at your local college store or at our preferred online store **www.cengagebrain.com**.

Printed in the United States of America
1 2 3 4 5 6 7 18 17 16 15 14

In memory of Fredda Blanchard-Fields, friend and collaborator,
who dedicated her life to educating students.

To Chris

BRIEF CONTENTS

CONTENTS

CHAPTER 12

CHAPTER 13

CHAPTER 14

PREFACE

People's experiences growing older in the 21st century differ dramatically from their parents' and grandparents' experience. The complex issues confronting individuals and societies are the reason a solid grounding in research and theory about adult development and aging is essential for even understanding news events. The health care debates from 2009 to the present bring many issues to the forefront, including Medicare, end-of-life issues, and longevity and the possibility of significant intergenerational policy issues. Other news stories about genetic breakthroughs, stem cell research, brain-imaging techniques, and the latest breakthroughs in treating dementia happen regularly. To understand why these issues are so critical, one must understand aging in a broader, rapidly changing context. That is why *Adult Development and Aging* is now in its seventh edition.

The first few decades of this century will witness a fundamental change in the face of the population—literally. Along with many countries in the industrialized world, the United States will experience an explosive growth in the older adult population due to the aging of the baby-boom generation. Additionally, the proportion of older adults who are African American, Latino, Asian American, and Native American will increase rapidly. To deal with these changes, new approaches need to be created through the combined efforts of people in many occupations—academics, gerontologists, social workers, health care professionals, financial experts, marketing professionals, teachers, factory workers, technologists, government workers, human service providers, and nutritionists, to mention just a few. Every reader of this book, regardless of his or her area of expertise, needs to understand older adults in order to master the art of living.

This seventh edition of *Adult Development and Aging* continues to provide in-depth coverage of the major issues in the psychology of adult development and aging. The seventh edition adds numerous topics and provides expanded coverage of many of the ones discussed in earlier editions.

Changes in *Adult Development and Aging* Seventh Edition

A new feature, **Adult Development in Action**, challenges students to think critically about decisions they might make as career professionals such as health care workers, gerontologists, and activities directors.

We also include more **glossary terms** highlighted throughout each chapter to increase accessibility and provide additional study tools.

Chapter-by-Chapter Additions and Enhancements

Chapter 1

- Introduces "emerging adulthood," the period between adolescence and full adulthood.

Chapter 2

- "Neuroimaging Techniques" explains how and why the ability to see inside the brain of living people has revolutionized our understanding of relations between the brain and our behavior.

- Increased explanation of the distinctions between structural neuroimaging and functional neuroimaging.

- Description of the brain's structure includes explanation of neurons, dendrites, axon, neurofibers, terminal branches, neurotransmitters, and synapse.

- A new diagram of a neuron illustrates dendrites, axon, neurofibers, and terminal branches.

- "What Age-Related Changes Occur in Neurons?" discusses the decrease in neurons as the brain declines.

- Increased discussion on neurotransmitters, their involvement in brain processes and cognitive aging especially in Alzheimer's patients.

- The section on "Age-Related Changes in Brain Structures" is enhanced so it now includes a discussion of white matter and the study of its structural health.

- New to the chapter is "Linking Structural Changes with Executive Functioning" examining older adults' ability to focus on relevant information and control their thoughts.

- "Linking Structural Changes with Memory" raises the question of whether Alzheimer's is an acceleration of aging rather than a separate process.

- Another section has been added; "Linking Structural Changes with Emotion"

- "How Do We Know?: The Aging Emotional Brain" studies Winecoff's research findings.

- "Linking Structural Changes with Socio-economic Cognition" examines how the aging brain processes complex situations such as those involving moral judgment.

- "Complex Development in the Prefrontal Cortex" examines the critical role of the prefrontal cortex plays on human behavior.

- Investigation of how older adults attempt to compensate for age-related changes to the brain.

- "The Parieto-Frontal Integration Theory" examines the notion that intelligence comes from a distributed and integrated network of neurons in the parietal and frontal areas of the brain.

- "Theories of Brain-Behavior Changes Across Adulthood" includes discussion of the HAROLD, CRUNCH, STAC methods.

- Section 2.4 "Neural Plasticity and the Aging Brain" has been significantly revised to include information on how nutrition influences brain changes and cognitive activity.

- "Current Controversies: Are Neural Stem Cells the Solution to Brain Aging?"

- "Social Policy Implications" asserts the importance of policymakers supporting neuroscience research.

Chapter 3

- Discussion of how chronic stress can accelerate changes in telomeres while moderate exercise can actually slow the rate at which telomeres shorten.

- Discussion and accompanying figure of cardiovascular disease as the leading cause of death in the United States.

- Cardiovascular health as it relates to ethnicity.

- The factors leading to hypertension including heredity, sodium intake, and obesity.

- Menopausal hormone therapy and how decreasing levels of estrogen can contribute to osteoporosis, urinary incontinence, and cardiovascular disease.

- Updated "Current Controversies: Menopausal Hormone Therapy" now discusses the circumstances under which a physician might recommend HRT.

- The nervous system builds on the age-related changes to the brain discussed in chapter 2.

- "Social Policy Implications" discusses preventing falls.

Chapter 4

- New examples of how self-ratings of health reflect socio-economic background.

- Enhanced discussion of how psychoneuroimmunology is being used as a framework to predict health outcomes.

- New discussion of the way Verbrugge and Jette's model is being used to identify disability in China.

- "How Does Disability in Older Adults Differ Globally?" discusses how adults with disabilities or functional limitations are on the rise around the world.

Chapter 5

- New section titled "Preventive and Corrective Proactivity (PCP) Model."

- Additional key words: preventative and corrective adaptations.

- New discussion on high-tech approaches to home modification, including "Granny pods."

- A discussion of "elderspeak" used in nursing homes.

- "How Do We Know?: Identifying different types of elderspeak in Singapore."

Chapter 6

- New Chapter opening vignette about Harry Lorayne's book "Ageless Memory."

- Additional emphasis on automatic and effortful processing.

- "Age Differences in Encoding versus retrieval" compares the differences in the attention processes of older and younger adults.

- "Neuroscience Evidence" discusses neuroimaging and cognitive neuroscience findings that show age related differences in encoding and retrieval.

- Enhanced discussion on memory includes a study of differences in age with regard to prospective memory, evidence of how memory changes across adulthood, and information on ways to preserve memory as we age.

- "How Do We Know?: Failing to Remember I Did What I Was Supposed to Do."

- Discussion of memory self-efficacy, the belief one will be able to perform a specific task.

- Stronger discussion of memory and health includes physical implications like temporary global amnesia.

- New "Current Controversies: Concussions and Athletes."

Chapter 7

- "Neuroscience Research and Intelligence in Young and Middle Adulthood."

- Discussion of the neural efficiency hypothesis that intelligent people process information more efficiently.

- "How Do We Know?: Age Differences in Information Search and Decision Making."

Chapter 8

- "Self-Perception and Social Beliefs" examines our self-perception of aging.

- "Attributional Biases" examines whether there are age differences in the tendency to rely more on dispositional attributions, situational attributions, or a combination of both when making casual attributions.

Chapter 9

- "How Do We Know?: Well-being reflected in brain function in emotion and depression."

- Social Policy Implications now has discussion of interaction between government policy and the experience of aging.

Chapter 10

- New figure: Action of beta-amyloid and tau proteins in relation to neurons.

- Discussion of proposed new diagnostic criteria for Alzheimer's disease.

- New figure: 12-month prevalence of depression among all U.S. residents by age.

- New figure: Clinical continuum of Alzheimer's disease showing types of changes over time.

Chapter 11

- New figure on the vulnerability-stress-adaptation model.

- New figure: Family expenditures on a child, by income level and age of child, 2011.

- "Current Controversies: New Diagnostic Criteria for Alzheimer's Disease."

Chapter 12

- "Current Controversies: Do women lean out when they should lean in?"

- Updated discussion about unemployment during/after the Great Recession.

Chapter 13

- Expanded discussion on "brain death" and how it is perceived in both the medical profession and also religion.

- "Discovering Development: A Self-Reflective Exercise on Death."

- Discussion of neuroimaging research about death anxiety.

- Discussion of insurance coverage with regard to Hospice.

- "Patient Self-Determination and Competency Evaluation" describes the Patient Self-Determination Act and why financial reimbursement for individual physician's discussion with patients about this issue was not included in the Affordable Care Act 2010.

- "How Do We Know?: Grief Processing and Avoidance in the United States and China."

- New discussion about college students and the expression of grief.

Chapter 14

- Discussion of the dependency ratio.

- Expanded discussion of Social Security and proposals for reform.

- "Current Controversies: What to do about Social Security and Medicare."

- New discussion of the way age impacts metabolism.

- "Approaches to Successful Aging" further emphasizes Vaillant's model.

Writing Style

Although *Adult Development and Aging* covers complex issues and difficult topics, we use clear, concise, and understandable language. All terms were examined to ensure their use is essential; otherwise, they were eliminated.

The text is aimed at upper-division undergraduate students. Although it will be helpful if students completed an introductory psychology or life-span human development course, the text does not assume this background.

Instructional Aids

The many pedagogical aids in the sixth edition have been retained and enhanced in the seventh edition.

- *Learning Aids in the Chapter Text.* Each chapter begins with a chapter outline. At the start of each new section, learning objectives are presented. These objectives are keyed to each primary subsection that follows, and they direct the students' attention to the main points to be discussed. At the conclusion of each major section are concept checks, one for each primary subsection, that help students spot-check their learning. Key terms are defined in context; the term itself is printed in boldface, with the sentence containing the term's definition in italic.

- *End-of-Chapter Learning Aids.* At the end of each chapter are summaries, organized by major sections and primary subsection heads. This approach helps students match the chapter outline with the summary. Numerous review questions, also organized around major sections and primary subsections, are provided to assist students in identifying major points. Integrative questions are included as a way for students to link concepts across sections within and across chapters. Key terms with definitions are listed.

- *Boxes.* Three types of boxes are included. Those titled *How Do We Know?* draw attention to specific research studies that were discussed briefly in the main body of the text. Details about the study's design, participants, and outcomes are presented as a way for students to connect the information about these issues in Chapter 1 with specific research throughout the text. *Current Controversies* boxes raise controversial and provocative issues about topics discussed in the chapter. These boxes get students to think about the implications of research or policy issues and may be used effectively as points of departure for class discussions. *Discovering Development* boxes give students a way to see developmental principles and concepts in the "real world" as well as some suggestions on how to find others. These boxes provide a starting point for applied projects in either individual or group settings, and help students understand how development is shaped by the interaction of biological, psychological, sociocultural, and life-cycle forces.

Instructor Companion Site

Everything you need for your course in one place! This collection of book-specific lecture and class tools is available online via www.cengage.com/login. Access and download an instructor's manual, test bank, and PowerPoint slides.

Cengage Learning Testing Powered by Cognero

The Test Bank is also available through Cognero, a flexible, online system that allows you to author, edit, and manage test bank content as well as create multiple test versions in an instant. You can deliver tests from your school's learning management system, your classroom, or wherever you want.

Acknowledgments

As usual, it takes many people to produce a textbook; such is the case with the seventh edition. The editorial group at Cengage is excellent.

I also want to thank the reviewers of the seventh edition, who provided extremely helpful and insightful commentary that improved the book: Leslie Adams Lariviere, Assumption College; Sandra Arntz, Carroll University; Hallie Baker, Muskingum University; Anita Glee Bertram, University of Central Oklahoma; Casey Catlin, University of Nevada-Reno; Lisa Connolly, University of Indianapolis; Alissa Dark-Freudeman, UNC-Wilmington; Mary Dolan, CSU San Bernardino; Lisa Emery, Appalachian State University; Daniella Errett, Pennsylvania Highlands Community College; Carolyn Grasse-Backman, Penn State-Harrisburg; Regina Hughes, Collin College; Bonnie Kin, Brenau University; Ryan Leonard, Gannon University; Donna Makowiecki, Holy Family University-Philadelphia; Sara Margolin, SUNY-Brockport; George Martinez, Somerset Community College; Rick Scheidt, Kansas State University; Gail Spessert, Frederick Community College, Carroll Community College; Virginia Tompkins, Ohio State University-Lima; Marcia Weinstein, Salem State University.

Finally to a group too often overlooked—the sales representatives. Without you, none of this would have any payoff. You are an extension of us and the whole Cengage editorial and production team. What a great group of hard-working folks you are!

Thanks to you all. Live long and prosper!

John C. Cavanaugh

ABOUT THE AUTHOR

Courtesy of John C. Cavanaugh

John C. Cavanaugh is President and CEO of the Consortium of Universities of the Washington Metropolitan Area. Previously, he was Chancellor of the Pennsylvania State System of Higher Education and President of the University of West Florida. A researcher and teacher of adult development and aging for more three decades, he has published more than 80 articles and chapters and authored, co-authored, or co-edited 19 books on aging, information technology, and higher education policy. He is a Past President of Division 20 (Adult Development and Aging) of the American Psychological Association (APA) and is a Fellow of APA (Divisions 1, 2, 3, and 20) and the Gerontological Society of America, and a Charter Fellow of the Association for Psychological Science. He has held numerous leadership positions in these associations, including Chair of the Committee on Aging for APA. He has served on numerous state and national committees for aging-related and higher education organizations. John is a devoted fan of *Star Trek* and a serious traveler, photographer, backpacker, cook, and chocoholic. He is married to Dr. Christine K. Cavanaugh.

CHAPTER 1

STUDYING ADULT DEVELOPMENT AND AGING

1.1 PERSPECTIVES ON ADULT DEVELOPMENT AND AGING
Discovering Development: Myths and Stereotypes about Aging • The Life-Span Perspective • The Demographics of Aging

1.2 ISSUES IN STUDYING ADULT DEVELOPMENT AND AGING
The Forces of Development • Interrelations among the Forces: Developmental Influences • Culture and Ethnicity • The Meaning of Age • Core Issues in Development • *Current Controversies: Does Personality in Young Adulthood Determine Personality in Old Age?*

1.3 RESEARCH METHODS
Measurement in Adult Development and Aging Research • General Designs for Research • Designs for Studying Development • *How Do We Know?: Conflicts between Cross-Sectional and Longitudinal Data* • Integrating Findings from Different Studies • Conducting Research Ethically

SOCIAL POLICY IMPLICATIONS
Summary • Review Questions • Integrating Concepts in Development • Key Terms • Resources

ALTHOUGH TIRED AND A BIT UNSTEADY, DIANA NYAD GOT OUT OF THE WATER AND WALKED UNDER HER OWN POWER ONTO THE BEACH AT KEY WEST, FLORIDA.

At age 64, she had just become the first person ever to swim the 110 miles from Havana, Cuba, to Key West, Florida without the protection of a shark cage. Her feat, completed on September 2, 2013, after more than 50 hours of open water swimming, is just one more in a growing list of accomplishments by people at a point in life once thought to be a time of serious decline in abilities. No more.

From athletes to politicians to people in everyday life, boundaries once thought fixed are being pushed every day. Consider that just since 2008, we have seen the oldest woman ever to compete in swimming in the Olympics, Dara Torres, win Olympic medals at age 41 in Beijing, thus redefining people's beliefs about world-class athletes and mothers (her daughter was aged two at the time). She won three silver medals, missing a gold by .01 second. Competing in her fifth Olympic Games, Torres clearly demonstrated that a combination of great genes and a highly rigorous training regimen enabled her to compete in a sport in which most world-class women swimmers' careers are over by the time they are in their mid-twenties.

We have also seen Senator John McCain, at age 72, become the oldest person to be nominated for a first term as president by a major political party. Senator McCain had a long, distinguished career as an officer in the U.S. Navy, was a prisoner of war for 5 years during the Vietnam conflict, and went on to be elected to Congress from Arizona. By his own admission, McCain was in better health than many other people of his age at the time of his campaign. When questioned about his age, he pointed out his 96-year-old mother, who accompanied him on many of his campaign trips. His (and his mother's) energy and stamina demonstrated that chronological age alone is a very poor index of people's capabilities.

Diana Nyad, Dara Torres, and John McCain are great examples of how middle-aged and older adults are being looked at differently today. They showed that adults are capable of doing things thought unimaginable or inappropriate just a few years ago. They also illustrate how the normal changes people experience as they age vary across individuals and why we need to rethink common stereotypes about age.

But there is also an entire generation poised to redefine what growing older really means.

ENRIQUE DE LA OSA/Reuters/Landov

U.S. long-distance swimmer Diana Nyad is pictured before attempting to swim to Florida from Havana August 31, 2013. Nyad jumped into the calm, turquoise waters of Cuba on Saturday and began making her way towards home, Key West Florida, in pursuit of a dream that she says nearly cost her life during a previous attempt in 2012. Her biggest challenges during the 103 mile (166-km) swim, apart from fatigue, were the poisonous jelly fish that float through the Florida Straits, the sharks, the man o'wars, storms, waves and the powerful and unpredictable Gulf Stream, the mighty ocean current that flows west to east between Cuba and Florida.

AP Images/David J. Phillip

Dara Torres of the United States celebrates winning the silver medal in the women's 4 × 100-meter medley relay final during the swimming competitions in the National Aquatics Center at the Beijing 2008 Olympics in Beijing.

Sen. John McCain, R-Ariz., at age 72 in 2008 was the oldest person to receive a nomination as a presidential candidate of a major political party.

The baby-boom generation, consisting of people born between 1946 and 1964, are on average the healthiest and most active generation to begin reaching old age in history. They are not content with playing traditional roles assigned to older adults, and are doing their best to change the way older adults are perceived and treated.

In this chapter, we examine a seemingly simple question: Who are older people? We will see that the answer is more complicated than you might think. We also consider the ways in which gerontologists study adults and how adults develop.

1.1 Perspectives on Adult Development and Aging

LEARNING OBJECTIVES

- What is gerontology? How does ageism relate to stereotypes of aging?
- What is the life-span perspective?
- What are the characteristics of the older adult population?
- How are they likely to change?

Roberto's great-grandmother Maria is 89 years old. Maria tells Roberto that when she was a young girl in El Paso, there were very few older women in either her family

or the neighborhood. Roberto knows there are many older people, mostly women, in his own neighborhood, and wonders when and why this changed over her lifetime.

Before you read any more, take a minute and think about your own grandparents or great-grandparents. How would you and other people describe them? Do you want to be like them when you are their age?

We are all headed toward old age. How do you want to be thought of and treated when you get there? Do you look forward to becoming old, or are you afraid about what may lie ahead? Most of us want to enjoy a long life like Maria's but don't think much about growing old in our daily lives.

Reading this book will give you the basic facts about growing older. You will learn how to organize these facts by putting them into two contexts: the bio-psychosocial framework and the life-span approach. By the time you are finished, you should have a new, different way of thinking about aging.

You already enjoy a major advantage compared with Maria. She and other people her age did not have the opportunity as young students to learn much about what is typical and what is not typical about aging. Until the last few decades, very little information was available about old age, which people generally thought to be characterized only by decline. Over the past 50 years, though, the science of gerontology, *which is the study of aging from maturity through old age, has flourished.* As you can imagine from reading the vignette about Dara Torres and John McCain, and as you will see throughout this book, aging reflects the individual differences you have come to expect across people as they change over time. Still, many myths about old people persist. These myths of aging lead to negative stereotypes of older people, which may result in ageism, *a form of discrimination against older adults based on their age.* Ageism has its foundations in myths and beliefs people take for granted, as well as in intergenerational relations (North & Fiske, 2012). It may be as blatant as believing that all old people are senile and are incapable of making decisions about their lives. It may occur when people are impatient with older adults in a grocery store checkout line. Or it may be as subtle as dismissing an older person's physical complaints with the question "What do you expect for someone your age?" As you will learn by doing the activities in the Discovering Development feature, such stereotypes surround us.

DISCOVERING DEVELOPMENT:

MYTHS AND STEREOTYPES ABOUT AGING

We are surrounded by misconceptions of older adults. We have all seen cartoons making jokes about older adults whose memories are poor or whose physical abilities have declined. Most damaging are the ideas portrayed in the media that older adults are incapable of leading productive lives and making a difference. For example, many greeting cards portray older people as having little memory, no teeth, and no desire for sex. As a way to discover something about development, try to find several examples of myths or stereotypes about aging. Look at those greeting cards, cartoons, advertisements, and articles in popular magazines, television shows, and music. Gather as many as you can, and then check them against the research on the topic discussed in this text. By the end of the course, see how many myths and stereotypes you can show to be wrong.

This book rebuts these erroneous ideas, but it does not replace them with idealized views of adulthood and old age. Rather, it paints an accurate picture of what it means to grow old today, recognizing that development across adulthood brings growth and opportunities as well as loss and decline. To begin, we consider the life-span perspective, which helps place adult development and aging into the context of the whole human experience. Afterward, we consider the fundamental developmental forces, controversies, and models that form the foundation for studying adult development and aging. In particular, we examine the biological, psychological, sociocultural, and life-cycle forces, and the nature–nurture and continuity–discontinuity controversies. We consider some basic definitions of age, and you will see that it can be viewed in many different ways. Finally, by examining various research methods we show how the information presented in this book was obtained.

The Life-Span Perspective

Imagine trying to understand, without knowing anything about his or her life, what your best friend is like. We cannot understand adults' experiences without appreciating what came before in childhood and adolescence. Placing adulthood in this broader context is what the life-span perspective is all about. *The* life-span perspective *divides human development into two phases:* *an early phase (childhood and adolescence) and a later phase (young adulthood, middle age, and old age).* The early phase is characterized by rapid age-related increases in people's size and abilities. During the later phase, changes in size are slow, but abilities continue to develop as people continue adapting to the environment (Baltes, Lindenberger, & Staudinger, 2006).

Viewed from the life-span perspective, adult development and aging are complex phenomena that cannot be understood within the scope of a single disciplinary approach. Understanding how adults change requires input from a wide variety of perspectives. Moreover, aging is a lifelong process, meaning that human development never stops.

One of the most important perspectives on life-span development is that of Paul Baltes (1987; Baltes et al., 2006), who identified four key features of the life-span perspective:

1. *Multidirectionality:* Development involves both growth and decline; as people grow in one area, they may lose in another and at different rates. For example, people's vocabulary ability tends to increase throughout life, but reaction time tends to slow down.

2. *Plasticity:* One's capacity is not predetermined or set in concrete. Many skills can be trained or improved with practice, even in late life. There are limits to the degree of potential improvement, however, as described in later chapters.

3. *Historical context:* Each of us develops within a particular set of circumstances determined by the historical time in which we are born and the culture in which we grow up. Maria's experiences were shaped by living in the 20th century in a Chicano neighborhood in southwest Texas.

4. *Multiple causation:* How people develop results from a wide variety of forces, which we consider later in this chapter. You will see that development is shaped by biological, psychological, sociocultural, and life-cycle forces.

The life-span perspective emphasizes that human development takes a lifetime to complete. It sets the stage for understanding the many influences we experience and points out that no one part of life is any more or less important than another.

Basing their theories on these principles, Baltes et al. (2006) argue that life-span development consists of the dynamic interactions among growth, maintenance, and loss regulation. In their view, four factors are critical:

1. As people grow older, they show an age-related reduction in the amount and quality of biologically based resources.

2. There is an age-related increase in the amount and quality of culture needed to generate continuously higher growth. Usually this results in a net slowing of growth as people age.

3. People show an age-related decline in the efficiency with which they use cultural resources.

4. There is a lack of cultural, "old-age friendly" support structures.

Taken together, these four factors create the need to shift more and more resources to maintain function and deal with biologically related losses as we grow old, leaving fewer resources to be devoted to continued growth. As we see throughout this book, this shift in resources has profound implications for experiencing aging and for pointing out ways to age successfully.

The Demographics of Aging

Take a look around at the people you see in your everyday life in your hometown. There have never been as many older adults as there are now, especially people over age 85. Why? Most important, health care improved during the 20th century, and many fewer women died during childbirth. Also, one of the largest generations ever, the baby boomers, began reaching age 65. Let's take a closer look.

Population Trends in the United States. Look closely at the age distributions in the U.S. population for 2000 and projections for 2025, 2050, and 2100. These show that the population is aging (see Figures 1.1, 1.2, 1.3, and 1.4). In 2000, there were many more people between their mid-30s and 40s than any other age group. Projections for 2025 (when nearly all the baby boomers will have reached age 65) show that the distribution will have changed dramatically; the baby boomers' aging makes the graph look much more rectangular. By 2050, the shape of the distribution will be more like a beehive, as more people continue to live into their 80s, 90s, and 100s. The biggest change by the year 2100 will be in the number of older men.

The coming dramatic change in the number of older adults has already had profound effects on everyone's lives. Through the first few decades of the 21st century, older adults, driven by the baby boomers, will be a major economic and political force. There is legitimate concern that the cost of entitlement programs that support older adults, such as Social Security and other pension systems

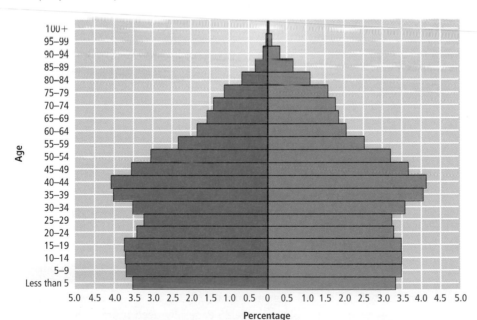

Figure 1.1

Resident population of the United States as of July 1, 2000.

Source: National Projections Program, Population Division, U.S. Census Bureau, Washington, D.C. 20233.

Figure 1.2
Projected resident population of the United States as of July 1, 2025.

Source: National Projections Program, Population Division, U.S. Census Bureau, Washington, D.C. 20233.

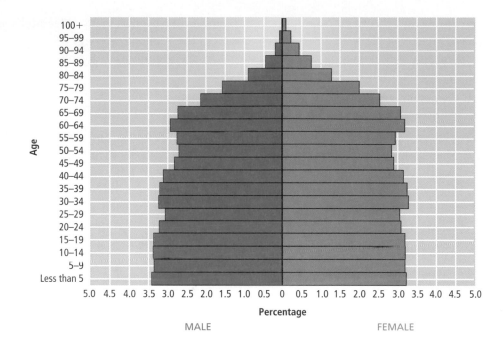

Figure 1.3
Projected resident population of the United states as of July 1, 2050.

Source: National Projections Program, Population Division, U.S. Census Bureau, Washington, D.C. 20233.

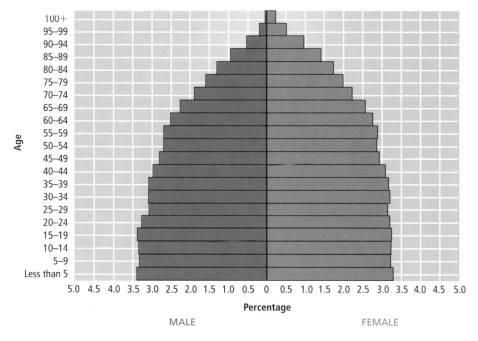

as well as Medicare, will become the largest expenditures in the federal and states' budgets, forcing intergenerational conflict over shrinking public resources. The costs for programs that support older adults will be borne by smaller groups of taxpayers in younger generations.

The strain on health and social services will be exacerbated because the most rapidly growing segment of the U.S. population is people over age 85. In fact, the number of such people will increase over threefold between 2010 and 2050 (from about 5.7 million to over 19 million), compared to a much smaller percentage increase in the number of 20 to 29-year-olds during the same period (from about 42 million to over 56 million) (U.S. Census Bureau, 2012a). As we discuss in Chapter 4, people over age 85 generally need more assistance with daily living than do people under age 85.

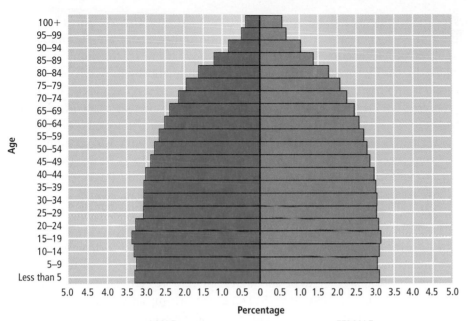

Figure 1.4

Projected resident population of the United States as of July 1, 2100.

Source: National Projections Program, Population Division, U.S. Census Bureau, Washington, D.C. 20233.

Diversity of Older Adults in the United States. Just like people your age, older adults are not all alike. The number of older adults among ethnic minority groups is increasing faster than among European Americans. For example, the number of Native American elderly has increased by nearly two-thirds in recent decades; Asian and Pacific Islander elderly have quadrupled; older adults are the fastest-growing segment of the African American population; and the number of Latino American elderly is also increasing rapidly (U.S. Census Bureau, 2012a). Projections for the future

diversity of the U.S. population are shown in Figure 1.5. You should note the very large increases in the number of Asian, Native, and Latino American older adults relative to European and African American older adults.

Future older adults will be better educated. In 2010, a little more than half of the people over age 65 have only a high school diploma or some college, and about 25% have a bachelor's degree or higher. By 2030 it is estimated that 85% will have a high school diploma, and 75% will have a college degree (U.S. Census Bureau, 2012a). These dramatic changes will be due mainly to

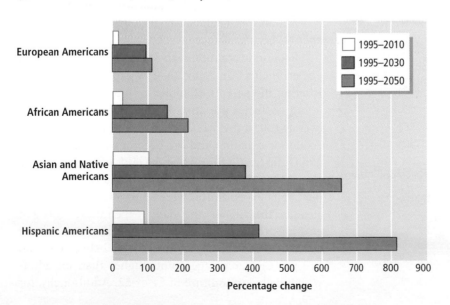

Figure 1.5

Projected growth of minority populations of older adults in the United States 1995–2050.

Source: Data from the U.S. Census Bureau.

better educational opportunities for more students and greater need for formal schooling (especially college) to find a good job. Also, better-educated people tend to live longer, mostly because they have higher incomes, which give them better access to good health care and a chance to follow healthier lifestyles. We examine these issues in more detail in Chapter 4.

You probably know some older adults who are fiercely independent, who view the challenges of aging as something you face mainly alone or with help from professionals. You also probably know others who view themselves as part of a larger unit, typically family, and see the same challenges as something one faces with other family members as a group. In more formal terms, the first group of people represents individualism, and the second group reflects collectivism (Ajrouch, 2008; Phillips, Ajrouch, & Hillcoat-Nalletamby, 2010).

As the number of ethnic minority older adults continues to increase, an important emerging issue will be the differences in these perspectives. This matters because the ways in which intervention is done differ a great deal. For those who emphasize individualism, the emphasis and approach is very much focused on only the person in question. In contrast, intervention with those who fit the collectivism approach needs to include the broader family or even friendship network. As the United States becomes more diverse, these views, which reflect different cultures globally, will increasingly need to be taken into account by all organizations.

John Lund/Sam Diephuis/Blend Images/Getty Images

This Latina older woman represents the changing face of older adults in the United States.

Population Trends Around the World. The population trends in the United States are not unique. As you can see in Figures 1.6 and 1.7 the number of older adults will increase dramatically in nearly all areas of the world over the next several decades. (The figures show the expected changes between 2000 and 2030.) Overall, the "oldest" area of the world will continue to be Europe. The "youngest" area will continue to be Africa, where overall poor access to health care and a high incidence of conflict and AIDS significantly shorten lives (U.S. Census Bureau, 2012b).

Economically powerful countries around the world, such as China, are trying to cope with increased numbers of older adults that strain the country's resources. Due to China's one child policy; by 2030 there are projected to be about 20 million more older adults than children under 15. The economic impact will be significant for China, and in general the aging of the world's workforce and population in general will have significant effects on the world economy (Krueger & Ludwig, 2007; Tyers & Shi, 2012). For example, pension and health care costs will increase dramatically, and there will be fewer workers to bear the burden in many industrialized countries. Canada leads the industrialized world in the rate of increase in the older adult population: between 2000 and 2030, it will increase by 126%.

But that's nothing compared to the explosive increase in the population of older adults that faces developing countries (U.S. Census Bureau, 2012b). For example, Egypt, Malaysia, and Singapore will see a fivefold increase in older adults by 2050, with many other countries, such as Brazil (fourfold), also experiencing very significant increases.

Economic conditions in different countries have a powerful effect on aging. One way to see this is to ask whether the parents of adults in households in developing countries are alive. Given that the parents are over age 50 (if they are alive), the relationship between economic situation and age becomes clearer. Banerjee and Duflo (2010) found that the odds of having a living parent was about the same for all adults whose daily per capita expenditures were $4 or less, and increased steadily the higher the daily expenditure got. For example, the probability of having a living parent for adults whose daily expenditures were between $6 and $10 was 36 percentage points higher than for adults with a daily expenditure of $1 or $2. Additionally, for

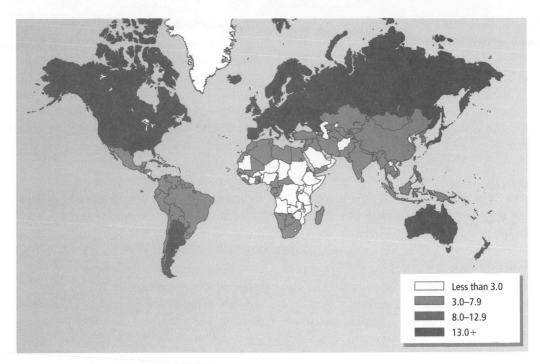

Figure 1.6
Percentage of people in countries globally aged 65 and over, 2000.

Source: U.S. Census Bureau, 2000a.

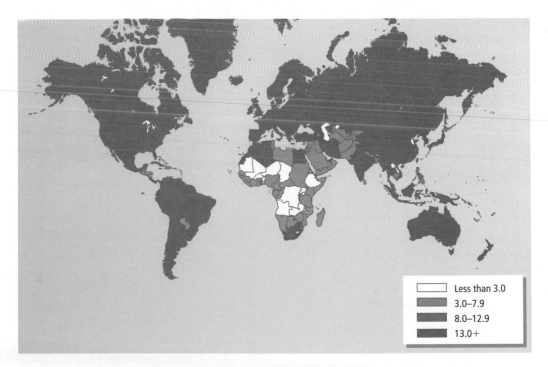

Figure 1.7
Percentage of people in countries globally aged 65 and over, 2030.

Source: U.S. Census Bureau, 2000a.

people living in India, Indonesia, or Vietnam, the odds that people over age 50 with daily expenditures of $1 or $2 will die within 5–7 years is at least three times greater than it is for people whose daily expenditures are $6–10. Clearly, poverty is strongly related to the odds of living a long life.

The worldwide implications of these population shifts are enormous. First, consider what will happen in countries such as Japan and throughout most of Europe, where the changes will result in net population decreases. Why? The main reason these countries are "aging" is a significantly lower birth rate. Once the large older-adult population dies, population decreases are inevitable. For them, it presents the problem of how their economies will handle a shrinking supply of workers (and consumers). In contrast, the dramatic increase in older adults (and population in general) of most of the rest of the world presents the multiple problems of financing the care of more older adults in health care systems that are already inadequate and strained, as well as trying to absorb more older workers in fragile economies (Lloyd, 2012; Phillips & Siu, 2012).

ADULT DEVELOPMENT IN ACTION

If you were a staff member for your congressional representative, what would you advise with respect to economic and social policy given the demographic changes in the U.S. population?

1.2 Issues in Studying Adult Development and Aging

LEARNING OBJECTIVES

- What four main forces shape development?
- What are normative age-graded influences, normative history-graded influences, and nonnormative influences?
- How do culture and ethnicity influence aging?
- What is the meaning of age?
- What are the nature–nurture, stability–change, continuity–discontinuity, and the "universal versus context-specific development" controversies?

Levar Johnson smiled broadly as he held his newborn granddaughter for the first time. So many thoughts *rushed into his mind. He could only imagine the kinds of things Devonna would experience growing up. He hoped that she would have a good neighborhood in which to play and explore her world. He hoped that she inherited the family genes for good health. He wondered how Devonna's life growing up as an African American in the United States would be different from his experiences.*

Like many grandparents, Levar wonders what the future holds for his granddaughter. The questions he considers are interesting in their own right, but they are important for another reason: They get to the heart of general issues of human development that have intrigued philosophers and scientists for centuries. You have probably wondered about many similar issues. How do some people manage to remain thin, whereas other people seem to gain weight merely by looking at food? Why do some people remain very active and mentally well into later life? How does growing up in a Spanish-speaking culture affect one's views of family caregiving? Answering these questions requires us to consider the various forces that shape us as we mature. Developmentalists place special emphasis on four forces: biological, psychological, sociocultural, and life cycle. These forces direct our development much as an artist's hands direct the course of a painting or sculpture.

Following from the forces that shape adult development and aging are questions such as: What is the relative importance of genetics and environment on people's behavior? Do people change gradually, or do they change more abruptly? Do all people change in the same way? These questions reflect controversies that historically underlie the study of human development (Lerner, 2001): the nature–nurture controversy, the change–stability controversy, the continuity–discontinuity controversy, and the "universal versus context-specific development" controversy.

Having a firm grasp on the forces and controversies of development is important because it provides a context for understanding why researchers and theorists believe certain things about aging or why some topics have been researched a great deal and others have been hardly studied at all. For example, someone who believes that a decline in intellectual ability is an innate and inevitable part of aging is unlikely to search for intervention techniques to raise performance. Similarly, someone who believes that personality characteristics change across adulthood would be likely to search for life transitions.

The Forces of Development

Gray hair, remembering, activity levels—Why do adults differ so much on these and other things? This question requires us to understand the basic forces that shape us. Developmentalists typically consider four interactive forces (shown in Figure 1.8):

1. **Biological forces** *include all genetic and health-related factors that affect development.* Examples of biological forces include menopause, facial wrinkling, and changes in the major organ systems.

2. **Psychological forces** *include all internal perceptual, cognitive, emotional, and personality factors that affect development.* Collectively, psychological forces provide the characteristics we notice about people that make them individuals.

3. **Sociocultural forces** *include interpersonal, societal, cultural, and ethnic factors that affect development.* Sociocultural forces provide the overall contexts in which we develop.

4. **Life-cycle forces** *reflect differences in how the same event or combination of biological, psychological, and sociocultural forces affects people at different points in their lives.* Life-cycle forces provide the context for the developmental differences of interest in adult development and aging.

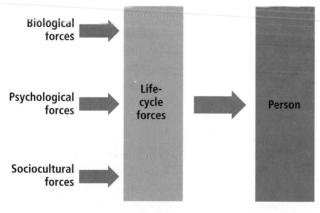

Figure 1.8

The biopsychosocial framework shows that human development results from interacting forces.

One useful way to organize the biological, psychological, and sociocultural forces on human development is with the biopsychosocial framework. Together with life-cycle forces, the biopsychosocial framework provides a complete overview of the shapers of human development. Each of us is a product of a unique combination of these forces. Even identical twins growing up in the same family eventually have their own unique friends, partners, occupations, and so on. To see why all these forces are important, imagine that we want to know how people feel about forgetting. We would need to consider several biological factors, such as whether the forgetting was caused by an underlying disease. We would want to know about such psychological factors as what the person's memory ability has been throughout his or her life and about his or her beliefs about what happens to memory with increasing age. We would need to know about sociocultural factors, such as the influence of social stereotypes about forgetting. Finally, we would need to know about the age of the person when a forgetting experience occurs. Focusing on only one (or even two or three) of the forces would provide an incomplete view of how the person feels. The biopsychosocial framework, along with life-cycle forces, will provide a way to understand all the developmental outcomes you will encounter in this text.

Interrelations among the Forces: Developmental Influences

All the forces we have discussed combine to create people's developmental experiences. One way to consider these combinations is to consider the degree to which they are common or unique to people of specific ages. An important concept in this approach is *cohort. A* **cohort** *is a group of people born at the same point or specific time span in historical time.* So everyone born in 1995 would be the 1995 cohort; similarly, those born between 1946 and 1964 represent the baby-boom cohort. Based on this approach, Baltes (1987; Baltes et al., 2006) identifies three sets of influences that interact to produce developmental change over the lifespan: normative age-graded influences, normative history-graded influences, and nonnormative influences.

Normative age-graded influences *are experiences caused by biological, psychological, and sociocultural forces that occur to most people of a particular age.* Some of these, such as puberty, menarche, and menopause, are biological. These normative biological events usually indicate a major change in a person's life; for example, menopause is an indicator that a woman can no longer bear children without medical intervention. Normative psychological events include focusing on certain concerns at different points in adulthood, such as a middle-aged person's concern with socializing the younger generation. Other normative age-graded influences involve sociocultural forces, such as the time when first marriage occurs and the age at which someone retires. Normative age-graded influences typically correspond to major time-marked events, which are often ritualized. For example, many younger adults formally celebrate turning 21 as the official transition to adulthood, getting married typically is surrounded with much celebration, and retirement often begins with a party celebrating the end of employment. These events provide the most convenient way to judge where we are on our social clock.

Normative history-graded influences *are events that most people in a specific culture experience at the same time.* These events may be biological (such as epidemics), psychological (such as particular stereotypes), or sociocultural (such as changing attitudes toward sexuality). Normative history-graded influences often give a generation its unique identity, such as the baby-boom generation, generation X (people born roughly between 1965 and 1975), and the millennial generation (sometimes called the Echo Boomers or generation Y, born between 1979 and 1994). These influences can have a profound effect across all generations. For example, the attacks on the World Trade Center on September 11, 2001, fundamentally changed attitudes about safety and security that had been held for decades.

Nonnormative influences *are random or rare events that may be important for a specific individual but are not experienced by most people.* These may be favorable events, such as winning the lottery or an election, or unfavorable ones, such as an accident or layoff. The unpredictability of these events makes them unique. Such events can turn one's life upside down overnight.

Life-cycle forces are especially key in understanding the importance of normative age-graded, normative history-graded, and nonnormative influences. For example, history-graded influences may produce generational differences and conflict; parents' and grandparents' experiences as young adults in the 1960s and 1970s (before AIDS, smartphones, and global terrorism) may have little to do with the complex issues faced by today's young adults. In turn, these interactions have important implications for understanding differences that appear to be age related. That is, differences may be explained in terms of different life experiences (normative history-graded influences) rather than as an integral part of aging itself (normative age-graded influences). We will return to this issue when we discuss age, cohort, and time-of-measurement effects in research on adult development and aging.

Culture and Ethnicity

Culture and ethnicity jointly provide status, social settings, living conditions, and personal experiences for people of all ages, and they influence and are influenced by biological, psychological, and life-cycle developmental forces. Culture can be defined as shared basic value orientations, norms, beliefs, and customary habits and ways of living. Culture provides the basic worldview of a society in that it gives it the basic explanations about the meanings and goals of everyday life (Matsumoto & Juang, 2013). Culture is such a powerful influence because it connects to biological forces through family lineage, which is sometimes the way in which members of a particular culture are defined. Psychologically, culture shapes people's core beliefs; in some cases this can result in ethnocentrism, or the belief that one's own culture is superior to others. Being socialized as a child within a culture usually has a more profound effect on a person than when one adopts a culture later in life, resulting in significant life-cycle timing effects. Culture is extremely important in gerontology because how people define basic concepts such as *person*, *age*, and *life course* varies a great deal across cultures.

Equally important is the concept of ethnicity, which is an individual and collective sense of identity based on historical and cultural group membership and related behaviors and beliefs (Matsumoto & Juang, 2013). Compared with culture, ethnic group identities have both solid and fluid properties, reflecting the fact that there are both unchanging and situation-specific aspects to ethnic identity (Jaspal & Cinnirella, 2012). An example of these properties is that the terms referring to an ethnic group can change over time; for example, the terms *colored people*, *Negroes*, *black Americans*, and *African Americans* have all been used to describe Americans of African ancestry. Ethnic identity is first influenced by biology through one's parents. However,

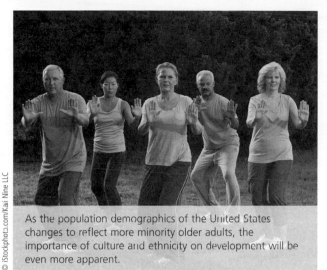

As the population demographics of the United States changes to reflect more minority older adults, the importance of culture and ethnicity on development will be even more apparent.

© iStockphoto.com/Kali Nine LLC

how one incorporates ethnic identity depends on numerous psychological factors as well as age.

Both culture and ethnicity are key dimensions along which adults vary. However, we know very little about how culture or ethnicity affects how people experience old age. Throughout the rest of this book, we explore areas in which culture and ethnicity have been studied systematically. Unfortunately, most research focuses only on European Americans. Given the demographic trends discussed earlier, this focus must change so we can understand the experience of growing older in the United States in the next few decades.

The Meaning of Age

When you are asked the question "How old are you?" what crosses your mind? Is it the number of years since the day of your birth? Is it how old you feel at that time? Is it defined more in terms of where you are biologically, psychologically, or socially than in terms of calendar time? You may not have thought about it, but age is not a simple construct (and in the case of people such as the !Kung, it has no meaning at all).

Likewise, aging is not a single process. Rather, it consists of at least three distinct processes: primary, secondary, and tertiary aging (Birren & Cunningham, 1985). **Primary aging** *is normal, disease-free development during adulthood.* Changes in biological, psychological, sociocultural, or life-cycle processes in primary aging are an inevitable part of the developmental process; examples include menopause, decline

in reaction time, and the loss of family and friends. Most of the information in this book represents primary aging. **Secondary aging** *is developmental changes that are related to disease, lifestyle, and other environmentally induced changes that are not inevitable (e.g., pollution).* The progressive loss of intellectual abilities in Alzheimer's disease and related forms of dementia are examples of secondary aging. Finally, **tertiary aging** *is the rapid losses that occur shortly before death.* An example of tertiary aging is a phenomenon known as terminal drop, in which intellectual abilities show a marked decline in the last few years before death.

Everyone does not grow old in the same way. Whereas most people tend to show usual patterns of aging that reflect the typical, or normative, changes with age, other people show highly successful aging in which few signs of change occur. For example, although most people tend to get chronic diseases as they get older, some people never do. What makes people who age successfully different? At this point, we do not know for sure. It may be a unique combination of genetics, optimal environment, flexibility in dealing with life situations, a strong sense of personal control, and maybe a bit of luck. For our present discussion, the main point to keep in mind is that everyone's experience of growing old is somewhat different. Although many people develop arthritis, how each person learns to cope is unique.

When most of us think about age, we usually think of how long we have been around since our birth; this way of defining age is known as chronological age. *Chronological age* is a shorthand way to index time and organize events and data by using a commonly understood standard: calendar time. Chronological age is not the only shorthand index variable used in adult development and aging. Gender, ethnicity, and socioeconomic status are others. No index variable itself actually causes behavior. In the case of gender, for example, it is not whether a person is male or female per se that determines how long he or she will live on average but rather the underlying forces, such as hormonal effects, that are the true causes. This point is often forgotten when age is the index variable, perhaps because it is so familiar to us and so widely used. However, age (or time) does not directly cause things to happen, either. Iron left out in the rain will rust, but rust is not caused simply by time. Rather, rust is a time-dependent process involving oxidation in which time is a measure of the rate at which rust is created. Similarly, human behavior is affected by experiences that occur with the passage of time, not by time itself. What we study in adult development and aging is the result of time- or age-dependent processes, not the result of age itself.

Describing a person's age turns out to be quite complicated. Here's why. *Perceived age* refers to the age you think of yourself as. The saying "You're only as old as you feel" captures perceived age. Where people are, relative to the maximum number of years they could possibly live, is their biological age. *Biological age* is assessed by measuring the functioning of the various vital, or life-limiting, organ systems, such as the cardiovascular system.

Psychological age refers to the functional level of the psychological abilities people use to adapt to changing environmental demands. These abilities include memory, intelligence, feelings, motivation, and other skills that foster and maintain self-esteem and personal control.

Finally, *sociocultural age* refers to the specific set of roles individuals adopt in relation to other members of the society and culture to which they belong. Sociocultural age is judged on the basis of many behaviors and habits, such as style of dress, customs, language, and interpersonal style. Sociocultural age is especially important in understanding many of the family and work roles we adopt. When to get married, have children, make career moves, retire, and so on often are influenced by what we think our sociocultural age is. Such decisions also play a role in determining our self-esteem and other aspects of personality. Many of the most damaging stereotypes about aging (e.g., that older people should not have sex) are based on faulty assumptions about sociocultural age.

A good example of the complexities of age is the concept of emerging adulthood. *Some human developmentalists view the period from the late teens to the mid- to late 20s as* emerging adulthood, *a period when individuals are not adolescents but are not yet fully adults* (Arnett, 2012). Emerging adulthood is a time to explore careers, self-identity, and commitments. It is also a time when certain biological and physiological developmental trends peak, and brain development continues in different ways.

In sum, a person's age turns out to be quite complex. Think about yourself. You probably have days when even though the calendar says you're a certain age, your exploits the day before resulted in your feeling much younger at the time and much older the next morning. How "old" anyone is can change from one moment to the next.

Core Issues in Development

Is it your genes or experiences that determine how intelligent you are? If a young adult woman is outgoing, does this mean she will be outgoing in late life? If people change, is it more gradual or sporadic? Is aging the same around the world? These and similar questions have occupied some of the greatest Western philosophers in history: Plato, Aristotle, René Descartes, John Locke, and Ludwig Wittgenstein, among many others. Four main issues occupy most of the discussion: nature versus nurture, stability versus change, continuity versus discontinuity, and universal versus context-specific development. Because each of these issues cuts across the topics we discuss in this book, let's consider each briefly.

The Nature–Nurture Issue. Think for a minute about a particular characteristic that you and several people in your family have, such as intelligence, good looks, or a friendly, outgoing personality.

Why is this trait so prevalent? Is it because you inherited the trait from your parents? Or is it because of where and how you and your parents were brought up? *Answers to these questions illustrate different positions on the* nature–nurture issue, *which involves the degree to which genetic or hereditary influences (nature) and experiential or environmental influences (nurture) determine the kind of person you are.* Scientists once hoped to answer these questions by identifying either heredity or environment as *the* cause of a particular aspect of development. The goal was to be able to say, for example, that intelligence was due to heredity or that personality was due to experience. Today, however, we know that virtually no features of life-span development are due exclusively to either heredity or environment. Instead, development is always shaped by both: Nature and nurture are mutually interactive influences.

For example, it is known that some forms of Alzheimer's disease are genetically linked. However, whether one actually gets Alzheimer's disease, and possibly even how the disease progresses, may be influenced by the environment. Specifically, an environmental trigger may be needed for the disease to occur. Moreover, evidence indicates that providing a supportive environment for people with Alzheimer's disease improves their performance on cognitive tasks (Hunter, Ward, & Camp, 2012).

So in order to understand a newborn's future we must simultaneously consider his or her inborn, hereditary characteristics and the environment. Both factors must be considered together to yield an adequate account of why we behave the way we do. To explain a person's behavior and discover where to focus intervention, we must look at the unique interaction for that person between nature and nurture.

The Stability–Change Issue. Ask yourself the following question: Are you pretty much the same as you were 10 years ago, or are you different? How so? Depending on what aspects of yourself you considered, you may have concluded that you are pretty much the same (perhaps in terms of learning style) or that you are different (perhaps in some physical feature such as weight). *The stability–change issue concerns the degree to which people remain the same over time*, as discussed in the Current Controversies feature. Stability at some basic level is essential for us (and others) to recognize that one is the same individual as time goes on. But we also like to believe that our characteristics are not set in concrete, that we can change ourselves if we so desire. (Imagine not being able to do anything to rid yourself of some character defect.)

Although there is little controversy about whether children change in some ways from birth through age 18, there is much controversy about whether adults do as well. Much of the controversy over stability and change across adulthood stems from how specific characteristics are defined and measured. How much we remain the same and how much we change, then, turns out to be a difficult issue to resolve in an objective way. For many gerontologists, whether stability or change is the rule depends on what personal aspect is being considered and what theoretical perspective one is adopting.

The Continuity–Discontinuity Controversy. The third major issue in developmental psychology is a

CURRENT CONTROVERSIES:

DOES PERSONALITY IN YOUNG ADULTHOOD DETERMINE PERSONALITY IN OLD AGE?

Lest you think the controversies underlying adult development and aging do not reflect ongoing debate, consider the case of personality in adulthood. Perhaps no other topic in gerontology has resulted in such heated debates as whether people's basic personality remains the same throughout adulthood or undergoes fundamental change. As we explore in detail in Chapter 9, numerous theories have been developed just to account for the data on this one topic.

Consider yourself and other adults you know. Is the person labeled "class clown" in high school likely to be as much of a fun-loving person 10, 20, or 30 years later? Will the shy person who would never ask anyone to dance be as withdrawn? Or will these people be hardly recognizable at their various class reunions? Probably in your experience you've encountered both outcomes; that is, some people seem to remain the same year after year, whereas some people seem to undergo tremendous change. Why is that?

For one thing, it depends on how specific you get in looking at aspects of a person's personality. In the case of a very specific trait, such as shyness, you will probably see overall stability across adulthood. But if you look at a more global aspect such as the degree to which a person is concerned with the next generation, then you are more likely to find change.

What does this mean? Certainly, it means you have to be very careful in making general statements about stability or change. It also means you have to be quite specific about what you are interested in measuring and at what level of complexity. We will encounter many more examples of both stability and change throughout the book that reflect both these needs.

derivative of the stability–change controversy. *The continuity–discontinuity controversy concerns whether a particular developmental phenomenon represents a smooth progression over time (continuity) or a series of abrupt shifts (discontinuity).* Continuity approaches usually focus on the amount of a characteristic a person has, whereas discontinuity approaches usually focus on the kinds of characteristics a person has. Of course, on a day-to-day basis, behaviors often look nearly identical, or continuous. But when viewed over the course of many months or years, the same behaviors may have changed dramatically, reflecting discontinuous change. Throughout this book, you will find examples of developmental changes that appear to be more on the continuities side and ones that appear to be more on the discontinuities side.

An example of continuity is discussed in Chapter 6: reaction time. As people grow older, the speed with which they can respond slows down. But in Chapters 8 you will read about an example of discontinuity: How people approach problems, especially ones with complex and ambiguous features, undergoes fundamental shifts from young adulthood through middle age.

Within the discontinuity view lies the issue of how adaptable people are in situations as they age. Baltes and colleagues (1998; Baltes et al., 1999) use the term *plasticity* to describe this in relation to people's capacity. Plasticity *refers to the belief that capacity is not fixed, but can be learned or improved with practice.* For example, people can learn ways to help themselves remember information, which in turn may help them deal with declining short-term memory ability with age. Although plasticity can be demonstrated in many arenas, there are limits to the degree of potential improvement, as we will see in later chapters.

The Universal versus Context-Specific Development Controversy.

The universal versus context-specific development controversy *concerns whether there is just one path of development or several.* Consider the !Kung tribe, who live in the Kalahari Desert of Botswana in southwest Africa (Lee, Hitchcock, & Biesele, 2002). If you were to ask an older !Kung "How old are you?" you would quickly learn that the question has no meaning. !Kung also do not keep track of the number of years they have been alive, the number of children they have, or how often they move. !Kung mothers can describe in detail each of their children's births, but they leave it to others to figure out how many children this adds up to. To the !Kung, age per se is unimportant; when asked to describe people who are "younger" or "older," they give the names of specific people. Social roles among the !Kung also do not differ by age; for example, women in their 20s and 60s all tend gardens, draw water from wells, and take care of children.

Members of the !Kung tribe experience development in ways very different from the ways most Americans do.

Peter Johnson/Corbis

Life among !Kung adults contrasts sharply with life among adults in the United States, where age matters a great deal and social roles differ accordingly. Can one theory explain development in both groups? Maybe. Some theorists argue that such differences are more apparent than real and that development worldwide reflects one basic process for everyone. According to this view, differences in development are simply variations on a fundamental developmental process, much as Hershey, Nestlé, Teuscher, and Godiva chocolates are all products of the same basic manufacturing process.

The opposing view is that differences between people may not be just variations on a theme. Advocates of this view argue that adult development and aging are inextricably intertwined with the context in which they occur. A person's development is a product of complex interactions with the environment, and these interactions are not fundamentally the same in all environments. Each environment has its own set of unique procedures that shape development, just as the "recipes" for chocolates, computers, and pens have little in common.

The view adopted in this book is that adult development and aging must be understood within the contexts in which they occur. In some cases, this means that contexts are sufficiently similar that general trends can be identified. In others, such as the !Kung and U.S. societies, these differences prevent many general statements. In Levar's case with his granddaughter, it may be a blend of the two.

ADULT DEVELOPMENT IN ACTION

How would understanding the forces and issues that shape human development help you be a better healthcare worker at a neighborhood clinic?

1.3 Research Methods

LEARNING OBJECTIVES

- What approaches do scientists use to measure behavior in adult development and aging research?
- What are the general designs for doing research?
- What specific designs are unique to adult development and aging research?
- What ethical procedures must researchers follow?

Leah and Sarah are both 75 years old and are in fairly good health. They believe their memory is not as good as it once was, so they both use various memory aids: Leah tries to think of images in her mind to remember her grocery list, whereas Sarah writes them down. Leah and Sarah got into a discussion recently about which technique works better.

You might be asking yourself why you need to know about research methods when you could just Google the topic and find out all sorts of things about it. Here's why—there is good research and bad research and everything else in between. The only way to tell the difference is by knowing what makes good research that results in trustworthy information.

Just as in any profession, gerontology has certain tools of the trade that are used to ensure good research.

That's what we will be considering in this section—the tools that gerontologists have used for decades in discovering the secrets of adult development and aging.

This section is so important that if you have trouble understanding the information after reading it a few times, ask your instructor.

So suppose Leah and Sarah know that you're taking a course in adult development and aging, and they ask you to settle the matter. You know research could show whose approach is better under what circumstances, but how? Gerontologists must make several key decisions as they prepare to study any topic. They need to decide how to measure the topic of interest, they must design the study, they must choose a way to study development, and they must respect the rights of the people who will participate in the study.

What makes the study of adult development and aging different from other areas of social science is the need to consider multiple influences on behavior. Explanations of development entail consideration of all the forces we considered earlier. This makes research on adult development and aging more difficult, if for no other reason than it involves examining more variables.

Measurement in Adult Development and Aging Research

Researchers typically begin by deciding how to measure the topic of interest. For example, the first step toward resolving Leah and Sarah's discussion about remembering grocery items would be to decide how to measure remembering. Gerontologists usually use one of three approaches: observing systematically, using tasks to sample behavior, and asking people for self-reports. In addition, researchers need to be concerned with how representative the participants in the study are of the larger group of people in question.

Regardless of the kind of method chosen, researchers must show it is both reliable and valid. *The reliability of a measure is the extent to which it provides a consistent index of the behavior or topic of interest.* A measure of memory is reliable to the extent that it gives a consistent estimate of performance each time you administer it. All measures used in gerontological research must be shown to be reliable, or they cannot be used. *The validity of a measure is the extent to which it measures what researchers think it measures.* For example, a measure of memory is valid only if it can be shown to actually measure memory (and not vocabulary ability, for example). Validity often is established by showing that the measure in question is closely related to another measure known to be valid. Because it is possible to have a measure that is reliable but not valid (a ruler is a reliable measure of length but not a valid measure of memory), researchers must ensure that measures are both reliable and valid.

Systematic Observation.

As the name implies, systematic observation *involves watching people and carefully recording what they say or do.* Two forms of systematic observation are common. In naturalistic observation, people are observed as they behave spontaneously in some real-life situation. For example, Leah and Sarah could be observed in the grocery store purchasing their items as a way to test how well they remember.

Structured observations differ from naturalistic observations in that the researcher creates a setting that is particularly likely to elicit the behavior of interest. Structured observations are especially useful for studying behaviors that are difficult to observe naturally. For example, how people react to emergencies is hard to study naturally because emergencies generally are rare and unpredictable events. A researcher could stage an emergency and watch how people react. However, whether the behaviors observed in staged situations are the same as would happen naturally often is hard to determine, making it difficult to generalize from staged settings to the real world.

Sampling Behavior with Tasks.

When investigators can't observe a behavior directly, another popular alternative is to create tasks that are thought to sample the behavior of interest. For example, one way to test older adults' memory is to give them a grocery list to learn and remember. Likewise, police training includes putting the candidate in a building in which targets pop up that may be either criminals or innocent bystanders. This approach is popular with gerontological researchers because it is so convenient. The main question with this approach is its validity: Does the task provide a realistic sample of the behavior of interest? For example, asking people to learn grocery lists would have good validity to the extent it matched the kinds of lists they actually use.

Self-Reports.

The last approach, self-reports, is a special case of using tasks to sample people's behavior. Self-reports *are simply people's answers to questions about the topic of interest.* When questions are posed in written form, the verbal report is a questionnaire; when they are posed verbally, it is an interview. Either way, questions are created that probe different aspects of the topic of interest. For example, if you think imagery and lists are common ways people use to remember grocery items, you could devise a questionnaire and survey several people to find out.

Although self-reports are very convenient and provide information on the topic of interest, they are not always good measures of people's behavior, because they are inaccurate. Why? People may not remember accurately what they did in the past, or they may report what they think the researcher wants to hear.

Representative Sampling.

Researchers usually are interested in broad groups of people called populations. Examples of populations are all students taking a course on adult development and aging or all Asian American widows. Almost all studies include only a sample of people, which is a subset of the population. Researchers must be careful to ensure that their sample is truly representative of the population of interest. An unrepresentative sample can result in invalid research. For example, what would you think of a study of middle-aged parents if you learned that the sample consisted entirely of two-parent households? You would, quite correctly, decide that this sample is not representative of all middle-aged parents and question whether its results apply to single middle-aged parents.

As you read on, you'll soon discover that most of the research we consider in this text has been conducted on middle-class, well-educated European Americans. Are these samples representative of all people in the United States? In the world? Sometimes, but not always. Be careful not to assume that findings from this group apply to people of other groups. In addition, some developmental issues have not been studied in all ethnic groups and cultures. For example, the U.S. government does not always report statistics for all ethnic groups. To change this, some U.S. government agencies, such as the National Institutes of Health, now require samples to be representative. Thus in the future we may gain a broader understanding of aging.

General Designs for Research

Having selected the way we want to measure the topic of interest, researchers must embed this measure in a research design that yields useful, relevant results. Gerontologists rely on primary designs in planning their work: experimental studies, correlational studies, and case studies. The specific design chosen for research depends in large part on the questions the researchers are trying to address.

Experimental Design. To find out whether Leah's or Sarah's approach to remembering works better, we could gather groups of older adults and try the following. We could randomly assign the participants into three groups: those who are taught to use imagery, those who are taught to use lists, and those who are not taught to use anything. After giving all the groups time to learn the new technique (where appropriate), we could test each group on a new grocery list to see who does better.

What we have done is an example of an experiment, which involves manipulating a key factor that the researcher believes is responsible for a particular behavior and randomly assigning participants to the experimental and control groups. In our case, the key variable being manipulated (termed the **independent variable***) is the instructions for how to study. In a study of memory, a typical behavior that is observed (termed the* **dependent variable***) is the amount of information actually remembered.*

More generally, in an experiment the researcher is most interested in identifying differences between groups of people. One group, the experimental group, receives the manipulation; another group, the control group, does not. This sets up a situation in which the level of the key variable of interest differs across groups. In addition, the investigator exerts precise control over all important aspects of the study, including the variable of interest, the setting, and the participants. Because the key variable is systematically manipulated in an experiment, researchers can infer cause-and-effect relations about that variable. In our example, we can conclude that type of instruction (how people

study) causes better or worse performance on a memory test. Discovering such cause-and-effect relations is important if we are to understand the underlying processes of adult development and aging.

Finally, we must note that age cannot be an independent variable, because we cannot manipulate it. Consequently, we cannot conduct true experiments to examine the effects of age on a particular person's behavior. At best, we can find age-related effects of an independent variable on dependent variables.

Correlational Design. *In a correlational study, investigators examine relations between variables as they exist naturally in the world.* In the simplest correlational study, a researcher measures two variables, and then sees how they are related. Suppose we wanted to know whether the amount of time spent studying a grocery list such as one that Sarah might create was related to how many items people remember at the store. To find out, the researcher would measure two things for each person in the study: the length of study time and the number of items purchased correctly.

The results of a correlational study usually are measured by computing a correlation coefficient, abbreviated r. Correlations can range from -1.0 to 1.0, reflecting three different types of relations between study time and number of groceries remembered.

1. When $r = 0$, the two variables are unrelated: Study time has no relation to remembering groceries.

2. When $r > 0$, the variables are positively related: As study time increases (or decreases), the number of grocery items remembered also increases (or decreases).

3. When $r < 0$, the variables are inversely related: When study time increases (or decreases), the number of groceries remembered decreases (or increases).

Correlational studies do not give definitive information about cause-and-effect relations; for example, the correlation between study time and the number of groceries remembered does not mean that one variable caused the other, regardless of how large the relation was. However, correlational studies do provide important information about the strength of the relation between variables, which is reflected in the absolute value of the correlation coefficient. Moreover, because developmental researchers are interested in how variables are related to factors that are very difficult, if not impossible, to manipulate, correlational techniques are used a great deal. In fact, most developmental research is correlational at some level because age cannot be manipulated within an individual. This means we can describe a great many developmental phenomena, but we cannot explain very many of them.

Case Studies. Sometimes researchers cannot obtain measures directly from people and are able only to watch them carefully. *In certain situations, researchers may be able to study a single individual in great detail in a case study.* This technique is especially useful when researchers want to investigate very rare phenomena, such as uncommon diseases or people with extremely high ability. Identifying new diseases, for example, begins with a case study of one individual who has a pattern of symptoms that is different from any known syndrome. Case studies are also very valuable for opening new areas of study, which can be followed by larger studies using other methods (e.g., experiments). However, their primary limitation is figuring out whether the information gleaned from one individual holds for others as well.

| Designs for Studying Development

Once the general design is chosen, most gerontologists must decide how to measure possible changes or age differences that emerge as people develop. For example, if we want to know how people continue (or fail) to use imagery or lists in remembering grocery items as they get older, we will want to use a design that is particularly sensitive to developmental differences. Such designs are based on three key variables: age, cohort, and time of measurement. Once we have considered these, we will examine the specific designs for studying development.

Age, Cohort, and Time of Measurement. Every study of adult development and aging is built on the combination of three building blocks: age, cohort, and time of measurement (Cavanaugh & Whitbourne, 2003).

Age effects *reflect differences caused by underlying processes, such as biological, psychological, or sociocultural changes.* Although usually represented in research by chronological age, age effects are inherent changes within the person and are not caused by the passage of time per se.

Cohort effects *are differences caused by experiences and circumstances unique to the generation to which one belongs.* In general, cohort effects correspond to the normative history-graded influences discussed earlier. However, defining a cohort may not be easy. Cohorts can be specific, as in all people born in one particular year, or general, such as the baby-boom cohort. As described earlier, each generation is exposed to different sets of historical and personal events (such as World War II, tablet computers, or opportunities to attend college). Later in this section we consider evidence of how profound cohort effects can be.

Time-of-measurement effects *reflect differences stemming from sociocultural, environmental, historical, or other events at the time the data are obtained from the participants.* For example, data about wage increases given in a particular year may be influenced by the economic conditions of that year. If the economy is in a serious recession, pay increases probably would be small. In contrast, if the economy is booming, pay increases could be large. Clearly, whether a study is conducted during a recession or a boom affects what is learned about pay changes. In short, the point in time in which a researcher decides to do research could lead him or her to different conclusions about the phenomenon being studied.

The three building-block variables (age, cohort, and time of measurement) can be represented in a single chart, such as the one shown in Table 1.1. Cohort is represented by the years in the first column, time of measurement is represented by the years across the top, and age is represented by the numbers in the

Table 1.1

THREE BASIC BUILDING BLOCKS OF DEVELOPMENTAL RESEARCH				
	TIME OF MEASUREMENT			
Cohort	2000	2010	2020	2030
1950	50	60	70	80
1960	40	50	60	70
1970	30	40	50	60
1980	20	30	40	50

Cohort is represented by the years in the first column, time of measurement by the years across the top, and age by the values in the cells.

individual cells. Note that age is computed by subtracting the cohort year from the time of measurement.

In conducting adult development and aging research, investigators have attempted to identify and separate the three effects. This has not been easy, because all three influences are interrelated. If one is interested in studying 40-year-olds, one must necessarily select the cohort that was born 40 years ago. In this case age and cohort are *confounded*, because one cannot know whether the behaviors observed occur because the participants are 40 years old or because of the specific life experiences they have had as a result of being born in a particular historical period. *In general, confounding is any situation in which one cannot determine which of two or more effects is responsible for the behaviors being observed.* Confounding of the three effects we are considering here is the most serious problem in adult development and aging research.

What distinguishes developmental researchers from their colleagues in other areas of psychology is a fundamental interest in understanding how people change. Developmental researchers must look at the ways in which people differ across time. Doing so necessarily requires that researchers understand the distinction between age change and age difference. An age change occurs in an individual's behavior over time. Leah's or Sarah's memory at age 75 may not be as good as it was at age 40. To discover an age change, one must examine the same person (in this case, Leah or Sarah) at more than one point in time. An age difference is obtained when at least two different people of different ages are compared. Leah and Sarah may not remember as many grocery items as a person of age 40. Even though we may be able to document substantial age differences, we cannot assume they imply an age change. We do not know whether Leah or Sarah has changed since she was 40, and of course we do not know whether the 40-year-old will be any different at age 75. In some cases age differences reflect age changes, and in some cases they do not.

If what we really want to understand in developmental research is age change (what happens as people grow older), we should design our research with this goal in mind. Moreover, different research questions necessitate different research designs. We next consider the most common ways in which researchers gather data about age differences and age changes: cross-sectional, longitudinal, time lag, and sequential designs.

Cross-Sectional Designs. *In a cross-sectional study, developmental differences are identified by testing people of different ages at the same time.* Any single column in Table 1.2 represents a cross-sectional design. Cross-sectional designs allow researchers to examine age differences but not age change.

Table 1.2

CROSS-SECTIONAL DESIGN				
TIME OF MEASUREMENT				
Cohort	2000	2010	2020	2030
1950	**50**	60	70	80
1960	**40**	50	60	70
1970	**30**	40	50	60
1980	**20**	30	40	50

Cohort is represented by the years in the first column, time of measurement by the years across the top, and age by the values in the cells.

Cross-sectional research has several weaknesses. Because people are tested at only one point in their development, we learn nothing about the continuity of development. Consequently, we cannot tell whether someone who remembers grocery items well at age 50 (in 2000) is still able to do so at age 80 (in 2030), because the person would be tested at age 50 or 80, but not both. Cross-sectional studies also are affected by cohort effects, meaning that differences between age groups (cohorts) may result as easily from environmental events as from developmental processes. Why? Cross-sectional studies assume that when the older participants were younger, they resembled the people in the younger age groups in the study. This isn't always true, of course, which makes it difficult to know why age differences are found in a cross-sectional study. In short, age and cohort effects are confounded in cross-sectional research.

Despite the confounding of age and cohort and the limitation of being able to identify only age differences, cross-sectional designs dominate the research literature in gerontology. Why? The reason is a pragmatic one: Because all the measurements are obtained at one time, cross-sectional research can be conducted more quickly and inexpensively than research using other designs. In addition, one particular variation of cross-sectional designs is used the most: the extreme age groups design.

Suppose you want to investigate whether people's ability to remember items at the grocery store differs with age. Your first impulse may be to gather a group of younger adults and compare their performance with that of a group of older adults. Typically, such studies compare samples obtained in convenient ways; younger adults usually are college students, and older adults often are volunteers from senior centers or church groups.

Although the extreme age groups design is very common (most of the studies cited in this book used this design), it has several problems (Hertzog & Dixon, 1996). Three concerns are key. First, the samples are not representative, so we must be very careful not to read too much into the results; findings from studies on extreme age groups may not generalize to people other than ones like those who participated. Second, age should be treated as a continuous variable, not as a category ("young" and "old"). Viewing age as a continuous variable allows researchers to gain a better understanding of how age relates to any observed age differences. Finally, extreme age group designs assume the measures used mean the same thing across both age groups. Measures may tap somewhat different constructs, so the reliability and validity of each measure should be checked in each age group.

Despite the problems with cross-sectional designs in general and with extreme age groups designs in particular, they can provide useful information if used carefully. Most importantly, they can point out issues that may provide fruitful avenues for subsequent longitudinal or sequential studies, in which case we can uncover information about age changes.

Longitudinal Designs. *In a longitudinal study, the same individuals are observed or tested repeatedly at different points in their lives.* As the name implies, a longitudinal study involves a lengthwise account of development and is the most direct way to watch growth occur. A longitudinal design is represented by any horizontal row in Table 1.3. A major advantage of longitudinal designs is that age changes are identified because we are studying the same people over time.

Usually the repeated testing of longitudinal studies extends over years, but not always. *In a microgenetic study, a special type of longitudinal design, participants*

Table 1.3

LONGITUDINAL DESIGN				
	TIME OF MEASUREMENT			
Cohort	2000	2010	2020	2030
1950	50	60	70	80
1960	**40**	**50**	**60**	**70**
1970	30	40	50	60
1980	20	30	40	50

Cohort is represented by the years in the first column, time of measurement by the years across the top, and age by the values in the cells.

are tested repeatedly over a span of days or weeks, typically with the aim of observing change directly as it occurs. For example, researchers might test children every week, starting when they are 12 months old and continuing until 18 months. Microgenetic studies are particularly useful when investigators have hypotheses about a specific period when developmental change should occur (Flynn, Pine, & Lewis, 2006), or in order to intensively document a behavior over time (e.g., Boom, 2012).

Microgenetic studies are particularly useful in tracking change as a result of intervention. For example, older adults could be given a series of measures of memory ability and then be interviewed about their use of memory strategies. A series of training sessions about how to improve memory could be introduced including additional memory tests and interviews, followed by a posttest to find out how well the participants learned the skills in which they were trained. The microgenetic method would look in detail at the performance of those who learned and improved after training, compared to those who did not, and search for differences in either the pattern of performance in the memory tests or in the details in the interviews for reasons why some people improved while others did not. This would provide a vivid portrait of change over the period of the intervention.

If age changes are found in longitudinal studies, can we say why they occurred? Because only one cohort is studied, cohort effects are eliminated as an explanation of change. However, the other two potential explanations, age and time of measurement, are confounded. For example, suppose we wanted to follow the 1990 cohort over time. If we wanted to test these individuals when they were 20 years old, we would have had to do so in 2010. Consequently, any changes we identify could result from changes in underlying processes or factors related to the time we choose to conduct our measurement. For instance, if we conducted a longitudinal study of salary growth, the amount of salary change in any comparison could stem from real change in the skills and worth of the person to the company or from the economic conditions of the times. In a longitudinal study we cannot tell which of these factors is more important.

Longitudinal studies have three additional potential problems. First, if the research measure requires some type of performance by the participants, we may have the problem of practice effects. Practice effects result from the fact that performance may improve over time simply because people are tested over and over again with the same measures. Second, we may have a problem with participant dropout because it is difficult to keep a group of research participants intact over the course of a longitudinal study. Participants may move, lose interest, or die. Participant dropout can result in two different outcomes. We can end up with positive selective survival if the participants at the end of the study tend to be the ones who were initially higher on some variable (e.g., the surviving participants are the ones who were the most healthy at the beginning of the study). In contrast, we could have negative selective survival if the participants at the conclusion of the study were initially lower on an important variable (e.g., the surviving participants may have been those who were initially less healthy).

The third problem with longitudinal designs is that our ability to apply the results to other groups is limited. The difficulty is that only one cohort is followed. Whether the pattern of results that is observed in one cohort can be generalized to another cohort is questionable. Thus researchers using longitudinal designs run the risk of uncovering a developmental process that is unique to that cohort.

Because longitudinal designs necessarily take more time and usually are expensive, they have not been used very often. However, researchers now recognize that we badly need to follow individuals over time to further our understanding of the aging process. Thus, longitudinal studies are becoming more common.

Sequential Designs. Thus far, we have considered two developmental designs, each of which has problems involving the confounding of two effects. These effects are age and cohort in cross-sectional designs, and age and time of measurement in longitudinal designs. These confounds create difficulties in interpreting behavioral differences between and within individuals, as illustrated in the How Do We Know? feature. Some of these interpretive dilemmas can be alleviated by using more complex designs called sequential designs, which are shown in Table 1.4. Keep in mind, though, that sequential designs do not cure the confounding problems in the three basic designs.

Table 1.4

SEQUENTIAL DESIGN				
	TIME OF MEASUREMENT			
Cohort	2000	2010	2020	2030
1950	50	60	70	80
1960	**40**	**50**	**60**	**70**
1970	30	**40**	**50**	**60**
1980	20	30	40	50

Cohort is represented by the years in the first column, time of measurement by the years across the top, and age by the values in the cells.

Sequential designs *represent different combinations of cross-sectional or longitudinal studies.* In the table, a cross-sequential design consists of two or more cross-sectional studies conducted at two or more times of measurement. These multiple cross-sectional designs include the same age ranges; however, the participants are different in each wave of testing. For example, we might compare performances on intelligence tests for people between ages 20 and 50 in 1980 and then repeat the study in 1990 with a different group of people aged 30 to 60.

Table 1.4 also depicts the longitudinal sequential design. A longitudinal sequential design consists of two or more longitudinal designs that represent two or more cohorts. Each longitudinal design in the sequence begins with the same age range and follows people for the same length of time. For example, we may want to begin a longitudinal study of intellectual development with a group of 50-year-olds in 1980, using the 1930 cohort. We would then follow this cohort for a period of years. In 1990, we would begin a second longitudinal study on 50-year-olds, using the 1940 cohort, and follow them for the same length of time as we follow

HOW DO WE KNOW?:

CONFLICTS BETWEEN CROSS-SECTIONAL AND LONGITUDINAL DATA

Who was the investigator, and what was the aim of the study? In the 1950s, little information was available concerning longitudinal changes in adults' intellectual abilities. What there was showed a developmental pattern of relative stability or slight decline, quite different from the picture of substantial across-the-board decline obtained in cross-sectional studies. To provide a more thorough picture of intellectual change, K. Warner Schaie began the Seattle Longitudinal Study in 1956.

How did the investigator measure the topic of interest? Schaie used standardized tests of primary mental abilities to assess a wide range of abilities such as logical reasoning and spatial ability.

Who were the participants in the study? Over the course of the study, more than 5,000 individuals have been tested at eight testing cycles (1956, 1963, 1970, 1977, 1984, 1991, 1998, and 2005). The participants were representative of the upper 75% of the socioeconomic spectrum and were recruited through a very large health maintenance organization in Seattle. Extensions of the study include longitudinal data on second-generation family members and on the grandchildren of some of the original participants.

What was the design of the study? To provide a thorough view of intellectual change over time, Schaie invented a new type of design—the sequential design.

Participants were tested every seven years. Like most longitudinal studies, Schaie's sequential study encountered selectivity effects—that is, people who return over the years for retesting tend to do better initially than those who fail to return (in other words, those who don't perform well initially tend to drop out of the study). However, an advantage of Schaie's sequential design is that by bringing in new groups of participants, he was able to estimate the importance of selection effects, a major improvement over previous research.

Were there ethical concerns with the study? The most serious issue in any study in which participants are followed over time is confidentiality. Because people's names must be retained for future contact, the researchers were very careful about keeping personal information secure.

What were the results? Among the many important findings from the study are differential changes in abilities over time and cohort effects. As you can see in Figure 1.9, scores on tests of primary mental abilities improve gradually until the late 30s or early 40s. Small declines begin in the 50s, increase as people age into their 60s, and become increasingly large in the 70s (Schaie & Zanjani, 2006).

Cohort differences were also found. Figure 1.10 shows that on some skills, such as inductive reasoning ability, but not others, more recently born younger and middle-aged cohorts performed better than cohorts born earlier. An example of the latter is that older cohorts outperformed younger ones on number skills (Schaie & Zanjani, 2006). These cohort effects probably

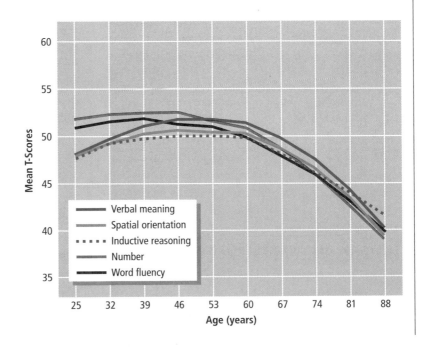

Figure 1.9

Longitudinal Changes in Intellectual Functions from Age 25 to 88.

Source: From "Intellectual Development Across Adulthood" by K. Warner Schaie and Faika A. K. Zanjani, in Handbook of Adult Development and Learning, *ed. by C. Hoare, p. 102. Copyright © 2006 by Oxford University Press.*

reflect differences in educational experiences; younger groups' education emphasized figuring things out on one's own, whereas older groups' education emphasized rote learning. Additionally, older groups did not have calculators or computers, so they had to do mathematical problems by hand.

Schaie uncovered many individual differences as well; some people showed developmental patterns closely approximating the overall trends, but others showed unusual patterns. For example, some individuals showed steady declines in most abilities beginning in their 40s and 50s, others showed declines in some abilities but not others, but some people showed little change in most abilities over a 14-year period. Such individual variation in developmental patterns means that average trends, like those depicted in the figures, must be interpreted cautiously; they reflect group averages and do not represent the patterns shown by each person in the group.

Another key finding is that how intellectual abilities are organized in people does not change over time (Schaie et al., 1998). This finding is important because it means that the tests, which presuppose a particular organizational structure of intellectual abilities, can be used across different ages. Additionally, Schaie (1994) identified several variables that appear to reduce the risk of cognitive decline in old age:

- Absence of cardiovascular and other chronic diseases
- Living in favorable environmental conditions (such as good housing)

- Remaining cognitively active through reading and lifelong learning
- Having a flexible personality style in middle age
- Being married to a person with high cognitive status
- Being satisfied with one's life achievements in middle age

What did the investigator conclude? Three points are clear. First, intellectual development during adulthood is marked by a gradual leveling off of gains, followed by a period of relative stability, and then a time of gradual decline in most abilities. Second, these trends vary from one cohort to another. Third, individual patterns of change vary considerably from person to person.

Overall, Schaie's findings indicate that intellectual development in adulthood is influenced by a wide variety of health, environmental, personality, and relationship factors. By attending to these influences throughout adulthood, we can at least stack the deck in favor of maintaining good intellectual functioning in late life.

What converging evidence would strengthen these conclusions? Although Schaie's study is one of the most comprehensive ever conducted, it is limited. Studying people who live in different locations around the world would provide evidence as to whether the results are limited geographically. Additional cross-cultural evidence comparing people with different economic backgrounds and differing access to health care would also provide insight into the effects of these variables on intellectual development.

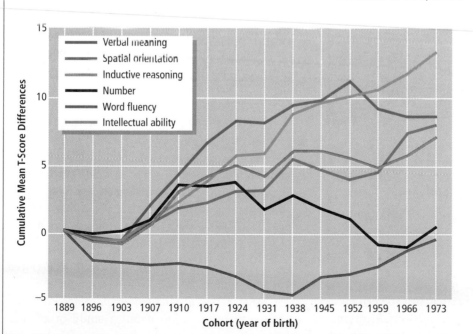

Figure 1.10

Cohort differences in intellectual functions from birth cohorts between 1889 and 1973.

Source: From "Intellectual Development Across Adulthood" by K. Warner Schaie and Faika A. K. Zanjani, in Handbook of Adult Development and Learning, *ed. by C. Hoare, p. 106. Copyright © 2006 by Oxford University Press.*

the first cohort. This design helps clarify whether the longitudinal effects found in a single longitudinal study are cohort-specific or are more general findings.

Although sequential designs are powerful and provide by far the richest source of information about developmental issues, few researchers use them, because they are costly. Trying to follow many people over long periods of time, generating new samples, and conducting complex data analyses are expensive and time consuming. Clearly, this type of commitment to one project is not possible for most researchers.

Integrating Findings from Different Studies

Several times in the past few pages, we've emphasized the value of using different methods to study the same phenomenon. The advantage of this approach is that conclusions are most convincing when the results are the same regardless of method.

In reality, though, findings are often inconsistent. Suppose, for example, many researchers find that people often share personal information with friends (e.g., through Facebook or Google+), some researchers find that people share occasionally with friends, and a few researchers find that people never share with friends. What results should we believe? What should we conclude? **Meta-analysis** *allows researchers to synthesize the results of many studies to estimate relations between variables* (Plonsky & Oswald, 2012). In conducting a meta-analysis, investigators find all studies published on a topic over a substantial period of time (e.g., 10 to 20 years), and then record and analyze the results and important methodological variables.

Thus, meta-analysis is a particularly powerful tool because it allows scientists to determine whether a finding generalizes across many studies that used different methods. In addition, meta-analysis can reveal the impact of those different methods on results.

Conducting Research Ethically

Choosing a good research design involves more than just selecting a particular method. Researchers must determine whether the methods they plan on using are ethical. That is, when designing a research study, investigators must do so in a way that does not violate the rights of people who participate. To verify that every research project has these protections, local panels of experts and community representatives review proposed studies before any data are collected. Only with the approval of this panel can scientists begin their study. If the review panel objects to some aspects of the proposed study, the researcher must revise those aspects and present them anew for the panel's approval. Likewise, each time a component of a study is changed, the review panel must be informed and give its approval.

To guide review panels, professional organizations (e.g., the American Psychological Association) and government agencies (e.g., the National Institutes of Health) have codes of conduct that specify the rights of research participants and procedures to protect these participants. The following essential guidelines are included in all of these codes:

- *Minimize risks to research participants.* Use methods that have the least potential for causing harm or stress for research participants. During the research, monitor the procedures to be sure to avoid any unforeseen stress or harm.

- *Describe the research to potential participants so they can determine whether they wish to participate.* Prospective participants must be told the purpose of the project, what they will be asked to do, whether there are any risks or potential harm, any benefits they may receive, that they are free to discontinue participation at any time without penalty, that they are entitled to a complete debriefing at the end of the project, and any other relevant information the review panel deems appropriate. After the study has been explained, participants sign a document that says they understand what they will do in the study. Special caution must be exercised in obtaining consent for the participation of children and adolescents, as well as people who have conditions that affect intellectual functioning (e.g., Alzheimer's disease, severe head injury). In these cases, consent from a parent, legal guardian, or other responsible person, in addition to the agreement of the person him- or herself, is necessary for participation.

- *Avoid deception; if participants must be deceived, provide a thorough explanation of the true nature of the experiment as soon as possible.* Providing complete information about a study in advance sometimes biases or distorts a person's responses.

Consequently, investigators may provide participants with partial information about the study or even mislead them about its true purpose. As soon as it is feasible—typically just after the experiment—any false information that was given to research participants must be corrected, and the reasons for the deception must be provided.

- *Results should be anonymous or confidential.* Research results should be anonymous, which means that people's data cannot be linked to their name. When anonymity is not possible, research results should be confidential, which means the identity of participants is known only to the investigator conducting the study.

The requirement for informed consent is very important. If prospective participants cannot complete the informed consent procedure themselves, perhaps because they are incapacitated or because they have a condition, such as Alzheimer's disease, that causes intellectual impairment, special cautions must be taken. The American Geriatrics Society (1998) and the Alzheimer's Association (2004), among other professional organizations, have published guidelines outlining some of these protections. For example, when the participant cannot understand the consent process, someone else (usually a family member) must complete it. In addition, the researcher must describe the procedures to the participant and still obtain the participant's assent. However, this process is task specific; some cognitively impaired people, particularly early in the disease process, can respond appropriately to certain types of consent. And researchers can obtain advance consent for future participation when the cognitive impairment is more severe. In all cases, though, researchers must take extra precautions to be sensitive to these individuals; for example, if it becomes apparent that the participant does not like the procedures, the researcher must stop collecting data from that individual.

These ethical principles provide important protections for participants and investigators alike. By treating research participants with respect, investigators are in a better position to make important discoveries about adult development and aging.

ADULT DEVELOPMENT IN ACTION

If you were responsible for making grants at your local United Way organization, how might you determine through research whether the programs you fund actually have the outcomes they claim?

SOCIAL POLICY IMPLICATIONS

Creating sound social policy requires good information. Elected officials and others who create policy rely on research findings to provide the basis for policy. In terms of social policies affecting older adults, the data obtained through the use of the research designs discussed earlier are critical.

For example, research such as Schaie's research on intellectual development described in the How Do We Know? feature had a major impact on the elimination of nearly all mandatory retirement rules in the 1980s. Research on worker satisfaction and post retirement lifestyles influenced decisions in corporations such as McDonald's and Wal-Mart to hire older adults, who are highly reliable employees. The buying power of older adults has resulted in major advertising campaigns for everything from calcium replacement medications to active lifestyles.

In each of the remaining chapters, we will be highlighting a particular social policy and how it relates to research. By making these ties, you will be able to understand better how research findings can be applied to address social issues.

SUMMARY

1.1 Perspectives on Adult Development and Aging

What is gerontology? How does ageism relate to stereotypes of aging?

- Gerontology is the study of aging from maturity through old age, as well as the study of older adults as a special group.

- Myths of aging lead to negative stereotypes of older people, which can result in ageism, a form of discrimination against older people simply because of their age.

What is the life-span perspective?

- The life-span perspective divides human development into two phases: an early phase (childhood and adolescence) and a later phase (young adulthood, middle age, and old age).

- There are four key features of the life-span perspective: multidirectionality, plasticity, historical context, and multiple causation.

What are the characteristics of the older adult population?

- The number of older adults in the United States and other industrialized countries is increasing rapidly because of better health care, including declines in mortality during childbirth. The large numbers of older adults have important implications for human services.

- The number of older Latino, Asian American, and Native American adults will increase much faster between now and 2050 than will the number of European American and African American older adults.

- Whether older adults reflect individualism or collectivism has implications for interventions.

- The increase in numbers of older adults is most rapid in developing countries.

1.2 Issues in Studying Adult Development and Aging

What four main forces shape development?

- Development is shaped by four forces. (1) Biological forces include all genetic and health-related factors. (2) Psychological forces include all internal perceptual, cognitive, emotional, and personality factors. (3) Sociocultural forces include interpersonal, societal, cultural, and ethnic factors.

(4) Life-cycle forces reflect differences in how the same event or combination of biological, psychological, and sociocultural forces affects people at different points in their lives.

What are normative age-graded influences, normative history-graded influences, and nonnormative influences?

- Normative age-graded influences are life experiences that are highly related to chronological age. Normative history-graded influences are events that most people in a specific culture experience at the same time. Nonnormative influences are events that may be important for a specific individual but are not experienced by most people

How do culture and ethnicity influence aging?

- Culture and ethnicity jointly provide status, social settings, living conditions, and personal experiences for people of all ages. Culture can be defined as shared basic value orientations, norms, beliefs, and customary habits and ways of living, and it provides the basic worldview of a society. Ethnicity is an individual and collective sense of identity based on historical and cultural group membership and related behaviors and beliefs.

What is the meaning of age?

- Three types of aging are distinguished. (1) Primary aging is normal, disease-free development during adulthood. (2) Secondary aging is developmental changes that are related to disease. (3) Tertiary aging is the rapid losses that occur shortly before death.

- Chronological age is a poor descriptor of time-dependent processes and serves only as a shorthand for the passage of calendar time. Time-dependent processes do not actually cause behavior.

- Perceived age is the age you think of yourself as being.

- Better definitions of age include biological age (where a person is relative to the maximum number of years he or she could live), psychological age (where a person is in terms of the abilities people use to adapt to changing environmental demands), and sociocultural age (where a person is in terms of the specific set of roles adopted in relation to other members of the society and culture).

What are the nature–nurture, stability–change, continuity–discontinuity, and the "universal versus context-specific development" issues?

- The nature–nurture issue concerns the extent to which inborn, hereditary characteristics (nature) and experiential, or environmental, influences (nurture) determine who we are. The focus on nature and nurture must be on how they interact.

■ The stability–change issue concerns the degree to which people remain the same over time.

■ The continuity–discontinuity issue concerns competing views of how to describe change: as a smooth progression over time (continuity) or as a series of abrupt shifts (discontinuity).

■ The issue of universal versus context-specific development concerns whether there is only one pathway of development or several. This issue becomes especially important in interpreting cultural and ethnic group differences.

1.3 Research Methods

What approaches do scientists use to measure behavior in adult development and aging research?

■ Measures used in research must be reliable (measure things consistently) and valid (measure what they are supposed to measure).

■ Systematic observation involves watching people and carefully recording what they say or do. Two forms are common: naturalistic observation (observing people behaving spontaneously in a real-world setting) and structured observations (creating a setting that will elicit the behavior of interest).

■ If behaviors are hard to observe directly, researchers often create tasks that sample the behavior of interest.

■ Self-reports involve people's answers to questions presented in a questionnaire or interview about a topic of interest.

■ Most research on adults has focused on middle-class, well-educated European Americans. This creates serious problems for understanding the development experiences of other groups of people.

What are the general designs for doing research?

■ Experiments consist of manipulating one or more independent variables, measuring one or more dependent variables, and randomly assigning participants to the experimental and control groups. Experiments provide information about cause and effect.

■ Correlational designs address relations between variables; they do not provide information about cause and effect but do provide information about the strength of the relation between the variables.

■ Case studies are systematic investigations of individual people that provide detailed descriptions of people's behavior in everyday situations.

What specific designs are unique to adult development and aging research?

■ Age effects reflect underlying biological, psychological, and sociocultural changes. Cohort effects are differences caused by experiences and circumstances unique to the generation to which one belongs. Time-of-measurement effects reflect influences of the specific historical time when one is obtaining information. Developmental research designs represent various combinations of age, cohort, and time-of-measurement effects. Confounding is any situation in which one cannot determine which of two or more effects is responsible for the behaviors being observed.

■ Cross-sectional designs examine multiple cohorts and age groups at a single point in time. They can identify only age differences and confound age and cohort. The use of extreme age groups (young and older adults) is problematic in that the samples may not be representative, age should be treated as a continuous variable, and the measures may not be equivalent across age groups.

■ Longitudinal designs examine one cohort over two or more times of measurement. They can identify age change but have several problems, including practice effects, dropout, and selective survival. Longitudinal designs confound age and time of measurement. Microgenetic studies are short-term longitudinal designs that measure behaviors very closely over relatively brief periods of time.

■ Sequential designs involve more than one cross-sectional (cross-sequential) or longitudinal (longitudinal sequential) design. Although they are complex and expensive, they are important because they help disentangle age, cohort, and time-of-measurement effects.

■ Meta-analyses examine the consistency of findings across many research studies.

What ethical procedures must researchers follow?

■ Investigators must obtain informed consent from their participants before conducting research.

REVIEW QUESTIONS

1.1 Perspectives on Adult Development and Aging

- What are the premises of the life-span perspective?
- How are population demographics changing around the world, and what difference does it make?

1.2 Issues in Studying Adult Development and Aging

- What are the four basic forces in human development?
- What are the major characteristics of normative age-graded, normative history-graded, and non-normative influences?
- How do nature and nurture interact?
- What are culture and ethnicity?
- In what ways can age be defined? What are the advantages and disadvantages of each definition?
- What is the stability–change issue?
- What is the continuity–discontinuity issue? What kinds of theories derive from each view?
- What is the universal versus context-specific development issue, and how does it relate to sociocultural forces?

1.3 Research Methods

- What are the reliability and validity of a measure?
- What are the three main approaches scientists use to measure behavior in adult development and aging research? What are the strengths and weaknesses of each?
- How do we know whether a sample is representative?
- What is an experiment? What information does it provide?
- What is a correlational design? What information does it provide?
- What is a case study? What information does it provide?
- What are age, cohort, and time-of-measurement effects? How and why are they important for developmental research?
- What is a cross-sectional design? What are its advantages and disadvantages?
- What is a longitudinal design? What are its advantages and disadvantages?
- What differences are there between cross-sectional and longitudinal designs in terms of uncovering age differences and age changes?
- What are sequential designs? What different types are there? What are their advantages and disadvantages?
- What are the limitations of the extreme age groups design?
- What steps must researchers take to protect the rights of participants?

INTEGRATING CONCEPTS IN DEVELOPMENT

- Analyze each of the four major controversies in development in terms of the four developmental forces. What real-world examples can you think of that are examples of each combination of controversy and force?
- Using yourself as an example, figure out your age using chronological, perceived, biological, psychological, and sociocultural definitions. How do they differ? Why?
- Using the Leah and Sarah vignette as an example, design cross-sectional, longitudinal, and sequential studies of two different styles of caring for people with Alzheimer's disease. What will you learn from each of the studies?

KEY TERMS

age effects One of the three fundamental effects examined in developmental research, along with cohort and time-of-measurement effects, which reflects the influence of time-dependent processes on development.

ageism The untrue assumption that chronological age is the main determinant of human characteristics and that one age is better than another.

biological forces One of four basic forces of development that includes all genetic and health-related factors.

biopsychosocial framework Way of organizing the biological, psychological, and sociocultural forces on human development.

case study An intensive investigation of individual people.

cohort A group of people born at the same point or specific time span in historical time.

cohort effects One of the three basic influences examined in developmental research, along with age and time-of-measurement effects, which reflects differences caused by experiences and circumstances unique to the historical time in which one lives.

confounding Any situation in which one cannot determine which of two or more effects is responsible for the behaviors being observed.

continuity–discontinuity controversy The debate over whether a particular developmental phenomenon represents smooth progression over time (continuity) or a series of abrupt shifts (discontinuity).

correlational study An investigation in which the strength of association between variables is examined.

cross-sectional study A developmental research design in which people of different ages and cohorts are observed at one time of measurement to obtain information about age differences.

dependent variable Behaviors or outcomes measured in an experiment.

emerging adulthood A period when individuals are not adolescents but are not yet fully adults.

experiment A study in which participants are randomly assigned to experimental and control groups and in which an independent variable is manipulated to observe its effects on a dependent variable so that cause-and-effect relations can be established.

gerontology The study of aging from maturity through old age.

independent variable The variable manipulated in an experiment.

life-cycle forces One of the four basic forces of development that reflects differences in how the same event or combination of biological, psychological, and sociocultural forces affects people at different points in their lives.

life-span perspective A view of the human life-span that divides it into two phases: childhood/adolescence and young/middle/late adulthood.

longitudinal study A developmental research design that measures one cohort over two or more times of measurement to examine age changes.

meta-analysis A technique that allows researchers to synthesize the results of many studies to estimate relations between variables.

microgenetic study A special type of longitudinal design in which participants are tested repeatedly over a span of days or weeks, typically with the aim of observing change directly as it occurs.

nature–nurture issue A debate over the relative influence of genetics and the environment on development.

nonnormative influences Random events that are important to an individual but do not happen to most people.

normative age-graded influences Experiences caused by biological, psychological, and sociocultural forces that are closely related to a person's age.

normative history-graded influences Events that most people in a specific culture experience at the same time.

plasticity The belief that capacity is not fixed, but can be learned or improved with practice.

primary aging The normal, disease-free development during adulthood.

psychological forces One of the four basic forces of development that includes all internal perceptual, cognitive, emotional, and personality factors.

reliability The ability of a measure to produce the same value when used repeatedly to measure the identical phenomenon over time.

secondary aging Developmental changes that are related to disease, lifestyle, and other environmental changes that are not inevitable.

self-reports People's answers to questions about a topic of interest.

sequential designs Types of developmental research designs involving combinations of cross-sectional and longitudinal designs.

sociocultural forces One of the four basic forces of development that include interpersonal, societal, cultural, and ethnic factors.

stability–change issue A debate over the degree to which people remain the same over time as opposed to being different.

systematic observation A type of measurement involving watching people and carefully recording what they say or do.

tertiary aging Rapid losses occurring shortly before death.

time-of-measurement effects One of the three fundamental effects examined in developmental research, along with age and cohort effects, which result from the time at which the data are collected.

universal versus context-specific development controversy A debate over whether there is a single pathway of development, or several.

validity The degree to which an instrument measures what it is supposed to measure.

RESOURCES

Access quizzes, glossaries, flashcards, and more at www.cengagebrain.com.

CHAPTER 2

NEUROSCIENCE AS A BASIS FOR ADULT DEVELOPMENT AND AGING

YOU SEE AND HEAR MORE AND MORE ADVERTISEMENTS AND LITERATURE TOUTING THE IMPORTANCE OF "BRAIN FITNESS." In the grocery store and on television, marketers and self-help solicitors encourage people to eat the right "brain foods" filled with antioxidants. *They promise that these* antioxidants *will protect your cells from the harmful effect of* free radicals, *substances that can damage cells, including brain cells, and play a role in cancer and other diseases as we grow older.* Similarly, advertisements promote exercising your brain through mental aerobics such as playing chess, reading the newspaper, and attending plays. There is an entire industry of online and computerized brain-training games, such as Lumosity.com, aimed at delaying the onset of cognitive decline and prolonging cognitive vitality. *This relatively recent phenomenon has coincided with the rapid surge of research in* neuroscience *or the study of the brain—in particular, plasticity of the aging brain.* Images such as the one shown below help us measure brain activity. Evidence that the brain can change for the better as we grow older sends an intriguing message to our aging population. However, there is danger in this. As in any relatively new field, descriptions in the media, especially the Internet, may extend well beyond the actual scope of our scientific understanding of the brain.

In this chapter we explore our understanding of the aging brain by examining contemporary theories and recent empirical findings of neuroscience and aging. First, we briefly review the various neuroscience theories underlying and techniques used in studying the brain. Next, we focus on cognitive neuroscience and aging including age-related change in brain structures, neurochemical properties, and brain function. Two contemporary areas of research are explored, including cultural influences on brain aging, as well as neural plasticity in later adulthood. Finally, we explore more recent developments in the area of social neuroscience and aging—in particular, intriguing findings that reveal the neurological underpinnings of enhanced emotional processing in older adulthood in contrast to declines in cognitive processing such as the ability to control information in the conscious mind.

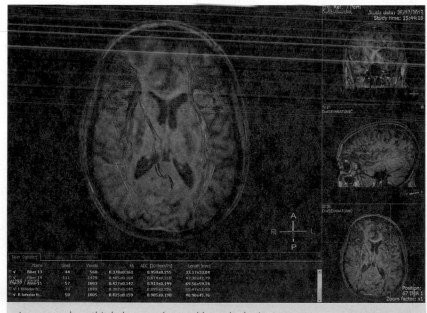

Images such as this help us understand how the brain operates.

2.1 The Neuroscience Approach

LEARNING OBJECTIVES

- What brain imaging techniques are used in neuroscience research?
- What are the main research methods used and issues studied in neuroscience research in adult development and aging?

At age 70, Margaret was having trouble moving the left side of her body. With the aid of accurate brain imaging techniques, she was diagnosed as having a tumor located at the front of the right motor cortex. (Because the brain is wired in general to control the side of the body opposite of the side of the brain in question, movement on one's left side is controlled by the right side of the brain in the area called the motor cortex.) With image-guided surgery, the tumor was removed, and Margaret recovered comfortably.

How did Margaret's physicians figure out what was wrong with her? We are learning a great deal about the relations between changes in the brain and changes in behavior through technological advances in noninvasive imaging and in assessing psychological functioning (Blanchard-Fields, 2010; Linden, 2012). Neuroimaging *is a set of techniques in which pictures of the brain are taken in various ways to provide understanding of both normal and abnormal cognitive aging.*

Neuroimaging Techniques

What neuroimaging does is allow us to see inside the brain of a living person to examine the various structures of the brain. Neuroimaging has revolutionized our understanding of the relations between the brain and our behavior, and it is responsible for an explosion of knowledge over the past few decades. Advances in neuroimaging have led to much of our understanding of such diseases as Alzheimer's disease (which we will consider in detail in Chapter 10) and to other key insights into age-related changes that occur to everyone and those changes that reflect disease or other abnormal changes.

But neuroimaging must be used carefully and ethically. For one thing, we are still figuring out which changes in the brain are normative and which ones are not. We need to know what a "healthy" brain looks like at different points in the human life span. So just because we observe a change does not mean anything

in and of itself unless additional research is done to place it in context.

Two neuroimaging techniques are used most often:

1. **Structural neuroimaging** *provides highly detailed images of anatomical features in the brain.* The most commonly used are X-rays, computerized tomography (CT) scans, and magnetic resonance imaging (MRI). Images from structural neuroimaging techniques are like photographs in that they document what a specific brain structure looks like at a specific point in time. Structural neuroimaging is usually effective at identifying such things as bone fractures, tumors, and other conditions that cause structural damage in the brain, such as strokes.

2. **Functional neuroimaging** *provides an indication of brain activity but not high anatomical detail.* The most commonly used neuroimaging techniques are single photon emission computerized tomography (SPECT), positron emission tomography (PET), functional magnetic resonance imaging (fMRI), magnetoencephalograpy (or multichannel encephalography), and near infrared spectroscopic imaging (NIRSI). In general, fMRI is the most commonly used technique in cognitive neuroscience research (Poldrack, 2012). Functional neuroimaging provides researchers with information about what parts of the brain are active when people are doing specific tasks. A typical image will show different levels of brain activity as different colors; for example, red on an image might indicate high levels of brain activity in that region, whereas blue might indicate low levels of activity.

These techniques, coupled with tests of behavior such as specific cognitive processing tasks (e.g., recognizing which pictures you studied from a deck containing pictures you saw and pictures you did not), have shown quite convincingly that age-related brain changes are responsible for age-related changes in performance (Blanchard-Fields, 2010; Guidotti Breting, Tuminello, & Han, 2012).

In Margaret's case, a magnetic resonance imaging (MRI) scan was conducted. This identified areas of the brain associated with specific functions. The scan produced an image showing the brain location of interest and the outline of a tumor in the area of the brain involved in controlling movement.

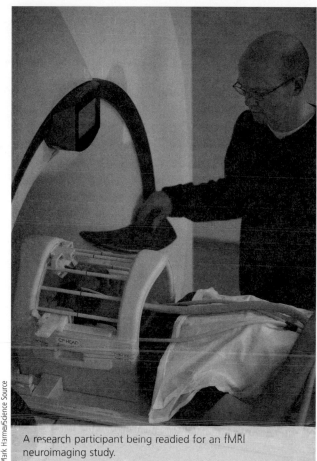

Mark Harmel/Science Source

A research participant being readied for an fMRI neuroimaging study.

In addition to using MRIs to locate brain tumors, we are interested in how neuroimaging techniques advance our understanding of how the brain changes as we grow older. Do the changes reflect decline, stability, or perhaps improvement and compensation? Is there plasticity or growth in the aging brain? These are important questions that researchers in the field of contemporary neuroscience and aging are exploring.

A neuroscientific approach to the study of aging has several advantages. For example, the neuroscience approach has resulted in the development of new, effective interventions that are enhancing the quality of life of older adults and that can be evaluated not only by observing behavioral change but also at the neurological level, such as the relationship between physical activity and cognitive aging (e.g., Jak, 2012).

These techniques and others can test models of cognitive aging. Neuroscience has become increasingly more relevant to cognitive aging research as the focus has expanded beyond studying pathologies of the aging brain, such as Alzheimer's or Parkinson's disease, toward investigating normative and healthy aging. In addition, neuroscientific data are more informative for models of cognitive aging and usher in increased progress in the field by testing established theories using cutting-edge methods. Furthermore, examination of the structure and function of the brain has become even more informative for cognitive aging research as the focus has shifted from describing brain activation patterns toward explaining them.

Neuroscience Perspectives

Researchers take three general methodological perspectives in tackling the neuroscience of aging: the neuropsychological, the neurocorrelational, and the activation imaging approach (see Cabeza, 2004). *The neuropsychological approach compares brain functioning of healthy older adults with adults displaying various pathological disorders in the brain.* In this approach researchers are interested in whether patients of any age with damage in specific regions of the brain show similar cognitive deficits to those shown by healthy older adults. If this is the case, then researchers can conclude that decline in cognitive functioning as we grow older may be related to unfavorable changes in the same specific regions of the brain observed in the brain-damaged patients.

Let's suppose this type of comparison is made between healthy older adults and persons showing frontal lobe damage. People with brain damage in the frontal lobe display lower levels of dopamine (a chemical substance we will consider a bit later in detail), which results in a decrease in how quickly mental processing occurs, termed speed of processing. Interestingly, this same slowing resembles what is observed in healthy older adults.

Another important objective of research using this approach is to isolate the neural or brain mechanisms that are associated with both normal and pathological decline in cognitive functions. These findings stimulate development of theories by identifying influential factors that warrant theoretical explanation as to how and why these factors may cause cognitive decline as we age.

Just as we saw in Chapter 1 in relation to adult development and aging research in general, neuroscience researchers use certain research designs to study changes in brain structures and processes.

The **neurocorrelational approach** *attempts to relate measures of cognitive performance to measures of brain structure or functioning.* For example, a researcher may be interested in the correlation between cognitive behavior, such as the ability to remember information over short periods of time, and neural structural measures, such as the volume of the brain or activity in specific areas of the brain (Cabeza & Dennis, 2013). Instead of direct measures of brain structure or functioning, some researchers investigate the correlation between behavioral tests that are associated with the function of specific brain regions (e.g., tests of frontal lobe functioning). However, this approach is speculative, in that we cannot be certain whether the tests accurately reflect the actual anatomical and functional activity of the specific brain region under investigation.

The **activation imaging approach** *attempts to directly link functional brain activity with cognitive behavioral data.* This approach allows real-time investigation of changes in brain function as they affect cognitive performance in older adults. As you may have surmised, this approach relies on functional neuroimaging techniques, such as fMRI. For example, studies using this approach have found that younger adults' brains show unilateral activation (i.e., activation in only one hemisphere of the brain) when they perform specific cognitive tasks, but older adults' brains tend to show increased activation in both brain hemispheres when performing the same tasks (see Cabeza, 2002; Grady, 2012). As we will discuss later, this difference in activation in younger and older adult brains may provide neurological evidence that older adults' brains compensate for age-related changes. **Compensatory changes** *are changes that allow older adults to adapt to the inevitable behavioral decline resulting from changes in specific areas of the brain.*

Overall, neuroscience has brought an important perspective to studying cognitive aging, influencing theories of adulthood in several ways. First, theories of brain-behavior relations can be tested using these approaches. For instance, age-related changes in how we selectively direct our attention to specific characteristics of our environment can be validated by examining how age-related changes in performance are associated with both functional and structural changes in the brain. In other words, we can explain how changes in performance map to changes in the brain.

Second, research methods that focus on the age-related changes in the structure and functioning of the brain can help to explain why certain cognitive functions, such as well-practiced tasks, vocabulary, and wisdom, can be preserved into old age while other functions, such as processing speed, decline rapidly as people age. By carefully tracking which brain structures and functions change in which direction—or in some cases remain the same—we can differentiate and explain seemingly contradictory patterns of behavior over time.

Neuroscientific methods, however, have limitations (Alam, Patel, & Giordano, 2012). Like any set of tools, neuroscience techniques must be used appropriately and ethically. Nevertheless, advances in the field of neuroscience have had a major impact on our understanding of cognitive aging because they have revealed new findings that psychological theories have to account for and be consistent with.

Before we explore some of the scientific research on age-related changes in the brain, complete the Discovering Development exercise. Compare your findings with the evidence described in the text that follows. What similarities and differences are revealed?

DISCOVERING DEVELOPMENT:

WHAT DO PEOPLE BELIEVE ABOUT BRAIN FITNESS?

With all the hype about keeping your brain fit, what do people believe you have to do to accomplish this? To find out, ask some people of different ages these questions:

- What happens to the brain as we grow older?
- What do you think causes these changes?
- What do you think you can do to make sure that the brain stays fit as you grow older?

Compile the results from your interviews and compare them with what you discover in this chapter. To what extent do people's beliefs correspond to the scientific evidence? In which areas are they completely off base?

ADULT DEVELOPMENT IN ACTION

How would a physician decide whether to use structural neuroimaging or functional neuroimaging to aid in a clinical diagnosis?

2.2 Neuroscience and Adult Development and Aging

LEARNING OBJECTIVES

- How is the brain organized structurally?
- What are the basic changes in neurons as we age?
- What changes occur in neurotransmitters with age?
- What changes occur in brain structures with age?
- What do age-related structural brain changes mean for behavior?

Samuel is 73, and he is worried about contracting Alzheimer's disease. He remembers that his father became disoriented at this age and had trouble remembering things that he had just been told. How can Samuel find out if his brain is aging normally or pathologically? Psychological tests are somewhat predictive of disease—but not completely. This is a dilemma older adults are facing in our society today.

Much adult development and aging research has focused on cognitive aging, both normal and pathological. Historically, this research was based on behavioral data, which in turn gave rise to the classic theories of cognitive aging (see Chapter 6; Salthouse, 1996; Schaie, 1996). More recently, though, the availability of neuroscientific methods has stimulated research that allows us to study cognitive processes—and changes in these processes—in the living brain, using noninvasive brain imaging techniques discussed earlier. For instance, brain activity involved in the identification of faces occurs in areas of the brain that are among the first affected by Alzheimer's

disease (Saavedra, Iglesias, & Olivares, 2012). And so changes in brain activity in these regions may signal the onset of the disease before other, more apparent changes, occur.

This is exactly the type of information in which Samuel, the man in the vignette, would be interested. To make these types of discoveries, we must first have a strong knowledge base of how the brain ages normally. Let's examine what the field of neuroscience and aging has contributed to our knowledge of the aging brain.

How Is the Brain Organized?

The human brain is an amazingly complex organ. It still remains more flexible and capable than any computer, handling billions of computations and providing us with the wide range of emotions we experience. Needless to say, the structure of such a complex organ is, well, complex. *At the most basic level, the brain is made up of cells called* neurons, *an example of which is shown in Figure 2.1. Key structural features of the neuron are the* dendrites, *which act like antennas to receive signals from other nearby neurons, the* axon, *which is part of the neuron containing the* neurofibers, *which are the structures that carry information inside the neuron from the dendrites to the* terminal branches, *which are the endpoints of the neuron. Neurons do not physically touch each other. In order for information to be passed from one neuron to another, the terminal branches release chemicals called* neurotransmitters, *that travel across the space between neurons, called the* synapse, *where they are received by the dendrites of the next neuron.*

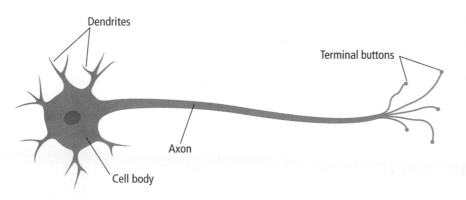

Dendrites

Terminal buttons

Axon

Cell body

Direction of information flow

Figure 2.1

A typical neuron showing dendrites, axon, neurofibers, and terminal branches.

© 2015 Cengage Learning

Now that we know the basic building block of the brain, let's take a look at how the neurons themselves are organized into various brain structures. Figure 2.2 shows the major structures of the brain that are the focus of neuroscience research in adult development and aging. *The study of the structure of the brain, called,* **neuroanatomy,** *is fundamental to neuroscience.* We will refer to a number of brain regions that exhibit age-related changes in both structure and function.

The **cerebral cortex** *is the outermost part of the brain. It consists of two hemispheres (left and right) that are connected by a thick bundle of neurons called the* **corpus callosum.** Most neuroscience research focuses on the cerebral cortex.

Each region of the brain has distinguishing features that relate to the specific functions those regions control. For example, in most people, language processing is associated primarily with the left hemisphere, whereas recognizing nonspeech sounds, emotions, and faces is associated with the right hemisphere. *The* **prefrontal and frontal cortex** *is intimately involved in higher-order* **executive functions** *such as the ability to make and carry out plans, switch between tasks, and maintain attention and focus, and connects*

with other key brain structures that are involved with emotion. In addition, the **cerebellum,** *at the back of the brain, controls equilibrium and the coordination of fine motor movements, and may be involved in some cognitive functions. The* **hippocampus,** *located in the middle of the brain, is a key structure associated with memory. The* **limbic system** *is a set of brain structures involved with emotion, motivation, and long-term memory, among other functions. For adult development and aging research, the most important components of the limbic system include the* **amygdala,** *and the hippocampus.*

Details regarding both additional brain structures and the functional aspects of the various regions of the brain will be discussed more fully with respect to specific age-related changes.

What Age-Related Changes Occur in Neurons?

Several changes occur with age in neurons (Juraska & Lowery, 2012). As we age, the number of neurons in the brain declines. Structural changes include decreases in the size and number of dendrites, the development of tangles in the fibers that make up the

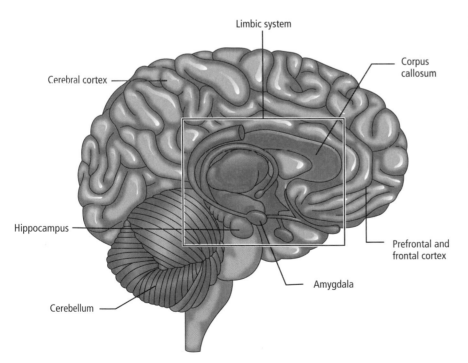

Cerebral cortex

Limbic system

Corpus callosum

Hippocampus

Cerebellum

Prefrontal and frontal cortex

Amygdala

Figure 2.2

Major structures of the human brain showing cerebral cortex, corpus callosum, prefrontal and frontal cortex, cerebellum hippocampus, limbic system, and amygdala.

© 2015 Cengage Learning

axon, and increases in the deposit of certain proteins. The number of potential connections also declines, as measured by the number of synapses among neurons.

Interestingly, these same changes occur but in much greater numbers in diseases such as Alzheimer's disease, leading some researchers to speculate that there may be a link between normal brain aging and pathological brain aging having to do with the speed and number of changes, not in the kind of changes that occur.

What Age-Related Changes Occur in Neurotransmitters?

As noted earlier, because neurons do not touch each other, much of the information transmission from one neuron to another occurs chemically via neurotransmitters. Advances have also been made in measuring changes in neurotransmitters in the aging brain. Let's explore some of the key findings.

Dopamine. One neurotransmitter that has received a great deal of attention is dopamine. Dopamine *is a neurotransmitter associated with higher-level cognitive functioning like inhibiting thoughts, attention, and planning, as well as emotion, movement, and pleasure and pain. Collectively, the neurons that use dopamine are called the* dopaminergic system. For example, high dopamine levels are linked to cognitive processing that is effortful and deliberate, but not to the processes that are more automatic and less effortful. To investigate dopamine, the majority of studies have used postmortem analyses (i.e., analyses during autopsies), results from neuropsychological tests, and simulated modeling and the imaging of dopamine activity. Bäckman et al. (2006) concluded that there is clear evidence that effective functioning of the dopaminergic system declines in normal aging. Exactly what does this mean?

Declines in the dopaminergic system are related to declines in several different aspects of memory (Nyberg, et al., 2012), such as episodic (short-term) memory and memory for information acquired in tasks that must be performed quickly, and the amount of information that can be held in mind at any given moment (called working memory). As we shall see in Chapter 6, these are cognitive tasks that are effortful and not automatic. Fewer age differences are observed in more automatic tasks, like judging the familiarity of

information. Overall, the studies using neuroscience methods to examine changes in the dopaminergic system with increasing age suggest that these changes play a role in cognitive aging.

Other Neurotransmitters. The neurotransmitter serotonin is involved in several types of brain processes, including memory, mood, appetite, and sleep. Abnormal processing of serotonin has been shown to be related to cognitive decline both in normal aging and in Alzheimer's disease, as well as other disorders such as schizophrenia (Rodriguez, Noristani, & Verkhratsky, 2012). In Chapter 10, we will return to the role of serotonin in mental disorders.

Another important neurotransmitter related to aging is acetylcholine. In the brain, acetylcholine has an important role in arousal, sensory perception, and sustaining attention (Ando, 2012). Damage to the brain structures that use acetylcholine is associated with serious memory declines such as those found in Alzheimer's disease.

What Age-Related Changes Occur in Brain Structures?

As you already know from observation or personal experience, our bodies undergo visible changes with age. Chapter 3 will provide additional detail. The brain is no exception. Documenting those changes, however, has not been direct until the past decade. As a result, the majority of studies examining structural changes in the brain as we grow older have applied a correlational approach by employing postmortem analyses of adults' brains.

More recently, researchers have been able to use cross-sectional and longitudinal designs to examine age differences in the brain using brain imaging techniques. In these studies, different regions of the brain are examined in terms of various structural changes and deficiencies, such as thinning and shrinkage in volume and density, and the declining health of the brain's white matter, or white matter hyperintensities (WMH). White matter *refers to neurons that are covered by myelin that serve to transmit information from one part of the cerebral cortex to another or from the cerebral cortex to other parts of the brain.* White matter hyperintensities (WMH) *are determined by the observation of high signal intensity or a bright spotty appearance on images, which indicate brain pathologies such as neural atrophy* (Nordahl, Ranganath, Yonelinas, DeCarli, Fletcher, & Jagust, 2006).

Overall, postmortem and neuroimaging studies demonstrate that many changes occur with age. One important change is that considerable shrinkage occurs in the brain by late life. However, this shrinkage is selective (Juraska & Lowry, 2012). For example, the prefrontal cortex, the hippocampus, and the cerebellum show profound shrinkage. In contrast, the areas of the brain related to sensory functions, such as the visual cortex, show relatively little shrinkage.

The white matter area also shows deterioration with increasing age. *A neuroimaging method* called *diffusion tensor imaging (DTI) assesses the rate and direction that water diffuses through the white matter.* This results in an index of the structural health of the white matter (Madden et al., 2012). By using DTI, studies examining WMH have demonstrated that deterioration of white matter may represent a cause of increased prefrontal cortex dysfunction in older adults. As we will see later, deterioration of the prefrontal cortex has important implications for cognitive functioning in late adulthood. Of equal importance is the fact that WMH are linked to cerebrovascular diseases (e.g., stroke resulting from hypertension), which are preventable and can be treated through medication and changes in lifestyle.

What Do Structural Brain Changes Mean?

As you were reading about the structural changes that occur in the brain with age, you probably were wondering what these changes mean in terms of behavior, especially cognitive functioning. As we will discover later in this book, with increasing age, many facets of thinking, learning, and remembering become less efficient and effective. So it should not be surprising that executive functioning and other aspects of cognition have received most of the attention in cognitive neuroscience and aging research.

Linking Structural Changes with Executive Functioning. Understanding how changes in brain structures affect behavior involves careful linking of specific brain structures to specific behaviors. First, it is necessary to carefully describe the target behavior. Second, careful documentation of structural changes in the brain is necessary. Third, the two sets of data need to be studied to establish the link.

Executive functioning is a good example, as its various aspects are well described. Among the most studied aspects of executive functioning are processes such as the ability to control what one is thinking about at any specific point in time, and the ability to focus on relevant information and eliminate the irrelevant. Executive functioning failures in older adults can result in the erroneous selection of irrelevant information as relevant, the inability to divert attention away from irrelevant information to the task at hand, and inefficiency in switching tasks, among others (Alexander et al., 2012). For example, when older adults are reading an article that is filled with information some of which is true and some of which is false, even if they are told which information is false they still have a difficult time factoring out the false information in their understanding of the article.

Poor performance on executive functioning tasks has been linked to decreased volume of the prefrontal cortex (Juraska & Lowery, 2012). Evidence also suggests that WMH in healthy older adults who show no signs of serious cognitive disease (such as Alzheimer's disease) have been linked to lower cognitive test scores and decreased executive functioning (Madden et al., 2012). Age-related decline in the functioning of blood vessels in the brain may affect white matter structures that underlie all the areas important to executive functioning. Finally, how well one acquires new skills has been linked to the volumes of the prefrontal cortex and cerebellum (Juraska & Lowery, 2012).

Driving a car involves complex, higher-order cognitive skills that involve executive functioning.

Linking Structural Changes with Memory. Similar research has examined links between memory and specific structural changes in the brain. For example, reductions in volume in the hippocampus are related to memory decline (Juraska & Lowery, 2012).

Much research has examined specific areas in the temporal lobe (located above the ear) and its influence on memory by examining people with Alzheimer's disease (a type of dementia described in detail in Chapter 10). For example, atrophy (very severe shrinkage), many types of abnormal neurons, and large losses of neurons are observed in this region of the brain in persons with Alzheimer's disease, who also show profound memory impairment (Juraska & Lowery, 2012). Interestingly, research on older adults who do not show serious cognitive declines like those seen in Alzheimer's disease, but who are older than those studied who had Alzheimer's disease, has found similar correlations between temporal lobe atrophy and typical declines in memory performance seen in late life. Could Alzheimer's disease be an acceleration of normal aging processes as opposed to a separate disease process? We will take up this question again in Chapter 10.

Linking Structural Changes with Emotion. As we have just seen, the typical age-related changes observed in executive functioning and memory map onto age-related deterioration in specific brain structures. Let's now take a closer look at another very important aspect of the human experience—emotion—and see how structural brain changes affect it. To begin, let's consider an example of how neuroimaging research helps establish linkages between brain structures and behavior, in this case, emotion. An excellent example of how this research is done is a study by Winecoff and her colleagues (2011) described in the How Do We Know? feature.

HOW DO WE KNOW?:

THE AGING EMOTIONAL BRAIN

Who were the investigators, and what was the aim of the study? Very little research has examined the specific underlying neural mechanisms of emotion. Winecoff and her colleagues (2011) decided to examine these mechanisms and discover whether they differed with age.

How did the investigators measure the topic of interest? Winecoff and her colleagues used a battery of tests to measure cognitive performance and emotional behavior. They tested participants' immediate recall, delayed recall, and recognition. They also administered a response-time test to measure psychomotor speed, and a digit-span test to measure working memory. (A digit-span test is one in which strings of random digits are presented and the participant has to remember them in order. The longest number of digits the person can remember is called the "digit-span.") The researchers also had participants complete three questionnaires to measure various types of emotions.

After these measures were obtained, participants were given the cognitive reappraisal task depicted in Figure 2.3. In brief, participants learned a reappraisal strategy that involved thinking of themselves as an emotionally detached and objective third party. During the training session, they told the experimenter how they were thinking about the image to ensure task compliance, but they were instructed not to speak during the scanning session. This instruction was given to ensure that the brain activity measured was related to thinking, and not to the brain activity necessary to move one's tongue and mouth during speech, for example. During the functional magnetic resonance imaging (fMRI) session, participants completed 60 positive image trials (30 "Experience" and 30 "Reappraise"), 60 negative image trials (30 "Experience" and 30 "Reappraise") trials, and 30 neutral image trials (all "Experience"). Within each condition, half of the images contained people, and the other half did not. The fMRI session provided images of ongoing brain activity.

Who were the participants in the study? The sample consisted of 22 younger adults (average age = 23 years, range = 19−33 years) and 20 older adults (average age = 69 years; range = 59−73 years). Participants were matched on demographic variables including education. Participants received the cognitive, memory, and emotion tests on one day, and the reappraisal task in the fMRI session on a second day. Participants were paid $55.

What was the design of the study? The study used a cross-sectional design, with testing of two age groups over two sessions.

Were there ethical concerns with the study? All participants provided written consent under a protocol approved by the Institutional Review Board of Duke University Medical Center.

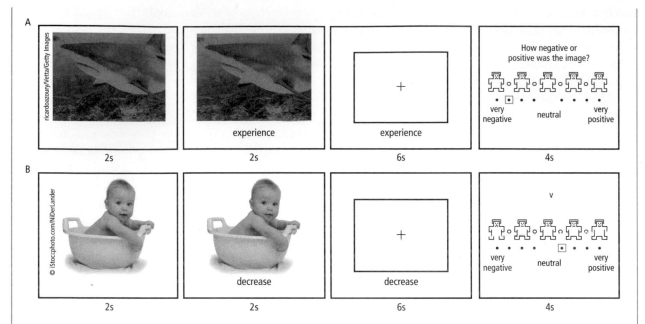

Figure 2.3

Cognitive reappraisal task. Participants were trained in the use of a reappraisal strategy for emotional regulation. (A) On "experience" trials, participants viewed an image and then received an instruction to experience naturally the emotions evoked by that image. The image then disappeared, but participants continued to experience their emotions throughout a 6-second delay period. At the end of the trial, the participants rated the perceived emotional valence of that image using an eight-item rating scale. (B) "Reappraise" trials had similar timing, except that the cue instructed participants to decrease their emotional response to the image by reappraising the image (e.g., distancing themselves from the scene). Shown are examples of images similar to those of the negative (A) and positive (B) images used in the study.

Source: Winecoff, A., LaBar, K. S. Madden, D. I., Cabeza, R., & Huettel, S. A. (in press). Cognitive and Neural Contributions to Emotion Regulation in Aging. Social Cognitive and Affective Neuroscience, 6. By permission of Oxford University Press.

What were the results? Younger and older adults performed the reappraisal tasks similarly; that is, in the reappraisal condition, positive images were reported as less positive and negative images were reported as less negative. However, older adults' reports of negative emotion were higher than those of younger adults in the negative reappraisal situation.

Examination of the fMRI results showed that reappraisals involved significant activation of specific areas in the prefrontal cortex for both positive and negative emotions. For both age groups, activity in the prefrontal area increased, and activity in the amygdala decreased during the reappraisal phase. These patterns are shown in Figure 2.4. As you can see in the top figure, certain areas in the prefrontal cortex showed a pattern of activation that followed participants' self-reports of emotion regulation. Shown here are activation patterns in the contrast between "Reappraise-Negative" and "Experience-Negative" conditions. The graph shows

that for both positive and negative stimuli, and for both younger and older adults, prefrontal activation increased in "Reappraise" (reap) trials compared to "Experience" (exp) trials. In contrast, the lower graph shows that in the amygdala (amy) there was a systematic decrease in activation during emotion regulation between "Experience-Negative" and "Reappraise-Negative" conditions.

Additional analyses of the fMRI data showed that emotion regulation modulates the functional interaction between the prefrontal cortex and the amygdala. Younger adults showed more activity in the prefrontal cortex during "Reappraise" trials for negative pictures than older adults did. Cognitive abilities were related to the degree of decrease in amygdala activation, independent of age.

What did the investigators conclude? Winecoff and her colleagues concluded that the prefrontal cortex plays a major role in emotional regulation, especially for older adults. In essence, the prefrontal

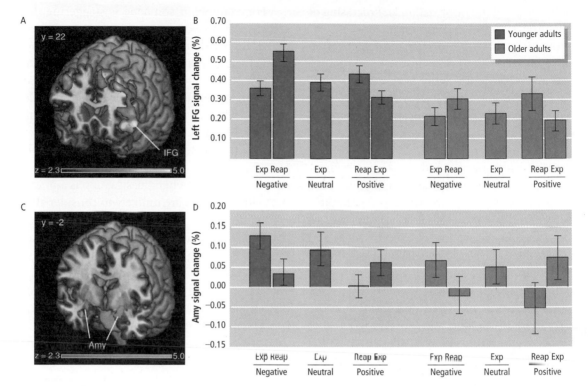

Figure 2.4

Modulation of prefrontal and amygdalar activation by emotion regulation.

Source: Winecoff, A., LaBar, K. S. Madden, D. J., Cabeza, R., & Huettel, S. A. (in press). Cognitive and Neural Contributions to Emotion Regulation in Aging. Social Cognitive and Affective Neuroscience, 6. By permission of Oxford University Press.

cortex may help suppress (regulate) emotions in the same way as that area of the brain is involved in inhibiting other behaviors. Importantly, the degree of emotional regulation was predicted by cognitive ability, with higher cognitive ability associated with higher emotional regulation. This may mean that as cognitive abilities decline, people may be less able to regulate their emotions, a pattern typical in such diseases as dementia. Thus, not only is there evidence of underlying brain structures playing critical roles in emotion regulation, but there may be a neurological explanation for the kinds of emotional outbursts that occur in dementia and related disorders.

What converging evidence would strengthen these conclusions? Winecoff and her colleagues studied only two age groups of healthy adults and did not include either old-old participants or adults with demonstrable cognitive impairment. It will be important to study these groups to map brain function changes and behavior more completely.

How does emotional processing change across adulthood? The quick answer is that it's complicated (Kaszniak & Menchola, 2012). In general, research shows that adults of all ages report about the same range and experience of emotion. But there is also evidence that changes in brain activity in the prefrontal cortex and the amygdala with age may be related to a decrease in processing of negative emotional information and an increase in processing of positive emotional information with age. These differences tend to be interpreted as reflecting increased emotional regulation with age;

in other words, older adults tend to be able to regulate their emotions better than younger adults. This may be due to a desire on the part of people as they age to develop closer, more meaningful relationships that generate positive emotions, while avoiding people and situations that generate negative ones.

Cognition and emotion interact. Kensinger and colleagues (Kensinger, 2012; Kensinger & Corkin, 2006) propose two distinct cognitive and neural processes that contribute to emotional processing and memory. The difference depends upon how emotionally arousing the information is. Processing of negative high-arousal information for memory is relatively automatic in nature and is linked to activation of the amygdala as it interacts with the hippocampus to support memory performance. For memory processing of negative low-arousal stimuli, more activation of the prefrontal cortex–hippocampus network is necessary.

Kensinger (2012) argues that whether emotional arousal enhances memory depends on the engagement in emotion-specific processes that are linked to these distinct neural processes. So when a person accurately remembers negative high-arousal items, this corresponds to increased activation of the amygdala and prefrontal cortex. Other studies support this conclusion. For instance, if the amygdala is damaged, individuals do not attend to arousing stimuli.

How do structural and functional changes in the brain affect these processes? The short answer is that it depends (Fossati, 2012; Lee & Siegle, 2012; Ray & Zald, 2012). Older adults show more brain activity between the prefrontal cortex and the medial temporal lobe than younger adults do, regardless of whether the content is emotionally positive or negative. These increases in connections may be due to age-related changes that occur in the prefrontal cortex that make it necessary for older adults to use more connections to process the information (Waring, Addis, & Kensinger, 2013). We'll return to this need for extra connections a bit later when we consider the notion of whether older adults compensate for brain changes.

Linking Structural Changes with Social-Emotional Cognition. What happens in the brain when things get even more complicated, such as when we have to process complex situations that involve social judgments, when memory, emotion, and previously learned information come together? The story begins in the early 2000s, when researchers first outlined a social cognitive neuroscience approach to attributional inferences, or how people make causal judgments about why social situations occur (e.g., Lieberman, Gaunt, Gilbert, & Trope, 2002). That work identified a social judgment process that involves a relatively automatic system in which people read cues in the environment quickly and easily, without deliberation, and then make social judgments.

For example, if someone is staggering down the hallway, we may automatically assume the person is intoxicated without taking into consideration many other factors that might cause someone to stagger (e.g., he is injured, he is experiencing a medical emergency). In other words, we have a tendency to automatically put the person into a preexisting social category. We base this judgment on easily activated, well-practiced categories of information based on our past experiences and current goals, and we do this most prominently when the situation is ambiguous. In such situations, we are unlikely to consider alternative explanations.

What's intriguing is that researchers have presented compelling evidence that drawing these kinds of quick conclusions in ambiguous situations is probably a result of how our brains are wired. It turns out that we have specialized areas in the brain, such as the lateral temporal cortex, amygdala, and basal ganglia, that are associated with automatic social cognition (Fossati, 2012; Lee & Siegle, 2012).

Researchers also have identified another system that underlies a more deliberative form of social cognitive judgments that employs symbolic logic and reflective awareness. The neural basis of these more reflective judgments appears to reside in the prefrontal cortex, the anterior cingulate cortex, and the hippocampus (Lee & Siegle, 2012).

So how do these different brain pathways change with age, and what difference does that make? The brain structures involved in more automatic processing (e.g., the amygdala) show less age-related deterioration, whereas those involved in more reflective processing (e.g., the prefrontal cortex) show more severe deterioration. Based on these findings, we would expect that older adults might tend to rely more on automatic processes.

Complex Development in the Prefrontal Cortex. There is no question that neuroscience research points to the central role played by the prefrontal cortex in adult development and aging. This part of the brain is intimately involved in the most important aspects of thinking and reasoning, including executive functioning, memory, and emotion. So it is probably not surprising to discover that at a detailed level, age-related changes in the prefrontal cortex are complex.

The most important arena in this complex pattern is in the interface between emotion and memory. We have already seen that brain pathways involved in memory tend to deteriorate with age, whereas key pathways involved in emotion do not. How is this explained?

Let's start by focusing on a well-documented effect, the positivity effect. *The positivity effect refers to the fact that older adults are more motivated to derive emotional meaning from life and to maintain positive feelings* (Isaacowitz & Blanchard-Fields, 2012; Scheibe & Carstensen, 2010). As a result, older adults are more likely than younger adults to attend to the emotional meaning of information.

Research shows that in addition to some common brain areas that process all emotion, there are also some unique pathways; for instance, positive emotional processing occurs in different brain regions from negative emotional processing (Fossati, 2012; Kensinger, 2012). Some of these pathways are the same for all adults. Specifically, the common pathways in emotion processing for adults of all ages include the amygdala and the part of the prefrontal cortex right behind the eyes (the lateral orbitofrontal cortex). For positive emotion processing, other parts of the front of the prefrontal cortex are involved. For negative emotion processing, the temporal region is brought into action instead.

But there are some important age-related differences in brain pathways, too, that help us understand age-related differences in emotion-related behaviors. When older adults process information that is emotionally positive, they also show increased activity in the middle portion of the prefrontal cortex, the amygdala, and the cingulate cortex (a structure that forms a "collar" around the corpus callosum). Bringing additional areas of the brain into play during processing is a phenomenon we will return to a bit later.

These age-related changes in how the brain processes positive and negative emotional information shows both that there are probably underlying structural changes in the brain that result in age-related differences in behavior, and that these structural changes can be quite nuanced and complex. Additionally, neuroimaging research has drawn attention to the truly central and critical role played by the prefrontal cortex in understanding why people are the way they are.

2.3 Making Sense of Neuroscience Research: Explaining Changes in Brain-Behavior Relations

LEARNING OBJECTIVES

- What is the Parieto-Frontal Integration Theory, and what does it explain?
- How do older adults attempt to compensate for age-related changes in the brain?
- What are the major differences among the HAROLD, CRUNCH, and STAC models of brain activation and aging?

We have considered evidence that structural and neurochemical changes occur in the brain as we grow older, and that these changes in the brain relate to changes in cognitive functioning. With that as background, let's now reconsider research that is based on the functional brain imaging techniques, such as fMRI, that we noted earlier.

The main point of functional brain imaging research is to establish how age-related deterioration in specific brain structures affects a person's ability to perform various tasks, measuring both at the same time.

A second aim of these types of studies, and the point of this section, is to identify patterns of how the brain is sometimes able to compensate for negative age-related changes by activating different or additional regions when tasks pose a distinct difficulty. In other words, older and younger adults may differ in terms of which regions of the brain are used in order to perform cognitive tasks more effectively. On the one hand, these compensation strategies could result in roughly equivalent performance despite other differences across age. On the other hand, these compensation strategies could be ineffective and could reveal the neurological underpinnings of the cognitive decline observed in older adults. Which of these outcomes occurs not only has important consequences for performance on research tasks, but also in how well older adults might adapt to challenges in their daily lives.

The Parieto-Frontal Integration Theory

The typical finding is reduced brain activity in older as compared to younger adults in prefrontal and temporal areas that support cognitive functioning, such as memory (Juraska & Lowery, 2012). However, we also know that there is a marked increase in activity in specific areas of the prefrontal cortex and other brain regions during certain tasks, specifically memory for emotional material, in older adults as compared to younger adults (Grady, 2012; Spaniol & Grady, 2012). We will come back to this discrepancy a bit later.

There's more, though. Grady (2012; Spaniol & Grady, 2012) points out that reduced prefrontal recruitment in aging is context-dependent. That is, older adults sometimes show reduced activation or recruitment of the appropriate prefrontal regions, and sometimes show the same or more recruitment compared to younger adults depending on the tasks they are doing at the time.

Given the pivotal role played by the prefrontal cortex in such a wide range of cognitive tasks, researchers are homing in on its role in explaining intelligence at a holistic level. Research now shows that the prefrontal cortex, along with the parietal lobe (an area of the brain at the top of the head), plays an important role in general intellectual abilities. Based on 37 studies using various types of neuroimaging techniques, Jung and Haier (2007) proposed the Parieto-Frontal Integration Theory. *The Parieto-Frontal Integration Theory (P-FIT) proposes that intelligence comes from a distributed and integrated network of neurons in the parietal and frontal areas of the brain.* Figure 2.5. Shows these key brain areas. In general, P-FIT accounts for individual differences in intelligence as having their origins in individual differences in brain structure and function.

The P-FIT model is an example of theories based on neuroscience research, and has been tested and supported in several studies. It is clear that performance on specific measures of intelligence, including many of those that we will consider in detail in Chapter 7, are quite likely related to specific combinations of brain structures (Haier et al., 2010).

Finally, there is also considerable research showing the central role that the prefrontal cortex plays in

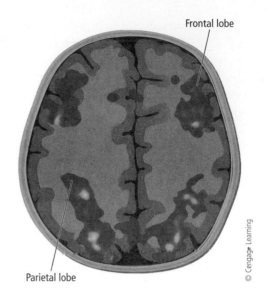

Figure 2.5
The P-FIT Model indicates that integration of the parietal and frontal lobes underlies intelligence.

integrating cognition and emotion (Ray & Zald, 2012): specifically, how different areas within the prefrontal cortex connect to two other key areas of the brain, the limbic system and the amygdala, influence how we process emotional content, as we have seen.

Given different patterns of brain activation across adulthood for certain tasks, the question arises whether these differences reflect adaptive behavior as people age. That's the issue we'll consider next.

Can Older Adults Compensate for Changes in the Brain?

We have seen that differences in brain activation have been documented between younger and older adults, and that these differences relate to differences in performance. There's an additional, and interesting, nuance to these findings. For example, it turns out that it is not simply that older adults show reduced activation in regions associated with a particular cognitive task. Rather, studies focusing on verbal working memory and long-term memory show focal, unilateral activity in the left prefrontal region in younger adults but bilateral activation (i.e., in both the left and right prefrontal areas) in older adults when performing the same tasks (Grady, 2012; Spaniol & Grady, 2012).

These findings surprised researchers, and ushered in much discussion and research as to what this meant for the aging brain. Is the older brain working to compensate for deterioration in these focal regions related to the cognitive task? Is the older brain working harder and recruiting more brain structures, or is the bilateral activation merely the inefficient operation of poor inhibition of irrelevant information that turns the activation into interference of optimal functioning (Park & Reuter-Lorenz, 2009)?

The answer appears to be yes—older adults are compensating. Researchers concluded that this bilateral activation in older adults may serve a functional and supportive role in their cognitive functioning (Grady, 2012; Park and Reuter-Lorenz, 2008). Supportive evidence comes from the association between bilateral activation in older adults and higher performance, evidence not found in younger adults, across a number of tasks including category learning tasks, visual field tasks, and various memory tasks.

Figure 2.6 shows that there is greater prefrontal bilateral activity in older adults during working memory tasks than in younger adults. On the left side of the figure, you can see that there is left-lateralized prefrontal engagement in younger adults, whereas older adults also engage the right prefrontal areas. The right side demonstrates that younger adults and low-performing older adults show right-lateralized activation during a long-term memory task. Interestingly, high-performing older adults still show bilateral prefrontal engagement. It may be that high functioning older adults are more adept at compensating for normative deterioration in the brain by utilizing other areas of the brain. Whether or not this is an accurate conclusion is still being debated.

Theories of Brain-Behavior Changes Across Adulthood

As we have seen, several studies have shown evidence for different patterns of brain activity in specific regions in older adults across numerous cognitive tasks, suggesting that the underlying brain changes are not overly specific to a narrow set of circumstances (e.g., Grady, 2012). Additional age-related neural activation (especially in prefrontal areas) may be functional and adaptive for optimal performance as people grow older. Researchers now suggest that these activation patterns may reflect an adaptive brain that functionally reorganizes and compensates for age-related changes (Spaniol & Grady, 2012; Sun, Tong, & Yang, 2012).

A number of models have been used to attempt to explain these findings. Three of the most prominent are the HAROLD model by Cabeza (2002), the CRUNCH model developed by Reuter-Lorenz and her colleagues (Reuter-Lorenz, 2002; Reuter-Lorenz & Mikels, 2006), and the STAC model (Park & Reuter-Lorenz, 2009). These models make a common assumption: The primary reason for greater activation in different brain regions, as well as for the different patterns within the prefrontal cortex, is the need for the recruitment of additional brain regions in order to successfully execute cognitive functions as one grows older.

The HAROLD Model. Numerous studies have documented the fact that younger adults show brain activation in one brain hemisphere when performing various cognitive tasks, but that older adults' brains tend to show increased activation in both brain hemispheres. Explaining this difference led to the development of the HAROLD model. *The HAROLD model stands for*

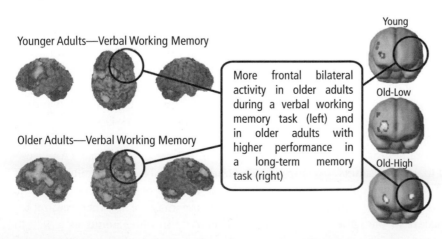

Younger Adults—Verbal Working Memory

Older Adults—Verbal Working Memory

More frontal bilateral activity in older adults during a verbal working memory task (left) and in older adults with higher performance in a long-term memory task (right)

Young

Old-Low

Old-High

Figure 2.6
Prefrontal bilateral activation increases with age.

Source: Park, D. C., & Reuter-Lorenz, P. (2008). The Adaptive Brain: Aging and Neurocognitive Scaffolding. Copyright 2009, Reprinted with permission from the Annual Review of Psychology, Volume 60, www.annualreviews.org

Hemispheric Asymmetry Reduction in OLDer adults that explains the empirical findings of reduced lateralization in prefrontal lobe activity in older adults (that is, the reduced ability of older adults to separate cognitive processing in different parts of the prefrontal cortex) (Cabeza, 2002; Collins & Mohr, 2013). It suggests that the function of the reduced lateralization is compensatory in nature; that is, additional neural units are being recruited and used to increase attentional resources, processing speed, or inhibitory control.

The HAROLD model has been supported by several studies that show how the brain creates and uses reserve abilities to lessen the impact of age-related changes in the brain (e.g., Cabeza & Dennis, 2013; Collins & Mohr, 2013; Steffener & Stern, 2012). What remains to be established, though, is where the line should be drawn separating normal age-related changes that can be compensated and changes that are so extensive or are happening so rapidly that compensation does not work.

The CRUNCH Model. *The CRUNCH model stands for Compensation-Related Utilization of Neural Circuits Hypothesis, and describes how the aging brain adapts to neurological decline by recruiting additional neural circuits (in comparison to younger adults) to perform tasks adequately* (DeCarli et al., 2012; Reuter-Lorenz, 2002; Reuter-Lorenz & Mikels, 2006). Like the HAROLD model, the CRUNCH model incorporates bilaterality of activation. But the CRUNCH model suggests this is not the only form of compensation. Two main mechanisms are suggested that the older brain uses to perform tasks: *more of the same* and *supplementary processes. More of the same* means that when task demands are increased, more activation can be found in the same brain region that is activated for processing easier tasks. This effect can be found in younger as well as older adults. However, in older adults, neural efficiency declines, so additional neuronal circuits are recruited earlier than they are in younger adults.

Supplementary processes take place when different brain regions are activated to compensate for lacking or insufficient processing resources. Reduced lateralization is one way of recruiting additional resources because both hemispheres are called into action rather than just one. In addition, however, compared to younger adults' brains older adults' brains also show overactivation in different brain regions. This happens when the activation level in older adults' brains occurs in the same

regions as in younger adults' brains, but at a significantly higher level. These patterns suggest that compensation can take different forms in the aging brain.

The CRUNCH model also has considerable support (e.g., DeCarli et al., 2012; Grady, 2012). However, just as is true about the HAROLD model, the point at which compensation breaks down is not well established under the CRUNCH model.

The STAC Model. How do we explain the specific patterns of age-related changes in prefrontal activity? To answer that question, Park and Reuter-Lorenz (2009) proposed the STAC model, shown in Figure 2.7. *The Scaffolding Theory of Cognitive Aging (STAC) model is based on the idea that age-related changes in one's ability to function reflect a life-long process of compensating for cognitive decline by recruiting additional brain areas* (Goh & Park, 2009). As we will see especially in Chapters 6 and 7, aging is associated with both decline as well as preservation of various cognitive abilities. The STAC model explains neuroimaging studies that show selective changes in the aging brain that reflect neural decline as well as compensatory neural recruitment, especially in the prefrontal cortex.

From the perspective of the STAC model, what's the purpose of the compensation? For one thing, there is growing evidence that the increase in frontal activity in older adults may be a response to decreased efficiency of neural processing in the perceptual areas of the brain (Park & Reuter-Lorenz, 2009).

There's another reason, too. Remember how the prefrontal region helps suppress irrelevant information that may interfere with the task one is actually performing? It turns out that older adults have trouble suppressing what's referred to as the default network of the brain. *The default network of the brain refers to regions of the brain that are most active when one is at rest.* One example of this would be the brain activity occurring when an individual lies quietly and is not directly engaged in a cognitive task (Andrews-Hanna, 2012). When a younger adult begins a demanding cognitive task, this default network is suppressed. But older adults display less suppression of this default network, resulting in poorer performance (Andrews-Hanna, 2012; Grady, 2012). Thus, this failure to shift from a resting state to a more active state to engage in cognitive processing may be another reason for increased frontal activity in older adults as a way to

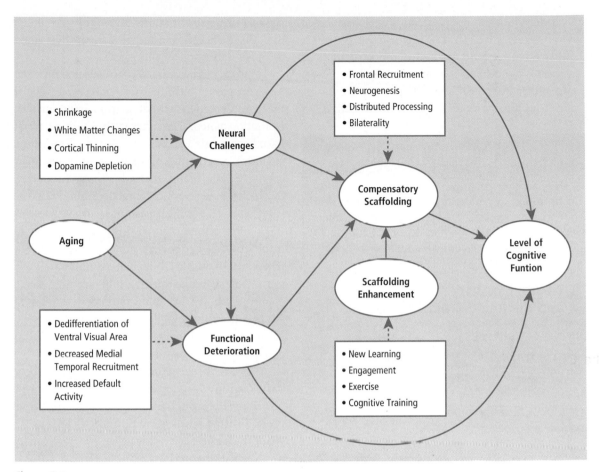

Figure 2.7

Conceptual model of the Scaffolding Theory of Cognitive Aging.

Source: Park, D. C., & Reuter-Lorenz, P. (2008). The Adaptive Brain: Aging and Neurocognitive Scaffolding. Copyright 2009, Reprinted with permission from the Annual Review of Psychology, Volume 64.

"work around" the lack of suppression (Grady, 2012; Juraska & Lowery, 2012).

The STAC model (Park & Reuter-Lorenz, 2009) suggests that the reason older adults continue to perform at high levels despite neuronal deterioration is because they create and rely on a back-up neural pathway. It works like this. When you learn a new task, learning moves from effortful processing (learning is hard work!) to overlearning (more automatic, less effortful processing). The neurological shift that happens in a young adult is from a broader dispersed network (which Park and Reuter-Lorenz call *the scaffold*) used while learning to a more focal, efficient, and optimal neural circuit. In older adults, though, the initial scaffolding remains available as a secondary, back-up circuit that can be counted on when necessary. Scaffolded networks are less efficient than the honed, focal ones they used as

young adults, so on average poorer performance is the result. But enough of the time, information is remembered eventually. The trade-off is that without the scaffolding, performance would be even worse because older adults would have to rely on the more focal areas.

The elegance of the STAC model is that older adults' performance can be understood in terms of factors that impact decline and those that impact compensation. As Park and Reuter-Lorenz (2009) argue, this integrative approach embraces a lifelong potential for plasticity and the ability to adapt to age-related changes.

In sum, neuroscience has opened new avenues of understanding aging. Advances in neuroscientific methods allow us to adequately test conditions under which age-related structural change in the brain is associated with decline, compensation, or even improvement in functioning. Rather than using general biological deterioration as the default explanation for behavioral changes, we can now identify specific brain mechanisms that are reflected in different structures of and activation patterns in the brain. These techniques have also allowed us to differentiate preserved areas of the brain from areas that are more prone to decline.

ADULT DEVELOPMENT IN ACTION

You are an activity therapist at a senior center, and want to design activities for the members that will help them compensate for typical age-related cognitive changes. Using the theories described in this section, what would an example of a good activity be?

2.4 Neural Plasticity and the Aging Brain

LEARNING OBJECTIVES

- What evidence is there for neural plasticity?
- How does aerobic exercise influence brain changes and cognitive aging?
- How does nutrition influence brain changes and cognitive activity?

Marisa has been playing incessantly with her latest Nintendo Wii video game. Her grandmother, Leticia, became captivated by her granddaughter's gaming and asked her granddaughter to teach her how to do it. Marisa was delighted and helped her grandmother learn the game. After months of practice, Marisa noted that her grandmother seemed stronger in her normal physical activities and her perceptual skills seemed to have improved. In addition, Leticia and her granddaughter Marisa had more in common than ever before.

There's an old saying that "You can't teach an old dog new tricks." Even if that's true for dogs, is it true for people? Neuroscience research helps provide some answers.

As discussed earlier in this chapter, there are certain situations in which the brain itself compensates for age-related changes. As was noted then, compensation is based on the notion that there is plasticity in both brain changes and behavior across the adult life span. Plasticity *involves the changes in the structure and function of the brain as the result of interaction between the brain and the environment.* In other words, plasticity is the result of people and their brains living in the world and accumulating and learning from experiences over

time. Leticia's observations of the positive changes that took place after she started playing the Wii video game are a good example of this plasticity.

Plasticity provides a way to understand compensatory changes in both the more observable behavior and the less observable (without neuroimaging, anyway) reorganization of neural circuitry in the brain. Many attempts have been made to assess the potential for plasticity in cognitive functioning by focusing on ways to improve cognitive performance through training (a good example of which would be Leticia's practice on the video game).

Baltes and colleagues' now classic research set the standard for documenting the range of plasticity in older adults' cognitive performance (e.g., Baltes & Kliegl, 1992; Willis, Bliezner, & Baltes, 1982). They found that whereas older adults are able to improve cognitive ability in memory tasks through tailored strategy training beyond the level of untrained younger adults, this is highly task-specific, and the ability-level gains are very narrow in focus.

Since these early findings, research has shown that basic cognitive processes affected by aging can indeed be improved through training, and that they transfer to multiple other kinds of functioning as long as the tasks share the same basic underlying functions (e.g., Dahlin, Neely, Larsson, Bäckman, & Nyberg, 2008). From a neural plasticity perspective, research on neural stem cells has revealed compelling evidence that demonstrates the effects of experience on various aspects of brain functioning in adulthood and aging (Fuentealba, Obernier, & Alvarez-Buylla, 2012; Ruckh et al., 2012). Neural stem cells *are cells that persist in the adult brain and can generate new neurons throughout the life span.* The discovery of neural stem cells proved wrong the long-standing belief that neurogenesis (i.e., the development of new neurons) dwindles away at the end of embryonic development. In practical terms, it means that you certainly *can* teach an old dog new tricks.

All of this research adds a new level of understanding to what happens to individuals as they grow older. For example, even though aging is associated with an overall decrease in the number of new neurons, this differs across regions of the brain and may be altered even at advanced ages.

The big question, of course, is whether the discovery of neural stem cells and the fact that neurons can regenerate even in late life means that neuroscience research could be used to cure brain diseases and essentially create "new brains" (Kazanis, 2012). Perhaps, that is likely many years from now. In the meantime, what we do know is that brain cells can regenerate, even in late life, under the right circumstances, and that the brain shows considerable plasticity to create ways for people to compensate with age-related declines in functioning. Still, this work is not without controversy, as discussed in the Current Controversies feature.

CURRENT CONTROVERSIES:

ARE NEURAL STEM CELLS THE SOLUTION TO BRAIN AGING?

Imagine if you could replace brain cells that had either died or had been damaged? That's the goal of researchers who study neural stem cells. Clearly, this research would fundamentally change our understanding of aging and of brain disease.

Research on the potential of neural stem cells took a major leap forward in 2007 with the founding of the New York Neural Stem Cell Institute. The Institute's mission is "to develop regenerative therapies for diseases of the central nervous system." Ongoing research programs include identifying potential uses of neural stem cells in treating such diseases as amyotrophic lateral sclerosis, Alzheimer's disease, brain injury and stroke, macular degeneration, multiple sclerosis, optic neuropathy, Parkinson's disease, retinitis pigmentosa, and spinal cord injury.

The National Human Neural Stem Cell Resource supplies researchers with neural stem cells obtained from the post-natal, postmortem, human brain.

Despite the great promise of this research, a basic question is whether it should be done at all. Several key ethical questions arise (Ramos-Zúñiga et al., 2012). This research requires that the human brain be used as an experimental object of study, and be manipulated in specific ways. Certainly, any such intervention, whether it is a treatment for a disease or a replacement of defective brain cells, requires the highest level of ethical principles. Perhaps the most difficult issue is that just because an intervention *can* be done, does not necessarily mean that is *should* be done.

As a result, researchers must go to great lengths to analyze the ethical implications of every research project involving neural stem cells, along with any potential clinical applications and outcomes. The usual medical standard of causing no harm is especially important in this research, as is a very careful assessment of the risk-benefit balance. But most important is keeping in the forefront of everything the fact that the research involves a human and a human brain.

Exercise and Brain Aging

Some of the most compelling work that has moved beyond the mere documentation of plasticity to the actual improvement of cognitive skills and concomitant changes in the brain focuses on the influence of aerobic exercise. Overall, research shows clearly that brain plasticity is enhanced as a result of aerobic exercise (Thomas, Dennis, Bandettini, & Johansen-Berg, 2012), and some studies have even shown that aerobic exercise can counter the declines in the hippocampus associated with Alzheimer's disease (Erickson et al., 2009; Intlekofer & Cotman, 2013).

An example of this line of research is a study by Erickson and his colleagues (2009). They were interested in learning whether aerobic exercise had any effect on the volume of the hippocampus, a key brain structure connected to memory. Erickson and colleagues had older adults exercise on a motorized treadmill, while their respiration, blood pressure, and

Aerobic exercise is good for maintaining brain health.

© iStockphoto.com/michellegibson

heart rate were continuously monitored. Participants also completed a spatial memory task and had an MRI to measure hippocampal volume. They found that higher aerobic fitness levels were associated with the preservation of greater hippocampal volume, which in turn was the best predictor of how well participants performed on the spatial memory task.

We will return to the many benefits of exercise in Chapter 4. As a preview, the positive effects on the brain are only one reason to get up and exercise.

Nutrition and Brain Aging

We began this chapter with a consideration of "brain food" and the claims that certain foods result in benefits for the brain. Thanks to neuroimaging studies, researchers are beginning to understand the relations between categories of nutrients and brain structures.

For example, Bowman and colleagues (2012) identified three nutrient biomarker patterns associated with cognitive function and brain volume. Two patterns were associated with better cognitive functioning and greater brain volume: one higher in blood plasma levels of vitamins B (B1, B2, B6, folate, and B12), C, D, and E, and another high in blood plasma levels of omega-3 fatty acids (usually found in seafood). A third pattern characterized by high trans fat was associated with less favorable cognitive function and less total cerebral brain volume. More detailed analyses have examined two different omega-3 fatty acids: eicosapentaenoic acid (EPA) and docosahexaenoic acid (DHA). Samieri and colleagues (2012) showed that only the EPA type was associated with maintaining better neuronal structure in the right part of the amygdala, and that atrophy of this part of the amygdala was associated with significant declines in memory and increases in symptoms of depression. Some additional research indicates that DHA may slow the progression of Alzheimer's disease, but once the disease has developed the effect disappears (Cunnane, Chouinard-Watkins, Castellano, & Barberger-Gateau, 2013).

Although researchers are only beginning to understand how nutrition affects brain structures, the findings to date clearly show that the effects could be substantial. As with exercise, we will return to the topic of nutrition and its effects on aging in Chapter 4.

SOCIAL POLICY IMPLICATIONS

The fact that the general view that the human brain gradually loses tissue from age 30 onward, and that those changes can mean poorer cognitive performance, combined with the projected rapid growth of an aging population present society with numerous public policy issues regarding the staggering costs of medical intervention and care for older adults. The good news is that advanced research in neuroscience tells us that this is an oversimplification of what really happens to the aging brain. Of importance to policy makers is that researchers are identifying ways in which such brain deterioration can be reduced or even reversed. In addition, researchers have identified areas of the brain that are relatively preserved and may even show growth. Thus, it is important for policy makers to obtain a more complete and accurate picture of aging. Why?

Research in neuroscience and aging is extremely important for a wide range of social policies from health care policies to laws pertaining to renewing drivers licenses and the age at which people should be eligible for retirement benefits, among others. Federal agencies such as the National Institute on Aging have focused much of their efforts onto better ways to assess and understand changes in the brain. These efforts demand more multidisciplinary research.

A good example is the compelling research regarding the effects of aerobic exercise and diet on the aging brain and how well it functions. The old saying of "use-it-or-lose-it" appears to be true.

What's at stake regarding policy? We are now talking about extending the vitality of older adulthood. Evidence from neuroimaging research provides a platform from which new interventions might be developed to make this a reality. However, policy makers must continue to support neuroscience research in order to keep our knowledge moving forward.

ADULT DEVELOPMENT IN ACTION

As the director of older adult services at a regional Area Office on Aging, you need to design websites about the benefits of exercise and good nutrition for older adults. What would the key information elements of the Website be?

SUMMARY

2.1 The Neuroscience Approach

What brain imaging techniques are used in neuroscience research?

- Structural neuroimaging such as computerized tomography (CT) and magnetic resonance imaging (MRI) provide highly detailed images of anatomical features in the brain.
- Functional neuroimaging such as single photon emission computerized tomography (SPECT), positron emission tomography (PET), functional magnetic resonance imaging (fMRI), magnetoencephalography, and near infrared spectroscopic imaging (NIRSI) provide an indication of brain activity but not high anatomical detail.

What are the main research methods used and issues studied in neuroscience research in adult development and aging?

- The neuropsychological approach compares brain-related psychological functioning of healthy older adults with adults displaying pathological disorders in the brain.
- The neuro-correlational approach links measures of behavioral performance to measures of neural structure or functioning.
- The activation imaging approach directly links functional brain activity with behavioral data.

2.2 Neuroscience and Adult Development and Aging

How is the brain organized structurally?

- The brain consists of neurons, which are comprised of dendrites, axon, neurofibers, and terminal branches. Neurons communicate across the space between neurons called the synapse via chemicals called neurotransmitters.
- Important structures in the brain for adult development and aging include the cerebral cortex, corpus callosum, prefrontal and frontal cortex, cerebellum, hippocampus, limbic system, and amygdala.

What are the basic changes in neurons as we age?

- Structural changes in the neuron include declines in number, decreases in size and number of dendrites, the development of tangles in neurofibers, and increases in deposits of certain proteins.

What changes occur in neurotransmitters with age?

- Important declines occur in the dopaminergic system (neurons that use dopamine) that are related to declines in memory, among others.
- Age-related changes in serotonin affect memory, mood, appetite, and sleep.
- Age-related changes in acetylcholine are related to arousal, sensory perception, and sustained attention.

What changes occur in brain structures with age?

- White matter (neurons covered by myelin) becomes thinner and shrinks, and does not function as well with age. White matter hyperintensities (WMH) are related to neural atrophy.
- Many areas of the brain show significant shrinkage with age.

What do age-related structural brain changes mean for behavior?

- Structural changes in the prefrontal cortex with age cause significant declines in executive functioning.
- Age-related structural changes in the prefrontal cortex and the hippocampus cause declines in memory function.
- Older and younger adults process emotional material differently. Older adults show more activity in more areas of the prefrontal cortex.
- Brain structures involved in automatic processing (e.g., amygdala) show less change with age, whereas brain structures involved in more reflective processing (e.g., prefrontal cortex) show more change with age.
- The positivity effect refers to the fact that older adults are more motivated to derive emotional meaning from life and to maintain positive feelings. Older adults activate more brain structures when processing emotionally positive material.

2.3 Making Sense of Neuroscience Research: Explaining Changes in Brain-Behavior Relations

What is the Parieto-Frontal Integration Theory, and what does it explain?

- The Parieto-Frontal Integration Theory (P-FIT) proposes that intelligence comes from a distributed and integrated network of neurons in the parietal and frontal areas of the brain.

How do older adults attempt to compensate for age-related changes in the brain?

■ Older adults compensate for brain changes by activating more areas of the brain than young adults when performing the same tasks.

What are the major differences among the HAROLD, CRUNCH, and STAC models of brain activation and aging?

■ The Hemispheric Asymmetry Reduction in Older Adults (HAROLD) model explains the finding of the reduced ability of older adults in separating cognitive processing in different parts of the prefrontal cortex.

■ The Compensation-Related Utilization of Neural Circuits Hypothesis (CRUNCH) model describes how the aging brain adapts to neurological decline by recruiting additional neural circuits (in comparison to younger adults) to perform tasks adequately. This model explains how older adults show overactivation of certain brain regions.

■ The Scaffolding Theory of Cognitive Aging (STAC) model is based on the idea that age-related changes in one's ability to function reflect a life-long process of compensating for cognitive decline by recruiting additional brain areas. This explains how older adults build and rely on back-up neural pathways.

2.4 Neural Plasticity and the Aging Brain

What evidence is there for neural plasticity?

■ Plasticity involves the changes in the structure and function of the brain as the result of interaction between the brain and the environment. Plasticity helps account for how older adults compensate for cognitive changes.

■ Neural stem cells are cells that persist in the adult brain and can generate new neurons throughout the life span.

How does aerobic exercise influence brain changes and cognitive aging?

■ Brain plasticity is enhanced through aerobic exercise.

How does nutrition influence brain changes and cognitive activity?

■ Maintaining good levels of certain nutrients in blood plasma helps reduce the levels of brain structural changes and cognitive declines.

REVIEW QUESTIONS

2.1 The Neuroscience Approach

■ Describe structural and functional neuroimaging techniques. How do they differ?

■ Describe the various neuroscience methodological perspectives used to study the aging brain. What are their strengths and their limitations?

■ How does the neuroscience level of examination contribute to our understanding of adult development and aging?

2.2 Neuroscience and Adult Development and Aging

■ Describe the basic structures in the brain.

■ What age-related changes are observed in neurons?

■ What happens to dopamine functioning in the aging brain? What age-related changes occur in other neurotransmitters?

■ What age-related changes occur in brain structures? What structures play major roles in the aging process?

■ What are the differences in brain activation during cognitive tasks for younger and older adults? What key differences have been identified in activity in the prefrontal cortex between younger and older adults?

■ What age-related differences have been documented in executive processing?

■ What differences are there in memory with age as they relate to brain activation?

■ How do younger and older adults process emotionally related material?

2.3 Making Sense of Neuroscience Research: Explaining Changes in Brain-Behavior Relations

■ What does P-FIT explain?

■ What evidence is there that older adults compensate for age-related changes in the brain?

■ Compare and contrast the HAROLD, CRUNCH, and STAC theories.

2.4 Neural Plasticity and the Aging Brain

■ What is neural plasticity? How might neural stem cells be used to increase neural plasticity?

- How does aerobic exercise affect age-related brain changes?
- How does nutrition affect age-related brain changes?

INTEGRATING CONCEPTS IN DEVELOPMENT

- Which of the theories of bilateral activation in older adults' brains makes the most sense to you? Why?
- What would you say about the stereotypes of aging now that you understand the plasticity of brain functioning?
- What does the work on brain plasticity imply for exercising the mind and body?
- How would you design a cognitive training program to take advantage of age-related changes in brain structures and plasticity?

KEY TERMS

activation imaging approach Attempts to directly link functional brain activity with cognitive behavioral data.

amygdala The region of the brain, located in the medial-temporal lobe, believed to play a key role in emotion.

antioxidants Compounds that protect cells from the harmful effects of free radicals.

axon A structure of the neuron that contains neurofibers.

cerebellum The part of the brain that is associated with motor functioning and balance equilibrium.

cerebral cortex The outermost part of the brain consisting of two hemispheres (left and right)

CRUNCH model A model that describes how the aging brain adapts to neurological decline by recruiting additional neural circuits (in comparison to younger adults) to perform tasks adequately.

compensatory changes Changes that allow older adults to adapt to the inevitable behavioral decline resulting from changes in specific areas of the brain.

corpus callosum A thick bundle of neurons that connects the left and right hemispheres of the cerebral cortex

default network of the brain The regions of the brain that are most active at rest.

dendrites A structural feature of a neuron that acts like antennas to receive signals from other nearby neurons.

diffusion tensor imaging (DTI) The measurement of the diffusion of water molecules in tissue in order to study connections of neural pathways in the brain.

dopamine A neurotransmitter associated with higher-level cognitive functioning.

dopaminergic system Neuronal systems that use dopamine as their major neurotransmitter.

executive functions Include the ability to make and carry out plans, switch between tasks, and maintain attention and focus.

free radicals Substances that can damage cells, including brain cells, and play a role in cancer and other diseases as we grow older.

functional neuroimaging Provides an indication of brain activity but not high anatomical detail.

HAROLD model A model that explains the empirical findings of reduced lateralization in prefrontal lobe activity in older adults (that is, the reduced ability of older adults to separate cognitive processing in different parts of the prefrontal cortex).

hippocampus Located in the medial-temporal lobe, this part of the brain plays a major role in memory and learning.

limbic system A set of brain structures involved with emotion, motivation, and long-term memory, among other functions.

neuro correlational approach An approach that attempts to relate measures of cognitive performance to measures of brain structure or functioning.

neural stem cells Cells that persist in the adult brain and can generate new neurons throughout the life span.

neuroanatomy The study of the structure of the brain.

neurofibers Structures in the neuron that carry information inside the neuron from the dendrites to the terminal branches.

neuroimaging A set of techniques in which pictures of the brain are taken in various ways to provide understanding of both normal and abnormal cognitive aging.

neurons A brain cell.

neuropsychological approach Compares brain functioning of healthy older adults with adults displaying various pathological disorders in the brain.

neuroscience The study of the brain.

neurotransmitters Chemicals that carry information signals between neurons across the synapse.

Parieto-Frontal Integration Theory (P-FIT) A theory that proposes that intelligence comes from a distributed and integrated network of neurons in the parietal and frontal areas of the brain.

plasticity Involves the interaction between the brain and the environment and is mostly used to describe the effects of experience on the structure and functions of the neural system.

positivity effect When an individual remembers more positive information relative to negative information.

prefrontal cortex Part of the frontal lobe that is involved in executive functioning.

Scaffolding Theory of Cognitive Aging (STAC) A model based on the idea that age-related changes in one's ability to function reflect a life-long process of compensating for cognitive decline by recruiting additional brain areas.

structural neuroimaging A set of techniques that provides highly detailed images of anatomical features in the brain.

synapse The gap between neurons across which neurotransmitters travel.

terminal branches The endpoints in a neuron that help transmit signals across the synapse.

White matter Neurons that are covered by myelin that serve to transmit information from one part of the cerebral cortex to another or from the cerebral cortex to other parts of the brain.

white matter hyperintensities (WMH) Abnormalities in the brain often found in older adults; correlated with cognitive decline.

RESOURCES

Access quizzes, glossaries, flashcards, and more at www.cengagebrain.com.

CHAPTER 3

PHYSICAL CHANGES

THE SUMMER OLYMPICS HELD IN BEIJING IN 2008 WERE SPECIAL FOR MANY REASONS.

Among the most important were accomplishments and milestones in swimming. Michael Phelps set the record for most gold medals won in a single Olympics (8) and overall (14). At age 23, he had reached the highest level of performance for a male swimmer. Phelps epitomized the fact that most world-class amateur and professional athletes reach their peak in their twenties. Indeed, his performance declined at the London Games in 2012, at which he won only four gold.

Then there are people who rewrite our beliefs about athletic performance. In Beijing, Dara Torres was competing in her fifth Olympics. As we noted in Chapter 1, she became, at age 41, the oldest

Although most Olympic athletes in events such as swimming are young adults like Michael Phelps, middle-aged adults like Dara Torres can also achieve world-class performance through a combination of good genes and a very healthy lifestyle.

swimmer ever to win an Olympic medal (she won three silver medals), and one of only a few who have won medals in five different Olympic games. Middle-aged adults everywhere were thrilled that someone who traditionally would have been written off as too old defeated women less than half her age.

Our beliefs about physical performance are changing. To be sure, athletic success is a combination of years of intense practice and excellent genes. But before Beijing, no one would have thought that a middle-aged woman could compete at that level. Before London, few thought the overall Olympic record for gold and for total medals could be broken.

Phelps and Torres represent the best. What about the rest of us? In this chapter, we will discover how physical abilities typically change across adulthood. What makes Phelps and Torres (and other world-class amateur and professional athletes) different is that because they stay in great physical condition, the normative changes tend to happen more slowly.

3.1 | Why Do We Age? Biological Theories of Aging

LEARNING OBJECTIVES

- How do rate-of-living theories explain aging?
- What are the major hypotheses in cellular theories of aging?
- How do programmed-cell-death theories propose that we age?
- How do the basic developmental forces interact in biological and physiological aging?

Before he started selling his Lean Mean Grilling Machine, George Foreman was a champion boxer. In fact, at age 44 he became, the oldest boxer ever to win the heavyweight championship. Foreman's success in the boxing ring came after a 10-year period when he did not fight and despite the belief that his career was finished.

Why is it that some people, like George Foreman and Dara Torres, manage to stay competitive in their sports into middle age and others of us experience significant physical decline? For that matter, why do we age at all? After all, some creatures, such as lobsters, do not age as humans do. (As far as scientists can tell,

Ezra Shaw/Getty Images

AP Images/Wong Maye-E

lobsters never show measurable signs of aging, such as changes in metabolism or declines in strength or health.) For millennia, scientists and philosophers have pondered the question of why people grow old and die. Their answers have spurred researchers to create a collection of theories based on basic biological and physiological processes. The search has included many hypotheses, such as metabolic rates and brain sizes, that haven't proved accurate. But as scientists continue unlocking the keys to our genetic code, hope is rising that we may eventually have an answer. To date, though, none of the more than 300 existing theories provides a complete explanation of all the normative changes humans experience (Vintildea & Miguel, 2007).

Before we explore some of the partial explanations from scientific research, complete the Discovering Development exercise. Compare your results for this exercise with some of the theories described next. What similarities and differences did you uncover?

DISCOVERING DEVELOPMENT:

WHY DO MOST PEOPLE THINK WE AGE?

What does the average person believe about how and why we age physiologically? To find out, list the various organ and body systems discussed in this chapter. Ask some people of different ages two sets of questions. First, ask them what they think happens to each system as people grow older. Then ask them what they think causes these changes. Compile the results from your interviews, and compare them with what you discover in this chapter. To what extent were your interviewees correct in their descriptions? Where were they off base? Does any of the misinformation match up with the stereotypes of aging we considered in Chapter 1? Why do you think this might be the case? How accurate are people in describing aging?

Rate-of-Living Theories

One theory of aging that makes apparent common sense postulates that organisms have only so much energy to expend in a lifetime. (Couch potatoes might like this theory, and may use it as a reason why they are not physically active.) The basic idea is that the rate of a creature's metabolism is related to how long it lives (Barzilai, Huffman, Muzumdar, & Bartke, 2012).

Several changes in the way that hormones are produced and used in the human body have been associated with aging, but none have provided a definitive explanation. Although some research indicates that significantly reducing the number of calories animals and people eat may increase longevity, research focusing on nonhuman primates shows that longer lives do not always result from restricting calories. Furthermore, the quality of life that would result for people on such a diet raises questions about how good a strategy calorie restriction is (Barzilai et al., 2012). That's because the caloric restrictions in this research tend to be extreme. Extrapolated to people, the restrictions could well cause a drop in humans' ability to engage in the kinds of activities we would consider important for a high quality of life.

Cellular Theories

A second family of ideas points to causes of aging at the cellular level. One notion focuses on the number of times cells can divide, which presumably limits the life span of a complex organism. Cells grown in laboratory culture dishes undergo only a fixed number of divisions before dying, with the number of possible divisions dropping depending on the age of the donor organism; this phenomenon is called the Hayflick limit, after its discoverer, Leonard Hayflick (Hayflick, 1996). For example, cells from human fetal tissue are capable of 40 to 60 divisions; cells from a human adult are capable of only about 20.

What causes cells to limit their number of divisions? *Evidence suggests that the tips of the chromosomes, called* telomeres, *play a major role in aging by adjusting the cell's response to stress and growth stimulation based on cell divisions and DNA damage* (Lin, Epel, & Blackburn, 2012). Healthy, normal telomeres help regulate the cell division and reproduction process.

An enzyme called telomerase *is needed in DNA replication to fully reproduce the telomeres when cells divide.* But telomerase normally is not present in somatic cells, so with each replication the telomeres become shorter. Eventually, the chromosomes become unstable and cannot replicate because the telomeres become too short.

Some researchers believe that in some cases cancer cells proliferate so quickly because telomeres are not able to regulate cell growth and reproduction (Lin et al., 2012; Londoño-Vallejo, 2008). Current thinking is that one effective cancer treatment may involve targeting telomerase (Harley, 2008). Other research indicating the telomeres can be lengthened is promising (Epel, 2012).

Chronic stress may accelerate the changes that occur in telomeres, and thereby shorten one's life span (O'Donovan, Tomiyama, Lin, Puterman, Adler, Kemeny et al., 2012). Research also shows that moderate levels of exercise may slow the rate at which telomeres shorten, which may help slow the aging process itself (Savela, Saijonmaa, Strandberg, Koistinen, Strandberg, Tilvis et al., 2013).

A second cellular theory is based on a process called cross-linking, in which certain proteins in human cells interact randomly and produce molecules that are linked in such a way as to make the body stiffer (Cavanaugh, 1999b). The proteins in question, which make up roughly one-third of the protein in the body, are called collagen. Collagen in soft body tissue acts much like reinforcing rods in concrete. The more cross-links there are, the stiffer the tissue. For example, leather tanning involves using chemicals that create many cross-links to make the leather stiff enough for use in shoes and other products. As we age, the number of cross-links increases. This process may explain why muscles, such as the heart, and arteries become stiffer with age. However, few scientific data demonstrate that cross-linking impedes metabolic processes or causes the formation of faulty molecules that would constitute a fundamental cause of aging (Hayflick, 1998). Thus, even though cross-linking occurs, it probably is not an adequate explanation of aging.

A third type of cellular theory proposes that aging is caused by unstable molecules called free radicals, which are highly reactive chemicals produced randomly in normal metabolism (Dutta, Calvani, Bernabei, Leeuwenburgh, & Marzetti, 2012). When these free radicals interact with nearby molecules, problems may result. For example, free radicals may cause cell damage to the heart by changing the oxygen levels in cells.

The most important evidence that free radicals may be involved in aging comes from research with substances that prevent the development of free radicals in the first place. These substances, called antioxidants, prevent oxygen from combining with susceptible molecules to form free radicals. Common antioxidants include vitamins A, C, and E, and coenzyme Q. A growing body of evidence shows that ingesting antioxidants postpones the appearance of age-related diseases such as cancer, cardiovascular disease, and immune system dysfunction (Dutta et al., 2012; Lu & Finkel, 2008), but there is no direct evidence yet that eating a diet high in antioxidants actually increases the life span (Berger, Lunkenbein, Ströhle, & Hahn, 2012).

Programmed-Cell-Death Theories

What if aging were programmed into our genetic code? This possibility seems more likely as the explosion of knowledge about human genetics continues to unlock the secrets of our genetic code. Even when cell death appears random, researchers believe that such losses may be part of a master genetic program that underlies the aging process (Freitas & de Magalhães, 2011; Mackenzie, 2012). Programmed cell death appears to be a function of physiological processes, the innate ability of cells to self-destruct, and the ability of dying cells to trigger key processes in other cells. At present, we do not know how this self-destruct program is activated, nor do we understand how it works. Nevertheless, there is increasing evidence that many diseases associated with aging (such as Alzheimer's disease) have genetic aspects.

It is quite possible that the other explanations we have considered in this section and the changes we examine throughout this text are the result of a genetic program. We will consider many diseases throughout the text that have known genetic bases, such as Alzheimer's disease. As genetics research continues, it is likely that we will have some exciting answers to the question, Why do we age?

Implications of the Developmental Forces

Although scientists do not yet have one unified theory of biological and physiological aging, the picture is becoming clearer. We know that there are genetic components, that the body's chemistry lab sometimes produces incorrect products, and that errors occur in the operation and replication of DNA (Freitas & de

Magalhães, 2011). From the perspective of the basic developmental forces, the biological theories provide ways to describe the biological forces. As we examine specific body systems in this chapter and health-related processes in Chapter 4, we will begin to integrate the biological forces with the psychological, sociocultural, and life-cycle forces. In those discussions, notice how changes in body systems and diseases are influenced by these other factors.

The implication of this dynamic, interactive process is that the diagnosis and treatment of health-related concerns must also include many perspectives. It is not enough to have your physical functioning checked to establish whether you are healthy. Rather, you need not only a typical bodily physical but also a checkup of psychological and sociocultural functioning. Finally, the results of all these examinations must be placed in the context of the overall life span.

So, a unified theory of aging would have to account for a wide array of changes relating not only to biological forces but to other forces as well. Perhaps then we'll discover why George Foreman was still successful in the boxing ring and Dara Torres was winning in the pool when most of their peers were watching them on television.

Or we just might discover how to reverse or stop aging. The business of "antiaging medicine," products designed to stop or prevent aging, is booming. Although most researchers who specialize in studying the fundamental mechanisms of aging largely dismiss such efforts, not all do. For example, research on the Chinese herb Sanchi (*Panax notoginsengs*) shows promise in reducing wrinkles (Rattan, Kryzch, Schnebert, Perrier, & Nizard, 2013). Healthy behaviors that delay the effects of aging are legitimate activities that have a research foundation; whether they should be called "antiaging" is another matter (Palmore, 2007). Exercise has been shown to delay many aspects of aging; cosmetic surgery aimed at making someone look younger does not, and is likely more related to aging stereotypes than healthy lifestyles.

There are three general research-based approaches to the work aimed at slowing or reversing aging. First, the goal is to delay the chronic illnesses of old age. Second, there is research aimed at slowing the fundamental processes of aging so that the average life span is increased to over 110 years (from roughly 78 now).

Third, some researchers seek to arrest or even reverse aging, perhaps by removing the damage inevitably caused by metabolic processes.

Research separating healthy behaviors from age denials is key (Palmore, 2007). Legitimate research sponsored by such agencies as the National Institutes of Health becomes confused with counterfeit antiaging interventions. If the legitimate research unlocks the secrets of aging, then a serious public discussion is needed to prepare society for the implications of a possible significant lengthening of the life span.

ADULT DEVELOPMENT IN ACTION

If you were a geriatric nurse, what advice would you give to your patients about living longer based on existing biological theories of aging?

3.2 Appearance and Mobility

LEARNING OBJECTIVES
- How do our skin, hair, and voices change with age?
- What happens to our body build with age?
- What age-related changes occur in our ability to move around?

By all accounts, Kristina is extremely successful. She was a famous model in her late teens and 20s, and by the time she was 36 she had learned enough about the business to start her own multinational modeling agency. The other day Kristina was very upset when she looked in the mirror and saw a wrinkle. "Oh no," she exclaimed, "I can't be getting wrinkles! What am I going to do?"

Kristina's experience isn't unique. We all see the outward signs of aging first in the mirror: gray hair, wrinkled skin, and an expanding waistline or hips. These changes occur gradually and at different rates; some of us experience all the changes in young adulthood, whereas others don't have them until late middle or old age. How we perceive the person staring back at us in the mirror says a great deal about how we feel about aging; positive feelings about the signs of aging are related to positive self-esteem.

How easily we move our changing bodies in the physical environment is also a major component of adaptation and well-being in adulthood. If we cannot get around, we must depend on others, which lowers our self-esteem and sense of competence. Having a body that moves effectively also lets us enjoy physical activities such as walking, swimming, and skiing.

Changes in Skin, Hair, and Voice

When we, like Kristina, see the first visible signs of aging, it makes no difference that these changes are universal and inevitable. Nor does it matter that our wrinkles are caused by a combination of changes in the structure of the skin and its connective and supportive tissue and the cumulative effects of exposure to sunlight. As normal as the loss of hair pigmentation is, we may still want to hide the gray (Aldwin & Gilmer, 2013). What matters on that day is that we have seen our first wrinkle and gray hair.

Changes in the Skin. Why does our skin wrinkle? Wrinkling is actually a complex, four-step process (Robert, Labat-Robert, & Robert, 2012). First, the outer layer of skin becomes thinner through cell loss, causing the skin to become more fragile. Second, the collagen fibers that make up the connective tissue lose much of their flexibility, making the skin less able to regain its shape after a pinch. Third, elastin fibers in the middle layer of skin lose their ability to keep the skin stretched out, resulting in sagging. Finally, the underlying layer of fat, which helps provide padding to smooth out the contours, diminishes.

It may surprise you to know that how quickly your face ages is largely under your control. Two major environmental causes of wrinkles are exposure to ultraviolet rays from the sun, which breaks down the skin's connective tissue, and smoking, which restricts the flow of blood to the skin around the lips (Mayo Clinic, 2012a). Using sunscreens and sunblocks properly and limiting your exposure to sunlight, as well as quitting smoking, may slow the development of wrinkles. The message is clear: Young adults who are dedicated sun-worshippers or are smokers eventually pay a high price.

Older adults' skin is naturally thinner and drier, giving it a leathery texture, making it less effective at

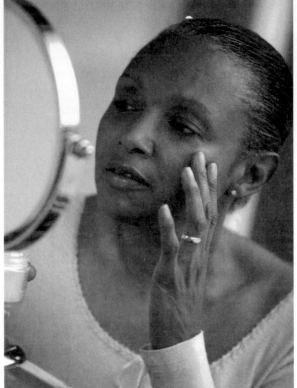

Getting gray hair and wrinkles is part of the normative aging process.

Ariel Skelley/Blend Images/Getty Images

regulating heat or cold, and making it more susceptible to cuts, bruises, and blisters. To counteract these problems, people should use skin moisturizers, vitamin E, and facial massages (Mayo Clinic, 2012a; Robert et al., 2012). The coloring of light-skinned people undergoes additional changes with age. The number of pigment-containing cells in the outer layer decreases, and those that remain have less pigment, resulting in lighter skin. In addition, age spots (areas of dark pigmentation that look like freckles) and moles (pigmented outgrowths) appear more often. Some of the blood vessels in the skin may become dilated and create small, irregular red lines. Varicose veins may appear as knotty, bluish irregularities in blood vessels, especially on the legs (Aldwin & Gilmer, 2004; Weiss, Munavalli, Choudhary, Leiva, & Nouri, 2012).

Changes in the Hair. Gradual thinning and graying of the hair of both men and women occur inevitably with age, although there are large individual differences in the rate of these changes. Hair loss is caused by destruction of the germ centers that produce the hair follicles, whereas graying results from a cessation of pigment production. Men usually do not lose facial hair as they age; you probably have seen many balding men with thick, bushy beards. In addition, men often develop bushy eyebrows and hair growth inside the ears. In contrast, women often develop patches of hair on the face, especially on the chin (Aldwin & Gilmer, 2004). This hair growth is related to the hormonal changes of the climacteric, discussed later in this chapter.

Changes in the Voice. The next time you're in a crowd of people of different ages, close your eyes and listen to the way they sound. You probably will be fairly accurate in guessing how old the speakers are just from the quality of the voices you hear. Younger adults' voices tend to be full and resonant, whereas older adults' voices tend to be thinner or weaker. Age-related changes in one's voice include lowering of pitch, increased breathlessness and trembling, slower and less precise pronunciation, and decreased volume. A longitudinal study of Japanese adults revealed that women have more changes in their fundamental frequency, and shimmer (i.e., frequent change from soft to loud volume) and glottal noise is characteristic of older voices (Kasuya et al., 2008). Some researchers report that these changes are due to changes in the larynx (voice box), the respiratory system, and the muscles controlling speech. However, other researchers contend that these changes result from poor health and are not part of normal aging.

Changes in Body Build

If you have been around the same older people, such as your grandparents, for many years, you undoubtedly have noticed that the way their bodies look changed over time. Two changes are especially visible: a decrease in height and fluctuations in weight. Height remains fairly stable until the 50s, but between the mid-50s and mid-70s men lose about 1 inch and women lose about 2 inches (Havaldar, Pilli, & Putti, 2012). This height loss usually is caused by compression of the spine from loss of bone strength, changes in the discs between the vertebrae in the spine, and changes in posture. Importantly, height loss of more than 3 cm is associated

with increased risk of dying from cardiovascular and respiratory diseases (Masunari, Fujiwara, Kasagi, Takahashi, Yamada, & Nakamura, 2012). We consider some specific aspects of changes in bone structure a bit later.

Weight gain in middle age followed by weight loss in later life is common. Typically, people gain weight between their 20s and their mid-50s but lose weight throughout old age. In part, the weight gain is caused by changes in body metabolism, which tends to slow down, and reduced levels of exercise, which in turn reduces the number of calories needed daily. Unfortunately, many people do not adjust their food intake to match these changes. The result is often tighter-fitting clothes. For men, this weight gain tends to be around the abdomen, creating middle-aged bulge. For women, this weight gain tends to be around the hips, giving women the familiar "pear-shaped" figure. By late life, though, the body loses both muscle and bone, which weigh more than fat, in addition to some fat, resulting in weight loss (Yang, Bishai, & Harman, 2008). Research on the relationships among body weight, health, and survival shows that older adults who have normal body weight at age 65 have longer life expectancy and lower rates of disability than 65-year-olds in other weight categories. Keeping your weight in the normal range for your height, then, may help you live longer.

Changes in Mobility

Being able to get around on one's own is an important part of remaining independent. As you will see, we all experience some normative changes that can affect our ability to remain mobile, but most of these changes do not inevitably result in serious limitations.

Muscles and Balance. Although the amount of muscle tissue in our bodies declines with age, this loss is hardly noticeable in terms of strength and endurance; even at age 70 the loss is no more than 20%. After that, however, the rate of change increases. By age 80 the loss in strength is up to 40%, and it appears to be more severe in the legs than in the arms and hands. However, some people retain their strength well into old age (Seene, Kaasik, & Riso, 2012). Research evidence suggests that muscle endurance also diminishes with age but at a slower rate. Men and women show no differences in the rate of muscle change.

This loss of muscle strength is especially important in the lower body (El Haber et al., 2008). As lower body strength declines, the likelihood of balance problems and falls increases, as do problems with walking. Exercise may help delay these changes.

Bones. You have probably seen commercials and advertisements aimed mostly at women for products that help maintain bone mass. If you surmise that such products reflect a serious and real health concern, you are correct. Normal aging is accompanied by the loss of bone tissue throughout the body. Bone loss begins in the late 30s, accelerates in the 50s (particularly in women), and slows by the 70s (Havaldar et al., 2012). The gender difference in bone loss is important. Once the process begins, women lose bone mass approximately twice as fast as men. The difference results from two factors. First, women have less bone mass than men in young adulthood, meaning that they start out with less ability to withstand bone loss before it causes problems. Second, the depletion of estrogen after menopause speeds up bone loss.

What happens to aging bones? The process involves a loss of bone mass inside the bone, which makes bones more hollow. In addition, bones tend to become porous. The changes result from body weight, genetics, and lifestyle factors such as smoking, alcohol use, and diet (Havaldar et al., 2012). All these bone changes cause an age-related increase in the likelihood of fractures, because hollow, porous bones are easier to break. Furthermore, broken bones in older people present more serious problems than in younger adults, because they are more likely to be clean fractures that are difficult to heal. Bones of younger adults fracture in such a way that there are many cracks and splinters to aid in healing. This is analogous to the difference between breaking a young, green tree branch (which is harder to do) and snapping an old, dry twig.

Women are especially susceptible to severe bone degeneration, a disease called osteoporosis, *in which the loss of bone mass and increased porosity create bones that resemble laced honeycombs.* You can see the result in Figure 3.1. Eventually, people with osteoporosis tend to develop a distinct curvature in their spines, as shown in Figure 3.2.

Osteoporosis is the leading cause of broken bones in older women (NIHSeniorHealth, 2011a). Although it is most common in older adults, osteoporosis can occur in people in their 50s.

Osteoporosis is more common in women than men, largely because women have less bone mass in general, because some girls and women do not consume enough dietary calcium to build strong bones when they are younger (i.e., build bone mass), and because the decrease in estrogen following menopause greatly accelerates bone loss.

Osteoporotic bone tissue

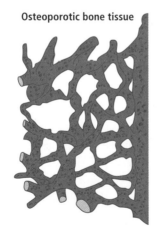

Normal bone tissue

Figure 3.1

Osteoporotic and normal bone structures. Notice how much mass the osteoporotic bone has lost.

© 2015 Cengage Learning

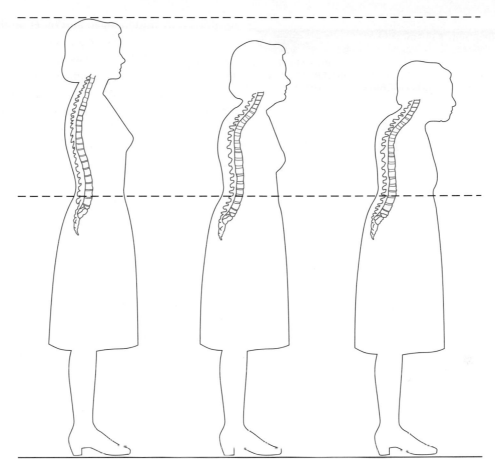

Figure 3.2

Changes in the curvature of the spine as a result of osteoporosis. These changes create the stooping posture common to older people with advanced osteoporosis.

Source: Reprinted with permission from Ebersole, P., & Hess, P., Toward Healthy Aging, 5e, (p. 395). Copyright © 1998 Mosby St. Louis; with permission from Elsevier.

Osteoporosis is caused in part by having low bone mass at skeletal maturity (the point at which your bones reach peak development), deficiencies in calcium and vitamin D, estrogen depletion, and lack of weight-bearing exercise that builds up bone mass. Other risk factors include smoking; high-protein diets; and excessive intake of alcohol, caffeine, and sodium. Women who are being treated for asthma, cancer, rheumatoid arthritis, thyroid problems, or epilepsy are also at increased risk because the medications used can lead to the loss of bone mass.

NIHSeniorHealth (2011b) recommends getting enough vitamin D and dietary calcium as ways to prevent osteoporosis. There is evidence that calcium supplements after menopause may slow the rate of bone

loss and delay the onset of osteoporosis, but benefits appear to be greater when the supplements are provided before menopause. People should consume foods (such as milk or broccoli) that are high in calcium and should also take calcium supplements if necessary. Recommended calcium intake for men and women of various ages are shown in Table 3.1. Data clearly show that metabolizing vitamin D directly affects rates of osteoporosis; however, whether supplementary dietary vitamin D retards bone loss is less certain (National Institute of Arthritis and Musculoskeletal and Skin Diseases, 2008b).

In terms of medication interventions, bisphosphonates are the most commonly used and are highly effective, but can have side effects if used over

Table 3.1

RECOMMENDED CALCIUM AND VITAMIN D INTAKES		
AGE	**CALCIUM (MILLIGRAMS)**	**VITAMIN D (INTERNATIONAL UNITS)**
Infants		
Birth to 6 months	200	400
6 months to 1 year	260	400
Children and Young Adults		
1 to 3 years	700	600
4 to 8 years	1,000	600
9 to 13 years	1,300	600
14 to 18 years	1,300	600
Adult Women and Men		
19 to 30 years	1,000	600
31 to 50 years	1,000	600
51- to 70-year-old males	1,000	600
51- to 70-year-old females	1,200	600
Over 70 years	1,200	800

Source: National Institute of Arthritis and Musculoskeletal and Skin Diseases, 2010d.

a long period of time (Salari & Abdollahi, 2012). Fosamax, Actonel, and Boniva are three common examples of this family of medications. Bisphosphonates slow the bone breakdown process by helping to maintain bone density during menopause. Research indicates that using bisphosphonates for up to five years appears relatively safe if followed by stopping the medication (called a "drug holiday"); there is evidence for protective effects lasting up to five years more.

Lowering the risk of osteoporosis involves dietary, medication, and activity approaches (NIHSeniorHealth, 2011b). Some evidence also supports the view that taking supplemental magnesium, zinc, vitamin K, and special forms of fluoride may be effective. Estrogen replacement is effective in preventing women's bone loss after menopause but is controversial because of potential side effects (as discussed later). There is also evidence that regular weight-bearing exercise (e.g., weight lifting, jogging, or other exercise that forces you to work against gravity) is beneficial.

Joints. Many middle-aged and older adults complain of aching joints. They have good reason. Beginning in the 20s, the protective cartilage in joints shows signs of deterioration, such as thinning and becoming cracked and frayed. Two types of arthritis can result: osteoarthritis and rheumatoid arthritis. These diseases are illustrated in Figure 3.3.

Over time the bones underneath the cartilage become damaged, which can result in osteoarthritis, *a disease marked by gradual onset and progression of pain and disability, with minor signs of inflammation* (National Institute of Arthritis and Musculoskeletal and Skin Diseases, 2010a). The disease usually becomes noticeable in late middle age or early old age, and it is especially common in people whose joints are subjected to routine overuse and abuse, such as athletes and manual laborers. Thus osteoarthritis is a wear-and-tear disease. Pain typically is worse when the joint is used, but skin redness, heat, and swelling are minimal or absent. Osteoarthritis usually affects the hands, spine, hips, and knees, sparing the wrists, elbows, shoulders, and ankles. Effective management approaches consist mainly of certain steroids and anti-inflammatory drugs, rest, nonstressful exercises that focus on range of motion, diet, and a variety of homeopathic remedies.

A second form of arthritis is rheumatoid arthritis, *a more destructive disease of the joints that also develops slowly and typically affects different joints and causes other types of pain than osteoarthritis* (National Institute of Arthritis and Musculoskeletal and Skin Diseases., 2009). Most often, a pattern of morning stiffness and aching develops in the fingers, wrists, and ankles on both sides of the body. Joints appear swollen.

The typical therapy for rheumatoid arthritis consists of aspirin or other nonsteroidal anti-inflammatory drugs, such as Advil or Aleve. Newer treatments include disease-modifying anti-rheumatic drugs (DMARDs) (such as hydroxycholorquine and methotrexate) that limit the damage occurring in the joints, and TNF-alpha inhibitors that act as an anti-inflammatory agent and have been shown to stop the disease's progression in some patients. Rest and passive range-of-motion exercises are also helpful.

Contrary to popular belief, rheumatoid arthritis is not contagious, hereditary, or self-induced by any

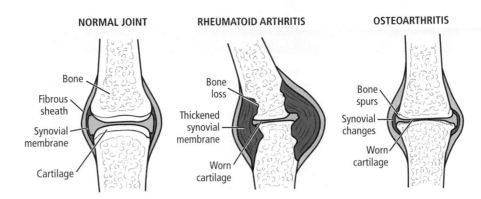

Figure 3.3

Rheumatoid arthritis versus osteoarthritis. Osteoarthritis, the most common form of arthritis, involves the wearing away of the cartilage that caps the bones in your joints. With rheumatoid arthritis, the synovial membrane that protects and lubricates joints becomes inflamed, causing pain and swelling. Joint erosion may follow.

Adapted from the MayoClinic.com article, "Arthritis" (http://www.mayoclinic.com/health/arthritis/DS01122)

known diet, habit, job, or exposure. Interestingly, the symptoms often come and go in repeating patterns (National Institute of Arthritis and Musculoskeletal and Skin Diseases, 2009). Although apparently not directly inherited, family history of rheumatoid arthritis plays a role because researchers think that you can inherit a predisposition for the disease.

Surgical interventions may be an option if medications do not provide relief. For example, *arthroplasty*, or the total replacement of joints damaged by arthritis, continues to improve as new materials help artificial joints last longer. When joints become inflamed, surgeons may be able to remove the affected tissue. Or in some cases cartilage may be transplanted into a damaged joint. These latter two approaches help patients avoid full joint replacement, generally viewed as the method of last resort.

Comparisons among osteoporosis, osteoarthritis, and rheumatoid arthritis can be seen in Table 3.2.

Psychological Implications

The appearance of wrinkles, gray hair, fat, and the like can have major effects on a person's self-concept (Aldwin & Gilmer, 2004) and reflect ageism in society (Clarke & Griffin, 2008). Middle-aged adults may still think of themselves as productive members of society and rebel against being made invisible. Because U.S. society places high value on looking young, middle-aged and older adults, especially women, may be regarded as inferior on a number of dimensions, including intellectual ability. Consequently, women report engaging in "beauty work" (dyeing their hair, cosmetic surgery, and the like) in order to remain visible in society. In contrast, middle-aged men with some gray hair often are considered distinguished, more experienced, and more knowledgeable than their younger counterparts.

Given the social stereotypes we examined in Chapter 1, many women (and increasingly, some men) use any available means to compensate for these changes. Some age-related changes in facial appearance can be disguised with cosmetics. Hair dyes can restore color. Surgical procedures such as face-lifts can tighten sagging and wrinkled skin. But even plastic surgery only delays the inevitable; at some point everyone takes on a distinctly old appearance.

Losses in strength and endurance in old age have much the same psychological effects as changes in

Table 3.2

SIMILARITIES AND DIFFERENCES AMONG OSTEOPOROSIS, OSTEOARTHRITIS, AND RHEUMATOID ARTHRITIS

	OSTEOPOROSIS	OSTEOARTHRITIS	RHEUMATOID ARTHRITIS
Risk Factors			
Age-related	x	x	
Menopause	x		
Family history	x	x	x
Use of certain medications such as glucocorticoids or seizure medications	x		
Calcium deficiency or inadequate vitamin D	x		
Inactivity	x		
Overuse of joints		x	
Smoking	x		
Excessive alcohol	x		
Anorexia nervosa	x		
Excessive weight		x	
Physical Effects			
Affects entire skeleton	x		
Affects joints		x	x
Is an autoimmune disease			x
Bony spurs		x	x
Enlarged or malformed joints	x	x	
Height loss	x		

Sources: National Institute of Arthritis and Musculoskeletal and Skin Diseases (2006), http://www.niams.nih.gov/Health_Info/Bone/Osteoporosis/Conditions_Behaviors/osteoporosis_arthritis.asp.

appearance (Aldwin & Gilmer, 2004). In particular, these changes tell the person that he or she is not as capable of adapting effectively to the environment. Loss of muscle coordination (which may lead to walking more slowly, for example) may not be inevitable, but it can prove embarrassing and stressful. Exercise and resistance training can improve muscle strength, even up to age 90, and may also reduce the odds of getting dementia (Andel et al., 2008). Interestingly, the rate of improvement does not seem to differ with age; older adults get stronger at the same rate as younger adults.

The changes in the joints, especially in arthritis, have profound psychological effects (Aldwin & Gilmer, 2004). These changes can severely limit movement, thereby reducing independence and the ability to complete normal daily routines. Moreover, joint pain is very difficult to ignore or disguise, unlike changes in appearance. Consequently, the person who can use cosmetics to hide changes in appearance cannot use the same approach to deal with constant pain in the joints. Older adults who suffer bone fractures face several other consequences in addition to discomfort. For example, a hip fracture may force hospitalization or even a stay in a nursing home. For all fractures, the recovery period is much longer than for a younger adult. In addition, older people who witness friends or relatives struggling during rehabilitation may reduce their own activities as a precaution.

ADULT DEVELOPMENT IN ACTION

If you were a personal exercise trainer, what regimen would you recommend for your older clients to help them maintain maximum health?

3.3 Sensory Systems

LEARNING OBJECTIVES

- What age-related changes happen in vision?
- How does hearing change as people age?
- What age-related changes occur in people's senses of touch and balance?
- What happens to taste and smell with increasing age?

Bertha has attended Sunday services in her local AME (African Methodist Episcopal) church for 82 years. Over the past few years, though, she has experienced greater difficulty in keeping her balance as she walks down the steps from her row house to the sidewalk. Bertha is noticing that her balance problems occur even when she is walking on level ground. Bertha is concerned that she will have to stop attending her beloved church because she is afraid of falling and breaking a bone.

You have probably seen people like Bertha walking slowly and tentatively along the sidewalk. Why do older people have these problems more often? If you said it is because the sensory system directly related to maintaining balance, the vestibular system, and muscle strength decline with age, you would only be partly correct. It turns out that keeping one's balance is a complex process in which we integrate input from several sources, such as vision and touch, as well as bones and joints. In this section we examine the changes that occur in our sensory systems. These changes challenge our ability to interact with the world and communicate with others.

| Vision

Have you ever watched middle-aged people try to read something that is right in front of them? If they do not already wear glasses or contact lenses, they typically move the material farther away so that they can see it clearly. This change in vision is one of the first noticeable signs of aging, along with the wrinkles and gray hair we considered earlier. Because we rely extensively on sight in almost every aspect of our waking life, its normative, age-related changes have profound and pervasive effects on people's everyday lives, especially feelings of sadness and loss of enjoyment of life (Mojon-Azzi, Sousa-Poza, & Mojon, 2008).

How does eyesight change with age? The major changes are best understood by grouping them into two classes: changes in the structures of the eye, which begin in the 40s, and changes in the retina, which begin in the 50s (Mojon-Azzi et al., 2008).

Structural Changes in the Eye. Two major kinds of age-related structural changes occur in the eye. One is a decrease in the amount of light that passes through the eye, resulting in the need for more light to do tasks such as reading (Andersen, 2012). As you might suspect, this change is one reason why older adults do not see as well in the dark, which may account in part for their reluctance to go places at night. One possible logical response to the need for more light would be to increase illumination levels in general. However, this solution does not work in all situations because we also become increasingly sensitive to glare. In addition, our ability to adjust to changes in illumination, called adaptation, declines. Going from outside into a darkened movie theater involves dark adaptation; going back outside involves light adaptation. Research indicates that the time it takes for both types of adaptation increases with age (Charman, 2008). These changes are especially important for older drivers, who have more difficulty seeing after confronting the headlights of an oncoming car.

The other key structural changes involve the lens (Andersen, 2012; Charman, 2008). As we grow older, the lens becomes more yellow, causing poorer color discrimination in the green–blue–violet end of the spectrum. Also, the lens's ability to adjust and focus declines as the muscles around it stiffen. *This is what causes difficulty in seeing close objects clearly (called* **presbyopia**), *necessitating either longer arms or corrective lenses.* To complicate matters further, the time our eyes need to change focus from near to far (or vice versa) increases. This also poses a major problem in driving. Because drivers are constantly changing their focus from the instrument panel to other autos and signs on the highway, older drivers may miss important information because of their slower refocusing time.

Besides these normative structural changes, some people experience diseases caused by abnormal structural changes. *First, opaque spots called* cataracts *may develop on the lens, which limits the amount of light transmitted.* Cataracts often are treated by surgical removal and use of corrective lenses. *Second, the fluid in the eye may not drain properly, causing very high pressure; this condition, called* glaucoma, *can cause internal damage and loss of vision.* Glaucoma, a fairly common disease in middle and late adulthood, is usually treated with eye drops.

Retinal Changes. The second major family of changes in vision result from changes in the retina. The retina lines approximately two-thirds of the interior of the eye. The specialized receptor cells in vision, the rods and the cones, are contained in the retina. They are most densely packed toward the rear and especially at the focal point of vision, a region called the macula. At the center of the macula is the fovea, where incoming light is focused for maximum acuity, as when you are reading. With increasing age, the probability of degeneration of the macula increases (Ambati & Fowler, 2012). Macular degeneration involves the progressive and irreversible destruction of receptors from any of a number of causes. This disease results in the loss of the ability to see details; for example, reading is extremely difficult, and television often is reduced to a blur. It is the leading cause of functional blindness in older adults.

A second age-related retinal disease is a by-product of diabetes, a chronic disease described in detail in

Chapter 4. Diabetes is accompanied by accelerated aging of the arteries, with blindness being one of the more serious side effects. Diabetic retinopathy, as this condition is called, can involve fluid retention in the macula, detachment of the retina, hemorrhage, and aneurysms (Bronson-Castain, Bearse, Neuville, Jonasdottir, King-Hooper, Barez et al., 2012). Because it takes many years to develop, diabetic retinopathy is more common among people who developed diabetes early in life.

The combined effects of the structural changes in the eye create two other types of changes. First, the ability to see detail and to discriminate different visual patterns, called acuity, declines steadily between ages 20 and 60, with a more rapid decline thereafter. Loss of acuity is especially noticeable at low light levels (Charman, 2008).

Psychological Effects of Visual Changes. Clearly, age-related changes in vision affect every aspect of older adults' daily lives and their well-being (Mojon-Azzi et al., 2008; Zimdars, Nazroo, & Gjonça, 2012). Imagine the problems people experience performing tasks that most young adults take for granted, such as reading a book, watching television, reading grocery labels, or driving a car. Fortunately, some of the universal changes, such as presbyopia, can be corrected easily through glasses or contacts. Surgery to correct cataracts is now routine. The diseased lens is removed and an artificial one is inserted in an outpatient procedure that usually lasts about 30 minutes, with little discomfort. Patients usually resume their normal activities in less than a week and report much improved daily lives.

If you want to provide environmental support for older adults, taking their vision changes into account, you need to think through your intervention strategies carefully. For example, simply making the environment brighter may not be the answer. For increased illumination to be beneficial, surrounding surfaces must not increase glare. Using flat latex paint rather than glossy enamel and avoiding highly polished floors are two ways to make environments "older adult–friendly." There should be high contrast between the background and operational information on dials and controls, such as on stoves and radios. Older adults may also have trouble seeing some fine facial details which may lead them to decrease their social contacts for fear of not recognizing someone.

Older drivers may miss information due to changes in vision.

Visual impairments with age change the relations between certain personality traits and emotion (Wahl, Heyl, & Schilling 2012). For instance, the relationship between extraversion and positive emotions is stronger in people with few or no impairments than in people with impairments. Visual problems also increase vulnerability to falls because the person may be unable to see hazards in his or her path or to judge distance very well. Thus, part of Bertha's concern about falling may be caused by changes in her ability to tell where the next step is or to see hazards along the sidewalk.

Hearing

Experiencing hearing loss is one of the most well-known normative changes with age (Li-Korotky, 2012). A visit to any housing complex for older adults will easily verify this point; you will quickly notice that television sets and radios are turned up fairly loud in most of the apartments. Yet you don't have to be old to experience significant hearing problems. When he began to find it difficult to hear what was being said to him, President Bill Clinton obtained two hearing aids. He was 51 years old at the time, and he attributed his hearing loss to too many high school bands and rock concerts when he was young. His situation is far from unique. Loud noise is the enemy of hearing at any age. You probably have seen people who work in noisy environments wearing protective gear on their ears so that they are not exposed to loud noise over extended periods of time.

But you can do serious damage to your hearing with short exposure, too; in 1988, San Francisco punk rock bassist Kathy Peck was performing with her all-female punk band "The Contractions" at the Oakland Coliseum and played so loudly that she had ringing in her ears for 3 days and suffered permanent hearing loss. As a result, she founded Hearing Education and Awareness for Rockers (HEAR; http://www.hearnet.com) shortly thereafter to educate musicians about the need to protect their ears (Noonan, 2005). You don't need to be at a concert to damage your hearing, either. Using headphones or earbuds, especially at high volume, can cause the same serious damage and should be avoided (Gilliver, Carter, Macoun, Rosen, & Williams, 2012). It is especially easy to cause hearing loss with headphones or earbuds if you wear them while exercising; the increased blood flow to the ear during exercise makes hearing receptors more vulnerable to damage. Because young adults do not see their music listening behavior as a risk (Gilliver et al., 2012), hearing loss from this and other sources of loud noise is on the rise. The worse news is that hearing loss is also likely to increase among older adults in the future (Agrawal, Platz, & Niparko, 2008).

The cumulative effects of noise and normative age-related changes create the most common age-related hearing problem: reduced sensitivity to high-pitched tones, called **presbycusis**, *which occurs earlier and more severely than the loss of sensitivity to low-pitched tones* (Agrawal et al., 2008). Research indicates that by the late 70s, roughly half of older adults have presbycusis. Men typically have greater loss than women, but this may be because of differential exposure to noisy environments. Hearing loss usually is gradual at first but accelerates during the 40s, a pattern shown clearly in Figure 3.4.

Presbycusis results from four types of changes in the inner ear (Punnoose, Lynm, & Golub, 2012): sensorineural, consisting of atrophy and degeneration of receptor cells or the auditory nerve, and is permanent; and conductive, consisting of obstruction of or damage to the vibrating structures in the outer or middle ear area. Knowing the cause of a person's presbycusis is important, because the different causes have different implications for other aspects of hearing (Punnoose et al., 2012). Sensory presbycusis has little effect on other hearing abilities. Neural presbycusis seriously affects the ability to understand speech. Metabolic presbycusis produces severe loss of sensitivity to all pitches. Finally, mechanical presbycusis also produces loss across all pitches, but the loss is greatest for high pitches.

Because hearing plays a major role in social communication, its progressive loss could have an equally important effect on people's quality of life (Heyl & Wahl, 2012). Dalton and colleagues (2003) found that people with moderate to severe hearing loss were significantly more likely to have functional impairments with tasks in daily life (e.g., shopping). In addition, they were more likely to have decreased cognitive functioning. Clearly, significant hearing impairment can result in decreased quality of life.

Loss of hearing in later life can also cause numerous adverse emotional reactions, such as loss of independence, social isolation, irritation, paranoia, and depression. Much research indicates hearing loss per se does not cause social maladjustment or emotional disturbance. However, friends and relatives of an older person with undiagnosed or untreated hearing

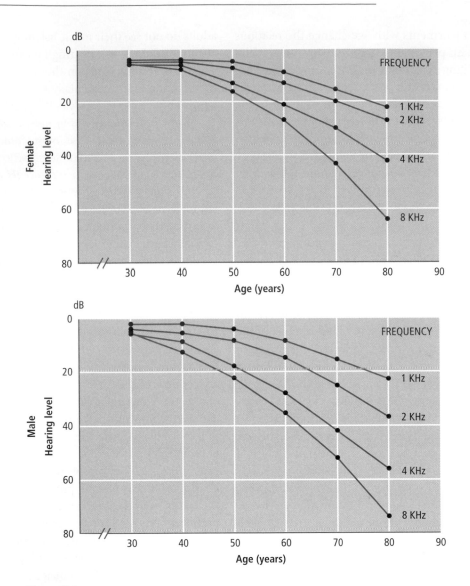

Figure 3.4

Gender differences in hearing loss. Notice that the changes in men are greater.

Source: J. M. Ordy, K. R. Brizzee, T. Beavers, & P. Medart. "Age differences in the Functional and Structural Organization of the Auditory System in Man," in J. M. Ordy & K. R. Brizzee (eds.), Sensory Systems and Communication in the Elderly. *Copyright © Lippincott, Williams & Wilkins, 1979.*

loss often attribute emotional changes to hearing loss, which strains the quality of interpersonal relationships (Li-Korotky, 2012). Thus, hearing loss may not directly affect older adults' self-concept or emotions, but it may negatively affect how they feel about interpersonal communication. By understanding hearing loss problems and ways to overcome them, people who have no hearing loss can play a large part in minimizing the effects of hearing loss on the older people in their lives.

Fortunately, many people with hearing loss can be helped through two types of amplification systems and cochlear implants, described in Table 3.3. Analog hearing aids are the most common and least expensive, but they provide the lowest-quality sound. Digital hearing aids include microchips that can be programmed for different hearing situations. Cochlear implants do not amplify sound; rather, a microphone transmits sound to a receiver, which stimulates auditory nerve fibers

Table 3.3

HELPING PEOPLE WITH HEARING LOSS	
TYPE OF DEVICE	**HOW IT WORKS**
Analog hearing aid	Although there are various styles, the basic design is always the same. A mold is placed in the outer ear to pick up sound and send it through a tube to a microphone. The microphone sends the sound to an amplifier. The amplifier enhances the sound and sends it to the receiver. The receiver sends the amplified sound to the ear.
Digital hearing aid	These are similar to analog hearing aids, but digital aids use directional microphones to control the flow of sound. Compression technology allows the sound to be increased or decreased as it rises and falls naturally in the room. Microchips allow hearing aids to be programmed for different hearing situations. This technology also uses multiple channels to deliver sound with varying amplification characteristics.
Cochlear implant	The main difference between hearing aids and cochlear implants is that implants do not make the sound louder. Rather, the implant is a series of components. A microphone, usually mounted behind the ear on the scalp, picks up sound. The sound is digitized by microchips and turned into coded signals, which are broadcast via FM radio signals to electrodes that have been inserted into the inner ear during surgery. The electrodes stimulate the auditory nerve fibers directly.

directly. Although technology continues to improve, none of these devices can duplicate your original equipment, so be kind to your ears.

Somesthesia and Balance

Imagine that you are locked in an embrace with a lover right now. Think about how good it feels when you are caressed lovingly, the tingly sensations you get. You can thank your somesthetic system for that; without it, you probably wouldn't bother. Remember Bertha, the older woman worried about falling? To maintain balance and avoid falls, your somesthetic system integrates a great deal of information about your body position.

Somesthesia. As you've probably discovered, a lover's touch feels different on various parts of your body. That's because the distribution of touch receptors is not consistent throughout the body; the greatest concentrations are in the lips, tongue, and fingertips. Although it takes more pressure with age to feel a touch on the smooth (nonhairy) skin on the hand such as the fingertips (Stevens, 1992), touch sensitivity in the hair-covered parts of the body is maintained into later life (Whitbourne, 1996a).

Older adults often report that they have more trouble regulating body temperature so that they feel comfortable (Guergova & Dufour, 2011). Changes in the perception of temperature are likely caused by aging

of the skin and reduction in the number of temperature receptors, as well as possible changes in the peripheral nerves. These changes are greater in the arms and legs.

Sensations from the skin, internal organs, and joints serve critical functions. They keep us in contact with our environment, help us avoid falling, help us communicate, keep us safe, and factor into our perception of pain. In terms of self-esteem, how well our body is functioning tells us something about how well we are doing. Losing bodily sensations can have major implications; loss of sexual sensitivity and changes in the ability to regulate one's body temperature affect the quality of life. How a person views these changes is critical for maintaining self-esteem. We can help by providing supportive environments that lead to successful compensatory behaviors. Despite years of research, we do not understand how or even whether our ability to perceive these sensations changes with age. Part of the problem has to do with how such sensations, including pain, are measured and how individual differences in tolerance affects people's reports.

Balance. Bertha, the older woman we met in the vignette, as well as anyone riding a bicycle, is concerned about losing balance and falling. Bertha (and each of us) gets information about balance mainly from the vestibular system, housed deep in the inner ear, but the eyes provide important cues, too. The vestibular system is designed to respond to the forces of gravity as they act on the head and then to provide this information to the parts of the brain that initiate the appropriate movements so that we can maintain balance. The eyes send signals to the back of the brain (the occipital cortex) and provide visual cues about maintaining balance. Importantly, changes in the white matter in the frontal cortex and in the occipital cortex that occur with age have been shown to be related to difficulty in maintaining proper balance (Van Impe, Coxon, Goble, Doumas, & Swinnen, 2012). The importance of white matter in aging was discussed in Chapter 2.

Dizziness (the vague feeling of being unsteady, floating, and light-headed) and vertigo (the sensation that one or one's surroundings are spinning) are common experiences for older adults. Although age-related structural changes in the vestibular system account for some of the problems, they do not entirely account for increases in dizziness and vertigo. Also, it takes older adults longer to integrate all the other sensory information coming to the brain to control posture (Aldwin & Gilmer, 2004). And dizziness can be a side effect of certain medications and physical illnesses.

Because of these changes, the likelihood of falling increases with age, especially after age 70 (Vereeck et al., 2008). Falls may be life-threatening events for older adults, especially for those with osteoporosis, because of the increased risk of broken bones. Environmental hazards such as loose rugs and slippery floors are more likely to be a factor for healthy, community-dwelling older adults, whereas disease is more likely to play a role in institutionalized people. Increases in body sway, the natural movement of the body to maintain balance, occur with increasing age. Connections between the degree of body sway and likelihood of falling have been shown, with people who fall often having more body sway (El Haber et al., 2008).

Because fear of falling has a real basis, it is important that concerns not be taken lightly (Granacher, Muehlbauer, & Gruber, 2012). Careful assessment of balance is important in understanding the nature and precise source of older adults' problems. People can also be trained to prevent falls through tai chi (Li et al., 2008), described in detail in the How Do We Know? feature.

HOW DO WE KNOW?:

PREVENTING FALLS THROUGH TAI CHI

Who were the investigators, and what were the aims of the studies? Helping older adults improve their balance is an important way to help lower the risk of falling. Tai chi, an ancient Chinese martial art, enhances body awareness. Previous research had shown that tai chi is an effective approach to improving balance, but whether it could be used with typical community-dwelling older adults was unknown. Li et al. (2008) examined whether using tai chi to improve balance could be implemented in a community-based senior center.

How did the investigators measure the topic of interest? Each Tai Chi—Moving for Better Movement class began with warm-up exercises, followed by teaching and practicing the 8-form variation of tai chi for 45 minutes, and ended with a 5-minute cooldown period. Program effectiveness was measured as the change in physical performance and quality of life as indexed by the functional reach test, the up-and-go test, time to rise from a chair, the 50-foot speed walk, and a 12-item physical and mental health scale. Frequency of falls was monitored monthly using a falls calendar in which participants marked when falls occurred. Long-term maintenance of the program was measured as the degree to

which participants continued during the 12 weeks after the formal program ended.

Who were the participants in the study? Participants were 140 community-dwelling adults in Oregon who were over age 60, in good health, physically mobile, and did not show any mental deficits. The study was conducted in senior centers.

What was the design of the studies? The researchers used a pretest-posttest design to measure change. Participants took the one-hour tai chi classes twice per week for 12 weeks.

Were there ethical concerns with the study? Participants in the study were provided with informed consent and were closely monitored throughout the study, so there were no ethical concerns.

What were the results? Results showed that participants improved on all measures during the course of the program. No loss of improvement was observed in the 12 weeks following the end of the formal program.

What did the investigators conclude? Li and colleagues concluded that tai chi represents an effective intervention to improve older adults' movement to lower the risk of falling. It was easily adapted in senior centers, making it a low-cost, high-payoff intervention. Because tai chi is a low-impact martial art, it is easily adapted for use by older adults.

Taste and Smell

Taste. There is an expression "too old to cut the mustard," which dates back to when people made mustard at home by grinding mustard seed and adding just the right amount of vinegar ("cutting the mustard") to balance the taste. If too much vinegar was added, the concoction tasted terrible, so the balance was critical. Many families found that older members tended to add too much vinegar.

Despite the everyday belief that taste ability changes with age, we do not have much data documenting what actually happens. We do know that the ability to detect different tastes declines gradually and that these declines vary a great deal from flavor to flavor and person to person and the amount of experience one has with particular substances (Bitnes et al., 2007). Whatever age differences we observe are not caused by a decline in the sheer number of taste buds; unlike other neural cells, the number of taste cells does not change appreciably across the life span (Imoscopi, Inelmen, Sergi, Miotto, & Manzato, 2012).

Despite the lack of evidence of large declines in the ability to taste, there is little question that older adults complain more about boring food and are at risk for malnutrition as a result (Henkin, 2008). The explanation may be that changes in the enjoyment of food are caused by psychosocial issues (such as personal adjustment), changes in smell (which we consider next), or disease. For instance, we are much more likely to eat a balanced diet and to enjoy our food when we feel well enough to cook, when we do not eat alone, and when we get a whiff of the enticing aromas from the kitchen.

Smell. "Stop and smell the roses." "Ooh! What's that perfume you're wearing?" "Yuck! What's that smell?" There is a great deal of truth in the saying "The nose knows." Smell is a major part of our everyday lives. How something smells can alert us that dinner is cooking, warn of a gas leak or a fire, let us know that we are clean, or be sexually arousing. Many of our social interactions involve smell (or the lack of it). We spend billions of dollars making our bodies smell appealing to others. It is easy to see that any age-related change in sense of smell would have far-reaching consequences.

Researchers agree that the ability to detect odors remains fairly intact until the 60s, when it begins to

There is little evidence to support age-related changes in taste.

© Monkey Business Images/Shutterstock.com

decline, but there are wide variations across people and types of odors (Nordin, 2012). These variations could have important practical implications. A large survey conducted by the National Geographic Society indicated that older adults were not as able to identify particular odors as younger people. One of the odors tested was the substance added to natural gas that enables people to detect leaks—not being able to identify it is a potentially fatal problem.

Abnormal changes in the ability to smell are turning out to be important in the differential diagnosis of probable Alzheimer's disease, resulting in the development of several quick tests such as the Pocket Smell Test (Steffens & Potter, 2008). According to several studies, people with Alzheimer's disease can identify only 60% of the odors identified by age-matched control participants; in more advanced stages of the disease, this further declined to only 40% compared with controls. These changes give clinicians another indicator for diagnosing suspected cases of Alzheimer's disease.

The major psychological consequences of changes in smell concern eating, safety, and pleasurable experiences. Odors play an important role in enjoying food and protecting us from harm. Socially, decreases in our ability to detect unpleasant odors may lead to embarrassing situations in which we are unaware that we have body odors or need to brush our teeth. Social interactions could suffer as a result of these problems. Smells also play a key role in remembering life experiences from the past. Who can forget the smell of cookies baking in Grandma's oven? Loss of odor cues may mean that our sense of the past suffers as well.

ADULT DEVELOPMENT IN ACTION

If you were a consultant asked to design the optimal home environment for older adults, what specific design features would you include that would provide support for normative age-related sensory changes? (Keep your answer and refer to it in Chapter 5.)

3.4 Vital Functions

LEARNING OBJECTIVES

- What age-related changes occur in the cardiovascular system? What types of cardiovascular disease are common in adult development and aging? What are the psychological effects of age-related changes in the cardiovascular system?
- What structural and functional changes occur with age in the respiratory system? What are the most common types of respiratory diseases in older adults? What are the psychological effects of age-related changes in the respiratory system?

Steve is an active 73-year-old man who walks and plays golf regularly. He smoked earlier in his life, but he quit years ago. He also watches his diet to control fat intake. Steve recently experienced some chest pains and sweating but dismissed it as simply age-related. After all, he thinks, I take care of myself. However, Steve's wife, Grace, is concerned he may have a more serious problem.

You cannot live without your cardiovascular (heart and blood vessels) and your respiratory (lungs and air passageways) systems; that's why they are called vital functions. Each undergoes important normative changes with age that can affect the quality of life. In this section, we'll find out whether Grace has reason to worry

about Steve's symptoms. We'll also discover why figuring out the pattern of age-related changes in the respiratory system is very difficult (here's a tip—it has to do with biological-psychological-environmental interactions).

Overall, the age-related changes in the cardiovascular and respiratory systems are excellent examples of how the forces of development interact. On the biological front, we know that some cardiovascular and respiratory diseases have important genetic links. Psychologically, certain personality traits have been linked with increased risk of disease. Socioculturally, some cardiovascular and respiratory diseases are clearly tied to lifestyle. The impact of both cardiovascular and respiratory diseases also differs as a function of age. Let's explore in more detail how these various forces come together.

Cardiovascular System

Tune into your pulse. The beating of your heart is the work of an amazing organ. In an average lifetime, the heart beats more than 3 billion times, pumping the equivalent of more than 900 million gallons of blood. Two important age-related structural changes in the heart are the accumulation of fat deposits and the stiffening of the heart muscle caused by tissue changes. By the late 40s and early 50s, the fat deposits in the lining around the heart may form a continuous sheet. Meanwhile, healthy muscle tissue is being replaced by connective tissue, which causes a thickening and stiffening of the heart muscle and valves. These changes reduce the amount of muscle tissue available to contract the heart. The net effect is that the remaining muscle must work harder. To top it off, the amount of blood that the heart can pump declines from roughly 5 liters per minute at age 20 to about 3.5 liters per minute at age 70 (National Institute on Aging, 2012a).

The most important change in the circulatory system involves the stiffening (hardening) of the walls of the arteries. These changes are caused by calcification of the arterial walls and by replacement of elastic fibers with less elastic ones.

The combination of changes in the heart and the circulatory system results in a significant decrease in a person's ability to cope with physical exertion, especially aerobic exercise. By age 65, the average adult has experienced a 60 to 70% decline in the aerobic capacity since young adulthood. However, if you stay in good shape throughout adulthood, the decline is much less (National Institute on Aging, 2012a). This decline is one reason why older adults who are not in good shape are more likely to have heart attacks while performing moderately exerting tasks such as shoveling snow. The changes that occur with aging in the heart related to exercise are shown in Figure 3.5.

Cardiovascular Diseases. In the United States, more than 30% of the people currently have some form of cardiovascular disease; by 2030 this will rise to over 40% (Roger, Go, Lloyd-Jones, Benjamin, Berry, Borden et al., 2012). It is the leading cause of death in all ethnic groups in the United States and in many other countries. The incidence of cardiovascular disease increases dramatically with age, with the rates for men higher until age 75 for coronary heart disease and for women higher for stroke. Incidence rates over age 75 tend to converge for men and women. How cardiovascular disease dominates causes of death in the United States in people under and over age 85 is shown in Figure 3.6.

In terms of ethnic differences in various types of cardiovascular disease, African Americans, American Indians, and Native Hawaiians have the highest rates of hypertension (high blood pressure; we will consider this condition a bit later), and Asian Americans have the lowest rate of heart disease (Roger et al., 2012). In part these differences are due to genetics, and in part they are due to life style and inadequate access to health care.

Rates of cardiovascular disease have been declining in the United States among men since the 1980s (Roger et al., 2012). These declines may be deceiving, though, because key risk factors are actually increasing; for example, roughly two-thirds of adults are classified as overweight, and rates of diabetes are going up.

Several types of cardiovascular disease are noteworthy. **Congestive heart failure** *occurs when cardiac output and the ability of the heart to contract severely decline, making the heart enlarge, pressure in the veins increase, and the body swell.* Congestive heart failure is

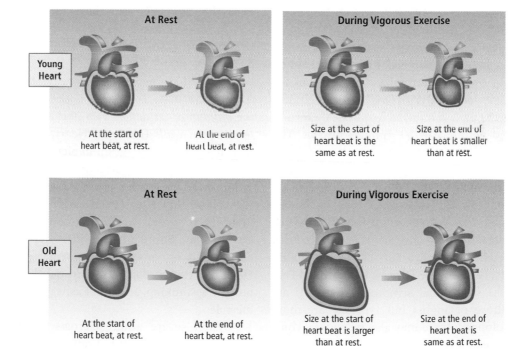

Figure 3.5
The Heart: Young and Old.

Source: National Institute on Aging (2008). Aging Hearts and Arteries: A Scientific Quest. Retrieved September 3, 2008, from http://www.nia.nih.gov/HealthInformation/Publications/AgingHeartsandArteries/default.htm. Design by Levine and Associates, Washington, DC.

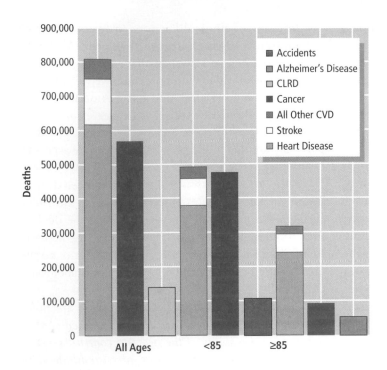

Figure 3.6

Cardiovascular disease (CVD) and other major causes of death: Total, <85 years of age, and ≥85 years of age.

Source: National Center for Health Statistics and National Heart, Lung, and Blood Institute.

the most common cause of hospitalization for people over age 65. **Angina pectoris** *occurs when the oxygen supply to the heart muscle becomes insufficient, resulting in chest pain.* Angina may feel like chest pressure, a burning pain, or a squeezing that radiates from the chest to the back, neck, and arms (Mayo Clinic, 2011b). In most cases the pain is induced by physical exertion and is relieved within 5 to 10 minutes by rest. The most common treatment of angina is nitroglycerine, although in some cases coronary arteries may need to be cleared through surgical procedures or replaced through coronary bypass surgery.

Heart attack, called **myocardial infarction (MI)**, *occurs when blood supply to the heart is severely reduced or cut off.* Mortality after a heart attack is much higher for older adults (Centers for Disease Control and Prevention, 2012a). The initial symptoms of an MI are identical to those of angina but typically are more severe and prolonged; there may also be nausea, vomiting, severe weakness, and sweating, which Steve experienced in the vignette. Thus, Grace is right to be concerned about Steve's symptoms. However, chest pain may be absent in women and older adults, resulting in so-called silent heart attacks (National Institutes

of Health, 2011). Treating heart attack victims of all ages includes careful evaluation and a prescribed rehabilitation program consisting of lifestyle changes in diet and exercise.

Atherosclerosis. *Is an age-related disease caused by the buildup of fat deposits on and the calcification of the arterial walls* (National Heart, Lung and Blood Institute, 2011). A diagram depicting atherosclerosis is shown in Figure 3.7. Much like sandbars in a river or mineral deposits in pipes, the fat deposits interfere with blood flow through the arteries. These deposits begin very early in life and continue throughout the life span. Some amount of fat deposit inevitably occurs and is considered a normal part of aging. However, excess deposits may develop from poor nutrition, smoking, and other aspects of an unhealthy lifestyle.

When severe atherosclerosis occurs in blood vessels that supply the brain, neurons may not receive proper nourishment, causing them to malfunction or die, a condition called cerebrovascular disease. *When the blood flow to a portion of the brain is completely cut off, a* **cerebrovascular accident**

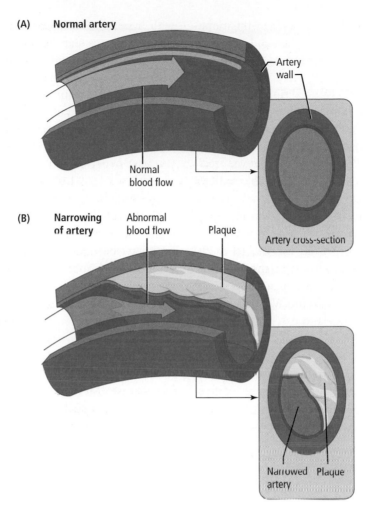

(A)   Normal artery

Artery
wall

Normal
blood flow

Artery cross-section

**(B)   Narrowing   Abnormal   Plaque
of artery   blood flow**

Narrowed   Plaque
artery

Figure 3.7
Normal artery and atherosclerosis. (A) shows a normal artery with normal blood flow. (B) shows an artery with plaque buildup.

Source: National Heart, Lung and Blood Institute (2011). Retrieved from http://www.nhlbi.nih.gov/health/health topics/topics/atherosclerosis/

(CVA), *or stroke, results.* Estimates are that every 40 seconds someone in the United States has a CVA, making stroke one of the most common forms of cardiovascular disease (Centers for Disease Control and Prevention, 2012b). Causes of CVAs include clots that block blood flow in an artery or the actual breaking of a blood vessel, which creates a cerebral hemorrhage. The severity of a CVA and likelihood of recovery depend on the specific area of the brain involved, the extent of disruption in blood flow, and the duration of the disruption. Consequently, a CVA may affect such a small area that it goes almost unnoticed, or it may be so severe as to cause death. Two common problems following a CVA are *aphasia* (problems with speech) and *hemiplegia* (paralysis on one side of the body).

The risk of a CVA increases with age; in fact, CVAs are among the leading causes of death and chronic disorders among older adults in the United States (Centers for Disease Control and Prevention, 2012b). In addition to age, other risk factors include being male, being African American, and having high blood pressure, heart disease, or diabetes. The higher risk among African Americans appears to be caused by a greater prevalence of hypertension in this population compounded by poorer quality and access to health care in general (Centers for Disease Control and Prevention, 2012c).

Treatment of CVA has advanced significantly. The most important advance is use of the clot-dissolving drug tissue plasminogen activator (tPA) to treat CVAs (Saver, Fonarow, Smith, Reeves, Grau-Sepulveda, Pan et al., 2013). Currently, tPA is the only approved treatment for CVAs caused by blood clots, which constitute 80% of all CVAs. Not every patient should receive tPA treatment, and tPA is effective only if given promptly, which is vitally important. So if you or a person you know thinks they are experiencing a CVA, get medical attention immediately, because tPA therapy must be started within 3 hours after the onset of a stroke to be most effective. Recovery from CVA depends on the severity of the stroke, area and extent of the brain affected, and patient age.

Besides blood clots, high blood pressure plays a major role in CVAs. (Do you know what yours is?) Blood pressure consists of measuring two types of pressure: the pressure during the heart's contraction phase when it is pumping blood through the body, called the systolic pressure, and the pressure during the heart's relaxation phase between beats, called the diastolic pressure. The systolic pressure is always given first. On average, a blood pressure of 120 over 80 mm Hg (millimeters of mercury, the scale on which the pressure is measured) is considered optimal for adults.

As we grow older, blood pressure tends to increase normally, mostly because of structural changes in the cardiovascular system. *When blood pressure increases become severe, defined as 140 mm Hg or more systolic pressure (the top number in a blood pressure reading) or 90 mm Hg or more diastolic pressure (the lower number in the reading), the disease* **hypertension** *results* (WebMD.com, 2012a). Nearly 30% of the population age 18 and older has some degree of hypertension (Yoon, Burt, Louis, & Carroll, 2012). This rate is roughly the same for European Americans and Mexican Americans, but jumps to about 40% among African Americans. This difference may be caused by a genetic mutation affecting enzymes that help control blood pressure and by environmental factors related to stress, poor access to health care, and poverty.

Hypertension is a disease you ignore at the risk of greatly increasing your chances of dying. Older adults

with hypertension have three times the risk of dying from cardiovascular disease, and it has important negative effects on cognitive abilities and a host of other organs including kidney function (Yoon et al., 2012). Because hypertension is a disease with no clear symptoms, most people with undiagnosed hypertension are not aware they have a problem. Regular blood pressure monitoring is the only sure way to find out whether you have hypertension. It could save your life.

What causes this silent killer? Several suspected causes are obesity, stress, lack of exercise, and dietary sodium (salt) (WebMD, 2011a). All of these causes are related to life style and are under one's control. Genetic links have been identified as well.

Too much sodium (salt) is a factor that many people overlook. Eating sodium in one's diet is essential for life because the body needs a certain amount each day to regulate blood pressure and blood volume properly (McGee, 2007). However, too much sodium can have several very bad effects on health: In addition to hypertension, it can cause congestive heart failure and kidney disease (McGee, 2007). Sodium occurs naturally in many foods, such as raw celery, many cheeses, and scallops. It is also present in nearly all processed foods, often in high concentrations; for example, one serving of typical saltine crackers contains 1,100 milligrams, pretzels have 1,650, and a hot dog about 1,100. When you consider that the American Heart Association (2011) recommends that adults should not consume more than 1,500 milligrams per day (about a teaspoon), it is clear that getting too much sodium is easy to do.

Another chronic cardiovascular condition that is discussed less often is *hypotension,* or low blood pressure. Symptoms of hypotension include dizziness or light-headedness that is caused most commonly when you stand up quickly after lying down or sitting, or sometimes after eating (WebMD, 2011b). Hypotension often is related to anemia and is more common in older adults. Although hypotension per se is not a dangerous condition, the resulting dizziness can increase the likelihood of fainting and falls, which may result in more serious injury.

Respiratory System

You probably don't pay much attention to your breathing unless you're gasping for breath after exercise—or you're an older adult. Older adults tend to notice their breathing a great deal more. Why? With increasing age, the rib cage and the air passageways become stiffer, making it harder to breathe. The lungs change in appearance over time, going gradually from their youthful pinkish color to a dreary gray, caused mainly by breathing in carbon particles (from air pollution). The maximum amount of air we can take into the lungs in a single breath begins to decline in the 20s, decreasing by 40% by age 85. And the rate at which we can exchange oxygen for carbon dioxide drops significantly as the membranes of the air sacs in the lungs deteriorate (Pride, 2005).

One of the difficulties in understanding age-related changes in the respiratory system is that it is hard to know how much of the change is caused specifically by normative developmental factors and how much is caused by environmental factors. For example, it is difficult to determine how much age-related change in respiratory function is due to air pollution.

Respiratory Diseases. *The most common and incapacitating respiratory disorder in older adults is* **chronic obstructive pulmonary disease (COPD)**, *a family of diseases that includes chronic bronchitis and emphysema.* By 2012, COPD was the third-leading-cause of death in the United States, with rates higher in women than in men. Smoking is the most important cause of COPD, but secondhand smoke, air pollution, and industrial dusts and chemicals can also cause it (American Lung Association, 2012).

Emphysema *is the most serious type of COPD and is characterized by the destruction of the membranes around the air sacs in the lungs* (WebMD, 2012b). This irreversible destruction creates holes in the lung, drastically reducing the ability to exchange oxygen and carbon dioxide. To make matters worse, the bronchial tubes collapse prematurely when the person exhales, thereby preventing the lungs from emptying completely. Emphysema is a very debilitating disease. In its later stages, even the smallest physical exertion causes a struggle for air. People with emphysema may have such poorly oxygenated blood that they become confused and disoriented. About 95% of the cases of emphysema are self-induced by smoking; the remaining cases are caused by a genetic deficiency of a protein known as an a1-antitrypsin (WebMD, 2012b). This protein, a natural "lung protector," is made by the liver;

when it is missing, emphysema is inevitable. Although some drugs are available to help ease breathing, lung transplantation remains a treatment of last resort for people with emphysema, especially in the genetic form of the disease.

Chronic bronchitis can occur at any age, but it is more common in people over age 45, especially among people who are exposed to high concentrations of dust, irritating fumes, and air pollution. Treatment usually consists of medication (called bronchodilators) to open bronchial passages and a change of work environment. Similarly, asthma is another very common respiratory disease that is increasing in prevalence. Treatment for asthma also involves the use of bronchodilators.

Overall, treatment for COPD needs to begin as soon as a problem is diagnosed. That may involve stopping smoking (the best treatment available for smokers). In other cases, supplemental oxygen or using glucocorticosteroid medications may provide some relief. The thing to remember, though, is that the damage caused by COPD is irreversible.

ADULT DEVELOPMENT IN ACTION

If you ran a training program for personal exercise trainers, what age-related changes in vital functions would you emphasize?

3.5 The Reproductive System

LEARNING OBJECTIVES
- What reproductive changes occur in women?
- What reproductive changes occur in men?
- What are the psychological effects of reproductive changes?

Helen woke up in the middle of the night drenched in sweat. She'd been feeling fine when she went to bed after her 48th birthday party, so she wasn't sure what was the matter. She thought she was too young to experience menopause. Helen wonders what other things she'll experience.

As you probably surmised, Helen has begun going through "the change," a time of life that many women look forward to and just as many see as the beginning of old age. For women like Helen, "the change" is the defining physiological event in middle age. Men do not endure such sweeping biological changes but experience several gradual changes instead. Beyond the physiological effects, these changes have important psychological implications because many people think midlife is a key time for redefining ourselves. Let's see how the experience differs for women and men.

Female Reproductive System

As Helen is beginning to experience, the major reproductive change in women during adulthood is the loss of the natural ability to bear children. *As women enter midlife, they experience a major biological process, called the* **climacteric,** *during which they pass from their reproductive to nonreproductive years.* **Menopause** *is the point at which menstruation stops.*

The major reproductive change in women during adulthood is the loss of the ability to bear children. This change begins in the 40s as menstrual cycles become irregular, and by age 50 to 55 it is usually complete (Vorvick, 2010). *This time of transition from regular menstruation to menopause is called* **perimenopause,** *and how long it lasts varies considerably.* The gradual loss and eventual end of monthly periods is accompanied by decreases in estrogen and progesterone levels, changes in the reproductive organs, and changes in sexual functioning

A variety of physical and psychological symptoms may accompany perimenopause and menopause with decreases in hormonal levels (WomensHealth. gov, 2010a): hot flashes, night sweats, headaches, sleep problems, mood changes, more urinary infections, pain during sex, difficulty concentrating, vaginal dryness, less interest in sex, and an increase in body fat around the waist. Many women report no symptoms at all, but most women experience at least some, and there are large differences across social, ethnic, and cultural groups in how they are expressed (Nosek, Kennedy, & Gudmundsdottir, 2012; Utian, 2005). For example, women in the Mayan culture of Mexico and Central America welcome menopause and its changes as a natural phenomenon and do not attach any stigma to aging (Mahady et al., 2008). In the United States, Latinas and African Americans, especially working-class women, tend to view menopause more positively,

whereas European American women describe it more negatively (Dillaway et al., 2008). Women in South American countries report a variety of symptoms that impair quality of life, many of which persist five years beyond menopause (Blümel, Chedraui, Baron, Belzares, Bencosme, Calle, et al., 2012).

The decline in estrogen that women experience after menopause is related to increased risk of osteoporosis, cardiovascular disease, stress urinary incontinence (involuntary loss of urine during physical stress, as when exercising, sneezing, or laughing), weight gain, and memory loss (Dumas et al., 2010; Mayo Clinic, 2012b). In the case of cardiovascular disease, at age 50 (prior to menopause) women have 3 times less risk of heart attacks than men on average. Ten years after menopause, when women are about 60, their risk equals that of men.

In response to these increased risks and to the estrogen-related symptoms that women experience, one approach is the use of **menopausal hormone therapy (MHT):** *women take low doses of estrogen, which is often combined with progestin (synthetic form of progesterone).* Hormone therapy is controversial and has been the focus of many research studies with conflicting results (Bach, 2010; Mayo Clinic, 2012b). There appear to be both benefits and risks with MHT, as discussed in the Current Controversies Feature.

CURRENT CONTROVERSIES:

MENOPAUSAL HORMONE THERAPY

For many years, women have had the choice of taking medications to replace the female hormones that are no longer produced naturally by the body after menopause. Hormone therapy may involve taking estrogen alone or in combination with progesterone (or progestin in its synthetic form). Research on the effects of menopause hormone therapy have helped clarify the appropriate use of such medications.

Until about 2003, it was thought that menopausal hormone therapy (MHT) was beneficial for most women, and results from several studies were positive. But results from the Women's Health Initiative research in the United States and from the Million Women Study in the United Kingdom indicated that, for some types of MHT, there were several potentially serious side effects. As a result, physicians are now far more cautious in recommending MHT.

The Women's Health Initiative (WHI), begun in the United States in 1991, was a very large study (National Heart, Lung, and Blood Institute, 2003). The estrogen plus progestin trial used 0.625 milligram of estrogen taken daily plus 2.5 milligrams of medroxyprogesterone acetate (Prempro) taken daily. This combination was chosen because it is the mostly commonly prescribed form of the combined hormone therapy in the United States and, in several observational studies, had appeared to benefit women's health. The women in the WHI estrogen plus progestin study were aged 50 to 79 when they enrolled in the study between 1993 and 1998. The health of study participants was carefully monitored by an independent panel called the Data and Safety Monitoring Board (DSMB). The study was stopped in July 2002 because investigators discovered a significant increased risk for breast cancer and that overall the risks outnumbered the benefits. However, in addition to the increased risk of breast cancer, heart attack, stroke, and blood clots, MHT resulted in fewer hip fractures and lower rates of colorectal cancer.

The Million Women Study began in 1996 and includes 1 in 4 women over age 50 in the United Kingdom, the largest study of its kind ever conducted. Like the Women's Health Initiative, the study examined how MHT (both estrogen/progestin combinations and estrogen alone) affects breast cancer, cardiovascular disease, and other aspects of women's health. Results from this study confirmed the Women's Health Initiative outcome of increased risk for breast cancer associated with MHT.

The combined results from the WHI and the Million Women Study led physicians to recommend that women over age 60 should not begin MHT to relieve menopausal symptoms or protect their health. In fact, women over age 60 who begin MHT are at increased risk for certain cancers.

In sum, women face difficult choices when deciding whether to use MHT as a means of combatting certain menopausal symptoms and protecting themselves against other diseases. For example, MHT can help reduce hot flashes and night sweats, help reduce vaginal dryness and discomfort during sexual intercourse, slow bone loss, and perhaps ease mood swings. On the other hand, MHT can increase a woman's risk of blood clots, heart attack, stroke, breast cancer, and gallbladder disease.

The best course of action is to consult closely with one's physician to weigh the benefits and risks. It's also a good idea to keep in mind several key points (WomensHealth.gov, 2010b):

- Once a woman reaches menopause, MHT is recommended only as a short-term treatment.
- Doctors very rarely recommend MHT to prevent certain chronic diseases like osteoporosis.
- Women who have gone through menopause should not take MHT to prevent heart disease.
- MHT should not be used to prevent memory loss, dementia, or Alzheimer's disease.

Women's genital organs undergo progressive change after menopause. The vaginal walls shrink and become thinner, the size of the vagina decreases, vaginal lubrication is reduced and delayed, and the external genitalia shrink somewhat. These changes have important effects on sexual activity, such as an increased possibility of painful intercourse and a longer time and more stimulation needed to reach orgasm. Failure to achieve orgasm is more common in midlife and beyond than in a woman's younger years. However, maintaining an active sex life throughout adulthood lowers the degree to which problems are encountered. Despite these changes, there is no physiological reason not to continue having an active and enjoyable sex life from middle age through late life. The vaginal dryness that occurs, for example, can be countered by using personal lubricants, such as *K-Y* or *Astroglide*.

Whether women continue to have an active sex life has a lot more to do with the availability of a suitable partner than a woman's desire for sexual relations. This is especially true for older women. The AARP *Modern Maturity* sexuality study (AARP, 1999), the *Sex in America* study (Jacoby, 2005), and the *Sex, Romance, and Relationships* (Fisher, 2010) studies all found that older married women were far more likely to have an active sex life than unmarried women. The primary reason for the decline in women's sexual activity with age is the lack of a willing or appropriate partner, not a lack of physical ability or desire (AARP, 1999; Fisher, 2010; Jacoby, 2005).

Male Reproductive System

Unlike women, men do not have a physiological (and cultural) event to mark reproductive changes, although there is a gradual decline in testosterone levels (Bribiescas, 2010) that can occur to a greater extent in men who are obese or have diabetes (Nigro & Christ-Crain, 2012). Men do not experience a complete loss of the ability to father children, as this varies widely from individual to individual, but men do experience a normative decline in the quantity of sperm (Dugdale, 2012). However, even at age 80 a man is still half as fertile as he was at age 25 and is quite capable of fathering a child.

With increasing age the prostate gland enlarges, becomes stiffer, and may obstruct the urinary tract. Prostate cancer becomes a real threat during middle age; annual screenings are often recommended for men over age 50 (American Cancer Society, 2012a).

Men experience some physiological changes in sexual performance. By old age, men report less perceived demand to ejaculate, a need for longer time and more stimulation to achieve erection and orgasm, and a much longer resolution phase during which erection is impossible (Saxon & Etten, 1994). Older men also report more frequent failures to achieve orgasm and loss of erection during intercourse (AARP, 1999; Fisher, 2010; Jacoby, 2005). However, the advent of Viagra, Cialis, and other medications to treat erectile dysfunction has provided older men with easy-to-use medical treatments and the possibility of an active sex life well into later life.

As with women, as long as men enjoy sex and have a willing partner, sexual activity is a lifelong option. Also as with women, the most important ingredient of sexual intimacy for men is a strong relationship with a partner (AARP, 1999; Fisher, 2010; Jacoby, 2005). For example, married men in early middle age tend to have intercourse four to eight times per month. The loss of an available partner is a significant reason frequency of intercourse drops on average by two and three times per month in men over age 50 and 60, respectively (Araujo, Mohr, & McKinlay, 2004).

Psychological Implications

Older adults say that engaging in sexual behavior is an important aspect of human relationships throughout adulthood (AARP, 1999; Fisher, 2010; Jacoby, 2005). Healthy adults at any age are capable of having and enjoying sexual relationships. Moreover, the desire to do so normally does not diminish. Unfortunately, one of the myths in our society is that older adults cannot and should not be sexual. Many young adults find it difficult to think about their grandparents having great sex.

Such stereotyping has important consequences. What do you think to yourself when we see an older couple being publicly affectionate? Can you envision your grandparents enjoying an active sex life? Many people feel that such behavior is cute. But observers tend not to refer to their own or their peers' relationships in this way. Many nursing homes and other institutions actively dissuade their residents from having sexual relationships and may even refuse to allow married couples to share the same room. Adult children may believe their widowed parent does not have the right to establish a new sexual relationship. The message we are sending is that sexual activity is fine for the young but not for the old. The major reason why older women do not engage in sexual relations is the lack of a socially sanctioned partner. It is not that they have lost interest; rather, they believe they are simply not permitted to express their sexuality any longer.

ADULT DEVELOPMENT IN ACTION

As a gerontologist, what do you think should be done to create a more realistic view of reproductive changes and interest in sex across the adult lifespan?

3.6 The Autonomic Nervous System

LEARNING OBJECTIVES
- What major changes occur in the autonomic nervous system?
- What are the psychological effects of changes in the autonomic nervous system?

Jorge is an active 83-year-old former factory worker who lives with his wife, Olivia, in a crowded apartment in Los Angeles. Over the past few years, Jorge has had increasing difficulty handling the heat of southern California summers. Olivia has noticed that Jorge takes more naps during the day and sleeps poorly at night. Jorge and Olivia wonder whether there is something wrong with him.

As we saw in Chapter 2, our brains are the most complex structures yet discovered in the universe. Everything that makes us individuals is housed in the brain, and we are only now beginning to unlock its mysteries through the techniques described in Chapter 2.

In this section, we build in the changes we encountered in Chapter 2 and turn our attention to the autonomic nervous system (nerves in the body outside the brain and spinal column). Jorge's experiences are related to changes in the autonomic nervous system; we'll discover whether Jorge's problems are normative.

Autonomic Nervous System

Do you feel hot or cold right now? Do your palms sweat when you get nervous? What happens when you get frightened? These and other regulation functions in your body are controlled by the autonomic nervous system. Fortunately, few changes occur in the autonomic nervous system as we age, but two changes do tend to get people's attention: body temperature control and sleep. Jorge, whom we met in the vignette, is experiencing both of these changes.

Regulating Body Temperature. Every year, newscasts around the world report that during very cold or very hot spells more older adults die than people in other age groups. Why does this happen? We considered evidence earlier in this chapter that cold and warm temperature thresholds may change little. If older people can feel cold and warm stimuli placed against them about as well as people of other age groups, what accounts for these deaths?

It turns out that older adults have difficulty telling that their core body temperature is low (Blatteis, 2012). In other words, older people are much less likely to notice that they are cold. Regulating body temperature involves nearly all body systems, most of which undergo declines with age. Because some of them respond to training (e.g., fitness training can help with declines in the musculoskeletal system), some causes of the declines can be addressed. However, changes in the skin and metabolic systems are inevitable. To make matters worse, older adults also have slower vasoconstrictor response, which is the ability to raise core body temperature (i.e., warm up) when the body's peripheral temperature drops (Blatteis, 2012; DeGroot & Kenney, 2007; Van Someren, 2007).

Similarly, older adults have trouble responding to high heat, because they do not sweat as much (Blatteis, 2012). Sweating decreases with age from the lower limbs up to the forehead, and is due to lower sweat production.

Taken together, the difficulties older adults have in regulating body temperature in extreme cold and heat are the primary reason why older adults are much more susceptible to hypothermia (body temperature below

Older people are less able to regulate their core body temperature because they have more difficulty noticing they are cold.

95°F over a long period) and hyperthermia (body temperature above 98.6°F that cannot be relieved by sweating) (Blatteis, 2012). This is why social service agencies are especially mindful of older adults during major weather events.

Sleep and Aging. How did you sleep last night? If you are older, chances are that you had some trouble. In fact, sleep complaints and problems are common in older adults (Wolkove et al., 2007a). These complaints most often concern difficulty in falling asleep, frequent or prolonged awakenings during the night, early morning awakenings, and a feeling of not sleeping very well. Effects of poor sleep are experienced the next day; moodiness, poorer performance on tasks involving sustained concentration, fatigue, and lack of motivation are some of the telltale signs.

Nearly every aspect of sleep undergoes age-related changes (Wolkove et al., 2007a). It takes older adults longer to fall asleep, they are awake more at night, they are more easily awakened, and they experience major shifts in their sleep–wake cycles, called circadian rhythms. Across adulthood, circadian rhythms move from a two-phase pattern of sleep (awake during the day and asleep at night for most people) to a multiphase rhythm reminiscent of that of infants (daytime napping and shorter sleep cycles at night). These changes are related to the changes in regulating core body temperature discussed earlier. Other major causes of sleep disturbance include sleep apnea (stopping breathing for 5 to 10 seconds), periodic leg jerks, heartburn, frequent need to urinate, poor physical health, and depression.

Older adults try lots of things to help themselves, such as taking daytime naps, without success (Wolkove et al., 2007b). As a result, many older adults are prescribed sleeping pills or hypnotic sedatives. But these medications must be used with great caution with older adults, and often do not help alleviate the problem in any case. Among the most effective treatments of sleep problems are increasing physical exercise, reducing caffeine intake, avoiding daytime naps, and making sure that the sleeping environment is as quiet and dark as possible (Passarella & Duong, 2008; Wolkove et al., 2007b).

Some research has linked the need for sleep to the amount of brain activity devoted to learning that occurred prior to sleep (Cirelli, 2012). So one hypothesis is that sleep needs decrease with age in relation to decreased new learning that occurs with age. However, research specifically examining this hypothesis remains to be done.

Research evidence also points to difficulties in regulating the optimal body temperature for good sleep may also be part of the issue for older adults (Romeijn, Raymann, Most, Te Lindert, Van Der Meijden, Fronczek, et al., 2012). Interestingly, this problem may in turn be related to changes in the frontal cortex, a key part of the brain that is involved in evaluating comfort. As we saw in Chapter 2, this part of the brain is involved in numerous age-related changes. Whether interventions that are aimed at helping insomniacs find their optimal body temperature for sleeping will work remains to be seen.

As we now know, Jorge's difficulty with heat and sleep reflect normative changes that occur with age. Olivia should be informed of these changes and encouraged to make sure Jorge drinks plenty of water and adopts good sleep habits.

Psychological Implications

Being able to maintain proper body temperature can literally be a matter of life and death. So the increased difficulty in doing that poses a real threat to older adults. Being in an environment that provides external means of temperature regulation (i.e., heating and air conditioning), and that has back-up systems in the event of emergency (e.g., generators in the event of power failures) are much more important for older adults.

Because thermoregulation involves so many of the body's systems, and because many of the age-related changes that occur are inevitable, it is important to focus on those systems that respond to intervention. By doing whatever is possible to keep those systems functioning as well as possible, people can lessen the overall problem of regulating body temperature.

A good night's sleep is also important for maintaining good overall health. Ensuring that the sleep environment is maximally conducive to sleeping and by providing whatever environmental supports possible, we can increase the odds of improving sleep.

BEGIN ADULT DEVELOPMENT IN ACTION:

ADULT DEVELOPMENT IN ACTIONS

What would be the best questions to ask an older adult client if you, as a social worker, were establishing whether the client had any problems with tolerating heat/cold or sleeping?

SOCIAL POLICY IMPLICATIONS

No one wants to fall and get hurt. That's true in any age group, but especially so with older adults, particularly older adults who live alone. The fear of falling is real, and even has been used as the basis for a famous television ad for an emergency alert system: An older woman is shown falling and saying, "I've fallen, and I can't get up." (Check out the original ad and the remixes on YouTube.)

Because of normative age-related changes in vision, hearing, balance, musculoskeletal changes, and other aspects of functioning, the risk of falling increases with age. As you can see in Figure 3.8, that increase is quite dramatic over age 75.

Falls can result in serious injuries or even death to older adults. People with osteoporosis are especially vulnerable to breaking their hip or pelvis, or may suffer a traumatic brain injury, any of which may necessitate a long rehabilitation. As a result, much attention has been paid to preventing falls. Some of these interventions are simple (such as removing loose floor rugs and ensuring that there is sufficient light and reduced glare). Others involve life style changes or technology.

The Centers for Disease Control and Prevention (2012d) have translated the research findings about increased risk and consequences of falls in older adults and have created several suggestions on how to prevent them. Among their suggestions are:

- Get exercise to strengthen muscles. Programs such as the Tai Chi program discussed in the How Do We Know? feature are effective.

- Be careful of medication side effects. Some medications may cause dizziness or drowsiness, which can increase the risk for falling.

- Correct any visual impairments to the extent possible.

- Remove hazards at home. Remove clutter you can trip over (books, clothes, and other materials on the floor). Install handrails on stairways. Use non-slip mats and grab bars in showers and bath tubs.

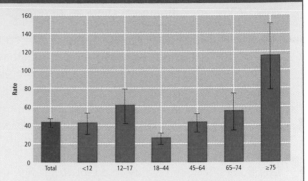

Figure 3.8

The figure shows the rate of nonfatal, medically consulted fall injury episodes, by age group, in the United States during 2010, according to the National Health Interview Survey. In 2010, the overall rate of nonfatal fall injury episodes for which a health-care professional was contacted was 43 per 1,000 population. Rates increased with age for adults aged ≥18 years. Persons aged 18–44 years had the lowest rate of medically consulted falls (26 per 1,000), and persons aged ≥75 years had the highest rate (115).

Source: Adams PF, Martinez ME, Vickerie JL, Kirzinger WK. Summary health statistics for the U.S. population: National Health Interview Survey, 2010. Vital Health Stat 2011;10(251). http://www.cdc.gov/mmwr/preview/mmwrhtml/mm6104a8.htm

The materials compiled by the Centers for Disease Control and Prevention include posters and brochures in Spanish and Chinese, as well as more formal booklets for community-based programs. These recommendations, if followed, would result in a safer environment for older adults.

SUMMARY

3.1 Why Do We Age? Biological Theories of Aging

How do rate-of-living theories explain aging?

- Rate-of-living theories are based on the idea that people are born with a limited amount of energy that can be expended at some rate unique to the individual.

- Metabolic processes such as eating fewer calories or reducing stress may be related to living longer.

- The body's declining ability to adapt to stress with age may also be a partial cause of aging.

What are the major hypotheses in cellular theories of aging?

- Cellular theories suggest that there may be a limit on how often cells may divide before dying (called the Hayflick limit), which may partially explain aging. The shortening of telomeres may be the major factor.

- A second group of cellular theories relate to a process called cross-linking that results when certain proteins interact randomly and produce molecules that make the body stiffer. Cross-links interfere with metabolism.

- A third type of cellular theory proposes that free radicals, which are highly reactive chemicals produced randomly during normal cell metabolism, cause cell damage. There is some evidence that ingesting antioxidants may postpone the appearance of some age-related diseases.

How do programmed-cell-death theories propose that we age?

- Theories about programmed cell death are based on genetic hypotheses about aging. Specifically, there appears to be a genetic program that is triggered by physiological processes, the innate ability to self-destruct, and the ability of dying cells to trigger key processes in other cells.

How do the basic developmental forces interact in biological and physiological aging?

- Although biological theories are the foundation of biological forces, the full picture of how and why we age cannot be understood without considering the other three forces (psychological, sociocultural, and life cycle).

3.2 Appearance and Mobility

How do our skin, hair, and voice change with age?

- Normative changes with age in appearance or presentation include wrinkles, gray hair, and thinner and weaker voice.

What happens to our body build with age?

- Normative changes include decrease in height and increase in weight in midlife, followed by weight loss in late life.

What age-related changes occur in our ability to move around?

- The amount of muscle decreases with age, but strength and endurance change only slightly.

- Loss of bone mass is normative; in severe cases, though, the disease osteoporosis may result, in which bones become brittle and honeycombed.

- Osteoarthritis and rheumatoid arthritis are two diseases that impair a person's ability to get around and function in the environment.

What are the psychological implications of age-related changes in appearance and mobility?

- Cultural stereotypes have an enormous influence on the personal acceptance of age-related changes in appearance.

- Loss of strength and endurance, and changes in the joints, have important psychological consequences, especially regarding self-esteem.

3.3 Sensory Systems

What age-related changes happen in vision?

- Several age-related changes occur in the structure of the eye, including decreases in the amount of light passing through the eye and in the ability to adjust to changes in illumination, yellowing of the lens, and changes in the ability to adjust and focus (presbyopia). In some cases these changes result in various diseases, such as cataracts and glaucoma.

- Other changes occur in the retina, including degeneration of the macula. Diabetes also causes retinal degeneration.

- The psychological consequences of visual changes include difficulties in getting around. Compensation strategies must take several factors into account; for example, the need for more illumination must be weighed against increased susceptibility to glare.

How does hearing change as people age?

- Age-related declines in the ability to hear high-pitched tones (presbycusis) are normative.
- Exposure to noise speeds up and exacerbates hearing loss.
- Psychologically, hearing losses can reduce the ability to have satisfactory communication with others.

What age-related changes occur in people's senses of touch and balance?

- Changes in sensitivity to touch, temperature, and pain are complex and not understood; age-related trends are unclear in most cases.
- Dizziness and vertigo are common in older adults and increase with age, as do falls. Changes in balance may result in greater caution in older adults when walking.

What happens to taste and smell with increasing age?

- Age-related changes in taste are minimal. Many older adults complain about boring food; however, these complaints appear to be largely unrelated to changes in taste ability.
- The ability to detect odors declines rapidly after age 60 in most people. Changes in smell are primarily responsible for reported changes in food preference and enjoyment.

3.4 Vital Functions

What age-related changes occur in the cardiovascular system?

- Some fat deposits in and around the heart and inside arteries are a normal part of aging. Heart muscle gradually is replaced with stiffer connective tissue. The most important change in the circulatory system is the stiffening (hardening) of the walls of the arteries.
- Overall, men have a higher rate of cardiovascular disease than women. Several diseases increase in frequency with age: congestive heart failure, angina pectoris, myocardial infarction, atherosclerosis (severe buildup of fat inside and the calcification of the arterial walls), cerebrovascular disease (cardiovascular disease in the brain), and hypertension (high blood pressure).

What structural and functional changes occur with age in the respiratory system?

- The amount of air we can take into our lungs and our ability to exchange oxygen and carbon dioxide decrease with age. Declines in the maximum amount of air we can take in also occur.
- Chronic obstructive pulmonary disease (COPD), such as emphysema, increases with age. Emphysema is the most common form of age-related COPD; although most cases are caused by smoking, a few are caused by secondhand smoke, air pollution, or genetic factors. Chronic bronchitis also becomes more prevalent with age.

3.5 The Reproductive System

What reproductive changes occur in women?

- The transition from childbearing years to the cessation of ovulation is called the climacteric; menopause is the point at which the ovaries stop releasing eggs. A variety of physical and psychological symptoms accompany menopause (e.g., hot flashes), including several in the genital organs; however, women in some cultures report different experiences.
- Menopausal hormone therapy remains controversial because of conflicting results about its long-term effects.
- No changes occur in the desire to have sex; however, the availability of a suitable partner for women is a major barrier.

What reproductive changes occur in men?

- In men, sperm production declines gradually with age. Changes in the prostate gland occur and should be monitored through yearly examinations.
- Some changes in sexual performance, such as increased time to erection and ejaculation and increased refractory period, are typical.

What are the psychological implications of age-related changes in the reproductive system?

- Healthy adults of any age are capable of engaging in sexual activity, and the desire to do so does not diminish with age. However, societal stereotyping creates barriers to free expression of such feelings.

3.6 The Autonomic Nervous System

What major changes occur in the autonomic nervous system?

- Regulating body temperature becomes increasingly problematic with age. Older adults have difficulty telling when their core body temperature drops, and their vasoconstrictor response diminishes. When they become very hot, older adults are less likely than are younger adults to drink the water they need.

- Sleep patterns and circadian rhythms change with age. Older adults are more likely to compensate by taking daytime naps, which exacerbates the problem. Effective treatments include exercising, reducing caffeine, avoiding daytime naps, and making the sleep environment as quiet and dark as possible.

What are the psychological implications of changes in the brain?

- Maintaining body temperature is essential to good health. Getting good sleep is also important for good functioning.

REVIEW QUESTIONS

3.1 Why Do We Age? Biological Theories of Aging

- What biological theories have been proposed to explain aging? What are their similarities and differences?

- Why do some people argue that diets high in antioxidants can prolong life?

- What are some of the sociocultural forces that operate on the biological theories? What are some examples of these forces?

3.2 Appearance and Mobility

- What age-related changes occur in appearance?

- How does body build change with age?

- How do muscle and bone tissue change with age?

3.3 Sensory Systems

- What age-related changes occur in vision? What are the psychological effects of these changes?

- What age-related changes occur in hearing? What are the psychological effects of these changes?

- What age-related changes occur in somesthesia and balance?

- What age-related changes occur in taste and smell?

3.4 Vital Functions

- What changes occur with age in the cardiovascular system? What gender differences have been noted? Which cardiovascular diseases increase in frequency with age?

- What changes occur with age in the respiratory system? How are respiratory diseases related to age?

3.5 The Reproductive System

- What age-related nges occur in women's and men's reproductive ability?

- How does interest in sexual activity change with age? What constraints operate on men and women?

3.6 The Nervous System

- What changes occur in people's ability to regulate body temperature?

- How does sleep change with age?

INTEGRATING CONCEPTS IN DEVELOPMENT

- How do the various biological theories of aging match with the major age-related changes in body systems? Which theories do the best job? Why?

- Given what you now know about normative changes in appearance, what would you say about the stereotypes of aging you identified in the Discovering Development exercise you did in Chapter 1?

- Why do you think the rates of death from cardiovascular disease are so much higher in industrialized countries than elsewhere?

- How might the age-related changes in the respiratory system be linked with societal policies on the environment?

KEY TERMS

angina pectoris A painful condition caused by temporary constriction of blood flow to the heart.

atherosclerosis A process by which fat is deposited on the walls of arteries.

cataracts Opaque spots on the lens of the eye.

cerebrovascular accident (CVA), An interruption of the blood flow in the brain.

chronic obstructive pulmonary disease (COPD), A family of age-related lung diseases that block the passage of air and cause abnormalities inside the lungs.

climacteric The transition during which a woman's reproductive capacity ends and ovulation stops.

congestive heart failure A condition occurring when cardiac output and the ability of the heart to contract severely decline, making the heart enlarge, increasing pressure to the veins, and making the body swell.

cross-linking Random interaction between proteins that produce molecules that make the body stiffer.

emphysema Severe lung disease that greatly reduces the ability to exchange carbon dioxide for oxygen.

free radicals, Deleterious and short-lived chemicals that cause changes in cells that are thought to result in aging.

glaucoma, A condition in the eye caused by abnormal drainage of fluid.

hypertension A disease in which one's blood pressure is too high.

menopausal hormone therapy (MHT) Low doses of estrogen, which is often combined with progestin (synthetic form of progesterone) taken to counter the effects of declining estrogen levels.

menopause The cessation of the release of eggs by the ovaries.

myocardial infarction (MI), A heart attack.

osteoarthritis, A form of rthritis marked by gradual onset and progression of pain and swelling, caused primarily by overuse of a joint.

osteoporosis, A degenerative bone disease more common in women in which bone tissue deteriorates severely to produce honeycomb-like bone tissue.

perimenopause The time of transition from regular menstruation to menopause.

presbycusis, A normative age-related loss of the ability to hear high-pitched tones.

presbyopia The normative age-related loss of the ability to focus on nearby objects, usually resulting in the need for glasses.

rheumatoid arthritis, A destructive form of arthritis involving more swelling and more joints than osteoarthritis.

telomerase An enzyme needed in DNA replication to fully reproduce the telomeres when cells divide.

telomeres, Tips of the chromosomes that shorten with each replication.

RESOURCES

Access quizzes, glossaries, flashcards, and more at www.cengagebrain.com.

CHAPTER 4

LONGEVITY, HEALTH, AND FUNCTIONING

4.1 HOW LONG WILL WE LIVE?
Discovering Development: Take the Longevity Test • Average and Maximum Longevity • Genetic and Environmental Factors in Average Longevity • Ethnic Differences in Average Longevity • Gender Differences in Average Longevity • International Differences in Average Longevity

4.2 HEALTH AND ILLNESS
Defining Health and Illness • Quality of Life • Changes in the Immune System • Chronic and Acute Diseases • The Role of Stress • *How Do We Know?: Negative Life Events and Mastery*

4.3 COMMON CHRONIC CONDITIONS AND THEIR MANAGEMENT
General Issues in Chronic Conditions • Common Chronic Conditions • *Current Controversies: The Prostate Cancer Dilemma* • Managing Pain

4.4 PHARMACOLOGY AND MEDICATION ADHERENCE
Patterns of Medication Use • Developmental Changes in How Medications Work • Medication Side Effects and Interactions • Adherence to Medication Regimens

4.5 FUNCTIONAL HEALTH AND DISABILITY
A Model of Disability in Late Life • Determining Functional Health Status • What Causes Functional Limitations and Disability in Older Adults?

SOCIAL POLICY IMPLICATIONS
Summary • Review Questions • Integrating Concepts in Development • Key Terms • Resources

JEANNE CALMENT WAS ONE OF THE MOST IMPORTANT PEOPLE TO EVER LIVE.

Her amazing achievement was not made in sports, government, or any other profession. When she died in 1996 at age 122 years and 164 days, she set the world record for the longest verified human life span. Jeanne lived her entire life in Arles, France. During her lifetime, she met Vincent Van Gogh, experienced the invention of the lightbulb, automobiles, airplanes, space travel, computers, and all sorts of everyday conveniences. She survived two world wars. Longevity ran in her family: Her older brother, François, lived to the age of 97, her father to 93, and her mother to 86. Jeanne was extraordinarily healthy her whole life, rarely being ill. She was also active; she learned fencing when she was 85, and still rode a bicycle at age 100. She lived on her own until she was 110, when she moved to a nursing home. Her life was documented in the 1995 film *Beyond* 120 *Years with Jeanne Calment*. Shortly before her 121st birthday, Musicdisc released *Time's Mistress*, a CD of Jeanne speaking over a background of rap and hip-hop music.

Did you ever wonder how long you would like to live? Would you like to live to be as old as Jeanne Calment? Scientific advances are happening so quickly in our understanding of the factors that influence longevity, many scientists think that numerous, perhaps most people could live to 120 years. Indeed, the May 2013 issue of *National Geographic* magazine devoted its main feature to the possibility the baby on the front cover and many of its peers would live to 120 years (or longer). Let's take a closer look at what we know about human longevity

Jeanne Calment lived more than 122 years.

Georges GOBET Agence France Presse/Newscom

4.1 How Long Will We Live?

LEARNING OBJECTIVES

- What is the average and the maximum longevity for humans?
- What genetic and environmental factors influence longevity?
- What ethnic factors influence average longevity?
- What factors create gender differences in average longevity

Susie is a 51-year-old Chinese American living in San Francisco. *Susie's mother (age 76), father (age 77), and grandmother (age 103), who are all in excellent health, live with her and her husband. Susie knows that several of her other relatives have lived long lives, but she wonders whether this has any bearing on her own life expectancy.*

As we saw in Chapter 1, many more people are living to old age today than ever before. Like Susie, people today have already seen far more older adults than their great-great-grandparents ever saw. The tremendous increase in the number of older adults has focused renewed interest in how long you may live. Susie's question about her own longevity exemplifies this interest. Knowing how long we are likely to live is important not only for us but also for government agencies, service programs, the business world, and insurance companies. Why? The length of life has an enormous impact on just about every aspect of life, from decisions about government health care programs (how much money should Congress allocate to Medicare?) to retirement policy (debates over the age at which people may collect maximum retirement benefits) to life insurance premiums (longer lives on average mean cheaper rates for young adults because they are now healthier for longer periods of their lives). Longer lives have forced changes in all these areas and will continue to do so for the next several decades.

Life expectancy can be examined from the perspective of the basic developmental forces, because how long we live depends on complex interactions among biological, psychological, socioeconomic, and life-cycle forces. For example, some people, like Susie, have many relatives who live to very old age, whereas others have relatives who die young. Tendencies toward long lives (or short ones, for that matter) tend to run in families. As you will see, our "long-life genes" play a major role in governing how long we are likely to live.

But the world in which we live can affect how long we live, too. Environmental factors such as disease and toxic chemicals modify our genetic heritage and shorten our lifetime, sometimes drastically. By the same token, environmental factors such as access to high-quality medical care can sometimes offset genetic defects that would otherwise have caused early death, thereby increasing our longevity. In short, no single developmental force can account for the length of life. Let's begin by exploring the concept of longevity. To get started, complete the exercise in the Discovering Development feature and see how long you might live. When you have finished, continue reading to discover the research base behind the numbers.

DISCOVERING DEVELOPMENT:

TAKE THE LONGEVITY TEST

Did you ever speculate about how long you might live? Are you curious? If you'd like a preview of several of the key influences on how long we live, try completing the questions at http://www.livingto100.com. Take notes about why you think each question is being asked. Once you're finished, submit your form. Take time to read about each of the topics, then read more about them in the text. Will you live to be 100? Only time will tell!

Average and Maximum Longevity

How long you live, called longevity, is jointly determined by genetic and environmental factors. Researchers distinguish between two different types of longevity: average longevity and maximum longevity. **Average longevity** *is commonly called average life expectancy and refers to the age at which half of the individuals who are born in a particular year will have died.* Average longevity is affected by both genetic and environmental factors.

Average longevity can be computed for people at any age. The most common method is to compute average longevity at birth, which is the projected age at which half of the people born in a certain year will have died. This computation takes into account people who die at any age, from infancy onward. The current average longevity is about 79 years at birth for people in the United States (National Center for Health Statistics, 2012a). This means that 79 years after a group of people are born, half of them will still be alive. When average longevity is computed at other points in the life span, the calculation is based on all the people who are alive at that age; people who died earlier are not included. For example, computing the average longevity for people currently 65 years old would provide a predicted age at which half of those people will have died. People who were born into the same birth cohort but who died before age 65 are not counted. Eliminating those who die at early ages from the computation of average longevity at a specific age makes projected average longevity at age 65 longer than it was at birth. In the United States, females currently aged 65 can expect to live on average about 20 more years; men about 18 more years.

For people in the United States, average longevity has been increasing steadily since 1900; recent estimates for longevity at birth and at age 65 are presented in Figure 4.1. Note in the figure that the most rapid increases in average longevity at birth occurred in the first half of the 20th century. These increases in average longevity were caused mostly by declines in infant mortality rates, brought about by eliminating diseases such as smallpox and polio and through better health care. The decrease in the number of women who died during childbirth was especially important in raising average life expectancies for women. Advances in medical technology and improvements in health care mean that more people survive to old age, thereby increasing average longevity in the general population.

Maximum longevity *is the oldest age to which any individual of a species lives.* Although the biblical character Methuselah is said to have lived to the ripe old age of 969 years, modern scientists are more conservative in their estimates of a human's maximum longevity. Even if we were able to eliminate all diseases,

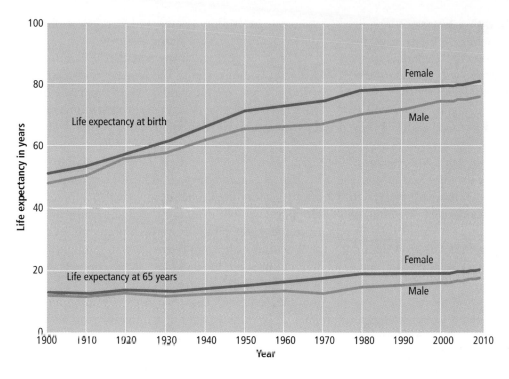

Figure 4.1

Average longevity for men and women in the United States 1900–2009.

Source: Data from Centers for Disease Control and Prevention, National Center for Health Statistics, National Vital Statistics System (2008).
© 2015 Cengage Learning

most researchers estimate the limit to be somewhere around 120 years because key body systems such as the cardiovascular system have limits on how long they can last (Hayflick, 1998). Genetic theories also place the human limit around 120 years (Barja, 2008; Rattan, 2012). The world record for longevity that can be verified by birth records was held by Jeanne Calment of France, who died in 1997 at age 122 years.

It remains to be seen whether maximum longevity will change as new technologies produce better artificial organs and health care. An important issue is whether extending the life span indefinitely would be a good idea. Because maximum longevity of different animal species varies widely (Barja, 2008; Rattan, 2012), scientists have tried to understand these differences by considering important biological functions such as metabolic rate or various changes at the molecular level (Rattan, 2012). But no one has figured out how to predict longevity. For example, why the giant tortoises of the Galapagos Islands typically live longer than we do remains a mystery.

Increasingly, researchers are differentiating between **active life expectancy** and **dependent life expectancy**; *the difference is between living to a healthy old age (active life expectancy) and simply living a long time (dependent life expectancy).* Said another way, it is the difference between adding years to life and adding life to years. One's active life expectancy ends at the point when one loses independence or must rely on others for most activities of daily living (e.g., cooking meals, bathing). The remaining years of one's life constitute living in a dependent state. How many active and dependent years one has in late life depends a great deal on the interaction of genetic and environmental factors, to which we now turn.

Genetic and Environmental Factors in Average Longevity

Let's return to Susie, who wonders whether she can expect to live a long life. What influences how long we will live on average? Our average longevity is influenced most by genetic, environmental, ethnic, and gender factors. Clearly, these factors interact; being from an ethnic minority group or being poor, for example, often means that one has a higher risk of exposure to a harmful environment and less access to high-quality health care. But it is important to examine each of these factors and see how they influence our longevity. Let's begin with genetic and environmental factors.

Genetic Factors. Living a long life has a clear, but complex, genetic link. We have known for a long time that a good way to have a greater chance of a long life is to come from a family with a history of long-lived individuals. Alexander Graham Bell (the same guy who received the credit for inventing the telephone) was one of the first people to demonstrate systematically the benefits of coming from a long-lived family. Bell considered 8,797 of William Hyde's descendants and found that children of parents who had lived beyond 80 survived about 20 years longer than children whose parents had both died before they were 60. Thus Susie's long-lived family sets the stage for Susie to enjoy a long life herself.

One exciting line of contemporary research, the Human Genome Project, completed in 2003, has mapped all our genes. This research and its spinoffs in microbiology and behavior genetics are continuing to produce astounding results in terms of genetic linkages to disease and aging (you can track these through the main website of the Project).

Based on this gene mapping work, attempts are being made to treat diseases by improving the way that medications work and even by implanting "corrected" genes into people in the hope that the good genes will in some cases reproduce and eventually wipe out the defective genes, and in others prevent the shortening of telomeres (discussed in Chapter 3; Boccardi & Herbig, 2012; Kanehisa et al., 2008). Payoffs from such research are helping us understand how increasing numbers of people are living to 100 or older. For example, research on people over age 100 (centenarians) in Sicily showed a connection between genetics and the immune system (Balistreri, Candore, Accardi, Bova, Buffa, Bulati et al., 2012). The oldest-old, such as Suzie's grandmother, are hardy because they have a high threshold for disease and show slower rates of disease progression than their peers who develop chronic diseases at younger ages and die earlier.

Environmental Factors. Although genes are a major determinant of longevity, environmental factors also affect the life span, often in combination with genes (Rando & Chang, 2012). Some environmental factors are more obvious; diseases, toxins, lifestyle, and social class are among the most important. Diseases, such as cardiovascular disease and Alzheimer's disease, and lifestyle issues, such as smoking and exercise, receive a great deal of attention from researchers. Environmental toxins, encountered mainly as air and water pollution, are a continuing problem. For example, toxins in fish, bacteria, and cancer-causing chemicals in drinking water, and airborne pollutants are major agents in shortening longevity.

Living in poverty shortens longevity. The impact of socioeconomic status on longevity results from reduced access to goods and services, especially medical care and diet, that characterizes most ethnic minority groups, the poor, and many older adults (Doubeni, Schootman, Major, Torres Stone, Laiyemo, Park et al., 2012). Most of these people have little or no health insurance, cannot access good health care, and cannot afford healthy food. For many living in urban areas, air pollution, poor drinking water, and lead poisoning from old water pipes are serious problems, but they simply cannot afford to move. Although longevity differences between high and low socioeconomic groups in the United States narrowed during the latter part of the 20th century, these improvements have stopped since 1990 due to continued differences in access to health care (Swanson & Sanford, 2012).

How environmental factors influence average life expectancy changes over time. For example, acquired immunodeficiency syndrome (AIDS) has had a devastating effect on life expectancy in Africa, where in some countries (e.g., Botswana, Namibia, South Africa, Zimbabwe) average longevity may have been reduced by as much as 30 years from otherwise expected levels (Kinsella & Phillips, 2005). In contrast, negative effects of cardiovascular diseases on average longevity are lessening as the rates of those diseases decline in many developed countries (National Center for Health Statistics, 2012a).

The sad part about most environmental factors is that we are responsible for most of them. Denying adequate health care to everyone, continuing to pollute our environment, and failing to address the underlying causes of poverty have undeniable consequences: These causes needlessly shorten lives and dramatically increase the cost of health care.

Ethnic Differences in Average Longevity

People in different ethnic groups do not have the same average longevity at birth. For example, although African Americans' average life expectancy at birth is about 6 years less for men and about 4 years less for women than it is for European Americans, by age 65 this gap has narrowed to about 2 and 1.5 years, respectively, for men and women. By age 85, African Americans tend to outlive European Americans. Why the shift over time?

Lower access to good-quality health care in general means that those African Americans who live to age 85 tend to be in better health on average than their European American counterparts. But this is just a guess. Latinos have higher average life expectancies than European Americans and African Americans at all ages despite having, on average, less access to health care (National Center for Health Statistics, 2012a). The full explanation for these ethnic group differences remains to be discovered.

Gender Differences in Average Longevity

Have you ever visited a senior center or a nursing home? If so, you may have asked yourself, "Where are all the very old men?" Women's average longevity is about 5 years more than men's at birth, narrowing to roughly 1 year by age 85 (National Center for Health Statistics, 2012b). These differences are fairly typical of most industrialized countries but not of developing countries. In fact, the female advantage in average longevity in the United States became apparent only in the early 20th century (Hayflick, 1996). Why? Until then, so many women died in childbirth that their average longevity as a group was no more than that of men. Death in childbirth still partially explains the lack of a female advantage in developing countries today; however, another part of the difference in some countries results from infanticide of baby girls. In industrialized countries, socioeconomic factors such as access to health care and improved lifestyle factors also help account for the emergence of the female advantage.

Many ideas have been offered to explain the significant advantage women have over men in average longevity in industrialized countries, and that emerging in developing countries (Roy, Punhani, & Shi, 2012). Overall, men's rates of dying from the top 15 causes of death are significantly higher than women's at nearly every age, and men are also more susceptible to infectious diseases. These differences have led some to speculate that perhaps it is not just a gender-related biological difference at work in longevity, but a more complex interaction of lifestyle, improved health care, greater susceptibility in men of contracting certain fatal diseases and dying prematurely (e.g., in war or through accidents at work), and genetics.

Other researchers disagree; they argue that there are potential biological explanations. These include the fact that women have two X chromosomes, compared with one in men; men have a higher metabolic rate; women have a higher brain-to-body weight ratio; and women have lower testosterone levels. However, none of these explanations has sufficient scientific support to explain why most women in industrialized countries can expect, on average, to outlive most men (Roy et al., 2012).

Despite their longer average longevity, women do not have all the advantages. Interestingly, older men who survive beyond age 90 are the hardiest segment of their birth cohort in terms of performance on cognitive tests (Perls & Terry, 2003). Between ages 65 and 89, women score higher on cognitive tests; beyond age 90, men do much better.

Coming from a family with many long-lived members increases your chances of having a long life yourself.

Stephen Simpson/Getty Images

International Differences in Average Longevity

Countries around the world differ dramatically in how long their populations live on average. As you can see in Figure 4.2, the current range extends from 38 years in Sierra Leone in Africa to over 82 years in Japan. Such a wide divergence in life expectancy reflects vast discrepancies in genetic, sociocultural and economic conditions, health care, disease, and the like across industrialized and developing nations.

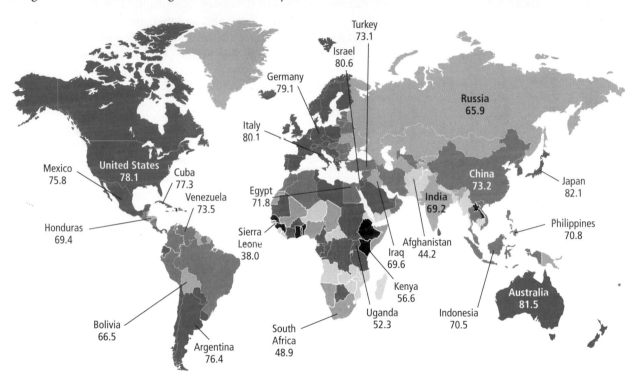

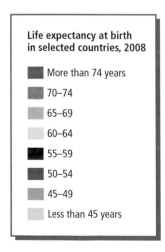

Life expectancy at birth in selected countries, 2008

- More than 74 years
- 70–74
- 65–69
- 60–64
- 55–59
- 50–54
- 45–49
- Less than 45 years

Figure 4.2

International data on life expectancy at birth. Note the differences between developed and developing countries.

Source: From International programs: International data base, by U.S. Census Bureau. Copyright © U.S. Census Bureau 2010.www.census.gov/ipc/ www/idb /tables.html

ADULT DEVELOPMENT IN ACTION

Suppose you are a financial planner for people who want to save for their retirement. Given what you have learned about longevity, how would you advise people in their 40s in terms of savings?

4.2 Health and Illness

LEARNING OBJECTIVES

- What are the key issues in defining health and illness?
- How is quality of life assessed?
- What normative age-related changes occur in the immune system?
- What are the developmental trends in chronic and acute diseases?
- What are the key issues in stress across adulthood?

Rosa is a 73-year-old immigrant from Mexico, living in a small apartment in a large city in the southwestern United States. For most of her life she has been very healthy, but lately she has noticed it is getting harder to get up every morning. In addition, when she gets a cold, she takes longer to recover than when she was younger. Rosa wonders whether these problems are typical or whether she is experiencing something unusual.

Each of us has had periods of health and of illness. Most people are like Rosa—healthy for nearly all our lives. In this section, we will tackle the difficult issue of defining health and illness. We will consider quality of life, an increasingly important notion as medical technology keeps people alive longer. We will see how the differences between acute and chronic disease become more important with age. Because our immune system plays such a central role in health and illness, we will examine key age-related changes in it. Finally, we will consider how stress can affect our health.

Defining Health and Illness

What does the term *health* mean to you? Total lack of disease? Complete physical, mental, and social well-being? Actually, scientists cannot agree on a comprehensive definition, largely because the term has been used in so many different contexts (Davies, 2007; Ogden, 2012). Many people now include biological, psychological, sociocultural, spiritual, and environmental components; as Davies (2007) puts it, health is an ongoing outcome from the processes of a life lived well.

The World Health Organization defines **health** *as a state of complete physical, mental, and social well-being, and not merely the absence of disease or infirmity* (World Health Organization, 2007). **Illness** *is the presence of a physical or mental disease or impairment.*

Think for a moment about your health. How would you rate it? Although this question looks simple, how people answer it turns out to be predictive of illness and mortality (Longest & Thoits, 2012). Why? There are several possibilities (Wolinsky & Tierney, 1998). One is that self-rated health captures more aspects of health than other measures. A second possibility is that poor self-rated health reflects respondents' belief that they are on a downward trajectory in functioning. A third is that people's self-ratings affect their health-related behaviors, which in turn affect health outcomes. Finally, self-rated health may actually represent an assessment of people's internal and external resources that are available to support health. Research data support all these ideas; a review of more than 30 years of research has shown that self ratings of health are very predictive of future health outcomes (Blazer, 2008).

Self-ratings also tend to be fairly stable over time. Wolinsky and colleagues (2008) followed 998 African Americans aged 49 to 65 for 4 years, and found that 55% had the same self-rating over time (25% improved and 20% declined). Even factoring in change in ratings does not improve the ability to predict mortality compared to a standard single indicator of health (Galenkamp, Deeg, Braam, & Huisman, in press). Overall, men rated their health worse than women did. Among the oldest-old, self-rated health is a powerful predictor of mortality across cultures; for example, a two-year study in China showed that self-rated health still predicted mortality even after socioeconomic status and health conditions had been accounted for (Chen & Wu, 2008). Similar results were obtained for men in India (Hirve, Juvekar, Sambhudas, Lele, Blomstedt, Wall et al., in press).

However, self-ratings of health do reflect differences in socioeconomic background in terms of how healthy people say they are. For example, indigenous Australians rate their health as significantly poorer than nonindigenous Australians, mainly due to differences in economic variables (e.g., access to health care) (Booth & Carroll, 2008). In the United States, African Americas are twice as likely, and Mexican Americans and Puerto Rican Americans three times more likely, to self-report their health as fair or poor than European Americans (Benjamins, Hirschman, Hirschtick, & Whitman, 2012).

Overall, given the strong relation between self-rated health and actual health-related outcomes, including one's own mortality, it should come as no surprise that researchers often include such measures in their studies of older adults. Such measures provide a good proxy (or stand-in) variable for health, avoiding a time-consuming (and possibly costly) assessment of health. This approach works most of the time; as we proceed, the times when it doesn't will be noted.

Quality of Life

We'll bet if you asked most people what they want out of life, they would say something about a good quality of life. But what does that mean? Precise definitions are hard to find. Sometimes people find it easier to say what quality of life is not: being dependent on a respirator while in a permanent vegetative state is one common example. Researchers, though, like to be more specific. They tend to look at several specific aspects of quality of life: health-related quality of life and non-health-related quality of life. Health-related quality of life includes all of the aspects of life that are affected by changes in one's health status. Non-health-related quality of life refers to things in the environment, such as entertainment, economic resources, arts, and so on that can affect our overall experience and enjoyment in life.

Most research on quality of life has focused on two areas: quality of life in the context of specific diseases or conditions and quality of life relating to end-of-life issues. We briefly lay out the issues here. We will return to them as we discuss specific situations in this chapter and in Chapters 5 (interventions that increase quality of life) and 13 (end-of-life issues).

In many respects, quality of life is a subjective judgment that can be understood in the context of broader models of adult development and aging.

One such model describes ways in which people select domains of relative strength, optimize their use of these strengths, and compensate for age-related changes (Baltes et al., 2006). In addition, one must also consider not only the physical health aspects but also mental health and the person's life situation in assessing quality of life (Brett, Gow, Corley, Pattie, Starr, & Deary, 2012). From this perspective, quality of life is a successful use of the selection, optimization, and compensation model (SOC) to manage one's life, resulting in successful aging. Applying this approach to research in health care, *quality of life* refers to people's perceptions of their position in life in context of their culture (Karim et al., 2008) and in relation to their goals, expectations, values, and concerns (Brett et al., 2012).

In general, research on health-related quality of life addresses a critical question (Lawton et al., 1999): To what extent does distress from illness or side effects associated with treatment reduce a person's wish to live? Lawton and colleagues (1999) set the standard for answering this question by showing that it depends a great deal on a person's valuation of life, the degree to which a person is attached to his or her present life. How much one enjoys life, has hope about the future, and finds meaning in everyday events, for example, have a great deal of impact on how long that person would like to live.

Narrowing the focus of the quality-of-life concept as it relates to specific conditions brings us to the domains of physical impairment or disability and of dementia. Quality of life in the former context includes issues of environmental design that improve people's functioning and well-being, such as handicapped accessible bathrooms and facilities (Pynoos, Caraviello, & Cicero, 2010). We examine environmental influences in Chapter 5.

Quality of life is more difficult to assess in people with dementia and chronic diseases, although new assessment instruments have been developed (Karim et al., 2008; Skevington & McCrate, 2012). We consider this issue in more detail in Chapter 10 when we focus on Alzheimer's disease.

Changes in the Immune System

Every day, our bodies are threatened by invaders: bacterial, viral, and parasitic infections (as well as their toxic by-products) and abnormal cells such as precancerous and tumor cells. Fortunately for us, we have a highly advanced defense system against foreign invaders: the immune system. The National Cancer Institute provides a Web-based overview of how our immune system works; check it out to learn how sophisticated our defense system is.

Many details of how our immune system works remain unknown. For instance, one great mystery is how the immune system learns to differentiate your own cells from invaders. Researchers think the mechanism involves recognizing certain substances, called *antigens*, on the surface of invading bacteria and cells that have been taken over by viruses. Regardless of how this actually happens, once the immune system has learned to recognize the invader, it creates a defense against that invader.

How does this defense system work? It's an amazing process that is based essentially on only three major types of cells, which form a network of interacting parts (Mak & Saunders, 2014): cell-mediated immunity (consisting of cells originating in the thymus gland, or *T-lymphocytes*), immunity based on the release of antibodies in the blood, such as those manufactured in bone marrow or acquired from immunization or previous infection (*B lymphocytes*), and nonspecific immunity (*monocytes* and *polymorphonuclear neutrophil leukocytes*)

The primary job of the T- and B-lymphocytes is to defend against malignant (cancerous) cells, viral infection, fungal infection, and some bacteria. Natural killer (NK) cells are another special type of lymphocytes that monitor our bodies to prevent tumor growth. These are our primary defense against cancer, although how this happens is not fully understood. NK cells also help fight viral infections and parasites. In addition, there are five major types of specialized antibodies called immunoglobulins (IgA, IgD, IgE, IgG, and IgM). For example, IgM includes the "first responders" in the immune system, IgE is involved in allergies and asthma, and IgG (also called g-globulin) helps fight hepatitis.

How does aging affect the immune system? Researchers are only beginning to understand this process, and there are large gaps in the literature (Mak & Saunders, 2014). Moreover, the immune system is sensitive to a wide variety of lifestyle and environmental factors, such as diet, stress, exercise, and disease, making it very difficult to isolate changes caused by aging alone (Effros, 2012; Goldstein, 2012).

Changes in health with age provide insights into immune functioning. Older adults are more susceptible to certain infections and have a much higher risk of cancer (both of which are discussed in more detail later in this chapter), so most researchers believe that the immune system changes with age. Indeed, NK cells and several other aspects of the immune system decrease in effectiveness with age (Effros, 2012). For one thing, older adults' immune systems take longer to build up defenses against specific diseases, even after an immunization injection. This is probably caused by the changing balance in T-lymphocytes and may partially explain why older adults need to be immunized earlier against specific diseases such as influenza.

Similarly, B-lymphocytes decrease in functioning. Research examining the administration of substances such as growth hormones to older adults to stimulate lymphocyte functioning indicates that some specific lymphocyte functioning returns to normal with treatment, and can regenerate the thymus gland, both of which are important in treating individuals with HIV (Chidgey, 2008). This process for T- and B-lymphocytes is described in Figure 4.3.

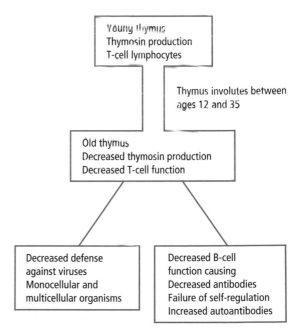

Figure 4.3

Process of aging of the immune system.

Source: Reprinted with permission from Ebersole, P., & Hess, P., Toward Healthy Aging (5e, p. 41). Copyright © 1998 Mosby St. Louis: with permission from Elsevier.
© 2015 Cengage Learning

Changes in immune system function have important implications (Effros, 2012; Goldstein, 2012). Older adults become more prone to serious consequences from illnesses—such as those caused by viruses—that are easily defeated by younger adults. Older adults also benefit less from immunizations. In addition, various forms of leukemia, which are cancers of the immune cells, increase with age, along with other forms of cancer. *Finally, the immune system can begin attacking the body itself in a process called* **autoimmunity.** Autoimmunity results from an imbalance of B- and T-lymphocytes, giving rise to autoantibodies, and is responsible for several disorders, such as rheumatoid arthritis (Goronzy & Weyand, 2012).

A growing body of evidence is pointing to key connections between our immune system and our psychological state. Over 20 years of research shows how our psychological state, or a characteristic such as our attitude, creates neurological, hormonal, and behavioral responses that directly change the immune system and make us more likely to become ill (Segerstrom, 2012). **Psychoneuroimmunology** *is the study of the relations between psychological, neurological, and immunological systems that raise or lower our susceptibility to and ability to recover from disease.*

Psychoneuroimmunology is increasingly being used as a framework to understand health outcomes and in predicting how people cope with and survive illness (Irwin, 2008; Yan, 2012). By considering the various factors influencing disease, interventions that optimally combine medication, diet, and mind-body strategies (e.g., meditation) can be devised.

HIV/AIDS and Older Adults. An increasing number of older adults have HIV/AIDS (HIV is the virus that causes the disease AIDS); the Administration on Aging (2012b) estimates that in the United States roughly 1.2 million people in the United States have HIV. By 2015, it is expected that about half of the people in the United States with HIV will be over age 50. Unfortunately, because of the social stereotype that older adults are not sexually active, many physicians do not test older patients; however, as HIV/AIDS rates increase among older adults, the importance of testing is being emphasized (Longo et al., 2008).

Although older men are at higher risk for AIDS, older women also are at significant risk. For men, the most common risk factor is homosexual or bisexual behavior. In contrast, AIDS usually is transmitted to older women through heterosexual contact with infected partners. Older adults may be more susceptible to HIV infection because of the changes in the immune system discussed earlier. For women, the thinning of the vaginal wall with age makes it more likely that it will tear, making it easier for the HIV to enter the bloodstream. Older adults may believe that condom use is no longer necessary, which also raises the risk (Tangredi et al., 2008). Older African Americans are 12 times more likely than their European American counterparts to have HIV, and Latinos are five times more likely (Gay Men's Health Crisis, 2010).

Once they are infected, the progression from HIV-positive status to AIDS is more rapid among older adults due to the changes in the immune system with age described earlier (Gay Men's Health Crisis, 2010). Once they are diagnosed with AIDS, older adults' remaining life span is significantly shorter than it is for newly diagnosed young adults, and mortality rates are higher.

Clearly, older adults need to be educated about their risk for HIV and AIDS, and about the continued need for condom use. However, ageism on the part of professionals, misconceptions about sexual activity among older adults, and older adults' lack of knowledge concerning HIV/AIDS are all barriers (Milaszewski, Greto, Klochkov, & Fuller-Thomson, 2012). Few media stories about the problem focus on older adults, who thus may mistakenly believe they have nothing to worry about. They are less likely to raise the issue with a physician, less likely to be tested, and, if diagnosed, less likely to seek support groups. In short, we need to change outmoded beliefs about older adults and sexuality and focus on health and prevention.

Chronic and Acute Diseases

Rosa, the immigrant from Mexico, is typical of older adults: She is beginning to experience some recurring health difficulties and is finding out that she does not recover as quickly from even minor afflictions. You probably have had several encounters with illnesses that come on quickly, may range from mild to very severe, last a few days, and then go away. Illnesses such as influenza and strep throat are examples. You also may have experienced conditions that come on more slowly, last much longer, and have long-term consequences. Kidney disease, diabetes, and arthritis are examples. Your experiences reflect the difference between acute and chronic diseases.

Acute diseases *are conditions that develop over a short period of time and cause a rapid change in health.* We are all familiar with acute diseases, such as colds, influenza, and food poisoning. Most acute diseases are cured with medications (such as antibiotics for bacterial infections) or allowed to run their course (the case with most viral infections). *In contrast,* **chronic diseases** *are conditions that last a longer period of time (at least 3 months) and may be accompanied by residual functional impairment that necessitates long-term management.* Chronic diseases include arthritis and diabetes mellitus.

What do you think happens to the incidence of acute and chronic diseases as people age? If you say that the rates of acute diseases go down whereas the rates of chronic diseases go up, you are correct. Contrary to what many people believe, older adults have fewer colds, for example, than younger adults. However, when they do get an acute disease, older adults tend to get sicker; recovery takes longer; and death from acute disease occurs more often (Centers for Disease Control and Prevention, 2012e). Thus, although they get fewer acute infections, older people may actually spend more days feeling sick than their younger (and, based on frequency of occurrence, "sicker") counterparts.

This is probably why many people mistakenly believe that the rates of acute disease increase with age. Because they have more problems fighting acute infections, older adults are more at risk from dying of an acute condition. For example, the rate of respiratory infection is about the same for younger and older adults, but people over age 65 account for nearly all deaths from pneumonia and influenza. For these reasons, health professionals strongly recommend that older adults be vaccinated against pneumonia and influenza.

Until the 1990s, chronic disease was simply viewed as a part of aging. With the publication in 1991 of the historic document *Healthy People 2000: National Health Promotion and Disease Prevention* (U.S. Department of Health and Human Services, 1991), the view shifted dramatically to one of prevention and wellness. As we see a bit later in this chapter, advances in understanding the causes of chronic disease have resulted in better

prevention in many cases, and better disease management in others.

The Role of Stress

You know what it feels like to be stressed. Whether it's from the upcoming exam in this course, the traffic jam you sat in on your way home yesterday, or the demands your children place on you, stress seems to be everywhere.

There is plenty of scientific evidence that over the long term, stress is very bad for your health. But despite thousands of scientific studies, scientists still cannot agree on a formal definition of stress. What is certain is that stress involves both physiological and psychological aspects (Gouin, Glaser, Malarkey, Beversdorf, & Kiecolt-Glaser, 2012).

The most widely applied approaches to stress involve (a) focusing on the physiological responses the body makes through the nervous and endocrine systems; and (b) the idea that stress is what people define as stressful. Let's consider each in more detail.

Stress as a Physiological State. There is widespread agreement across many research studies that people differ in their physiological responses to stress (Campbell & Ehlert, 2012). Prolonged exposure to stress results in damaging influences from the sympathetic nervous system (which controls such things as heart rate, respiration, perspiration, blood flow, muscle strength, and mental activity) and a weakening of the immune system (Cohen, Janicki Deverts, Doyle, Miller, Frank, Rabin et al., 2012). These effects have a direct causative effect on susceptibility to a wide range of diseases, from the common cold to cardiovascular disease, to cancer, and may play a role in shortening telomeres (see Chapter 3; O'Donovan et al., 2012).

Gender differences in stress responses have also been documented. There is some evidence that the hormone oxytocin plays a different role in women than in men. Oxytocin is the hormone important in reproductive activities, such as breast feeding, and for establishing strong bonds with one's children (Campbell, 2008). Researchers speculate that when stressed, men opt for a "flight or fight" approach whereas women opt for a "tend and befriend" approach (Taylor, 2006). Fisher-Shofty, Levkovitz, and Shamay-Tsoory (in press) showed that oxytocin improves accurate perception of social interactions, but in different ways in men and women. In men, performance improved only for competition recognition, whereas in women it improved for kinship recognition.

The Stress and Coping Paradigm. Suppose you are stuck in a traffic jam. Depending on whether you are late for an important appointment or have plenty of time on your hands, you will probably feel very different about your situation. *The stress and coping paradigm views stress not as an environmental stimulus or as a response but as the interaction of a thinking person and an event* (Lazarus, 1984; Lazarus et al., 1985; Lazarus & Folkman, 1984). How we interpret an event such as being stuck in traffic is what matters, not the event itself or what we do in response to it. Put more formally, stress is "a particular relationship between the person and the environment that is appraised by the person as taxing or exceeding his or her resources and endangering his or her well-being" (Lazarus & Folkman, 1984, p. 19). Note that this definition states that stress is a transactional process between a person and the environment, that it takes into account personal resources, that the person's appraisal of the situation is key, and that unless the situation is considered to be threatening, challenging, or harmful, stress does not result. A diagram of the transactional model is shown in Figure 4.4.

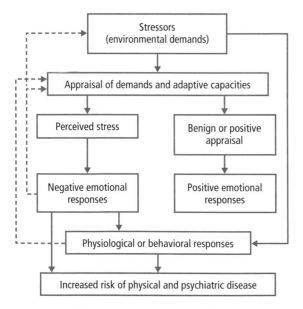

Figure 4.4

An example of a transactional model of stress.

Source: From Measuring Stress: A Guide For Health And Social Scientists, *edited by Sheldon Cohen, Kessler & Gordon. Copyright © 1995 by Oxford University Press, Inc. Used with permission from Oxford University Press, Inc.*

Appraisal. Lazarus and Folkman (1984) describe three types of appraisals of stress. **Primary appraisal** *categorizes events into three groups based on the significance they have for our well-being: irrelevant, benign or positive, and stressful.* Primary appraisals filter the events we experience. Specifically, any event that is appraised as either irrelevant (things that do not affect us) or as benign or positive (things that are good or at least neutral) is not stressful. So, we literally decide which events are potentially stressful and which ones are not. This is an important point for two reasons. First, it means we can effectively sort out the events that may be problems and those that are not, allowing us to concentrate on dealing with life's difficulties more effectively. Second, it means that we could be wrong about our reading of an event. A situation that may appear at first blush to be irrelevant, for example, may actually be very important, or a situation deemed stressful initially may turn out not to be. Such mistakes in primary appraisal could set the stage for real (or imagined) crises later on.

If a person believes that an event is stressful, a second set of decisions, called secondary appraisal, is made. **Secondary appraisal** *evaluates our perceived ability to cope with harm, threat, or challenge.* Secondary appraisal is the equivalent of asking three questions: "What can I do?" "How likely is it that I can use one of my options successfully?" and "Will this option reduce my stress?" How we answer these questions sets the stage for addressing them effectively. For example, if you believe there is something you can do in a situation that will make a difference, then your perceived stress may be reduced, and you may be able to deal with the event successfully. In contrast, if you believe there is little that you can do to address the situation successfully or reduce your feelings of stress, then you may feel powerless and ineffective, even if others around you believe there are steps you could take.

Sometimes, you learn additional information or experience another situation that indicates you should reappraise the original event. **Reappraisal** *involves making a new primary or secondary appraisal resulting from changes in the situation.* For example, you may initially dismiss an accusation that your partner is cheating on you (i.e., make a primary appraisal that the event is irrelevant), but after being shown pictures of your partner in a romantic situation with another person, you reappraise the event as stressful. Reappraisal can either increase stress (if your partner had initially denied the encounter) or lower stress (if you discovered that the photographs were fakes).

The three types of appraisals demonstrate that determining whether an event is stressful is a dynamic process. Initial decisions about events may be upheld over time, or they may change in light of new information or personal experience. Different events may be appraised in the same way, and the same event may be appraised differently at any two points in time. This dynamic process helps explain why people react the way they do over the life span. For example, as our physiological abilities change with increasing age, we may have fewer physical resources to handle particular events. As a result, events that were appraised as not stressful in young adulthood may be appraised as stressful in late life.

Coping. During the secondary appraisal of an event labeled stressful in primary appraisal, we may believe there is something we can do to deal with the event effectively. *Collectively, these attempts to deal with stressful events are called* coping. Lazarus and Folkman (1984) view coping more formally as a complex, evolving process of dealing with stress that is learned. Much like appraisals, coping is seen as a dynamic, evolving process that is fine-tuned over time. Our first attempt might fail, but if we try again in a slightly different way we may succeed. Coping is learned, not automatic. That is why we often do not cope very well with stressful situations we are facing for the first time (such as the end of our first love relationship). The saying "practice makes perfect" applies to coping, too. Also, coping takes time and effort. Finally, coping entails only managing the situation; we need not overcome or control it. Indeed, many stressful events cannot be fixed or undone; many times the best we can do is to learn to live with the situation. It is in this sense that we may cope with the death of a spouse.

People cope in different ways. At a general level we can distinguish between problem-focused coping and emotion-focused coping. **Problem-focused coping** *involves attempts to tackle the problem head-on*. Taking medication to treat a disease and spending more time studying for an examination are examples of problem-focused coping with the stress of illness or failing a prior test. In general, problem-focused coping entails doing something directly about the problem at hand. **Emotion-focused coping** *involves dealing with one's feelings about the stressful event*. Allowing oneself to express anger or frustration over becoming ill or failing an exam is an example of this approach. The goal here is not necessarily to eliminate the problem, although this may happen. Rather, the purpose may be to help oneself deal with situations that are difficult or impossible to tackle head-on.

Several other behaviors can also be viewed in the context of coping. Many people use their relationship with God as the basis for their coping (Bade, 2012; Kinney, Ishler, Pargament, & Cavanaugh, 2003). For believers, using religious coping strategies usually results in positives outcomes when faced with negative events.

How well we cope depends on several factors. For example, healthy, energetic people are better able to cope with an infection than frail, sick people. Psychologically, a positive attitude about oneself and one's abilities is also important. Good problem-solving skills put one at an advantage by creating several options with which to manage the stress. Social skills and social support are important in helping one solicit suggestions and assistance from others. Finally, financial resources are important; having the money to pay a mechanic to fix your car allows you to avoid the frustration of trying to do it yourself.

The number of stressful events, per se, is less important than one's appraisal of them and whether the person has effective coping skills to deal with them. Of course, should the number of stressful issues exceed one's ability to cope, then the number of issues being confronted would be a key issue.

Aging and the Stress and Coping Paradigm. Two important age-related differences in the stress and

Religiosity and spirituality are important aspects of a person's lifestyle that must be considered in holistic approaches to health and wellness.

Kevin Fleming/CORBIS

coping paradigm are the sources of stress and the choice of coping strategies. In terms of stress, three national surveys in the United States (1983, 2006, and 2009) showed that younger adults, and those with lower levels of education and income reported higher stress than older adults and those with higher levels of education and income (Cohen & Janicki-Deverts, 2012).

Age differences in coping strategies across the life span are consistent (Martin et al., 2008; Meléndez, Mayordomo, Sancho, and Tomás, 2012). One key difference is that older adults are less likely to use active coping strategies and are more likely to use past experience, emotion-focused, and religious coping strategies.

We explore the relation between age and stress in more detail in the How Do We Know? feature. Cairney and Krause (2008) use data from a large Canadian study to show that the experience of negative life events matters in the lives of older adults.

HOW DO WE KNOW?:

NEGATIVE LIFE EVENTS AND MASTERY

Who were the investigators, and what was the aim of the study? How older adults cope with the effects of stressful events related to personal mastery (whether people feel in control of things in their life) is important in understanding how people manage their lives. John Cairney and Neal Krause (2008) decided to see if exposure to life events affects age-related decline in feelings of mastery.

How did the investigators measure the topic of interest? To get a broad assessment of the key variables, Cairney and Krause used several self-report measures. *Mastery* was measured by a seven-item self-report questionnaire that is widely used in this type of research (a sample item is "You have little control over the things that happen to you."). *Recent life events* were measured by the number of negative life events that the respondent or someone close to the respondent had experienced in the previous 12 months. *Physician contact* was measured by asking the respondent how many times he or she had seen or talked with a family physician or general practitioner in the past 12 months. *Physical health concerns* were measured by asking respondents about 21 chronic health conditions, and by asking about limitations in daily activities. *Social support* was measured by asking whether respondents had someone (a) to confide in, (b) to count on, (c) who could give them advice, and (d) who made them feel loved. *Socioeconomic measures* included the highest education level the respondent had obtained and a five-level measure of income adequacy.

Who were the participants in the study? The sample was drawn from the longitudinal biennial National Population Health Survey (NPHS) conducted by Statistics Canada. This telephone survey consists of a national probability sample of Canadian residents across all 10 provinces every 2 years beginning in 1994 (Wave 1). For Wave 1, of the 18,342 possible respondents aged 12 and over, 17,626 participated (96.1%); 16,291 were over

age 18. After eliminating cases with missing data, the final sample consisted of 15,410 respondents. Wave 4 (in 2000) included the same set of measures as Wave 1 for mastery, allowing a comparison over time. Of the respondents who completed Wave 1,840 died and 5,049 could not be relocated, declined to participate, or provided incomplete data in Wave 4. This left 9,521 respondents for this longitudinal study.

What was the design of the study? Cairney and Krause used a longitudinal design with two times of measurement: 1994 and 2000.

Were there ethical concerns in the study? Because people had the right not to participate, and data were not identifiable by individual and only reported in aggregate, there were no ethical concerns with the study.

What were the results? Because of the problems inherent in longitudinal designs (see Chapter 1), Cairney and Krause checked for systematic differences in participants in the Wave 1 and Wave 4 data. They found that men, those from higher income groups, those with only a high school education, older adults, and those with more physical disabilities or health problems were more likely to have died by Wave 4. Single individuals, those with lower income adequacy, with more physical disability, and with higher levels of social support were more likely to drop out by Wave 4.

An analysis of the effects of stress on perceived mastery was done by comparing outcomes at ages 25, 45, and 65. This analysis showed that at each time of measurement for people in all three age groups, exposure to more negative life events was associated with decline in mastery, with this outcome being strongest with the age 65 group. Looking at the data longitudinally, the effects of more negative life events over time was greatest for the group that was age 65 in Wave 1.

What did the investigators conclude? These findings show that experiencing negative life events is a major source of age-related declines in feelings of personal mastery. In turn, loss of personal mastery may explain why older adults are more vulnerable to the negative effects of stress.

Effects of Stress on Health. How does stress affect us? If the stress is short, such as being stuck in a traffic jam for an hour when we're already late in an otherwise relaxed day, the answer is that it probably will have little effect other than on our temper. But if the stress is continuous, or chronic, then the picture changes dramatically.

Chronic stress has many serious effects (Ogden, 2012), including pervasive negative effects on the immune system that cause increased susceptibility to viral infections, increased risk of atherosclerosis and hypertension, and impaired memory and cognition (Webster-Marketon & Glaser, 2008). Effects can last for decades; severe stress experienced in childhood has effects that last well into adulthood (Shonkoff, Garner et al., 2012).

Research indicates that different types of appraisals that are interpreted as stressful create different physiological outcomes (Webster-Marketon & Glaser, 2008). This may mean that how the body reacts to stress depends on the appraisal process; the reaction to different types of stress is not the same. In turn, this implies that changing people's appraisal may also be a way to lower the impact of stress on the body.

ADULT DEVELOPMENT IN ACTION

Design an education program for adults regarding health and the immune system, with special focus on stress and coping.

4.3 Common Chronic Conditions and Their Management

LEARNING OBJECTIVES

- What are the most important issues in chronic disease?
- What are some common chronic conditions across adulthood?
- How can people manage chronic conditions?

Moses is a 75-year-old African American man who worked as a lawyer all his life. Recently, he was diagnosed as having prostate cancer. Moses has heard about several treatment options, such as surgery and radiation therapy, and he is concerned about potential side effects, such as impotence. Moses wonders what he should do.

Every day, millions of older adults get up in the morning and face another day of dealing with chronic diseases such as diabetes and arthritis. Although medical advances are made every year, true cures for these conditions probably are not imminent. We considered some chronic diseases in Chapter 3 in the context of discussing age-related changes in major body systems; arthritis and cardiovascular disease were among them. In this section, we will consider other chronic conditions, such as diabetes and cancer. We will see that Moses's concern about how to deal with his prostate cancer is one facing many men. As Moses will discover, in many situations there is no clear-cut "right" way to proceed. We will also examine some ways to help alleviate the effects of some chronic conditions and consider some ways in which we may be able to prevent such diseases or at least reduce our chances of getting them.

General Issues in Chronic Conditions

Having a chronic disease does not mean that one immediately becomes incapacitated. Even though the type and severity of chronic conditions vary across people, most older adults manage to accomplish the necessary tasks of daily living despite having a chronic condition.

Chronic conditions can make life unpleasant and in some cases can increase susceptibility to other diseases. Understanding chronic conditions requires understanding how the four developmental forces interact. We saw in Chapter 3 that researchers are beginning to understand genetic connections with chronic conditions such as cardiovascular disease and cancer. Other biological aspects include the changes in physical systems with age, including the immune system, which can set the stage for chronic conditions. Key psychological aspects of chronic disease include the coping skills people bring to bear on their conditions; we consider some of these later in this chapter. Sociocultural factors include the lack of adequate health care, which creates barriers to treatment. The ethnic group differences in some chronic conditions, such as hypertension, are also important to keep in mind. Finally, life-cycle factors help us understand why reactions to the same chronic condition vary with the age of onset. Moreover, some conditions, such as rheumatoid arthritis, can occur at any point in adulthood, whereas others, such as prostate cancer, tend to occur mostly after midlife. As the number of older adults increases rapidly, so will the extent of chronic conditions as health problems. This will necessitate a fundamental change in health care, reflecting a shift from an acute care focus to one that focuses much more on managing chronic conditions.

Common Chronic Conditions

Nearly half of adults in the United States have a chronic health condition (Centers for Disease Control and Prevention, 2012f). Some of the most common, such as cardiovascular disease and arthritis, were considered in Chapter 3. We will consider three other common conditions, diabetes mellitus, cancer, and incontinence, in this section.

Diabetes Mellitus. *The disease* diabetes mellitus *occurs when the pancreas produces insufficient insulin.* The primary characteristic of diabetes mellitus is above-normal sugar (glucose) in the blood and urine caused by problems in metabolizing carbohydrates. People with diabetes mellitus can go into a coma if the level of sugar gets too high, and they may lapse into unconsciousness if it gets too low.

There are two general types of diabetes (American Diabetes Association, 2012). Type I diabetes *usually develops earlier in life and requires the use of insulin, hence it is sometimes called insulin-dependent diabetes.* Type II diabetes *typically develops in adulthood and is often effectively managed through diet.* There are three groups of older adults with diabetes: those who developed diabetes as children, adolescents, or young adults; those who developed diabetes in late middle age and also typically developed cardiovascular problems; and those who develop diabetes in late life and usually show mild problems. This last group includes the majority of older adults with diabetes mellitus. In adults, diabetes mellitus is often associated with obesity. The symptoms of diabetes seen in younger people (excessive thirst, increased appetite and urination, fatigue, weakness, weight loss, and impaired wound healing) may be far less prominent or absent in older adults. As a result, diabetes mellitus in older adults often is diagnosed during other medical procedures, such as eye examinations or hospitalizations for other conditions.

Overall, diabetes is more common among older adults and members of minority groups (Centers for Disease Control and Prevention, 2011b). The chronic effects of increased glucose levels may result in serious complications. The most common long-term effects include nerve damage, diabetic retinopathy (discussed in Chapter 3), kidney disorders, cerebrovascular accidents (CVAs), cognitive dysfunction, damage to the coronary arteries, skin problems, and poor circulation in the arms and legs, which may lead to gangrene. Diabetes also increases the chance of having a stroke or developing atherosclerosis and coronary heart disease.

Although it cannot be cured, diabetes can be managed effectively through a low-carbohydrate and low-calorie diet; exercise; proper care of skin, gums, teeth, and feet; and medication (insulin). For older adults, it is important to address potential memory difficulties with the daily testing and management regimens. Education about diabetes mellitus is included in Medicare coverage, making it easier for older adults to learn how to manage the condition.

Cancer. Cancer is the second leading cause of death in the United States, behind cardiovascular disease (Centers for Disease Control and Prevention, 2012g). Over the life span, nearly one in two American men and one in three American women will develop cancer (American Cancer Society, 2012b). The risk of getting cancer increases markedly with age. About one in four men and one in five women will die from cancer. The good news is that the death rates for most types of cancer have been falling since the 1990s.

Many current deaths caused by cancer are preventable. Some forms of cancer, such as lung and colorectal cancer, are caused in large part by unhealthy lifestyles. Smoking causes more preventable health conditions than any other lifestyle issue. Most skin cancers can be prevented by limiting exposure to the sun's ultraviolet rays. Clearly, changes in lifestyle would have a major impact on cancer rates.

The incidence and mortality rates of some common forms of cancer in men and women are shown in Figure 4.5. Notice that prostate cancer is the most common form of cancer in men, and breast cancer is the most common form in women (American Cancer Society, 2012b).

Death rates from various forms of cancer differ: Lung cancer kills more than three times as many men as prostate cancer and considerably more women than breast cancer (in women). Five-year survival rates for these cancers also differ dramatically. Whereas only 15% of patients with lung cancer are still living 5 years after diagnosis, nearly 90% of female patients with

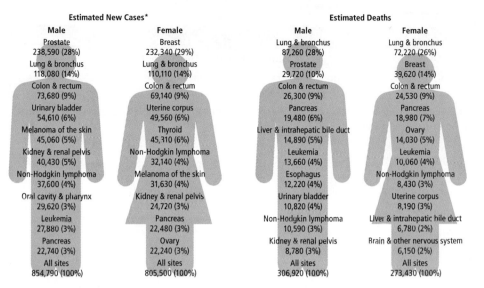

Estimated New Cases*

Male	Female
Prostate 238,590 (28%)	Breast 232,340 (29%)
Lung & bronchus 118,080 (14%)	Lung & bronchus 110,110 (14%)
Colon & rectum 73,680 (9%)	Colon & rectum 69,140 (9%)
Urinary bladder 54,610 (6%)	Uterine corpus 49,560 (6%)
Melanoma of the skin 45,060 (5%)	Thyroid 45,310 (6%)
Kidney & renal pelvis 40,430 (5%)	Non-Hodgkin lymphoma 32,140 (4%)
Non-Hodgkin lymphoma 37,600 (4%)	Melanoma of the skin 31,630 (4%)
Oral cavity & pharynx 29,620 (3%)	Kidney & renal pelvis 24,720 (3%)
Leukemia 27,880 (3%)	Pancreas 22,480 (3%)
Pancreas 22,740 (3%)	Ovary 22,240 (3%)
All sites 854,790 (100%)	All sites 805,500 (100%)

Estimated Deaths

Male	Female
Lung & bronchus 87,260 (28%)	Lung & bronchus 72,220 (26%)
Prostate 29,720 (10%)	Breast 39,620 (14%)
Colon & rectum 26,300 (9%)	Colon & rectum 24,530 (9%)
Pancreas 19,480 (6%)	Pancreas 18,980 (7%)
Liver & intrahepatic bile duct 14,890 (5%)	Ovary 14,030 (5%)
Leukemia 13,660 (4%)	Leukemia 10,060 (4%)
Esophagus 12,220 (4%)	Non-Hodgkin lymphoma 8,430 (3%)
Urinary bladder 10,820 (4%)	Uterine corpus 8,190 (3%)
Non-Hodgkin lymphoma 10,590 (3%)	Liver & intrahepatic bile duct 6,780 (2%)
Kidney & renal pelvis 8,780 (3%)	Brain & other nervous system 6,150 (2%)
All sites 306,920 (100%)	All sites 273,430 (100%)

*Excludes basal and squamous cell skin cancers and in situ carcinoma except urinary bladder.
©2013, American Cancer Society, Inc., Surveillance Research

Figure 4.5
Leading new cancer cases and deaths—2012 estimates.

breast cancer and over 95% of men with prostate cancer are (American Cancer Society, 2012b).

Why older people have a much higher incidence of cancer is not understood fully. Part of the reason is the cumulative effect of poor health habits over a long period of time, such as cigarette smoking and poor diet. In addition, the cumulative effects of exposure to pollutants and cancer-causing chemicals are partly to blame. As noted earlier in this chapter, some researchers believe that normative age-related changes in the immune system, resulting in a decreased ability to inhibit the growth of tumors, may also be responsible.

Research in molecular biology and microbiology is increasingly pointing to genetic links, likely in combination with environmental factors (Battista, Blancquaert, Laberge, van Schendel, & Leduc, 2012). The National Cancer Institute initiated the Cancer Genome Anatomy Program and an online journal and database has begun, called the Atlas of Genetics and Cytogenetics in Oncology and Haematology, in order to provide a comprehensive list of all genes responsible for cancer.

For example, two breast cancer susceptibility genes that have been identified are *BRCA1* on chromosome 17 and *BRCA2* on chromosome 13. When a woman carries a mutation in either *BRCA1* or *BRCA2*, she is at a greater risk of being diagnosed with breast or ovarian cancer at some point in her life. Similarly, a potential susceptibility locus for prostate cancer has been identified on chromosome 1, called *HPC1*, which

may account for about 1 in 500 cases of prostate cancer. An additional rare mutation of *HOXB13*, on chromosome 17, has also been identified.

Although genetic screening tests for breast and prostate cancer for the general population are not yet warranted, such tests may one day be routine. Genetics is also providing much of the exciting new research on possible treatments by giving investigators new ways to fight the disease. Age-related tissue changes have been associated with the development of tumors, some of which become cancerous; some of these may be genetically linked as well. The discovery that the presence of telomerase causes cells to grow rapidly and without limits on the number of divisions they can undergo provides additional insights into how cancer develops (Londoño-Vallejo, 2008; see Chapter 3). What remains to be seen is how these genetic events interact with environmental factors, such as viruses or pollutants. Understanding this interaction process, predicted by the basic developmental forces, could explain why there are great differences among individuals in when and how cancer develops.

The most effective way to address the problem of cancer is through increased use of screening techniques and preventive lifestyle changes. The American Cancer Society (2012c) strongly recommends these steps for people of all ages, but older adults need to be especially aware of what to do. Table 4.1 shows guidelines for the early detection of some common forms of cancer.

Table 4.1

AMERICAN CANCER SOCIETY GUIDELINES FOR THE EARLY DETECTION OF CANCER

THE AMERICAN CANCER SOCIETY RECOMMENDS THESE SCREENING GUIDELINES FOR MOST ADULTS	
Breast cancer	■ Yearly mammograms are recommended starting at age 40 and continuing for as long as a woman is in good health ■ Clinical breast exam (CBE) about every 3 years for women in their 20s and 30s and every year for women 40 and over ■ Women should know how their breasts normally look and feel and report any breast change promptly to their health care provider. Breast self-exam (BSE) is an option for women starting in their 20s.
Colorectal cancer and polyps	Beginning at age 50, both men and women should follow one of these testing schedules: **Tests that find polyps and cancer** ■ Flexible sigmoidoscopy every 5 years, or ■ Colonoscopy every 10 years, or ■ Double-contrast barium enema every 5 years, or ■ CT colonography (virtual colonoscopy) every 5 years **Tests that primarily find cancer** ■ Yearly fecal occult blood test (gFOBT), or ■ Yearly fecal immunochemical test (FIT) every year, or ■ Stool DNA test (sDNA)
Cervical cancer	■ **Cervical cancer screening (testing) should begin at age 21**. Women under age 21 should *not* be tested. ■ **Women between ages 21 and 29** should have a Pap test every 3 years. Now there is also a test called the HPV test. HPV testing should *not* be used in this age group unless it is needed after an abnormal Pap test result. ■ **Women between the ages of 30 and 65** should have a Pap test plus an HPV test (called "co-testing") every 5 years. This is the preferred approach, but it is also OK to have a Pap test alone every 3 years. ■ **Women over age 65** who have had regular cervical cancer testing with normal results should *not* be tested for cervical cancer. Once testing is stopped, it should not be started again. Women with a history of a serious cervical pre-cancer should continue to be tested for at least 20 years after that diagnosis, even if testing continues past age 65. ■ **A woman who has had her uterus removed (and also her cervix)** for reasons not related to cervical cancer and who has no history of cervical cancer or serious pre-cancer should *not* be tested. ■ **A woman who has been vaccinated against HPV** should still follow the screening recommendations for her age group.
Lung cancer	The American Cancer Society does not recommend tests to screen for lung cancer in people who are at average risk of this disease. However, the ACS does have screening guidelines for individuals who are at high risk of lung cancer due to cigarette smoking.
Prostate cancer	The American Cancer Society recommends that men make an informed decision with their doctor about whether to be tested for prostate cancer. Research has not yet proven that the potential benefits of testing outweigh the harms of testing and treatment. The American Cancer Society believes that men should not be tested without learning about what we know and don't know about the risks and possible benefits of testing and treatment.

Take control of your health, and reduce your cancer risk	■ Stay away from tobacco.
	■ Stay at a healthy weight.
	■ Get moving with regular physical activity.
	■ Eat healthy with plenty of fruits and vegetables.
	■ Limit how much alcohol you drink (if you drink at all).
	■ Protect your skin.
	■ Know yourself, your family history, and your risks.
	■ Have regular check-ups and cancer screening tests.
	■ For information on how to reduce your cancer risk and other questions about cancer, please call us anytime, day or night, at 1-800-227-2345 or visit us online at www.cancer.org.

Source: http://www.cancer.org/healthy/findcancerearly/cancerscreeningguidelines/american-cancer-society-guidelines-for-the-early-detection-of-cancer

As Moses is learning, one of the biggest controversies in cancer prevention concerns screening and treatment for prostate cancer. The Current Controversies feature summarizes the issues: lack of data about the causes and the course of the disease and disagreement over treatment approaches. This controversy mirrors similar debates over the treatment of breast cancer, contrasting the relative merits of regular screening mammography, and treatment approaches including radical mastectomy (removal of the breast and some surrounding tissue) versus lumpectomy (removal of the cancerous tumor only) and how chemotherapy, radiation, and drugs such as tamoxifen fit into the overall treatment approach.

CURRENT CONTROVERSIES:

THE PROSTATE CANCER DILEMMA

Roughly the size of a walnut and weighing about an ounce, the prostate gland is an unlikely candidate to create a major medical controversy. The prostate is located in front of the rectum and below the bladder and wraps around the urethra (the tube carrying urine out through the penis). Its primary function is to produce fluid for semen, the liquid that transports sperm. In half of all men over age 60, the prostate tends to enlarge, which may produce such symptoms as difficulty in urinating and frequent nighttime urination.

Enlargement of the prostate can happen for three main reasons: prostatitis (an inflammation of the prostate that is usually caused by an infection), benign prostatic hyperplasia (BPH), and prostate cancer. BPH is a noncancerous enlargement of the prostate that affects the innermost part of the prostate first. This often results in urination problems as the prostate gradually squeezes the urethra, but it does not affect sexual functioning.

Prostate cancer often begins on the outer portion of the prostate, which seldom causes symptoms in the early stages. Each year, more than 240,000 men in the United States are diagnosed with prostate cancer; nearly 30,000 die (National Cancer Institute, 2012). For reasons we do not yet understand, African American men such as Moses have a 40% higher chance of getting prostate cancer. In addition, a genetic link is clear: A man whose brother has prostate cancer is four times more likely to get prostate cancer than a man with no brothers having the disease.

Part of the controversy surrounding prostate cancer relates to whether early detection reduces mortality from the disease. Research investigating whether screening for early detection of prostate cancer saved lives indicated that, overall, it did not, and may actually create problems such as unnecessary treatment because most forms of prostate cancer are very slow growing. This lack of data led the U.S. Preventive Services Task Force, the Canadian Task Force on the Periodic Health Examination, and others to recommend abandoning routine prostate cancer screening because of the cost and the uncertain benefits associated with it.

The American Cancer Society and the National Comprehensive Cancer Network jointly created a guide to prostate cancer screening and treatment to help men negotiate the confusing state of affairs (American Cancer Society, 2012a; National Comprehensive Cancer Network, 2012). The background information provided by these organizations can help men decide what, if any, screening and treatment options are best for them.

The sharp division among medical experts highlights the relation between carefully conducted research and public health policy. At present, there has been insufficient comparison of various treatment options (which include surgery, radiation, hormones, and drugs), and we do not fully understand the natural course of prostate cancer in terms of which types of tumors grow rapidly or spread to other organs and the typical type that grows slowly and does not. Given that some of the side effects of surgery include urinary incontinence and impotence, and that some of the other therapies may produce other unpleasant effects, there is debate on whether the disease should be treated at all in most patients (National Cancer Institute, 2012).

At present, men who experience prostate-related symptoms are left to decide for themselves, in consultation with their physician, what to do. Many men opt for immediate treatment and learn how to live with any subsequent side effects. Support groups for men with prostate cancer are becoming more common, and many encourage the patient's partner to participate.

The controversy surrounding early screening and detection of prostate cancer is unlikely to subside soon because the necessary research concerning effective treatment and survival will take years to conduct. Until then, if you or someone you know is over 50 or is in a high-risk group, the decision still must be made. Talk at length with a physician who is up-to-date on the topic and educate yourself about the alternatives.

In general, cancer treatment involves several major approaches that are typically used in combination: surgery, chemotherapy, radiation, and others (e.g., biological therapy, gene therapy, bone marrow transplant). In addition, numerous alternative therapies, such as herbal approaches, exist. Continued advances in genetic research probably will result in genetically engineered medications designed to attack cancer cells. As with any health care decision, people with cancer need to become as educated as possible about the options.

Incontinence. *For many people, the loss of the ability to control the elimination of urine and feces on an occasional or consistent basis, called* incontinence, *is a source of great concern and embarrassment.* As you can imagine, incontinence can result in social isolation and lower quality of life if no steps are taken to address the problem.

Urinary incontinence, the most common form, increases with age and varies across ethnic groups as a function of gender (Shamliyan, Wyman, & Kane, 2012; Tennstedt et al., 2008). Among community-dwelling older adults, roughly 20% of women and 10% of men have urinary incontinence. But rates are much higher if the person has dementia and is living in the community (about 35%) or if the person is living in a nursing home (roughly 70%). European American women report a higher rate of urinary incontinence than either African American or Latina women; rates for men do not vary across ethnic groups.

Urinary incontinence occurs most often for four major reasons (Mayo Clinic, 2012d). Stress incontinence *happens when pressure in the abdomen exceeds the ability to resist urinary flow.* This may occur when a person coughs, sneezes, exercises, or lifts a heavy object. Urge incontinence *usually is caused by a central nervous system problem after a stroke or urinary tract infection.* People feel the urge to urinate but cannot get to a toilet quickly enough. Overflow incontinence *results from improper contraction of the kidneys, causing the bladder to become overdistended.* Certain drugs, tumors, and prostate enlargement are common causes of overflow incontinence. Functional incontinence *occurs when the urinary tract is intact but because of physical disability or cognitive impairment the person is unaware of the need to urinate.* This is the most common form in people with dementia, Parkinson's disease, or arthritis.

Most types of incontinence can be alleviated with interventions. Among the most effective are behavioral interventions, which include diet changes, relearning to recognize the need to toilet, and pelvic floor muscle training for stress incontinence (Shamliyan et al., 2012; Zahariou, Karamouti, & Papaioannou, 2008). Certain medications and surgical intervention may be needed in some cases. Numerous products such as protective undergarments and padding also are available to help absorb leaks. All these options help alleviate the psychological and social effects of incontinence and help people live better lives (Markland, Vaughan, Johnson, Burgio, & Goode, 2012).

Managing Pain

People do not like to be in pain, and they fear pain more than almost any other aspect of disease. Perhaps that is because pain is one of the most unpleasant aspects of many chronic diseases. Pain is disruptive, saps energy, negatively affects quality of life, and can lead to an ever-intensifying cycle of pain, anxiety, and anguish. Pain is also one of the most common complaints of older adults, affecting more than 40% of community-dwelling elderly on a regular basis (Shega, Dale, Andrew, Paice, Rockwood, & Weiner, 2012). Pain does not necessarily reflect the same things as pain in younger adults; for older adults it is not only an indication that something is wrong, but can also be responsible for depression, sleep disorders, decreased social interaction, impaired mobility, and increased health care costs (Karp et al., 2008).

Unfortunately, many myths exist about pain in older adults, such as that older adults should simply accept the physical pain they experience as part of growing older. Failure to understand the real nature of pain in older adults can lead to a failure to relieve it.

How do people manage pain? Perhaps the most important aspects are to understand that pain is not a necessary part of treatment, people can control their pain, no one approach is likely to be sufficient, and asking for pain relief is to be expected. There are two general pain management techniques: pharmacological and nonpharmacological (WebMD, 2010). These approaches often are used together for maximum pain relief.

Pharmacological approaches to pain management include nonnarcotic and narcotic medications. Nonnarcotic medications are best for mild to moderate pain, while narcotic medications are best for severe pain. Nonnarcotic medications include NSAIDs (nonsteroidal anti-inflammatory drugs), such as ibuprofen and acetaminophen. However, these drugs must be used with caution because they may cause toxic side effects in older adults. Narcotic drugs that work well in older adults include morphine and codeine; other commonly used drugs, such as meperidine and pentazocine, should be avoided because of age-related changes in metabolism. Patients taking any of these medications must be monitored very closely.

Many people manage the pain of arthritis through medication.

Fuse/Getty Images

Nonpharmacological pain control includes a variety of approaches, all of which are effective with some people; the trick is to keep trying until the best approach is found. Common techniques include the following:

- Deep and superficial stimulation of the skin through therapeutic touch, massage, vibration, heat, cold, and various ointments
- Electrical stimulation over the pain site or to the spine
- Acupuncture and acupressure
- Biofeedback, in which a person learns to control and change the body processes responsible for the pain
- Distraction techniques such as soft music that draw a person's attention away from the pain
- Relaxation, meditation, and imagery approaches that rid the mind of tension and anxiety
- Hypnosis, either self-induced or induced by another person

The most important point is that pain is not a necessary part of growing old or having a disease. Pain relief is an important part of recovery and should be included in any treatment regimen for adults of all ages.

ADULT DEVELOPMENT IN ACTIONS

Given the higher frequency of chronic disease with age, what issues would you, as a professional human resources expert, need to include in creating support programs for employees?

4.4 Pharmacology and Medication Adherence

LEARNING OBJECTIVES

- What are the developmental trends in using medication?
- How does aging affect the way the medications work?
- What are the consequences of medication interactions?
- What are the important medication adherence issues?

Lucy is an 80-year-old woman who has several chronic health problems. As a result, she takes 12 medications every day. She must follow the regimen very carefully; some of her medications must be taken with food, some on an empty stomach, and some at bedtime. Lucy's daughter is concerned that Lucy may experience serious problems if she fails to take her medications properly.

One of the most important health issues for older adults is the use of both prescription and over-the-counter medications. In fact, older adults take more medications on average than any other age group, roughly half of all drugs prescribed in the United States. When over-the-counter drugs are included, this translates into about six or seven medications per older adult; Lucy takes more than the average. Like Lucy, most people take these drugs to relieve pain or related problems resulting from chronic conditions.

Patterns of Medication Use

The explosion of new prescription and over-the-counter medications over the past few decades has created many options for physicians in treating disease, especially chronic conditions. Although advances in medication are highly desirable, there are hidden dangers for older adults (U.S. Food and Drug Administration, 2012).

Until the late 1990s, clinical trials of new medications were not required to include older adults. Thus, for most of the medications currently on the market, we do not know whether they are as effective for older adults as they are for younger or middle-aged adults. Equally important, because of normative changes in metabolism with age, the effective dosage of medications may change as people get older, which can mean a greater risk of overdose with potentially serious consequences, including death, or the need to increase the dose in order to get the desired effect.

When one considers that many of these newer, often more effective medications are very expensive, the ability of many older adults to afford the best medication treatments is questionable. The prescription drug insurance most older Americans have through Medicare still leaves significant deductibles and co-payments that are too high for many low income older adults. Additionally, figuring out which option is best can be quite complex, serving as a further barrier. (You can get much more information from the official Medicare prescription drug coverage website.)

As even more medications are developed and approved, the use of multiple medications will continue and likely increase. When used appropriately, medications can improve people's lives; when used inappropriately, they can cause harm. Understanding how medications work and how these processes change with age is extremely important.

Developmental Changes in How Medications Work

When Lucy takes her medications every day, what happens? Understanding how medications work involves knowing the developmental changes in absorption, distribution, metabolism, and excretion of medications (Hacker, Messer, & Bachmann, 2009).

Absorption *is the time needed for one of Lucy's medications to enter the bloodstream.* For drugs taken orally, a key factor is the time it takes for the medication to go from the stomach to the small intestine, where maximum absorption occurs. This transfer may take longer than expected in older adults, resulting in too little or too much absorption, depending on the drug. For example, if a drug takes longer to transfer from the stomach to the small intestine in older adults, too little of the drug may be left to be effective. However, once in the small intestine, absorption does not appear to differ among older, middle-aged, or younger adults (Hacker et al., 2009).

Once in the bloodstream, the medication is distributed throughout the body. How well distribution occurs depends on the adequacy of the cardiovascular system. Maximal effectiveness of a drug depends on the balance between the portions of the drug that bind with plasma protein and the portions that remain free. As we grow older, more portions of the drug remain free; this means that toxic levels of a drug can build up more easily in older adults.

Similarly, drugs that are soluble in water or fat tissue can also build up more easily in older adults because of age-related decreases in total body water or possible increases in fat tissue. The effective dosage of a drug depends critically on the amount of free drug in the body; thus, whether the person is young or old, thin or obese, is very important to keep in mind (Lilley, Rainforth Collins, & Snyder, in press)

Getting rid of medications in the bloodstream is partly the job of the liver, a process called drug metabolism. There is much evidence that this process is slower in older adults, meaning that drugs stay in the body longer as people grow older (Le Couteur, McLachlan, & de Cabo, 2012). Slower drug metabolism can also create the potential for toxicity if the medication schedule does not take this into account.

Sometimes drugs are decomposed into other compounds to help eliminate them. Drug excretion *occurs mainly through the kidneys in urine, although some elimination occurs through feces, sweat, and saliva.* Changes in kidney function with age, related to lower total body water content, are common. This means that drugs often are not excreted as quickly by older adults, again setting the stage for possible toxic effects (Le Couteur et al., 2012).

What do these changes mean? Most important, the dosage of a drug needed to get the desired effect may be different for older adults than for middle-aged or younger adults. In many cases, physicians recommend using one-third to one-half the usual adult dosage when the difference between the effective dosages

and toxic dosages is small or there is a high rate of side effects (Le Couteur et al., 2012). In addition, because of age-related physiological changes, several drugs are not recommended for use by older adults. In general, a dosage strategy of "start low and go slow" is best.

Medication Side Effects and Interactions

Because of their high rate of medication use, older adults also have the highest risk of adverse drug effects (Le Couteur et al., 2012; Lilley et al., in press; U.S. Food and Drug Administration, 2012). In part, these problems result from physiological changes that occur with age in how drugs are absorbed into the body, how long they remain, and how well they work. For example, changes in the stomach may slow down the rate at which drugs enter the body, meaning that achieving the effective level of the drug in the body may take longer. Changes in liver and kidney functioning affect how rapidly the drug is removed and excreted from the body, meaning that levels of the drug may remain high for longer periods of time.

As we have seen, age-related increases in the frequency of chronic conditions means that older adults are likely to have more than one medical problem for which they take medications. In this regard, Lucy is fairly typical. *Treating multiple conditions results in* polypharmacy, *the use of multiple medications.* Polypharmacy is potentially dangerous because many drugs do not interact well; the action of some drugs is enhanced in combination with others, whereas other drugs may not work at all in combination. Drug interactions may create secondary medical problems that in turn need to be treated, and the primary condition may not be treated as effectively. Moreover, drug interactions can produce symptoms that appear to be caused by other diseases; in some cases they may cause confusion and memory loss that mimics Alzheimer's disease. Professionals and family members need to monitor the situation closely (Arnold, 2008).

Lucy's daughter is correct in worrying about her mother taking her medications as prescribed. Analyzing a person's medication regimen, including both prescription and over-the-counter medications, and asking the patient or caregiver to describe how they are taken is important in diagnosing health problems. Given the high level of medication use among older adults, what can be done to minimize

Table 4.2

EXAMPLE OF A COMPLEX MEDICATION REGIMEN			
	Morning	Dinner	Bedtime
Large yellow pill	Take 1 each day with food		
Small blue pill	Take 1 every other day		
Small white pill	Take 2 per day for two days, then 1 per day; repeat		
Round pink tablet		Take 1 every other day	
Oval white pill			Take 2 each night with plenty of water
Small yellow pill			Take one per week

drug interaction effects? Physicians play a key role, but other health care professionals also must be alert because older adults typically go to more than one physician. Accurate medication histories including all types of medicines are essential. Inappropriate use of drugs, such as antipsychotics to control behavior, must also be monitored.

Adherence to Medication Regimens

The likelihood of adverse drug reactions increases as the number of medications increases. Taking more drugs also means that keeping track of each becomes more difficult. Imagine having to keep track of six different medications, each of which has a different schedule, as presented in Table 4.2.

Medication adherence (taking medications correctly) becomes less likely the more drugs people take and the more complicated the regimens are. Combined with sensory, physical, and cognitive changes in older adults, medication adherence is a significant problem in this age group (Shea, 2006). Prospective memory, remembering to take one's medication at a future time, is critical to good adherence to a medication regimen (Zogg, Woods, Sauceda, Wiebe, & Simoni, 2012). The oldest old are especially at risk; the most common problem is that they simply forget to take the medication. (We consider ways to help people remember to take their medications in Chapter 7.) Yet adherence is crucial to treatment success. Christensen and Johnson (2002) present an interactive model that describes the context of patient adherence. This model is shown in Figure 4.6.

The best approach, of course, is to keep the number of medications to a minimum (Shea, 2006). If the use of drugs is determined to be essential, then periodic reevaluations should be conducted and the medication discontinued when possible. In addition, the lowest effective dosage should be used. In general, medication use by older adults should get the same careful consideration as by any other age group.

Figure 4.6

Conceptual representation of the patient-by-treatment-context interactive framework. The dashed lines reflect the fact that research generally does not find that patient characteristics or contextual features have a significant effect on adherence.

© 2015 Cengage Learning

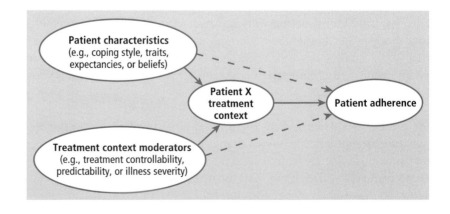

ADULT DEVELOPMENT IN ACTION

If you were a home health aide, what would you do to help your clients remember to take their medications? (Write down your answer and then see if you came up with similar ideas as you will read about in Chapter 7.)

4.5 Functional Health and Disability

LEARNING OBJECTIVES

- What factors are important to include in a model of disability in late life?
- What is functional health?
- What causes functional limitations and disability in older adults?

Brian is a 68-year-old former welder who retired 3 years ago. He and his wife, Dorothy, had planned to travel in their RV and see the country. But Brian's arthritis has been getting worse lately, and he is having increasing difficulty getting around and doing basic daily tasks. Brian and Dorothy wonder what the future holds for them.

Brian and Dorothy are not alone. Many couples plan to travel or to do other activities after they retire, only to find health issues complicating the situation. As the focus on health has shifted over the past several decades to chronic disease, researchers have increasingly focused on how well people can function in their daily lives. In this section, we examine how functional health is determined and how disability occurs.

A Model of Disability in Late Life

As we saw earlier in this chapter, one defining characteristic of a chronic condition is that it lasts a long time. This means that for most adults, the time between the onset of a chronic condition and death is long, measured in years and even decades. Chronic diseases typically involve some level of discomfort, and physical limitations are common, everyday issues for most people, as they are for Brian. Over the course of the disease, these problems usually increase, resulting in more efforts by patients and health care workers to try to slow the progress of the disease. In many cases, these efforts allow people to resume such activities as

daily walks and shopping and to feel optimistic about the future (Verbrugge, 1994, 2005). This is especially true for the oldest old (Fauth, Zarit, & Malmberg, 2008). Social context also matters for older adults, as disablement is associated with much higher loneliness on one hand, and positive marital relationships are associated with lower impairment (Warner & Kelley-Moore, 2012).

In the context of chronic conditions, disability *is the effects of chronic conditions on people's ability to engage in activities that are necessary, expected, and personally desired in their society* (Verbrugge, 1994, 2005). When people are disabled as a result of a chronic condition, they have difficulty doing daily tasks, such as household chores, personal care, job duties, active recreation, socializing with friends and family, and errands. One of the most important research efforts related to health and aging is seeking to understand how disability results from chronic conditions and what might be done to help prevent it. For these reasons, it is important to understand the changing context of disability in the United States.

Researchers point out that as the age at which disablement occurs in late life gets closer to the end of life, these changes create what is called the compression of morbidity (Andersen, Sebastiani, Dworkis, Feldman, & Perls, 2012; Lindley, 2012). Compression of morbidity *refers to the situation in which the average age when one becomes disabled for the first time is postponed, causing the time between the onset of disability and death to be compressed into a shorter period of time.* This implies that older adults in the United States are becoming disabled later in life than previously, and are disabled a shorter time before dying than in past generations.

Verbrugge and Jette (1994) originally proposed an excellent comprehensive model of disability resulting from chronic conditions, a model that has greatly influenced research (see Figure 4.7). The model consists of four main parts. The main pathway emphasizes the relations between pathology (the chronic conditions a person has), impairments of organ systems (such as muscular degeneration), functional limitations in the ability to perform activities (such as restrictions in one's mobility), and disability.

The model also includes risk factors and two types of intervention strategies: environmental and health

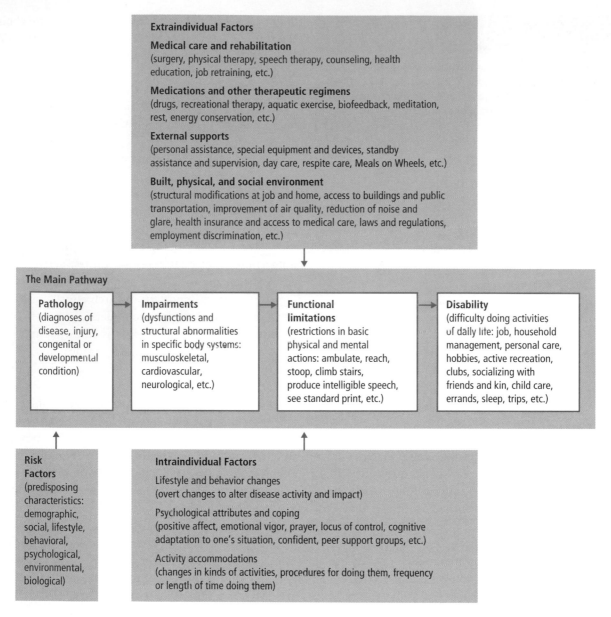

Figure 4.7
A model of the disablement process.

Source: Verbrugge, L.M., & Jette, A.M. (1994). The disablement process. Social Science and Medicine, 38, *4. Reprinted with permission.*

care (*extraindividual factors*) and behavioral and personality (*intraindividual factors*). **Risk factors** *are long-standing behaviors or conditions that increase one's chances of functional limitation or disability.* Examples of risk factors include low socioeconomic status, chronic health conditions, and health-related behaviors such as smoking. Extraindividual factors include

interventions such as surgery, medication, social support services (e.g., Meals on Wheels), and physical environmental supports (e.g., wheelchair ramps). The presence of these factors often helps people maintain their independence and may make the difference between living at home and living in a long-term care facility. Intraindividual factors include such things as beginning an exercise program, keeping a positive outlook, and taking advantage of transportation programs to increase mobility.

Extraindividual and intraindividual interventions are both aimed at reducing the restrictions and difficulties resulting from chronic conditions. Unfortunately, sometimes they do not work as intended and may even create problems of their own. For example, a prescribed medication may produce negative side effects that, instead of alleviating the condition, create a new problem. Or social service agencies may have inflexible policies about when a particular program is available, which may make it difficult for a person who needs the program to participate. *Such situations are called* exacerbators, *because they make the situation worse than it was originally.* Although they may be unintended, the results of exacerbators can be serious and necessitate additional forms of intervention.

One of the most important aspects of Verbrugge and Jette's (1994) model is the emphasis on the fit between the person and the environment, a topic we explore in detail in Chapter 5. When a person's needs are met by the environment, the person's quality of life and adaptation are optimal.

Verbrugge and Jette's model has been extended and validated in several ways. For example, the basic aspects of the model were extended to explain the disablement process in osteoarthritis (Wang, Chern, & Chiou, 2005). Femia, Zarit, and Johansson (2001), and Fauth and colleagues (2008) validated the model in research on older adults over age 79 in Sweden. Among the most important results were the mediating role of psychosocial factors such as mastery, depression, and loneliness on risk factors for disability; for example, higher feelings of mastery resulted in lower levels of disability. And the model is helping in the development of a new approach to classifying disability in China (Purser, Feng, Yi, & Hoenig, 2012).

Determining Functional Health Status

How can we determine where a person can be categorized along Verbrugge and Jette's continuum? *The answer to this question describes a person's* functional health status, *that is, how well the person is functioning in daily life.* Determining functional health status requires very careful assessment in order to differentiate the tasks a person reports he or she can do, tasks a person can demonstrate in a laboratory or clinic that simulate the same tasks at home, and tasks the person actually does at home (Kingston, Collerton, Davies, Bond, Robinson, & Jagger, 2012).

Most of the time, assessing functional health status is done for a very practical reason: to identify older adults who need help with everyday tasks. **Frail older adults** *are those who have physical disabilities, are very ill, and may have cognitive or psychological disorders and need assistance with everyday tasks.* They constitute a minority of older adults, but the size of this group increases a great deal with age.

Frail older adults are people whose competence is declining. However, they do not have one specific problem that differentiates them from their active, healthy counterparts; rather, they tend to have several (Rockwood et al., 2004). To identify the areas in which people experience limited functioning, researchers have developed observational and self-report techniques to measure how well people can accomplish daily tasks.

Everyday competence assessment consists of examining how well people can complete activities of daily living and instrumental activities of daily living (Gold, 2012). **Activities of daily living (ADLs)** *include basic self-care tasks such as eating, bathing, toileting, walking, or dressing.* A person can be considered frail if he or she needs help with one or more of these tasks. **Instrumental activities of daily living (IADLs)** *are actions that entail some intellectual competence and planning.* Which activities constitute IADLs varies widely across cultures. For example, for most adults in Western culture, IADLs would include shopping for personal items, paying bills, making telephone calls, taking medications appropriately, and keeping appointments. In other cultures, IADLs might include caring for animal herds, making bread, threshing grain, and tending crops.

The number of older adults who need assistance with ADLs and IADLs has declined somewhat since the early 1990s, as you can see in Figure 4.8 (AgingStats.gov, 2012b). About 26% of older adults enrolled in Medicare need assistance with at least one ADL, about 12% need help with at least one IADL, and about 4% are sufficiently impaired that they live in an assisted living or nursing home facility.

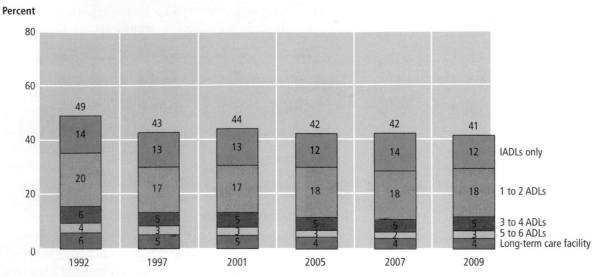

NOTE: A residence is considered a long-term care facility if it is certified by Medicare or Medicaid; has three or more beds, is licensed as a nursing home or other long-term care facility, and provides at least one personal care service; or provides 24-hour, 7-day-a-week supervision by a caregiver. ADL limitations refer to difficulty performing (or inability to perform for a health reason) one or more of the following tasks: bathing, dressing, eating, getting in/out of chairs, walking, or using the toilet. IADL limitations refer to difficulty performing (or inability to perform for a health reason) one or more of the following tasks: using the telephone, light housework, heavy housework, meal preparation, shopping, or managing money. Percents are age-adjusted using the 2000 standard population. Estimates may not sum to the totals because of rounding. Reference population: These data refer to Medicare enrollees.

Figure 4.8

Percentage of Medicare enrollees age 65 and over who have limitations in activities of daily living (ADLs) or instrumental activities of daily living (IADLs), or who are in a facility, selected years 1992–2009.

Source: http://www.census.gov/ipc/www/idb/tables.html.

As you can see in Figure 4.9, the percentage of people needing assistance increases with age, from 8.2% of people aged 65–69 to 30% of those over age 80 (Administration on Aging, 2012a). The percentage of people needing assistance also varies across ethnic groups, with Asian Americans and European Americans having the lowest rate, African Americans and American Indian/Alaska Native/Native Hawaiian/Other Pacific Islander having the highest, and Latinos being in the middle (National Center for Health Statistics, 2012c).

In addition to basic assistance with ADLs and IADLs, frail older adults have other needs. Research shows that these individuals are also more prone to depression and anxiety disorders (AgingStats.gov, 2012b). Although frailty becomes more likely with increasing age, especially during the last year of life, there are many ways to provide a supportive environment for frail older adults. We take a closer look at some of them in Chapter 5.

What Causes Functional Limitations and Disability in Older Adults?

As you were reading about the Verbrugge and Jette (1994) model, you may have been thinking about Brian's situation and those of other adults you know. If you and your classmates created a list of all the conditions you believe cause functional limitations and disabilities in older adults, the list undoubtedly would be long. (Try it and see for yourself.) But by strategically combining a large representative sample of conditions with sophisticated statistical analyses, this list can be shortened greatly. If these steps are taken, what conditions best predict future problems in functioning?

In a classic longitudinal study conducted over three decades, Strawbridge and colleagues (1998) found that smoking, heavy drinking, physical inactivity, depression, social isolation, and fair or poor perceived health predicted who would become disabled in some way. As

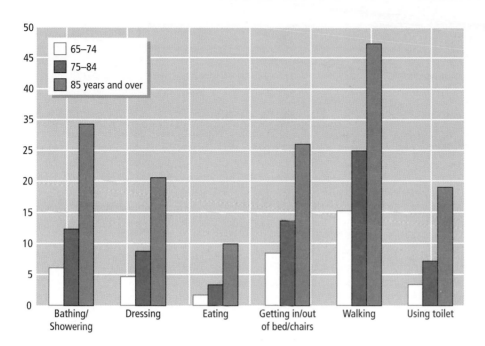

Figure 4.9
Percent of persons with limitations in activities of daily living by age group: 2009.

Source: http://www.aoa.gov/AoARoot/Aging_Statistics/Profile/2011/16.aspx

predicted by Verbrugge and Jette (1994), lack of physical activity is a powerful predictor of later disability and with higher rates of cancer, cardiovascular disease, diabetes, and obesity, all of which result in higher rates of disability and premature death (Gretebeck, Ferraro, Black, Holland, & Gretebeck, 2012).

How Important Are Socioeconomic Factors? Once we have identified the specific conditions that are highly predictive of future functional limitations, an important question is whether the appropriate intervention and prevention programs should be targeted at particular groups of people. That is, would people who are well educated and have high incomes have the same rate of key chronic conditions as people in lower socioeconomic groups? If not, then people with different socioeconomic backgrounds have different needs.

Research indicates a fairly strong and consistent relationship between socioeconomic status and health-related quality of life. Across all racial and ethnic groups, more affluent older adults have lower levels of disability and higher health-related quality of life than individuals in lower socioeconomic groups (Administration on Aging, 2012a; National Center for Health Statistics, 2012c). A Canadian study showed that this difference appears to be set in early adulthood and maintained into late life (Ross, Garner, Bernier, Feeny, Kaplan, McFarland et al., 2012).

How Does Disability in Older Adults Differ Globally? Throughout this and previous chapters, we have encountered important differences between men and women and between various ethnic/racial and socioeconomic groups. Do these patterns hold globally?

Not surprisingly, the answer is "yes" (World Health Organization, 2012). As the number of older adults rises around the world, the number of people with disabilities or functional limitations does, too. Also, the rates of disabilities are higher in low-income countries and among women. Early detection and treatment of chronic disease can lower these rates.

Looked at more closely, some interesting patterns emerge. The United States, for example, has higher rates of most chronic diseases and functional impairment than England or the rest of Europe (National Institute on Aging, 2012a). An important difference is access to health care, in terms of whether everyone is guaranteed access by the government or not.

ADULT DEVELOPMENT IN ACTION

If you were a social policy leader, what national policies need to be addressed to best prepare the United States for the coming rapid increase in older adults and the resulting increase in functional limitations in this population?

SOCIAL POLICY IMPLICATIONS

Two demographic trends will create the potential for significant worldwide change over the next few decades. First, increasing longevity in developed countries will result in many more older adults. This means that societies and governments will have increased pressure to provide services tailored to older adults. Such services are often much more expensive. For example, health care for older adults costs more because it involves treating more chronic diseases and more intensive intervention over time.

Second, the size of various generations will affect the scope of this change. For instance, the large baby-boom generation, combined with increased longevity, will make the issue of more older adults acute; the lower birth rate of the subsequent generation will lessen the pressures in future decades by lowering the relative proportion of the population that is over age 65.

What does this mean? For the next few decades there will be increased emphasis on social policies and services that directly benefit older adults, and they are likely to demand them. While they have the numbers, and the concomitant political power, such policies are likely to be adopted, perhaps to the detriment of younger generations.

This changing political climate plays out in elections. You may remember that in the 2012 presidential election campaign there was great debate over changing the rules by which Medicare operates (e.g., changing the age of eligibility, switching from a defined benefit program to a defined contribution program, etc.). The commentary on both sides of the issue was loud, even from older adults who would not have been affected by any of the proposed changes.

As the baby boomers age and die, though, two further things will occur. First, there will be a tremendous transfer of wealth to a smaller generation, with the likely outcome of concentrating wealth in fewer hands. Second, policies generally favorable to older adults may get changed as the next large generation (the baby boomers' children and grandchildren) enters middle age.

These shifts in policy could have major implications for everything from housing (e.g., more state and federal support for subsidized housing for older adults) to health care (e.g., substantially more expenditures for older adults' health care). If the policies change to reflect the demographic needs of the day, then such policies may need to be undone in the future, which is often politically difficult to accomplish. Close attention to all these issues is necessary for the best policies to be enacted.

So what do you think? What policies need to be changed? How?

SUMMARY

4.1 How Long Will We Live?

What is the average and maximum longevity for humans?

- Average longevity is the age at which half of the people born in a particular year will have died. Maximum longevity is the longest time a member of a species lives. Active longevity is the time during which people are independent. Dependent life expectancy is the time during which people rely on others for daily life tasks.

- Average longevity increased dramatically in the first half of the 20th century, but maximum longevity remains at about 120 years. The increase in average longevity resulted mainly from the elimination of many diseases and a reduction in deaths during childbirth.

What genetic and environmental factors influence longevity?

- Having long- or short-lived parents is a good predictor of your own longevity.

- Living in a polluted environment can dramatically shorten longevity; being in a committed relationship lengthens it. Environmental effects must be considered in combination with each other and with genetic influences.

What ethnic factors influence average longevity?

- Different ethnic groups in the United States have different average longevity. However, these differences result primarily from differences in nutrition, health care, stress, and socioeconomic status.

In late life, people in some ethnic minority groups live longer than European Americans.

What factors create gender differences in average longevity?

- Women tend to live longer than men, partly because men are more susceptible to disease and environmental influences. Numerous hypotheses have been offered for this difference, but none have been supported strongly.

4.2 Health and Illness

What are the key issues in defining health and illness?

- Health is the absence of acute and chronic physical or mental disease and impairments. Illness is the presence of a physical or mental disease or impairment.
- Self-rated health is a good predictor of illness and mortality. However, gender and cultural differences have been found.

How is the quality of life assessed?

- Quality of life is a multidimensional concept that encompasses biological, psychological, and socio-cultural domains at any point in the life cycle.
- In the context of health, people's valuation of life is a major factor in quality of life.

What normative age-related changes occur in the immune system?

- The immune system is composed of three major types of cells, which form a network of interacting parts: cell-mediated immunity (consisting of thymus-derived, or T-lymphocytes), humoral immunity (B-lymphocytes), and nonspecific immunity (monocytes and polymorphonuclear neutrophil leukocytes). Natural killer (NK) cells are also important components.
- The total number of lymphocytes and NK cells does not change with age, but how well they function does.
- The immune system can begin attacking itself, a condition called autoimmunity.
- Psychoneuroimmunology is the study of the relations between psychological, neurological, and immunological systems that raise or lower our susceptibility to and ability to recover from disease.
- HIV and AIDS are growing problems among older adults.

What are the developmental trends in chronic and acute diseases?

- Acute diseases are conditions that develop over a short period of time and cause a rapid change in health. Chronic diseases are conditions that last a longer period of time (at least 3 months) and may be accompanied by residual functional impairment that necessitates long-term management.
- The incidence of acute disease drops with age, but the effects of acute disease worsen. The incidence of chronic disease increases with age.

What are the key issues in stress across adulthood?

- The stress and coping paradigm views stress, not as an environmental stimulus or as a response, but as the interaction of a thinking person and an event.
- Primary appraisal categorizes events into three groups based on the significance they have for our well-being: irrelevant, benign or positive, and stressful. Secondary appraisal assesses our ability to cope with harm, threat, or challenge. Reappraisal involves making a new primary or secondary appraisal that results from changes in the situation.
- Attempts to deal with stressful events are called *coping*. Problem-focused coping and emotion-focused coping are two major categories. People also use religion as a source of coping.
- There are developmental declines in the number of stressors and in the kinds of coping strategies people use.
- Stress has several negative consequences for health.

4.3 Common Chronic Conditions and Their Management

What are the most important issues in chronic disease?

- Chronic conditions are the interaction of biological, psychological, sociocultural, and life-cycle forces.
- What are some common chronic conditions across adulthood?
- Arthritis is the most common chronic condition. Arthritis and osteoporosis can cause mild to severe impairment.
- Cardiovascular and cerebrovascular diseases can create chronic conditions after stroke.
- Diabetes mellitus occurs when the pancreas produces insufficient insulin. Although it cannot be cured, it can be managed effectively. However, some serious problems, such as diabetic retinopathy, can result.

- Many forms of cancer are caused by lifestyle choices, but genetics also plays an important role. The risk of developing cancer increases markedly with age. Prostate and breast cancer involve difficult treatment choices.

- For many people, the inability to control the elimination of urine and feces on an occasional or consistent basis, called incontinence, is a source of great concern and embarrassment. Effective treatments are available.

How can people manage chronic conditions?

- Effective pain management can be achieved through pharmacological and nonpharmacological approaches. Pain is not a normal outcome of aging and is not to be dismissed.

4.4 Pharmacology and Medication Adherence

What are the developmental trends in using medication?

- Older adults use nearly half of all prescription and over-the-counter drugs. The average older adult takes six or seven medications per day. However, the general lack of older adults in clinical trials research means we may not know the precise effects of medications on them.

- How does aging affect the way that medications work?

- The speed with which medications move from the stomach to the small intestine may slow with age. However, once drugs are in the small intestine, absorption rates are the same across adulthood.

- The distribution of medications in the bloodstream changes with age.

- The speed of drug metabolism in the liver slows with age.

- The rate at which drugs are excreted from the body slows with age.

What are the consequences of medication interactions?

- Older adults are more prone to harmful side effects of medications.

- Polypharmacy is a serious problem in older adults and may result in serious drug interactions.

What are the important medication adherence issues?

- Polypharmacy leads to lower rates of correct adherence to medication regimens.

4.5 Functional Health and Disability

What factors are important to include in a model of disability in late life?

- Disability is the effects of chronic conditions on people's ability to engage in activities in daily life.

- A model of disability includes pathology, impairments, functional limitations, risk factors, extraindividual factors, and intraindividual factors. This model includes all four main developmental forces.

What is functional health?

- Frail older adults are those who have physical disabilities, are very ill, or may have cognitive or psychological disorders and who need assistance with everyday tasks.

- Activities of daily living (ADLs) include basic self-care tasks such as eating, bathing, toileting, walking, and dressing.

- Instrumental activities of daily living (IADLs) are actions that entail some intellectual competence and planning.

- Rates of problems with ADLs and IADLs increase dramatically with age.

What causes functional limitations and disability in older adults?

- The chronic conditions that best predict future disability are arthritis and cerebrovascular disease. Other predictors include smoking, heavy drinking, physical inactivity, depression, social isolation, and fair or poor perceived health.

- Being wealthy helps increase average longevity but does not protect one from developing chronic conditions, meaning that such people may experience longer periods of disability late in life.

- Women's health generally is poorer across cultures, especially in developing countries.

- Ethnic group differences are also important. The validity of measures of functioning sometimes differs across ethnicity and gender.

REVIEW QUESTIONS

4.1 How Long Will We Live?

- What is the difference between average longevity and maximum longevity?

- What genetic and environmental factors influence average longevity?

- What ethnic and gender differences have been found?

4.2 Health and Illness

- How are the definitions of health and illness linked?
- How is quality of life defined generally, especially in relation to health?
- What are the major age-related changes in the immune system? How do they affect health and illness?
- What is the difference between acute and chronic diseases? How do the rates of each change with age?
- How does the stress and coping paradigm explain the experience of stress? What age-related changes occur in the process?

4.3 Common Chronic Conditions and Their Management

- What are the general issues to consider in managing chronic disease?
- What are some common chronic diseases experienced by older adults?
- How is pain managed?

4.4 Pharmacology and Medication Adherence

- What is the typical pattern of medication use in older adults?
- What changes occur with age that influence how well medications work?
- What are the major risks for side effects and drug interactions?
- How can adherence to medication regimens be improved?

4.5 Functional Health and Disability

- What are the key components in a model of disability in older adults?
- What are ADLs and IADLs? How does the number of people needing assistance change with age?
- What conditions result in disability most often?
- How do socioeconomic status, ethnicity, and gender affect health and disability?

INTEGRATING CONCEPTS IN DEVELOPMENT

- What physiological changes described in Chapter 2 are important in understanding health?
- Based on information in Chapters 2 and 3, how might a primary prevention program be designed to prevent cardiovascular disease? (Compare your answer with the intervention types described in Chapter 5.)
- How do the ethnic differences in average longevity and in health relate to the diversity issues we examined in Chapter 1?

KEY TERMS

absorption The time needed for a medication to enter a patient's bloodstream.

active life expectancy The age to which one can expect to live independently.

activities of daily living (ADLs) Basic self-care tasks such as eating, bathing, toileting, walking, and dressing.

acute diseases Conditions that develop over a short period of time and cause a rapid change in health.

autoimmunity The process by which the immune system begins attacking the body.

average longevity The length of time it takes for half of all people born in a certain year to die.

chronic diseases Conditions that last a longer period of time (at least 3 months) and may be accompanied by residual functional impairment that necessitates long-term management.

compression of morbidity The situation in which the average age when one becomes disabled for the first time is postponed, causing the time between the onset of disability and death to be compressed into a shorter period of time.

coping In the stress and coping paradigm, any attempt to deal with stress.

dependent life expectancy The age to which one can expect to live with assistance.

diabetes mellitus A disease that occurs when the pancreas produces insufficient insulin.

disability The effects of chronic conditions on people's ability to engage in activities that are necessary, expected, and personally desired in their society.

drug excretion The process of eliminating medications, usually through the kidneys in urine, but also through sweat, feces, and saliva.

drug metabolism The process of getting rid of medications in the bloodstream, partly in the liver.

emotion-focused coping A style of coping that involves dealing with one's feelings about the stressful event.

exacerbators Situations that makes a situation worse than it was originally.

frail older adults Older adults who have physical disabilities, are very ill, and may have cognitive or psychological disorders and need assistance with everyday tasks.

functional health status How well a person is functioning in daily life.

functional incontinence A type of incontinence usually caused when the urinary tract is intact but due to physical disability or cognitive impairment the person is unaware of the need to urinate.

health The absence of acute and chronic physical or mental disease and impairments.

Illness The presence of a physical or mental disease or impairment.

incontinence The loss of the ability to control the elimination of urine and feces on an occasional or consistent basis.

instrumental activities of daily living (IADLs) Actions that entail some intellectual competence and planning.

maximum longevity The maximum length of time an organism can live—roughly 120 years for humans.

overflow incontinence A type of incontinence usually caused by improper contraction of the kidneys, causing the bladder to become overdistended.

polypharmacy The use of multiple medications.

primary appraisal First step in the stress and coping paradigm in which events are categorized into three groups based on the significance they have for our well-being—irrelevant, benign or positive, and stressful.

problem-focused coping A style of coping that attempts to tackle a problem head-on.

psychoneuroimmunology The study of the relations between psychological, neurological, and immunological systems that raise or lower our susceptibility to and ability to recover from disease.

reappraisal In the stress and coping paradigm, this step involves making a new primary or secondary appraisal resulting from changes in the situation.

risk factors Long-standing behaviors or conditions that increase one's chances of functional limitation or disability.

secondary appraisal In the stress and coping paradigm, an assessment of our perceived ability to cope with harm, threat, or challenge.

stress and coping paradigm A model that views stress, not as an environmental stimulus or as a response, but as the interaction of a thinking person and an event.

stress incontinence A type of incontinence that happens when pressure in the abdomen exceeds the ability to resist urinary flow.

Type I diabetes A type of diabetes that tends to develop earlier in life and requires the use of insulin; also called insulin-dependent diabetes.

Type II diabetes A type of diabetes that tends to develop in adulthood and is effectively managed through diet.

urge incontinence A type of incontinence usually caused by a central nervous system problem after a stroke or urinary tract infection in which people feel the urge to urinate but cannot get to a toilet quickly enough.

RESOURCES

Access quizzes, glossaries, flashcards, and more at www.cengagebrain.com.

CHAPTER 5

WHERE PEOPLE LIVE:
PERSON–ENVIRONMENT INTERACTIONS

5.1 DESCRIBING PERSON–ENVIRONMENT INTERACTIONS
Competence and Environmental Press • *Discovering Development: What's Your Adaptation Level?* • Preventive and Corrective Proactivity (PCP) Model • Stress and Coping Framework • Common Theoretical Themes and Everyday Competence

5.2 THE ECOLOGY OF AGING: COMMUNITY OPTIONS
Aging in Place • Deciding on the Best Option • Home Modification • Adult Day Care • Congregate Housing • Assisted Living

5.3 LIVING IN NURSING HOMES
Types of Nursing Homes • *Current Controversies: Financing Long-Term Care* • Who Is Likely to Live in Nursing Homes? • Characteristics of Nursing Homes • Special Care Units • Can a Nursing Home Be a Home? • Communicating with Residents • *How Do We Know?: Identifying Different Types of Elderspeak in Singapore* • Decision-Making Capacity and Individual Choices • New Directions for Nursing Homes

SOCIAL POLICY IMPLICATIONS
Summary • Review Questions • Integrating Concepts in Development • Key Terms • Resources

YOU ENCOUNTER THEM EVERY DAY—DEVICES SUCH AS GRIP BARS IN BATHROOMS, WIDER DOORWAYS, AND RAMPS LEADING TO BUILDING ENTRANCES.

You may not pay much attention to them and even take them for granted, but these environmental modifications matter. They may mean the difference between living independently and living somewhere else. Supportive environments for adults, especially older adults with significant physical or cognitive impairment, are key to providing continuing quality of life. Research on how people deal with the settings where they reside has revolutionized the way we design houses and care facilities. The rapidly increasing need for alternatives to nursing homes has resulted in the creation of a wide range of options for families. These changes began with the simple observation that behavior is a function of the environment in which it occurs and the interaction with the individual's personal characteristics.

In this chapter, we explore how differences in the interaction between personal characteristics and the living environment can have profound effects on our behavior and feelings about ourselves. Several theoretical frameworks are described that help us understand how to interpret person–environment interactions in a developmental context. Next, we consider the ecology of aging and discover how people can age in place, along with the support systems that underpin that goal. We consider the role of adult day care and

Home adaptations help people age in place.

Laurent Repotel/Alamy

several housing options that help people stay in the community as much as possible. Because some people need intensive support, we take a close look at nursing homes. Sometimes we must consider the person separately from the environment, but keep in mind throughout the chapter that in the end it is the interaction of the two we want to understand.

5.1 Describing Person–Environment Interactions

LEARNING OBJECTIVES

- What is the competence and environmental press model?
- What is the preventive and corrective proactivity (PCP) model?
- What are the major aspects of stress and coping theory relating to person–environment interactions?
- What are the common themes in the theories of person–environment interactions?

Hank has lived in the same poor neighborhood all of his 75 years. He has lived alone for the past several months since his wife, Marilyn, had a stroke and was placed in a nursing home. Hank's oldest daughter expressed concern about her father and has been pressing him to move in with her. Hank is reluctant; he likes knowing his neighbors, shopping in familiar stores, and being able to do what he wants. He wonders how well he could adapt to living in a new neighborhood after all these years. He realizes it might be easier for him to cope if he lived with his daughter, but it's a tough decision.

To appreciate the roles different environments play in our lives, we need a framework for interpreting how people interact with them. Theories of person–environment interactions help us understand how people view their environments and how these views may change as people age. These views have been described since the 1930s and have significant impact on the study of adults (Pynoos, Caraviello, & Cicero, 2010). We consider four that affect views of adult development and aging: competence and environmental press, congruence, stress and coping, and everyday competence.

All these theories can be traced to a common beginning. In 1936, Kurt Lewin conceptualized person–environment interactions in the equation: $B =$ f(P, E). *This relationship defining* **person–environment interactions** *means behavior (B) is a function of both the person (P) and the environment (E).* More recent theorists took Lewin's equation and described the components in the equation in more detail. Specifically, their speculations concern the characteristics of people and environments that combine to form behavior.

Most of these models emphasize the importance of people's perceptions of their environments. Although objective aspects of environments (i.e., crime, housing quality) are important, personal choice plays a major role. For example, many people deliberately choose to live in New York or Atlanta, even though certain crime rates in those cities are higher than in Selma or Walla Walla. The importance of personal perception in environments is similar to the role of personal perception in social cognition and in concepts such as personal control (see Chapter 9). As you will see, these ideas, especially the notion of personal control, are included in many approaches to understanding person–environment interactions.

Competence and Environmental Press

Understanding psychosocial aging requires attention to individuals' needs rather than treating all older adults alike. One method focuses on the relation between the person and the environment (Aldwin & Igarashi, 2012). The competence–environmental press approach is a good example of a theory incorporating elements of the biopsychosocial model into the person–environment relation (Lawton & Nahemow, 1973; Nahemow, 2000; Pynoos et al., 2010). **Competence** *is defined as the upper limit of a person's ability to function in five domains: physical health, sensory-perceptual skills, motor skills, cognitive skills, and ego strength.* These domains are viewed as underlying all other abilities and reflect the biological and psychological forces. **Environmental press** *refers to the physical, interpersonal, or social demands that environments put on people.* Physical demands might include having to walk up three flights of stairs to your apartment. Interpersonal demands may require adjusting your behavior patterns to different types of people. Social demands involve dealing with laws or customs that place certain expectations on people. These

aspects of the theory reflect biological, psychological, and social forces. Both competence and environmental press change as people move through the life span; what you are capable of doing as a 5-year-old differs from what you are capable of doing as a 25-, 45-, 65-, or 85-year-old. Similarly, the demands put on you by the environment changes as you age. Thus, the competence–environmental press framework reflects life-cycle factors as well.

The competence and environmental press model depicted in Figure 5.1 shows how the two are related. Low to high competence is represented on the vertical axis, and weak to strong environmental press is

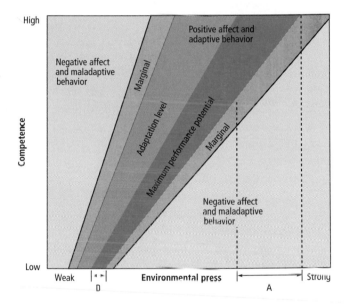

Figure 5.1

Behavioral and emotional outcomes of person–environment interactions are based on the competence and environmental press model. This figure indicates a person of high competence will show maximum performance over a larger range of environmental conditions than will a person with lower levels of competence. The range of optimal environments occurs at a higher level of environmental press (A) for the person with the most competence than it does for the person with the lowest level of competence (B).

Source: Lawton, M. P. & L. Nahemow. Ecology of the Aging Process. In C. Eisdorfer & M. P. Lawton (Eds.), The Psychology of Adult Development and Aging, p. 661.

displayed on the horizontal axis. Points in the figure represent various combinations of the two. Most important, the shaded areas show adaptive behavior and positive affect can result from many different combinations of competence and environmental press levels. Adaptation level *is the area where press level is average for a particular level of competence; this is where behavior and affect are normal. Slight increases in press tend to improve performance; this area on the figure is labeled the* zone of maximum performance potential. *Slight decreases in press create the* zone of maximum comfort, *in which people are able to live happily without worrying about environmental demands.* Combinations of competence and environmental press that fall within either of these two zones result in adaptive behavior and positive emotion that translate into a high quality of life.

As a person moves away from these areas, behavior becomes increasingly maladaptive and affect becomes negative. Notice that these outcomes can result from several different combinations and for different reasons. For example, too many environmental demands on a person with low competence and too few demands on a person with high competence both result in maladaptive behaviors and negative emotion.

What does this mean with regard to late life? Is aging merely an equation relating certain variables? The important thing to realize about the competence–environmental press model is that each person has the potential of being happily adapted to some living situations, but not to all. Whether people function well depends on if what they are able to do fits what the environment forces them to do. When their abilities match the demands, people adapt; when there is a mismatch, they don't. In this view, aging is more than an equation, because the best fit must be determined on an individual basis.

How do people deal with changes in their particular combinations of environmental press (such as adjusting to a new living situation) and competence (perhaps reduced abilities due to illness)? People respond in two basic ways (Lawton, 1989; Nahemow, 2000). *When people choose new behaviors to meet new desires or needs, they exhibit* proactivity *and exert control over their lives. In contrast, when people allow the situation to dictate the options they have, they demonstrate* docility *and have little control.* Lawton (1989)

argues that proactivity is more likely to occur in people with relatively high competence, and docility in people with relatively low competence.

The model has considerable research support. For example, the model accounts for why people choose the activities they do (Lawton, 1982), how well people adhere to medication regimens (LeRoux & Fisher, 2006), and how they adapt to changing housing needs over time (Iwarsson, Slaug, & Fänge, 2012; Pynoos, Steinman, Do Nguyen, & Bressette, 2012). This model helps us understand how well people adapt to various care settings, (Golant, 2012; Moore, 2005). In short, there is considerable merit to the view that aging is a complex interaction between a person's competence level and environmental press, mediated by choice. This model can be applied in many different settings.

As an example of the Lawton and Nahemow model, consider Rick. Rick works in a store in an area of Chicago where the crime rate is moderately high, representing a moderate level of environmental press. Because he is good at self-defense, he has high competence; thus he manages to cope. Because the Omaha police chief wants to lower the crime rate in that area, she increases patrols, thereby lowering the press level. If Rick maintains his high competence, maladaptive behavior may result because he has more competence than is optimal for the new environment. But if a street gang moved in instead of the police, Rick would have to increase his competence and be more prepared to maintain his adaptation level. Other changes in the environment (such as arson threats) or in his competence (such as a broken arm) would create different combinations.

Before leaving Lawton and Nahemow's model, we need to note an important implication for aging. The less competent the person is, the greater the impact of environmental factors. To the extent people experience declines in health, sensory processes, motor skills, cognitive skills, or ego strength, they are less able to cope with environmental demands. Personal competence predicts how well older adults adapt after being discharged from a hospital or when provided assistive technology (Lichtenberg et al., 2000; Peterson, Prasad, & Prasad, 2012). Thus, for older adults to maintain good adaptational levels, changes to lower environmental press or raise competence are needed. This point is made clearer in the Discovering Development feature. Take some time to complete it.

DISCOVERING DEVELOPMENT:

WHAT'S YOUR ADAPTATION LEVEL?

Lawton and Nahemow's competence and environmental press model has wide applicability, as indicated in the examples of Hank and Rick. The model provides an excellent introduction to the importance of considering people's capabilities and the environmental demands made of them. To understand how the model works, consider yourself. Make a list of the different aspects of your life, such as school, social activities, work, and so forth. Think about each of these areas and rate yourself in terms of your abilities. For example, in the case of school, consider each course you are taking and rate how capable you are in each. Then consider the number and kinds of demands made on you in each area. For instance, think about the many demands put on you in each course. Now look at how the rating of your competence intersects with the kinds and number of demands. Does it place you in the position of feeling bored? In this case, you would fall in the left side of the graph. Are you feeling stressed out and under pressure? Then you would fall on the right side of the graph. Feeling just about right? You've experienced your adaptation level. Doing this analysis for the various aspects of your life will help you understand why you feel more competent in some areas than others.

Because most older adults prefer to live at home, assessing competence and environmental press in that context is very important (Chin & Quine, 2012; Iwarsson et al., 2012). Given the importance of making as many living arrangement options available as possible, it is critical we understand how the environment affects people's day-to-day functioning in them. For example, the changing balance between competence and environmental press is a major factor in older adults' decisions to relocate (Sergeant & Ekerdt, 2008). Additionally, the competence and environmental press model has been the basis for evaluating and optimizing living situations with people who have severe cognitive impairments, such as those of Alzheimer's disease (Dalton & Harrison, 2012). To manage severe cognitive impairment effectively, caregivers must identify the right level of environmental support based on the patient's level of competence.

For example, people with mild cognitive impairment may be able to live independently, but as the impairment increases additional levels of support are needed. The model has provided the basis for designing special care units for people with Alzheimer's disease. In these units, environmental supports such as color-coded room doors, help people with dementia identify where they belong.

Preventive and Corrective Proactivity (PCP) Model

Maintaining a high quality of life is a key goal for adults of all ages. From the competence-environmental press approach we saw proactivity, exerting control over one's life, is central to achieving that goal. Because proactivity is so important, Kahana and Kahana (2003; Kahana, Kahana, & Zhang, 2006) built a model of successful aging on the core concept of proactivity. The model is shown in Figure 5.2.

The PCP model explains how life stressors (such as life events, chronic illnesses) and lack of good congruence in person–environment interactions (Component B), especially when the person has nothing to help buffer or protect against these things, result in poor life outcomes (Component F). The helpful buffers include external resources (Component E) such as friends or home modifications, internal resources or dispositions (Component C) such as a positive outlook on life, and specific proactive behaviors (Component D), such as physical exercise, work to lower the negative impact of the stressors and prepare people to cope better in the future. In brief, the PCP model proposes proactive adaptations and helpful external resources reduce the effect of life stressors on quality-of-life outcomes.

What kinds of actions reflect proactive adaptations? Kahana et al. (2006) described two types of proactive adaptations: preventive and corrective. **Preventive adaptations** *are actions that avoid stressors and increase or build social resources.* An example of a preventive adaptation would be increasing one's social network by adding friends. **Corrective adaptations** *are actions taken in response to stressors and can be facilitated by internal and external resources.* An example of a corrective adaptation is changing one's diet after having a heart attack.

Older adults tend to engage in more corrective adaptations than preventive adaptations, at least

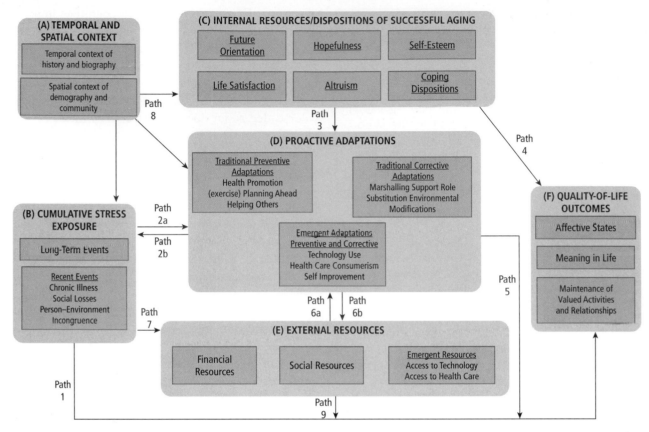

Figure 5.2
Model of emerging proactive options for successful aging.

Source: Kahana, E., Kahana, B., & Zhang, J. (2006). Motivational antecedents of preventive proactivity in late life: Linking future orientation and exercise. Motivation and Emotion, *29, 438–459 (Figure 1). DOI: 10.1007/s11031-006-9012-2. Retrieved from http://www.springerlink.com/content/61304201gm163778// fulltext.html#Fig1.*

initially. However, many actions that start as corrective adaptations turn into preventive adaptations. A great example of this is exercise. Many people begin an exercise program only after they are told to, perhaps as part of a recovery regimen after a health crisis. However, continued exercise becomes preventive by helping the person avoid future recurrences of the original health problem and avoid other problems altogether.

Research supports the importance of proactivity as described in the PCP model. Kahana, Kelley-Moore, & Kahana (2012) showed life stressors can still have a negative effect on quality-of-life outcomes four years after they occur, but proactive adaptations (such as exercise, planning ahead, and gathering support) significantly reduce this negative impact. Longitudinal research in China also showed the importance of

proactivity and other external and internal resources in improving quality-of-life outcomes in the oldest old residents in the community and in long-term care facilities (Liu, Dupre, Gu, Mair, & Chen (2012).

We consider the PCP model again in Chapter 14 when we focus specifically on successful aging. In the meantime, keep it in mind as you learn about specific behaviors and situations that help people adapt successfully to the changes that occur with age.

Stress and Coping Framework

As you know from your own experience, sometimes your interaction with the environment is stressful. Schooler (1982) has applied Lazarus and Folkman's cognitive theory of stress and coping, described in Chapter 4, to the understanding of the older person's interaction with the environment. The basic premise of Lazarus' theory is that people evaluate situations to assess their potential threat value. Situations can be evaluated as harmful, beneficial, or irrelevant. When situations are viewed as harmful or threatening, people also establish the range of coping responses they have at their disposal for avoiding the harmful situation. This process results in a coping response. Outcomes of coping may be positive or negative depending on many contextual factors.

Schooler (1982) argues this perspective is especially helpful in understanding older adults like Hank because of their greater vulnerability to social and physical hazards. To test his ideas, Schooler evaluated retest data on a sample of 521 people drawn from a national sample of 4,000 older adults living in long-term care facilities. In particular, he examined the impact of three potential stressors (environmental change, residential mobility, and major life events) on health or morale. He also examined the buffering, or protective effects of social support systems and ecological factors on the relationships between the stressors and outcomes. Consistent with the theory, Schooler showed the presence of social support systems affected the likelihood that particular situations would be defined as threatening. For example, living alone is more likely to be viewed as stressful when people have little social support than when they have many friends who live nearby.

Schooler's initial work provides an important theoretical addition because it deals with the relation between everyday environmental stressors and the adaptive response of community-dwelling individuals. His ideas have been extended to other contexts. When certified nurse aides (CNAs) working in nursing homes were provided with training and empowered as a way to deal with environmental stressors, the result was better care for residents, better cooperation between CNAs and nurses, and reduced turnover (Yeatts & Cready, 2008). Caregivers of persons with dementia also show resilience when they have effective ways of dealing with environmental stressors (Gaugler, Kane, & Newcomer, 2007).

Common Theoretical Themes and Everyday Competence

The three theories we have considered have much in common. Most important, all agree the focus must be on the interaction between the person and the environment, not on one or the other. Another important

Older adults' ability to perform typical daily activities is essential for assessing everyday competence.

Leland Bobbé/CORBIS

common theme is no single environment meets everyone's needs. Rather, a range of potential environments may be optimal.

Several researchers built on these ideas and focused on people's everyday competence (e.g., Heyl & Wahl, 2012; Lou & Ng, 2012). *Everyday competence is a person's potential ability to perform a wide range of activities considered essential for independent living; it is not the person's actual ability to perform the tasks.* Everyday competence also involves a person's physical, psychological, and social functioning, that interact in complex ways to create the person's day-to-day behavior. Lou & Ng (2012) showed cognitive competence, closeness to family, and relationship-based coping are helping Chinese older adults who live alone deal effectively with loneliness. Additionally, an older person's competence in the psychological domain includes cognitive problem-solving abilities, beliefs about personal control and self-efficacy, and styles of coping (Diehl et al., 2005, 2012).

Although everyday competence is most often considered in the context of activities of daily living (ADLs) and instrumental activities of daily living (IADLs; see Chapter 4), it can also be considered more broadly. The reason is a behavior must not be viewed in isolation; behavior is expressed in a particular environmental context. In particular, researchers and clinicians need to be sensitive to cultural and contextual differences in everyday competence across different environments (Diehl et al., 2005, 2012).

Using these ideas, Willis (1991, 1996a; Allaire & Willis, 2006; Jones et al., 2012; Schaie & Willis, 1999) developed a model of everyday competence incorporating all the key ideas discussed earlier. Willis distinguishes between antecedents, components, mechanisms, and outcomes of everyday competence. Antecedents include both individual (e.g., health, cognition) and sociocultural (e.g., cultural stereotypes, social policy, health care policy) factors. These influence the intraindividual and contextual components, the particular domains and contexts of competence. Which components are most important or exert the most influence depends on the overall conditions under which the person lives. These elements of the model reflect the basic ideas in both the competence and environmental press model and the person-environment model we considered earlier. The mechanisms involve factors that moderate the way competence is actually expressed; such as whether one believes he or she is in control of the situation, influences how competent the person turns out to be. Finally, the model proposes the primary outcomes of everyday competence are psychological and physical well-being, two of the major components of successful aging.

Understanding the complexities of everyday competence is important as a basis for considering whether people, especially some older adults, are capable of making certain decisions for themselves. This issue often arises in terms of competence to make key health care and other decisions, a topic we consider in more detail later in this chapter. Willis' model also points out the health outcomes of one episode of everyday competence are the antecedents of the next, illustrating how future competence is related to current competence. Research on cognitive training from this perspective shows that training on reasoning, maintained over time, can attenuate age-related change (Jones et al., 2012). Finally, decline in older adults' ability to handle everyday problems predicts mortality, indicating everyday competence may be a reasonable indicator of health status (Allaire & Willis, 2006).

All of this research supports the idea that older adults can age in place to the extent their everyday competence permits. Aging in place requires whatever necessary services and supports an older adult needs in order to live in the community be provided or made available. This approach has been adopted by governments (e.g., Australia in relation to disability; Bigby, 2008; Disability Policy Research Working Group, 2011), and is the goal for much of the smart technology available for older adults, such as cognitive wellness systems (Meza-Kubo & Morán, in press). We consider aging in place in more detail in the next section.

ADULT DEVELOPMENT IN ACTION

How would a thorough understanding of competence and environmental press influence your work as a housing planner for older adults?

5.2 The Ecology of Aging: Community Options

LEARNING OBJECTIVES

- What is aging in place?
- How do people decide the best option?
- How can a home be modified to provide a supportive environment?
- What options and services are provided in adult day care?
- What is congregate housing?
- What are the characteristics of assisted living?

Mark was diagnosed as having vascular dementia about six months ago. Because he now has difficulty in remembering to turn off his gas stove, his daughter and son-in-law think it may be best for him to move into an assisted living facility. They had Mark evaluated by his physician, who indicates she thinks for safety reasons assisted living is a good idea, especially because Mark's family lives several hundred miles away.

Most people go through young adulthood, middle age, and into later life performing routine daily tasks without much thought. As we grow older, the normative changes that occur often result in more challenges in dealing with environments that were once not a problem at all. Even our homes, formerly a comfortable supportive place, can present difficult challenges; the walk up the stairs to a bedroom may become an equivalent of climbing a mountain.

Mark is typical of a growing number of older adults in the United States and other countries—he experiences a significant decline in function, lives alone, and his adult child and family live in another city some distance away. As a result, he, like many older adults, needs a different living situation. He does not need full-time nursing care at this point, but does need a more supportive environment.

Changes in functional status and how these changes are helped or hurt by the environments we live in are an important aspect of the experience of growing older for many people. *These changes are studied in a field called the ecology of aging or environmental psychology, which seeks to understand the dynamic relations between older adults and the environments they inhabit* (Scheidt & Schwarz, in press). It is important to understand how seemingly small changes in a person's environment can result in major changes in behavior, changes that can make the difference between a person being able to live independently or needing a more supportive situation.

In this section, we consider options for older adults that help them maintain as much independence as possible. First, we evaluate the concept of aging in place. Then we present three approaches to helping people live in the community as long as possible: home modification, and two living situations that provide various levels of support—congregate housing and assisted living.

Aging in Place

Imagine you are an older adult who has difficulty cooking meals and getting around. If you had a choice of where you wanted to live, where would it be? Maybe some of your family members urge you to move to a place where your meals are provided and you can be driven where you need to go, while others suggest you to stay in your own place even though there will be challenges. What do you do?

Based on the competence–environmental press model described earlier, older adults have options (Scheidt & Schwarz, 2010). As the environment in which one lives becomes more restrictive, many older adults engage in selection and compensation to cope. They may select a different place to live or they may adapt their behaviors in order to compensate for their limitations, such as using microwaveable prepared foods instead of cooking meals from scratch. Using a cane or other device to assist in walking is another example of compensation.

The idea of aging in place reflects a balancing of environmental press and competence through

selection and compensation. Being able to maintain one's independence in the community is often important for people, especially in terms of their self-esteem and ability to continue engaging in meaningful ways with friends, family, and others. This is important psychologically (Rowles, Oswald, & Hunter, 2004). Older adults who age in place form strong emotional and cognitive bonds with their residences that help transform a "house" into a "home." Having a "home" provides a strong source of self-identity.

Throughout adulthood, people adapt to changes in the places where they live, sometimes severing connections with past settings (Rowles & Watkins, 2003). Making a change in where people live, and having to psychologically disconnect with a place where they may have lived for many decades, can be difficult and traumatic. There is no question people develop attachments to place, deriving a major portion of their identity from it and feeling they own it.

Rowles (2006) discusses the process of how a place becomes a home. Because of the psychological connections, the sense that one is "at home" becomes a major concern in relocation, especially if the relocation involves giving up one's home. Later in this chapter, we consider how a nursing home might become a home, but for now the important idea is that a key factor is a sense of belonging.

Aging in place is a major goal for the majority of older adults.

Take A Pix Media/Blend Images/Getty Images

Feeling one is "at home" is a major aspect of aging in place. Providing older adults a place to call their own that supports the development of the psychological attachments necessary to convert the place to a home is key for successful aging in place (Scheidt & Schwarz, 2010). Aging in place provides a way for older adults to continue finding aspects of self-identity in where they live, and to take advantage of support systems that are established and familiar.

The growing understanding of the importance of aging in place has resulted in a rethinking of certain housing options that provide a way for frail older adults to stay in their communities. Such options are important for fragile older adults who are poor and cannot afford more expensive formal assisted living or nursing home facilities (discussed later). One alternative is cluster housing that combines the aging in place philosophy with supportive services (de Jong, Rouwendal, van Hattum, & Brouwer, 2012; Golant, 2008).

Golant (2008) describes several types of affordable cluster housing care. A key feature is that services are provided to the residents by staff hired by the owner or a service provider under contract. These services might range from having only a service case manager or to actually providing information, caregiving assistance (e.g., meals, housekeeping), transportation, or health care. The aging in place philosophy in these settings emphasizes individual choice on the part of residents in terms of what services to use. This approach is being adopted in other countries, such as the Netherlands (de Jong et al., 2012).

Although cluster housing and other approaches to aging in place make sense as lower-cost alternatives to nursing homes that keep people in their communities, affording them is often difficult. Unlike long-term care facilities, cluster housing developments are not covered by Medicaid or other insurance. Finding solutions to the funding issue will be an important aspect for keeping costs down and providing supporting environments for older adults who need support. For many, making modifications to their existing housing represents a more cost-effective option, and provides a research-based way to remain in a familiar environment. We consider this approach later in this section.

Deciding on the Best Option

One of the most difficult decisions individuals and families have to make is where an older member should live. Such decisions are never easy and can be quite wrenching. Figuring out the optimal "fit" where the individual's competence and the environmental press are in the best balance rests on the ability of all concerned to be objective about the individual's competence and the ability of the lived-in environment to provide the level of support necessary. This balance requires a degree of honesty in communication with all family members that is sometimes challenging

There are several key decision points in addressing the issue of the optimal housing environment. First, it must be determined whether the individual has significant cognitive or physical impairment requiring intervention or support. Next, an assessment of the ability of family members or friends to provide support or care must be made. Once that information is understood, a series of decisions can be made about the best way to provide the necessary environmental supports to create the optimal "fit." Assuming all information shows the need for some sort of intervention, the next critical decision is whether there is an option for providing that intervention in the current home situation or if other options need to be pursued. Later, we consider several living options for individuals needing support ranging from minor modifications of the present home to skilled care nursing homes.

Throughout this process, the individual in question needs to be an integral part of decision making to the extent possible. This is especially important when the outcome is likely to be a placement that involves moving from the person's current residence. The degree the person actually understands the options available, why the options are being pursued, and the long-term meaning of the decision being considered is an integral part of the person's right to determine his or her own life outcome (a point considered in more detail later).

Individuals and families facing these decisions should consult with the person's physician after a thorough diagnostic evaluation. Additionally, objective information about available housing options can be obtained from local senior centers, offices on aging, and other nonprofit service providers.

Home Modification

The competence–environmental press model provides two options for people who experience difficulties dealing with the tasks of daily life. On one hand, people can increase their competency and develop better or new skills for handling. To better remember where you put your car keys, you can learn a new memory strategy. On the other hand, people can lower the environmental press by modifying the environment to make the task easier; putting a hook for the car keys next to the door you exit so you see them on your way out.

These two options represent applications of theory to real-world settings that also apply to helping people deal with the challenges they face in handling tasks of daily living in their homes. When it comes to these kinds of issues, the most frequent solution involves modifying one's home (i.e., changing the environment) in order to create a new optimal balance or better "fit" between competence and environmental press (Scheidt & Schwarz, 2010).

Many strategies are available for modifying a home to help a person accommodate changing competencies. Minor structural changes, such as installing assistive devices (e.g., hand rails in bathrooms and door handles that are easier to grip), are common strategies. In other cases, more extensive modifications may be needed to make a home fully accessible, such as widening doorways, lowering countertops, and constructing wheelchair ramps.

Although minor alterations can often be done at low cost, more extensive modifications needed by people with greater limitations may be unaffordable for low-income individuals. Even though the cost of such interventions is significantly lower than placement in long-term care facilities or assisted living, many people simply cannot afford them. As a result, many older adults with functional impairments experience a mismatch between their competency and their environment (Iwarsson et al., 2012; Wahl, Fänge, Oswald, Gitlin, & Iwarsson, 2009; Wahl, Iwarsson, & Oswald, 2012).

Research indicates home modifications done to address difficulties with accomplishing activities of daily living (ADLs) typically reduce disability-related outcomes (Iwarsson et al., 2012; Wahl et al., 2009, 2012). Whether these modifications help older adults who are prone to falling remains inconclusive.

An emerging high-tech approach to home modification is the auxiliary dwelling unit (ADU). The ADU is a portable hospital room that is a separate dwelling placed next to a family's main dwelling to give an older relative both privacy and proximity to family (Kunkle, 2012). Colloquially known as *granny pods*, the dwelling contains a number of "smart" devices that do everything from serving as a virtual companion, providing special knee-level lighting to reduce the risk of falls, and offering better mobility through ceiling mounted lifts. A diagram of a typical unit is shown in Figure 5.3.

The advantage to ADUs is that they can be as temporary or permanent as needed, and they provide both independence and support for aging in place. As technology improves, it is likely solutions like ADUs will increase in popularity and decrease in cost.

Adult Day Care

In some cases, older adults need more support than is possible with just home modification, but still do not need assistance on a full-time basis. For them, one possible option may be adult day care. **Adult day care** *is designed to provide support, companionship, and certain services during the day.* This situation arises most often when the primary caregiver is employed or has other obligations and is unavailable during the day.

The primary goal of adult day care is to delay placement into a more formal care setting. It achieves this goal by providing alternative care that enhances the client's self-esteem and encourages socialization. Three general types of adult day care are available (National Adult Day Services Association, 2012). The first provides only social activities, meals, and recreation, with minimal health services. The second type is adult day health care that provides more intensive health and therapy intervention and social services for people with more serious medical problems or who require intensive nursing care for a specific medical condition. The third provides specialized care to particular populations, such as people with dementia or developmental disabilities.

Adult day care centers can be independent or sponsored by a profit (22%) or nonprofit (78%) organizations. They may provide transportation to and from the center. Depending on the services received, Medicaid or other insurance may cover some of the

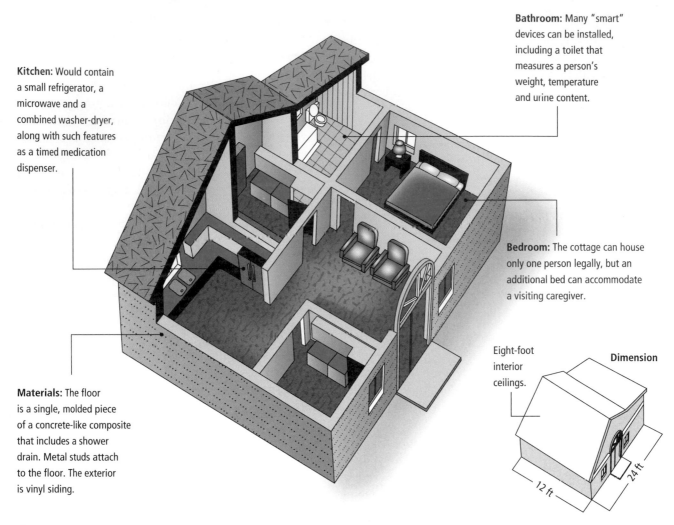

Kitchen: Would contain a small refrigerator, a microwave and a combined washer-dryer, along with such features as a timed medication dispenser.

Bathroom: Many "smart" devices can be installed, including a toilet that measures a person's weight, temperature and urine content.

Bedroom: The cottage can house only one person legally, but an additional bed can accommodate a visiting caregiver.

Materials: The floor is a single, molded piece of a concrete-like composite that includes a shower drain. Metal studs attach to the floor. The exterior is vinyl siding.

Eight-foot interior ceilings.

Dimension

12 ft

24 ft

Figure 5.3
An example of an auxiliary dwelling unit.
© 2015 Cengage Learning

expenses (Medicare does not). Because some states do not license adult day care centers, careful screening of a particular center is advised.

About 35% of adult day care clients live with an adult child and 20% with a spouse or partner. The average age of clients is over 70, and about two-thirds are women (National Adult Day Services Association, 2012). Family members choosing adult day care (and can afford it) typically do so because they need occasional assistance with caregiving, have safety concerns about the care recipient when the caregiver is not around, take increasing amounts of time off from work for caregiving, are experiencing problems in their

relationship with the care recipient, or the care recipient could benefit from more contact with other older adults (MetLife, 2010).

For people with cognitive impairment, changes in routine can result in confusion or disruptive behavior. It is especially important for them, as it is for all older adults who may become adult day care clients, to inform them of this choice. A good strategy is to engage in a few trials to find out how well the person acclimates to the different surroundings and activities.

Research demonstrates adult day care is a viable and important option for caregivers. Caregivers are interested in programs that meet the needs of their loved ones and are generally satisfied with the services provided (Madeo, Feld, & Spencer, 2008). Family members clearly seek what is best for their loved one in searching for and helping make the transition to adult day care centers (Bull & McShane, 2008; Musolf, 2012). However, as a study in Australia demonstrated, family caregivers can be overwhelmed by the amount of information and confused by the process of placing their family member (Robinson et al., 2012).

Evidence is clear that compared with keeping relatives with cognitive impairment at home, good adult day care programs can reduce problematic behaviors and lower the need for psychotropic medication in clients, and result in lower reports of caregiving burden among caregivers (Mosello et al., 2008; MetLife, 2010). However, a key factor in the success of day care programs is having culturally appropriate programs in interventions, as demonstrated in studies of Korean (Park, 2008) and Chinese (Yeung, Wong, & Mok, 2011) clients who benefitted most when programs took their cultural background into account.

Congregate Housing

Congregate housing includes a range of living options from those providing only housing to those providing some level of medical services (Howe, Jones, & Tilse, in press). The most common form is an apartment complex of older adults that provides a level of support such as shared meals. Congregate housing is often the least expensive form of supported living for older adults, because the cost is typically subsidized by various government agencies and nonprofit organizations. Because of its affordability, it is an especially important option for low-income older adults who need support to remain out of a nursing home. However, there is a shortage of congregate housing in the United States.

Traditional congregate housing differs from assisted living in terms of the level of services provided. Although many traditional congregate housing complexes do not include individual kitchens and provide shared meals, the level of medical assistance, for example, is lower than in assisted living. Congregate housing facilities do not provide 24-hour medical services on site. Currently, newer congregate housing complexes are including higher levels of other service, so the distinction with assisted living is being blurred.

The service coordination provided in congregate living accomplishes several things: interface with housing officials, individual service plans for residents, coordination of shared activities (e.g., cleaning common spaces), and mediation of resident conflicts. Most congregate housing complexes require residents be capable of independent living and not require continual medical care, be medically stable, know where they are and oriented to time (e.g., know today's date and other key time-related information), show no evidence of disruptive behavior, be able to make independent decisions, and be able to follow any specific service plan developed for them. If at some point a resident no longer meets one of the criteria, he or she is usually required to move out.

The decision to move into congregate housing is usually done in conjunction with one's family, and is typically a response to a significant decline in functioning or other health-related problem (Sergeant & Ekerdt, 2008). The best decisions about where one should live in late life are those that lead to outcomes that are congruent to the person's needs and goals (Golant, 2011); congregate living can work for those seeking specific types of social engagement.

Assisted Living

Given that maintaining a sense of place, a home, is important to older adults, it should not come as a surprise that they prefer living options that foster that desire. That is how the option of assisted living came into being (Scheidt & Schwarz, 2010). **Assisted living facilities** *are housing options for older adults that provide a supportive living arrangement for people needing assistance with personal care (such as bathing or taking medications) but who are not so impaired physically or cognitively that they need 24-hour care.*

An ideal assisted living situation has three essential attributes (Scheidt & Schwarz, 2010). First, the physical environment where a person lives is designed to be as much like a single-family house as possible. That way, the setting has a residential appearance, a small scale, and personal privacy that includes at a minimum a private room and a full bath that is not shared with other residents unless the resident explicitly wishes. The public spaces in the facility are designed to provide indoor and outdoor access, which enhances a resident's autonomy and independence.

Second, the philosophy of care at an ideal assisted living facility emphasizes personal control, choice, dignity, and autonomy, and promotes a preferred lifestyle residents and their families consider to be a "normal," good quality of life. This philosophy is implemented by understanding residents' personal preferences and priorities, and allowing residents to exert control over their lives, schedules, and private dwellings.

Third, ideal assisted living facilities should meet residents' routine services and special needs. It is important to keep in mind that assisted living facilities foster residents' autonomy, so the levels of support provided are not meant to deal with high level, intensive nursing or other complex needs (Thomas, Guihan, & Mambourg, 2011). Supports tend to include transportation, socialization, and daily checks to establish how residents are doing that day. For some families, a choice may need to be made between the greater autonomy in assisted living and greater support in long-term care facilities.

Despite the fact assisted living facilities have existed for more than 20 years, there are serious gaps in service and in regulations (Scheidt & Schwarz, 2010). For example, no national consensus or federal guidelines exist to govern the characteristics of the people who can and should be served in these facilities, the services provided, or minimum staffing standards. The different combinations of housing and service arrangements that today are called assisted living "make simple generalizations about either their physical settings or their care environments particularly challenging—and inevitably contribute to consumer confusion" (Golant, 2008, 7).

Despite the problems with precisely defining assisted living facilities, the number of them continues to grow. In the United States, there are over 30,000 assisted living facilities with over 1 million residents, and there is continued expectation for growth over the next few decades as the baby boom generation ages. One important reason for this growth is that assisted living offers a more cost-effective approach than long-term care facilities for those older adults who cannot live independently but do not need the level of nursing care provided in a long-term care facilities.

Residents in assisted living facilities are in independent apartments or similar units. The services they provide vary, but usually include monitoring and management of health care, assistance with activities of daily living, housekeeping and laundry, reminders or assistance with medication, recreation and entertainment activities, transportation, and security (Eldercare.gov, 2012). Before choosing an assisted living facility, you should check several things:

- Think ahead. What will the resident's future needs be and how will the facility meet those needs?

- Is the facility close to family and friends? Are there any shopping centers or other businesses nearby (within walking distance)?

- Do admission and retention policies exclude people with severe cognitive impairments or severe physical disabilities?

- Does the facility provide a written statement of the philosophy of care?

- Visit each facility more than once, sometimes unannounced.

- Visit at meal times, sample the food, and observe the quality of mealtime and the service.

- Observe interactions among residents and staff.

- Check to see if the facility offers social, recreational, and spiritual activities.

- Talk to residents.

- Learn what types of training staff receive and how frequently they receive training.

- Review state licensing reports.

Residents generally pay the costs of assisted living facilities, which ranged between $25,000 and $50,000 per year in 2012 (Eldercare.gov, 2012). Medicare does not pay for either living costs or any of the services provided. In some cases, Medicaid may pay for services depending on the situation. Given that assisted living is usually less expensive than nursing homes, the lack of broad financial support for these programs means that the cost of care is not as low as it could be.

Research on assisted living increased as more assisted living options appeared. Residents' well-being is related to whether the decision to live there was under their control and to the quality of relationships formed with co-residents (Street & Burge, 2012). A review of housing needs for older adults in Western Europe revealed a serious need for a range of alternatives, especially in assisted living (Stula, 2012). Because of an anticipated increase in number of older adults who will need assistance and an increase in the range of functional impairments that older adults will experience, living facilities will need to have more flexible designs.

One of the main future challenges will be the blurring of congregate (independent) living, assisted living, and long-term care facilities into hybrids of these arrangements (Scheidt & Schwarz, 2010). The hope is more stringent regulations will follow the blending of these forms of housing, and services will not destroy the special characteristics of assisted living. Another challenge, both now and in the future, is the cost of assisted living, which is already out of the reach of many elderly Americans. Finally, researchers point to the need for updating our views of residential options for older adults (Golant, 2012). Because the future role of the government in providing funds for affordable shelter and care will continue to be limited, individuals and families will assume the largest financial burden of providing long-term care funds for their loved ones. Having access to the resources that this requires will be a major issue.

ADULT DEVELOPMENT IN ACTION

As a gerontological social worker, what key factors would you consider when making recommendations about the best housing/living options for your older adult clients?

5.3 Living in Nursing Homes

LEARNING OBJECTIVES

- What are the major types of nursing homes?
- Who is most likely to live in nursing homes?
- What are the key characteristics of nursing homes?
- What are special care units?
- How can a nursing home be a home?
- How should people communicate with nursing home residents?
- How is decision-making capacity assessed?
- What are some new directions for nursing homes?

The last place Maria thought she would end up was a bed in one of the local nursing homes. "That's a place where old people go to die," she used to say. "It's not gonna be for me." But here she is. Maria, 84 and living alone, fell and broke her hip. She needs to stay for a few weeks while she recovers. She hates the food; "tasteless goo," she calls it. Her roommate, Arnetta, calls the place a "jail." Arnetta, 79 and essentially blind, has Alzheimer's disease.

Maria and Arnetta may be the kind of people you think of when you conjure up images of nursing homes. To be sure, you will probably find some people like them there. But for each Maria or Arnetta, there are many more that come to terms with their situation and struggle to make sense of their lives. Nursing homes are indeed places where people who have serious health problems go, and for many it is their final address. Yet if you visit a nursing home, you will find many inspiring people with interesting stories to tell.

Misconceptions about nursing homes are common. Contrary to what some people believe, only about 5% of older adults live in nursing homes on any given day. As you can see in Figure 5.4, the percentage of older adults enrolled in Medicare who live in a long-term care facility at any given point in time increases from 2% in those aged 65–74 to about 14% of adults over age 85 (AgingStats. gov, 2012); however, over their lifetime, over 50% of older women and about 30% of older men will spend at least some time in a long-term care facility (Georgia Health Care Association, 2012). The gender difference is because older women take care of their husbands at home, but in turn need to relocate to a long-term care facility for their own care because their husbands are, on average, deceased.

Long-term care settings are different environments from those we have considered so far. The residents of such facilities differ in many respects from their community-dwelling counterparts. Likewise, the environment itself is dissimilar from neighborhood and community contexts. But because many aspects of the environment in these facilities are controlled, they offer a unique opportunity to examine person–environment interactions in more detail.

In this section we examine types of long-term care settings, the typical resident, the psychosocial environment, and residents' ability to make decisions for themselves.

Types of Nursing Homes

Nursing homes house the largest number of older residents of long-term care facilities. They are governed by

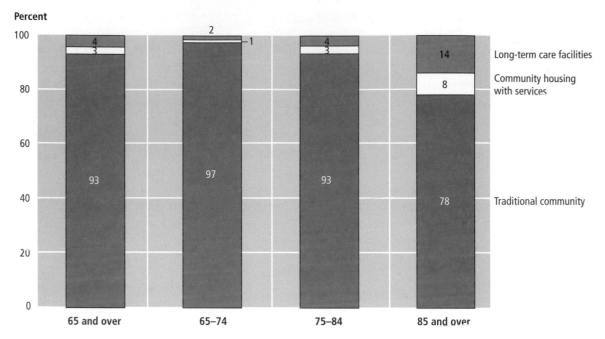

Figure 5.4

Percentage of Medicare enrollees age 65 and over in selected residential settings by age group, 2009.

Source: Centers for Medicare and Medicaid Services, Medicare Current Beneficiary Survey.

state and federal regulations that establish minimum standards of care. Two levels of care in nursing homes are defined in U.S. federal regulations (Allen, 2011). Skilled nursing care consists of 24-hour care including skilled medical and other health services, usually provided by nurses. Intermediate care is also 24-hour care including nursing supervision, but at a less intense level. In actual practice, the major differences between the two are the types and numbers of health care workers on the staff. Perhaps for this reason, the distinction between skilled and intermediate care often is blurred.

The cost of nursing home care is high. With the aging of the baby-boom generation, how this cost will be met is an issue confronting millions of families. As noted in the Current Controversies feature, funding for nursing homes will be an increasingly important political issue in the coming decades.

CURRENT CONTROVERSIES:

FINANCING LONG-TERM CARE

The current system of financing long-term care in the United States is in serious trouble. The average cost of a private room is about $90,500 per year at the beginning of 2013 (MetLife, 2012) and is by far the leading catastrophic health care expense. The Centers for Medicare and Medicaid Services (2012) estimates that by 2021 national expenditures for nursing home care will rise about $100 billion per year to $255 billion. Contrary to popular belief, Medicare does not cover nursing home care but does have limited nursing home and home care benefits for people who need skilled nursing services and who meet other criteria. Private insurance plans pay less than 10% of the costs nationally. About 25% of the expense is paid directly by nursing home residents. When residents become impoverished (a definition that varies widely from state to state), they become dependent on Medicaid, that pays the bulk of the total. (In 2010, the total Medicaid expenditures for skilled nursing home care were roughly $45.1 billion, or 31.5% of the total national expenditure on nursing home care.) Given these expenses and the lack of insurance coverage, how will we be able to finance the long-term health care system?

Several options have been proposed, taking the Affordable Health Care Act into account (Pettinato, 2013). Four main strategies are possible:

- A strategy that promotes private long-term care insurance and keeps public financing as a safety net. This approach spreads the financial risk without expanding the demands on federal or state budgets and taxpayers to pay fully for long-term care. Still, a public safety net would be essential as a last resort.

- A strategy to expand the public safety net for people with low to moderate incomes, with people from higher-income brackets expected to provide for themselves through private financing. This approach is a needs-tested model that targets the people with the greatest need and the fewest resources for government assistance.

- A strategy to establish public catastrophic long-term care insurance and support complementary private insurance to fill the gap along with the public safety net. This approach spreads the risk and the burden on a greater number of people, reducing the cost of private insurance, but still pricing it beyond the means of many older adults.

- A strategy to establish universal public long-term care insurance supplemented with private financing and a public safety net. This approach spreads the burden over the greatest number of people,

thereby addressing the problem of affordability of private insurance.

Despite the wide range of options, many of them still place the burden on individuals to devise ways of financing their own care. Given the cost, and the fact that millions of Americans do not have access to health insurance, large subsidies from the government will still be needed for long-term care regardless of what the private sector does.

Given that government subsidies for long-term care will be needed for the foreseeable future, the question becomes how to finance them. Under the current Medicaid system, older adults are not protected from becoming impoverished, and in essence are required to have few assets in order to qualify. With the aging of the baby-boom generation, many more people will spend their assets, causing Medicaid costs to skyrocket. If we want to continue the program in its current form, additional revenues will be needed, either in the form of taxes or dramatic spending reductions in other areas of public budgets.

The questions facing us are whether we want to continue forcing older adults to become totally impoverished when they need long-term care, the government to continue subsidy programs, encourage those who can afford it to buy long-term care insurance, and if we are willing to pay higher taxes for better coverage. How we answer these questions will have a profound impact on the status of long-term care over the next few decades.

Who Is Likely to Live in Nursing Homes?

Who is the typical resident of a nursing home? She is over age 85, European American, recently admitted to a hospital, living in a retirement home rather than being a homeowner, is cognitively impaired, has problems with IADLs, is probably widowed or divorced, and has no siblings or children living nearby. Maria and Arnetta, whom we met in the vignette, reflect these characteristics. However, this profile is changing rapidly (Feng, Fennell, Tyler, Clark, & Mor, 2011). Latino American and Asian residents increased roughly 55 percent each between 1999 and 2008, and African American residents increased nearly 11 percent. Meanwhile, European American residents declined 10 percent.

What are the health issues and functional impairments of typical nursing home residents? For the most part, the average nursing home resident has significant mental and physical problems. The main reason

for placing almost 80% of nursing home residents is significant health problems (AgingStats.gov, 2012). Estimates show nearly 80% of residents have mobility problems, and more than one third have mobility, eating, and incontinence issues. In addition, the rates of mental health and cognitive impairment problems are high, with between 30 and 50% of residents showing signs of clinical depression.

As you may surmise from the high level of impairment among nursing home residents, frail older people and their relatives do not see nursing homes as an option until other avenues have been explored. This may account for the numbers of truly impaired people who live in nursing homes; the kinds and number of problems make life outside the nursing home difficult for them and their families and beyond the level of assistance provided by assisted living facilities. For these reasons, the decision to place a family member in a nursing home is a difficult one (Beaulieu, 2012; Caron, Ducharme, & Griffith, 2006), even when the family member in question has serious cognitive impairment (Klug, Volkov, Muus, & Halaas, 2012). Placement decisions are often made quickly in reaction to a crisis, such as a person's impending discharge from a hospital or other health emergency. The decision tends to be made by partners or adult children, a finding generalized across ethnic groups such as European Americans, Mexican Americans, and Koreans, especially when there is evidence of cognitive impairment (Almendarez, 2008; Klug et al., 2012; Kwon & Tae, in press).

Characteristics of Nursing Homes

Nursing homes vary a great deal in the amount and quality of care they provide. One useful way of evaluating them is by applying the competence–environmental press model. When applied to nursing homes, the goal is to find the optimal level of environmental support for people who have relatively low levels of competence.

Selecting a nursing home should be done carefully. The Centers for Medicare and Medicaid Services of the U.S. Department of Health and Human Services provides a detailed *Nursing Home Quality Initiative* website that is a guide for choosing a nursing home based on several key quality factors. Among the most important things to consider are:

- Quality of life for residents (e.g., whether residents are well groomed, the food is tasty, and rooms contain comfortable furniture);

- Quality of care (whether staff respond quickly to calls, whether staff and family are involved in care decisions);

- Safety (whether there are enough staff, whether hallways are free of clutter); and

- Other issues (whether there are outdoor areas for residents to use).

These aspects of nursing homes reflect those dimensions considered by states in their inspections and licensing process.

Individuals and families should also keep several other things in mind:

- Skilled nursing care is usually available only for a short time following hospitalization, whereas custodial care may be an option for a much longer period. If a facility offers both types, it may or may not be possible to shift level of care without relocating to another room.

- Nursing homes that only take Medicaid residents may offer longer term but less intensive care levels. Nursing homes that do not accept Medicaid may force the resident to leave when Medicare or private funds run out.

- Ensure the facility and its administrator are fully licensed, and a full array of staff training is available on such topics as recognizing abuse and neglect, how to deal with difficult residents, and how to investigate and report your complaints.

- Ensure the resident's care plan is put together by a team of professionals, and residents have choices, can exert some control over their routines and care, and have appropriate assistance with ADLs and IADLs.

- Ask questions about staff educational levels (including continuing education) and turnover.

Based on the various theories of person–environment interaction discussed earlier in this chapter, the best nursing homes use what researchers recommend—a "person-centered care" approach to nursing home policies (Morgan & Yoder, 2012), especially when working with people who have cognitive impairment (Lawlor & York, 2007). Although there is not yet complete consensus about the underlying characteristics of person-centered care (Morgan & Yoder, 2012), in general this approach is based on promoting residents' well-being through increasing their perceived level of personal control and treating them with respect. An example of this approach includes such things as residents getting to decorate their own rooms, choosing what they want to eat from a buffet, and deciding whether they want to take a shower or a bath. Person-centered planning focuses on the individual, and does not use a one-size-fits-all approach. Most important, this approach involves a team who knows and cares about the individual who work together with the person to create the best supportive environment possible.

Such policies are grounded in classic research showing that residents who have higher perceived personal control show significant improvement in well-being and activity level, and actually live longer (Langer & Rodin, 1976; Rodin & Langer, 1977).

Nursing homes using the person-centered planning approach also note major decreases in the need for certain medications (e.g., sleep and anti-anxiety drugs) and soft restraints, as well as substantial declines in the number of residents who are incontinent (Reese, 2001). Feelings of self-efficacy are crucial to doing well and adjusting to life in a long-term care facility (Brandburg, Symes, Mastel-Smith, Hersch, & Walsh, in press).

Although the person-centered care approach has been around for years, many nursing homes still rely on a traditional approach of rules, routines, and requirements (Robinson & Gallagher, 2008). Perhaps the best way to begin changing the culture from one where residents are expected to be passive to one that includes them in their own care is to focus on activities related to dining. Choosing what one eats, being able to socialize with one's friends, and interacting with staff while enjoying a meal is one way to create the level of personal involvement and trust necessary to implement a person-centered approach.

Today, person-centered care is considered a best practice in nursing homes (Dellefield, 2008; Toles & Anderson, 2011). Including nursing home residents in the planning of their own care represents a major shift in culture, and is an example of the application of research to practice.

Special Care Units

Most residents of nursing homes have cognitive impairment, and the majority of those individuals have dementia. Providing a supportive environment for people with moderate to severe dementia requires certain specialized design and intervention features. This need has resulted in the development of special care units in many nursing homes.

Well-designed special care units for people with dementia provide a supportive and therapeutic set of programs that help the person function at the highest level possible. Optimally, staff working in special care units receive specific training to work with persons with dementia. The best units have physical design elements that take functional limitations into account; for example, the hallways of some facilities are designed so if residents wander, they merely follow the interior halls or exterior path in a circle so they do not leave the building or the complex, and the decorating is done in a way to minimize confusion. Most facilities

have residents with cognitive impairment wear wrist or ankle bands that trigger alarms if they wander beyond a certain point or exit the facility, another safe way to provide opportunities for residents to move about freely but safely. The best facilities also permit residents to bring a few personal items as reminders of their past in order to provide a more homelike environment. They also provide a private dining area in a family-like setting in order to minimize possible negative interactions between residents with dementia and residents without cognitive impairment.

Selecting the right special care unit for a person with dementia must be done carefully by the family with proper input from health care professionals (Gillick, 2012; Paris, 2008). As noted in the competence–environmental press model, as competence declines the environment must provide more support in order for behavior to be optimized. So the special care unit must have the right level of environmental support at the placement, as well as the availability of additional levels of support when the person's competence level continues to decline. Memory aids should be built into the unit, such as color-coded halls. Staffing levels and training are key as is the range of intervention programs and activities available. Such programs should be research based, such as those based on the Montessori techniques discussed in Chapter 10.

The research-based staff training required at the best special care units includes several aspects of caring for older adults with moderate to severe cognitive impairment:

- Appropriate and effective communication techniques (as discussed later in this section)
- Behavioral management techniques to address aggressive or agitated behavior (a common symptom in dementia)
- Appropriate techniques for assisting with personal health and hygiene that protect residents' dignity
- Appropriate methods for dealing with incontinence
- Appropriate techniques for handling sexuality in persons with dementia
- Effective techniques for controlling wandering (in addition to physical design aspects of the facility)
- Appropriate ways of supervising or assisting with eating

- Appropriate techniques and interventions to address memory failure and disorientation

- Appropriate techniques for assisting with mobility (e.g., walking, using a wheelchair)

Training in these areas will not guarantee high-quality care, but it increases the likelihood of it.

Research indicates that upon admission, residents of special care units are younger, more behaviorally impaired, and less likely to be minority than general nursing home residents when both exist in the same facility (e.g., Gruneir et al., 2008a; Sengupta, Decker, Harris-Kojetin, & Jones, 2012). Residents of special care units tend to have lower hospitalization rates, were less likely to have serious other health issues (e.g., be tube fed), and have family members who were satisfied with the quality of care than residents of non-special care units (Cadigan, Grabowski, Givens, & Mitchell, 2012). The increased quality of care residents of special care units receive is more the result of a difference in philosophy of care between nursing homes with and without special care units than it is due to the special care unit itself (Cadigan et al., 2012; Gruneir et al., 2008b). Given the use of physical restraints is associated with higher morbidity (Reid, 2008), it may be nursing homes that include special care units also have different approaches for dealing with problem behaviors that help avoid the use of or need for physical restraints.

Can a Nursing Home Be a Home?

One key aspect of nursing homes has been largely overlooked: To what extent do residents consider a nursing home to be home? This gets to the heart of what makes people feel the place where they live is

Nursing home residents benefit from social activities and interaction with residents and staff.

more than just a dwelling. On the surface, it appears nursing homes are full of barriers to this feeling. After all, they may have regulations about the amount of furnishings and other personal effects residents may bring, and residents are in an environment with plenty of structural reminders that it is not a house in suburbia. Not having their own refrigerator, for example, means they can no longer invite friends over for a home-cooked meal (Shield, 1988).

Can nursing home residents move beyond these barriers and reminders and achieve a sense of home? The answer is yes, but with some important qualifications. In a groundbreaking series of studies, Groger (1995, 2002) proposed a nursing home can indeed be perceived as a home. She interviewed older African American adults, some who lived in nursing homes and others who were home care clients, along with a sample of the nursing home residents' caregivers. Groger's analyses of her interviews revealed that nursing home residents can feel at home. The circumstances fostering this feeling include having the time to think about and participate in the placement decision, even if only minimally; having prior knowledge and positive experience with a specific facility; defining home predominantly in terms of family and social relationships rather than in terms of place, objects, or total autonomy; and being able to establish a kind of continuity between home and nursing home either through activities or similarities in living arrangements.

Groger (2002) points out that residents pull from their repertoire of coping strategies to help them come to terms with living in a nursing home. Groger (1995) also reports that getting nursing home residents to reminisce about home actually facilitates adjustment. Some residents concluded only after long and detailed reflection on their prior home that the nursing home was now home. In addition, it may be easier for nursing home residents to feel at home on some days than others and from one situation to another, depending on the events or stimuli at the time.

Helping nursing home residents feel at home is an important issue that must be explored in more detail. Perhaps having people think about what constitutes a home, before and after placement, may make the transition from community to the facility easier to face. For those needing the care provided in a nursing home, anything done to ease the transition is a major benefit. Assessing the degree to which residents feel at home is possible (Molony, McDonald, & Palmisano-Mills, 2007), and can be used to document functional changes after placement into a facility (Molony, Evans, Jeon, Rabig, & Straka, 2011).

At a general level, nursing home residents' satisfaction relates to several key variables: facility, staff, and resident factors, as shown in Figure 5.5 (Chou et al., 2003). Research indicates that staff satisfaction plays a crucial role in nursing home residents' satisfaction. In contrast, providing more care does not (Chou et al., 2003). In addition, when residents have a voice in determining the quality of care, irrespective of their functional abilities, their quality of life improves (Moyle & O'Dwyer, 2012). As we will see next, how people communicate with residents is also key.

Communicating with Residents

Have you ever been to a nursing home? If so, one of the things you may have found difficult is talking with the residents, especially when interacting with residents who are cognitively impaired. Unfortunately, this uneasiness often results in people relying on stereotypes of older adults in general and nursing home residents in particular in speaking to them and results in inappropriate communication styles.

The communication style most people adopt is one in which younger adults over accommodate their speech based on their stereotyped expectations of dependence and incompetence. This style is described as a general "communication predicament" of older adults (Ryan

et al., 1986). Such speech conveys a sense of declining abilities, loss of control, and helplessness, which, if continued, may cause older adults to lose self-esteem and withdraw from social interactions. As time goes on, older adults who are talked to in this way may even begin behaving in ways that reinforce the stereotypes.

Inappropriate speech to older adults that is based on stereotypes of incompetence and dependence is called patronizing speech. Patronizing speech is slower speech marked by exaggerated intonation, higher pitch, increased volume, repetitions, tag and closed-end questions, and simplification of vocabulary and grammar. Speaking in this way can be conceptualized as "secondary baby talk," which is baby talk inappropriately used with adults (Mohlman, Sirota, Papp, Staples, King, & Gorenstein, 2012). *Secondary baby talk, also called* infantilization or elderspeak, *also involves the unwarranted use of a person's first name, terms of endearment, simplified expressions, short imperatives, an assumption that the recipient has no memory, and cajoling as a way to demand compliance.*

In a classic study, Whitbourne and colleagues (1995) established that infantilizing speech is viewed extremely negatively by some older adults. They found community-dwelling older adults rated infantilizing speech especially negatively and were particularly resentful of its intonation aspects as indicative of a lack of respect. Nursing home residents were less harsh in their judgments, giving support to the idea that being exposed to infantilizing speech lowers one's awareness of its demeaning qualities. Whitbourne and colleagues

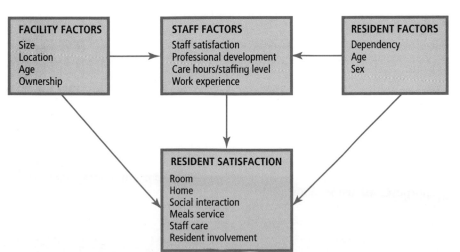

Figure 5.5
Major factors influencing resident satisfaction in nursing homes.

Source: Chou, S-C., Boldy, D. P., & Lee, A. H. (2003). Factors influencing residents' satisfaction in residential aged care. The Gerontologist 43, 459–472, Copyright © Reprinted with permission from the Gerontological Society of America.

FACILITY FACTORS
Size
Location
Age
Ownership

STAFF FACTORS
Staff satisfaction
Professional development
Care hours/staffing level
Work experience

RESIDENT FACTORS
Dependency
Age
Sex

RESIDENT SATISFACTION
Room
Home
Social interaction
Meals service
Staff care
Resident involvement

also found no evidence that infantilizing speech is high in nurturance, as some previous authors had suggested.

Residents with dementia tend to be more resistive to care when they are the targets of elderspeak (Williams et al., 2008). In younger adults, use of patronizing speech appears to be related to the amount of interaction they have had with unrelated older adults (i.e., older adults who are not their relatives), with more experience being related to lower use of patronizing speech (Hehman, Corpuz, & Bugental, 2012).

It turns out there may be different types of elderspeak, with different effects on the targets of the communications. In a study described in more detail in the How Do We Know? feature, Chee (2011) examined elderspeak in an eldercare facility in Singapore. Choi discovered there may be at least two types of elderspeak, what she terms "right" and "wrong." She also demonstrated elderspeak is a common approach used in a variety of settings, but that it is used toward older women most often.

HOW DO WE KNOW?:

IDENTIFYING DIFFERENT TYPES OF ELDERSPEAK IN SINGAPORE

Who were the investigators, and what was the aim of the study? Older adults who attend day services programs face many difficulties with the way people talk to (or about) them. The concept of patronizing speech, discussed in the text, captures the essence of the problem. Felicia Yi Tian Chee (2011) decided to establish the different kinds of patronizing speech used in such settings.

How did the investigator measure the topic of interest? Chee initially spent significant amounts of time at the adult day care center in Singapore to establish rapport with the clients. Data were gathered through observations and note taking during normal interactions between staff and clients. A coding system was developed to reflect different aspects of speech toward the older adult clients: (a) limited vocabulary, mirroring the limited vocabulary and sentence structure used when children are learning to speak; (b) infantilizing and over-parenting, when the staff member assumes the role of "parent" and treats the client as if he/she were the "child," an approach used most in conversations about toileting, displays of verbal affection, and reprimanding; and (c) repetition, which includes expansion, semantic elaboration, and comprehension checks.

Who were the participants in the study? Participants were 30 older adult clients (8 males, 22 females) with a variety of health conditions. Most of the clients were ethnic Chinese, but there were 3 ethnic Indians. Older adults' first languages varied, with most speaking Mandarin Chinese. For purposes of data analyses, clients were grouped into three clusters: those who were healthy and ambulatory, those who were healthy and wheelchair-bound, and those with dementia.

What was the design of the study? The design was naturalistic observation. Chee observed verbal communication interactions without participating herself.

Were there ethical concerns with the study? All participants were volunteers.

What were the results? Chee observed greater use of elderspeak with those clients who had greater physical or cognitive dependency on the caregiving staff. Thus, clients in wheelchairs and those with dementia were the targets of elderspeak more often than healthy clients. Although clients with dementia received all three types of elderspeak, they received the least reprimanding or domineering speech, perhaps because the staff perceived them as more in need of care. Clients in wheelchairs received nearly as much elderspeak as those with dementia. Female clients received more elderspeak than male clients.

More elderspeak occurred in situations in which clients were dependent on staff to help them perform some function, such as toileting or feeding. Situations in which clients were being encouraged to perform a task were also common ones in which elderspeak was used.

Clients did not appear to react strongly to elderspeak. Chee surmises that they either resigned themselves to it or chose not to respond.

What did the investigators conclude? Elderspeak occurs in a wide variety of interactions with clients in day services centers, but is related to level of physical or cognitive ability.

Chee concluded elderspeak aimed at comprehension checking and encouragement, when no other elements of elderspeak are present, may enhance clients' performance. In contrast, other forms of elderspeak tended to result in poorer performance of the task at hand.

So how should people talk to older adults, especially those needing services or living in long-term care facilities? Ryan and her colleagues (1995) initially proposed the communication enhancement model as a framework for appropriate exchange. This model is based on a health promotion model that seeks opportunities for health care providers to optimize outcomes for older adults through more appropriate and effective communication. As you can see from Figure 5.6, this model emphasizes communication with older adults must be based on recognizing individualized cues, modifying communication to suit individual needs and situations, appropriately assessing health and social problems, and empowering both older adults and health care providers.

Combining the communication enhancement model with the person-centered care model discussed earlier provides a way for paraprofessional staff in long-term care facilities to communicate more effectively with residents, including those living on dementia special care units (Passalacqua & Harwood, 2012). Such strategies are important if the culture in long-term care facilities is to change.

Ryan and colleagues' model and research can be readily applied to interactions with older adults from different ethnic groups and with older adults who have cognitive impairments. An analysis of intergenerational communication comparing Western and Eastern cultures showed complex cultural variability, including the occurrence of less positive perceptions of conversations in some cases from respondents in Korea, Japan, China, Hong Kong, and the Philippines than in some Western countries (Williams et al., 1997). But cultural norms also influence communication. As the persons

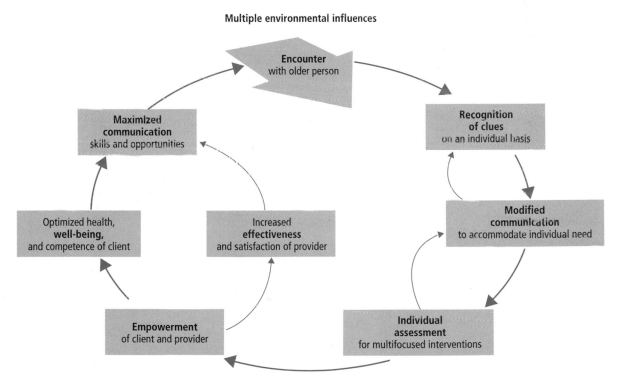

Figure 5.6

The communication enhancement model. Note that this model is dynamic in that there are opportunities to modify communication interactions and to have the outcomes of one interaction serve as input for another.

Source: E. B. Ryan, S. D. Meredith, M. J. MacLean, and J. B. Orange, 1995. Changing the way we talk with elders: Promoting health using the Communication Enhancement Model. International Journal of Aging and Human Development 41, 89–107. Reproduced by permission.

they were talking to grew older, younger adult Thais and Japanese increased their communicative respect and deference (Ota, McCann, & Honeycutt, 2012).

In general, an approach to communication based on the communication enhancement model promotes mental, social, and physical well-being among older adults and counters the fostering of dependence that follows from the traditional medical model discussed earlier. When patronizing speech occurs in nursing homes, active steps should be taken to eliminate it (Dobbs et al., 2008). Most important, this research reminds us we must speak to all older adults in a way that conveys the respect they deserve.

So what should you do as a visitor? The first time most people visit a nursing home, they are ill-prepared to talk to family members who are frail, have trouble remembering, and cannot get around easily. The hardest part is trying to figure out what to say in order to avoid patronizing speech. However, visiting residents of nursing homes is a way to maintain social contacts and provide a meaningful activity. Even if the person you are visiting is frail, has a sensory impairment, or some other type of disability, visits can be uplifting. As noted earlier in the chapter, high-quality social contacts help older adults maintain their life satisfaction. Here are several suggestions for making visits more pleasant (Papalia & Olds, 1995; adapted from Davis, 1985), along with guidance from the Gerontological Society of America (2012):

- Face older adults when you speak to them, with your lips at the same level as theirs.

- Ask open-ended questions and genuinely listen.

- Concentrate on the older adult's expertise and wisdom, as discussed in Chapter 14, by asking for advice on a life problem he or she knows a lot about, such as dealing with friends, cooking, or crafts.

- Ask questions about an older adult's living situation and social contacts.

- Allow the older person to exert control over the visit: where to go (even inside the facility), what to wear, what to eat (if choices are possible).

- Listen attentively, even if the older person is repetitive. Avoid being judgmental, be sympathetic to complaints, and acknowledge feelings.

- Talk about things the person likes to remember, such as raising children, military service, growing up, work, courtship, and so on.

- Do a joint activity, such as putting a jigsaw puzzle together, arranging a photograph album, or doing arts and crafts.

- Record your visit on audiotape or videotape. This is valuable for creating a family history you will be able to keep. The activity may facilitate a life review as well as provide an opportunity for the older person to leave something of value for future generations by describing important personal events and philosophies.

- Bring children when you visit, if possible. Grandchildren are especially important, because many older adults are happy to include them in conversations. Such visits also give children the opportunity to see their grandparents and learn about the diversity of older adults.

- Stimulate as many senses as possible. Wearing bright clothes, singing songs, reading books, and sharing foods (as long as they have been checked and approved with the staff) help to keep residents involved with their environment. Above all, though, hold the resident's hands. There's nothing like a friendly touch.

Always remember your visits may be the only way the residents have of maintaining social contacts with friends and family. By following these guidelines, you will be able to avoid difficulties and make your visits more pleasurable.

Decision-Making Capacity and Individual Choices

Providing high-quality care for nursing home residents means putting into practice the various competence-enhancing interventions we have discussed relating to personal control and communication. Doing so means residents participate in making decisions about their care. But how can we make sure residents understand what they are being asked to decide, especially when a majority of them have cognitive impairment?

The need to address this question became apparent in 1991 with the enactment of the Patient Self-Determination Act (PSDA). This law mandated all facilities receiving Medicare and Medicaid funds comply with five requirements regarding advance care planning, referred to as advance directives (Emanuel, 2008):

- Providing written information to people at the time of their admission about their right to make medical treatment decisions and to formulate advance directives (i.e., decisions about life-sustaining treatments and who can make medical decisions for them if they are incapacitated);

- Maintaining written policies and procedures regarding advance directives;

- Documenting the completion of advance directives in the person's medical chart;

- Complying with state law regarding the implementation of advance directives; and

- Providing staff and community education about advance directives.

The PSDA mandates work well with most people. However, assessing a person's capacity to make medical decisions is a tremendous challenge for medical ethics (American Geriatrics Society Ethics Committee, 1996; Rich, 2013). In theory, advance directives enable people to choose the type of medical treatment they prefer in advance of a medical crisis. However, numerous studies show the theory does not hold up well in practice: Most people, especially older adults, see such planning as a family process. They engage in informal advance care planning, preferring to allow family members to make decisions for them when the need arises and to give them leeway in interpreting advance directives even when they exist (Allen & Shuster, 2002). Thus it is unlikely a person being admitted to a nursing home will have completed a formal advance directive.

Because placement in a nursing home is already stressful and likely to occur in the context of a medical crisis, the new resident is unlikely to understand the information presented as mandated by the PSDA. To make matters worse, if new residents are cognitively impaired, they may be thought to be unable to act in their own behalf in communicating treatment preferences and end-of-life wishes and understanding the consequences of their choices (Allen et al., 2003), although there still may be ways to assist them in

expressing their preferences (Moriarty, Rutter, Ross, & Holmes, 2012). The degree to which cognitive impairment interferes with a person's ability to decide their treatment raises important ethical questions concerning whether physicians can trust any advance directive signed by such individuals after they move to a nursing home (Gillick, 2012; Kapp, 2008).

Assessing a nursing home resident's ability to make medical treatment decisions can be conceptualized as a problem involving the fit between the original intent of the law and the resident's cognitive capacity (Allen et al., 2003; Smyer & Allen-Burge, 1999). Several researchers have tackled the problem of how to assess decision-making capacity with varying results. Most important, a careful assessment of the resident's capacity to understand treatment and intervention options is necessary (Gillick, 2012; Kapp, 2008).

Still, many problems remain. No uniform approach to determining residents' cognitive competence exists, although progress is being made through the establishment of guidelines (American Bar Association/American Psychological Association, 2005, 2006, 2008). One barrier to a common approach is that each state sets the criteria needed to demonstrate cognitive competence (which is usually approached from the opposite side—what it takes to establish incompetence). To complicate matters further, research also shows lack of agreement between what nursing home residents want and what their families think they would want, and this also varies with ethnicity (Connolly, Sampson, & Purandare, 2012; Winter & Parks, 2012). Resolving the problem involves using the various approaches we considered for determining person–environment interactions, combined with strong clinical assessment (see Chapter 10), in the context of specific treatment goals and maintaining quality of life. Clearly, creating an optimal solution takes an interdisciplinary team of professionals, residents, and family members working together.

One solution may be to assess key members of the family (who serve as proxies in completing the forms) as to their beliefs as well as careful observation of the resident's capacity by the staff (Allen et al., 2003). Health care staff also need to sit down with family members and talk with them directly about treatment options so better decisions are made (Feltz & Samayoa, in press).

New Directions for Nursing Homes

Nursing homes are not static entities. New ways of approaching care continue to be developed. Three interesting new developments are the Eden Alternative, the Green House Project, and the Pioneer Network.

The Eden Alternative. Imagine an approach to caring for frail older adults starting from the premise that skilled care environments are habitats for people rather than facilities for the frail. Such an environment has the potential to address issues such as boredom, loneliness, and helplessness. The Eden Alternative takes this approach.

Founded by Dr. William and Judy Thomas, the Eden Alternative approaches care from the perspective of protecting the dignity of each person. It is based on the following 10 principles:

1. The three plagues of loneliness, helplessness, and boredom account for the bulk of suffering among our elders.

2. An elder-centered community commits to creating a human habitat where life revolves around close and continuing contact with plants, animals, and children. It is these relationships that provide the young and old alike with a pathway to a life worth living.

3. Loving companionship is the antidote to loneliness. Elders deserve easy access to human and animal companionship.

4. An elder-centered community creates opportunity to give as well as receive care. This is the antidote to helplessness.

5. An elder-centered community imbues daily life with variety and spontaneity by creating an environment where unexpected and unpredictable interactions and happenings can take place. This is the antidote to boredom.

6. Meaningless activity corrodes the human spirit. The opportunity to do things that we find meaningful is essential to human health.

7. Medical treatment should be the servant of genuine human caring, never its master.

8. An elder-centered community honors its elders by de-emphasizing top-down bureaucratic authority, seeking instead to place the maximum possible decision-making authority into the hands of the elders or into the hands of those closest to them.

9. Creating an elder-centered community is a never-ending process. Human growth must never be separated from human life.

10. Wise leadership is the lifeblood of any struggle against the three plagues. For it, there can be no substitute.

Arguably, the Eden Alternative helped launch a culture change in nursing homes that improved residents' quality of life (Kapp, in press; Rahman & Schnelle, 2008) by blending person-centered care with relational care (care that takes unintended actions into account) (Rockwell, 2012). The main outcomes of this movement are resident-directed care and staff empowerment. Research indicates the cultural changes resulting from the Eden Alternative are associated with less feelings of boredom and helplessness and improved quality of life (Bergman-Evans, 2004; Kapp, in press).

Green House Project. The Green House concept is grounded in the Eden Alternative. It is a radical departure from the concept that skilled nursing care is best provided in large residential facilities. In contrast, a Green House aims to provide older adults who need skilled nursing care a small, homelike environment that shifts the focus from a large facility to a more homelike setting. Only 6–10 residents live there, in a dwelling that blends architecturally with houses in the neighborhood, making it much more homelike (Kapp, in press; Rabig et al., 2006; Zarit & Reamy, in press).

The Green House concept emphasizes the importance of encouraging residents to participate in their care by helping with daily tasks such as cooking and gardening, assisted by specially trained staff (Johnson & Rhodes, 2007). By emphasizing participation in one's own care to the extent possible, personal dignity is maintained, and quality of life improved (Kane et al., 2007). As a result, the Green House concept is spreading across the United States as a viable alternative to large nursing homes.

The Pioneer Network. The Pioneer Network is also dedicated to changing the way older adults are treated in society, particularly in care facilities. The Pioneer Network focuses on changing the culture of aging in America regardless of where older adults live. Like the Eden Alternative, this approach focuses on respecting older adults and providing maximally supportive environments for them. Their values are also similar in spirit:

- Know each person.
- Each person can and does make a difference.
- Relationship is the fundamental building block of a transformed culture.
- Respond to spirit, as well as mind and body.
- Risk taking is a normal part of life.
- Put the person before the task.
- All elders are entitled to self-determination wherever they live.
- Community is the antidote to institutionalization.
- Do unto others as you would have them do unto you.
- Promote the growth and development of all.
- Shape and use the potential of the environment in all its aspects: physical, organizational, psychosocial, and spiritual.
- Practice self-examination, searching for new creativity and opportunities for doing better.
- Recognize culture change and transformation are not destinations but a journey, always a work in progress.

The Pioneer Network, as part of the larger cultural change in caring for older adults, advocates a major emphasis on making nursing homes more like a home, and works in cooperation with the Centers for Medicare and Medicaid Services to work for revisions in nursing home regulations (Schoeneman, 2008). This work is aimed at creating a new culture of aging.

What the Eden Alternative, the Green House concept, and the Pioneer Network have in common is a commitment to viewing older adults as worthwhile members of society regardless of their physical limitations. Treating all people with dignity is an important aspect in maintaining a person's quality of life. Everyone deserves that.

ADULT DEVELOPMENT IN ACTION

As a nursing home administrator, what changes would you predict in resident demographics, nursing home design, and the types of services offered based on what you know about the aging population?

SOCIAL POLICY IMPLICATIONS

One recurring theme in this chapter is the problem of financing health care interventions in later life for people in the United States. The Current Controversies feature raises several key points about the costs of nursing homes in the United States and the lack of ways to finance those costs. With the aging of the baby-boom generation, it is possible the coming wave of older adults will be unable to afford the level and quality of care they expect to receive.

This is not the way it is in other countries. For example, U.S. health care expenditures as a percentage of its gross domestic product are nearly 5 times greater than they are in Singapore, but Singapore's health care is more effective as measured by the World Health Organization in terms of health attainment of the average resident, affordability, and responsiveness (Murray & Evans, 2003). As such, mere expenditures are not a good indicator of quality.

International funding models for long-term care reflect a wide variety of approaches, including social insurance, universal coverage through public services, financial need based systems, and hybrid approaches. Similarly, there is an equally wide array of ways for limiting expenses. Many countries provide services ranging from in-home care through skilled nursing care, and have formal evaluation procedures to determine the best approach to care for each individual.

It is clear there is an array of successful models of providing long-term care to older adults that range from those completely supported by taxes to those that combine public and private contributions. Each has advantages (and disadvantages) that could inform discussions in the United States. It is equally clear the current U.S. model is not sustainable financially, and without serious attention there will be major difficulties faced by the coming generation of aging baby boomers.

SUMMARY

5.1 Describing Person–Environment Interactions

What is the competence–environmental press model?

- Competence is the upper limit on one's capacity to function.

- Environmental press reflects the demands placed on a person.

- Lawton and Nahemow's model establishes points of balance between the two, called adaptation levels. One implication of the model is the less competent a person is, the more impact the environment has.

- People can show proactivity (doing something to exert control over their lives) or docility (letting the situation determine their lives).

What is the proactive and corrective proactivity (PCP) model?

- The preventive and corrective proactivity (PCP) model explains how life stressors and lack of good congruence in person–environment interactions, especially when the person has nothing to help buffer or protect against these things, result in poor life outcomes.

- Preventive adaptations are actions that avoid stressors and increase or build social resources. Corrective adaptations are actions taken in response to stressors, and can be facilitated by internal and external resources.

What are the major aspects of stress and coping theory relating to person–environment interaction?

- Schooler applied Lazarus's model of stress and coping to person–environment interactions. Schooler claims older adults' adaptation depends on their perception of environmental stress and their attempts to cope. Social systems and institutions may buffer the effects of stress.

What are the common themes in the theories of person–environment interactions?

- All theories agree the focus must be on interactions between the person and the environment. No single environment meets everyone's needs.

- Everyday competence is a person's potential ability to perform a wide range of activities considered essential for independent living.

- Everyday competence forms the basis for deciding whether people are capable of making decisions for themselves.

5.2 The Ecology of Aging: Community Options

What is aging in place?

- Aging in place reflects the balance of environmental press and competence through selection and compensation. Feeling "at home" is a major aspect of aging in place.

- Throughout adulthood people compensate for change; aging in place represents a continuation of that process.

- Aging in place has resulted in a rethinking of housing options for older adults.

How do people decide the best option?

- The best placement options are based on whether a person has cognitive or physical impairment, the ability of family or friends to provide support, and whether intervention, if needed, can be provided in the current residence or a move is necessary.

How can a home be modified to provide a supportive environment?

- Modifying a home can be a simple process (such as adding hand rails in a bathroom) or extensive (such as modifying doorways and entrances for wheelchair access).

- Home modifications are usually done to address difficulties with activities of daily living (ADLs).

What options are provided in adult day care?

- Adult day care provides support, companionship, and certain types of services. Programs include social, health care, and specialized services.

- Introduction of adult day care needs to be done carefully with persons who have cognitive impairment.

What is congregate housing?

- Congregate housing includes a range of options, that provide social support and meals, but not ongoing medical care.

What are the characteristics of assisted living?

- Assisted living provides options for adults needing a supportive living environment, assistance with activities of daily living, and a modest level of medical care.

- Assisted living situations have three essential attributes: a home-like environment; the philosophy of care emphasizes personal control, choice, and dignity; and facilities meet residents' routine services and special needs.

- Research shows assisted living is especially helpful for frail older adults.

5.3 Living in Nursing Homes

- At any given time, only about 5% of older adults are in nursing homes. Such facilities are excellent examples of the importance of person–environment fit.

What are the major types of nursing homes?

- A distinction within nursing homes is between skilled nursing care and intermediate care.
- Costs of nursing home care are high, and only certain types of insurance cover part of the costs. Future funding is a major concern.

Who is likely to live in nursing homes?

- The typical resident is female, European American, very old, financially disadvantaged, widowed/divorced or living alone, has no children or family nearby, and has significant problems with activities of daily living. However, the number of minorities in nursing homes is increasing rapidly.
- Placement in nursing homes is seen as a last resort and is often based on the lack of other alternatives, lack of other caregivers, or policies governing the level of functioning needed to remain in one's present housing. It often occurs quickly in the context of a medical crisis.

What are the key characteristics of nursing homes?

- Selection of nursing homes must be done carefully and take the person's health conditions and financial situation into account.
- Person-centered planning is the best approach, especially for people who have cognitive impairment.

What are special care units?

- Special care units provide a supportive environment for people with specific problems such as dementia.
- Residents of special care units tend to be younger and more impaired than the rest of the nursing home residents.

Can a nursing home be a home?

- Residents of nursing homes can come to the conclusion that this can be home. Home is more than simply a place to live: Coming to the feeling that one is at home sometimes entails reflection on what one's previous home was like and recognizing a nursing home can have some of the same characteristics.

How should people communicate with nursing home residents?

- Inappropriate speech to older adults is based on stereotypes of dependence and lack of abilities. Patronizing and infantilizing speech are examples of demeaning speech, that are rated negatively by older adults. The communication enhancement model has been proposed as a framework for appropriate exchange. This model is based on a health promotion model that seeks opportunities for health care providers to optimize outcomes for older adults through more appropriate and effective communication.

How is decision-making capacity assessed?

- The Patient Self-Determination Act (PSDA) requires people to complete advance directives when admitted to a health care facility. A major ethical issue concerns how to communicate this information to people with cognitive impairment in nursing homes.

What are some new directions for nursing homes?

- The Eden Alternative, the Green House concept, and the Pioneer Network have a commitment to viewing older adults as worthwhile members of society regardless of their physical limitations.

REVIEW QUESTIONS

5.1 Describing Person–Environment Interactions

- What are person–environment interactions?
- Describe Lawton and Nahemow's theory of environmental press. In their theory, what is adaptation level?
- Describe the preventive and corrective proactivity (PCP) model.
- Describe the application of the stress and coping model to person–environment interactions. What kinds of things buffer stress?
- What are the common themes expressed by the various theories of person–environment interactions?
- What are the key components of everyday competence?

5.2 The Ecology of Aging: Community Options

- What is aging in place?
- What factors should people use to make decisions about the most supportive environment in which to live?

- How can homes be modified to support older adults? What is an auxiliary dwelling unit?
- What services are provided at adult day care centers?
- What is congregate housing?
- What services are provided at assisted living facilities?

5.3 Living in Nursing Homes

- How many older adults live in long-term care facilities at any given time?
- What types of nursing homes are there?
- Who is most likely to live in a nursing home? Why?
- How have the characteristics of nursing homes been studied?
- Why do special care units often reflect better placement for people with significant physical or cognitive impairment?
- How does a resident of a nursing home come to view it as a home?
- What are the characteristics of inappropriate speech aimed at older adults? What is an alternative approach?
- How does the Patient Self-Determination Act relate to residents' decision-making capacity?
- What do the Eden Alternative, the Green House concept, and the Pioneer Network have in common?

INTEGRATING CONCEPTS IN DEVELOPMENT

- What do the demographics about the aging of the population imply about the need for long-term care through the first few decades of the 21st century?
- How do the theories of person–environment interaction include the basic developmental forces?
- How might a better financing arrangement for alternative living environments be designed?

KEY TERMS

adaptation level In Lawton and Nahemow's model, the point at which competence and environmental press are in balance.

adult day care Designed to provide support, companionship, and certain services during the day.

assisted living facilities Housing options for older adults that provide a supportive living arrangement for people who need assistance with personal care (such as bathing or taking medications) but are not so impaired physically or cognitively they need 24-hour care.

competence In the Lawton and Nahemow model, the theoretical upper limit of a person's ability to function.

corrective adaptations Actions taken in response to stressors and can be facilitated by internal and external resources.

docility When people allow the situation to dictate the options they have and exert little control.

ecology of aging Also called environmental psychology, a field of study that seeks to understand the dynamic relations between older adults and the environments they inhabit.

environmental press In the Lawton and Nahemow model, the demands put on a person by the environment.

everyday competence A person's potential ability to perform a wide range of activities considered essential for independent living.

infantilization or elderspeak Also called secondary baby talk, a type of speech that involves the unwarranted use of a person's first name, terms of endearment, simplified expressions, short imperatives, an assumption that the recipient has no memory, and cajoling as a means of demanding compliance.

patronizing speech Inappropriate speech to older adults based on stereotypes of incompetence and dependence.

person–environment interactions The interface between people and the world they live in that forms the basis for development, meaning behavior is a function of both the person and the environment.

preventive adaptations Actions that avoid stressors and increase or build social resources.

proactivity When people choose new behaviors to meet new desires or needs and exert control over their lives.

zone of maximum comfort In competence–environmental press theory, the area where slight decreases in environmental press occur.

zone of maximum performance potential In competence–environmental press theory, the area where increases in press tend to improve performance.

RESOURCES

CHAPTER 6

ATTENTION AND MEMORY

IF YOU ARE LIKE MOST PEOPLE, YOU PROBABLY HAVE TROUBLE REMEMBERING THE NAMES OF EVERY PERSON YOU MEET. Not Harry

Lorayne (born 1926). Harry was able to meet as many as 1500 people for the first time, hear their name once, and remember each one perfectly. The book *Ageless Memory* (2008) is the culmination of his more than 40-year career training people how to remember information and dazzling audiences with his own abilities. Thousands of people bought his books and videos and attended his programs.

Why did Lorayne have such an impact? As we shall see, how well we remember things takes on considerable importance in our lives. Memory is such a pervasive aspect of our daily lives and reflects a cognitive ability that is quite public; we use it as a measure for whether our "minds" are still intact. From remembering where we put our keys, cooking our favorite food, and taking our medications, we rely on memory to get us through our day. Most important, we use memory to construct our personal biography; our story gives us a sense of identity. Imagine how frightening it would be to wake up and have no memory what-soever—no recollection of your name, address, parents, or anything else.

Harry Lorayne

Perhaps that is why we put so much value on maintaining a good memory in old age and why memory training, as espoused by Lorayne, is so important. Older adults are stereotyped as people whose memory is on the decline, people for whom forgetting is not to be taken lightly. Many people think forgetting to buy a loaf of bread when they are 25 is all right, but forgetting it when they are 65 is cause for concern ("Do I have Alzheimer's disease?"). We will see that forgetting is part of daily life, and the belief it only happens in late life is wrong. In fact, older adults are quite adept at using strategies in their everyday life contexts to remember what they need to know.

In this chapter, we focus on both attention and memory, since they go hand in hand. We examine how people process information from the world around them and make sense out of it. We then discover cognition is a highly dynamic thing; lower-order processes such as attention create and influence higher-order thought, and higher-order thought determines where we focus our attention. People need to notice things in order to build knowledge and remember, because what we already know shapes what we notice. Thus, current research emphasizes changes in the different qualitative ways we process information and the quantitative differences in the amount of processing that occurs as we grow older. This research proves the traditional stereotype about memory and aging is wrong.

An important aspect of this research is whether or not we observe age-related decline in cognitive processes such as memory and attention and depends on the type of task being administered or the context wherein the memory operates. Some tasks, such as memorizing long lists of unrelated words, show large declines in performance with age, whereas others, such as remembering emotionally charged or personally relevant information, show no decline, and at times, improvement with age.

These task-related differences bring us back to the life-span perspective. A key issue is the extent research on attention and memory reflects the everyday cognitive functioning of older adults. In other words, what are the practical implications of age-related changes in cognitive functioning in specific situations?

We use memory not only as an end, when the goal is what and how much we remember, but also as a means to an end. For example, we use memory as an end when we summarize the most recent episode of our favorite television show, tell other people about ourselves, or remember to make specific points in a discussion. In these situations we use memory, but the point is not just what or how much we remember. In these and many other situations, memory is also a means to facilitate social exchange, allow other people to get to know us, or give ourselves a shared past with others. We return to this idea when we examine cognition in context later in the chapter.

Throughout this chapter, we consider results from experiments with responses made by people using computers. Although there is substantial evidence for age differences in some of the ways young and older adults process information, part of the difference may be due to cohort effects (see Chapter 1). Specifically, older adults in general are much less used to working on computers than younger adults, making the task less familiar to older adults. Consequently, they may not perform up to their maximum. Whether this experiential difference accounts for part of the age differences researchers uncovered remains to be seen; however, given the research is cross-sectional, meaning that age and cohort effects are confounded (see Chapter 1), this explanation remains a possibility.

6.1 Information Processing and Attention

LEARNING OBJECTIVES

- What are the primary aspects of the information-processing model?
- What are the basic components of attention?
- How does speed of processing relate to cognitive aging?
- What types of processing resources relate to attention and memory?
- What is automatic and effortful processing?

Trey strolled into a car dealership and convinced the salesperson to let him take one of the sports cars on the lot for a spin around the block. When he climbed behind the wheel, his excitement almost got the better of him. As he started the engine and eased into first gear, he became filled with utter terror. He suddenly realized he must pay complete attention to what he was doing. Why? The car had—a clutch. He had never driven a manual transmission before. Now he was faced with the need to filter out everything—people's conversations, the radio, and the sound of the wind whipping through his hair.

How can Trey filter everything out? More importantly, what abilities can he use to pay attention? If something happened on the road, how quickly could he respond? Would these abilities be any different in a younger adult than in an older adult? Have you ever had this experience? If so, how did you access this knowledge?

How do we learn, remember, and think about things? Psychologists do not know for sure. About the best they can do is create models or analogues of how they believe our cognitive processes work. In this section, we consider the most popular model: the information-processing model.

Information-Processing Model

The **information-processing model** *uses a computer metaphor to explain how people process stimuli.* As with a computer, information enters the system (people's brains) and is transformed, coded, and stored in various ways. Information enters storage temporarily, as in a computer's buffer, until it becomes stored more permanently, as on a computer storage device (USB, hard drive, cloud storage, etc.). At a later time, information can be retrieved in response to some cue, such as a command to open a file. Let's see how this works more formally.

The information-processing model is based on three long-held assumptions (Neisser, 1976): (1) People are active participants in the process; (2) both quantitative (how much information is remembered) and qualitative (what kinds of information are remembered) aspects of performance can be examined; and (3) information is processed through a series of processes. First, incoming information is transformed based on what a person already knows about it. The more one knows, the more easily the information is incorporated. Second, researchers look for age differences in both how much information is processed and what types of information are remembered best under various conditions. Third, researchers in adult development and aging focus on several specific aspects of information processing: early aspects, including a brief sensory memory and attention; and active processing that transfers information into a longer term store (e.g., long-term memory).

Using the information-processing model poses three fundamental questions for adult development and aging: (1) What areas of information processing show evidence of age differences (e.g., early stages of processing such as attention, working memory, long-term memory)? (2) How can we explain variability when we find age differences in information processing? (3) What are the practical implications of age-related changes in information processing?

Sensory Memory. All memories start as sensory stimuli—a song heard, a person seen, a hand felt. We need to experience these things for only a small fraction of a second in order to process the information. This ability is due to the earliest step in information processing, sensory memory, where new, incoming information is first registered. Sensory memory *is a brief and almost identical representation of the stimuli that exists in the observable environment.* Sensory memory takes in large amounts of information rapidly. It does not appear to have the limits other processes do when attentional focus is applied. This type of memory is as if the representation exists in your mind in the absence of the stimuli itself.

However, unless we pay attention to sensory information, the representation will be lost quickly. Try drawing either side of a U.S. penny in detail. (Those who are not from the United States can try drawing a common coin in their own country.) Most of us find this task difficult despite seeing the coins every day. Much detailed information about pennies has passed through our sensory memory repeatedly, but because we failed to pay attention, it was never processed to a longer lasting store. Age differences are not typically found in sensory memory (Nyberg, Lövdén, Riklund, Lindenberger, & Bäckman, 2012).

Attention: The Basics

Each of us have experienced being in a situation when our thoughts drift off and someone snaps at us, "Pay attention to me." We come back into focus, and realize we had not been paying attention.

But what exactly does it mean to "pay attention?" One way to look at it is to think of attention from a functional perspective (McDowd & Shaw, 2000). From the functual perspective, attention is composed of separate dimensions serving different functions. The complex tasks we engage in when processing information usually require more than one attentional function. In Trey's case, he must selectively attend to or focus on the clutch, shifting gears, the road and its obstacles, and at the same time filter out distracting information. This kind of changing focus is how we control attention. In addition, attentional processes are influenced by the capacity to sustain attention, as well as the speed that information is processed.

Attentional control is linked to the processes in the parieto-frontal lobes discussed in Chapter 2 (Ptak, 2012). As we know, the parieto-frontal integration processes undergo significant change with age. Not surprisingly, then, age differences emerge in various aspects of attention. Let's consider these in more detail.

Speed of Processing

Imagine you are sitting quietly watching a video on your iPad. Suddenly, the fire alarm goes off. How quickly can you respond?

That quick response refers to a notion in cognitive psychology known as speed of processing. Speed of processing *is how quickly and efficiently the early steps in information processing are completed.*

At one time, researchers believed decline in speed of processing explained age-related changes in cognitive functioning (e.g., Salthouse, 1996). This theory generally fell out of favor because research shows

As adults grow older, how quickly and efficiently information processing occurs slows down.

whether or not you observe slowing depends on what the task is because all components of mental processing do not slow equivalently.

Evidence including neuroimaging studies indicates age-related slowing depends on what adults are being asked to do (e.g., choosing which response to make; Dirk & Schmiedek, 2012; Grady, 2012; Nyberg et al., 2012). Interestingly, the amount of beta-amyloid protein found in the central nervous system, a biomarker linked with the possible subsequent development of dementia (see Chapter 2), has been shown to be related to the degree processing speed slows (Rodrigue, Kennedy, Devous, Rieck, Hebrank, Diaz-Arrastia et al., 2012).

Processing Resources

Many theorists and researchers believe with increasing age comes a decline in the amount of cognitive "energy" one deploys on a task. This idea is described in terms of processing resources. **Processing resources** *refers to the amount of attention one has to apply to a particular situation.*

The idea of a decline in general processing resources is appealing because it would account for poorer performance not only on attention but also on a host of other areas (Dirk & Schmiedek, 2012). However there is a nagging problem about the processing resource construct: At this general level it has never been clearly defined and is too broad. Two more precise approaches to processing resources are inhibitory loss and attentional resources.

Inhibitory Loss. One popular hypothesis is older adults have reduced processing resources because they have difficulty inhibiting the processing of irrelevant information (Aslan & Bäuml, 2012). Evidence indicates the oldest-old (people aged 85 or older) have more task-irrelevant thoughts during processing and have trouble keeping them out of their minds. This difference could explain why they tend to have trouble with changing and dividing their attention.

The inhibition idea has considerable support (Kimbler, Margrett, & Johnson, 2012). Not only do older adults have difficulty inhibiting irrelevant information in laboratory tasks, it matters with respect to everyday problem-solving. Kimbler and colleagues (2012) showed emotionally supportive messages reduce distracting thoughts and improve performance on everyday tasks for middle-aged and older adults.

There are simple strategies to compensate for older adults' difficulties with inhibiting irrelevant information. For example, simply asking older adults to close their eyes or avert their gaze away from irrelevant information improves performance. Using this strategy, older adults were just as good as young adults in attending to auditory stimuli (Einstein, Earles, & Collins, 2002).

Finally, researchers are asking whether there is a beneficial effect for the lack of inhibition of information under the right circumstances. It turns out there is. When information that was initially distracting but later became relevant, older adults performed better than young adults (Kim, Hasher, & Zacks, 2007; Thomas & Hasher, 2012). In such cases, the inability to inhibit distracting information turned into an advantage as the nature of relevant information changed.

Once again, we embrace a life-span perspective: adult developmental changes in cognitive functioning are characterized by both gains and losses. It is important to consider inhibitory loss in both ways. Under certain conditions it can be a hindrance, and in others it can be helpful. It all depends on the situation (Healey, Campbell, & Hasher, 2008; Thomas & Hasher, 2012).

Attentional Resources. Another way of looking at processing resource issues is through the lens of attention. In particular, a key issue is how well adults can perform more than one task at a time. Such multitasking requires us to spread our attention across all the tasks. **Divided attention** *concerns how well people perform multiple tasks simultaneously.* Driving a car is a classic divided attention task—you pay attention to other cars, the gauges in your car, pedestrians along the side of the street, and perhaps your passengers as you have a conversation with them.

Although it is widely believed older adults have more trouble than younger adults at dividing attention, it turns out the age differences observed are due to older adults' difficulties with the individual tasks and not to spreading their attention across them per se (Rizzuto, Cherry, & LeDoux, 2012). Observations in the workplace show older workers are just as able to multitask, but perform each task a bit more slowly than younger workers. However, when the tasks become complex, older adults encounter difficulties dividing their attention and their performance suffers as a result.

Age differences on divided-attention tasks can be minimized if older adults are given training, thereby reducing the demands on attention. Such training can even be through online computer games (van Muijden, Band, & Hommel, 2012). These results imply that older adults may be able to learn through experience how to divide their attention effectively between tasks. Check out this idea by completing the Discovering Development feature.

DISCOVERING DEVELOPMENT:

HOW GOOD ARE YOUR NOTES?

Divided attention tasks are encountered all the time. You are familiar with one of them—taking notes while listening to a lecture (either on video or live). An interesting developmental question is whether the quality of the notes differs with age. One way to find out informally is to compare the notes taken in the same class by younger and older students. If there are no older adults in your class, there may be some in other courses. Ask them if you can compare their notes with those of someone younger. What predictions would you make based on the research evidence you have read thus far? What role would practice play in these differences? Whose notes are actually better? Why do you think this is?

So, you may ask, when do older adults have difficulty performing multiple tasks simultaneously? You may have observed older adults having difficulty trying to remember something as they are walking down a staircase, or trying to simply walk and talk at the same time. Li and colleagues (Li et al., 2001) found older adults prioritize walking and maintaining balance at the expense of memory. In other words, older adults focused on the task most important to them; walking and balancing to prevent falls. Younger adults, on the other hand, optimized their memory performance and ignored walking and balancing. Older adults and children perform more poorly than younger adults when executing a memory task while walking (Krampe, Schaefer, Lindenberger, & Baltes, 2011).

Automatic and Effortful Processing

There are two other constructs that round out our understanding of attention and cognitive processing: automatic and effortful processing. **Automatic processing** *places minimal demands on attentional capacity and gets information into the system largely without us being aware of it.* Some automatic processes appear to be "prewired" in the sense they require no attentional capacity and do not benefit from practice; others are learned through experience and practice (Apperly, 2012). For example, those who have been driving a car for many years stop at a stop sign without really thinking about it. We will see that performance on tasks that depend on automatic processes do not demonstrate significant age differences.

In contrast, **effortful processing** *requires all of the available attentional capacity.* Most of the tasks involving deliberate memory, such as learning the words on a list, require effortful processing. In these cases, we are typically aware of what we are doing. When we first learn how to drive a car with a clutch, we are aware of the information we process (e.g., how much to let up on the clutch versus how hard to press the accelerator pedal). It is with effortful processing that age differences tend to emerge.

Finally, when considering attentional resources, it is extremely important to ask the question: Is attention a fixed capacity that decreases with age? Researchers observed decline in older adults' performance on laboratory tasks assessing memory. However, a different picture may emerge when we consider the functional capacity or resources necessary in specific task contexts can be modified depending on the relevance, accessibility of knowledge, and expertise related to the cognitive processes required (Hertzog, 2008). Under conditions where the task requirement is to simply have a familiarity with the information, there are no age differences. However, when there is effort and deliberate processing involved to remember the information, age differences emerge. Because age differences are sensitive to the conditions under which they are measured, the key question for researchers today is: When and under what circumstances will we observe age-related change in cognitive functioning, and when is that change problematic?

If you are an employee at an Apple store who shows people how to use the new device they bought, what principles would you apply from this section when instructing older adults?

6.2 Memory Processes

LEARNING OBJECTIVES

- What is working memory? What age differences have been found in working memory?
- How does implicit memory and explicit memory differ across age?
- Within long-term memory, how does episodic and semantic memory performance differ across age?
- What age differences have been found in encoding versus retrieval?

Susan is a 75-year-old widow who feels she does not remember recent events, such as if she took her medicine, as well as she used to. She also occasionally forgets to turn off the gas on her stove and sometimes does not recognize her friend's voice on the phone. However, she has no trouble remembering things from her 20s. Susan wonders if this is normal or if she should be worried.

Memory researchers have long focused on three general steps in memory processing as potential sources of age differences: encoding, storage, and retrieval (Weisberg & Reeves, 2013). Encoding *is the process of getting information into the memory system.* Storage *involves the manner in which information is represented and kept in memory. Getting information back out of memory is termed* retrieval. Because there is no evidence for age differences in how information is organized in storage, most research has examined encoding and retrieval as sources of age differences (Naveh-Benjamin & Ohta, 2012).

Working Memory

Think about a time when you asked a friend for their mobile phone number so you could send them text messages. You don't have a pen and paper, and you don't have an app like Bump on your phone to help. So you work to keep the phone number in your mind until you can type it in.

To successfully complete the task, you have to use your working memory. Working memory *is the active processes and structures involved in holding information in mind and simultaneously using that information, sometimes in conjunction with incoming information, to solve a problem, make a decision, or learn new information.*

Researchers typically consider working memory an umbrella term for many similar short-term holding and computational processes relating to a wide range of cognitive skills and knowledge domains (Baddeley, 2012). This places working memory right in the thick of things—it plays an active, critical, and central role in encoding, storage, and retrieval.

Recall that sensory memory has a large capacity to deal with incoming information. In contrast, researchers generally agree working memory has a relatively small capacity. This capacity limitation of working memory operates like a juggler who can only keep a small number of items in the air simultaneously.

Because working memory deals with information being processed right at this moment, it also acts as a kind of mental scratchpad. This means unless we take direct action to keep the information active, the page we are using will be used up quickly and tossed away. For this reason, we need to have some way to keep information in working memory. That process is known as rehearsal. Rehearsal *is the process that information is held in working memory, either by repeating items over and over or by making meaningful connections between the information in working memory and information already known.*

Most evidence indicates there is significant age-related decline in working memory (McCabe & Loaiza, 2012), although the extent of the decline is still in doubt. These data are important because working memory is the key to understanding age differences in memory. The loss of some of the ability to hold items in working memory may limit older adults' overall cognitive functioning. If information becomes degraded or is only partially integrated into one's knowledge base due to problems in working memory, it will be difficult to remember it.

However, some evidence suggests age differences in working memory are not universal. Working memory appears to depend on the type of information being used and may vary across different tasks (McCabe & Loaiza, 2012). For example, age-related decline in spatial working memory tends to be greater than that in verbal working memory, although there is decline in both types of working memory (Oosterman, Morel, Meijer, Buvens, Kessels, & Postma, 2011).

Why does working memory ability decline with age? There are several reasons, including alertness at different times of the day, order of the tasks, and task interference (Rowe, 2011). Another idea is older adults have more trouble juggling all of the elements once they are accessed (McCabe & Loaiza, 2012).

Although the evidence for age-related decline in working memory is not entirely clear, there is compelling evidence for how age differences in working memory relate to performance on more complex cognitive tasks. For example, researchers have begun to show working memory may be key to understanding the age differences in recall performance (McCabe & Loaiza, 2012).

Implicit versus Explicit Memory

In addition to working memory, we can further divide memory systems into two other types: implicit memory and explicit memory. **Implicit memory** *(sometimes called procedural memory) involves retrieval of information without conscious or intentional recollection.* **Explicit memory** *(sometimes called declarative memory), is intentional and conscious remembering of information learned and remembered at a specific point in time.*

Implicit memory is much like getting into a routine—we do things from memory but we do not have to think about them. The exact way we brush our teeth tends not to be something we consciously think about at the time. We just remember how to do it. Whether age differences in implicit memory are observed depend on the specific kind of implicit memory task in question (Howard & Howard, 2012). Learning sequences tend to show age differences, whereas learning spatial context does not. Interestingly, neuroscience imaging research shows the kind of over-activity in the frontal cortex in older adults that is typical in situations when older adults are compensating for declines (see Chapter 2 for more details).

By far, most research on memory aging focuses on explicit memory. In general, performance on explicit memory tasks declines with age, although there are many exceptions and qualifications to this conclusion (Light, 2012). This research typically concerns our next topic, long-term memory.

Long-Term Memory

When most people think about memory, they think about having to remember something over time, whether a few minutes or many days. Everyday life is full of examples—remembering routines, performing on an exam, summarizing a book or movie, and remembering an appointment. These types of situations constitute what memory researchers call long-term memory (Rutherford, Markopoulos, Bruno, & Brady-Van den Bos, 2012). **Long-term memory** *refers to the ability to remember rather extensive amounts of information from a few seconds to a few hours to decades.*

Memory researchers have created a wide variety of tasks requiring individuals to remember all sorts of information for varying lengths of time. Well over a century of research indicates long-term memory represents a relatively large-capacity store where information can be kept for long periods. Mounting evidence in cognitive neuroscience suggests long-term memory is not a unitary construct, but consists of distinct, functionally different multiple systems and are served by different brain structures (see Chapter 2).

As we delve into the various aspects of long-term memory, let us focus first on the more deliberate and effortful systems of explicit long-term memory. Two important types of long-term memory are semantic and episodic memory. **Semantic memory** *concerns learning and remembering the meaning of words and concepts not tied to specific occurrences of events in time.* Examples of semantic memory include knowing the definitions of words in order to complete crossword puzzles, being able to translate this paragraph from English into French, and understanding what the instructor is saying in a lecture.

Episodic memory *is the general class of memory having to do with the conscious recollection of information from a specific event or point in time.* Examples of episodic memory include learning the material in this course so you will be able to reproduce it on an examination in the future, remembering what you did on your summer vacation last year, and memorizing a speech for a play.

Like implicit versus explicit memory, episodic and semantic memory appear to be impacted differently by aging (Rönnlund, Nyberg, Bäckman, & Nilsson, 2005; Spaniol & Voss, 2006). Episodic memory stays fairly stable until around 55–60 years of age and then shows a precipitous decline beginning around age 65. In contrast, semantic memory increases from 35–55 years of age and then levels off. Although semantic memory starts to decline at age 65, the decline is much less substantial than for episodic memory (Rönnlund et al., 2005).

Semantic Memory. As indicated previously, semantic memory is relatively spared in normal aging. Evidence suggests there are no deficits in semantic memory processes such as language comprehension, the structure of knowledge, and the activation of general knowledge (Grady, 2012; Nyberg et al., 2012). Semantic memory retrieval typically does not tax working memory, and thus older adults can draw upon experience in word meanings and/or general world knowledge. In addition, whereas retrieval of episodic memories is based on cues to the original experience, semantic memories are retrieved conceptually as part of our world knowledge. This connection between semantic memory and world knowledge will come up again in Chapter 7 when we consider certain types of intelligence show little, if any, decline with age.

However, research also shows age changes in semantic memory can happen if it becomes hard to access and retrieve. One reason for access problems is if the knowledge in semantic memory is not used on a regular basis (Hertzog et al., 2003). You may have experienced this already, if you learned another language in childhood, but now have trouble with it if you didn't use it.

A second reason is simple momentary retrieval failure for information that is otherwise accessible. A common example is when adults have a "tip-of-the-tongue" experience (Brown, 2012). A tip-of-the-tongue (TOT) experience is when you try to retrieve a name or word you are certain you know, but it is not quite accessible at the moment. Imagine you are at a party and see someone familiar; you "know" that person's name, but you simply cannot retrieve it. Another aspect of this TOT experience is you can retrieve partial information such as the number of syllables in that person's name, the initial sounds or letters.

Older adults not only experience more TOT's, but also report less partial information about the target, both in the laboratory and in everyday life (Facal, Juncos-Rabadán, Rodriguez, & Pereiro, 2012). Such TOT problems indicate even highly familiar information can become more difficult to retrieve as we grow older.

Episodic Memory. Because episodic memory includes so many of the day-to-day activities adults perform, it has been the focus of more research than any other single topic in memory development (Light, 2012; Morcom & Friston, 2012). Typically, researchers study episodic memory by having people learn information, such as a list of words, and then asking them to recall or recognize the items. In a **recall** test, *people are asked to remember information without hints or cues.* Everyday examples of recall include telling everything you can remember about a movie or taking an essay exam with no notes or access to materials. **Recognition,** on the other hand, *involves selecting previously learned information from among several items.* Everyday examples of recognition include taking multiple-choice tests and picking out the names of your high school friends from a complete list of your classmates.

Many factors influence adults' performance on episodic memory tests, and whether age differences are found. Consider how the information to be learned is presented (organized with cues may be better than randomly), how fast it is presented (slower may be better), how familiar people are with the material (familiar may be better), and how the test is given (recognition is usually better) all make a difference.

The results from hundreds of studies point to several conclusions. Overall, older adults perform worse than younger adults on recall tests of episodic memory because they omit more information, include more intrusions, and repeat more previously recalled items (Light, 2012; Morcom & Friston, 2012).

On recognition tests, differences between older and younger adults are reduced. However, in comparison with young adults, older adults are more likely to say they recognize items that were never-presented, especially if they share a conceptual meaning or perceptual resemblance to the items actually presented (Light, 2012).

One thing that helps people remember information in episodic memory tests is using internal study strategies, such as rehearsal or organizing information into categories. Older adults tend to be less efficient at spontaneously using these strategies. But they can and do use them when instructed to do so, and show significant improvement in performance. However, these improvements are not sufficient, in general, to eliminate age differences in recall, indicating age differences in recall of episodic information is caused more by retrieval problems than poor encoding during study (Hertzog, Fulton, Mandviwala, & Dunlosky, 2013).

Age differences between older and younger adults can be reduced (but not eliminated) in several other ways: allowing older adults to practice or perform a similar task before learning a new list; using material more familiar to older adults; and using compensatory strategies to help themselves remember (we will examine this later in the chapter).

Although it would be easy to conclude episodic memory does nothing but decline with age, that would be wrong. It turns out there is one episodic memory process relatively spared with age: autobiographical memory, that we will consider a bit later.

Age Differences in Encoding versus Retrieval

As we saw earlier, encoding is the process of getting information into memory, and retrieval is the process of getting that information out. What key changes occur in these processes with age?

Encoding. Results from years of research suggest an age-related decrement in encoding processes (Craik & Rose, 2012). The most important reason for these changes is adults' spontaneous use of strategies during the learning of new information declines with age. *A strategy is anything people do to make the task easier and increase the efficiency of encoding or retrieval.*

Compared to younger adults, older adults tend not to behave as strategically when studying information to be remembered (Dunlosky, Bailey, & Hertzog, 2011). However, when instructed or taught to do so, older adults can use encoding strategies well. So, the age changes observed reflect more a decrease in the degree the strategies are used spontaneously, rather than a decrease in the ability to use strategies.

Certainly, if information does not get encoded well, it is less likely to be there or to be as accessible for remembering later. So, at least part of the reason older adults perform more poorly than younger adults on tests of memory recall is because of poorer encoding.

Retrieval. We have already seen one of the most supported research findings is older adults do more poorly than younger adults at recalling information. Besides potential encoding difficulties, what else might account for this difference?

Research evidence clearly points to the fact older adults tend to spontaneously use fewer retrieval strategies (Hertzog et al., 2013; Light, 2012). Moreover, even when encoding strategies are provided, and the opportunity to apply them during recall is allowed, older adults still do worse.

Based on extensive research evidence, researchers generally concluded most of the reason memory performance declines with age has to do with retrieval problems (e.g., Hertzog et al., 2013).

Neuroscience Evidence. Cognitive neuroscience (discussed in Chapter 2) presents evidence suggesting age differences in encoding and retrieval. Neuroimaging studies indicate during encoding, older adults' prefrontal cortex shows over-activity, indicating the usual pattern of compensatory processes with age (see Chapter 2 for more details) (Kalpouzos & Nyberg, 2012; Kalpouzos, Persson, & Nyberg, 2012).

In terms of retrieval, neuroimaging studies show age-related differences in how the prefrontal cortex and hippocampus work together (Giovanello & Schacter, 2012). In younger adults, activity in these areas depends on the extent the retrieval task requires relations to be made between the information being remembered, whereas activity in these regions in older adults stayed equivalent irrespective of relational processing. Other research indicates age-related compensatory brain activity for retrieval, similar to that seen in other cognitive processing (Oedekoven, Jansen, Kircher, & Leube, 2013). Specifically, younger adults have extensive neural network connections in the parietal and frontal regions involved in retrieval than older adults. However, older adults show higher levels of brain activity in these regions, indicating a likely compensatory strategy for less extensive networks.

Overall, these data support the view, described in Chapter 2, that older adults process information in their brains differently than younger adults. These differences in part represent attempts at working around, or compensating for, the normal age-related changes occurring in information processing.

In summation, the research on encoding and retrieval processes is important for two key reasons. First, it emphasizes age-related decrements in memory are complex; they are not due to changes in a single process. Second, memory intervention or training programs must consider both encoding and retrieval.

ADULT DEVELOPMENT IN ACTION

Suppose you are a geriatric physician. Based on what you learned in this section, what would be a good way to test for normative age-related changes in memory?

6.3 Memory in Context

LEARNING OBJECTIVES

- What age differences are there in prospective memory?
- How does autobiographical memory change across adulthood?
- How does source memory and processing of misinformation change across adulthood?
- What are some factors that preserve memory as we grow older?

Tyler, an elderly man of 80, has exercised his memory abilities since he reached his 60th birthday. He made sure to read voraciously, done crossword puzzles religiously, and kept up on current events. At a recent family gathering, it was quite evident such behavior paid off. In a game of trivial pursuit, he was the ultimate winner. However, when his grandson told him nonstop about a car he wanted to buy, Tyler later had trouble recalling all of the details.

As noted at the beginning of this chapter, memory is so integral to our everyday life we take it for granted. In the case of Tyler, using his memory of previously studied knowledge proved extremely important in participating in family games. However, he still had

trouble remembering the details of recently learned information. This difference in memory ability has been the focus of research on age differences and how memory operates in everyday life (Dismukes, 2012; Ossher, Flegal, & Lustig, 2013).

This research is extremely important for three reasons. First, it may shed some light that generalize findings based on laboratory tasks such as word-list recall. Second, new or alternative variables affecting performance could be uncovered, such as factors that enhance memory functioning in older adults could be identified. Third, research on everyday memory may force us to re-conceptualize memory itself.

Prospective Memory

One area receiving increasing attention is prospective memory. **Prospective memory** *involves remembering to remember something in the future, such as an action or event* (Dismukes, 2012). Everyday life is full of examples, such as remembering to pick up one's children after school and remembering you have a dinner date next Friday evening.

A theoretical model of how prospective memory works is shown in Figure 6.1 (Zogg, Woods, Sauceda, Wiebe, & Simoni, 2012). Note the process starts with the intention to remember something in the future, and depends critically on monitoring both event and time cues. This distinction, first introduced by Einstein and McDaniel (1990), is critical for understanding why people do and do not perform the actual task they are attempting to remember to do.

In event-based tasks, an action is to be performed when a certain external event happens, such as giving a certain person a message when they provide a secret word. A time-based task involves performing an action after a fixed amount of time, such as remembering an appointment at 1:00 pm.

Researchers found time-based tasks showed more age differences as long as people used self-generated strategies to remember, as these tend to decline with age; the cues that typically accompany event-based tasks helped reduce or eliminate age differences (Rummel, Hepp, Klein, & Silberleitner, 2012). Adults of all ages benefit from the use of reminders, but older adults especially benefit from clear prioritization of

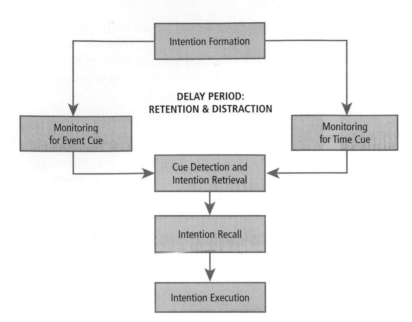

Figure 6.1

Conceptual model of the component processes of prospective memory.

Source: Zogg, J. B., Woods, S. P., Sauceda, J. A., Wiebe, J. S., & Simoni, J. M. (2012). The role of prospective memory in medication adherence: A review of an emerging literature. Journal of Behavioral Medicine, 35, 47–62. http://link .springer.com/article/10.1007/s10865-011-9341-9/fulltext .html#Sec1, Figure 1.

tasks (i.e., ranking tasks from most to least important) (Ihle, Schnitzspahn, Rendell, Luong, & Kliegel, 2012).

Of course, it's clearly important to remember things one is supposed to do in the future. But once all of those tasks are complete, it's equally important to remember *that fact*. Interestingly, little research has been done examining age differences in people's ability to remember all of the tasks they are supposed to complete have, in fact, been completed. One of these, showing important age differences, is described in the "How Do We Know?" feature.

HOW DO WE KNOW?:

FAILING TO REMEMBER I DID WHAT I WAS SUPPOSED TO DO

Who were the investigators, and what was the aim of the study? Most research on prospective memory focuses on whether people remember to *do* something in the future. Scullin, Bugg, and McDaniel (2012) realized it is also important for people to *stop* doing something once all of the tasks are done. They investigated whether there are age differences in people's ability to remember to stop doing an action when it is no longer necessary to do it.

How did the investigators measure the topic of interest? The study had two phases. In the first, younger and older adults were told to perform a task, that they subsequently did. In Phase 2, participants were told the task was finished, yet still received the cue to perform the task, and measured as to whether they still did it despite being told not to.

Who were the participants in the study? Younger adult university students (average age = 19 years) and community-dwelling older adults (average age = 75 years) participated.

What was the design of the study? The experiment was a 2 × 3 between-subjects design that included age group (younger or older) and condition (nonsalient-cue/task-match, salient-cue/task-match, or salient-cue/task-mismatch). The nonsalient-cue/task-match condition had a cue that did not signal the need to do the task. The salient-cue/task match had a cue that was the signal to perform the task. The salient-cue/task-mismatch had the cue that formerly signaled the need to do the task, but no longer indicated that. Participants were randomly assigned to the three conditions.

Were there ethical concerns with the study? There were no ethical concern because all of the participants were volunteers and had the experiment fully explained.

What were the results? In Phase 1, younger and older adults performed equivalently by correctly remembering to perform the task when cued. In Phase 2, though, older adults were more likely to continue attempting to perform the task when the cue occurred even though they had been told it was no longer necessary. Thus, older adults had more errors of commission.

What did the investigators conclude? Careful analyses of the results indicated older adults who made commission errors were less able to inhibit the task response than those who did not make commission errors. Inhibition is an important part of executive functioning, the higher level cognitive processes that control decision making (in this case the decision to complete the task). Additionally, older adults who made commission errors were more likely to get stuck making the task response in ways that implied they might have had trouble stopping even if they wanted to.

Autobiographical Memory. We noted earlier one main function of memory is to create one's sense of identity (Prebble, Addis, & Tippett, 2013). In other words, some of the information people learn and keep for a long time concerns information and events that happen to us. When we put all those incidents and information together, we create our autobiography. *Autobiographical memory involves remembering information and events from our own life.*

Testing autobiographical memory is tricky. To do it correctly requires having independent verification a remembered event actually happened in the way claimed. That's fine if there is a video of the event. But much of our lives are not on video making it difficult to validate event recall. Plus, just because a person doesn't remember something could be due to memory failure, certainly, or because they never learned it in the first place. Some ingenious researchers, though, managed to circumvent these problems and figured out how to study autobiographical memory.

Autobiographical memory is primarily a form of episodic memory, although it can also involve semantic memory. The episodic component of autobiographical memory is the recollection of temporal and spatial events from one's past (e.g., birthday parties, vacations, graduations). The semantic component consists of knowledge and facts of one's past (e.g., personal characteristics, knowledge that an event occurred) without having to remember exactly what or when things occurred.

Autobiographical memories change over time for all adults, with certain specific details (e.g., what objects are next to each other) being forgotten first, and other information (e.g., the main focus of the event) being remembered best (Talamini & Gorree, 2012). The number of autobiographical memories increases fastest during young adulthood (ages 18–25), especially those involving social interaction (Fuentes & Desrocher, 2012).

As you may have experienced, details for autobiographical events change over time. You might think details for events would get fuzzier or fewer over time. For many events, that's true. But, surprisingly, that's not what always happens.

How memory for details of autobiographical events changes over time can only be studied when an independent record exists, made at the time the events happened. Biological/medical data, such as height or age at menarche (when a girl first menstruates) provide such a source. In a classic study, Casey, Dwyer, Coleman, Krall, Gardner, & Valadian (1991) examined records available from the Harvard Longitudinal Studies of Child Health and Development on individuals from birth to age 50. Detailed information was collected over the years on such things as what childhood diseases the participants had, whether they smoked cigarettes, and what kinds and how much food they ate. At age 50, participants completed a lengthy questionnaire about these issues, and their responses were compared with similar reports made 10 and 20 years earlier, as well as with the official records. Casey and colleagues found half of the memories elicited at age 50 were more accurate than the memories for the same information elicited 10 years earlier at age 40. However, information about amounts of food consumed or individual episodes was not remembered well. Apparently, these events tend to get blended together and are not stored as separate incidents. Long-term accuracy for medical information has been validated by several other studies (e.g., Kyulo, Knutsen, Tonstad, Fraser, & Singh, 2012).

What distinguishes memorable events from those that aren't? What makes a moment we will remember the rest of our lives? Many people think highly traumatic or surprising and unexpected events are ones indelibly etched in our memories. Events such as September 11, 2001, or the unexpected death of a loved one are examples. *Researchers label memories for personally traumatic or unexpected events* **flashbulb memories.**

Flashbulb memories tend to feel real to people, who believe their recollections are highly accurate down to small details (Neisser, 2012). It turns out, though, when researchers compare what people claim they remember with independent records of actual events, the memories are often wrong. Many people feel absolutely certain they remember exact details of the events on September 11, 2001. President George Bush often related his detailed recollection of how and what he heard about the terrorist attacks. However, comparison with actual historical records indicate his memory was inaccurate in important ways concerning the details (Greenberg, 2004). Nevertheless, people tend to get the gist of the story correct, and highly emotional events do tend to be remembered better than unemotional ones (Neisser, 2012). The errors and influences on autobiographical memory help explain why eyewitness testimony is often unreliable (Roediger, Wixted, & DeSoto, 2012).

Given autobiographical memory is the basis for identity, what events do people remember and when did they occur across the life span? What Susan experienced in the vignette, and as can be seen in Figure 6.2, is typical. For both younger and older adults, when asked to remember life events, vivid memories experienced earlier in life (between 10 and 30 years of age) are reported more often than those occurring during middle adulthood (between 30 and 50 years of age; Fitzgerald, 1999; Willander & Larsson, 2006). Events form less-remembered periods can be recalled if given additional context (such as news headlines

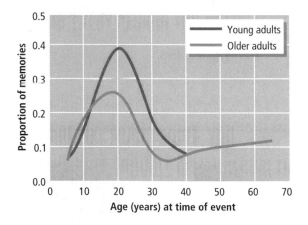

Figure 6.2

Both younger and older adults remember more life events from their teens and 20s than from any other period of life.

Source: Based on Fitzgerald, J. (1999). Autobiographical memory and social cognition. In T. M. Hess & F. Blanchard-Fields (Eds.), Social cognition and aging.

from specific years) (Mace & Clevinger, 2013). It may be this earlier period of life contains more key events important in creating one's personal history (Conway & Holmes, 2004; Pasupathi & Carstensen, 2003).

Source Memory and Processing of Misinformation

Why are some autobiographical memories that seem so vivid actually inaccurate at the detail level? Two main reasons have to do with how we remember the source of information and how susceptible we are to false information.

Source Memory. Think about a familiar event in your life. Now attempt to remember how you obtained your memory of it. Did you actually experience the event? Are you sure?

Source memory refers to the ability to remember the source of a familiar event as well as the ability to determine if an event was imagined or actually experienced. Remembering the source of information is important in many contexts. It is important for people to be able to discriminate whether they actually remembered to take medication or only thought to do it. The ability to discriminate between these two events requires one to retrieve information about the context in which the event in question originally occurred. By reconstructing the original event accurately, the adults will remember whether they actually took the medication or not.

Research on age differences in source memory reveals older adults are less accurate at a number of source-memory tasks (Dulas & Duarte, 2012; Spaniol & Grady, 2012). The problem appears to be younger adults are better than older adults at connecting the item to be remembered with the context in which it is learned (Boywitt, Kuhlmann, & Meiser, 2012). A large cross-sectional study of source memory with adults between 21 and 80 years revealed a linear decrease in performance, implying the decrements in performance happen gradually across the adult life span (Cansino, Estrada-Manilla, Hernández-Ramos, Martinez-Galindo, Torres-Trejo, Gómez-Fernández et al., 2013). The main exception to these age differences is when the source memory information is emotional; in some cases both younger and older adults show identical patterns of performance, perhaps because emotional information is processed differently than the information in pure memory tasks (Nashiro, Sakaki, Huffman, & Mather, 2013).

Benjamin (2010) proposed older adults have a global deficit in memory causing problems in source memory and the inability to exclude irrelevant information. The Density of Representations Yields Age-related Deficits (DRYAD) model proposes older adults are presumed to have less valid representations of events and objects than are young adults. To date, research support has been obtained in some studies (Benjamin, Diaz, Matzen, & Johnson, 2012).

Neuroimaging research indicates older adults show over-activation of areas in the prefrontal cortex (Giovanello & Schacter, 2012; Spaniol & Grady, 2012), a pattern we saw in Chapter 2 reflecting compensatory behavior. Some research supports the notion the brain regions in which source memory is processed may even change with increasing age (Dulas & Duarte, 2012).

We can relate these findings to the role retrieval cues play in older adults' memory functioning. Old and Naveh-Benjamin (2008) suggest contextual details can serve as retrieval cues and without access to them older adults may have more difficulty in remembering events. Furthermore, episodic memory is more highly dependent upon contextual information that could explain why older adults have difficulties with that kind of task.

False Memory. At times in our lives, we may be repeatedly told stories about us by relatives or friends that we could not have personally experienced. However, if we hear them enough, we may start believing the events are real and falsely incorporate them into our autobiographical memory. False memory *is when one remembers items or events that did not occur.*

The focus in false memory research is on memory errors. One way to study false memory in the laboratory is to present participants with information (e.g., a list of related words, a video of an event) and test people's memory for both the information actually presented and information that was not (e.g., words related to those in the list but never studied, details that could plausibly have happened in the event but were not actually seen).

People tend to falsely recall and incorrectly recognize such plausible information and feel confident about it (Johnson, Raye, Mitchell, & Ankudowich, 2012). Important events may not be remembered at all, or may be remembered with the right kinds of cues. And, even highly emotional events can be accurate or highly inaccurate depending on the circumstances surrounding how they are remembered. Older adults tend to be more susceptible to these issues than younger adults (Benjamin, 2001; Jacoby & Rhodes, 2006; Karpel et al., 2001).

Once again, an explanation for this effect is older adults have more difficulty in correctly identifying information as false because they have trouble linking content information to its context, as noted earlier. Moreover, older adults have more difficulty separating misleading context from relevant context, that also explains why older adults are more susceptible to misleading information in general (Jacoby, Rogers, Bishara, & Shimizu, 2012).

Factors That Preserve Memory

As indicated by some of the results in everyday memory, older adults perform quite well at certain everyday memory tasks in certain situations. *These findings imply there may be specific factors that help preserve memory performance, termed* cognitive reserve. Let's investigate some of them.

Exercise. A major meta-analytic study showed conclusively physical fitness training improves cognitive performance in older adults regardless of the training method or the older adults' personal characteristics (Colcombe & Kramer, 2003). Neuroscience research also clearly demonstrates regular exercise has a wide range of effects on the brain, such as increased neural plasticity (i.e., flexibility and adaptability of brain functioning), and can be viewed as an intervention alternative for diseases such as Parkinson's, Alzheimer's, and stroke, and may prevent some of the normative decline typically associated with aging (Marques-Aleixo, Oliveira, Moreira, Magalhães, & Ascensão, 2012).

Multilingualism and Cognitive Functioning. In an intriguing study, Kavé, Eyal, Shorek, and Cohen-Mansfield (2008) explored whether the number of languages a person speaks positively influences the cognitive state of older adults. In fact, older adults from 75 to 95 years of age who spoke four languages or more showed the best cognitive state. Similarly, Bialystock,

Regular exercise has been shown to improve cognitive functioning in older adults.

© bikeriderlondon/Shutterstock.com

Craik, and Luk (2012) found bilingualism plays a large role in protecting older adults from cognitive decline. These findings suggest speaking multiple languages might be a protective factor for maintaining our cognitive state as we age.

Semantic Memory in Service of Episodic Memory. Given that semantic memory is relatively unimpaired as we grow older (as discussed earlier), it may have an enhancement effect on episodic memory for older adults. Several studies show older adults perform better when they can use previously learned semantic information to support episodic knowledge (Badham, Estes, & Maylor, 2012; Naveh-Benjamin, Craik, Guez, & Kreuger, 2005). The more associations are made, the stronger the effect and the more performance is improved.

Negative Stereotypes and Memory Performance. Older adults may not perform at optimal levels because they are aware of and threatened by the typical belief that aging hampers memory ability (Hess, Auman, Colcombe, & Rahhal, 2003). Specifically, negative or threatening stereotypes suppress older adults' controlled or conscious use of memory while increasing the likelihood they will use automatic response instead (Mazerolle, Régner, Morisset, Rigalleau, & Huguet, 2012). We will explore this psychosocial factor influencing cognition in Chapter 8.

ADULT DEVELOPMENT IN ACTION

How might autobiographical memory be used in therapeutic settings?

6.4 Self-Evaluations of Memory Abilities

LEARNING OBJECTIVES

- What are the major types of memory self-evaluations?
- What age differences have been found in metamemory and memory monitoring?

Eugene just reached his 70th birthday. However, he is greatly concerned. He believed since he was young this is the age when memory really goes downhill. He has a great fear of losing his memory completely. He asks people to repeat things to him over and over for fear he will forget them. This fear takes a toll on his self-concept. He doesn't feel he has control over his life the way he used to.

How good is your memory? Do you forget where you put your keys? Or are you like the proverbial elephant who never forgets anything? Like most people, you probably tend to be your own harshest critic when it comes to evaluating your memory performance. We analyze, scrutinize, nitpick, and castigate ourselves for the times we forget; we rarely praise ourselves for all the things we do remember, and continue to be on guard for more memory slips. The self-evaluations we make about memory may affect our daily life in ways traditionally were unrecognized. This is exactly what is happening to Eugene. His negative evaluations of his memory ability are creating much undue stress in his life.

The self-evaluations we make about memory are complex (Cavanaugh, 1996; Castel, McGillivray, &

Freidman, 2012). They are based not only on memory and performance per se but also on how we view ourselves in general, our theories about how memory works, what we remember from past evaluations, and our attributions and judgments of our effectiveness.

Aspects of Memory Self-Evaluations

Researchers of memory self-evaluation have focused primarily on two types of awareness about memory. *The first type involves knowledge about how memory works and what we believe to be true about it; this type of self-evaluation is referred to as* metamemory. For instance, we may know recall is typically harder than recognition memory strategies are often helpful, and working memory is not limitless. We may also believe memory declines with age, appointments are easier to remember than names, and anxiety impairs performance. Metamemory is most often assessed with questionnaires asking about these various facts and beliefs.

The second type of self-evaluation, called memory monitoring, *refers to the awareness of what we are doing with our memory right now.* We can be aware of the process of remembering in many ways. At times we know how we study, search for some particular fact, or keep track of time for an appointment. At other times we ask ourselves questions while doing a memory task. For example, when faced with having to remember an important appointment later in the day, we may consciously ask ourselves whether the steps we have taken (e.g., making a note in our smartphone) are sufficient.

Age Differences in Metamemory and Memory Monitoring

Researchers explored age differences in metamemory mainly by using questionnaires (see Castel et al., 2012; Tonković & Vranić, 2011). These questionnaires tap several dimensions of knowledge about memory and reflect the complexity memory itself. Older adults seem to know less than younger adults about the internal workings of memory and its capacity, view memory as less stable, expect memory will deteriorate with age, and perceive they have less direct control over memory (Blatt-Eisengart & Lachman, 2004; Hertzog & Dunlosky, 2011; Horhota, Lineweaver, Ositelu, Summers, & Hertzog, 2012). Do these beliefs affect how well people actually remember information? Does what you believe about yourself matter?

The Role of Memory Self-Efficacy. Belief in one's ability to accomplish things is an old, pervasive theme in literature, religion, psychotherapy, and many other diverse arenas (Berry, 1999; Cavanaugh & Green, 1990). One of the most beloved children's books is *The Little Engine that Could*. The train engine keeps telling itself, "I think I can. I think I can." and, of course, it performs successfully.

As it applies to memory, belief in oneself is referred to as memory self-efficacy; *it is the belief one will be able to perform a specific task.* This is an important construct in understanding how memory changes with age (Berry, West, & Cavanaugh, 2013). Memory self-efficacy is an important type of memory belief distinct from general knowledge about memory; one may know a great deal about how memory works but still believe one's ability to perform in a specific situation is poor.

Memory self-efficacy emerged as one of the key aspects of metamemory because of its importance in accounting for performance in several different types of situations, as well as helping to explain how people make performance predictions in the absence of direct experience with tasks (Berry et al., 2013). Overall, studies show older adults with lower memory self-efficacy perform worse on memory tasks. Yet older adults with low memory self-efficacy compensate for poor memory performance by using people for assistance and compensatory strategies to aid in their memory performance (de Frias et al., 2003; Lachman & Agrigoroaei, 2012).

Age Differences in Memory Monitoring. Memory monitoring involves knowing what you are doing with your memory right now. The ability to monitor one's memory does not appear to decline with age (Hertzog & Dunlosky, 2011). This is important, as memory monitoring may provide a basis for compensating for real age-related declines in episodic memory through the use of memory strategies. Older adults who are better at monitoring are more likely to use effective strategies (Hertzog, Price, & Dunlosky, 2012), and apply strategies learned in training to other, appropriate situations (Hertzog & Dunlosky, 2012).

Metamemory is important in understanding how people formulate predictions of how well they are likely to perform; monitoring and using data from one's performance may be more important for subsequent predictions on the same task. The good news is evidence suggests in older adulthood, the ability to monitor multiple aspects of memory functioning is relatively spared (Hertzog & Dunlosky, 2011).

ADULT DEVELOPMENT IN ACTION

How might you use self-evaluations of memory in your job as a director of a senior center?

6.5 Memory Training

LEARNING OBJECTIVES

- What are the major ways memory skills are trained? How effective are these methods?

After retirement, Alison and Charlie noticed they had trouble remembering things more than they used to. They worried that given their advanced age there was nothing they could do about it. However, one night they saw an advertisement on television suggesting we have control over our memory fitness. As fate would have it, the next day there was a flyer posted in their condominium recreation room for a memory training class to help older adults overcome memory failures. They immediately signed up.

Imagine you have problems remembering where you left your keys. Or suppose someone you love has gone through a comprehensive diagnostic process, and a memory problem was discovered. Can anything be done to help people remember? In most cases, the answer is yes. Fortunately for Alison and Charlie they learned of this. Researchers developed different types of memory training programs; many are effective for healthy older adults, even for persons with severe memory impairments (Gross, Parisi, Spira, Kueider, Ko, Saczynski et al., 2012; Hunter, Ward, & Camp, 2012). In this section we examine the attempts at remediating memory problems and the individual differences affecting the success of these programs.

Training Memory Skills

The notion memory can be improved through acquiring skills and practicing them is old, dating back to prehistory (Yates, 1966). For example, the story related in *The Iliad* was told for generations through the use of mnemonic strategies before it was finally written down. Self-help books teach readers how to improve their own memory have also been around for a long time (e.g., Grey, 1756). Interestingly, the old how-to books taught techniques virtually identical with those advocated in more contemporary books such as those generated by Harry Lorayne, who we encountered at the beginning of this chapter.

Training people how to remember information better, especially through the use of memory strategies, can be aimed at any adult. As you may have realized in our earlier discussion about memory strategies, most of the best strategies share several things in common. First, they require paying attention to the incoming information. Second, they rely on already-stored information to facilitate making new connections with the new material in semantic memory. Finally, in the process of encoding, strategies provide the basis for future retrieval cues. Additionally, putting training for memory strategies in the context of healthy life styles tends to enhance the positive outcomes (Miller, Siddarth, Gaines, Parrish, Ercoli, Marx et al., 2012).

Memory aids or strategies can be organized into meaningful groups. Among the most useful of these classifications is Camp and colleagues' (1993) E-I-E-I-O framework. The E-I-E-I-O framework combines two types of memory, explicit memory and implicit memory, with two types of memory aids; external aids and internal aids.

As discussed earlier, explicit memory involves the conscious and intentional recollection of information; remembering this definition on an exam is one example. Implicit memory involves effortless and unconscious recollection of information such as knowing stop signs are red octagons is usually not something people need to exert effort to remember when they see one on the road.

External aids *are memory aids that rely on environmental resources, such as notebooks or calendars.* **Internal aids** *are memory aids that rely on mental processes, such as imagery.* The Aha! or Oh! experience in the framework is the one that comes with suddenly remembering something. As you can see in Table 6.1, the E-I-E-I-O framework helps organize how different types of memory can be combined with different kinds of memory aids to provide a broad range of intervention options to help people remember.

Table 6.1

THE E-I-E-I-O MODEL OF MEMORY HELPS CATEGORIZE DIFFERENT TYPES OF MEMORY AIDS		
TYPE OF MEMORY	**TYPE OF MEMORY AID**	
	External	Internal
Explicit	Appointment book Grocery list	Mental imagery Rote rehearsal
Implicit	Color-coded maps Sandpaper letters	Spaced retrieval Conditioning

© 2015 Cengage Learning

Smartphones can serve as powerful external memory aids.

© StockLite/Shutterstock.com

We can use Camp and colleagues' approach to examine research on external and internal memory aids. In addition, we briefly review two alternatives, memory exercises and medications.

External Memory Aids. External memory aids are objects such as diaries, address books, calendars, notepads, microcomputers, and other devices commonly used to support memory in everyday situations like taking notes during a visit to the physician (McGuire, Morian, Codding, & Smyer, 2000; Watson & McKinstry, 2009). Some external aids involve actually using external device to store information (e.g., smartphones or paper calendars), whereas others involve the use of external aids to cue action (e.g., setting a book out by the door so you won't forget it).

In general, explicit-external interventions, especially those involving smartphones or other computer-based devices, are the most frequently used, because they are easy to use, widely available, and work well with adults affected by a wide variety of physical or mental disorders (Bäckman, 2012; Thompson, Koorenhof, & Kapur, 2012; Wallace & Morris, 2012). Many of the apps on a smartphone are aimed at relieving us of memory burden (e.g., contacts, calendars, maps). These explicit-external interventions have potential value for improving older adults' cognitive performance in real-world settings.

The problem of remembering one's complex medication schedule is best solved with an explicit-external intervention: a pillbox divided into compartments corresponding to days of the week and different times of the day. Research shows this type of pillbox is the easiest to load and results in the fewest errors, and works for people with mild cognitive impairment (Ownby, Hertzog, & Czaja, 2012). Memory interventions like this can help older adults maintain their independence. Nursing homes also use explicit-external interventions, such as bulletin boards with the date and weather conditions, to help residents keep in touch with current events.

Advocating the use of external aids in memory rehabilitation is becoming increasingly popular as well as extensively grounded in research. Camp, Zeisel, and Antenucci (2011) advocate external aids should be relied on alone or in combination with other techniques (e.g., Montessori methods) in working with Alzheimer's patients. Research also indicates for external cues to be most effective, they should (1) be given close to the time action is required, (2) be active rather than passive, (3) be specific to the particular action, (4) be portable, (5) fit a wide range of situations, (6) store many cues for long periods, (7) be easy to use, and (8) not require a pen or pencil.

External-implicit combinations, more widely used with children, nevertheless have applicability with older adults in some situations. Many nursing homes use different color schemes to designate different wings or sections of the building. Because people process the color-coded aspects of the building automatically, the implicit nature of this external cue makes it ideal for people who may otherwise have difficulty learning and remembering new information.

Internal Memory Aids. Looking at Camp and colleagues' examples of internal memory aids may trigger some personal experiences. Many people use rote rehearsal in preparing for an examination (e.g., repeating Camp—E-I-E-I-O over and over), or use mental imagery in remembering the location of their car in a parking lot (we're parked near the giraffe on the light post).

Most research on memory training discussed earlier concerns of improving people's use of these and other internal strategies that supply meaning and help organize incoming information. Classic examples of formal internal strategies include the method of loci (remembering items by mentally placing them in locations in a familiar environment), mental retracing (thinking about all the places you may have left your keys), turning letters into numbers, and forming acronyms out of initial letters (such as NASA from **N**ational **A**eronautic and **S**pace **A**dministration). Most memory improvement courses train people to become proficient at using one of these internal strategies.

Getting proficient at explicit internal memory strategies is hard work. As noted earlier, explicit strategies require effortful processing that is more taxing on older adults. Thus, explicit memory intervention would most likely work best with older adults who are least likely to suffer memory failures or for young adults. In fact, healthy older adults are less willing to use effortful internal strategies. In addition, older adults with dementia are unlikely to benefit from these types of strategies (Camp et al., 2011). Thus, Camp argues older adults would benefit more from preserved implicit memory abilities.

One implicit-internal memory aid proven quite powerful is based on a technique called spaced retrieval. Camp and colleagues (Camp, 2005; Hunter et al., 2012; Bourgeois et al., 2003) relate even people with Alzheimer's disease can learn new things with this technique. Spaced retrieval involves teaching persons with dementia or other serious cognitive impairment to remember new information by gradually increasing the time between retrieval attempts. This easy, almost magical technique has been used to teach names of staff members and other information, and it holds considerable potential for broad application. It is superior to other techniques (Haslam, Hodder, & Yates, 2011), and combining spaced retrieval with additional memory encoding aids helps even more (Kinsella et al., 2007).

Memory Drugs. Although considerable research has focused on the underlying neurological mechanisms in memory, little definitive information is available that can be easily translated into treatment approaches, though this is not for lack of trying. Many attempts at enhancing memory through the use of drugs that affect neurotransmitters have been made, but so far have produced only modest, short-term improvements with no long-term changes.

Most of the medications approved by the United States Food and Drug Administration work through neurotransmitters (see Chapter 2). Two groups of medications receiving most of the attention are cholinesterase inhibitors (e.g., Aricept, Exelon). Side effects include nausea, vomiting, and diarrhea. A second group of medications are memantine, target glutamate, another neurotransmitter. The most common side effect of this medication is dizziness. Unfortunately, neither class of medications works well, especially as dementia worsens.

Many medications have side effects that can cause memory problems. Although alcohol is one widely known drug having this outcome, many over-the-counter and prescription medications can create symptoms that mimic various types of memory problems, and can be quite severe if left unaddressed. Medications commonly used to lower cholesterol (statins) can cause memory problems such as forgetfulness. Clearly, if one is taking medications and experiencing memory difficulties, a thorough analysis of whether the medication is causing the side effect should be conducted.

ADULT DEVELOPMENT IN ACTION

As a nursing home administrator, how could you apply the principles of memory training to improve the quality of life of your residents?

6.6 Clinical Issues and Memory Testing

LEARNING OBJECTIVES

- What is the difference between normal and abnormal memory aging?
- What are the connections between memory and physical and mental health?
- How is memory affected by nutrition?

Latarra's children are concerned. Latarra is 80 and is becoming more and more forgetful. With the scare of Alzheimer's disease so salient in our society, they are concerned their mother is its next victim. What should they do? A friend tells them memory decline is normal with aging. But to ease their concerns they make an appointment for a clinical screening for their mother. This could reassure them it is only normal aging causing her forgetfulness, and not Alzheimer's disease.

To this point we have been trying to understand the changes that occur in normal memory with aging. But what about situations where people have serious memory problems that interfere with their daily lives? How do we tell the difference between normal and abnormal memory changes? These are two of the issues clinicians face. Latarra's children face this critical issue. Like Latarra's children, clinicians are often confronted with relatives of clients who complain of serious memory difficulties. Clinicians must differentiate the individuals who have no real reason to be concerned from those with some sort of disease. What criteria should be used to make this distinction? What diagnostic tests would be appropriate to evaluate adults of various ages?

Unfortunately, there are no easy answers to these questions. First, as we have seen, the exact nature of normative changes in memory with aging is not yet understood completely. This means we have few standards to compare for people who may have problems. Second, there are few comprehensive batteries of memory tests specifically designed to tap a wide variety of memory functions (Mayes, 1995). Too often clinicians are left with hit-or-miss approaches and have little choice but to piece together their own assessment battery (Edelstein & Kalish, 1999).

Fortunately, the situation is changing. Since the mid-1980s researchers and clinicians began to work closely to devise better assessments (Mayes, 1995). This collaboration is producing results to help address the key questions in memory assessment: Has something gone wrong with memory? Is the loss normal? What is the prognosis? What can be done to help the client compensate or recover?

In this section we consider the efforts being made to bridge the gap between laboratory and clinic. We begin with a brief look at the distinction between normal and abnormal memory changes. Because abnormal memory changes could be the result of a psychological or physical condition, we consider links between memory and mental health. After that, we discuss how memory is affected by nutrition and drugs.

Normal versus Abnormal Memory Aging

Many normative changes take place in memory as people grow old, such as those in working memory and episodic memory. Still, many aspects of memory functioning do not change, such as the ability to remember the gist of a story. Increasingly forgetting names or what one needs at the supermarket, though annoying, appears to be part of aging. However, some people experience far greater changes, such as forgetting where they live or their spouse's name. Where is the line dividing normative memory changes from abnormal ones?

From a functional perspective, one way to distinguish normal and abnormal changes is to ask whether the changes disrupt a person's ability to perform daily living tasks. The normative changes we encountered in this chapter usually do not interfere with a person's ability to function in everyday life. When problems appear, however, it would be appropriate to find out what is the matter. A person who repeatedly forgets to turn off the stove or how to get home is clearly experiencing changes affecting personal safety and interferes with his or her daily life. Such changes should be brought to the attention of a physician or psychologist.

As indicated in Chapter 2, recent advances in neuroscience, especially the study of brain–behavior relations through neuroimaging, led to an explosion in our knowledge of specific diseases and brain changes that can create abnormal memory performance. Such brain-imaging techniques also allow researchers to find tumors, strokes, and other types of damage or disease that could account for poorer-than-expected memory performance.

Mapping the normative age-related changes in memory we have considered in this chapter is not easy, mainly because numerous parts of the brain are involved in processing information that eventually ends up in memory (Eichenbaum, 2012; Sasson, Doniger, Pasternak, Tarrasch, & Assaf, 2012). We know from Chapter 2, the prefrontal cortex, parietal region, and hippocampus are involved in memory. There are also structural changes in the white and gray matter that occur during learning that can also be measured (Zatorre, Fields, & Johansen-Berg, 2012). Local atrophy in these structures has been shown to be related to memory decrements in older adults (Kalpouzos et al., 2012).

Some diseases, especially the dementias, are marked by massive changes in memory. For example, Alzheimer's disease involves the progressive destruction of memory beginning with recent memory and eventually including the most personal—self-identity. Wernicke-Korsakoff syndrome, often accompanies long-term alcoholism, and involves major loss of recent memory and sometimes a total inability to form new memories after a certain point in time.

The most important point to keep in mind is telling the difference between normal and abnormal memory aging, and in turn, between memory and other cognitive problems, is often difficult (Fisher, Plassman, Heeringa, & Langa, 2008). There is no magic number of times someone must forget something before getting concerned. Because serious memory problems can also be due to underlying mental or physical health problems, these must be thoroughly checked out in conjunction with obtaining a complete memory assessment. A good general rule, though, is this. Forgetting where you parked the car in a large parking lot is a typical memory problem. Forgetting that you drove is another matter.

Memory and Physical and Mental Health

Several psychological disorders involve distorted thought processes that sometimes result in serious memory problems. The two disorders that are the main focus of research are depression and dementia; but other disorders, such as amnesia following a major seizure in epilepsy, head injury, or brain disease (e.g., stroke), are also important. We consider depression and dementia in detail in Chapter 10.

Damage to the brain resulting from physical or mental health disorders can result in profound decrements in different types of memory. For example, severe seizures in epilepsy can result in damage to the hippocampus and is heavily involved in creating associations between incoming information and information already in memory (Warren Duff, Magnotta, Capizzano, Cassell, & Tranel, 2012). This usually makes it difficult for people to learn and remember new facts and events, typically resulting in serious disruption of everyday life. Damage to the medial temporal lobe usually results in severe impairment of long-term memory, but few, if any, other cognitive problems (Warren et al., 2012).

Occasionally, people temporarily experience a complete loss of memory and are disoriented in time, a condition known as temporary global amnesia or TGA. The condition is most common in middle-aged adults. Currently, the cause is unknown, and neuroimaging studies have not provided definitive evidence of specific involvement of particular brain structures, nor is there consensus on the behavioral signs other than the memory problems, heightened anxiety, and depression (Hainselin, Quinette, Desgranges, Martinaud, De La Sayette, Hannequin et al., 2012). Persons who experience TGA are often aware of their problem but underestimate its severity. TGA has been associated with malfunctions of the valve in the jugular vein allowing blood to flows in the wrong direction (Baracchini, Tonello, Farina, Viaro, Atzori, Ballotta et al., 2012).

Memory impairment as a result of concussion, or traumatic brain injury, is the focus of a great deal of research, especially following concussion injuries received playing sports. Research clearly indicates there are a variety of negative effects on cognitive functioning following concussion, but adolescents are more likely to show longer-term effects than children or adults (Baillargeon, Lassonde, Leclerc, & Ellemberg, 2012). Memory deficits observed immediately following concussion in adolescents injured playing sports could still be detected six months later. The effects of concussion and its relation to continuing to participate in sports is highly controversial, as discussed in the Current Controversies feature.

CURRENT CONTROVERSIES:

CONCUSSIONS AND ATHLETES

Traumatic brain injury (TBI), such as concussion, can happen in just about any sport, as well as in combat injuries, exposure to explosions, automobile accidents, falls, or any other type of situation when one's head is hit hard. In essence, the brain slams against the skull, resulting in various levels of at least temporary damage and impairment. When you consider that between 2 and 4 million Americans are treated for mild TBI, with many more untreated, it is clear that TBI is a major concern.

Two situations brought TBI to the forefront: wars in Afghanistan and Iraq since 2001 and sports injuries. Estimates are about 30% of the military troops deployed in Iraq and Afghanistan who have suffered a TBI have permanent cognitive impairments in attention, memory, or self-awareness (Jagoda, 2012). Despite each state having legislation governing how soon athletes can return to playing after experiencing a concussion, there is little agreement on the diagnosis, treatment, and prognosis for patients.

There are several approaches to the diagnosis of concussion. In the United States, the American Congress of Rehabilitation Medicine established criteria in 1993: any loss of consciousness, loss of memory before or after the event, and feeling disoriented. The American Academy of Neurology has also developed criteria for evaluating sports concussions, depending on whether there was loss of consciousness or amnesia. Globally, the Consensus Statement on Concussion in Sport, developed in Zurich in 2008, governs the decision-making process (McCrory, Meeuwisse, Johnston, Dvorak, Aubry, Molloy et al., 2009). These criteria include (Jagoda, 2012) the definition of concussion: Concussion is defined as a complex pathophysiological process affecting the brain, induced by traumatic biomechanical forces. Several common features are:

- Caused either by a direct blow to the head, face, neck, or elsewhere on the body with an "impulsive" force transmitted to the head
- Typically results in the rapid onset of short-lived impairment of neurologic function that resolves spontaneously
- May result in neuropathological changes but the acute clinical symptoms largely reflect a functional disturbance rather than a structural injury
- Results in a graded set of clinical symptoms that may or may not involve loss of consciousness. Resolution of the clinical and cognitive symptoms typically follow a sequential course; it is important to note in a small percentage of cases, post-concussive symptoms may be prolonged
- No abnormality on standard structural neuro-imaging

The difficulty with all of these criteria is determining the seriousness of a TBI is often not easy. A significant percentage of people with a mild TBI based on the behavioral symptoms will show a significant lesion on a brain scan (Jagoda, 2012). Similarly, individuals such as Natasha Richardson, who died after hitting her head in a fall on a ski slope in 2009, showed few immediate signs she was actually experiencing bleeding between her brain and her skull.

Ignoring TBIs, especially repeated ones, can be deadly. A brain autopsy following the suicide at age 50 of former NFL player Dave Duerson in 2011 revealed he suffered from chronic traumatic encephalopathy (CTE), a form of dementia caused by repeated head trauma. Duerson suffered 10 known concussions, and reported symptoms well after he retired from football. Other former players who died relatively young also may have had the disease. Researchers at the Boston University School of Medicine Center for the Study of Traumatic Encephalopathy reported that 14 of 15 brains for former NFL players they examined showed evidence of CTE (Smith, 2011).

Clearly, there is more awareness of the problems associated with repeated TBI. Whether sports, or at least certain sports involving physical contact, should now be considered dangerous remains to be seen. What is certain, though, is the effects of repeated TBI last well into adulthood, and can cause serious cognitive impairment, and perhaps death, at a relatively early age.

Former NFL standout Dave Duerson suffered brain injury from repeated concussions.

Michael J. Minardi/Hulton Archive/Getty Images

| Memory and Nutrition

Researchers and clinicians often overlook nutrition as a cause of memory failures in adulthood (King, 2012). Evidence points to several compounds in healthy diets essential for well-functioning memory. Considerable research indicates flavonoids, found in green tea and blueberries, among other foods, may reverse age-related deficits in spatial memory (Rendeiro,

Guerreiro, Williams, & Spencer, 2012). Dietary iron intake in midlife has also been associated with better verbal memory, even after other potential explanations for the data were taken into account (Rickard, Chatfield, Powell, Stephen, & Richards, 2012). Finally, several vitamins, especially B vitamins 6, 9 (folic acid), and 12, have been associated with memory and other cognitive functions (de Jager, 2012).

These data indicate it is important to consider older adults' diets when assessing their memory performance. What may appear to be serious decrements in functioning may, in fact, be induced by poor nutrition or specific medications. Too often, researchers and clinicians fail to inquire about eating habits. Adequate assessment is essential to avoid diagnostic errors.

ADULT DEVELOPMENT IN ACTION

As a family member with older relatives living in your home, how can you help them maintain good memory?

SOCIAL POLICY IMPLICATIONS

With the graying of America we will see more and more older adults with memory-related problems. Thus, one important implication of this demographic trend is to meet the needs of this growing issue. The number of outreach memory and aging centers is growing in the United States. Such centers attract individuals with any level of memory impairment. These outreach programs connect to local communities and provide educational and referral opportunities along with skill development and training and resource development. The centers are important because they can bridge the gap between research, education, and patient care. Many of these centers are interdisciplinary in nature and thus have the benefit of collaborations with researchers in aging, neurologists, neuropsychologists, nurses, and pharmacists. They serve as catalysts to facilitate interactions among local networks of researchers and other applied centers such as chapters of the Alzheimer's Disease Association to enhance education and information dissemination. Thus, the implications of memory and aging research are becoming more important in our society. With the aging of the baby boomers, the social implications of understanding the memory competencies of our newest older generation have only begun to become apparent.

SUMMARY

6.1 Overview of Information Processing

What are the primary aspects of the information-processing model?

- The information-processing model is based on a computer metaphor and assumes an active participant, both quantitative and qualitative aspects of performance, and processing of information transformed through a series of systems.

- Sensory memory is the first level of processing incoming information from the environment. Sensory memory has a large capacity, but information only lasts there a short time.

What are the basic components of attention?

- From a functional perspective, attention consists of processing different aspects of stimuli.

How does speed of processing relate to cognitive aging?

- Speed of processing refers to how quickly and efficiently the early steps in information processing are performed. In general, older adults are slower.

What types of processing resources relate to attention and memory?

- Some researchers claim older adults have fewer processing resources than younger adults. However, this conclusion is suspect because processing resources is ill defined.

- Processing resources refers to the amount of attention one has to apply to a particular situation.

- Older adults have more difficulty filtering out or inhibiting irrelevant information (called inhibitory loss) than younger adults, but this may also have a beneficial effect under certain circumstances.

- Divided attention assesses attentional resources and involves doing more than one task that demands attention. Age differences in divided attention depend on the degree of task complexity and practice.

What are automatic and effortful processing?

- Automatic processing places minimal demands on attentional capacity whereas effortful processing requires all of the available attentional capacity. There are relatively no age differences in the former and pronounced age differences in the latter.

6.2 Memory Processes

What is working memory? What age differences have been found in working memory?

- Working memory refers to the processes and structures involved in holding information in mind and simultaneously using that information, sometimes in conjunction with incoming information, to solve a problem, make a decision, or learn. Information is kept active through rehearsal.

- In general, working memory capacity and rehearsal decline with age, although the extent of the decline is still in doubt. There is some evidence age differences in working memory are not universal.

How does implicit and explicit memory differ across age?

- Implicit memory involves retrieval of information without conscious or intentional recollection.

- Explicit memory is intentional and conscious remembering of information learned and remembered at a specific point in time.

- Older adults are generally better at implicit memory tasks than explicit memory tasks.

- Within long-term memory, how does episodic and semantic memory performance differ across age?

- Long-term memory refers to the ability to remember extensive amounts of information from a few seconds to a few hours to decades.

- In episodic memory, age-related decrements are typically found on recall tests but not on recognition tests. Older adults tend not to use memory strategies spontaneously as often or as well as younger adults.

- Semantic memory concerns learning and remembering the meaning of words and concepts not tied to specific occurrences of events in time. Fewer age differences are found in semantic memory.

What age differences have been found in encoding versus retrieval?

- Age-related decrements in encoding may be due to decrements in rehearsal within working memory and being slower at making connections with incoming information. Older adults do not spontaneously organize incoming information as well as younger adults, but they can use organizational helps when told to do so. However, the benefits of this approach are short-lived. Although older adults tend not to use optimal encoding strategies, this does not account for poor memory performance.

- Age-related decline in retrieval is related to both poorer encoding to some degree as well as failure to use retrieval strategies. Older adults also have more tip-of-the-tongue experiences than younger adults.

6.3 Memory in Context

What age differences are there in prospective memory?

- Age differences are less likely on event-based prospective memory tasks than on time-based prospective memory tasks. How accurately prospective memory tasks are performed depends on the time of day. Processing speed may help explain these age differences.

How does autobiographical memory change across adulthood?

- Some aspects of autobiographical memory remain intact for many years whereas other aspects do not. More memories are present from young adulthood than later in life. Verification of autobiographical memories is often difficult.

- Older adults have fewer flashbulb memories and their impact is restricted to particular points in the life span.

How does source memory and processing misinformation change across adulthood?

- The ability to remember the source of a familiar event or whether the event was imagined or experienced declines with age.

- Older adults are more susceptible to false memories in that they remember items or events that did not occur under specific conditions of plausibility and are more likely to believe false information as true.

What are some factors that help preserve memory as we grow older?

- Exercise, multilingualism, use of semantic memory, and avoiding the application of memory stereotypes are all factors that can enhance memory in older adults and delay cognitive decline.

6.4 Self-Evaluations of Memory Abilities

What are the major types of memory self-evaluations?

- There are two general categories of memory self-evaluations. Metamemory refers to knowledge about how memory works and what one believes to be true about it. Memory monitoring refers to the awareness of what we are doing with our memory right now.

What age differences have been found in metamemory and memory monitoring?

- Metamemory is typically assessed with questionnaires. Older adults seem to know less than younger adults about the workings of memory and its capacity, view memory as less stable, believe their memory will decline with age, and feel they have little control over these changes. Memory self-efficacy is an important predictor of performance in several settings.

- The ability to monitor one's performance on memory tasks does not usually decline with age. Memory monitoring may provide a basis for compensating for actual performance declines.

6.5 Memory Training

What are the major ways memory skills are trained? How effective are these methods?

- The E-I-E-I-O framework, based on explicit-implicit aspects of memory and external-internal types of strategies, is a useful way to organize memory training.

- Older adults can learn new internal memory strategies but, like all adults, usually abandon them over time.

- External-explicit strategies (such as lists and calendars) are common, but internal-implicit strategies are effective even with persons who have Alzheimer's disease.

- Use of memory enhancing drugs does not work over the long run.

6.6 Clinical Issues

What is the difference between normal and abnormal memory aging?

- Whether memory changes affect daily functioning is one way to separate normal from abnormal aging. Brain-imaging techniques allow localization of problems with more precision.

- Some diseases are marked by severe memory impairments. However, in many cases, telling the difference between normal changes and those associated with disease or other abnormal events is difficult.

- Different areas of the brain control different aspects of memory.

What is the connection between memory and physical and mental health?

- Dementia (such as Alzheimer's disease) and severe depression both involve memory impairment.

- Temporary global amnesia, more common in middle age than in younger or older adulthood, may be related to blood flow in the brain.

- Traumatic brain injury (TBI) can have serious consequences, as seen in the long-term potential damage from repeated concussions.

How is memory affected by nutrition?

- Flavonoids, iron, and B vitamins have all been shown to be related to memory functioning.

REVIEW QUESTIONS

6.1 Information Processing and Attention

- What is working memory? What is inhibition loss? What age differences have been found? What role do these processes play in understanding age differences in memory?

- What is episodic memory? What is semantic memory? How are they tested? What patterns of age differences have been found? What happens to the use of memory strategies with age?

- What is sensory memory?

- How do processing speed and processing resources affect older adults' information processing?

- In what way do older adults have difficulty filtering out information?

- How do automatic and effortful processing contribute to age differences in information processing?

- Why are attentional resources important to our understanding of age differences in memory?

6.2 Memory Processes

- What are working memory processes and how do they differ with increasing age?
- What is the difference between implicit and explicit memory? How do they change with age?
- Why are there age differences in episodic but not semantic memory?
- What are the relative contributions of encoding and retrieval in understanding age differences in memory?

6.3 Memory in Context

- What types of prospective memory have been distinguished? What age differences are there in prospective memory?
- What is autobiographical memory and how does it differ with age?
- How do source memory and processing of misinformation change with age?
- What are factors preventing decline in memory functioning? How do they work?

6.4 Self-Evaluations of Memory Abilities

- What major types of self-evaluations have been described?
- What age differences are there in metamemory and memory self-efficacy?
- What age differences have been found in memory monitoring?

6.5 Memory Training

- What is the E-I-E-I-O framework? How does it help organize memory training programs?
- How much do older adults benefit from each of the major types of memory training programs?
- What kinds of memory interventions work over time?

6.6 Clinical Issues

- What criteria are used to determine the difference between normal and abnormal changes in a person's memory?

- What physical and mental health conditions involve significant memory problems?
- What effect does nutrition have on memory?

INTEGRATING CONCEPTS IN DEVELOPMENT

- Based on material in Chapter 2 on cognitive neuroscience and the material in this chapter, what are the major factors involved in understanding age-related differences in memory?
- What aspects of neurological functioning would be important to consider in designing memory training programs?
- How could you design a good set of observations for family members to help them tell whether a relative's memory failures were normal or abnormal?
- Based on information in Chapters 3 and 4, what health promotion principles would help keep memory functioning better?
- How would you design an informational brochure for older adults to maximize their ability to remember it?

KEY TERMS

autobiographical memory Remembering information and events from your own life.

automatic processing Processes that are fast, reliable, and insensitive to increased cognitive demands.

cognitive reserve Factors that provide flexibility in responding and adapting to changes in the environment.

divided attention The ability to pay attention and successfully perform more than one task at a time.

effortful processing It requires all of the available attentional capacity when processing information.

encoding The process of getting information into the memory system.

episodic memory The general class of memory having to do with the conscious recollection of information from a specific event or point in time.

explicit memory The conscious and intentional recollection of information.

external aids Memory aids that rely on environmental resources.

false memory When one remembers items or events that did not occur.

flashbulb memories Memories for personally traumatic or unexpected events.

implicit memory The effortless and unconscious recollection of information.

information-processing model The study of how people take in stimuli from their environment and transform them into memories; the approach is based on a computer metaphor.

internal aids Memory aids that rely on mental processes.

long-term memory The aspects of memory involved in remembering rather extensive amounts of information over relatively long periods of time.

memory monitoring The awareness of what we are doing in memory right now.

memory self-efficacy The belief in one's ability to perform a specific memory task.

metamemory Memory about how memory works and what one believes to be true about it.

processing resources The amount of attention one has to apply to a particular situation.

prospective memory Process involving remembering to remember something in the future.

recall Process of remembering information without the help of hints or cues.

recognition Process of remembering information by selecting previously learned information from among several items.

rehearsal Process by which information is held in working memory, either by repeating items over and over or by making meaningful connections between the information in working memory and information.

retrieval The process of getting information back out of memory.

semantic memory Learning and remembering the meaning of words and concepts that are not tied to specific occurrences of events in time.

sensory memory A very brief and almost identical representation of the stimuli that exists in the observable environment.

source memory The ability to remember the source of a familiar event as well as the ability to determine if an event was imagined or actually experienced.

speed of processing How quickly and efficiently the early steps in information processing are completed.

storage The manner in which information is represented and kept in memory.

strategies Various techniques that make learning or remembering easier and that increase the efficiency of storage.

temporary global amnesia or TGA Temporary experience of a complete memory loss and disorientation in time.

working memory Refers to the processes and structures involved in holding information in mind and simultaneously using that information, sometimes in conjunction with incoming information, to solve a problem, make a decision, or learn new information.

RESOURCES

Access quizzes, glossaries, flashcards, and more at www.cengagebrain.com.

CHAPTER 7

INTELLIGENCE, REASONING, CREATIVITY, AND WISDOM

7.1 DEFINING INTELLIGENCE

Intelligence in Everyday Life • The Big Picture: A Life-Span View • Research Approaches to Intelligence • *Discovering Development: How Do People Show Intelligence?*

7.2 DEVELOPMENTAL TRENDS IN PSYCHOMETRIC INTELLIGENCE

The Measurement of Intelligence • Primary and Secondary Mental Abilities • Fluid and Crystallized Intelligence • Neuroscience Research and Intelligence in Young and Middle Adulthood • Moderators of Intellectual Change • *Current Controversies: Problems in Detecting Education and Life Style Effects on Intellectual Functioning* • Modifying Primary Abilities

7.3 QUALITATIVE DIFFERENCES IN ADULTS' THINKING

Piaget's Theory • Going beyond Formal Operations: Thinking in Adulthood • Integrating Emotion and Logic

7.4 EVERYDAY REASONING AND PROBLEM SOLVING

Decision Making • *How Do We Know?: Age Differences in Information Search and Decision Making* • Problem Solving • Expertise • Creativity and Wisdom

SOCIAL POLICY IMPLICATIONS

Summary • Review Questions • Integrating Concepts in Development • Key Terms • Resources

THE DALAI LAMA, SPIRITUAL LEADER OF THE TIBETAN PEOPLE, WAS THE RECIPIENT OF THE 1989 NOBEL PEACE PRIZE, AND IS RECOGNIZED AS A LEADER IN BUDDHIST PHILOSOPHY, HUMAN RIGHTS, AND GLOBAL ENVIRONMENTAL PROBLEMS. He reached this stature as a simple Buddhist monk, and claims he is "no more, no less." To the world, the Dalai Lama is recognized for his great wisdom and insight into the human condition. A sample of this wisdom is in his plea for "a new way of thinking … for responsible living and acting. If we maintain obsolete values and beliefs, a fragmented consciousness and a self-centered spirit, we will continue to hold to outdated goals and behaviors. Such an attitude by a large number of people would block the entire transition to an interdependent yet peaceful and cooperative global society." He also states as a Buddhist monk, he tries to develop compassion within, not simply as religious practice, but at a human level. To facilitate this he "sometimes finds it helpful to imagine himself standing as a single individual on one side, facing a huge gathering of all other human beings on the other side. Then he asks himself, 'Whose interests are more important?' To him it is quite clear however important he feels he is, he is just one individual while others are infinite in number and importance."

The Dalai Lama drives home the point that wisdom has long been associated with age. Surprisingly, psychologists only recently became interested in wisdom, perhaps because they were busy studying a related topic—intelligence. Another reason for not researching wisdom was the widespread belief it would be a waste of time. At one time, researchers and theorists were convinced all intellectual abilities inevitably declined as people aged, because of biological deterioration. For instance, Wechsler (1958) wrote "nearly all studies have shown that most human abilities decline progressively after reaching a peak somewhere between ages 18 and 25" (135).

In the decades since Wechsler stated this pessimistic view, many things changed. Researchers discovered intellectual development is an extremely complex process. We cannot give a simple yes or no answer to the question "Does intelligence decline with age?" and we continue to move farther away, rather than closer to, a simple answer.

Controversy raged for decades. Considering methodological comparisons between cross-sectional and longitudinal studies, Baltes and Schaie (1974) concluded "general intellectual decline is largely a myth"(p. 35). Botwinick (1977) countered with "decline in intellectual ability is clearly a part of the aging picture"(p. 580).

Who is right? Where do we stand now? Does intelligence decline, or is that a myth? Does wisdom come with age? Answering these questions will be our goal in this chapter. Such widely divergent conclusions about age-related changes in intelligence reflect different sets of assumptions about the nature of intelligence that are then translated into different theoretical and methodological approaches. We examine three avenues of research on intelligence and age: psychometric approach, life-span approach, and the cognitive-structural approach. Along the way we look at some attempts to modify intellectual abilities through training programs, but first we need to consider what intelligence is.

The Dalai Lama

AP Images/Chuck Robinson

7.1 Defining Intelligence

LEARNING OBJECTIVES

- How do people define intelligence in everyday life?
- What are the major components of the life-span approach?
- What are the major research approaches for studying intelligence?

When Toni graduated from high school she decided to start her own pet-sitting business. She started small, but ultimately cornered the market in her city. She lives a comfortable and wealthy lifestyle. After high school, her classmate Stacey went to college and majored in math. She pursued her doctorate and now lives a comfortable and modest lifestyle as a university professor. In comparing Toni and Stacey on intellectual ability, who would come out on top?

In terms of intelligence, the distinction between Toni and Stacey's success points to an important question to ask: What do we mean by intelligence? Is intelligence being able to learn new things quickly? Knowing a great deal of information? The ability to adapt to new situations or create new things or ideas? Or is intelligence the ability to make the most of what we have and to enjoy life? Intelligence encompasses all these abilities and more as we see in the different pathways Toni and Stacey took. It is all in the sense that people who stand out on these dimensions are often considered smart, or intelligent. It is more than just these abilities because intelligence also involves the qualitative aspects of thinking style, or how one approaches and conceptualizes problems.

Intelligence in Everyday Life

Robert Sternberg and his colleagues agree intelligence involves more than just a particular fixed set of characteristics (Sternberg, Jarvin, & Grigorenko, 2010). His approach is based on a list of behaviors that laypeople at a train station, supermarket, or college library reported to be distinctly characteristic of exceptionally intelligent, academically intelligent, everyday intelligent, or unintelligent people. This list of behaviors was given to experts in the field of intelligence and to a new set of laypeople. They were asked to rate either how distinctively characteristic each behavior was, or how important each behavior was in defining the four types of intelligence: exceptional, academic, everyday, or unintelligent people. Ratings were analyzed separately for the experts and the laypeople.

There is extremely high agreement between experts and laypeople on ratings of the importance of particular behaviors in defining intelligence. The two groups agreed intelligence consisted of three major clusters of related abilities: problem-solving ability, verbal ability, and social competence. Problem-solving ability consists of behaviors such as reasoning logically, identifying connections among ideas, seeing all aspects of a problem, and making good decisions. Verbal ability comprises such things as speaking articulately, reading with high comprehension, and having a good vocabulary. Social competence includes behaviors such as accepting others for what they are, admitting mistakes, displaying interest in the world at large, and being on time for appointments.

In a classic study, Berg and Sternberg (1992) wanted to know how these conceptions of intelligence differed across the adult life span. To find out, people aged 22 to 85 were asked to rate 55 behaviors they viewed as characteristic of exceptionally intelligent 30-, 50-, or 70-year-olds. Behaviors such as motivation, intellectual effort, and reading were said to be important indicators of intelligence for people of all ages. Other behaviors were specific to particular points in the life span. For example, a 30 year-old planning for the future and being open-minded were listed most often. The intelligent 50- and 70-year-olds were described as acting responsibly, adjusting to life situations, being verbally fluent, and displaying wisdom.

The Big Picture: A Life-Span View

One thing is clear about the ways people view intelligence—everyone has an idea of what intelligence is, and everyone considers it a complex construct. In the big picture, then, intelligence consists of many different skills. *Theories of intelligence, therefore, are* **multidimensional**; *that is, they specify many domains of intellectual abilities.* Although people disagree on the number of dimensions, they agree no single generic type of intelligence is responsible for all the mental activities we perform.

Baltes and colleagues (1993; 2006) take a broad view of intellectual development. The life-span concepts discussed in Chapter 1 including multidirectionality, plasticity, and interindividual variability play an important role in this conceptualization of intellectual change. Overall, this perspective asserts intellectual decline may be seen with age but stability and growth in mental functioning also can be seen across adulthood. The life-span perspective emphasizes the role of intelligence in human adaptation and daily activity.

The first concept, multidirectionality, *refers to the distinct patterns of change in abilities over the life span, with these patterns differing for different abilities.* For example, developmental functions for specific abilities differ, meaning the directional change in intelligence depends on the skills in question. As you will see later on, everyday knowledge accumulates over time and thus increases with age. However, basic cognitive mechanisms show more declines, especially into older age.

The term plasticity *refers to the range of functioning within an individual and the conditions under which a person's abilities can be modified within a specific age range.* Plasticity implies what may appear to be declines in some skills may in part represent a lack of practice in using them. Current studies examining brain plasticity and behavior find experience alters the brain across the life span (see Chapter 2). For example, Reuter-Lorenz (2002; Park & Reuter-Lorenz, 2009; Reuter-Lorenz & Mikels, 2006) found older and young adults show different activation patterns in the brain when they perform cognitive tasks. As we saw in Chapter 2, older adults activate areas in the brain that compensate for decline in their performance, resulting in better performance than would otherwise be the case. In other words, older adults activate new areas in the brain to compensate for decline in other areas. Finally, the research on training cognitive abilities described later in this chapter supports this view because older adults who show decline in cognitive functioning can be trained to perform at a higher level.

The last concept, interindividual variability, *acknowledges adults differ in the direction of their*

intellectual development. Schaie's (2008) sequential research indicates within a given cohort or generation, some people show longitudinal decline in specific abilities whereas other people show stability of functioning, and display improvements in those same abilities. Consequently, a single representation of typical or average changes with age may not really represent how the various individuals in a group function.

Using these four concepts of multidimensionality, plasticity, multidirectionality, and interindividual variability, Baltes and his colleagues proposed the dual-component model of intellectual functioning. Two interrelated types of developmental processes are postulated. *The first component, termed the* mechanics of intelligence, *concerns the neurophysiological architecture of the mind* (Baltes et al., 2006). This architecture provides the bases for cognitive abilities, including basic forms of thinking associated with information processing and problem solving such as reasoning, spatial orientation, or perceptual speed. Intellectual change in this first component is greatest during childhood and adolescence, as we acquire the requisite skills to handle complex cognitive tasks such as those encountered in school.

The second component, pragmatic intelligence, *concerns acquired bodies of knowledge available from and embedded within culture.* In other words, it includes everyday cognitive performance and human adaptation. Such abilities include verbal knowledge, wisdom, and practical problem solving. Pragmatic intellectual growth dominates adulthood.

These different trajectories of development are illustrated in Figure 7.1. As the figure suggests, different weightings of the forces of intelligence lead to specific predictions regarding the developmental pathway they take across the adult life span. If biological-genetic forces are considered to govern the mechanics more, a downward trajectory appears with age. However, if the pragmatics of intelligence is considered to be governed more by environmental-cultural factors, an upward trajectory is maintained across the adult life span.

This broad view of intellectual development in adulthood provides the background for asking more specific questions about particular aspects of

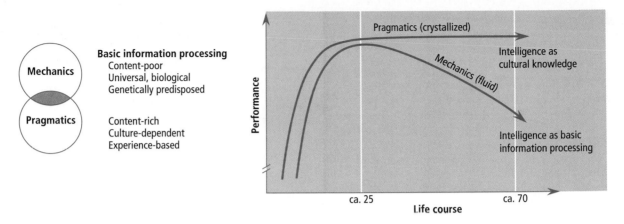

Figure 7.1

Life-span conceptualization of the mechanics and pragmatics of intelligence. The mechanics of intelligence correspond to fluid intelligence and the pragmatics to crystallized intelligence, as described later.

Source: Baltes, P. B. (1993). The aging mind: Potential and limits. The Gerontologist, 33, 580–594. The figure is Figure 1, p. 582.

intelligence. As we will see, three primary research approaches have emerged.

Research Approaches to Intelligence

Sternberg's and Baltes' work point out many different skills are involved in intelligence, depending on one's point of view. Interestingly, the behaviors listed by Sternberg's participants and the organizational structure provided by Baltes fit nicely with the more formal attempts at defining intelligence we encounter later in this chapter. Researchers have studied these skills from many perspectives, depending on their theoretical orientation. For example, some investigators approach these skills from a factor analysis approach and study them as separate pieces that can be added together to form intelligence. Others take a more holistic view and think of intelligence as a way or mode of thinking. These various theoretical orientations result in different means of studying intelligence.

Some investigators have concentrated on measuring intelligence as performance on standardized tests; this view represents the psychometric approach. For example, the problem-solving and verbal abilities in Sternberg and colleagues' study would be assessed by tests specifically designed to assess these skills. These tests focus on getting correct answers and tend to give less emphasis on the thought processes used to arrive at them.

Other researchers focus on information-processing mechanisms reviewed in Chapter 6. This approach aims at a detailed analysis of aging-associated changes in components of cognitive mechanisms and their interactions.

Finally, a number of researchers focused their efforts on reconceptualizing the meaning and measurement of intelligence by taking a cognitive-structural approach. *In the* cognitive-structural approach *researchers have been more concerned with the ways people conceptualize and solve problems than with scores on tests.* Such approaches to intelligence emphasize developmental changes in the modes and styles of thinking.

In this chapter, we consider these approaches and the research they stimulated. We discover each approach has its merits and whether age-related changes in intelligence are found depends on how intelligence is defined and measured. Before you continue, complete the exercise in the Discovering Development feature. The information you uncover will be useful as you read the rest of the chapter.

DISCOVERING DEVELOPMENT:

HOW DO PEOPLE SHOW INTELLIGENCE?

Earlier in this section, we encountered Sternberg and colleagues' research on people's implicit theories of intelligence. However, that study only examined broad categories of behavior that could be considered intelligent. Moreover, it was not conducted in such a way as to permit comparisons with research-based approaches to intelligence.

You and your classmates could address these shortcomings in the following way. Ask adults of different ages what they think constitutes intelligent behavior, much the same as Sternberg and colleagues did. However, be careful to make sure people are specific about the abilities they nominate. In addition, ask them about what makes adults' thinking different from adolescents' thinking and whether they believe there might be different stages of adults' thinking. Again, try to get your respondents to be as specific as possible.

Collate all the data from the class. Look for common themes in specific abilities, as well as in the qualitative aspects of thinking. As you read the rest of the chapter, see to what extent your data parallels that from more formal investigations.

ADULT DEVELOPMENT IN ACTION

If you were responsible for revising social policy regarding aging (say, criteria for living independently in the community), how would you approach that problem from the different perspectives of defining intelligence?

7.2 Developmental Trends in Psychometric Intelligence

LEARNING OBJECTIVES

- What is intelligence in adulthood?
- What are primary and secondary mental abilities? How do they change?
- What are fluid and crystallized intelligence? How do they change?
- How has neuroscience research furthered our understanding of intelligence in adulthood?

Ashley, a 35-year-old woman recently laid off from her job as an administrative assistant, slides into her seat on her first day of classes at the community college. She is clearly nervous. "I'm worried I won't be able to compete with these younger students, that I may not be smart enough," she sighs. "Guess we'll find out soon enough, though, huh?"

Many returning adult students like Ashley worry they may not be "smart enough" to keep up with 18- or 19-year-olds. Are these fears realistic? We see how the answer to this question depends on the types of intellectual skills being used.

As seen earlier, people naturally view intelligence as consisting of many components. One traditional way to measure intelligence, then, is to focus on individuals' performances on various tests of these component intellectual abilities and how these performances are interrelated. This approach to intelligence has a long history; the ancient Chinese and Greeks used this method to select people for certain jobs, such as master horseman (Doyle, 1974; DuBois, 1968). Tests also served as the basis for Alfred Binet's (1903) pioneering work in developing standardized intelligence tests, as well as many modern theories of intelligence.

Because of this long history of research in psychometric intelligence, we probably know more about this area than any other area in cognitive aging except for episodic memory. Yet this still provided no sense of closure as to how intelligence changes with age. There is substantial agreement on descriptions of change in different intellectual abilities (as we discuss later) and agreement on the methodological issues needing to be addressed when studying intellectual change.

However, there is little consensus on the proper interpretation of the data. For example, what does it mean that changes in intellectual abilities are related to increasing age? Remember in Chapter 1 we noted age does not cause change, that age is related to intellectual abilities is not the same thing as "aging" per se. As we shall see, age-related intellectual change is also related to important variables such as health, activity level, and educational achievements. It is in these areas that much of the controversy is still brewing.

The Measurement of Intelligence

Because the psychometric approach focuses on the interrelationships among intellectual abilities, the

Cognitive abilities are assessed across the life span using standardized tests.

So exactly how do researchers construct this theoretical hierarchy? The structure of intelligence is uncovered through sophisticated statistical detective work using factor analysis. First, researchers obtain people's performances on many types of problems. Second, the results are examined to determine whether performance on one type of problem, such as filling in missing letters in a word, predicts performance on another type of problem, like unscrambling letters to form a word. *If the performance on one test is highly related to the performance on another, the abilities measured by the two tests are interrelated and are called a* factor.

Most psychometric theorists believe intelligence consists of several factors. However, we should note although factor analysis is a sophisticated statistical technique, it is not an exact technique. Thus, estimates of the exact number of factors vary from a few to over 100. Most researchers and theorists believe the number to be relatively small. We examine two factors: primary and secondary mental abilities.

Primary and Secondary Mental Abilities

Since the 1930s, researchers agreed intellectual abilities can be studied as groups of related skills (such as memory or spatial ability) organized into hypothetical constructs called primary mental abilities. *In turn, related groups of primary mental abilities can be clustered into a half dozen or so broader skills termed* secondary mental abilities.

Roughly 25 primary mental abilities have been identified (Horn, 1982). Because it is difficult to study all of them, researchers focused on five representative ones:

- *Number*: the basic skills underlying our mathematical reasoning

- *Word fluency*: how easily we produce verbal descriptions of things

- *Verbal meaning*: our vocabulary ability

- *Inductive reasoning*: our ability to extrapolate from particular facts to general concepts

- *Spatial orientation*: our ability to reason in the three-dimensional world

Even with a relatively small number of primary mental abilities, it is still hard to discuss intelligence

major goal has long been to describe the ways these relationships are organized (Sternberg, 1985). *This organization of interrelated intellectual abilities is termed the* structure of intelligence. The most common way to describe the structure of intelligence is to picture it as a five-level hierarchy (Cunningham, 1987).

Each higher level of this hierarchy represents an attempt to organize components of the level below in a smaller number of groups. The lowest level consists of individual test questions—the specific items people answer on an intelligence test. These items or questions can be organized into tests at the second level.

The third level, primary mental abilities, reflects interrelationships among performances on intelligence tests. The interrelationships uncovered among the primary mental abilities produce the secondary mental abilities at the fourth level. Finally, general intelligence at the top refers to the interrelationships among the third-order abilities.

Keep in mind each time we move up the hierarchy we move away from people's actual performance. Each level above the first represents a theoretical description of how things fit together. Thus, there are no tests of primary abilities per se; primary abilities represent theoretical relationships among tests, that in turn represent theoretical relationships among actual performance.

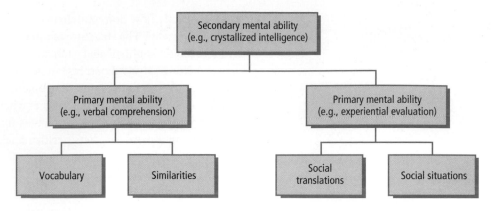

Figure 7.2

Secondary mental abilities reflect several primary mental abilities and their respective measurements. This figure shows those relations regarding crystallized intelligence.

© 2015 Cengage Learning

by focusing on separate abilities. As a result, theories of intelligence emphasize clusters of related primary mental abilities as a framework for describing the structure of intelligence. Because they are one step removed from primary mental abilities, secondary mental abilities are not measured directly. This can be seen in Figure 7.2 for the secondary mental ability crystallized intelligence, one of two secondary mental abilities we will consider next: fluid and crystallized intelligence.

Fluid and Crystallized Intelligence

As noted earlier, primary abilities are themselves organized into clusters of secondary mental abilities. A summary of the major secondary mental abilities is presented in Table 7.1. Two secondary mental abilities have received a great deal of attention in adult developmental research: fluid intelligence and crystallized intelligence (Horn, 1982).

Fluid intelligence *consists of the abilities that make you a flexible and adaptive thinker, allow you to make inferences, and enable you to understand the relations among concepts.* It includes the abilities you need to understand and respond to any situation, but especially new ones: inductive reasoning, integration, abstract thinking, and the like (Horn, 1982). An example of a question that taps fluid abilities is the following: What letter comes next in the series *d f i m r x e*?[1]

Crystallized intelligence *is the knowledge you have acquired through life experience and education in a particular culture.* Crystallized intelligence includes your breadth of knowledge, comprehension of communication, judgment, and sophistication with information (Horn, 1982). Many popular television game shows (such as *Jeopardy* and *Wheel of Fortune*) are based on contestants' accumulated crystallized intelligence.

Developmentally, fluid and crystallized intelligence follow two different paths, as you can see in Figure 7.3. Notice, fluid intelligence declines throughout adulthood, whereas crystallized intelligence improves. Although we do not yet fully understand why fluid intelligence declines, it may be related to underlying changes in the brain (Horn & Hofer, 1992). In contrast, the increase in crystallized intelligence (at least until late life) indicates people continue adding knowledge every day.

What do these different developmental trends imply? First, they indicate that—although it continues through adulthood—learning becomes more difficult with age.

[1]The next letter is *m*. The rule is to increase the difference between adjacent letters in the series by one each time and use a continuous circle of the alphabet for counting. Thus, *f* is two letters from *d*, *i* is three letters from *f*, and *e* is seven letters from *x*.

Table 7.1

DESCRIPTIONS OF MAJOR SECONDARY MENTAL ABILITIES

Crystallized intelligence (Gc)

This form of intelligence is indicated by a very large number of performances indicating breadth of knowledge and experience, sophistication, comprehension of communications, judgment, understanding of conventions, and reasonable thinking. The factor that provides evidence of Gc is defined by primary abilities such as verbal comprehension, concept formation, logical reasoning, and general reasoning. Tests used to measure the ability include vocabulary (What is a word near in meaning to *temerity*?), esoteric analogies (Socrates is to Aristotle as Sophocles is to _____?), remote associations (What word is associated with *bathtub*, *prizefighting*, and *wedding*?), and judgment (Determine why a foreman is not getting the best results from workers). As measured, the factor is a fallible representation of the extent to which a person has incorporated, through the systematic influences of acculturation, the knowledge and sophistication that constitutes the intelligence of a culture.

Fluid intelligence (Gf)

The broad set of abilities of this intelligence includes those of seeing relationships between stimulus patterns, drawing inferences from relationships, and comprehending implications. The primary abilities that best represent the factor, as identified in completed research, include induction, figural flexibility, integration, and, cooperatively with Gc, logical reasoning and general reasoning. Tasks that measure the factor include letter series (What letter comes next in the series *d t i m r x e*?), matrices (Discern the relationships between elements of 3-by-3 matrices), and topology (From among a set of figures in which circles, squares, and triangles overlap in different ways, select a figure that will enable one to put a dot within a circle and a square but outside a triangle). The factor is a fallible representation of such fundamental features of mature human intelligence as reasoning, abstracting, and problem solving. In Gf these features are not imparted through the systematic influences of acculturation but instead are obtained through learning that is unique to an individual or is in other ways not organized by the culture.

Visual organization (Gv)

This dimension is indicated by primary mental abilities such as visualization, spatial orientation, speed of closure, and flexibility of closure, measured by tests such as gestalt closure (Identify a figure in which parts have been omitted), form board (Show how cutout parts fit together to depict a particular figure), and embedded figures (Find a geometric figure within a set of intersecting lines). To distinguish this factor from Gf, it is important that relationships between visual patterns be clearly manifest so performances reflect primarily fluency in perception of these patterns, not reasoning in inferring the process.

Auditory organization (Ga)

This factor has been identified on the basis of several studies in which primary mental abilities of temporal tracking, auditory cognition of relations, and speech perception under distraction of distortion were first defined among other primary abilities and then found to indicate a broad dimension at the second order. Tasks that measure Ga include repeated tones (Identify the first occurrence of a tone when it occurs several times), tonal series (Indicate which tone comes next in an orderly series of tones), and cafeteria noise (Identify a word amid a din of surrounding noise). Like Gv, this ability is best indicated when the relationships among stimuli are not such that one needs to reason for understanding but instead are such that one can fluently perceive patterns among the stimuli.

Short-term acquisition and retrieval

This ability comprises processes of becoming aware and processes of retaining information long enough to do something with it. Almost all tasks that involve short-term memory have variance in this factor. Span memory, associative memory, and meaningful memory are primary abilities that define the factor, but measures of primary and secondary memory can also be used to indicate the dimension.

Long-term storage and retrieval

Formerly this dimension was regarded as a broad factor among fluency tasks, such as those of the primary abilities called associational fluency, expressional fluency, and object flexibility. In recent work, however, these performances have been found to align with others indicating facility in storing information and retrieving information that was acquired in the distant past. It seems, therefore, that the dimension mainly represents processes for forming encoding associations for long-term storage and using these associations, or forming new ones, at the time of retrieval. These associations are not so much correct as they are possible and useful; to associate *teakettle* with *mother* is not to arrive at a truth so much as it is to regard both concepts as sharing common attributes (e.g., warmth).

Source: Horn, J. L. (1982). The aging of human abilities. In B. B. Wolman (Ed.), Handbook of Developmental Psychology (pp. 847–870). Englewood Cliffs, NJ: Prentice Hall. Reprinted with permission.

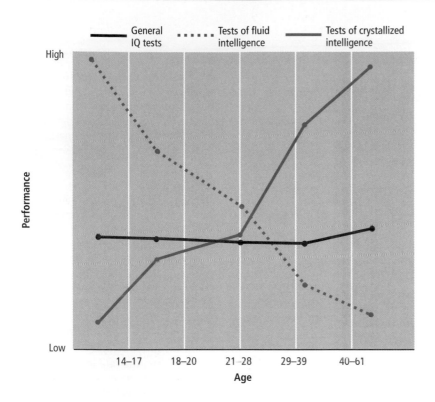

| General IQ tests | Tests of fluid intelligence | Tests of crystallized intelligence |

Figure 7.3

Performances on tests used to define fluid, crystallized, and general intelligence, as a function of age.

Source: Horn, J. L. (1970). Organization of data on life-span development of human abilities. In L. R. Goulet & P. B. Baltes (Eds.), Life-span Development Psychology: Research and Theory *(p. 463). Copyright © 1970 by Academic Press, reproduced by permission of the publisher.*

Second, intellectual development varies a great deal from one set of skills to another. Whereas individual differences in fluid intelligence remain relatively uniform over time, individual differences in crystallized intelligence increase with age, largely because maintaining crystallized intelligence depends on being in situations that require its use (Horn, 1982; Horn & Hofer, 1992). For example, few adults get much practice in solving complex letter series tasks like the one on page 192, but because people improve their vocabulary skills by reading and vary considerably in how much they read, differences are likely to emerge.

Neuroscience Research and Intelligence in Young and Middle Adulthood

As you might suspect from Chapters 2 and 6, considerable research shows specific areas in the brain are associated with intellectual abilities, and developmental changes in these areas are related to changes in performance. On the basis of 37 studies using various brain imaging techniques, Jung and Haier (2007) originally proposed the Parieto-Frontal Integration Theory that we encountered in Chapter 2. Remember

the Parieto-Frontal Integration Theory (P-FIT) proposes intelligence comes from a distributed and integrated network of neurons in the parietal and frontal lobes of the brain. (The parietal lobe is at the top of the head; the frontal lobe is behind the forehead.) In general, P-FIT accounts for individual differences in intelligence as having their origins in individual differences in brain structure and function.

The P-FIT model has been tested in several studies. Results indicate support for the theory when measures of fluid, crystallized, and spatial intelligence are related to brain structures assessed in young adults through neuroimaging (Brancucci, 2012; Shih & Jung, 2009). It is also clear performance on measures of specific abilities is likely related to specific combinations of brain structures (Haier et al., 2010).

A second theory of intelligence based on neuroscience evidence is based on how efficiently the brain works (Brancucci, 2012). *The neural efficiency hypothesis, states intelligent people process information more efficiently, showing weaker neural activations in a smaller number of areas than less intelligent people.* Research evidence is mounting that this idea holds merit, and with greater intelligence does come demonstrably increased efficiency in neural processing (e.g., Lipp, Benedek, Fink, Koschutnig, Reishofer, Bergner et al., 2012). However, how this neural efficiency develops is not yet known, nor are its developmental pathways understood.

It is clear neuroscience and related research on intelligence will continue to provide many insights into the bases for both the development of fluid and crystallized intelligence as well as understanding individual differences in each (Nisbett et al., 2012).

Finally, intellectual abilities have long been known to correlate with mortality in late life, but recent evidence increasingly shows this relation also holds in middle age based on research in Sweden (Batty et al., 2009). and Britain (Sabia et al., 2010).

Moderators of Intellectual Change

Based on the research we considered thus far, two different developmental trends emerge: we see gains in experience-based processes but losses in information-processing abilities. The continued growth in some areas is viewed as a product of lifelong learning. The losses are viewed as an inevitable result of the decline of physiological processes with age.

A number of researchers, though, emphasize individual differences in the rate of change in intellectual aging (Baltes et al., 2006; MacDonald et al., 2004; Schaie, 2008). These researchers do not deny that some adults show intellectual decline. Based on large individual differences in intellectual performance over time, they simply suggest these decrements may not happen to everyone to the same extent. They argue many reasons besides age explain performance differences. In this section, we explore some of the social and physiological factors proposed as modifiers of intellectual development. These include cohort differences, education level, social variables, personality, health and lifestyle, and relevancy and appropriateness of tasks.

Cohort Differences. Do the differences in intellectual performance obtained in some situations reflect true age-related change or mainly cohort, or generational, differences? This question gets right to the heart of the debate over interpreting developmental research on intelligence. On one hand, dozens of cross-sectional studies document significant differences in intellectual

performance with age. On the other hand, several longitudinal investigations show either no decrement or even an increase in performance (Hertzog, Dixon et al., 2003; Schaie, 2005, 2008, 2011; Zelinski, Kennison, Watts, & Lewis, 2009).

The way to resolve the discrepancy between the two approaches involves comparing data collected over long periods of time from several samples and analyzed simultaneously in both cross-sectional and longitudinal designs as discussed in Chapter 1. When this is done, the results indicate part of the apparent decline with age in performance on intelligence tests is because of generational differences rather than age differences (Schaie, 2005, 2011; see also the How Do We Know? feature earlier in this chapter). These trends reflect better education opportunities, healthier lifestyles, better nutrition, and improved health care.

The complex pattern of cohort differences indicates interpreting data from cross-sectional studies is difficult. Recall from Chapter 1 cross-sectional studies confound age and cohort; and because there are both age- and cohort-related changes in intellectual abilities, drawing any meaningful conclusions is nearly impossible. Schaie (2005, 2008, 2011) argues the trends indicate a leveling off of cohort differences, that may come to a halt in the early part of the 21st century. This conclusion is supported by a study of 531 adult parent–offspring pairs indicating generational (cohort) improvements were becoming smaller for more recently born pairs (Schaie et al., 1992).

Information Processing. A number of researchers suggest general processing constraints that occur with aging (discussed in Chapter 6) may help identify mechanisms underlying decline in fluid intelligence abilities with age (Baltes et al., 2006; Zimprich & Martin, 2002, 2009). For example, evidence suggests perceptual speed accounts for much of the age-related decline in both fluid and crystallized mental abilities. Similarly, working memory decline with increasing age accounts for poor performance on the part of older adults when the tasks involve coordinating both new incoming information and stored information such as those found in the fluid and/or mechanic component of intelligence. Finally, evidence suggests the inability to inhibit actions and thoughts or to avoid interference typically found in older adults may also account for efficient functioning in fluid and/or mechanic abilities.

Social and Life Style Variables. Numerous social and life style variables have been identified as important correlates of intellectual functioning. Think for a minute about the kind of job you currently have or would like to get. What kind of intellectual skills does it demand? What similarities or differences are there between your chosen job (e.g., school counselor) and a different one (say, accountant)? An interesting line of research concerns how the differences in cognitive skills needed in different occupations makes a difference in intellectual development (Bosma, van Boxtel, Ponds, Houx, & Jolles, 2003; de Grip, Bosma, Willems, & van Boxtel, 2008). To the extent a job requires you to use certain cognitive abilities a great deal, you may be less likely to show declines in them as you age.

Other social demographic variables implicated in slower rates of intellectual decline include a higher socioeconomic status, exposure to stimulating environments, the utilization of cultural and educational resources throughout adulthood, and not feeling lonely (Schaie, 2008). For example, research examining loneliness suggests it is associated with more rapid

People in cognitively demanding jobs may be less likely to show noticeable declines in cognitive functioning with increasing age.

© 41/Shutterstock.com

cognitive decline (Wilson, Krueger, Arnold, Schneider, Kelly, Barnes et al., 2007) and for having a mental health problem later in life (Coyle & Dugan, 2012).

Finally, although research suggests education and life style factors are a predictor of intellectual functioning, it is still a matter of debate whether it helps slow cognitive change in late life (Hertzog et al., 2009; Zahodne, Glymour, Sparks, Bontempo, Dixon, MacDonald et al., 2011). We examine this debate in the Current Controversies feature.

CURRENT CONTROVERSIES:

PROBLEMS IN DETECTING EDUCATION AND LIFE STYLE EFFECTS ON INTELLECTUAL FUNCTIONING

The fact that having more formal education is positively correlated to one's intelligence is well established in the research literature. Similarly, there is evidence certain life style factors, such as cognitive engagement and social engagement, are also correlated with intellectual functioning (Small, Dixon, McArdle, & Grimm, 2012).

Education is an important predictor of both fluid and crystallized abilities (Constantinidou, Christodoulou, & Prokopiou, 2012). In some studies, it also predicts survivorship, in some cases to age 100 or beyond (Martin, Hagberg, & Poon, 2012).

These findings led some researchers to speculate education may provide protection against abnormal cognitive aging, such as Alzheimer's disease, perhaps by creating extra cognitive reserve or by changing the brain to have thicker cortex. The evidence is mixed. There is little evidence of structural brain changes, such

as cortical thickening, with higher levels of education (Pillai, McEvoy, Hagler, Holland, Dale, Salmon et al., 2012). However, other research documents increased white matter volume in some brain regions (Foubert-Samier, Catheline, Amieva, Dilharreguy, Helmer, Allard et al., 2012). There is also growing evidence higher levels of education results in lower rates of dementia, but paradoxically, once cognitive decline begins and is noticeable it proceeds more rapidly and there is evidence of greater damage in the brain (Meng & D'Arcy, 2012).

Research examining cognitive engagement in adulthood shows that reductions in such engagement are correlated with declines in verbal speed, episodic memory, and semantic memory (Small et al., 2012). In turn, cognitive decline is associated with decreases in social engagement. What's not clear though is what comes first. Is it the case that the memory declines are the *result* of lower cognitive engagement, or is it the reverse (that memory declines are the reason for decreases in cognitive engagement)? We cannot tell from the research, because the nature of the research design, correlational, does not permit such determinations to be made (see Chapter 1).

So how do we reconcile these data? On one hand, education is related to increased performance on intelligence tests, and becoming less cognitively active is related to performance declines. One would expect education and cognitive activity to protect people against cognitive decline. But that's not what happens in the long run. What's going on?

One possibility is that education per se is not what is at work. Rather, there are two other possibilities. Because education is correlated with a healthier life style on average, perhaps it is the latter that is responsible for the data. For example, research showing shorter telomere length (see Chapter 3), an indicator of biological aging, is related to low educational levels that in turn relate to less healthy life style (Kingma, de Jonge, van der Harst, Ormel, & Rosmalen, 2012). Also, because education does produce some level of cognitive reserve, it is likely the amount of cognitive decline necessary for others to notice is greater than it is for people with less education. That would explain why, once cognitive decline in highly educated people becomes noticeable, it appears to proceed rapidly.

Overall, we need more carefully conducted research to understand the role played by education and life style and their relation to intelligence and cognitive changes with age. Only when we separate education from its related variables (e.g., health) will we understand its actual role.

Personality. Several aspects of personality have been proposed as important for understanding intellectual change. Similar to research we examined in Chapter 6 on memory, one of these aspects concerns self-efficacy (Hayslip & Cooper, 2012). Older adults perceive what they do to help maintain their intellectual abilities can make a difference. Specifically, high initial levels of fluid abilities and a high sense of internal control led to positive changes in people's perceptions of their abilities; low initial levels led to decreases in perceptions of ability and behavior (Lachman & Andreoletti, 2006).

Neuroticism and chronic psychological distress have been implicated in rapid cognitive decline (Wilson, Arnold et al., 2006; Wilson, Bennett et al., 2005). This makes sense given neuroticism is strongly associated with frequency of negative emotions. Negative emotions and psychological distress go hand-in-hand. Furthermore, neurobiological research suggests chronic psychological distress may cause deteriorative changes in the limbic system of the brain that regulates emotion and cognition (Dwivedi et al., 2003; Webster et al., 2002). These deteriorative changes could cause cognitive impairment. However, this area is still in its infancy and further research is needed.

On a more upbeat note, positive beliefs and attitudes also have important indirect effects on cognitive enrichment. This indirect effect is reflected in the influence of these beliefs and attitudes on desirable behaviors such as exercise and mental stimulation known to be associated with enrichment effects on intelligence (Hertzog et al., 2009). Research indicates people with flexible attitudes at midlife tend to experience less decline in intellectual competence than people who are more rigid in middle age (Lachman, 2004; Willis & Boron, 2008).

Health. The most obvious relationship between health and intelligence concerns the functioning of the brain itself. We noted in Chapter 2 several normative changes in brain structure with age affect functioning. We also noted in Chapter 6 brain injuries, nutrition, and other factors can also affect functioning. Diseases such as dementia wreak havoc in the brain, and others, such as cardiovascular disease, can have serious negative effects.

Cardiovascular disease and its implications for intellectual functioning have been studied extensively. These diseases are linked to a pattern of cognitive impairment that looks like what is typically observed in "normal" cognitive aging. Some researchers suggest the effects of age on intelligence and cognition are related at least in part to vascular disease that selectively affects the prefrontal brain (Spiro & Brady, 2008).

Finally, we noted in Chapters 3 and 6 physical exercise has considerable benefit. In this context, exercise helps maintain cognitive fitness as well as slow down cognitive decline once it has begun (Amoyal & Fallon, 2012). This alone should be enough reason to get up and get moving!

Modifying Primary Abilities

As you have seen, older adults do not perform as well on tests of some primary abilities as younger adults, even after taking the moderators of performance into account (Schaie, 2005). In considering these results, investigators began asking whether there was a way to slow down or even reverse the declines. There has been much research examining the effects of lifestyle, health, and personality, among other variables, on intelligence.

Pursuing this issue further, we ask a number of relevant questions regarding training. Are the age-related differences remaining after cohort and other effects are removed permanent, or might these differences be reduced or even eliminated if older adults are given appropriate training? Can we modify adults' intelligence? This again addresses the important issue of plasticity in intellectual functioning, one of the life-span tenets discussed in Chapter 1.

The most common training research focuses on those intellectual abilities that constitute primary mental abilities, especially those clustered into fluid intelligence. These are the intellectual abilities most likely to decline with age. Middle-aged and older adults can be successfully taught to increase their speed of processing, and this training transfers to tasks not included in the training sessions (Simpson, Camfield, Pipingas, Macpherson, & Stough, 2012).

Two large-scale projects examined training of primary abilities over extended periods of time. These projects adopt the view that aging in healthy adults has great potential for cognitive growth (Lövdén et al., 2012), with the research largely being conducted within the Selective Optimization with Compensation (SOC) framework described in Chapter 1. Let's see what researchers discovered in Project ACTIVE.

Project ACTIVE. Sherry Willis has revolutionized our understanding of how far researchers can go to investigate the impact of training primary mental abilities. She designed a longitudinal research project named Advanced Cognitive Training for Independent and Vital Elderly (ACTIVE) to provide answers to key questions about whether the age-related changes observed in intelligence research were inevitable or could be modified through training (Unverzagt, Smith, Rebok, Marsiske, Morris, Jones et al., 2009; Willis & Schaie, 2009).

Begun in the mid-1990s, the ACTIVE study was a multicenter, randomized, controlled clinical research project that investigates the long-term effectiveness of cognitive training on enhancing mental abilities (memory, reasoning, and attention) and preserving instrumental activities of daily living (managing finances, taking medication, using the telephone, and driving) in older adults. Six centers across the eastern United States enrolled nearly 3000 people initially. Participants underwent detailed assessments of mental and functional ability on multiple occasions over several years of follow-up. The design of Project ACTIVE is shown in Figure 7.4.

The ACTIVE project findings show cognitive training interventions improved mental abilities and daily functioning in older independent living adults (e.g., Ball, Berch, Helmers, Jobe, Leveck, Marsiske et al., 2002). ACTIVE also showed positive effects of cognitive training at 5 years post-intervention for basic mental abilities, health-related quality of life, and improved ability to perform instrumental activities of daily living (IADL) (Unverzagt et al., 2009).

There is an important caveat, though. A subgroup analysis through 2 years of follow-up suggested participants who showed mild cognitive impairment (MCI) did not benefit from memory training; interestingly though, they did benefit to the same degree as cognitively normal participants from training in reasoning and speed of processing. This finding suggests MCI may interfere with a person's ability to benefit from some, but not all forms of cognitive enhancement.

Additional findings from Project ACTIVE indicate cognitive training aimed initially at improving specific primary mental abilities, such as speed of processing or reasoning, can also have positive effects on participants' sense of control over one's life (Wolinsky, Vander Weg, Martin, Unverzagt, Willis, Marsiske et al., 2010).

The results from Project ACTIVE allow us to conclude declines in fluid abilities may be reversible. Perhaps the best news is the training effects are relatively enduring. Depending on the ability trained and the training method, effects last at least between two and five years (Ball et al., 2002; Willis, Tennstedt, Marsiske, Ball, Elias, Koepke et al., 2006).

What can we conclude from these findings? First, there is strong evidence in the normal course of development, no one is too old to benefit from training and training reduces the rates of decline for those fluid abilities examined. Second, transfer of training occurs, but evidence is lacking that it occurs across a wide range of materials unless training involves executive functioning and working memory, when the effects generalize to many different tasks (Basak, Boot, Voss, & Kramer, 2008; Dahlin, Stigsdotter, Larsson, Bäckman, & Nyberg., 2008). Finally, training gains are durable and last up to several years (Ball et al., 2002; Willis et al., 2006).

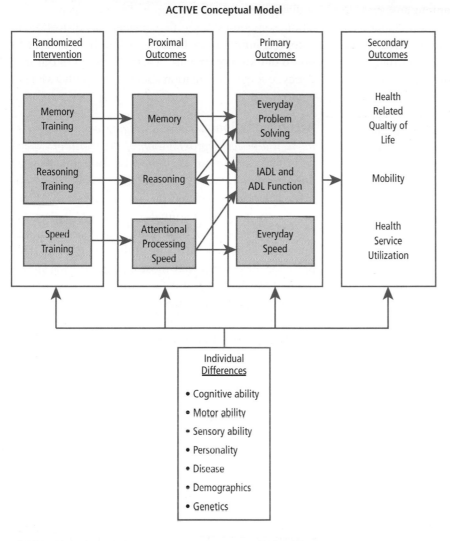

ACTIVE Conceptual Model

Figure 7.4
Experts in any field handle tasks in those fields differently than novices.

Source: Unverzagt, F. W., Smith, D. M., Rebok, G. W., Marsiske, M., Morris, J. N., Jones, R. et al. (2009). The Indiana Alzheimer Disease Center's Symposium on Mild Cognitive Impairment. Cognitive training in older adults: Lessons from the ACTIVE Study. Current Alzheimer Research, 6, *375–383.* Retrieved from *http://www.ncbi.nlm.nih.gov/pmc/articles/PMC2729785/figure/F1/*

ADULT DEVELOPMENT IN AGING

If you were a director of a human resources department, how would the research on intelligence across adulthood influence your decisions about employee training programs?

7.3 Qualitative Differences In Adults' Thinking

LEARNING OBJECTIVES

- What are the main points in Piaget's theory of cognitive development?
- What evidence is there for continued cognitive development beyond formal operations?

- What is the role of both emotion and cognition in cognitive maturity?

Eddie, a student at a local university, thought the test he had just taken in his math course was unfair because the instructors simply marked the answers to complex problems right or wrong. He complained he deserved partial credit for knowing how to set up the problem and being able to figure out some of the steps.

Although Eddie did not know it, his argument parallels one in the intelligence literature—the debate on whether we should pay attention mainly to whether an answer is right or wrong or to how the person reasons the problem through. The psychometric approach we considered earlier does not focus on the thinking processes underlying intelligence; rather, psychometrics concentrates on interrelationships among answers to test questions. In contrast, cognitive-structural approaches focus on the ways in which people think; whether a particular answer is right or wrong is not important.

We will consider two theories that represent cognitive-structural approaches. First, we examine Piaget's theory as a foundation for this approach. Second, we explore the discussions concerning possible extensions of it, post-formal theory. Both these approaches postulate intellectual changes are mainly qualitative, even though they differ on many points.

Piaget's Theory

According to Piaget (1970, 1980), intellectual development is adaptation through activity. We create the ways our knowledge is organized and, ultimately, how we think. Piaget believed development of intelligence stems from the emergence of increasingly complex cognitive structures. He organized his ideas into a theory of cognitive development that changed the way psychologists conceptualize intellectual development.

Basic Concepts. For Piaget, thought is governed by the principles of adaptation and organization. Adaptation is the process of adjusting thinking to the environment. Just as animals living in a forest feed differently from the way animals living in a desert feed, how we think changes from one developmental context to another. Adaptation occurs through organization; that is how the organism is put together. Each component part has its own specialized function that is coordinated into the whole. In Piaget's theory, the organization of thought is reflected in cognitive structures that change over the life span. Cognitive structures determine how we think. It is the change in cognitive structures, the change in the fundamental ways we think, Piaget tried to describe.

What processes underlie intellectual adaptation? Piaget defined two: assimilation and accommodation. **Assimilation** *is the use of currently available knowledge to make sense out of incoming information.* It is the application of cognitive structures to the world of experience that makes the world understandable. A child who only knows the word *dog* may use it for every animal she encounters. So, when the child sees a cat and calls it a dog, she is using available knowledge, the word *dog*, to make sense out of the world—in this case the cat

walking across the living room. The process of assimilation sometimes leads to considerable distortion of incoming information, because we may have to force-fit it into our knowledge base. This is apparent in our tendency to forget information about a person that violates a stereotype.

Accommodation. *involves changing one's thought to make it a better approximation of the world of experience.* The child in our example who thought cats were dogs eventually learns cats are cats. When this happens, she accommodated her knowledge to incorporate a new category of animal.

The processes of assimilation and accommodation serve to link the structure of thought to observable behavior. Piaget believed most changes during development involved cognitive structures. His research led him to conclude there were four structures (i.e., four stages) in the development of mature thought: sensorimotor, preoperational, concrete operational, and formal operational. We consider the major characteristics of each stage briefly. Because we are most interested in Piaget's description of adult thought, we emphasize that.

Sensorimotor Period. In this first stage of cognitive development, intelligence is seen in infants' actions. Babies and infants gain knowledge by using their sensory and motor skills, beginning with basic reflexes (sucking and grasping) and eventually moving to purposeful, planned sequences of behavior (such as looking for a hidden toy). The most important thing infants learn during the sensorimotor period is that objects continue to exist even when they are out of sight; this ability is called object permanence.

Preoperational Period. Young children's thinking is best described as egocentric. This means young children believe all people and all inanimate objects experience the world just as they do. Young children believe dolls feel pain. Although young children can sometimes reason through situations, their thinking is not based on logic. A young child may believe his father's shaving causes the tap water to be turned on, because the two events always happen together.

Concrete Operational Period. Logical reasoning emerges in the concrete operational period. Children become capable of classifying objects into groups, such as fruits or vegetables, based on a logical principle; mentally reversing a series of events; realizing when changes occur in one perceptual dimension and they are compensated for in another, no net change occurs (termed conservation); and understanding the concept of transitivity (for instance, if A > B and B > C, then A > C). However, children are still unable to deal with abstract concepts such as love; to children love is a set of concrete actions and not an ill-defined abstract concept.

Formal Operational Period. For Piaget, the acquisition of formal operational thought during adolescence marks the end of cognitive development. Because he argues formal operational thinking characterizes adult thought, we will consider this level in some detail. Piaget and other commentators (e.g., Lemieux, 2012) agree on four aspects of formal operational thought: (1) It takes a hypothesis-testing approach (termed hypothetico-deductive) to problem solving; (2) thinking is done in one framework at a time; (3) the goal is to arrive at one correct solution; and (4) it is unconstrained by reality.

Piaget describes the essence of formal operational thought as a way of conceiving abstract concepts and thinking about them in a systematic, step-by-step way. Formal operational thought is governed by a generalized logical structure that provides solutions to problems people have never seen and may never encounter. Hypothetico-deductive thought is similar to using the scientific method; it involves forming a hypothesis and testing it until the hypothesis is either confirmed or rejected. Just as scientists are systematic in testing experimental hypotheses, formal operational thinking allows people to approach problem solving in a logical, methodical way.

Consider the situation when your car breaks down. When you take it for repairs, the mechanic forms hypotheses about what may be wrong based on a description of the trouble. The mechanic then begins to test each hypothesis systematically. The compression of each cylinder may be checked, one cylinder at a time. This ability to hold other factors constant while testing a particular component is one of the hallmarks of formal operational thought. By isolating potential causes of the problem, the mechanic efficiently arrives at a correct solution.

When we use hypothetico-deductive thought, we do so to arrive at one unambiguous solution to the problem. Formal operational thought is aimed at resolving ambiguity; one and only one answer is the goal. When more than one solution occurs, there is a feeling of uneasiness and people begin a search for clarification. This situation can be observed in high school classes when students press their teacher to identify the right theory (from among several equally good ones) or the right way to view a social issue (such as abortion). Moreover, when people arrive at an answer, they are quite certain about it because it was arrived at through the use of logic. When answers are checked, the same logic and assumptions are typically used, that sometimes means the same mistake is made several times in a row. For example, a person may repeat a simple subtraction error time after time when trying to figure out why his or her checkbook failed to balance.

Formal operational thinking knows no constraints (Piaget, 1970, 1980). It can be applied just as easily to real or imaginary situations. It is not bound by the limits of reality (Labouvie-Vief, 1980). Whether one can implement a solution is irrelevant; what matters is one can think about it. This is how people arrive at solutions to disarmament, for example, such as getting rid of all nuclear warheads tomorrow. To the formal operational thinker, that this solution is logistically impossible is no excuse. The lack of reality constraints is not all bad, however. Reasoning from a "Why not?" perspective may lead to the discovery of completely new ways to approach a problem or the invention of new solutions.

One serious problem for Piaget's theory is many adults apparently do not attain formal operations. Piaget (1972) himself admitted formal operations were probably not universal but tended to appear only in those areas that individuals were highly trained or specialized. This inspired a number of researchers to look beyond formal operations in determining pathways of adult cognitive development.

Going Beyond Formal Operations: Thinking In Adulthood

Suppose you are faced with the following dilemma:

You are a member of your college's or university's student judicial board and are currently hearing a case involving plagiarism. The student handbook states plagiarism is a serious offense resulting in expulsion. The student accused of plagiarizing a paper admits copying from Wikipedia but says she has never been told she needed to use a formal citation and quotation marks.

When confronted with real world dilemmas, young adults think differently about them than adolescents do.

© Stuart Jenner/Shutterstock.com

Do you vote to expel the student?

When this and similar problems are presented to older adolescents and young adults, interesting differences emerge. Adolescents tend to approach the problem in formal-operational terms and point out the student handbook is clear and the student ignored it, concluding the student should be expelled. Formal-operational thinkers are certain such solutions are right because they are based on their own experience and are logically driven.

But many adults are reluctant to draw conclusions based on the limited information in the problem, especially when the problem can be interpreted in different ways (Sinnott, 1998). They point out there is much about the student we don't know: Has she ever been taught the proper procedure for using sources? Was the faculty member clear about what plagiarism is? For adults, the problem is more ambiguous. Adults may eventually decide the student is (or is not) expelled, but they do so only after considering aspects of the situation that go well beyond the information given in the problem.

Based on numerous investigations, researchers concluded this different type of thinking represents a qualitative change beyond formal operations (Kitchener, King, & DeLuca, 2006; Lemieux, 2012; Sinnott, 2009). **Postformal thought** *is characterized by recognition that truth (the correct answer) may vary from situation to situation, solutions must be realistic to be reasonable, ambiguity and contradiction are the rule rather than the exception, and emotion and subjective factors usually play a role in thinking.* In general, the research evidence indicates post formal thinking has its origins in young adulthood (Kitchener et al., 2006; Sinnott, 2009).

Several research-based descriptions of the development of thinking in adulthood have been offered. *One of the best is the description of the development of* **reflective judgment**, *a way adults reason through dilemmas involving current affairs, religion, science, personal relationships, and the like.* Based on decades of longitudinal and cross-sectional research, King and Kitchener (2002; Kitchener et al., 2006) refined descriptions and identified a systematic progression of reflective judgment in young adulthood. A summary of these stages is shown in Table 7.2.

The first three stages in the model represent prereflective thought. People in these stages typically do not acknowledge and may not even perceive that knowledge is uncertain. Consequently, they do not understand some problems exist when there is not a clear and absolutely correct answer. A student pressuring her instructor for the "right" theory to explain human development reflects this stage. She is also likely to hold firm positions on controversial issues and does so without acknowledging other people's ability to reach a different (but nevertheless equally logical) position.

About halfway through the developmental progression, students think differently. In Stages 4 and 5, students are likely to say nothing can be known for certain and to change their conclusions based on the situation and the evidence. At this point, students argue knowledge is quite subjective. They are also less persuasive with their positions on controversial issues: "Each person is entitled to his or her own view; I cannot force my opinions on anyone else." Kitchener and King refer to thinking in these stages as "quasi-reflective" thinking.

As students continue their development into Stages 6 and 7, they begin to show true reflective judgment, understanding people construct knowledge using evidence and argument after careful analysis of the problem or situation. They once again hold firm convictions but reach them only after careful consideration of several points of view. They also realize they must continually reevaluate their beliefs in view of new evidence.

Even though people are able to think at complex levels, do they? Not usually (King & Kitchener, 2004). Why? Mostly because the environment does not provide the supports necessary for using one's highest-level thinking, especially for issues concerning knowledge and experience you already have. People may not always purchase the product with the least impact

Table 7.2

DESCRIPTION OF THE STAGES OF REFLECTIVE JUDGMENT

Prereflective Reasoning (Stages 1–3): Belief that "knowledge is gained through the word of an authority figure or through firsthand observation, rather than, for example, through the evaluation of evidence. [People who hold these assumptions] believe that what they know is absolutely correct, and that they know with complete certainty. People who hold these assumptions treat all problems as though they were well-structured" (King & Kitchener, 2004, p. 39). *Example statements typical of Stages 1–3:* "I know it because I see it." "If it's on Fox News it must be true."

Quasi-Reflective Reasoning (Stages 4 and 5): Recognition "that knowledge—or more accurately, knowledge claims—contain elements of uncertainty, which [people who hold these assumptions] attribute to missing information or to methods of obtaining the evidence. Although they use evidence, they do not understand how evidence entails a conclusion (especially in light of the acknowledged uncertainty), and thus tend to view judgments as highly idiosyncratic" (King & Kitchener, 2004, p. 40). *Example statements typical of stages 4 and 5:* "I would believe in climate change if I could see the proof; how can you be sure the scientists aren't just making up the data?"

Reflective Reasoning (Stages 6 and 7): People who hold these assumptions accept "that knowledge claims cannot be made with certainty, but [they] are not immobilized by it; rather, [they] make judgments that are 'most reasonable' and about which they are 'relatively certain,' based on their evaluation of available data. They believe they must actively construct their decisions, and that knowledge claims must be evaluated in relationship to the context in which they were generated to determine their validity. They also readily admit their willingness to reevaluate the adequacy of their judgments as new data or new methodologies become available" (King & Kitchener, 2004, p. 40). *Example statements typical of stages 6 and 7:* "It is difficult to be certain about things in life, but you can draw your own conclusions about them based on how well an argument is put together based on the data used to support it."

on the environment, such as a fully electric car, even though philosophically they are strong environmentalists, because recharging stations are currently not widely available. However, if pushed and if given the necessary supports (e.g., easily available charging stations), people demonstrate a level of thinking and performance far higher than they typically show on a daily basis.

Absolutist, Relativistic, and Dialectical Thinking.

A growth in reflective judgment is not the only aspect of post-formal thought researchers examined. Kramer, Kahlbaugh, and Goldston (1992; see also Kallio, 2011) identified three distinct styles of thinking: absolutist, relativistic, and dialectical. Absolutist thinking involves firmly believing there is only one correct solution to problems and personal experience provides truth. Adolescents and young adults typically think this way. Relativistic thinking involves realizing there are many sides to any issue and the right answer depends on the circumstances. Young and early middle-aged adults often think this way. One potential danger is relativistic thinking can lead to cynicism or an "I'll do my thing, and you do yours" approach to life. Because relativistic thinkers reason things out on a case-by-case basis, they are not likely to be strongly committed to any one position. The final step, dialectical thinking, clears up this problem. Dialectical thinkers see the merits in the different viewpoints but synthesize them into a workable solution. This synthesis often produces strong commitment and a definite plan of action.

Since Kramer et al.'s proposal, other researchers extended the notion of dialectical thinking to connect it to wisdom (Kross & Grossmann, 2012), coping flexibility (Cheng, 2009), and the ability to deal with a wide array of everyday problems effectively (Kallio, 2011).

Reflective judgment and dialectical thinking have much in common (Kallio, 2011). The key to postformal thought is the ability to think integratively, to pull together various lines of thought into one integrated whole. That gives adults the ability to understand different points of view and less likely to think from only one ideological perspective. One aspect of this integration involves bringing together logic and emotion.

Integrating Emotion and Logic

In addition to an increased understanding there is more than one "right" answer, adult thinking is characterized by the integration of emotion with logic (Jain & Labouvie-Vief, 2010; Labouvie-Vief, 2006; Labouvie-Vief, Grühn, & Studer, 2010). As they mature, adults tend to make decisions and analyze problems not so much on logical grounds as on pragmatic and emotional grounds. Rules and norms are viewed as relative, not absolute. Mature thinkers realize thinking is an inherently social enterprise that demands making compromises with other people and tolerating contradiction and ambiguity. Such shifts mean one's sense of self also undergoes a fundamental change.

A good example of this developmental shift is the difference between how late adolescents or young adults view an emotionally charged issue—such as unethical behavior at work—compared to the views of middle-aged adults. Younger people may view such behavior as completely inexcusable, with firing of the employee an inescapable outcome. Middle-aged adults may take contextual factors into account and consider what factors may have forced the person to engage in the behavior. Some might argue this is because the topic is too emotionally charged for adolescents to deal with intellectually whereas young adults are better able to incorporate emotion into their thinking.

The integration of emotion with logic in adulthood provides the basis for decision making in the personal and sometimes difficult arenas of love and work that we examine in detail in Chapters 11 and 12, respectively. In the present context, integration sets the stage for envisioning one's future life, a topic we take up later in this chapter.

Implicit Social Beliefs. The developmental integration of thought and emotion during young adulthood and middle age turns out to be influenced by life-cycle forces and cohort effects (see Chapter 1). How strongly people hold beliefs vary as a function of how particular generations were socialized.

Social cognition researchers argue individual differences in the strength of social representations of rules, beliefs, and attitudes are linked to specific situations (Blanchard-Fields, 2009; Labouvie-Vief et al., 2010). Such representations can be both cognitive (how we think about the situation) and emotional (how we react to the situation). When we encounter a specific situation, our cognitive belief system triggers an emotional reaction and related goals tied to the content of that situation demands integration of cognition and emotion. This, in turn, drives social judgments.

Research exploring social beliefs finds age differences in the types of social rules and evaluations evoked in different types of situations (Blanchard-Fields, 2009). When participants considered a husband who chooses to work long hours instead of spending more time with his wife and children, different evaluations about the husband and the marriage emerged. The belief that "marriage is more important than a career" tended to increase in importance with age. As can be seen in Figure 7.5, this is particularly evident from age

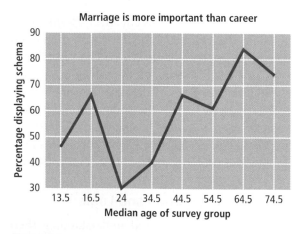
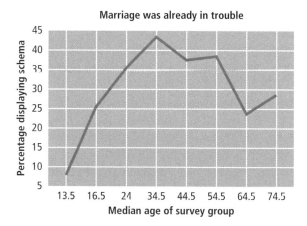

Figure 7.5

There are age differences in social rules and relationships evoked in different situations. As people grow older, there is an increase in the belief that marriage is more important than achievement in a career; also, older and younger couples may have explanations different from those of middle-aged adults as to why marriages fail.

24 to age 65. The social evaluation "the marriage was already in trouble" was also evident and yielded an inverted U-shaped graph; adults between ages 30 and 55 years were most likely to give this evaluation.

One possible explanation for these findings is cohort effects or generational differences (as discussed in Chapter 1) influenced whether strong family social rules would be activated (i.e., how cognition and emotion interact). Alternatively, the results could also reflect issues concerning different life stages of the respondents; the pressures of providing for children may influence how one responds in midlife more so than in early or later adulthood. In any case, social beliefs, as expressed through social rules and evaluations, are powerful influences on how we behave in everyday life. Either way, the developmental shift in the integration of cognition and emotion is an important determinant of age differences in social problem solving.

Neuroimaging Evidence. Evidence from neuroimaging research indicates emotion and logic processing is indeed integrated in adults (Gu, Liu, Van Dam, Hof, & Fan, 2013). This integration occurs in the prefrontal cortex and the anterior insula (an area of the brain deep inside the cortex). Additional research reviewed in Chapter 2 indicates the amygdala is also involved in processing emotion, and this information is also integrated with thought. This type of integration has been shown to be aberrant in some forms of mental disorders (e.g., schizophrenia; Anticevic, Repovs, & Barch, 2012). This means logic and emotion processing share at least some common brain pathways in healthy adults, and these pathways are disrupted in mental disorders..

The integration of emotion with logic that happens in adulthood provides the basis for decision making in the personal and sometimes difficult arenas of love and work that we examine in detail in Chapters 11 and 12, respectively. It also provides the basis for broader perspectives about life, and the ability to see points of view different from one's own.

ADULT DEVELOPMENT IN ACTION

For what types of jobs would an assessment of psychometric intelligence be more appropriate than of reflective judgment? What about the other way around?

7.4 Everyday Reasoning and Problem Solving

LEARNING OBJECTIVES

- What are the characteristics of older adults' decision making?
- What are optimally exercised abilities and unexercised abilities? What age differences have been found in practical problem solving?
- What is expertise and how does experience factor in?
- What are creativity and wisdom, and how do they relate to age and life experience?

Kim is a 75-year-old grandmother visiting her 14-year-old grandson. When he asks her to help with his algebra homework, she declines, stating she just does not have enough schooling to understand it. However, when he has trouble communicating with his parents, Kim can give him excellent advice on how to understand things from both their perspective and his. He ends up getting what he wanted and is delighted to know he can always go to his grandma for advice.

So far, our consideration of intellectual abilities includes examinations of how people's performance on standardized tests and their modes of thinking differ with age. But what we have not considered in detail is how people actually use their intellectual abilities and demonstrate characteristics we associate with intelligent people: solving problems, making decisions, gaining expertise, and becoming wise. This contrast in intellectual abilities is illustrated in Kim's lack of algebraic skills, yet wisdom in her interpersonal skills and the conduct of life. What we discovered in this chapter to this point is people's crystallized intelligence, reflecting life experience, continues to grow (or at least not decline) until later in life, and one hallmark of adults' thinking is the integration of emotion and logic. One might expect, then, the ability to make decisions and solve real-life problems would not decline until late adulthood, that expertise would increase and wisdom would be related to age. Are these expectations correct? Let's find out.

As we discussed, there are many age-related declines in basic cognitive and sensory mechanisms. We also learned there are age-related increases in experience that continues to build semantic memory and crystallized intelligence, as well as postformal thinking. Given these two perspectives on aging, an important distinction must be made. Although there are various age-related declines in the structure and processes of cognitive functioning, it is also important to consider the functional context of everyday behavior that is cognitively demanding. Thus, even though older adults may experience decline in memory, they may have appropriate skills and knowledge adequate for tasks in their daily lives. In other words, we cannot necessarily take information we learn in laboratory experiments on cognitive and intellectual aging and easily apply it to everyday life. Let's explore this distinction first in the area of everyday decision making.

Decision Making

At first glance, the research on decision making suggests older adults make less effective decisions (Besedeš, Deck, Sarangi, & Shor, 2012; Sanfey & Hastie, 2000). Older adults use less optimal strategies when deciding what options to select to best meet their needs (Besedeš et al., 2012). When decision making involves a high degree of working memory capacity (e.g., a lot of information must be held in memory simultaneously in order to make quick decisions), older adults do not perform as well (Peters et al., 2007). However, many everyday decision making situations do not necessarily reflect the firm time constraints and cognitive demands studied in typical laboratory research. Let's examine these situations.

A common everyday decision-making situation involves choosing one best option from a number of choices. These range from assessing automobiles for future purchase (Lambert-Pandraud, Laurent, & Lapersonne, 2005) and treatment decisions for breast cancer (Meyer et al., 2007), to retirement and financial planning (Hershey, Jacobs-Lawson, & Austin, 2013). Findings are quite comparable. Older adults search for less information in order to arrive at a decision, require less information to arrive at a decision, tend to avoid risk, and rely on easily accessible information (Shivapour, Nguyen, Cole, & Denburg, 2012).

When decision-making taps into relevant experience or knowledge, older adults tend to be just as effective or better in making decisions as younger adults. Experience and knowledge tend to make older adults less susceptible to irrational biases in their decision making in comparison to younger adults (Hess, Queen, & Ennis, 2012). It may be when decisions are personally relevant it bolsters older adults' attentional focus on important cues resulting in efficient decisions (Hess et al., 2012; Meyer et al., 2007). How information search strategies matter is discussed in more detail in the How Do We Know? feature.

HOW DO WE KNOW?:

AGE DIFFERENCES IN INFORMATION SEARCH AND DECISION MAKING

Who was the investigator and what was the aim of the study? Hess, Queen, and Ennis (2013) were interested in finding out how adults change their information search strategies as the self-relevance of the information changed. That is, when the information pertains to you personally, it is possible adults use different search strategies than when the information is not personally relevant.

How did the investigator measure the topic of interest? Hess and colleagues used two different decision tasks presented as complex arrays of 48 cells. The two decision tasks involved choosing a wireless phone plan or a prescription drug plan; both are decisions people make in everyday life. Both tasks had eight choice options (the columns in the matrix) and six attributes (the rows in the matrix). Attribute dimensions for the wireless phone plan included: monthly cost, number of minutes, messaging availability, data allowance, overage fees, and geographical coverage. Attributes for the prescription drug plan included: premium, deductible, copay, coverage-gap availability, pharmacy convenience, and formulary breadth. Cells within matrices contained values describing the choices on each of these dimensions. Clicking on the box for the copay attribute for Plan A in the prescription drug plan condition revealed a specific monetary value.

Alternatives were presented in eight different orders to control for effects associated with choice position. A handout describing each attribute dimension for both tasks was provided to eliminate the possibility choice attributes were completely unfamiliar to participants. Only one cell in the matrix could be viewed at a time, mimicking the experience of viewing one webpage at a time in Internet searches.

Participants in the high-accountability condition were told the following: "As an informed consumer, it is important you make good decisions and can justify the basis for these decisions. Therefore, after you have searched through the information in the array and made your choice, I will also ask you to orally justify the decision you made, including the strategy you used to search through the information and the reasons for choosing the alternative you did."

Participants in the low-accountability condition were not given any additional instructions.

Intrinsic motivation was measured with the Personal Need for Structure and the Need for Cognition scales. Participants also completed self-reported health and demographics measures, as well as measures of working memory and verbal ability. Finally, they rated the importance of each attribute in the decision tasks and whether they had experience with decisions like the ones they had to make in the experiment.

Who were the participants in the study? 79 younger (aged 21–41 years) and 81 older (aged 64–90 years) community-dwelling adults participated. Each participant was paid $30.

What was the design of the study? Participants were randomly assigned to a 2 × 2 × 2 (age group × accountability × task) experimental design.

Were there ethical concerns with the study? Participants were volunteers and were provided informed consent, so there were no ethical concerns.

What were the results? The accountability instructions had a disproportionate impact on older adults, who searched the matrices longer than younger adults. All participants viewed more cells in the matrix in the high-accountability than in the low-accountability conditions. The relevance of the information had a bigger impact on older adults' searches than on younger adults' searches. In low relevance tasks, both younger and older adults tended to use an attribute-based approach; participants chose an attribute and compared different alternatives along the same attribute dimension (e.g., compared different phones along the same dimension of number of minutes in the plan). The high relevance task increased the use of alternative-based strategies; respondents compare the same alternative across different attributes (e.g., look at the same phone across multiple attributes such as minutes, messaging, and cost).

What did the investigators conclude? Hess and colleagues concluded older adults are adaptive decision makers, adjusting their strategies based on task demands. Both the relevance of the information and the accountability of the decision affect search strategies.

An area that received considerable attention is the role emotion plays in age differences in decision making. Negative emotions such as anger and fear can be evoked when making a decision. Health related decisions are particularly distasteful because they can involve threat, are high in personal relevance and high importance to the individual (Lockenhoff & Carstensen, 2007). In support of the idea older adults are motivated to reduce the experience of negativity and enhance the experience of positivity (Carstensen & Mikels, 2005), research shows older adults focused more on positive information when making a health decision (Lockenhoff & Carstensen, 2007). Interestingly Kim and colleagues (2008) found older adults focused more on positive information than younger adults did when making a decision only when they were asked to explicitly evaluate their options before making a choice. If not asked to do so, there were no age differences in decision making.

Furthermore, these researchers asked participants how satisfied they were with their decision. For the older adult group asked to evaluate their options, their focus on the positive and satisfaction with their decision remained high over two weeks. In other words, older adults' high level of satisfaction with their decisions increased and persisted over two weeks by simply asking them to spend a few minutes evaluating their options. This did not happen for younger adults. Kim et al. (2008) comment on how advertisements or interventions having a positive impact on one age group may have a completely different impact on another.

Problem Solving

One of the most important ways people use their intellectual abilities is to solve problems. Think for a minute about everyday life and the number of problem-solving situations you encounter in school, on the job, in relationships, driving a car, and so forth. Each of these settings requires you to analyze complex situations quickly, to apply knowledge, and to create solutions, sometimes in a matter of seconds.

Some people tend to be better at dealing with certain problems more than with others. Why is that? One possible explanation has to do with the kinds of abilities we use regularly versus the abilities we use only occasionally. Nancy Denney proposed a more formal version of this explanation that we consider next.

Denney's Model of Unexercised and Optimally Exercised Abilities. Denney (1984) postulates intellectual abilities relating to problem solving follow two types of developmental functions. One of these functions represents unexercised or unpracticed ability, and the other represents optimally trained or optimally exercised ability. Unexercised ability *is the ability a normal, healthy adult would exhibit without practice or training.* Fluid intelligence is thought to be an example of untrained ability, because by definition, it does not depend on experience and is unlikely to be formally trained (Horn & Hofer, 1992). Optimally exercised ability *is the ability a normal, healthy adult would demonstrate under the best conditions of training or practice.* Crystallized intelligence is an example of optimally exercised ability, because the component skills (such as vocabulary ability) are used daily.

Denney argues the overall developmental course of both abilities is the same: They tend to increase until late adolescence or early adulthood and slowly decline thereafter. At all age levels there is a difference in favor of optimally exercised ability, although this difference is less in early childhood and old age. As the developmental trends move away from the hypothetical ideal, Denney argues the gains seen in training programs will increase. As we noted earlier in our discussion of attempts to train fluid intelligence, it appears this increase occurs.

Practical Problem Solving. Denney's model spurred considerable interest in how people solve practical problems. Based on the model, adults should perform better on practical problems than on abstract ones like those typically used on standardized intelligence tests. Tests of practical problem solving would use situations such as the following (Denney et al., 1982): "Let's say that a middle-aged woman is frying chicken in her home when, all of a sudden, a grease fire breaks out on top of the stove. Flames begin to shoot up. What should she do?" (116).

One way to assess practical problem solving in more focused terms is to create measures with clearly identifiable dimensions that relate to specific types of problems (Allaire, 2012). This is what Diehl, Willis, and Schaie (1995) did by creating the Observed Tasks of Daily Living (OTDL) measure. The OTDL consists of three dimensions that reflect three specific problems in everyday life: food preparation, medication intake, and telephone use. Each of these dimensions also reflects important aspects of assessing whether people can live independently, a topic we explored in Chapter 5. Diehl et al. showed performance on the OTDL is directly influenced by age, fluid intelligence, and crystallized intelligence and indirectly by perceptual speed, memory, and several aspects of health. These results provide important links between practical problem solving and basic elements of psychometric intelligence and information processing. However, more recent study findings indicate basic measures of inductive reasoning, domain-specific knowledge, memory, and working memory were related to everyday assessments of each of these abilities (Allaire, 2012; Thornton & Dumke, 2005). Allaire and Marsiske (1999, 2002) conclude everyday problems reflecting well-structured challenges from activities of daily living show a strong relationship to traditional psychometric abilities.

The search for relations between psychometric intelligence and practical problem-solving abilities is only one way to examine the broader linkages with intellectual functioning. It focuses on the degree of how everyday problem solving is a manifestation of underlying intellectual abilities (Berg, 2008). However, recall post-formal thinking is grounded in the ways people conceptualize situations. Indeed, much of the research that led to the discovery of post-formal thought involved presenting adults with lifelike problems. This approach enlarges the scope of what we consider everyday problem solving to include not just cognitive abilities, but also social, motivational, and cultural factors influencing how we solve problems (Berg, 2008).

Another important factor that influences the way we solve everyday problems is the context in which the problem occurs. Do we use the same strategies when solving a family conflict between two siblings as we do when solving a conflict over the leading role in a project at work? The answer is no. Interestingly, however, age differences reveal younger adults are more likely to use a similar strategy across problem-solving contexts: self-action in order to fix the problem. Older adults, on the other hand, are more likely to vary their strategy given the problem-solving context. In interpersonal conflict problems (e.g., family conflict) they use more emotion-regulating strategies (i.e., managing their emotions) whereas in instrumental situations (e.g., dealing with defective merchandise) they use self-action strategies (return the product) (Blanchard-Fields et al., 1997). Blanchard-Fields et al. (1997) argue as we grow older and accumulate more everyday experience, we become more sensitive to the problem context and use strategies accordingly.

There are also individual differences in the way the same problem situation is interpreted. How individuals represent problems differs and could vary across the life span as developmental life goals change (Berg et al., 1998). Berg and colleagues (Berg et al., 1998; Strough et al., 1996) find there are age differences in how individuals define their own everyday problems. Overall, middle-aged older adults defined problems more in terms of interpersonal goals (e.g., getting along with a person or spending more time with an individual), whereas adolescents and young adults focused more on competence goals (e.g., losing weight or studying for an exam). Furthermore, problem-solving strategies fit the problem definitions. Older adults defined problems more in terms of interpersonal concerns and subsequently reported strategies such as regulating others or including others, whereas competence goals resulted in strategies that involved more self-action. Along these lines Artistico, Cervone, and Pezzuti (2003) found older adults were more confident and generated more effective solutions to problems typical of the life stage of older adults. Finally, Blanchard-Fields, Mienaltowski, and Seay (2007) found older adults were rated as more effective in their everyday problem-solving strategy use than younger adults across all types of problem situations.

What can we conclude from the research on practical problem solving? First, practical problem-solving abilities are multidimensional and may not interrelate strongly with each other. Second, the developmental functions of these abilities are complex and may differ across abilities. Third, the relations between practical problem-solving abilities and psychometric intelligence are equally complex. Finally, the close connection between solving practical problems and emotion and motivation may prove fruitful in furthering our understanding of individual differences in abilities. In short, solving practical problems offers an excellent way to discover how all the topics we have considered in this chapter come together to produce behavior in everyday life.

Expertise

We saw earlier in this chapter aspects of intelligence grounded in experience (crystallized intelligence) tend to improve throughout most of adulthood. In a real-world experiential perspective, each of us becomes an expert at something important to us, such as our work, interpersonal relationships, cooking, sports, or auto repair. In this sense, an expert is someone who is much better at a task than people who have not put much effort into it. We tend to become selective experts in some areas while remaining amateurs or novices at others.

What makes experts better than novices? It's how experts handle the problem (Ericsson & Towne, 2010). For novices, the goal for accomplishing the activity is to reach as rapidly as possible a satisfactory performance level that is stable and "autonomous." In contrast, experts build up a wealth of knowledge about alternative ways of solving problems or making decisions. These well-developed knowledge structures are the major difference between experts and novices, and they enable experts to bypass steps needed by novices (Chi, 2006). Experts don't always follow the rules as novices do; they are more flexible, creative, and

Experts in any field handle tasks in those fields differently than novices.

Ariel Skelley/Blend Images/Getty Images

curious; and they have superior strategies grounded on superior knowledge for accomplishing a task (Ericsson & Towne, 2010). Even though experts may be slower in terms of raw speed because they spend more time planning, their ability to skip steps puts them at a decided advantage. In a way, this represents "the triumph of knowledge over reasoning" (Charness & Bosman, 1990).

What happens to expertise over the adult life span? Research evidence indicates expert performance tends to peak by middle age and drops off slightly after that (Masunaga & Horn, 2001). However, the declines in expert performance are not nearly as great as they are for the abilities of information processing, memory, and fluid intelligence that underlie expertise, and expertise may sometimes compensate for declines in underlying cognitive abilities (Masunaga & Horn, 2001; Taylor et al., 2005).

Such compensation is seen in expert judgments about such things as how long certain figure skating maneuvers will take. Older people who were experts were as good as younger adults who were still skating at predicting the amount of time skating moves take (Diersch, Cross, Stadler, Schütz-Bosbach, & Rieger, 2012). Thus, it appears knowledge based on experience is an important component of expertise. But how do people keep acquiring knowledge? That's achieved through lifelong learning.

Lifelong Learning. Many people work in occupations where information and technology change rapidly. To keep up with these changes, many organizations and professions now emphasize the importance of learning how to learn, rather than learning specific content that may become outdated in a couple of years. For most people, a college education will probably not be the last educational experience they have in their careers. Workers in many professions—such as medicine, nursing, social work, psychology, auto mechanics, and teaching—are now required to obtain continuing education credits to stay current in their fields. Online learning has made lifelong learning more accessible to professionals and interested adults alike (Fretz, 2001; Ranwez, Leidig, & Crampes, 2000), but open access to computers for these programs needs to be in supportive, quiet environments (Eaton & Salari, 2005).

Lifelong learning is gaining acceptance as the best way to approach the need for keeping active cognitively, and is viewed as critical part of aging globally (Swindell, 2012), but should lifelong learning be approached as merely an extension of earlier educational experiences? Knowles, Swanson, and Holton (2005) argue teaching aimed at children and youth differs from teaching aimed at adults. Adult learners differ from their younger counterparts in several ways:

- Adults have a higher need to know why they should learn something before undertaking it.

- Adults enter a learning situation with more and different experience on which to build.

- Adults are most willing to learn those things they believe are necessary to deal with real-world problems rather than abstract, hypothetical situations.

- Most adults are more motivated to learn by internal factors (such as self-esteem or personal satisfaction) than by external factors (such as a job promotion or pay raise).

Lifelong learning is becoming increasingly important, but educators need to keep in mind learning styles change as people age. Effective lifelong learning requires smart decisions about how to keep knowledge updated and what approach works best among the many different learning options available (Janssen et al., 2007).

Creativity and Wisdom

Two additional aspects of cognition examined for age-related differences are creativity and wisdom. Each has been the focus of stereotypes: creativity is assumed to be a function of young people, whereas wisdom is assumed to be the province of older adults. Let's see whether these views are accurate.

Creativity. What makes a person creative? Is it exceptional productivity? Does creativity mean having a career marked by precocity and longevity?

Researchers define creativity in adults as the ability to produce work that is novel, high in demand, and task appropriate (Sternberg & Lubart, 2001). Creative output, in terms of the number of creative ideas a person has or the major contributions a person makes, varies across the adult life span and disciplines (Jones,

2010; Kozbelt & Durmysheva, 2007; Simonton, 2012). When considered as a function of age, the overall number of creative contributions a person makes tends to increase through one's 30s, peak in the early 40s, and decline thereafter. The age-related decline does *not* mean people stop being creative altogether, just that they produce fewer creative ideas than when they were younger (Dixon & Hultsch, 1999). In fact, the age when people made major creative contributions, such as research that resulted in winning the Nobel Prize, increased throughout the 20th century (Jones, 2010).

Exciting neuroimaging research is supporting previous research that one's most innovative contribution tends to happen most often during the 30s or 40s, as well as showing that creative people's brains are different. This new research shows white matter brain structures that connect distant brain regions, and coordinate the cognitive control of information among them, are related to creativity and are more apparent in creative people (Jung et al., 2010; Takeuchi et al., 2010). Additional neuroimaging research shows different areas of the prefrontal and parietal areas are responsible for different aspects of creative thinking (Abraham, Beudt, Ott, & von Cramon, 2012). This research supports the belief creativity involves connecting disparate ideas in new ways, as different areas of the brain are responsible for processing different kinds of information. Because white matter tends to change with age, this finding also suggests there are underlying brain maturation reasons why innovative thinking tends to occur most often during late young adulthood and early middle age.

Wisdom. For thousands of years, cultures around the world greatly admired people who were wise. Based on years of research using in-depth think-aloud interviews with young, middle-aged, and older adults about normal and unusual problems people face, Baltes and colleagues (Ardelt, 2010; Baltes & Staudinger, 2000; Scheibe, Kunzmann, & Baltes, 2007) describe four characteristics of wisdom:

- Wisdom deals with important or difficult matters of life and the human condition.

- Wisdom is truly "superior" knowledge, judgment, and advice.

- Wisdom is knowledge with extraordinary scope, depth, and balance that is applicable to specific situations.

- Wisdom, when used, is well intended and combines mind and virtue (character).

Researchers used this framework to discover that people who are wise are experts in the basic issues in life (Ardelt, 2010; Baltes & Staudinger, 2000). Wise people know a great deal about how to conduct life, how to interpret life events, and what life means. Kunz (2007) refers to this as the strengths, knowledge, and understanding learned only by living through the earlier stages of life.

Research studies indicate contrary to what many people expect, there is no association between age and wisdom (Ardelt, 2010; Baltes & Staudinger, 2000; De Andrade, 2000; Hartman, 2001). As envisioned by Baltes and colleagues, whether a person is wise depends on whether he or she has extensive life experience with the type of problem given and has the requisite cognitive abilities and personality. Thus, wisdom could be related to crystallized intelligence, knowledge that builds over time and through experience (Ardelt, 2010).

Culture matters, though, in understanding wisdom. Younger and middle-aged Japanese adults use more wisdom-related reasoning strategies (e.g., recognition of multiple perspectives, the limits of personal knowledge, and the importance of compromise) in resolving social conflicts than younger or middle-aged Americans (Grossman, Karasawa, Izumi, Na, Varnum, Kitayama et al., 2012). However, older adults in both cultures used similar wisdom-related strategies.

So what specific factors help one become wise? Baltes (1993) identified three factors: (1) *general personal conditions* such as mental ability; (2) *specific expertise conditions* such as mentoring or practice; and (3) *facilitative life contexts* such as education or leadership experience. Personal growth during adulthood, reflecting Erikson's concepts of generativity and integrity also fosters the process, as do facing and dealing with life crises (Ardelt, 2010). All of these factors take time. Thus, although growing old is no guarantee of wisdom, it does provide the time, if used well, creates a supportive context for developing wisdom.

Becoming wise is one thing; having one's wisdom recognized is another. Interestingly, peer ratings of wisdom are better indicators of wisdom than self-ratings (Redzanowski & Glück, 2013). It appears people are better at recognizing wisdom in others than they are in themselves. Perhaps it is better that way.

Interestingly, there is a debate over whether with wisdom comes happiness. There is research evidence that wise people are happier (Bergsma & Ardelt, 2012; Etezadi & Pushkar, 2013). Wise people tend to have higher levels of perceived control over their lives and use problem-focused and positive reappraisal coping strategies more often than people who are not wise. On the other hand, some evidence indicates the attainment of wisdom brings increased distress (Staudinger & Glück, 2011). Perhaps because with the experience that brings wisdom comes an understanding that life does not always work out the way one would like.

ADULT DEVELOPMENT IN ACTION

If you were the director of a senior center, how would you capitalize on the wisdom of your members?

SOCIAL POLICY IMPLICATIONS

In the section on training, evidence suggests a cognitively enriched lifestyle can positively influence intellectual change as we grow older. This suggests there is promise in developing long-term cognitive enrichment programs to reduce morbidity and dependence in older adults. For example, it may be the case we can defer the need for assisted living, improve well-being, and reduce health care costs. Projects aimed at training intellectual abilities in older adult populations thus have important public policy implications in terms of funding priorities and reducing the burden on public funding for disabilities in senior citizens. The long-term goals of projects such as ACTIVE is to reduce public health problems associated with the increasing need for more formal care and hospitalization along with the loss of independence in the growing number of American senior citizens.

Richard M. Suzman, Ph.D., Director for the Behavioral and Social Research Program at the National Institute on Aging (NIA), says,

The trial (*ACTIVE trials*) was highly successful in showing that we can, at least in the laboratory, improve certain thinking and reasoning abilities in older people. The findings here were powerful and very specific. Although they did not appear to make any real change in the actual, daily activities of the participants, I think we can build on these results to see how training ultimately might be applied to tasks that older people do every day, such as using medication or handling finances. This intervention research, aimed at helping healthy older people maintain cognitive status as they age, is an increasingly high priority of the NIH/National Institute on Aging.

SUMMARY

7.1 Defining Intelligence

How Do People Define Intelligence In Everyday Life?

- Experts and laypeople agree intelligence consists of problem-solving ability, verbal ability, and social competence. Motivation, exertion of effort, and reading are important behaviors for people of all ages; however, some age-related behaviors are also apparent.

What are the major components of the life-span approach?

- The life-span view emphasizes there is some intellectual decline with age, primarily in the mechanics, but there is also stability and growth, primarily in the pragmatics. Four points are central. Plasticity concerns the range within one's abilities are modifiable. Multidimensionality concerns the many abilities that underlie intelligence. Multidirectionality concerns the many possible ways individuals may develop. Interindividual variability acknowledges people differ from each other.

What are the major research approaches for studying intelligence?

- Three main approaches are used to study intelligence. The psychometric approach focuses on performance on standardized tests. The cognitive-structural approach emphasizes the quality and style of thought. The information-processing approach emphasis basic cognitive mechanisms.

7.2 Developmental Trends in Psychometric Intelligence

What is intelligence in adulthood?

- Intellectual abilities fall into various related abilities that form the structure of intelligence.
- Intelligence in adulthood focuses on how it operates in everyday life.

What are primary mental abilities and how do they change across adulthood?

- Primary abilities comprise the several independent abilities that form factors on standardized intelligence tests. Five have been studied most: number, word fluency, verbal meaning, inductive reasoning, and spatial orientation.
- Primary mental abilities show normative declines with age that may affect performance in everyday life after around age 60, although declines tend to be small until the mid-70s. However, within individual differences show few people decline equally in all areas.

What are fluid and crystallized intelligence? How do they change?

- Fluid intelligence involves innate abilities that make people flexible and adaptive thinkers and underlie the acquisition of knowledge and experience. Fluid intelligence normally declines with age. Crystallized intelligence is knowledge acquired through life experience and education. Crystallized intelligence does not normally decline with age until late life. As age increases, individual differences remain stable with fluid intelligence but increase with crystallized intelligence.
- Age-related declines in fluid abilities have been shown to be moderated by cohort, education, social variables, personality, health, lifestyle, and task familiarity. Cohort effects and familiarity have been studied most. Cohort differences are complex and depend on the specific ability. Age differences in performance on familiar tasks are similar to those on standardized tests. Although taking both into account reduces age differences, they are not eliminated.
- Several studies show that fluid intelligence abilities improve after direct training and after anxiety reduction. Improvements in performance match or exceed individuals' level of decline. Training effects appear to last for several years regardless of the nature of the training, but generalization of training to new tasks is rare.

7.3 Qualitative Differences in Adults' Thinking

What are the main points in Piaget's theory of cognitive development?

- Key concepts in Piaget's theory include adaptation to the environment, organization of thought, and the structure of thought. The processes of thought are assimilation (using previously learned knowledge to make sense of incoming information) and accommodation (making the knowledge base conform to the environment). According to Piaget, thought develops through four stages: sensorimotor, preoperations, concrete operations, and formal operations.

What evidence is there for continued cognitive development beyond formal operations?

- Considerable evidence shows the style of thinking changes across adulthood. The development of reflective judgment in young adulthood occurs as a result of seven stages. Other research identified a progression from absolutist thinking to relativistic thinking to dialectical thinking. A key characteristic of post-formal thought is the integration of emotion and logic. Much of this research is based on people's solutions to real-world problems. Although there have been suggestions that women's ways of knowing differ from men's, research evidence does not provide strong support for this view.

7.4 Everyday Reasoning and Problem Solving

What are the characteristics of older adults' decision making?

- Older adults make decisions in a qualitatively different way from younger adults. They tend to search for less information, require less information, and rely on preexisting knowledge structures in making everyday decisions. Older adults perform more poorly when asked to create or invent new decision rules, in unfamiliar situations, and when the decision task requires high cognitive load.

What age differences are found in practical problem solving?

- In Denney's model, both unexercised and optimally exercised abilities increase through early adulthood and slowly decline thereafter. Performance on practical problem solving increases through middle age. Research indicates sound measures of practical problem solving can be constructed, but these measures do not tend to relate to each other, indicating problem solving is multidimensional. The emotional salience of problems is an important feature that influences problem-solving style with older adults performing better when problems involve interpersonal and emotional features.

What is the role of experience in expertise and problem solving?

■ Older adults can often compensate for declines in some abilities by becoming experts that allows them to anticipate what is going to be required on a task. Knowledge encapsulation occurs with age, when the processes of thinking become connected with the products of thinking. Encapsulated knowledge cannot be decomposed and studied component by component.

What is wisdom and how does it relate to age and life experience?

■ Wisdom involves four general characteristics: it deals with important matters of life; consists of superior knowledge, judgment, and advice; is knowledge of exceptional depth; and is well intentioned. Five specific behavioral criteria are used to judge wisdom: expertise, broad abilities, understanding how life problems change, fitting the response with the problem, and realizing life problems are often ambiguous. Wisdom also entails integrating thought and emotion to show empathy or compassion. Wisdom may be more strongly related to experience than age.

REVIEW QUESTIONS

7.1 Defining Intelligence

■ How do laypeople and researchers define intelligence?

■ What are the two main ways intelligence has been studied? Define each.

7.2 Developmental Trends in Psychometric Intelligence

■ What are primary mental abilities? Which ones have been studied most? How do they change with age?

■ Define fluid and crystallized intelligence. How does each change with age?

■ What factors moderate age changes in fluid intelligence? What role does cohort play? What role do health and lifestyle play?

■ What benefits do older people get from intervention programs aimed at improving fluid abilities? What training approaches have been used? How well do trained skills generalize?

■ Are there any limitations on the extent that older adults can improve their cognitive performance?

7.3 Qualitative Differences in Adults' Thinking

■ What are the key concepts in Piaget's theory?

■ What stages of cognitive development did Piaget identify? Do adults use formal operations?

■ What is reflective judgment? What are the stages in its development? What are absolutist, relativistic, and dialectical thinking?

■ How do emotion and logic become integrated?

■ What evidence is there for gender differences in post-formal thinking?

7.4 Everyday Reasoning and Problem Solving

■ How do older adults differ from younger adults in everyday decision making?

■ What are unexercised and optimally exercised abilities? How do their developmental paths differ from each other?

■ What are the developmental trends in solving practical problems? How does emotional salience of problems influence problem-solving style?

■ What is an expert? How is expertise related to age?

■ What is knowledge encapsulation?

■ What criteria are used to define wisdom? How is wisdom related to age?

INTEGRATING CONCEPTS IN DEVELOPMENT

■ How are the primary and secondary mental abilities related to the aspects of information processing considered in Chapters 6 and 7?

■ What do you think an integrated theory linking post-formal thinking, practical problem solving, expertise, and wisdom would look like?

■ What aspects of secondary mental abilities do you think would be most closely linked to expertise? Why?

■ How does effective social cognitive functioning considered in Chapter 9 relate to wisdom-related behaviors?

KEY TERMS

accommodation Changing one's thought to better approximate the world of experience.

assimilation Using currently available knowledge to make sense out of incoming information.

cognitive-structural approach An approach to intelligence that emphasizes the ways people conceptualize problems and focuses on modes or styles of thinking.

crystallized intelligence Knowledge acquired through life experience and education in a particular culture.

factor The interrelations among performances on similar tests of psychometric intelligence.

fluid intelligence Abilities that make one a flexible and adaptive thinker, that allow one to draw inferences, and allow one to understand the relations among concepts independent of acquired knowledge and experience.

interindividual variability An acknowledgment adults differ in the direction of their intellectual development.

mechanics of intelligence The aspect of intelligence that concerns the neurophysiological architecture of the mind.

multidimensional The notion intelligence consists of many dimensions.

multidirectionality The distinct patterns of change in abilities over the life span, with these patterns being different for different abilities.

neural efficiency hypothesis States intelligent people process information more efficiently, showing weaker neural activations in a smaller number of areas than less intelligent people.

optimally exercised ability The ability a normal, healthy adult would demonstrate under the best conditions of training or practice.

plasticity The range of functioning within an individual and the conditions under which a person's abilities can be modified within a specific age range.

post-formal thought Thinking characterized by a recognition that truth varies across situations, solutions must be realistic to be reasonable, ambiguity and contradiction are the rule rather than the exception, and emotion and subjective factors play a role in thinking.

pragmatic intelligence The component of intelligence that concerns acquired bodies of knowledge available from and embedded within culture.

primary mental abilities Independent abilities within psychometric intelligence based on different combinations of standardized intelligence tests.

psychometric approach An approach to intelligence involving defining it as performance on standardized tests.

reflective judgment Thinking that involves how people reason through dilemmas involving current affairs, religion, science, and the like.

secondary mental abilities Broad-ranging skills composed of several primary mental abilities.

structure of intelligence The organization of interrelated intellectual abilities.

unexercised ability The ability a normal, healthy adult would exhibit without practice or training.

RESOURCES

Access quizzes, glossaries, flashcards, and more at www.cengagebrain.com.

CHAPTER 8

SOCIAL COGNITION

8.1 STEREOTYPES AND AGING
Content of Stereotypes • Age Stereotypes and Perceived Competence • Activation of Stereotypes • Stereotype Threat • *Current Controversies: Are Stereotypes of Aging Associated with Lower Cognitive Performance?*

8.2 SOCIAL KNOWLEDGE STRUCTURES AND BELIEFS
Understanding Age Differences in Social Beliefs • Self-Perception and Social Beliefs • *How Do We Know?: Age Differences in Self-Perception*

8.3 SOCIAL JUDGMENT PROCESSES
Impression Formation • Knowledge Accessibility and Social Judgments • A Processing Capacity Explanation for Age Differences in Social Judgments • Attributional Biases

8.4 MOTIVATION AND SOCIAL PROCESSING GOALS
Personal Goals • Emotion as a Processing Goal • Cognitive Style as a Processing Goal

8.5 PERSONAL CONTROL
Multidimensionality of Personal Control • *Discovering Development: How Much Control Do You Have over Your Cognitive Functioning?* • Control Strategies • Some Criticisms Regarding Primary Control

8.6 SOCIAL SITUATIONS AND SOCIAL COMPETENCE
Collaborative Cognition • Social Context of Memory

SOCIAL POLICY IMPLICATIONS
Summary • Review Questions • Integrating Concepts in Development • Key Terms • Resources

WHEN A PROMINENT DEMOCRAT MARRIED A PROMINENT REPUBLICAN IN 1992,

both of whom were the top consultants to the competing presidential candidates that year, people had difficulty making sense of it. Many thought the marriage of Mary Matalin (George H. W. Bush's political director) and James Carville (Bill Clinton's campaign strategist) was doomed because they were political "opposites." In contrast, the newlyweds saw their passion for politics as a core similarity, and, more than 20 years later, are still married and consulting for different political parties (you may have seen them on various news networks).

The public wonderment about the Matalin–Carville relationship and marriage illustrates how people try to make sense of other people's behavior. Just as James and Mary are viewed through the stereotypes of political affiliation, all of us use social cognition as a way to make sense of the people and the world around us. As we will see, this is the essence of social cognitive functioning.

In this chapter, we consider how the social context is involved in our cognitive processes. We take a closer look at how our basic cognitive abilities influence our social cognitive processing. We examine how our past experiences and beliefs influence our social judgment processes such as how people make impressions and explain behavior (causal attributions). Finally we examine four aspects of social cognition: the role of motivation and emotion as processing goals, the way stereotypes affect how we judge older adults' behavior, the amount of personal control people feel they have, and how cognition is affected when we communicate with others in a social context.

First we need to highlight the importance of social-contextual aspects of cognition in terms of stereotypes. We are confronted with images of older adults all the time through cartoons, advertisements for medical products, jokes on greeting cards, and art. Many of these images are negative (e.g., older adults are terribly forgetful, slow, and easily confused) but some are positive (e.g., older adults are wise). The impact of these stereotypes on our lives is more pervasive than you may think. We'll explore some of these influences.

James Carville and Mary Matalin

Alex Wong/Newsmakers/Getty Images

Additionally, social cognition research raised some important issues for aging research such as how our life experiences and emotions, as well as changes in our pragmatic knowledge, social expertise, and values, influence how we think and remember. To address these issues, we must consider both the basic cognitive architecture of the aging adult (identified in Chapter 6) and the functional architecture of everyday cognition (discussed in Chapter 7). Even if basic cognitive mechanisms decline (such as episodic memory recall or speed of processing) older adults still have the social knowledge and skills that allow them to function effectively. In fact, by taking into consideration social and emotional factors, researchers find older adults' cognitive functioning often remains intact and may even improve across the life span (Blanchard-Fields, Horhota, & Mienaltowski, 2008; Carstensen & Mikels, 2005; Hess, 2005). This approach reinforces the perspective of this textbook that views effective development as a lifelong adaptive process.

8.1 Stereotypes and Aging

LEARNING OBJECTIVES

- How does the content of stereotypes about aging differ across adulthood?
- How do younger and older adults perceive the competence of the elderly?
- How do negative stereotypes about aging unconsciously guide our behavior?

Mark, a 70-year-old man, was getting ready to go home from a poker game at his friend's house. However, he could not find his keys. Down the street, Guy, a 20-year-old college student, was ready to pick up his girlfriend and he could not find his keys. Each of their respective friends at the two social events had different perceptions of Mark and Guy. Mark's friends started to worry whether Mark was becoming senile, speculating it might be all downhill from now on. They wondered whether this was serious enough to call the doctor. However, Guy's friends attributed his forgetfulness to being busy, under a lot of stress, and nervous about his upcoming date.

What accounts for these different explanations of losing one's keys for Mark and Guy? An explanation for the attributions Mark's friends made involves the negative stereotype of aging that older adults are slow-thinking and incompetent. Negative stereotypes of aging are extremely pervasive throughout our culture. Just peruse your local greeting card store and you will find humorous birthday cards capitalizing on our negative expectations about aging. Jokes run amuck about the older adult who keeps losing his or her memory. This captures all our negative stereotypes about memory and aging.

In contrast, the same behavior in a young adult holds very different meaning for most people; stress, preoccupation, lack of attention, and other explanations are used. Rarely is the cause attributed to a young adult's declining cognitive ability.

Fortunately, positive expectations about aging coexist with the negative ones, and stereotypes can be changed (Wurtele & Maruyama, 2013). Older adults are subjected to conflicting stereotypes. On the one hand, older adults are seen as grouchy, forgetful, and losing physical stamina and sexual abilities. On the other hand, older adults are seen as wise, generous, and responsible. The important question researchers ask is what effect stereotypes have on our social judgments and our behavior toward others, such as those in Mark's situation.

Content of Stereotypes

Stereotypes *are a special type of social knowledge structure or social belief. They represent socially shared beliefs about characteristics and behaviors of a particular social group.* We all have stereotypes of groups of people and beliefs about how they will act in certain situations,

such as "Older adults are more rigid in their point of view" or "Older adults talk on and on about their past."

These beliefs affect how we interpret new information. In other words, we use stereotypes to help us process information when engaged in social interactions. Just as with the literature on impression formation discussed earlier, we use stereotypes to size up people when we first meet them. This categorizing helps us understand why they behave the way they do and guides us in our behavior toward other people. Remember, stereotypes are not inherently negative in their effect. However, too often they are applied in ways that underestimate the potential of the person we are observing. This becomes more evident as we explore age-related stereotypes.

Much research has examined adult developmental changes in the content and structure of stereotypes (e.g., Hayslip, Caballero, Ward-Pinson, & Riddle, 2013). From a developmental perspective we ask if there are changes in the nature and strength of our stereotypes as we grow older. Overall, the consensus is growing that adults of all ages have access to multiple stereotypes of older adults (Cuddy & Fiske, 2002; Truxillo, McCune, Bertolino, & Fraccaroli, 2012).

There are also age differences in how we perceive older adults. The consensus on stereotype categories across age groups just depicted above is accompanied by developmental changes in the complexity of age stereotype beliefs. The ability to estimate the age of someone by seeing their face decreases with age, but older adults are better with their age group than are younger adults at judging older faces (Voelkle, Ebner, Lindenberger, & Riediger, 2012). Other studies show older adults identify more categories that fit under the superordinate category "older adult" than do younger and middle-aged adults (Hayslip et al., 2013). Overall, these findings suggest as we grow older, our ideas and age stereotypes become more elaborate and rich as we integrate our life experiences into our beliefs about aging (Baltes et al., 2006; O'Brien & Hummert, 2006).

Are there age differences in how negatively or positively people view older adults? Research indicates older adults have a more positive view of aging in comparison to younger adults (Wentura & Brandtstädter, 2003), a finding that holds cross-culturally, such as in Brazil (de Paula Couto & Koller, 2012). As the baby boom generation ages and redefines what being old means, it will be interesting to see whether stereotypes about older adults also change.

Age Stereotypes and Perceived Competence

Stereotypes are not simply reflected in our perceptions of what we think are representative personality traits or characteristics of older adults. We also make appraisals or attributions of older adults' competence when we observe them perform tasks and we assess whether we can count on them to perform important tasks. No area is more susceptible to negative stereotyped attributions of aging than memory competence. As we discussed in Chapter 6, people of all ages believe memory decreases with age and we have less and less control over current and future memory functioning as we grow older.

The interesting question is, how does this strong belief in age-related loss of memory affect our attributions (explanations) about older adults' competencies? In an elegant and classic series of studies, Joan Erber (e.g., Erber & Prager, 1999) found an age-based double standard in judging the competence of old versus young adults. *The age-based double standard is operating when an individual attributes an older person's failure in memory as more serious than a memory failure observed in a young adult.* So if an older woman cannot find her keys, this is seen as a much more serious memory problem (e.g., possibly attributed to senility) than if a younger woman cannot find her keys. The age-based double standard is most evident when younger people are judging the memory failure.

In contrast, when older people observe the same memory failure, they tend to judge both young and old targets of the story more equally. In fact, most of the time older adults are more lenient toward memory failures in older adults. However, in other types of competence judgments, older adults also display the age-based double standard. When assessing the *cause* of a memory failure, both younger and older people felt the failure was due to greater mental difficulty in the case of an older adult, whereas for younger adults participants attributed it to a lack of effort or attention (Erber et al., 1990).

The preceding tasks involve global explanations of memory failures in younger and older adults. However, what happens when you are asked to decide if an older adult should get a job or perform a task that demands memory capabilities? In several studies Erber and colleagues presented younger and older participants with an audiotaped interview of people applying for various volunteer positions, such as in a museum (Erber & Long, 2006; Erber & Szuchman, 2002). The applicant was either old or young, and either forgetful or not forgetful. They found despite the age-based double standard in judging older adults' memory failures found in earlier studies, people (both young and old) had more confidence in and would assign tasks or jobs to nonforgetful people irrespective of age.

What accounts for this apparent discrepancy in findings? Maybe, when forming an impression about someone's capability, people take other factors into consideration. For example, traits could come into play, such as how responsible the person is. Remember stereotypes about older adults included many positive ones, including being responsible. In fact, young adults were asked whom they would choose to be a neighbor they could rely on. Despite forgetfulness ratings, they consistently chose older neighbors over younger ones. They also judged older neighbors to be more responsible, reliable, dependable, and helpful than younger ones. Thus, being able to access these positive traits may have compensated for older neighbors' forgetfulness. In a recent follow-up study, younger and older adults rated both younger and older targets similarly on negative traits such as forgetfulness; however, only the older targets were rated higher on desirable traits such as responsibility (Erber & Szuchman, 2002).

What can we conclude from the trait studies of stereotypes and the attribution studies of stereotypes? First, when more individualized information (e.g., providing an audiotaped interview of the person) is provided and the individual is considered in a social setting (e.g., a volunteer position interview, a neighborly interaction), people consider more than just negative trait-based stereotypes in making social judgments. As in the neighborly interaction, we consider additional and more positive trait information such as reliable or dependable. The volunteer position may be perceived as a context that older adults would be effective regardless of their memory competence. In fact, research is drawing on these findings to identify what types of social environments will facilitate older adults' social competence. We examine this later.

Activation of Stereotypes

From the preceding review of research we know stereotypes of older adults exist regarding personality traits and perceptions of competence. They also influence our judgments about how capable older adults will be in memory-demanding situations. However, it is not enough to know the stereotypes exist; we need to know under what conditions they are activated, and if activated, how they affect our behavior and social judgments. Why do negative stereotypes of older adults influence our behaviors (e.g., talking down to older adults as if they were children) and attitudes (Hehman et al., 2012)? Considerable research in social cognition focuses on stereotype activation as a relatively unconscious and automatic process that guides our behavior and social judgments (e.g., Kunda & Spencer, 2003; Yen, Jewell, & Hu, 2013).

Social psychologists suggest the reason stereotypes are automatically activated is they become overlearned and thus are spontaneously activated when we encounter a member or members of a stereotyped group, such as African American or Muslim (Stojnov, 2013). *The activation of strong stereotypes, called* implicit stereotyping, *is not only automatic but also unconscious.* Thus it is more likely they influence our behavior without our being aware of it.

The effects of such implicit stereotyping are illustrated in a clever and classic study conducted by John Bargh and colleagues (Bargh et al., 1996). They demonstrated if you subliminally (outside of conscious awareness) prime young people with the image of an elderly person, the young people's actual behavior is influenced in an age-related manner (where age-related refers to the target person's age). In this case, the implicitly primed young adults walked down the hall more slowly after the experiment than did young adults who were not primed with the elderly image. This is a powerful demonstration of how our unconscious stereotypes of aging can influence our behavior.

Measuring implicit aging stereotyping is a challenge because by definition it is inaccessible. However, research using a technique called the Young-Old Implicit Attitudes Test (Crisp & Turner, 2012; Hummert et al., 2002) overcame this challenge. In this test, individuals categorize photographs of faces by

Implicit stereotyping of people, such as of older adults, can have a profound effect on people's behavior.

JGI/Tom Grill/Blend Images/Getty Images

indicating as fast as they can whether the photo is a younger or older person. They are asked to press a button with their right hand to indicate young and with their left hand to indicate old. Then they categorize other photographs as pleasant or unpleasant with the right hand indicating pleasant and the left hand indicating unpleasant. Next is the two-part test of implicit aging stereotypes. Part one consists of a combination of the young-old and pleasant-unpleasant categorization task using the same hands as just indicated. In this test, the right hand is associated with both young and pleasant, whereas the left hand is associated with both old and unpleasant. The second part reverses the hands for young-old. Now the right hand is associated with old and the left hand is associated with young. The right hand is still associated with pleasant, and the left hand with unpleasant. The logic is this: If you have a negative stereotype regarding aging, you will be much slower in your response during the second test.

It becomes difficult to use your right hand to indicate old because it is also associated with pleasant. This difficulty slows your response down.

Using this methodology, researchers (e.g., Crisp & Turner, 2012; Hummert et al., 2002) found people of all ages were faster to respond to young-pleasant and old-unpleasant trials than to old-pleasant and young-unpleasant trials. Furthermore, all individuals had implicit age attitudes that strongly favored the young over the old. If you would like to experiment with this test, it is available on the Internet.

Implicit stereotyping is illustrated in different domains of our behavior toward others as well. In many situations nursing staff or younger adults in general are trying to instruct or communicate with older adults, as seen in the photo. Much evidence suggests younger people engage in patronizing talk toward older adults in these situations (Hehman et al., 2012). As we saw in Chapter 5, patronizing speech can be detrimental to old adults' well-being.

Why do people engage in patronizing speech? Again, implicit stereotyping may be the answer. When communicating to others, we try to accommodate our audience so they understand what we are trying to say. In this case, when communicating to an older adult, negative stereotypes of older adults as less competent, less able to hear, and having poor memories may be activated and unconsciously and inadvertently result in an inaccurate assessment of how to accommodate our speech (see Chapter 5).

Stereotype Threat

Another important question to ask is whether implicit negative stereotypes of aging influence the cognitive functioning of older adults. This possibility is raised in the context of widely cited social psychological research on stereotype threat. Stereotype threat *is an evoked fear of being judged in accordance with a negative stereotype about a group to which you belong.* For example, if you are a member of a socially stigmatized group such as Latinos or Muslims, you are vulnerable to cues in your environment that activate stereotype threat about academic ability. In turn, you may perform more poorly on a task associated with that stereotype regardless of high competence in academic settings.

Substantial attention has focused on understanding the harmful effects of negative aging stereotypes on memory performance in older adults (Levy, Zonderman, Slade, & Ferrucci, 2012). Do older adults belong to a stigmatized group that is vulnerable to stereotype threat? Some researchers suggested that negative stereotypes do adversely affect older adults' cognitive functioning and may contribute to our perception of age-related decline in cognitive functioning (see Chapter 6). The initial studies examining this possibility used techniques similar to our discussion of stereotype activation: assessing implicit stereotyping. Becca Levy's nearly two decades of research has caused some controversy in this area. Read the Current Controversies feature. What do you think?

CURRENT CONTROVERSIES:

ARE STEREOTYPES OF AGING ASSOCIATED WITH LOWER COGNITIVE PERFORMANCE?

A major controversial issue in the cognitive aging literature is whether living in a society that equates old age with memory decline, senility, and dependency produces what Langer (1989) calls a "premature cognitive commitment" early in life. As children, we acquire ideas of what it means to be old, ideas that are usually negative, that become stereotypes guiding and influencing our behavior later in life. Thus, the question is the degree that negative societal beliefs, attitudes, and expectations determine the cognitive decline we observe in older adults.

When Levy and Langer (1994) first compared memory performance and attitudes on aging of Chinese older adults, hearing American older adults, and deaf American older adults, they found the Chinese older adults outperformed both groups of American older adults on several memory tasks. In addition, the deaf American older adults outperformed their hearing American counterparts. Attitudes on aging held by the different cultures were related to memory performance (Chinese had more positive attitudes, whereas Americans had more negative attitudes). Levy and Langer concluded negative stereotypes in American culture accounted for this difference.

However, there were several concerns with this correlational study. Does enhanced memory performance lead to more positive attitudes, or do positive attitudes lead to enhanced memory performance? Are there educational differences between the two cultural groups? Are the memory tests really the same given that they had to be translated into Chinese?

To further test this notion, Levy (1996) subliminally primed younger and older adults with negative stereotypes of an older adult (e.g., the word *senile*) or positive stereotypes (e.g., the word *wise*). She found when older adults were primed with negative aging stereotypes, their performance was worse on memory tests than older adults primed with positive stereotypes. Other researchers confirmed this result (e.g., Stein, Blanchard-Fields, & Hertzog, 2002; von Hippel & Henry, 2012).

Levy's most important and controversial finding goes well beyond results from laboratory task results in a one-time testing experience. She and her colleagues (Levy et al., 2012) showed adults over age 60 with more negative age stereotypes demonstrated over 30% greater decline in memory performance over 38 years than those with fewer negative age stereotypes.

It is intriguing and intuitive to believe a self-fulfilling prophecy operates with respect to older adults' memory performance. If society portrays older adults as declining in cognitive capacity and you are socialized to believe so at a young age, and if you believe these stereotypes, then it makes sense this will influence your memory performance as an older adult. All in all, negative stereotypes of aging exist. They have an effect on cognitive performance. Thus, although you may not be able to eliminate the decline in performance, interventions for improving attitudes and outlook on aging have the potential to improve the quality of performance relative to one's own level of functioning (Cherry, Brigman, Reese-Melancon, Burton-Chase, & Holland, 2013).

There is also evidence middle-aged adults are susceptible to negative age stereotypes (O'Brien & Hummert, 2006). Middle-aged adults who identified with older adulthood showed poorer memory performance if they were told their performance would be compared with other older adults. Middle-aged adults with more youthful identities did not show differences in memory performance regardless of whether they were told they would be compared to younger or older individuals.

Although most of the research in this area focused on the detrimental effects of negative stereotypes, some evidence also exists for the beneficial effects of positive stereotypes on older adults' cognitive performance. Compared to Milanese, Sardinians hold more positive attitudes about memory aging and perform better on memory tasks (Cavallini, Bottirolli, Fastame, & Hertzog, 2013).

The influence of stereotypes on performance is not restricted to just memory. Levy and Leifheit-Limson (2009) found subliminally inducing physical negative aging stereotypes had a harmful effect on older adults' balance performance. In contrast, presenting older adults with positive physical aging stereotypes resulted in better balance performance. Similarly, Levy and colleagues (2000) found that older adults exposed to negative aging stereotypes showed a heightened cardiovascular response to a stressful situation compared to older adults exposed to positive aging stereotypes. Levy argues negative aging stereotypes can be viewed as direct stressors.

Positive aging stereotypes, in contrast, could potentially have the ability to reduce cardiovascular stress. Finally, Levy, Slade, and Kasl (2002) found in a longitudinal study older adults who maintained positive perceptions of themselves as aging individuals tended to be healthier over time than those who held a negative self-perception of aging. Similarly, Jeste, Savla, Thompson, Vahia, Glorioso, Martin and colleagues (2013) report the stereotype of aging may be changing. It was the oldest-old who had the most positive view of successful aging. Thus it is important to recognize the role of positive stereotypes on older adults. Remember, however, this is correlational data. It does not tell us whether positive stereotypes cause people to be healthy across their adult life span. Nevertheless, the findings discussed here demonstrate how pervasive and powerful stereotypes can be on our behavior.

ADULT DEVELOPMENT IN ACTION

How would knowledge about the effects of negative stereotypes on older adult's cognition affect your approach to assessing them in a healthcare setting?

Social Knowledge Structures and Beliefs

LEARNING OBJECTIVES

- What are social knowledge structures?
- What are social beliefs, and how do they change with age?
- What are self-perceptions of aging, and what influences them across adulthood?

Anna is going on her first date since the death of her husband one year ago. She is 62 years old and was married for 30 years, so she is extremely nervous about what to do and how to act. When her date, Eric, picks her up, he announces he has made reservations at a nice Italian restaurant and afterward they will go to a late movie. Although Anna is nervous, she makes it through the date with few problems. To her delight, how she needs to act and what she should do came flooding back to her without an ounce of effort.

Similar to our knowledge of how a supervisor should act, on her date Anna experienced the easy accessibility of a well-learned social script or social knowledge on how to behave on a date. Social cognitive research has paid considerable attention to how social knowledge structures and social beliefs guide behavior.

Social knowledge structures and social beliefs are defined in terms of how we represent and interpret the behavior of others in a social situation (Frith & Frith, 2012). They come in many different forms. We have scripted knowledge structures regarding everyday activities such as what people should do when they go to the doctor's office or a restaurant. We are socialized to adhere to and believe in social rules, or how to behave in specific social situations, such as how a husband should act toward his wife.

Understanding Age Differences in Social Beliefs

Two interesting developmental questions arise with respect to social knowledge structures. First, does the content of our social knowledge and beliefs change as we grow older? And second, how do our knowledge structures and beliefs affect our social judgments, memory, problem solving, and more?

There are many types of belief systems that differ in content across age groups and also influence behavior. Understanding age differences in social belief systems has three important aspects (Blanchard-Fields & Hertzog, 2000; Blanchard-Fields et al., 2012; Blanchard-Fields & Horhota, 2006). First, we examine the specific content of social beliefs (i.e., the particular beliefs and knowledge individuals hold about rules, norms, and patterns of social behavior). Second, we consider the strength of these beliefs to know under what conditions they may influence behavior. Third, we need to know the likelihood these beliefs are automatically activated when a person is confronted with a situation when these beliefs are being violated or questioned. If these three aspects of the belief system are understood, it is possible to explain when and why age differences occur in social judgments.

Older adults may hold different beliefs than other age groups (e.g., different rules for appropriate social behavior during Anna's situation of dating). Such differences may stem from cohort differences (see Chapter 1). Additionally, how strongly individuals hold these beliefs may vary as a function of how particular generations were socialized. Although younger and older generations may both believe people should not live together before marriage, the oldest generation may be more adamant and rigid about this belief. However, evidence of age differences in the content of social beliefs does not provide a sufficient basis for understanding age differences in how and when such beliefs are activated and how they influence behavior.

Social cognition researchers argue there are individual differences in the strength of social representations of rules, beliefs, and attitudes linked to specific situations (Frith & Frith, 2012). Such representations can be both cognitive (how we conceptualize the situation) and emotional (how we react to the situation). When encountering a specific situation, the individual's belief system predictably triggers an emotional reaction and related goals tied to the content of that situation. This in turn drives social judgments.

Let's take the rule "You should never live with a romantic partner before you are married." If you were socialized from childhood to believe in this rule, you would negatively evaluate anyone violating it. If you were told Allen was putting pressure on Joan to live with him before they were married, and they subsequently broke up, you might have a negative emotional response and blame Allen for the breakup of the relationship because he was lobbying for cohabitation.

In a series of classic studies exploring social beliefs, age differences were found in the types of social rules evoked in different types of situations (Blanchard-Fields, 1996, 1999). Consider the situation we encountered in Chapter 7 about the influence of social rules on cognition (see page 204) in a situation that a husband chooses to work long hours instead of spending more time with his wife and family. As we saw in Figure 7.5, adults of different ages invoke the social rule "Marriage is more important than a career" more with increasing age. This was particularly evident from age 24 to age 65. Figure 7.5 also shows the social rule "The marriage was already in trouble" has an inverted U-shaped relationship. In other words, adults around ages 35 to 55 years as compared to 24- to 35-year-olds and those over 65 years produced this social rule the most.

In the present context, these findings indicate the influence of cohort effects on how different generations were socialized with respect to the important social rules of marriage. The oldest generation was probably socialized differently from the current younger adult generation as to what is appropriate behavior on the part of husbands and wives.

Alternatively, viewing marriage as more important than one's career may relate to the particular life stage and life circumstances different age groups confront rather than cohort differences. In this view, irrespective of cohort, making a living and proving oneself in a career may take precedence during mid-career/mid-family stages (Schaie, 1977–1978). In contrast, during the retirement/empty nest phase, the importance of a marital relationship may reemerge.

Still another interpretation might be the middle-aged group may not have relied on social rules to guide their thinking about the problem situation and focused more on the marital conflict itself. This could possibly reflect a by-product of the 1960s focus on communication of feelings. These are only a few examples of the complex sociocultural experiential factors that may influence different social beliefs.

Let's consider another scenario, this time involving a youthful couple who eloped despite the objections of their parents. The social rules "Parents should have talked to, not provoked, the young couple" and "They were too young" also displayed an inverted U-shaped relationship with age. Middle-aged individuals endorsed these rules, whereas younger and older age groups did not.

In contrast, the social rule "You can't stop true love" displayed a U-shaped relationship with age. Younger and older age groups endorsed this rule whereas individuals in middle adulthood did not. It may be the case in middle adulthood, between the ages 30 and 45, people are not focusing on issues of "Love conquers all." This makes sense given they are in the stage of life where the pragmatic aspects of building a career are more important than the passion of love. Middle-aged adults also emphasized the pragmatics of age (e.g., being too young) as an important factor in marriage decisions.

In summary, how social rules are invoked in making social judgments is a complex process. To some extent, the process reflects generational differences, and it reflects life experience. How these judgments influence our judgments about personal responsibility for behavior is a topic we turn to next.

Self-Perception and Social Beliefs

An important facet for understanding the impact of social beliefs on people is to understand how we form impressions of ourselves. It's our personal answer to the question, "How old do you feel?" that creates our self-perception of aging. Self-perception of aging *refers to individuals' perceptions of their own age and aging.*

Researchers have been curious about how people see themselves on this dimension for many years. In Chapter 14, how we view ourselves is an important predictor of whether we age successfully (or not). We know that positive self-perceptions are correlated with many good outcomes, such as better well-being, better health, and longer life (Kotter-Grühn & Hess, 2012).

Without doubt, what we think is true about the process of aging affects what we think of ourselves. The social stereotypes we associate with aging influence what we believe is true about us.

There are two major frameworks to explain how this influence works. Labeling theory *argues when we confront an age-related stereotype, older adults are more likely to integrate it into their self-perception.* Research on impression formation and priming of stereotypes supports this view. Resilience theory *argues confronting a negative stereotype results in a rejection of that view in favor of a more positive self-perception.* This view comes from people's tendency to want to distance themselves from the negative stereotype. Research shows older adults dissociate themselves from their age group when negative stereotypes become relevant to them (e.g., Weiss & Lang, 2012).

A good example of this line of research is highlighted in the How Do We Know? feature. Kotter-Grühn and Hess (2012) studied how negative views of aging were or were not assimilated into adults' views of themselves.

What's so different about self-perceptions of age and aging is it is one of the few areas we go from looking at old people and aging as something that happens to someone else rather than something happening to us (Kornadt & Rothermund, 2012). Research on how we incorporate societal views of age and aging indicate the extent to which that happens depends critically on our own old age and aging in specific domains of life (e.g., health). When we consider the influence stereotypes have on our thinking, we return to the ways self-perception affects how well we do things like remember information and even our health and longevity.

ADULT DEVELOPMENT IN ACTION

If you are a taking a poll on attitudes toward specific social issues, how would you design the survey to uncover the reasons for any age differences that were found?

HOW DO WE KNOW?:

AGE DIFFERENCES IN SELF-PERCEPTION

Who were the investigators and what was the aim of the study? Kotter-Grühn and Hess (2012) knew people's self-perceptions are important predictors of well-being and health. They wanted to find out what the specific indicators of self-perceptions of aging across adulthood are, and whether specific stereotypes about aging influenced self-perceptions.

How did the investigators measure the topic of interest? Personal satisfaction with aging was measured through a well-researched scale, the Philadelphia Geriatric Center Morale Scale. Respondents also indicated their "felt age," "desired age," and "perceived age." Physical health was assessed by a health survey. Age-related stereotypes were activated through a priming approach of rating faces described with either positive, negative, or neutral terms.

Who were the participants in the study? 183 adults aged 18–92 years volunteered to participate. There were 60 younger adults, 62 middle-aged adults, and 61 older adults. Overall, participants averaged over 14 years of education, and were paid $15/hour.

Were there ethical concerns with the study? Because the study used volunteers and were provided informed consent, there were no ethical concerns.

What were the results? As participant age increased, participants increasingly indicated they felt, wanted to be, and believed they looked proportionally younger than their actual age. Younger adults wanted to be about 4% older than they actually were, and older adults wanted to be about 33% younger than they were.

Following the priming task, older adults were the only age group to feel older regardless of whether the priming was positive or negative. For desired age, participants in all age groups who were in bad health reported they wanted to be a younger age after experiencing the negative priming task (but no change otherwise). For perceived age, all participants in poor health reported themselves as looking older after receiving the negative priming task.

All adults reported being relatively satisfied with their aging process.

What did the investigators conclude? Kotter-Grühn and Hess concluded that people's perceptions of their own aging are not made more positive by presenting them with positive images of aging. Actually, the opposite effect occurred for younger and middle-aged adults in good health—when given positive stereotypes, those groups reported feeling *older* than before the priming task. Their conclusion was negative images of aging have more powerful effects than positive ones in determining self-perceptions of aging.

8.3 Social Judgment Processes

LEARNING OBJECTIVES

- What is the negativity bias in impression formation, and how does it influence older adults' thinking?
- Are there age differences in accessibility of social information?
- How does processing context influence social judgments?
- To what extent do processing capacity limitations influence social judgments in older adults?

Alexandra and Klaus were taking care of their grandchildren for the weekend. They took them to the zoo for an outing. When they passed the gift shop, the children would not stop whining that they wanted a present. This frustrated Alexandra and Klaus, and they both tried to come up with an explanation for this distressing behavior. At first, they were worried because it seemed the behavior of their grandchildren indicated they were, in essence, selfish children. But on further reflection, they considered other factors. The parents always bought the children a gift at the zoo, and so the children naturally expected it to happen again. The grandparents felt better about the situation after considering the parents' role in it and bought the gifts for the children.

In this situation, Alexandra and Klaus were making important social judgments. They carefully analyzed the situation to understand their grandchildren's behavior by focusing on all the factors involved in it. Alexandra and Klaus show how we can correct our initial assessments of others if we take the time to reflect about all of the extenuating circumstances.

But what would have happened if they did not have the time to think about it, and instead had multiple distractions, such as dealing with the emotional outbursts of their grandchildren as well as their own emotional reactions? Their judgments could also have been influenced by strong beliefs about how children should behave in a social situation such as this one.

We consider the influence of both of these factors on making social judgments: the role played by cognitive capacity, or having enough time and making the effort to reflect on a situation, and social knowledge and beliefs. However, first let us explore the age differences in making social judgments.

Many laboratory studies examined abstract cognitive skills and how they change as we get older (see Chapter 6). Like the everyday cognition research discussed in Chapter 7, an important question in social cognition research is: to what extent do the findings from the lab translate into understanding behavior in everyday contexts as people grow older? The social cognition perspective provides a way of examining how basic cognitive abilities operate in social situations. The basic goal of the social cognition approach is to understand how people make sense of themselves, others, and events in everyday life (Frith & Frith, 2012).

Impression Formation

When people meet each other, we tend to immediately come to conclusions about them on many dimensions. Researchers (e.g., Adams, Nelson, Soto, Hess, & Kleck, 2012; Hess & Emery, 2012) examine age differences in social judgments by examining impression formation. **Impression formation** *is the way we form and revise first impressions about others.* Researchers examine how people use diagnostic trait information (aspects about people that appear critical or unique) in making initial impressions of an individual, and how this process varies with age. A common way of studying this is to have two groups of adults presented with information about a person, either through descriptions or inferences. One group gets positive information first, such as evidence of honesty. The other group is presented with negative information first, such as incidents of dishonest behavior. Each group then subsequently gets the opposite information about the

Older adults tend to hold onto first impressions longer when meeting new people.

Jupiterimages/Comstock Images/Getty Images

person (e.g., the group that got positive information first then gets negative information).

What happens to people's first impressions as a function of age is a well-established finding. As you can see from Figure 8.1, in a study that helped create this area of research focus, Hess and Pullen (1994) found all study participants modified their impressions. When new negative information was presented after the initial positive portrayal of the target person, older adults modified their impression of the target from positive to negative. Interestingly, however, they modified their first impression *less* when the negative portrayal was followed by positive information. Older adults make impressions influenced by all the information they receive.

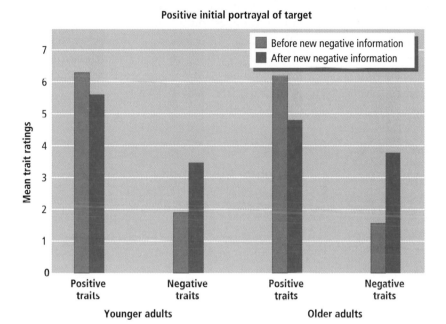

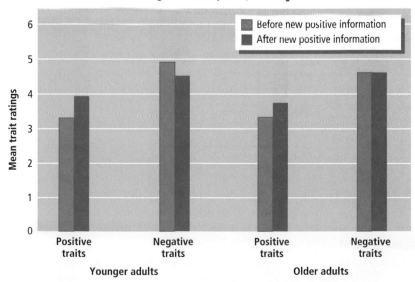

Figure 8.1

Mean trait ratings before and after presentation of new negative or positive information.

Source: A modified graph of the Hess, T. M., & Pullen, S. M. (1994). Adult age differences in impression change processes. Psychology and Aging 9, *p. 239.*

In contrast, younger adults did not show this pattern. Instead, they were more concerned with making sure the new information was consistent with their initial impression. To do so, they modified their impressions to correspond with the new information regardless of whether it was positive or negative. Younger adults, then, make their impression based on the most recent information they have.

Why do younger and older adults differ? Hess and Pullen suggest older adults may rely more on life experiences and social rules of behavior when making their interpretations, whereas younger adults may be more concerned with situational consistency of the new information presented. They also suggest older adults may be more subject to a negativity bias in impression formation. Negativity bias *occurs when people allow their initial negative impressions to stand despite subsequent positive information because negative information was more striking to them and thus affected them more strongly.*

This bias corresponds well with other studies demonstrating older adults pay attention to and seek out emotional information more than do younger people (Isaacowitz & Blanchard-Fields, 2012; von Hippel & Henry, 2012). We discuss this further later in the chapter. This bias suggests decline in cognitive functioning limits the ability of older adults to override the impact of their initial impressions.

Further evidence shows the social judgments older adults make appear to be more sensitive to the diagnosticity of the available information (Hess, 2006). If young adults receive new information about a person that contradicts their original impression, they are likely to adjust the initial impression. However, older adults are more selective in the information they choose to use in forming their judgments. They focus more on the relevant details to make those judgments, and change their initial impression only if the new information is *diagnostic*, that is relevant and informative (Hess & Emery, 2012; Hess, Germain, Rosenberg, Leclerc, & Hodges, 2005). It appears for older adults to invest information-processing resources in making a judgment, they need to be invested in the social situation that the judgment is made.

In some situations, older adults may be at a disadvantage when processing social information. Researchers have found although younger and older adults can process social information similarly, older adults are at a disadvantage when the social context is cognitively demanding (Hess & Emery, 2012; von Hippel & Henry, 2012). A cognitively demanding situation is similar to Alexandra and Klaus's situation where they were trying to understand their grandchildren's behavior under conditions of time pressure and multiple distractions. Researchers find when older adults take their time to make a social judgment, they process information similarly to younger adults and take into consideration all of the relevant information. However, when given a time limit, they have difficulty remembering the information they need to make their social judgments (Ybarra & Park, 2002; Ybarra, Winkielman, Yeh, Burnstein, & Kavanagh, 2011).

In the next section, we examine processes involved in accessing knowledge used to make social judgments.

Knowledge Accessibility and Social Judgments

Although we make judgments about people upon initial meeting and novel situations all the time, we tend not to be aware of exactly how those judgments are made. *When we are faced with new situations, we draw on our previous experiences stored in memory, in other words, our* social knowledge.

The stored knowledge about previous situations that might be similar and how easily we can retrieve it, affects what types of social judgments we make and how we behave in social situations. If you are attending your first day of work, for example, in order to act appropriately you draw on social knowledge that tells you "how to behave in a job setting." This process includes having available stored representations of the social world or memories of past events, how to apply those memories to various situations, and easy access to the memories.

We draw on implicit theories of personality (our personal theories of how personality works) to make judgments. For example, how a supervisor should behave at work. If the supervisor's behavior is inconsistent with our implicit theory of how he or she should act, this affects the impression we form of the supervisor. If a supervisor dresses in shorts and T-shirt and makes casual references to the party he attended last night, this may violate our implicit theory that supervisors should dress and act professionally. Research supports that implicit personality theories we have about people, in general, influence the impressions we form about specific individuals (Uleman & Saribay, 2012; von Hippel & Henry, 2012).

However, the fact social information in memory is available does not necessarily imply it is always easy to access to the information. The degree to which information in memory is easily accessible and remembered determines the extent that information will guide social judgments and/or behavior.

As we saw in Chapter 7, easy access to information will be influenced by several variables. First, accessibility depends on the strength of the information stored in memory. If you have extensive past experience with people who are aggressive, retrieving and applying the specific personality trait "aggressive," will be a highly accessible social knowledge structure representing features of this particular personality trait (e.g., dominance in social situations, highly competitive, and so on). Thus, you would judge a person as "aggressive" by interpreting the collection of behaviors you associate with "aggressive" as clearly diagnostic of aggressiveness.

In contrast, the personality trait construct "aggressive" would not be easily accessible for people who have little or no experience with aggressive people because the trait of aggressiveness may not have been retrieved often. These people would be likely to interpret the behavior differently (Uleman & Saribay, 2012). They may see the dominant or aggressive behavior a person exhibits as indicative of positive leadership.

Age differences in the accessibility of social knowledge influence social judgments across adulthood. First, as we saw in the case of impression formation, older adults rely on easily accessible social knowledge structures such as the initial impression made about an individual. Second, *age differences in knowledge accessibility also depend on the extent people rely on* source judgments, *in other words, when they try to determine the source of a particular piece of information.* Suppose you and a friend were introduced to two new people last week. Jane is an athlete and Sereatha is a bookworm. Sereatha revealed to you she loves to play tennis. Today, your friend asks you whether it was Jane or Sereatha that loves to play tennis. This is a source judgment.

Mather and colleagues (Mather, 2012; Nashiro, Sakaki, Huffman, & Mather, 2013) found when making source judgments, older adults rely more on easily accessible knowledge than younger adults. In the example of meeting Jane and Sereatha, older adults would be more likely to erroneously remember Jane loves to play tennis, as they would rely on an easily accessible stereotype the athlete is more likely to love tennis than the bookworm.

Finally, older adults make more social judgment biases because they have trouble distinguishing between true and false information (Chen, 2002; Wang & Chen, 2006). In studies by Chen and colleagues, older adults were instructed to disregard false information (printed in red) and pay attention to true information (printed in black) when reading criminal reports. The older adults had difficulty in doing so, and the false information (e.g., information exacerbating the nature of the crime) biased their judgments about how dangerous the criminal was and this affected their determination of the criminal's prison sentence.

Neuroimaging research indicates damage to or age-related changes in certain parts of the prefrontal cortex may be responsible for increased susceptibility to false information (Asp, Manzel, Koestner, Cole, Denburg, & Tranel, 2012). Therefore, there may be an age-related neurological reason why older adults are more likely to believe misleading information, such as that used in advertising or political campaigns.

A Processing Capacity Explanation for Age Differences in Social Judgments

Based on the research discussed so far, it appears processing resource limitations play an important role in understanding how older adults process and access social information. In fact, social cognitive researchers have long used information-processing models to describe how individuals make social judgments. In one of the best known models, Gilbert and Malone (1995) established the ability to make unbiased social judgments depends on the cognitive demand accompanying those judgments. We all make snap initial judgments, but then we reconsider and evaluate possible extenuating circumstances to revise those judgments. This revision takes processing resources, and if we are busy thinking about something else we may not be able to revise our initial judgments.

As we consider in more depth in the section on causal attributions, Blanchard-Fields and colleagues (Blanchard-Fields & Beatty, 2005; Blanchard-Fields, Hertzog, & Horhota, 2012) found older adults consistently hold to their initial judgments or conclusions of why negative events occur more often than younger adults. They appear not to adjust their initial judgments by considering other factors, as Alexandra and Klaus were able to do when they revised their interpretation of their grandchildren's behavior.

Because older adults typically exhibit lower levels of cognitive processing resources (see Chapter 6), it is possible this decline in resource capacity might impact social judgment processes. In the case of impression formation, older adults may have limited cognitive resources to process detailed information presented after the initial impression is formed. Use of such information overworks processing resources. Similarly, source judgments and selectively attending to only true information also places demands on one's cognitive resources.

If processing resource capacity is the major factor explaining social judgment biases, then it should affect all types of situations older people encounter. However, it also may be the extent social information is accessible, operates independently of a processing resource limitation to influence social judgments.

Attributional Biases

Consider the following scenario:

Erin is cleaning up after her infant son who spilled his dinner all over the table and floor. At the same time, she is listening on the phone to her coworker, Brittany, describing how anxious she was when she gave the marketing presentation in front of their new clients that day. Brittany is also describing how her supervisor told her the company depended on this presentation to obtain a contract from the new clients. After the phone call, Erin reflected on Brittany's situation. She decided Brittany is an anxious person and should work on reducing her anxiety in these types of situations.

Erin was interested in what caused Brittany's anxiety when presenting information at work. Was it something about Brittany, such as being an anxious person? Or was it due to some other reason, such as luck or chance? Or was it because of the pressure placed on Brittany by her supervisor?

Answers to these questions provide insights into particular types of social judgments people make to explain their behavior that are referred to as causal attributions. **Causal attributions** *are explanations of why behaviors occur.* A **dispositional attribution** *is a causal attribution that concludes the cause resides within the actor.* An explanation such as "Brittany is just an anxious person" would be a dispositional attribution of why Brittany is nervous. A **situational attribution** *is an explanation that the cause resides outside the actor.* An explanation such as "Brittany is succumbing to pressures from her supervisor and that's why she's nervous" would be a situational attribution.

In this vignette, Erin made a dispositional attribution about Brittany. In this section, we explore if there are age differences in the tendency to rely more on dispositional attributions, situational attributions, or on a combination of both when making causal attributions.

Historically, the study of attributions and aging has been confined to studying attributional judgments made about the aging population, usually involving competence in some domain such as memory. We discuss these issues when we examine research on stereotypes and attributions about older adults' mental competence. In that case, attributions about older persons' successes and failures are compared to similar successes and failures of younger adults. Such attributions go hand-in-hand with the stereotyping of older adults.

However, more recently the focus in attribution and aging research turned to the examination of changes in the nature of attributional processes, per se, from an adult developmental context. Thus, the question can be asked whether findings typically discovered in social psychological attribution theory and research hold true beyond the college years (Blanchard-Fields et al., 2008).

For many years, we have known college students typically produce informational distortions when making causal attributions about problem solving, called **correspondence bias** (e.g., Gilbert & Malone, 1995). In this case, youth rely more on dispositional information in explaining behavior and ignore compelling situational information such as extenuating circumstances.

Suppose you tried to approach your psychology professor yesterday. She did not acknowledge you were there but kept walking with her face buried in a manuscript. You might decide because your professor ignored your question, she is arrogant (a dispositional attribution). At the same time, you may have ignored important situational information, such as if she has recently been overwhelmed by upcoming deadlines. Thus you did not consider all the pertinent information to make a more accurate judgment. This type of finding has been primarily documented with college youths. However, it may be the case the life experience accumulated by middle-aged and older adults causes them to reach different conclusions and they consider equally both types of information in explaining why things happen the way they do.

In a series of creative investigations, Blanchard-Fields (Blanchard-Fields & Beatty, 2005; Blanchard-Fields & Horhota, 2005; Blanchard-Fields et al., 2007; Blanchard-Fields et al., 2012) studied the differences in causal attributions across the adult life span. Blanchard-Fields presented participants with different situations having positive or negative outcomes and asked them to decide whether something about the main character in the story (dispositional attributions), the situation (situational attributions), or a combination of both (interactive attributions) was responsible for the event. The vignettes represented situations such as that described earlier where Allen was pressuring Joan to live with him before marriage, Joan protested but Allen continued to pressure her, and the relationship ended up falling apart.

When the target events were ambiguous as to what was the specific cause of the outcome, as with Allen and Joan, all adults tended to make interactive attributions, but older adults did so at a higher rate. However, as can be seen from Figure 8.2, older adults paradoxically also blamed the main character more (dispositional attributions) than younger groups, especially in negative relationship situations.

In her research, Blanchard-Fields took a sociocultural perspective in explaining why older adults were more predisposed to making dispositional attributions and engaged in less postformal/dialectical reasoning in negative relationship situations. She notes the correspondence bias in older adults only occurred in negative relationship situations. In this case, older adults appeared to apply specific social rules about relationships in making their attributional judgments, apparently because of their stage in life and the

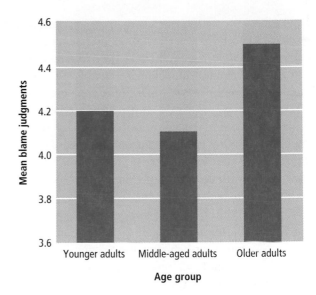

Figure 8.2

Dispositional attributions as a function of age.

© Cengage Learning

cohort in which they were socialized (such as the rule "Marriage comes before career"). In these situations, strong beliefs about how one should act in relationship situations appeared to be violated for the older adults, particularly older women. Therefore, these women made snap judgments about the main character that violated their strong beliefs and did not feel it was necessary to engage in conscious, deliberate analyses. They *knew* the character was wrong, as in the husband who chose to work long hours and not spend time with his family.

The interesting question arises, however, as to whether these attributional biases in older adults are truly due to activated belief systems that strongly impact their judgments or whether the older adults are deficient in conducting a causal analysis. This deficiency could take the form of limited cognitive resources that might prevent them from processing all details of the situation (e.g., extenuating situational circumstances). The vignette involving Erin shows how, on the one hand, we can rely on our experience as older adults to guide us through uncomfortable situations; but on the other hand, a reduction in our capacity does not allow us to consider all the relevant information in this case to make an accurate judgment about Brittany's behavior.

Earlier we questioned whether a processing resource hypothesis was the best explanation of social judgment biases. Again, this is particularly important because in Blanchard-Fields's attribution studies, the dispositional bias was only found for older adults when they were presented with negative relationship situations. Researchers have found everyday reasoning biases in older adults occur not because of declining cognitive ability, but because older adults are more likely than younger adults to base their judgments on their own beliefs (Blanchard-Fields et al., 2012; Klaczynski and Robinson, 2000).

These findings indicate the explanations people create to account for behavior vary depending on the type of situation (e.g., relationship or achievement situations), the age of the person, and whether strong social beliefs have been violated by a person in the situation. What is also emerging is the importance of the sociocultural context where people are socialized, since this appears to create different social rules that are then used to make causal attributions. Additional research supports this idea.

Blanchard-Fields and colleagues (2007) examined causal attributions in younger and older Chinese adults in comparison to younger and older American adults. Interestingly, they found older Americans showed a greater correspondence bias than younger Americans. However, both younger and older Chinese performed similarly and showed less correspondence bias. Older Americans may focus their attributions on the individual due to a lifelong experience of an individualistic orientation.

In order to adjust this initial judgment, the contextual information must be made salient to them in a socially meaningful manner. Support for this idea comes from studies showing when there is a plausible motivation for the target's behavior; older adults can correct their judgments to be less biased than in a standard attitude attribution paradigm (Blanchard-Fields & Horhota, 2005).

For older Americans to correct their attributions, the constraint needs to provide a meaningful reason why a person would contradict his or her own beliefs. For Chinese older adults, the meaningful nature of the situation does not need to be emphasized because to them situational influences and constraints represent a naturally occurring manner to approach any judgment situation and they have a lifelong experience of a collectivist orientation. More research is needed to shed additional light on how these age differences are created and under what circumstances they appear.

ADULT DEVELOPMENT IN ACTION

How might older adults' impression formation behavior be important to you as a political candidate?

8.4 Motivation and Social Processing Goals

LEARNING OBJECTIVES

- How do goals influence the way we process information, and how does this change with age?
- How do emotions influence the way we process information, and how does this change with age?
- How does a need for closure influence the way we process information, and how does it change with age?

Tracy and Eric are visiting their children and all their grandchildren on Cape Cod. All are having a good time until their son, Eddie, brings up the hot topic of the upcoming presidential election. The debate between family members regarding the best candidate becomes heated. Tracy and Eric are concerned about the negative feelings generated in the debate and encourage everyone to change the topic. However, the brothers and sisters are more interested in settling the issue now rather than later. Tracy and Eric cannot handle the negative energy and retire to bed early.

Why did Tracy and Eric focus on the emotional side of the problem (the increase in negative feelings), whereas the siblings focused on the more instrumental side of the problem (e.g., whom to vote for)?

The different foci of Tracy and Eric in contrast to the children resulted in different problem-solving strategies. Much like the research on social rules and social judgments, there is a growing area of research suggesting change in the relative importance of social goals and motivation across the life span profoundly influence how we interpret and use social information or direct attention and effort to certain aspects of the problem situation (Hess, 2006).

Goals change with age as a function of experience and time left in the life span. This can influence the degree we observe age differences in social cognitive functioning, such as the desire to focus on preserving ones' resources or eliminating negative affect in problem situations. Let's explore these further.

Personal Goals

Personal goals play a major role in creating direction in our lives. They consist of underlying motivations for our behavior and how we perceive our own ever-changing environment. Across the life span, personal goals change to match our needs, with young adults striving mainly for achievement, like completing a college degree or starting a career, and middle-aged and older adults seeking a balance between functioning independently and sharing their lives with others (e.g., children, spouses).

Selective optimization with compensation (SOC; see Chapter 1) is an important theoretical model that suggests development occurs as we continuously update our personal goals to match our appraisal of available resources to obtain those goals (Baltes et al., 2006). We choose manageable goals based on our interests as well as physical and cognitive strengths and limitations. As we grow older our limitations become more salient and require us to reevaluate our interests. Therefore, in older adulthood, research suggests interests shift toward physical health and socio emotional domains (Carstensen & Mikels, 2005; Isaacowitz & Blanchard-Fields, 2012).

This shift in priorities means goals for the same event may be perceived differently by older and younger adults. An example of the shift in goal selection can be seen in research that examines how younger and older adults prioritize how they want to perform in a dual-task situation. In a classic study, younger and older adults were asked to memorize a list of words while simultaneously maintaining their balance as they walked through an obstacle course (Li, Lindenberger, Freund, & Baltes, 2001). Although age differences in performing two tasks at the same time were more costly for the memory task than the walking task, older adults chose to forgo aids to improve their memory (e.g., a list) and instead chose to use aids designed to optimize walking performance (e.g., a handrail). When deciding which was more important

to them, memory performance versus balance, older adults displayed a preference for their physical safety even if it meant they would perform badly on a cognitive test. From this example, we see life-span shifts in personal goals can be both helpful and harmful.

Goal selection requires we thoughtfully choose where we invest our resources. In the laboratory, younger adults are primarily motivated to achieve maximum performance on any cognitive task presented to them. Older adults take a different perspective. They prefer to maintain steady performance by optimizing their current resources rather than risking loss with an unknown strategy (Baltes & Rudolph, 2012; Ebner, Freund, & Baltes, 2006).

Thus, although older adults are less willing than younger adults to invest energy into improving their cognitive performance, their strategy choice is more optimal for them because they are more interested in retaining their autonomy by maintaining abilities at their current level. Although this does not directly translate into cognitive gains, it does help older adults optimize their cognitive performance in those domains they prioritize in their lives (Baltes & Rudolph, 2012; Riediger, Freund, & Baltes, 2005). Although we cannot compensate for all of the resource limitations that come with advancing age, we can invest the resources we have into goals that maximize an independent life-style and a positive sense of well-being.

Along these lines, recent work by Carstensen and her colleagues suggests the pursuit of emotionally gratifying situations becomes a primary motivation that substantially influences cognition in the latter half of the life span (Carstensen & Mikels, 2005; Reed & Carstensen, 2012). We therefore turn to the impact of emotional processing goals on cognition.

Emotion as a Processing Goal

Emotional goals become increasingly important and salient as we grow older (Carstensen & Fried, 2012). It is primarily a motivational model that posits the degree an individual construes time as limited or expansive that leads to the ranking of emotional or knowledge-seeking goals as higher in priority, respectively. Thus, given limited time left in the life span, older adults may be more motivated to emphasize emotional goals and aspects of life. We examine this motivational factor in the context of maintaining and choosing intimate relationships in Chapter 10. However, it also can be applied in the context of social information processing.

A growing number of studies suggest older adults avoid negative information and focus more on positive information when making decisions and judgments and when remembering events, a phenomenon called the positivity effect (Carstensen & Fried, 2012; Carstensen, Mikels, & Mather, 2006). Older adults remember positive images more than negative ones, whereas younger adults remember both positive and negative images equally well (Isaacowitz & Blanchard-Fields, 2012; Reed & Carstensen, 2012). When examining what types of stimuli younger and older adults initially attend to, older adults allocate less attention to negative stimuli (e.g., angry faces) than younger adults. Older adults also remember more positive information when recalling their own autobiographical information and remember the positive aspects of their decisions more than the negative ones.

An alternative perspective proposes focusing on negative information is adaptive because it signals danger and vulnerability and thus is important for survival. This emphasis on negativity has been found in both the social and cognitive neuroscience literature for many years (e.g., Lane & Nadel, 2000; Rozin & Royzman, 2001). Within the social cognitive aging literature, some studies demonstrate older adults spend more time viewing negative stimuli (Charles et al., 2003) and display a negativity effect (Thomas & Hasher, 2006; Wood & Kisley, 2006).

With respect to memory, Grühn and colleagues (2005) found no evidence for a positivity effect; instead they found evidence for reduced negativity effect in older adults when remembering a list of words with negative, positive, and neutral valence. When incidentally encoding pictures, both younger and older adults recalled the central element more than peripheral elements for only negative scenes. However, when instructed to attend to this difference, only younger adults overcame this encoding bias, whereas older adults could not overcome the memory trade-off (Kensinger, Piguet, Krendl, & Corkin, 2005).

Emotional goals appear to help older adults because they create a supportive context for their cognitive functioning. In Chapter 6, we discussed the fact older adults create more false memories than younger adults do. Research on the interface between emotions

Older adults tend to remember more positive than negative information, such as good traits of their spouse/partner rather than negative ones.

Image Source/Getty Images

and cognition suggest the distinctiveness of emotions helps older adults reduce the number of false memories produced (May, Rahhal, Berry, & Leighton, 2005; Sakaki, Niki, & Mather, 2012).

However, it is important to recognize there are times when emotions may impede information processing. For example, highly arousing situations require a great amount of executive control processing (discussed in Chapter 6) that may lead older adults to be poorer at remembering and processing information (Kensinger & Corkin, 2004; Reed & Carstensen, 2012). In addition, a focus on only positive information can interfere with decision making by leading older adults to miss out on important negative information necessary to make a quality decision (Reed & Carstensen, 2012).

Cognitive Style as a Processing Goal

Another type of motivational goal that influences our thinking comes from our cognitive style, or how we approach solving problems. Examples include a need for closure and the inability to tolerate ambiguous situations. People with a high need for closure prefer order and predictability, are uncomfortable with ambiguity, are closed-minded, and prefer quick and decisive answers (Bar-Tal, Shrira, & Keinan, 2013). Empirical research on this construct resulted in the development of well-validated questionnaires such as the Need for Closure Scale (Webster & Kruglanski, 1994) and the Personal Need for Structure Scale (Thompson et al., 1992).

The question is whether cognitive resources or need for closure are implicated in biased judgments. As discussed earlier, situations that require substantial cognitive resources (i.e., require a lot of effort in cognitive processing such as processing information under time pressure) result in an increase in inaccuracies and biases in how we represent social information. However, biased judgments can also be caused by motivational differences such as an increase in need for closure. In fact, research using Need for Closure instruments suggests a high need for closure and/or structure is related to attributional biases, the tendency to make stereotyped judgments, formation of spontaneous trait inferences, and the tendency to assimilate judgments to primed constructs (e.g., Bar-Tal et al., 2013).

It may also be the case limited cognitive resources and motivational differences are both age-related and influence social judgments in interaction with each other (Stanley & Isaacowitz, 2012). Researchers argue changes in resources with aging (as in the declines we observed in working memory in Chapter 6) may lead to an increase in a need for closure with age. This leads to biases in the way older adults process social information.

Research documents a high need for closure does not influence susceptibility to emotional priming influences on neutral stimuli of young and middle aged adults. However, priming effects increased with higher need for structure in older adults. In other words, older adults with a high need for closure could not inhibit the effects of an emotional prime (e.g., a subliminally presented negative word) on their subsequent behavior (e.g., whether they liked or disliked an abstract figure). Because of age-related changes in personal resources (social and cognitive), motivational factors such as coming to quick and decisive answers to conserve resources become important to the aging adult.

ADULT DEVELOPMENT IN ACTION

If you were designing an advertisement for adults of different ages, how would you approach the suggestion to use emotion in the ad?

8.5 Personal Control

LEARNING OBJECTIVES

- What is the multidimensionality of personal control?
- How do assimilation and accommodation influence behavior?
- What is primary and secondary control?
- What is the primacy of primary control over secondary control?

Daniel did not perform as well as he thought he would on his psychology exam. He then had the unhappy task of determining why he did poorly. Was it his fault? Was the exam too picky? To add insult to injury, Daniel needed to raise his grades to maintain his scholarship grant. He decided the exam was too picky. This helped Daniel motivate himself to study for his next exams.

How Daniel answered such questions sheds light on how we tend to explain, or attribute our behavior, as in the earlier discussion of causal attributions. Among the most important ways we analyze the cause of events is in terms of who or what is in control in a specific situation. **Personal control** *is the degree one believes one's performance in a situation depends on something that one personally does.* A high sense of personal control implies a belief that performance is up to you, whereas a low sense of personal control implies your performance is under the influence of forces other than your own.

Personal control has become an extremely important idea in a wide variety of settings because of the way it guides behavior and relates to well-being (Brandtstädter, 1997; Lachman, 2006). Personal control is thought to play a role in memory performance (see Chapter 6), in intelligence (see Chapter 7), in depression (see Chapter 10), and in adjustment to and survival in different care settings (see Chapter 5).

Multidimensionality of Personal Control

The general consensus about personal control is that it is multidimensional (Lachman, Rosnick, & Röcke, 2009). Specifically, one's sense of control depends on which domain, such as intelligence or health, is being assessed. Lachman and colleagues (2009) found interesting changes in control beliefs depending on the domain being examined. They found no changes in a sense of control over one's health up to the early 70s. However, when older adults transition from the early 70s to the mid-70s and 80s, their sense of control over their health declines. This makes sense given the oldest-old experience accumulated losses in their reserved capacity to function. Similarly, positive beliefs about personal control are associated with lower stress across adulthood (Pearlin & Bierman, 2013).

Personal control beliefs are also important in cognitive domains. Cavallini and colleagues (2013) showed Sardinians who had a higher sense of personal control over their cognitive changes in later life performed better on memory tasks than their Milanese counterparts who had a lower sense of personal control.

In summation, researchers found maintaining a sense of control throughout adulthood is linked to better quality of social relationships, better health, and higher cognitive functioning. They suggest a sense of control may operate as a protective factor for one's well-being in the face of declining health and other losses associated with the oldest-old.

The same is true in an academic context such as college, where attributions of control are particularly important in determining the causes of success and failure in school. It would be interesting to explore the notion of control in regard to class performance among older and younger students. The exercise in the Discovering Development feature examines this question.

DISCOVERING DEVELOPMENT:

HOW MUCH CONTROL DO YOU HAVE OVER YOUR COGNITIVE FUNCTIONING?

As you progress through college, you are concerned with your grade-point average, how much you will learn relative to your profession of choice, and your performance on exams. The more control you perceive you have over the situation, the more confident you feel. There are two types of control attributions you can make. You can make an "entity" attribution about your performance in school. This means you attribute control to your innate ability to perform. Or you can hold a "skill" perspective. You now attribute control over your performance in terms of how much effort you exert, such as how much you study for an exam.

Are there age differences in these control beliefs? To find out, talk to students at your university ranging from first-year students to seniors and also ranging in age. There are a lot of older students coming back to school. Find out what they believe is the major cause of the successes and failures in school. Bring your results to class and pool them. See if there are college-level differences and/or age differences in perceptions of control over academic performance. Compare your findings to age differences reported in the text.

Control Strategies

The research just reviewed primarily examined control-related beliefs such as the belief control is in one's own hands or in the hands of others. However, a number of theoretical approaches and empirical work examined control-related strategies.

Brandtstädter (1999) first proposed the preservation and stabilization of a positive view of the self and personal development in later life involve three interdependent processes. *First, people engage in* assimilative activities *that prevent or alleviate losses in domains that are personally relevant for self-esteem and identity.* People may use memory aids more if having a good memory is an important aspect of self-esteem and identity. *Second, people make* accommodations *and readjust their goals and aspirations as a way to lessen or neutralize the effects of negative self-evaluations in key domains.* If a person notices the time it takes to walk a mile at a brisk pace increased, then the target time can be increased to help lessen the impact of feelings of failure. *Third, people use* immunizing mechanisms *that alter the effects of self-discrepant evidence.* In this case, a person who is confronted with evidence his or her memory performance has declined can look for alternative explanations or simply deny the evidence.

Taking a similar approach, Heckhausen, Wrosch, and Schulz (2010) view control as a motivational system that regulates human behavior over the life span, in other words, individuals' abilities to control important outcomes. These researchers define control-related strategies in terms of primary control and secondary control.

Primary control strategies. *involve bringing the environment in line with one's desires and goals.* Much like in Brandtstädter's assimilative activities, action is directed toward changing the external world. So, for example, if you lost your job, and thus your income, primary control strategies would entail an active search for another job (changing the environment so you once again have a steady income).

Secondary control strategies. *involve bringing oneself in line with the environment.* Much like Brandtstädter's accommodative activities, it typically involves cognitive activities directed at the self. Secondary control strategies could involve appraising the situation in terms of how you really did not enjoy that particular job.

An important part of this theoretical perspective is that primary control has functional primacy over secondary control. In other words, primary control lets people shape their environment to fit their goals and developmental potential. Thus, primary control has more adaptive value to the individual. The major function of secondary control is to minimize losses or expand levels of primary control.

This relation is depicted in Figure 8.3. Notice that primary control striving is always high across the life span, but the capacity to achieve primary control

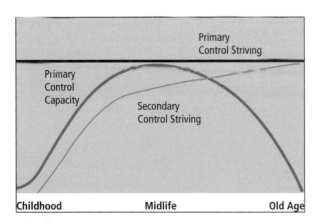

Figure 8.3

Hypothetical life-span trajectories for primary control potential and primary and secondary control striving.

Source: Heckhausen, J., Wrosch, C., & Schulz, R. (2010). A motivational theory of life-span development. Psychological Review, 117(1), 32–60 (p. 36). doi:10.1037/a0017668 http://www.ncbi.nlm.nih.gov/pmc/articles/PMC2820305/figure/F1/.
© 2015 Cengage Learning

peaks in midlife. As people continue to age, secondary control striving continues to increase, eventually approaching primary control striving.

Heckhausen and colleagues (2010) believe this has important implications for aging. They find in childhood much development is directed at expanding the child's primary control potential, and they predict stability in primary control striving through most of adult life. However, as we enter old age, the maintenance of primary control increasingly depends on secondary control processes. This is because of threats to primary control as a function of biological decline that occurs as we grow older. Thus secondary control increases with age. Research shows secondary control does indeed increase with age (Pfeiffer, 2013).

A particularly important question is how control strategies and beliefs affect emotional well-being. A growing number of studies suggest control beliefs are important contributors to both positive and negative well-being. If someone perceives he or she has control over desirable outcomes, this control is associated with high emotional well-being (Heckhausen et al., 2010; Pfeiffer, 2013). However, how adaptive control beliefs relate to well-being varies with life stage. For young and middle-aged adults, a strong sense of control relates to how we compensate for failure, for example, "We can overcome this momentary failure." Older adults focus a sense of control on how to master everyday demands (Heckhausen et al., 2010). Finally, for all age groups, planning for the future enhances one's sense of perceived control, and this in turn relates to high life satisfaction (Lachman et al., 2009).

Some Criticisms Regarding Primary Control

The notion of increases in accommodative strategies (Brandtstädter, 1999) and secondary strategies (Heckhausen et al., 2010) in older age is not without its criticisms. Carstensen and Freund (1994; Freund & Ritter, 2009) question whether losses people experience, though real, actually threaten the self. In addition, these authors argue age-related changes in goals could also be the result of natural movement through the life cycle, not simply of coping with blocked goals.

Criticisms also can be launched against these approaches to control by considering the globalization of so many aspects of our functioning. From a sociocultural perspective (e.g., cross-cultural research), there is much criticism regarding a bias toward Western cultures in the development of theories such as primary and secondary control, and in particular, the primacy of primary control over secondary control. Stephen J. Gould (1999) suggests in collectivist societies such as those found in Asia, the emphasis is not on individualistic strategies such as those found in primary control. Instead, the goal is to establish interdependence with others, to be connected to them and bound to a larger social institution. He cites studies showing throughout adulthood, Asian cultures exceed Western cultures in levels of secondary control and emotion-focused coping. Chang (2012) also noted Asian cultures use more secondary control than Latino cultures, but they also show greater social anxiety.

Thus one's sense of personal control is a complex, multidimensional aspect of personality. Consequently, general normative age-related trends might not be found. Rather, changes in personal control may well depend on one's experiences in different domains and the culture one grows up in, and may differ widely from one domain to another.

ADULT DEVELOPMENT IN ACTION

As a professional working with older adults, how would you combine your knowledge of the effects of stereotyping with your knowledge of the importance of personal control beliefs to create an intervention program?

8.6 Social Situations and Social Competence

LEARNING OBJECTIVES

- What is the social facilitation of cognitive functioning?
- What is collaborative cognition, and does it facilitate memory in older adults?
- How does the social context influence memory performance in older adults?

Brandon and Stephanie's granddaughter asked them what happened when they first met. Stephanie recalled *they met at a social gathering for World War II soldiers but couldn't remember the name of the person who introduced them; she could only describe him as tall and dark-haired. However, this cued Brandon; he remembered the man's name was Tucker. This back-and-forth remembering continued until, to their own amazement, they successfully reconstructed the whole gathering. Their granddaughter was delighted and complimented them on their good memories.*

When we typically think about the memories of older adults, we don't usually think of these kinds of successes. Brandon and Stephanie's reliance on each other to remember a past event shows how our social cognitive processes serve adaptive functions. In fact, there is a growing interest in how the social context can compensate for memory loss and facilitate memory performance. In this section, we examine two approaches to this issue: collaborative cognition and facilitative social contexts.

Similar to practical intelligence, wisdom, and everyday problem solving discussed in Chapter 7, the social cognition perspective offers us an enriched understanding of social competence in older adulthood. We are interested in how changes in social cognitive functioning both reflect the changing life contexts of the individual and affect adaptation to these changing contexts. In the previous sections, we primarily focused on how developmental changes in representations of self or other (such as social beliefs and self-beliefs) influence social cognitive processes such as making attributional judgments. In this section we focus on social cognition as it relates to the dynamic interplay between self, others, and context. A less researched but extremely important domain of social cognition and aging is how the particular types of social settings where we communicate with others, influence our cognitive processing. This relates to a different aspect of social cognition and aging research: the social facilitation of cognitive functioning.

Collaborative Cognition

There has been a recent focus in the social cognition and aging literature to examine cognition in social contexts, that is, how cognition works when we are interacting with others. This can be seen in work on the benefits and costs of collaborative cognition on cognitive performance (e.g., memory and problem solving) (Dixon, 2011; Meade, Nokes, & Morrow, 2009). **Collaborative cognition** *occurs when two or more people work together to solve a cognitive task.*

Research shows collaborative cognition enhances older adults' performance on a variety of memory and problem-solving tasks (Dixon, 2011; Meade et al., 2009; Strough & Margrett, 2002), thus serving an important adaptive function for older adults. Following the old saying "Two heads are better than one," researchers are interested in examining how this type of collaborative context could mitigate deficits in memory we typically see when assessing older adults in the laboratory (see Chapter 6).

Research shows older adults can collaborate on story recall as well as problem-solving performance and their performance is better than the average performance of older adults in individual settings (Dixon, 2011). In other words, cognitive performance improves with a collaborative context. On a recall task, by using a cognitive style together that minimizes working memory demands, older married couples performed just as well as younger couples. It is rare to find older adults' cognitive performance equal to that of younger adults.

Another way to look at the benefits of collaborative cognition is to examine how groups accomplish what they want to accomplish. What kinds of processes do older adults use to effectively remember an event as Brandon and Stephanie did? How do older adults divide up the cognitive work when they cooperate on a task?

Older married couples produce more statements resulting from a shared discussion, and provide richer descriptions when working together (Hoppmann & Gerstorf, 2009; Rauers, Riediger, Schmiedek, & Lindenberger, 2011). Unacquainted older adult pairs produced more sociability or support statements. Sociability statements were about agreeing with the partner's recall or comparing the story with events in their own lives. However, older married couples know each other well and can skip this step and get right down to the business of remembering. Older unacquainted couples are more concerned with being sociable and polite to the other member of the dyad. Older married couples are experienced enough with

one another to bypass the sociability concern and concentrate on better strategies to improve their performance. Overall, findings indicate well-acquainted older couples demonstrate an expertise to develop an adaptive pattern of recalling information that includes both social support issues and strategic efforts.

There is also growing evidence of the positive outcomes of collaboration when older adults tackle everyday problem-solving tasks such as errand running and planning a vacation (Allaire, 2012; Kimbler et al., 2012). Interestingly, older adults prefer to collaborate in their problem solving when they perceive deficiencies in their own functioning but prefer to work alone when they feel competent in the area (Strough et al., 2002). Collaborators of all ages report the benefits include optimizing the decision, enhancing the relationship, and compensating for individual weaknesses (Dixon, 2012; Kimbler et al., 2012). However, collaboration is not without its costs, such as selfishness,

Older adults tend to use compensatory strategies for declining memories by jointly remembering events with others.

withholding of one's honest opinion, and not meeting the other partner's needs.

Because collaborative cognition is such a common experience and likely to be grounded in the nuances of the relationship people develop over time, it will be a rich area to learn more about the developmental trajectory of memory across adulthood. Most people do remembering in collaborative situations multiple times a day, whether with a spouse/partner or with other family or friends. As we will see in Chapter 11, the quality of the relationship where this cognitive activity occurs probably has important influences on actual performance. Whether this is true, though, awaits more research.

Social Context of Memory

Another approach to identifying conditions when social facilitation of cognition in older adults occurs is in examining contextual variables that influence memory performance. Adams argues memory performance is influenced when the task approximates a real-world learning and social memory experience (Adams et al., 2002). Others have pointed out that prior knowledge (Stein-Morrow & Miller, 2009) and how and how often memories are practiced together (Coman & Hirst, 2012) also influence performance. In this case, what happens to memory performance when the assessment situation approximates the kinds of memory demands that naturally occur in a real-life situation?

A typical and relevant cognitive task for older adults is to transmit sociocultural information to younger generations (Birditt, Tighe, Fingerman, & Zarit, 2012; Quéniart & Charpentier, 2013). In this context, the older adult would be motivated to communicate effectively.

A storytelling situation is a good example. This kind of context is different from the traditional laboratory context, when the demand is to reproduce as much of the content of a text as possible. Adams et al. (2002) found when they placed older adults in a storytelling situation where they were asked to learn and retell a story from memory to a young child, their retellings of the story contained more detail and were more fluent than those of younger adults. Perhaps this superior performance stems from increased motivation in a social context where their concerns were directed at producing an interesting and coherent story for the child. This is a demonstration of how the social-communicative context or experience enhances what is most salient to the individual. Again, this finding illustrates the importance of taking into consideration the social context of a task situation when examining change in cognitive functioning as we grow older.

ADULT DEVELOPMENT IN ACTION

How might the research on collaborative cognition be used in therapeutic situations you might design if you were working in a long-term care facility?

SOCIAL POLICY IMPLICATIONS

The research on social cognition and aging further accentuates why it is important to consider social factors to explain cognitive functioning in older adulthood. Factors such as the social context we communicate in, the emotions we feel, and the strength of our beliefs and values drive our decisions and social judgments in important ways. Thus it is important not to limit explanations of changes in thinking and decision making to cognitive processing variables.

Important social factors influence how and when an individual attends to specific information and when this information influences social cognitive functioning. These factors include those we discussed earlier: motivational goals, cognitive style, attitudes, and values. By not considering these factors, we run the risk of underestimating the competence of older adults. By considering these factors we can explore the conditions under which older adults flourish and the conditions where we need to focus aid and attention.

This has important policy implications with respect to how we treat older adults in the workforce, establishing health policies, and enhancing the treatment of our older adult population. We can be optimistic about the future promise of research on aging and social cognition for identifying and probing such important social components of information processing. To summarize, by looking at cognition in a social context we get a more complete picture of how cognition operates in an everyday social environment.

SUMMARY

8.1 Stereotypes and Aging

How does the content of stereotypes about aging differ across adulthood?

- The content of stereotypes varies by age: older adults include more positive stereotypes along with negative ones.

How do younger and older adults perceive the competence of the elderly?

- An age-based double standard operates when judging older adults' failures in memory.
- Younger adults rate older adults as more responsible despite their memory failures.

How do negative stereotypes about aging unconsciously guide our behavior?

- Automatically activated negative stereotypes about aging guide behavior beyond the individual's awareness.
- Implicit stereotyping influences the way we patronize older adults in our communications.

What are the ways the positive and negative aging stereotypes influence older adults' behavior?

- Stereotypic beliefs have a negative impact on the cognitive performance of older adults.
- Stereotypic beliefs influence older adults' health and physical behavior.

8.2 Social Knowledge Structures and Beliefs

What are social knowledge structures?

- To understand age differences in social beliefs, we must first examine content differences.
- Second, we must assess the strength of the beliefs.
- Third, we need to know the likelihood beliefs will affect behavior.

What are social beliefs, and how do they change with age?

- Age differences in social beliefs can be attributed to generational differences and life-stage differences.

What are self-perceptions of aging, and what influences them across adulthood?

- Labeling theory (the incorporation of negative stereotypes) and resilience theory (distancing from negative stereotypes) both operate to create self-perceptions of aging.

8.3 Social Judgment Processes

What is the negativity bias in impression formation, and how does it influence older adults' thinking?

- When forming an initial impression, older adults rely heavily on preexisting social structures.
- Older adults weigh negative information more heavily in their social judgments than do younger adults.
- Older adults use less detailed information in forming impressions than do younger adults.

Are there age differences in accessibility of social information?

- Social knowledge structures must be available to guide behavior.
- Social information must be easily accessible to guide behavior.
- Accessibility depends on the strength of the information stored in memory.
- How the situation is framed influences what types of social knowledge will be accessed.

How does processing context influence social judgments?

- Age-related changes in processing capacity influence social judgments.
- Stages of processing suggest we make initial snap judgments and later correct or adjust them based on more reflective thinking.

To what extent do processing capacity limitations influence social judgments in older adults?

- Older adults tend to make more snap judgments because of processing resource limitations.

How do causal attributions and the correspondence bias change with age?

- Older adults display a dispositional bias when confronted with negative relationship situations.
- Older adults display more interactive attributions in negative relationship situations.
- The dispositional bias on the part of older adults can be attributed to both processing resource limitations and differences in social knowledge that influence their attributional judgments.
- Older adults display a higher level of social expertise than younger adults do when forming impressions.

8.4 Motivation and Social Processing Goals

How do goals influence the way we process information, and how does this change with age?

- Life-span shifts in goal orientation show interests shift toward physical health and socio-emotional domains increase with age.

How do emotions influence the way we process information, and how does this change with age?

- Older adults tend to focus their processing on positive emotional information more than negative information.

How does a need for closure influence the way we process information, and how does it change with age?

- Need for closure is a need for a quick and decisive answer with little tolerance for ambiguity.
- Older adults' social judgment biases are predicted by the degree they need quick and decisive closure. This is not so for younger age groups.

8.5 Personal Control

What is personal control, and what age differences exist in this area?

- Personal control is the degree that one believes performance depends on something one does.
- Age differences in the degree of personal control depend on the domain being studied. Some evidence suggests people develop several strategies concerning personal control to protect a positive self-image.

What is the multidimensionality of personal control?

- Older adults perceive less control over specific domains of functioning such as intellectual changes with aging.
- Perceived control over health remains stable until it declines in old age.
- Older adults perceive less control over social issues and personal appearance.

How do assimilation and accommodation influence behavior?

- Assimilative strategies prevent losses important to self-esteem.
- Accommodative strategies readjust goals.
- Immunizing mechanisms alter the effects of self-discrepant information.

What is primary and secondary control?

- Primary control helps change the environment to match one's goals.
- Secondary control reappraises the environment in light of one's decline in functioning.

What is the primacy of primary control over secondary control?

- Primary control has functional primacy over secondary control.
- Cross-cultural perspectives challenge the notion of primacy of primary control.

8.6 Social Situations and Social Competence

What is the social facilitation of cognitive functioning?

- Particular types of social settings where we communicate with others, influence our cognitive processing.

What is collaborative cognition, and does it facilitate memory in older adults?

- Collaborating with others in recollection helps facilitate memory in older adults.
- Collaborating with others enhances problem solving in older adults.

How does the social context influence memory performance in older adults?

- The social context can serve a facilitative function in older adults' memory performance.

REVIEW QUESTIONS

8.1 Stereotypes and Aging

- What are stereotypes?
- How is the content of stereotypes similar across age groups?
- How does the content of stereotypes differ across age groups?
- What is the age-based double standard of perceived competence in younger and older adults?
- What do older and younger adults perceive as the cause of memory failure in older individuals?
- How does perceived competence influence the way tasks are assigned to older and younger targets?
- What other factors besides competence are taken into consideration when judging older adults' future performance?
- What evidence supports the notion that stereotypes can be automatically activated out of conscious awareness?
- What is implicit stereotyping?
- Under what conditions are stereotypes activated?
- How do negative stereotypes of aging influence young adults' behavior?

8.2 Social Knowledge Structures and Beliefs

- What three important factors need to be considered to understand implicit social beliefs?
- Describe evidence for age differences in the content of social beliefs.
- What are labeling theory and resilience theory? What influences self-perceptions of aging across adulthood?

8.3 Social Judgment Processes

- What are the stages in attributional processing?
- What is the negativity bias, and what are the age differences in its impact?
- Describe the age differences in the extent that trait information is used in forming an impression.
- How does processing capacity affect social cognitive processing?
- What influences the accessibility of social information?
- What is the status of processing resource limitations as an explanation for social judgment biases?
- What are causal attributions?
- What is a correspondence bias?
- Are there age differences in the correspondence bias? If so, under what conditions?
- What accounts for the age differences in the correspondence bias?

8.4 Motivation and Social Processing Goals

- How do personal goals influence behavior?
- To what extent are there age differences in emotion as a processing goal in social cognitive functioning?
- What is need for closure?
- How does need for closure influence the processing of social information?
- Are there age differences in the degree to which need for closure influences social information processing?

8.5 Personal Control

- What evidence is there of age differences in personal control beliefs?
- In what domains do older adults exhibit low perceived control, and in what domains do they exhibit higher levels of perceived control?

- How are assimilative and accommodative strategies adaptive in older adults' functioning?
- Why is primary control viewed as having more functional primacy than secondary control?
- What cross-cultural evidence challenges the notion of primary control as functionally more important?
- How does personal control influence older adults' emotional well-being?

8.6 Social Situations and Social Competence

- What is collaborative cognition?
- What evidence suggests collaborative cognition compensates for memory failures in older adults?
- How does collaborative cognition facilitate problem-solving behavior?
- How do marital relationships influence collaborative cognition?
- How does a storytelling context influence age differences in memory for stories?
- What does it mean to say the social context facilitates cognitive performance?

INTEGRATING CONCEPTS IN DEVELOPMENT

- To what degree are declines in processing resource capacity discussed in Chapter 6 as ubiquitous in their effects on social cognitive processes?
- What relations can be found among dispositional traits, personal concerns, and life narratives?
- How does emotion as a processing goal relate to socio-emotional selectivity theory in Chapter 10?
- How does social cognition relate to post-formal thought as discussed in Chapter 7?
- How does personal control relate to concepts such as memory self-efficacy discussed in Chapter 6?

KEY TERMS

accommodations Readjustments of goals and aspirations as a way to lessen or neutralize the effects of negative self-evaluations in key domains.

age-based double standard When an individual attributes an older person's failure in memory as more serious than a memory failure observed in a young adult.

assimilative activities Exercises that prevent or alleviate losses in domains that are personally relevant for self-esteem and identity.

causal attributions Explanations people construct to explain their behavior, that can be situational, dispositional, or interactive.

cognitive style A trait-like pattern of behavior one uses when approaching a problem-solving situation.

collaborative cognition Cognitive performance that results from the interaction of two or more individuals.

correspondence bias Relying more on dispositional information in explaining behavior and ignoring compelling situational information such as extenuating circumstances.

dispositional attribution An explanation for someone's behavior that resides within the actor.

immunizing mechanisms Control strategies that alter the effects of self-discrepant evidence.

implicit stereotyping Stereotyped beliefs that affect your judgments of individuals without your being aware of it (i.e., the process is unconscious).

impression formation The way people combine the components of another person's personality and come up with an integrated perception of the person.

labeling theory Argues that when we confront an age-related stereotype, older adults are more likely to integrate it into their self-perception.

negativity bias Weighing negative information more heavily than positive information in a social judgment.

personal control The belief that what one does has an influence on the outcome of an event.

positivity effect The tendency to attend to and process positive information over negative information.

primary control The act of bringing the environment into line with one's own desires and goals, similar to Brandtstädter's assimilative activities.

resilience theory Argues that confronting a negative stereotype results in a rejection of that view in favor of a more positive self-perception.

secondary control The act of bringing oneself in line with the environment, similar to Brandtstädter's accommodative activities.

self-perception of aging Refers to individuals' perceptions of their own age and aging.

situational attribution An explanation for someone's behavior that is external to the actor.

social knowledge A cognitive structure that represents one's general knowledge about a given social concept or domain.

source judgments Process of accessing knowledge wherein one attempts to determine where one obtained a particular piece of information.

stereotypes Beliefs about characteristics, attributes, and behaviors of members of certain groups.

stereotype threat An evoked fear of being judged in accordance with a negative stereotype about a group to which an individual belongs.

RESOURCES

Access quizzes, glossaries, flashcards, and more at www.cengagebrain.com.

CHAPTER 9

PERSONALITY

9.1 DISPOSITIONAL TRAITS ACROSS ADULTHOOD
The Case for Stability: The Five-Factor Model • What Happens to Dispositional Traits Across Adulthood? • Conclusions about Dispositional Traits • *Current Controversies: Intraindividual Change and the Stability of Traits*

9.2 PERSONAL CONCERNS AND QUALITATIVE STAGES IN ADULTHOOD
What's Different about Personal Concerns? • Jung's Theory • Erikson's Stages of Psychosocial Development • Theories Based on Life Transitions • Conclusions about Personal Concerns

9.3 LIFE NARRATIVES, IDENTITY, AND THE SELF
Discovering Development: Who Do You Want to Be When You "Grow Up"? • McAdams's Life-Story Model • Whitbourne's Identity Theory • Self-Concept and Well-Being • *How Do We Know?: Brain Function in Emotion and Depression* • Possible Selves • Religiosity and Spiritual Support • Conclusions about Narratives, Identity, and the Self

SOCIAL POLICY IMPLICATIONS
Summary • Review Questions • Integrating Concepts in Development • Key Terms • Resources

MAYA ANGELOU MAINTAINS, "THERE IS NO AGONY LIKE BEARING AN UNTOLD STORY INSIDE OF YOU."

True to her conviction, she has spent a lifetime writing her story in numerous books, poems, and other literary works. She describes an incredible developmental path of oppression, hatred, and hurt that is ultimately transformed into self-awareness, understanding, and compassion. For example, in her later years she realized in confronting the atrocities of the world, if she accepts the fact of evil, she must also accept the fact of good, providing her with as little fear as possible for the anticipation of death. Another example involves integrating spirituality into her self-perception. Author Ken Kelley once asked her how spirituality fits into a way of life. She answered, "There is something more, the spirit, or the soul. I think that that quality encourages our courtesy, and care, and our minds. And mercy, and identity" (Kelley, 1995).

Maya Angelou's writings reflect some of the key issues involved in personality development we will examine in this chapter. First, we consider whether personality changes or remains stable

Maya Angelou

across adulthood. We examine this from two perspectives: a trait perspective, as well as personal concerns perspective. Then we discuss how we construct life narratives and our identity and self.

One of the oldest debates in psychology concerns whether personality development continues across the life span. From the earliest days, prominent people argued both sides. William James and Sigmund Freud believed personality was set by the time we reach adulthood. In contrast, Carl Jung asserted personality was continually shaped throughout our lives.

Although we still have these two theoretical camps, one arguing for stability and the other for change, there is a movement in the field to reconcile these differences. Although the data can be viewed as contradictory, results often depend on what specific measures researchers use and the aspect of personality investigated.

Why is the area of personality controversial? The answer lies in how we use personality in daily life. At one level we all believe and base our interactions with people on the presumption their personality remains relatively constant over time. Imagine the chaos that would result if every week or so everyone woke up with a brand new personality: The once easygoing husband is now a real tyrant, trusted friends become completely unpredictable, and our patterns of social interaction are in shambles. Clearly, to survive in day-to-day life we must rely on consistency of personality.

Still, we also believe people can change, especially with respect to undesirable aspects of their personalities. Picture what it would be like if we could never overcome shyness; if anxiety was a lifelong, incurable curse; or if our idiosyncratic tendencies causing others to tear their hair out could not be eliminated. The assumption of the modifiability of personality is strong indeed. The existence of psychotherapy is a formal verification of that assumption.

So in important ways, our personal theories of personality incorporate both stability and change. Is it any wonder, then, formal psychological theories of personality do the same? Let's see how those views are described.

Levels of Analysis and Personality Research. Sorting out the various approaches to personality helps us understand what aspects of personality the various researchers describe. Drawing on the work of several theorists and researchers, McAdams (1999) describes three parallel levels of personality structure and function, each containing a wide range of personality constructs: dispositional traits, personal concerns, and life narrative.

- **Dispositional traits** *consist of aspects of personality consistent across different contexts and can be compared across a group along a continuum representing high and low degrees of the characteristic.* Dispositional traits are the level of personality most people think of first, and they include commonly used descriptors such as shy, talkative, authoritarian, and the like.
- **Personal concerns** *consist of things important to people, their goals, and their major concerns in life.* Personal concerns are usually described in motivational, developmental, or strategic terms; they reflect the stage of life a person is in at the time.
- **Life narrative** *consists of the aspects of personality pulling everything together, those integrative aspects that give a person an identity or sense of self.* The creation of one's identity is the goal of this level.

In an extension of McAdams's model of personality, Karen Hooker (Bolkan & Hooker, 2012; Hooker & McAdams, 2003) added three processes that act in tandem with the three structural components of personality proposed by McAdams. **State processes** *act with dispositional traits to create transient, short-term changes in emotion, mood, hunger, anxiety, and so on.* **Personal concerns** *act in tandem with self-regulatory processes that include such processes as primary and secondary control* (discussed in Chapter 8). *Finally,* **cognitive processes** *act jointly with life narratives to create natural interaction that occur between a storyteller and listener, processes central in organizing life stories.*

Finally, as one moves from examining dispositional traits to personal concerns to life narrative (and their corresponding processes), it becomes more likely observable change will take place (Graham & Lachman, 2012; Newton & Stewart, 2012). In a sense, the level of dispositional traits can be viewed as the "raw stuff" of personality, whereas each successive level must be constructed to a greater extent. In the following sections, we use McAdams's levels to organize our discussion of adulthood personality. Let's begin with the "raw stuff" and see how dispositional traits are structured in adulthood.

9.1 Dispositional Traits across Adulthood

LEARNING OBJECTIVES

- What is the five-factor model of dispositional traits?
- What happens to dispositional traits across adulthood?
- What can we conclude from theory and research on dispositional traits?

Abby was attending her high school reunion. She hadn't seen her friend Michelle in 20 years. Abby remembered that in high school Michelle was always surrounded by a group of people. She always walked up to people and initiated conversations, was at ease with strangers, pleasant, and often described as the "life of the party." Abby wondered if Michelle would be the same outgoing person she was in high school.

Many of us eventually attend a high school reunion. It is amusing, so it is said, to see how our classmates changed over the years. In addition to noticing gray or missing hair and a few wrinkles, we should pay attention to personality characteristics. The questions that surfaced for Abby are similar to the ones we generate ourselves. For example, will Katy be the same outgoing person she was as captain of the cheerleaders? Will Ted still be as concerned about social issues at 48 as he was at 18?

To learn as much about our friends as possible we could make careful observations of our classmates' personalities over the course of several reunions. Then, at the gathering marking 60 years since graduation, we could examine the trends we observed. Did our classmates' personalities change substantially or did they remain essentially the same as they were 60 years earlier?

How we think these questions will be answered provides clues to our personal biases concerning personality stability or change across adulthood. As we will see, biases about continuity and discontinuity are more obvious in personality research than in any other area of adult development.

In addition to considering the old debate of whether Michelle's personality characteristics remained stable or have changed, Abby's description of Michelle suggests Michelle is an outgoing, or extroverted, person. How did Abby arrive at this judgment? She probably combined several aspects of Michelle's behavior into a concept that describes her rather concisely. What we have done is use the notion of a personality trait. Extending this same reasoning to many areas of behavior is the basis for trait theories of personality. More formally, people's characteristic behaviors can be understood through attributes that reflect underlying dispositional traits that are relatively enduring aspects of personality. We use the basic tenets of trait theory when we describe ourselves and others with such terms as calm, aggressive, independent, friendly, and so on.

Three assumptions are made about traits (Costa & McCrae, 2011). First, traits are based on comparisons of individuals, because there are no absolute quantitative standards for concepts such as friendliness. Second, the qualities or behaviors making up a particular trait must be distinctive enough to avoid confusion. Imagine the chaos if friendliness and aggressiveness had many behaviors in common and others were vastly different! Finally, the traits attributed to a specific person are assumed to be stable characteristics. We normally assume people who are friendly in several situations are going to be friendly the next time we see them.

These three assumptions are all captured in the classic definition of a trait: "*A trait is any distinguishable, relatively enduring way that one individual differs from others*" (Guilford, 1959, p. 6). *Based on this definition*, trait theories *assume little change in personality occurs across adulthood.*

Most trait theories have several common guiding principles. An important one for this discussion concerns the structure of traits. Like it does for intelligence (see Chapter 7), structure concerns the way traits are organized within the individual. This organization is usually inferred from the pattern of related and unrelated personality characteristics, and is generally expressed in terms of dimensions. Personality structures can be examined over time to see whether they change with age.

The Case for Stability: The Five-Factor Model

Although many trait theories of personality have been proposed over the years, few have been concerned with or have been based on adults of different ages. A major exception to this is the five-factor model proposed by Costa and McCrae (1994; Costa & McCrae, 2011). Their model is strongly grounded in cross-sectional, longitudinal, and sequential research. *The five-factor model consists of five independent dimensions of personality: neuroticism, extraversion, openness to experience, agreeableness, and conscientiousness.*

The first three dimensions of Costa and McCrae's model—neuroticism, extraversion, and openness to experience—have been the ones most heavily researched. Each of these dimensions is represented by six facets reflecting the main characteristics associated with it. The remaining two dimensions were added to the original three in the late 1980s to account for more data and to bring the theory closer to other trait theories. Let's consider each of the five dimensions briefly.

- **Neuroticism.** The six facets of neuroticism are anxiety, hostility, self-consciousness, depression, impulsiveness, and vulnerability. Anxiety and hostility form underlying traits for two fundamental emotions: fear and anger. Although we all experience these emotions at times, the frequency and intensity with which they are felt vary from one person to another. People who are high in trait anxiety are nervous, high-strung, tense, worried, and pessimistic. Besides being prone to anger, hostile people are irritable and tend to be hard to get along with.

  The traits of self-consciousness and depression relate to the emotions shame and sorrow. Being high in self-consciousness is associated with being sensitive to criticism, teasing, and feelings of inferiority. Trait depression involves feelings of sadness, hopelessness, loneliness, guilt, and low self-worth.

  The final two facets of neuroticism—impulsiveness and vulnerability—are most often manifested as behaviors rather than as emotions. Impulsiveness is the tendency to give in to temptation and desires because of a lack of willpower and self-control. Consequently, impulsive people often do things in excess, such as overeating and overspending, and they are more likely to smoke, gamble, and use drugs. Vulnerability involves a lowered capability to deal effectively with stress. Vulnerable people tend to panic in a crisis or emergency and highly dependent on others for help.

Costa and McCrae (1998, 2011) note, in general, people high in neuroticism tend to be high in each of the traits involved. High neuroticism typically results in violent and negative emotions that interfere with people's ability to handle problems or to get along with other people. We can see how this cluster of traits operates. A person gets anxious and embarrassed in a social situation such as a class reunion; the frustration in dealing with others makes the person hostile, leading to excessive drinking at the party, and may result in subsequent depression for making a fool of oneself, and so on.

■ **Extraversion.** The six facets of extraversion can be grouped into three interpersonal traits (warmth, gregariousness, and assertiveness) and three temperamental traits (activity, excitement seeking, and positive emotions). Warmth, or attachment, is a friendly, compassionate, intimately involved style of interacting with other people. Warmth and gregariousness (a desire to be with other people) make up what is sometimes called sociability. Gregarious people thrive on crowds; the more social interaction the better. Assertive people make natural leaders, take charge easily, make up their own minds, and readily express their thoughts and feelings.

Temperamentally, extraverts like to keep busy; they are the people who seem to have endless energy, talk fast, and want to be on the go. They prefer to be in stimulating, exciting environments and often go searching for a challenging situation. This active, exciting lifestyle is evident in the extravert's positive emotion; these people are walking examples of zest, delight, and fun.

An interesting aspect of extraversion is that this dimension relates well to occupational interests and values. People high in extraversion tend to have people-oriented jobs, such as social work, business administration, and sales. They value humanitarian goals and a person-oriented use of power. People low in extraversion tend to prefer task-oriented jobs, such as architecture or accounting.

■ **Openness to Experience.** The six facets of openness to experience represent six different areas. In the area of fantasy, openness means having a vivid imagination and active dream life. In aesthetics, openness is seen in the appreciation of art and beauty, sensitivity to pure experience for its own sake. When open to action, people exhibit a willingness to try something new such as a new kind of cuisine, movie, or a travel destination. People who are open to ideas and values are curious and value knowledge for the sake of knowing. Open people also tend to be open-minded in their values, often admitting what may be right for one person may not be right for everyone. This outlook is a direct outgrowth of individuals' willingness to think of different possibilities in addition to their tendency to empathize with others in different circumstances. Open people also experience their own feelings strongly and see them as a major source of meaning in life.

Not surprisingly, openness to experience is also related to occupational choice. Open people are likely to be found in occupations that place a high value on thinking theoretically or philosophically and less emphasis on economic values. They are typically intelligent and tend to subject themselves to stressful situations. Occupations such as psychologist or minister, for example, appeal to open people.

■ **Agreeableness.** The easiest way to understand the agreeableness dimension is to consider the traits characterizing antagonism. Antagonistic people tend to set themselves against others; they are skeptical, mistrustful, callous, unsympathetic, stubborn, and rude; and they have a defective sense of attachment. Antagonism may be manifested in ways other than overt hostility. Some antagonistic people are skillful manipulators or aggressive go-getters with little patience.

Scoring high on agreeableness, the opposite of antagonism, may not always be adaptive either, however. These people may tend to be overly dependent and self-effacing, traits that often prove annoying to others.

- **Conscientiousness.** Scoring high on conscientiousness indicates one is hardworking, ambitious, energetic, scrupulous, and persevering. Such people have a strong desire to make something of themselves. People at the opposite end of this scale tend to be negligent, lazy, disorganized, late, aimless, and not persistent.

What Happens to Dispositional Traits Across Adulthood?

Costa and McCrae investigated whether the traits that make up their model remain stable across adulthood (e.g., Costa & McCrae, 1988, 1994, 1997, 2011). They suggest personality traits stop changing by age 30; then appear to be "set in plaster" (Costa & McCrae, 1994, p. 21). The data from the Costa, McCrae, and colleagues' studies came from the Baltimore Longitudinal Study of Aging for the 114 men who took the Guilford-Zimmerman Temperament Survey (GZTS) on three occasions, with each of the two follow-up tests about six years apart.

What Costa and colleagues found was surprising. Even over a 12-year period, the 10 traits measured by the GZTS remained highly stable; the correlations ranged from .68 to .85. In much of personality research we might expect to find this degree of stability over a week or two, but to see it over 12 years is noteworthy.

We would normally be skeptical of such consistency over a long period. But similar findings were obtained in other studies. In a longitudinal study of 60-, 80-, and 100-year-olds, Martin and colleagues (2003) found

Steven Rubin/The Image Works

Will you recognize your classmates at a reunion years from now by their personalities?

there were no significant changes across overall personality patterns. However, some interesting changes did occur in the very old. There was an increase in suspiciousness and sensitivity and could be explained by increased wariness of victimization in older adulthood.

Stability was also observed in past longitudinal data conducted over a 7-year period (Mõttus, Johnson, & Deary, 2012; Roberts & DelVecchio, 2000), to as long as a 30-year span (Leon, Gillum, Gillum, & Gouze, 1979). According to this evidence, it appears individuals change little in self-reported personality traits over periods of up to 30 years long and over the age range of 20 to 90 years of age.

However, there is growing evidence both stability and change can be detected in personality trait development across the adult life span (Allemand, Zimprich, & Hendriks, 2008; Caspi, Roberts, & Shiner, 2005; Mathias, Allemand, Zimprich, & Martin, 2008; Mõttus, Johnson, & Deary, 2012). These findings came about because of advances in statistical techniques. Researchers find the way people differ in their personality becomes more pronounced with older age (Allemand et al., 2008; Mõttus, Johnson, & Deary, 2012). For example, studies (e.g., Donnellan & Lucas, 2008) find extraversion and openness decrease with age whereas agreeableness increases with age. Conscientious appears to peak in middle age. Most interestingly, neuroticism often disappears or is much less apparent in late life. Such changes are found in studies that examine larger populations across a larger age range (e.g., 16 to mid-80s) and greater geographical regions (e.g., United States and Great Britain).

Despite the impressive collection of research findings for personality stability using the five-factor model, there is growing evidence for personality change. Ursula Staudinger and colleagues have a perspective that reconciles these differences (Mühlig-Versen, Bowen, & Staudinger, 2012; Staudinger & Kunzman, 2005; Staudinger & Kessler, 2008). They suggest personality takes on two forms: adjustment and growth. **Personality adjustment** *involves developmental changes in terms of their adaptive value and functionality, such as functioning effectively within society, and how personality contributes to everyday life running smoothly.* **Personality growth** *refers to ideal end states such as increased self-transcendence, wisdom, and integrity.* Examples of this will be discussed later and includes Erikson's theory.

Both of these personality dimensions interact because growth cannot occur without adjustment. However, Staudinger argues while growth in terms of ideal end states does not necessarily occur in everyone, since it is less easily acquired, strategies for adjustment develops across the latter half of the life span. This framework can be used to interpret stability and change in the Big Five personality factors.

First, the most current consensus of change in the Big Five with increasing age is the absence of neuroticism and the presence of agreeableness and conscientiousness. These three traits are associated with personality adjustment, especially in terms of becoming emotionally less volatile and more attuned to social demands and social roles (Mühlig-Versen et al., 2012; Staudinger & Kunzmann, 2005). These characteristics allow older adults to maintain and regain levels of well-being in the face of loss, threats, and challenges; common occurrences in late life.

Studies also show a decrease in openness to new experiences with increasing age (e.g., Graham & Lachman, 2012; Helson & Kwan, 2000; Roberts et al., 2006; Srivastava et al., 2003). Staudinger argues openness to experience is related to personal maturity because it is highly correlated with ego development, wisdom, and emotional complexity. Evidence suggests these three aspects of personality (ego level, wisdom, and emotional complexity) do not increase with age and may show decline (Staudinger, Dörner, & Mickler, 2005; Grühn, Lumley, Diehl, & Labouvie-Vief, 2013, Mühlig-Versen et al., 2012). Staudinger concludes personal growth in adulthood appears to be rare rather than normative.

To summarize, there appears to be increases in adjustment aspects of personality with increasing age, and it could be normative. At the same time, however, the basic indicators of personality growth tend to show stability or decline. You might ask, what's going on?

The most likely answer is personality growth or change across adulthood does not normally occur unless there are special circumstances and with an environmental push for it to occur. Thus, the personality-related adjustment grows in adulthood does so in response to ever-changing developmental challenges and tasks, such as establishing a career, marriage, and family.

Conclusions about Dispositional Traits

What can we conclude about the development of dispositional traits across adulthood? Clearly, the overwhelming evidence supports the view personality traits remain stable throughout adulthood when data are averaged across many different kinds of people. However, if we ask about specific aspects of personality in specific kinds of people, we are more likely to find evidence of both change and stability.

A reasonable resolution to the trait debate is to understand the answer to the basic question depends on how the data are analyzed (Hill, Turiano, Mroczek, & Roberts, 2012; Mõttus et al., 2012; Mroczek & Spiro, 2003). Mroczek and colleagues challenge the conclusions drawn from the typical longitudinal studies on stability and change in personality by examining personality across the adult life span at the level of the individual. We describe this challenge in more detail in the Current Controversies feature.

CURRENT CONTROVERSIES:

INTRAINDIVIDUAL CHANGE AND THE STABILITY OF TRAITS

The controversy continues today as to if personality remains stable across the life span or changes. Given personality traits have shown to be important predictors of mental and physical health as well as psychological well-being, potential changes in personality can have important implications for gains and declines in life outcomes. However, as this chapter indicates, there is no clear evidence for one position or the other.

An important aspect to consider in this controversy is the level of analysis stability and change is determined.

Typically, stability and change are examined through average (mean) level comparisons over time. In other words, does an age group's mean level on a particular personality trait such as extraversion remain stable from one point in time to another (say 10 years apart) or does it change?

Several researchers (e.g., Hill et al., 2012; Mõttus et al., 2012; Mroczek & Spiro, 2003) suggest examining change in mean levels of a personality trait does not adequately address stability and change at the level of the individual. A group mean hides the extent individual people change. In an alternative approach, they also examine the extent each person in their longitudinal studies changes or remains the same over time. This allows them to ask the questions, "Do some people remain stable whereas others change?" and, if there are people who change, "Do some people change more than others?" Data addressing these questions indicate important individual differences in the extent people do or do not change.

This approach allows a more detailed answer to questions of stability and change. When we rely on group level analyses in major longitudinal approaches such as McCrae and Costa's (1994), we see there is primarily stability. However, when we examine individuals' respective growth curves, we see a more complex picture of personality development. Whereas a large proportion of individuals may remain stable, there is a substantial group of individuals whose personality traits either increase or decrease over time. Perhaps we can see a resolution to this debate in the future as more intraindividual studies on personality development emerge.

Another important issue for future research is the role of life experiences. If a person experiences few events inducing him or her to change, then change is unlikely. In this view a person will be at 60 much the same as he or she is at 30, all other factors being held constant. As we show later, this idea has been incorporated formally into other theories of personality.

What about that high school reunion? On the basis of dispositional traits, then, we should have little difficulty knowing our high school classmates many years from now.

ADULT DEVELOPMENT IN ACTION

If you were a counselor, how would you use research on stability and dispositional traits to understand why it is difficult for people to change their behavior?

9.2 Personal Concerns and Qualitative Stages in Adulthood

LEARNING OBJECTIVES

- What are personal concerns?
- What are the main elements of Jung's theory?
- What are the stages in Erikson's theory? What types of clarifications and extensions of it have been offered? What research evidence is there to support his stages?
- What are the main points and problems with theories based on life transitions?
- What can we conclude about personal concerns?

Andy showed all the signs. He divorced his wife of nearly 20 years to enter into a relationship with a woman 15 years younger, sold his ordinary-looking mid-size sedan for a red sports car, and began working out regularly at the health club after years of being a couch potato. Andy claims he hasn't felt this good in years; he is happy to be making this change in middle age. All of Andy's friends agree: This is a clear case of midlife crisis— or is it?

Many people believe strongly middle age brings with it a normative crisis called the midlife crisis. There would appear to be lots of evidence to support this view, based on case studies like Andy's. But is everything as it seems? We'll find out in this section. First we consider the evidence people's priorities and personal concerns change throughout adulthood, requiring adults to reassess themselves from time to time. This alternative position to the five-factor model discussed earlier claims change is the rule during adulthood.

What does it mean to know another person well? McAdams and Olson (2010) believe to know another person well takes more than just knowing where he or she falls on the dimensions of dispositional traits. Rather, it means knowing what issues are important to a person, that is, what the person wants, how the individual goes about getting what he or she wants, what the person's plans are for the future, how the person interacts with others who provide key personal relationships, and so forth. In short, we need to know something about a person's personal concerns. Personal concerns reflect what people want during particular times of their lives and within specific domains; they are the strategies, plans, and defenses people use to get what they want and avoid getting what they don't.

What's Different about Personal Concerns?

Many researchers began analyzing personality in ways explicitly contextual, in contrast to work on dispositional traits that ignores context. This work emphasizes the importance of sociocultural influences on development that shape people's wants and behaviors (Hooker & McAdams, 2003). Röcke and Lachman (2008) showed a person-centered approach that focuses on personal control and social relationship qualityis better than dispositional traits in understanding life satisfaction.

Although relatively little research has been conducted on the personal concerns level of personality, a few things are clear (Hooker & McAdams, 2003; McAdams & Olson, 2010). Personality constructs at this level are not reducible to traits. Rather, such constructs need to be viewed as conscious descriptions of what a person is trying to accomplish during a given period of life and what goals and goal-based concerns the person has.

As Cantor (1990) initially noted and others (e.g., Norem, 2012) summarized, these constructs speak directly to the question of what people actually do and the goals they set for themselves in life. Moreover, we expect considerable change would be seen at this level of personality, given the importance of sociocultural influences and the changing nature of life-tasks as people mature. Accompanying these goals and motivations that define personal concerns are the self-regulation processes implemented to effect change in personal concerns. The transition from primary control to secondary control or from assimilative to accommodative coping discussed in Chapter 8 enables people to recalibrate their goals and personal concerns in later life. This process serves the important function of maintaining satisfaction and meaningfulness in life (Hooker & McAdams, 2003; McAdams & Olson, 2010).

In contrast to the limited empirical data on the development of personal concerns, the theoretical base is arguably the richest. For the better part of a century, the notion that people's personality changes throughout the life span has been described in numerous ways, typically in theories postulating qualitative stages that reflect the central concern of that period of life. In this section, we consider several of these theories and evaluate the available evidence for each. Let's begin with Carl Jung's theory—the theory that started people thinking about personality change in midlife.

Jung's Theory

Jung represents a turning point in the history of psychoanalytic thought. Initially allied with Freud, he soon severed the tie and developed his own ideas that have elements of both Freudian theory and humanistic psychology. He was one of the first theorists to believe in personality development in adulthood; this marked a major break with Freudian thought, that argued personality development ended in adolescence.

Jung's theory emphasizes each aspect of a person's personality must be in balance with all the others. This means each part of the personality will be expressed in some way, whether through normal means, neurotic symptoms, or in dreams. Jung asserts the parts of the personality are organized in such a way as to produce two basic orientations of the ego. One of these orientations is concerned with the external world; Jung labels it extraversion. The opposite orientation, toward the inner world of subjective experiences, is labeled introversion. To be psychologically healthy, both of these orientations must be present, and they must be balanced. Individuals must deal with the external world effectively and also be able to evaluate their inner feelings and values. When people emphasize one orientation over another, they are classified as extraverts or introverts.

Jung advocates two important age-related trends in personality development. The first relates to the introversion–extraversion distinction. Young adults are more extraverted than older adults, perhaps because of younger people's needs to find a mate, have a career, and so forth. With increasing age, however, the need for balance creates a need to focus inward and explore personal feelings about aging and mortality. Thus, Jung argued with age comes an increase in introversion.

The second age-related trend in Jung's theory involves the feminine and masculine aspects of our personalities. Each of us, according to Jung, has elements of both masculinity and femininity. In young adulthood, however, most of us express only one of them while working hard to suppress the other. In other words, young adults most often act in accordance with gender-role stereotypes appropriate to their culture. As they grow older, people begin to let out the suppressed parts of their personality. This means men begin to behave in ways that earlier in life they would have considered feminine, and women behave in ways that they formerly would have thought masculine. These changes achieve a better balance that allows men and women to deal more effectively with their individual needs rather than being driven by socially defined stereotypes. This balance, however, does not mean a reversal of sex roles. On the contrary, it represents the expression of aspects of ourselves that have been there all along but we have simply not allowed showing. We return to this issue at the end of the chapter when we consider gender-role development.

Jung's ideas that self and personality are organized by symbols and stories and the notion we transcend the dualities of femininity masculinity and conscious–unconscious, among others, have now become active areas of research (Grühn et al., 2013; Labouvie-Vief, 2008; Labouvie-Vief, Grühn, & Mouras, 2009). However, as Labouvie-Vief and colleagues point out, most empirical evidence suggests these reorganizations proposed by Jung are more indicative of advanced or exceptional development.

Jung stretched traditional psychoanalytic theory to new limits by postulating continued development across adulthood. Other theorists took Jung's lead and argued not only personality development occurred in adulthood but also it did so in an orderly, sequential fashion. We consider the sequences developed by Erik Erikson.

Erikson's Stages of Psychosocial Development

The best-known life-span theorist is Erik Erikson (1982), who called attention to cultural mechanisms involved in personality development. According to him, personality is determined by the interaction between an inner maturational plan and external societal demands. He proposes the life cycle has eight stages of development, summarized in Table 9.1. Erikson believed the sequence of stages is biologically fixed.

Each stage in Erikson's theory is marked by a struggle between two opposing tendencies and both are experienced by the person. The names of the stages reflect the issues that form the struggles. The struggles are resolved through an interactive process involving both the inner psychological and the outer social influences. Successful resolutions establish the basic areas of psychosocial strength; unsuccessful resolutions impair ego development in a particular area and adversely affect the resolution of future struggles. Thus each stage in Erikson's theory represents a kind of crisis.

The sequence of stages in Erikson's theory is based on the **epigenetic principle,** *meaning each psychosocial strength has its own special time of ascendancy, or period of particular importance.* The eight stages represent the order of this ascendancy. Because the stages extend across the whole life span, it takes a lifetime to

Table 9.1

SUMMARY OF ERIKSON'S THEORY OF PSYCHOSOCIAL DEVELOPMENT, WITH IMPORTANT RELATIONSHIPS AND PSYCHOSOCIAL STRENGTHS ACQUIRED AT EACH STAGE			
Stage	**Psychosocial Crisis**	**Significant Relations**	**Basic Strengths**
1. Infancy	Basic trust versus basic mistrust	Maternal person	Hope
2. Early childhood	Autonomy versus shame and doubt	Paternal people	Will
3. Play age	Initiative versus guilt	Basic family	Purpose
4. School age	Industry versus inferiority	"Neighborhood," school	Competence
5. Adolescence	Identity versus identity confusion	Peer groups and outgroups; models of leadership	Love
6. Young adulthood	Intimacy versus isolation	Partners in friendship, sex competition, cooperation	Love
7. Adulthood	Generativity versus stagnation	Divided labor and shared household	Care
8. Old age	Integrity versus despair	Humankind, "my kind"	Wisdom

Source: From The Life Cycle Completed: A Review *by Erik H. Erikson. Copyright © 1982 by Rikan Enterprises, Ltd. Used by permission of W. W. Norton & Company, Inc.*

acquire all of the psychosocial strengths. Moreover, Erikson realizes present and future behavior must have its roots in the past, because later stages build on the foundation laid in previous ones.

Erikson argues the basic aspect of a healthy personality is a sense of trust toward oneself and others. Thus the first stage in his theory involves trust versus mistrust, representing the conflict an infant faces in developing trust in a world it knows little about. With trust come feelings of security and comfort.

The second stage, autonomy versus shame and doubt, reflects children's budding understanding they are in charge of their own actions. This understanding changes them from totally reactive beings to ones who can act on the world intentionally. Their autonomy is threatened, however, by their inclinations to avoid responsibility for their actions and to go back to the security of the first stage.

In the third stage, the conflict is initiative versus guilt. Once children realize they can act on the world and are somebody, they begin to discover who they are. They take advantage of wider experience to explore the environment on their own, ask many questions about the world, and imagine possibilities about themselves.

The fourth stage is marked by children's increasing interests in interacting with peers, their need for acceptance, and their need to develop competencies. Erikson views these needs as representing industry versus inferiority, and is manifested behaviorally in children's desire to accomplish tasks by working hard. Failure to succeed in developing self-perceived competencies results in feelings of inferiority.

During adolescence, Erikson believes we deal with the issue of identity versus identity confusion. The choice we make—the identity we form—is not so much who we are but who we can become. The struggle in adolescence is choosing from among a multitude of possible selves the one we will become. Identity confusion results when we are torn over the possibilities. The struggle involves trying to balance our need to choose a possible self and the desire to try out many possible selves.

During young adulthood the major developmental task, achieving intimacy versus isolation, involves establishing a fully intimate relationship with another. Erikson (1968) argues intimacy means the sharing of all aspects of oneself without fearing the loss of identity. If intimacy is not achieved, isolation results. One way to assist the development of intimacy is to choose a mate who represents the ideal of all one's past experiences. The psychosocial strength that emerges from the intimacy–isolation struggle is love.

With the advent of middle age the focus shifts from intimacy to concern for the next generation, expressed as generativity versus stagnation. The struggle occurs between a sense of generativity (the feeling people must maintain and perpetuate society) and a sense of stagnation (the feeling of self-absorption). Generativity is seen in such things as parenthood; teaching, like the man in the photograph; or providing goods and services for the benefit of society. If the challenge of generativity is accepted, the development of trust in the next generation is facilitated, and the psychosocial strength of care is obtained. We examine generativity in more detail a bit later in this chapter.

In old age, individuals must resolve the struggle between ego integrity and despair. This last stage begins with a growing awareness of the nearness of the end of life, but it is actually completed by only a small number of people (Erikson, 1982). According to Erikson (1982), this struggle comes about as older adults try to understand their lives in terms of the future of their family and community. Thoughts of a person's own death are balanced by the realization they live on through children, grandchildren, great-grandchildren, and the community as a whole. This realization produces what Erikson calls a "life-affirming involvement" in the present.

To achieve integrity, a person must come to terms with the choices and events that made his or her life

Erikson's stage of integrity is achieved when older adults understand that they will live on through future generations of their family and community.

unique. There must also be an acceptance of the fact one's life is drawing to a close. Research shows a connection between engaging in a life review and achieving integrity, so life review forms the basis for effective mental health interventions (Westerhof, Bohlmeijer, & Webster, 2010).

Who reaches integrity? Erikson (1982) emphasizes people who demonstrate integrity made many different choices and follow different lifestyles; the point is everyone has this opportunity to achieve integrity if they strive for it. Those who reach integrity become self-affirming and self-accepting; they judge their lives to have been worthwhile and good. They are glad to have lived the lives they did.

Clarifications and Expansions of Erikson's Theory. Erikson's theory made a major impact on thinking about life-span development. However, some aspects of his theory are unclear, poorly defined, or unspecified. Traditionally, these problems led critics to dismiss the theory as untestable and incomplete. However, the situation is changing. Other theorists tried to address these problems by identifying common themes, specifying underlying mental processes, and reinterpreting and integrating the theory with other ideas. These ideas are leading researchers to reassess the usefulness of Erikson's theory as a guide for research on adult personality development.

Logan (1986) points out Erikson's theory can be considered as a cycle that repeats: from basic trust to identity and from identity to integrity. In this approach the developmental progression is trust → achievement → wholeness. Throughout life we first establish we can trust other people and ourselves. Initially, trust involves learning about ourselves and others, represented by the first two stages (trust vs. mistrust and autonomy vs. shame and doubt). The recapitulation of this idea in the second cycle is seen in our struggle to find a person with whom we can form a close relationship yet not lose our own sense of self (intimacy vs. isolation).

In addition, Logan shows how achievement—our need to accomplish and to be recognized for it—is a theme throughout Erikson's theory. During childhood this idea is reflected in the two stages initiative versus guilt and industry versus inferiority, whereas in adulthood it is represented by generativity

versus stagnation. Finally, Logan points out the issue of understanding ourselves as worthwhile and whole is first encountered during adolescence (identity vs. identity confusion) and is re-experienced during old age (integrity vs. despair). Logan's analysis emphasizes psychosocial development, although complicated on the surface, may actually reflect only a small number of issues. Moreover, he points out we do not come to a single resolution of these issues of trust, achievement, and wholeness. Rather, they are issues we struggle with our entire lives.

Slater (2003) expanded on Logan's reasoning, suggesting the central crisis of generativity versus stagnation includes struggles between pride and embarrassment, responsibility and ambivalence, career productivity and inadequacy, as well as parenthood and self-absorption. Each of these conflicts provides further knowledge about generativity as the intersection of society and the human life cycle.

Researchers focusing on emerging adulthood raised the possibility of an additional stage specific to this phase of life. Patterson (2012) speculates a fifth stage she labels incarnation versus impudence is needed between adolescence (identity vs. role confusion) and young adulthood (intimacy vs. isolation). For Patterson, this crisis is "resolved through experimental sexuality, temporal and spatial social and intimate relationships, interdependence and self-sufficiency and dependence and helplessness, and relativist and absolutist ideological experimentation."

Some critics argue Erikson's stage of generativity is much too broad to capture the essence of adulthood. Kotre (1999, 2005) contends adults experience many opportunities to express generativity that are not equivalent and do not lead to a general state. Rather, he sees generativity more as a set of impulses felt at different times and in different settings, such as at work or in grandparenting. More formally, Kotre describes five types of generativity: biological and parental generativity, that concerns raising children; technical generativity, relating to the passing of specific skills from one generation to another; cultural generativity, referring to being a mentor (discussed in more detail in Chapter 12); agentic generativity, the desire to be or to do something that transcends death; and communal generativity, manifesting as a person's participation in a mutual, interpersonal reality. Only rarely, Kotre contends, is there a continuous state of generativity in adulthood. He asserts the struggles identified by Erikson are not fought constantly; rather, they probably come and go. We examine this idea in more detail in the next section.

Research on Generativity. Perhaps the central period in adulthood from an Eriksonian perspective is the stage of generativity versus stagnation. One of the best empirically based efforts to describe generativity is McAdams's model (McAdams, 2001; McAdams & Olson, 2010; Wilt, Cox, & McAdams, 2010) shown in Figure 9.1.

This multidimensional model shows how generativity results from the complex interconnections among societal and inner forces. The tension between creating a product or outcome that outlives oneself and selflessly bestowing one's efforts as a gift to the next generation (reflecting a concern for what is good for society) results in a concern for the next generation and a belief in the goodness of the human enterprise. The positive resolution of this conflict finds middle-aged adults developing a generative commitment that produces generative actions. A person derives personal meaning from being generative by constructing a life story or narration that helps create the person's identity.

The components of McAdams's model relate differently to personality traits. Generative *concern* is a general personality tendency of interest in caring for younger individuals, and generative *action* is the actual behaviors that promote the well-being of the next generation. Generative concern relates to life satisfaction and overall happiness, whereas generative action does not. For example, new grandparents may derive satisfaction from their grandchildren and are greatly concerned with their well-being but have little desire to engage in the daily hassles of caring for them on a regular basis.

Although they can be expressed by adults of all ages, certain types of generativity are more common at some ages than others. Middle-aged and older adults show a greater preoccupation with generativity themes than do younger adults in their accounts of personally meaningful life experiences (McAdams & Olson, 2010). Middle-aged adults make more generative commitments (e.g., "save enough money for my daughter to go to medical school"), reflecting a major difference in the inner and outer worlds of middle-aged and older adults as opposed to younger adults.

Similar research focusing specifically on middle-aged women yields comparable results. Hills (2013) argues leaving a legacy, a major example of generativity in practice, is a core concern in midlife, more so than at

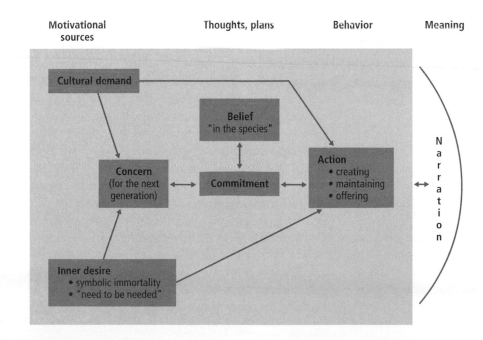

| Motivational sources | Thoughts, plans | Behavior | Meaning |

Figure 9.1

McAdams' model of generativity.

Source: McAdams, D. P., Hart, H. M., & Maruna, S. (1998). The anatomy of generativity. In D. P. McAdams & F. de St. Aubin (Eds.), Generativity and Adult Development: How and Why We Care for the Next Generation (p. 7).

any other age. Schoklitsch & Bauman (2012) point out the capacity of generativity peaks during midlife, but people continue to accomplish generative tasks into late life (e.g., great-grandparenthood).

These data demonstrate the personal concerns of middle-aged adults are fundamentally different from those of younger adults. In fact, generativity may be a stronger predictor of emotional and physical well-being in midlife and old age (Gruenewald, Liao, & Seeman, 2012; McAdams & Olson, 2010; Wilt et al., 2010). Among women and men, generativity is associated with positive emotion and satisfaction with life and work, and predicts physical health. Considered together, these findings provide considerable support for Erikson's contention the central concerns for adults change with age. However, the data also indicate generativity is much more complex than Erikson originally proposed and, while peaking in middle age, may not diminish in late life.

Theories Based on Life Transitions

Jung's belief in a midlife crisis and Erikson's belief personality development proceeds in stages laid the foundation for other theorists' efforts. For many laypeople, the idea adults go through an orderly sequence of stages that includes both crises and stability reflects their own experience. This is probably why books such as Sheehy's *Passages* (1976), *Pathfinders* (1981), *New Passages* (1995), and *Understanding Men's Passages* (1998) met with instant acceptance, or why Levinson's (Levinson et al., 1978) and Vaillant's works (Vaillant, 1977; Vaillant & Vaillant, 1990) have been applied to everything from basic personality development to understanding how men's occupational careers change.

A universal assumption of these theories is people go through predictable age-related crises. Some life transition theories (e.g., Levinson's) also propose these crises are followed by periods of relative stability. The overall view is adulthood consists of a series of alternating periods of stability and change.

Compared with the theories we considered to this point, however, theories based on life transitions are built on shakier ground. Some are based on small, highly selective samples (such as men who attended Harvard) or surveys completed by readers of particular

magazines. This is in contrast to the large databases used to test the five-factor model. These theories are associated with psychometrically sound measures and are well researched. Thus, the research methods used in studies of life transitions are questionable. Still, the intuitive appeal of these theories makes them worth a closer look.

An important question about life transition theories is the extent they are real and actually occur to everyone. Life transition theories typically present stages as if everyone universally experiences them. Moreover, many have specific ages tied to specific stages (such as age-30 or age-50 transitions). As we know from cognitive developmental research reviewed in Chapter 7, this is a tenuous assumption. Individual variation is the rule, not the exception. What actually happens may be a combination of expectations and socialization. Dunn and Merriam (1995) examined data from a large, diverse national sample and found less than 20% of people in their early 30s experienced the age-30 transition (which encompasses the midlife crisis) that forms a cornerstone of Levinson and colleagues' (1978) theory. The experience of a midlife crisis, discussed next, is an excellent case in point.

In Search of the Midlife Crisis. One of the most important ideas in theories that consider the importance of life transitions (subsequent to periods of stability) is middle-aged adults experience a personal crisis that results in major changes in how they view themselves. During a midlife crisis, people are supposed to take a good hard look at themselves and, they hope, attain a much better understanding of who they are. Difficult issues such as one's own mortality and inevitable aging are supposed to be faced. Behavioral changes are supposed to occur; we even have stereotypic images of the middle-aged male, like Andy, running off with a much younger female as a result of his midlife crisis. In support of this notion, Levinson and his colleagues (1978; Levinson & Levinson, 1996) write that middle-aged men in his study reported intense internal struggles much like depression.

However, far more research fails to document the existence, and more importantly, the universality of a particularly difficult time in midlife (Lachman, 2004). In fact, those who actually experience a crisis may be suffering from general problems of psychopathology (Goldstein, 2005; Labouvie-Vief & Diehl, 1999). Studies extending Levinson's theory to women have not found strong evidence of a traumatic midlife crisis either (Harris et al., 1986; Reinke et al., 1985; Roberts & Newton, 1987).

Researchers point out the idea of a midlife crisis became widely accepted as fact because of the mass media (Sterns & Huyck, 2001). People take it for granted they will go through a period of intense psychological turmoil in their 40s.

The problem is there is little hard scientific evidence of it. The data suggest midlife is no more or no less traumatic for most people than any other period in life. Perhaps the most convincing support for this conclusion comes from research conducted by Farrell and Rosenberg (Rosenberg et al., 1999). These investigators initially set out to prove the existence of a midlife crisis because they were firm believers in it. After extensive testing and interviewing, they emerged as nonbelievers.

However, Labouvie-Vief and colleagues (e.g., Labouvie-Vief & Diehl, 1999; Labouvie-Vief et al., 2009; Grühn et al., 2013) offer good evidence for a reorganization of self and values across the adult life span. They suggest the major dynamic that drives such changes may not be age dependent, but follow general cognitive changes. As discussed in Chapter 8, individuals around middle adulthood show the most complex understanding of self, emotions, and motivations. Cognitive complexity also is shown to be the strongest predictor of higher levels of complexity in general. From this approach, a midlife "crisis" may be the result of general gains in cognitive complexity from early to middle adulthood.

Abigail Stewart (Newton & Stewart, 2012; Peterson & Stewart, 1996; Torges, Stewart, & Duncan, 2008) found that women who have regrets about adopting traditional roles (e.g., wife/mother) but later pursue an education or career at midlife report higher well-being than either women who experience regret but do not make a change or women who never experienced regrets about their roles. *Stewart suggests rather than a midlife crisis, such an adjustment may be more*

Midlife is a time when one's sense of personal control and purpose peaks, and physical abilities begin to decline.

Stockbroker/MBI/Alamy

appropriately considered a **midlife correction**, *reevaluating one's roles and dreams and making the necessary corrections.*

Perhaps the best way to view midlife is as a time of both gains and losses (Lachman 2004). That is, the changes people perceive in midlife can be viewed as representing both gains and losses. Competence, ability to handle stress, sense of personal control, purpose in life, and social responsibility are all at their peak, whereas physical abilities, such as women's ability to bear children, and physical appearance in men and women are examples of changes many view as negative. This gain–loss view emphasizes two things. First, the exact timing of change is not fixed but occurs over an extended period of time. Second, change can be both positive and negative at the same time. Thus, rather than seeing midlife as a time of crisis, one may want to view it as a period when several aspects of one's life acquire new meanings.

Finally, we cannot overlook examining midlife crises from a cross-cultural perspective (Tanner & Arnett, 2009). Menon and Shweder (1998; Menon, 2001; Sterns & Huyck, 2001) suggest midlife crisis is a cultural invention. They present anthropological evidence suggesting the concept of midlife itself is limited to adults studied in the United States. In other cultures, transitions and crises are linked to role relations such as marriage and relocation into the spouse's family. Major transitions are defined by such events as children's marriages and mothers-in-law moving into the older adult role of observer (Menon, 2001; Tanner & Arnett, 2009). Again, this is a good reminder the cultural context plays an important role in adult development.

Conclusions about Personal Concerns

The theories and research evidence we considered show substantive change in adults' personal concerns definitely occurs as people age. This conclusion is in sharp contrast to the stability observed in dispositional traits but does support McAdams's (e.g., McAdams & Olson, 2010) contention this middle level of personality should show some change. What is also clear, is a tight connection between such change and specific ages is not supported by the bulk of the data. Rather, change appears to occur in wide windows of time depending on many factors, including one's sociocultural context. Finally, more research is needed in this area, especially investigations that provide longitudinal evidence of change within individuals.

ADULT DEVELOPMENT IN ACTION

As a director of human resources at a major corporation, how would knowledge about generativity help you understand your middle-aged employees better?

9.3 Life Narratives, Identity, and the Self

LEARNING OBJECTIVES

- What are the main aspects of McAdams's life-story model?
- What are the main points of Whitbourne's identity theory?
- How does self-concept come to take adult form? What is its development during adulthood?
- What are possible selves? Do they show differences during adulthood?
- What role does religion or spiritual support play in adult life?
- What conclusions can be drawn from research using life narratives?

Antje is a 19-year-old sophomore at a community college. She expects her study of early childhood education to be difficult but rewarding. She figures along the *way she will meet a great guy she will marry soon after graduation. They will have two children before she turns 30. Antje sees herself getting a good job teaching preschool children and someday owning her own day care center.*

Who are you? What kind of person are you trying to become? These are the kinds of questions Antje is trying to answer. Answering these questions requires concepts of personality going beyond dispositional traits and personal concerns. The aspects of personality we discussed thus far are important, but they lack a sense of integration, unity, coherence, and overall purpose (McAdams & Olson, 2010). For example, understanding a person's goals (from the level of personal concerns) does not reveal who a person is trying to be, or what kind of person the person is trying to create. What is lacking in other levels of analysis is a sense of the person's identity or sense of self.

In contrast to Erikson's (1982) proposition that identity formation is the central task of adolescence, many researchers now believe the important ways identity and the creation of the self continue to develop throughout adulthood (e.g., Graham & Lachman, 2012; Grühn et al., 2013; Newton & Stewart, 2012). This emerging field of how adults continue constructing identity and the self relies on life narratives, or the internalized and evolving story that integrates a person's reconstructed past, perceived present, and anticipated future into a coherent and vitalizing life myth (Cox & McAdams, 2012; Curtin & Stewart, 2012). Careful analysis of people's life narratives provides insight into their identity.

In this section, we consider two evolving theories of identity. Dan McAdams is concerned with understanding how people see themselves and how they fit into the adult world. Susan Krauss Whitbourne investigated people's own conceptions of the life course and how they differ from age norms and the expectations for society as a whole. To round out our understanding of identity and the self, we also examine related constructs. Before beginning, though, take time to complete the exercise in the Discovering Development feature. This exercise will give you a sense of what a life narrative is and how it might be used to gain insight into identity and the sense of self.

DISCOVERING DEVELOPMENT:

WHO DO YOU WANT TO BE WHEN YOU "GROW UP"?

From the time you were a child, people have posed this question to you. In childhood, you probably answered by indicating some specific career, such as firefighter or teacher. But now that you are an adult, the question takes on new meaning. Rather than simply a matter of picking a profession, the question goes much deeper to the kinds of values and the essence of the person you would like to become.

Take a few minutes and think about who you would like to be in another decade or two (or maybe even 50 years hence). What things will matter to you? What will you be doing? What experiences will you have had? What lies ahead?

This exercise can give you a sense of the way researchers try to understand people's sense of identity and self through the use of personal narrative. You might want to keep what you have written and check it when the appropriate number of years elapse.

McAdams's Life-Story Model

McAdams (2001; Cox & McAdams, 2012; Lilgendahl & McAdams, 2011) argues a person's sense of identity cannot be understood using the language of dispositional traits or personal concerns. Identity is not just a collection of traits, nor is it a collection of plans, strategies, or goals. Instead, it is based on a story of how the person came into being, where the person has been, where he or she is going, and who he or she will become, much like Antje's story. McAdams argues people create a life story that is an internalized narrative with a beginning, middle, and an anticipated ending. The life story is created and revised throughout adulthood as people change and the changing environment places different demands on them.

McAdams's research indicates people in Western societies begin forming their life story in late adolescence and early adulthood, but it has roots in the development of one's earliest attachments in infancy. As in Erikson's theory, adolescence marks the full initiation into forming an identity, and thus, a coherent life story begins. In early adulthood it is continued and refined, and from midlife and beyond it is refashioned

in the wake of major and minor life changes. Generativity marks the attempt to create an appealing story "ending" that will generate new beginnings for future generations.

Paramount in these life stories is the changing personal identity reflected in the emotions conveyed in the story (from tragedy to optimism or through comic and romantic descriptions). In addition, motivations change and are reflected in the person repeatedly trying to attain his or her goals over time. The two most common goal themes are agency (reflecting power, achievement, and autonomy) and communion (reflecting love, intimacy, and a sense of belonging). Finally, stories indicate one's beliefs and values, or the ideology a person uses to set the context for his or her actions.

Every life story contains episodes that provide insight into perceived change and continuity in life. People prove to themselves and others they have either changed or remained the same by pointing to specific events supporting the appropriate claim. The main characters in people's lives represent idealizations of the self, such as "the dutiful mother" or "the reliable worker." Integrating these various aspects of the self is a major challenge of midlife and later adulthood. Finally, all life stories need an ending so the self can leave a legacy that creates new beginnings. Life stories in middle-aged and older adults have a clear quality of "giving birth to" a new generation, a notion essentially identical to generativity.

One of the more popular methods for examining the development of life stories is through autobiographical memory (Lilgendahl & McAdams, 2011; McLean & Pasupathi, 2012). When people tell their life stories to others, the stories are a joint product of the speaker and the audience (Pasupathi, 2001, 2013; McLean & Pasupathi, 2012). Pasupathi finds the responses of the audience affect how the teller remembers his or her experiences. This is a good example of conversational remembering, much like collaborative cognition discussed in Chapter 8.

Overall, McAdams (2001; McAdams & Olson, 2010) believes the model for change in identity over time is a process of fashioning and refashioning one's life story. This process appears to be strongly influenced by culture. At times, the reformulation may be at a conscious level, such as when people make explicit decisions about changing careers. At other times, the revision process is unconscious and implicit, growing out of everyday activities. The goal is to create a life story that is coherent, credible, open to new possibilities, richly differentiated, reconciling of opposite aspects of oneself, and integrated within one's sociocultural context.

Whitbourne's Identity Theory

A second and related approach to understanding identity formation in adulthood is Whitbourne's (e.g., 1987, 1996c, 2010) idea that people build their own conceptions of how their lives should proceed. *The result of this process is the* **life-span construct**, *the person's unified sense of the past, present, and future.*

There are many influences on the development of a life-span construct: identity, values, and social context are a few. Together, they shape the life-span construct and the ways it is manifested. The life-span construct has two structural components that in turn are the ways it is manifested. The first of these components is the scenario, consisting of expectations about the future. The scenario translates aspects of our identity that are particularly important at a specific point into a plan for the future. The scenario is strongly influenced by age norms defining key transition points; such as graduating from college, a transition normally associated with the early 20s. In short, a scenario is a game plan for how we want our lives to go.

Kim, a typical college sophomore, may have the following scenario: She expects her course of study in nursing will be difficult but she will finish on time. She hopes to meet a nice guy along the way who she will marry shortly after graduation. She imagines she will get a good job at a major medical center that offer her opportunities for advancement. She and her husband will probably have a child, but she expects to keep working. Because she feels she will want to advance, she assumes at some point she will earn a master's degree. In the more distant future she hopes to be a department head and well respected for her administrative skills.

Tagging certain expected events with a particular age or time we expect to complete them creates a social clock (see Chapter 1). Kim will use her scenario to evaluate her progress toward her goals. With each major transition she will check how she is doing

against where her scenario says she should be. If she achieves her goals earlier than expected, she will feel proud of being ahead of the game. If things work out more slowly than she planned, she may chastise herself for being slow. If she begins to criticize herself a great deal, she may end up changing her scenario altogether; for example, if she does not get a good job and makes no progress, she may change her scenario to one that says she should stay home with her child.

As Kim starts moving into the positions laid out in her scenario, she begins to create the second component of her life-span construct, her life story. The life story is a personal narrative history organizing past events into a coherent sequence. The life story gives events personal meaning and a sense of continuity; it becomes our autobiography. Because the life story is what we tell others when they ask about our past, it eventually becomes somewhat over-rehearsed and stylized. An interesting aspect of the life story, and autobiographical memory in general, is that distortions occur with time and retelling (Lilgendahl & McAdams, 2011; McLean & Pasupathi, 2012; Pasupathi, 2001). In life stories, distortions allow the person to feel he or she was on time, rather than off time in terms of past events in the scenario. In this way, people feel better about their plans and goals and are less likely to feel a sense of failure.

Whitbourne grounded her theory on a fascinating cross-sectional study of 94 adults ranging in age from 24 to 61 (Whitbourne, 1986). The subjects came from all walks of life and represented a wide range of occupations and life situations. Using data from detailed interviews, Whitbourne was able to identify what she believes is the process of adult identity development based on equilibrium between identity and experience. Her model is presented in Figure 9.2. As the figure shows, there is continuous feedback between identity and experience; this explains why we evaluate ourselves positively at one point in time, yet appear defensive and self-protective at another.

As you can see, the processes of equilibrium are based on Piaget's concepts of assimilation and accommodation (see Chapter 7). Whitbourne explicitly attempted to integrate concepts from cognitive development with identity development to understand how identity is formed and revised across adulthood. The assimilation process involves using already

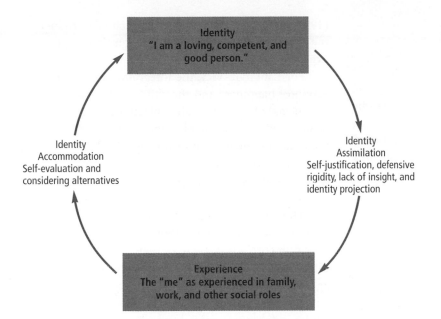

Identity
"I am a loving, competent, and good person."

Identity Accommodation
Self-evaluation and considering alternatives

Identity Assimilation
Self-justification, defensive rigidity, lack of insight, and identity projection

Experience
The "me" as experienced in family, work, and other social roles

Figure 9.2
Whitbourne's model of adult identity processes.

Source: Whitbourne, S. K. (1986). The psychological construction of the life span. In J. E. Birren & K. W. Schaie (Eds.), Handbook of the Psychology of Aging *(pp. 594–619). New York: Van Nostrand Reinhold. All rights reserved. Reproduced by permission of the author.*

existing aspects of identity to handle present situations. Over-reliance on assimilation makes the person resistant to change. Accommodation, in contrast, reflects the willingness of the individual to let the situation determine what he or she will do. This often occurs when the person does not have a well-developed identity around a certain issue.

Not surprisingly, Whitbourne found the vast majority of adults listed family as the most important aspect of their lives. Clearly, adults' identity as a loving person constitutes the major part of the answer to the question "Who am I?" Consequently, a major theme in adults' identity development is refining their belief that "I am a loving person." Much of this development is based in acquiring and refining deep, emotional relationships.

Another major source of identity for Whitbourne's participants was work. In this case, the key seemed to be keeping work interesting. As long as individuals had an interesting occupation that enabled them to become personally invested, their work identity was more central to their overall personal identity. This is a topic we pursue in Chapter 12.

Although Whitbourne found evidence of life transitions, overall she found scant evidence these transitions occurred in a stage-like fashion or were tied to specific ages. Rather, she found people tend to go through transitions when they feel they needed to and to do so on their own time line. Whitbourne, Sneed, and Skultety (2002) developed the Identity and Experiences Scale–General to measure identity processes in adults. This scale assesses an individual's use of assimilation and accommodation in forming identity in a general sense, and is based on her earlier work. Her model has expanded to incorporate how people adapt more generally to middle age and the aging process (Whitbourne, 2010).

In a series of studies, Whitbourne (e.g., Sneed & Whitbourne, 2003, 2005) reported identity assimilation and identity accommodation change with age. Identity assimilation was higher in older adulthood and identity accommodation was higher in younger adulthood. Furthermore, identity assimilation in older adulthood was associated with maintaining and enhancing positive self-regard through the minimization of negativity. In contrast, a changing identity (e.g., through accommodation) in older adulthood was associated more with poor psychological health. The ability to integrate age-related changes into one's identity and maintain a positive view of oneself is crucial to aging successfully (Whitbourne, 2010). This suggests people make behavioral adjustments to promote healthy adaptation to the aging process (see Chapter 3).

Self-Concept and Well-Being

As we have seen, an important aspect of identity in adulthood is how one integrates various aspects of the self. Self-perceptions and how they differ with age have been examined in a wide variety of studies and are related to many behaviors. Changes in self-perceptions are often manifested in changed beliefs, concerns, and expectations. Self-concept *is the organized, coherent, integrated pattern of self-perceptions.* Self-concept includes the notions of self-esteem and self-image.

Kegan's Theory of Self-Concept.

Kegan (1982, 1994, 2009) attempted to integrate the development of self-concept and cognitive development. He postulated six stages of the development of self, corresponding to stages of cognitive development described in Chapter 7. Kegan's first three stages—incorporative, impulsive, and imperial—correspond to Piaget's sensorimotor, preoperational, and concrete operational stages (see Chapter 7). During this time, he believes children move from knowing themselves on the basis of reflexes to knowing themselves through needs and interests.

He argues at the beginning of formal operational thought during early adolescence (see Chapter 7), a sense of interpersonal mutuality begins to develop; he terms this period the interpersonal stage. By late adolescence or young adulthood, people move to a mature sense of identity based on taking control of their own life and developing an ideology; Kegan calls this period the institutional stage.

Finally, with the acquisition of post-formal thought (see Chapter 7) comes an understanding that the self is a complex system that takes into account other people; Kegan terms this period the interindividual stage.

Kegan's work emphasizes that personality development does not occur in a vacuum. Rather, we must remember a person is a complex integrated whole. Consequently, an understanding of the development of self-concept or any other aspect of personality is enhanced by an understanding of how it relates to other dimensions of development.

Labouvie-Vief's Dynamic Integration Theory.

The integration of cognitive and personality development has also been a major focus of Gisela Labouvie-Vief (1997, 2003, 2005). She argues the self is a product of the integration of emotion and cognition, topics we explored in Chapters 7 and 8.

For Labouvie-Vief, the integration of the optimization of happiness and the ability to tolerate tension and negativity to maintain objectivity that creates a healthy self-concept in adulthood. She builds the case the dynamic integration of this optimization and differentiation is what creates a healthy balance. The ability to accomplish this integration increases from young through middle adulthood, but decreases in late life.

This point was clearly demonstrated by Labouvie-Vief and colleagues (1995). Working within a cognitive-developmental framework, they documented age differences in self-representation in people ranging in age from 11 to 85 years. Specifically, they found mature adults move from representations of the self in young adulthood that are relatively poorly differentiated from others or from social conventions and expectations, to highly differentiated representations in middle age, to less differentiated representations in old age. An important finding was the degree of differentiation in self-representation was related to the level of cognitive development, thereby providing support for Kegan's position.

Other Research on Self-Concept.

In addition to research integrating cognitive and emotional development, researchers also focused on other sources for creating the self across adulthood. In Chapter 8, we saw the incorporation of aging stereotypes strongly influences people's self-concept (e.g., Kornadt & Rothermund, 2012; Weiss & Lang, 2012).

Some research documents how people organize the various facets of their self-concept. That research shows older adults compartmentalize the different aspects of self-concept (e.g., various positive and negative aspects) more than either younger or middle-aged adults (Ready, Carvalho, & Åkerstedt, 2012).

In general, research examining self-concept shows it is significantly related to a wide variety of variables such as health and longevity. We return to this issue in Chapter 14 when considering successful aging.

Well-Being and Emotion.

How is your life going? Are you reasonably content, or do you think you could be doing better? Answers to these questions provide

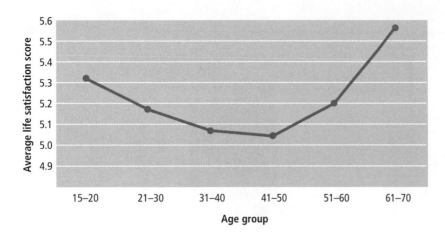

Figure 9.3

The pattern of a typical person's happiness through life in the United Kingdom.

Source: From Happiness, health, and economics, by A. Oswald. Copyright © Warwick University. http://imechanica.org/files/andrew_oswald_presentation_071129.pdf.

insight into your **subjective well-being**, *an evaluation of one's life associated with positive feelings.* Subjective well-being is usually assessed by measures of life satisfaction, happiness, and self-esteem (Oswald & Wu, 2010).

Overall, young-older adults are characterized by improved subjective well-being compared to earlier in adulthood (Charles & Carstensen, 2010). The differences in people's typical level of happiness across adulthood are illustrated in results from the United Kingdom, shown in Figure 9.3. These happiness-related factors hold across cultures as well; a study of Taiwanese and Tanzanian older adults showed similar predictors of successful aging (Hsu, 2005; Mwanyangala et al., 2010).

Emotion focused research in neuroscience provides answers to the question of why subjective well-being tends to increase with age (Cacioppo et al., 2011). A brain structure called the amygdala, an almond-shaped set of nuclei deep in the brain, helps regulate emotion. Evidence is growing that age-related changes in how the amygdala functions may

play a key role in understanding emotional regulation in older adults. Here's how. In young adults, arousal of the amygdala is associated with negative emotional arousal. When negative emotional arousal occurs, memory for events associated with the emotion are stronger. But the situation is different for older adults—both amygdala activation and emotional arousal are lower. That may be one reason why older adults experience less negative emotion, lower rates of depression, and better well-being (Cacioppo et al., 2011; Winecoff et al., 2011).

That's not the whole story. As described in Chapter 2, neuroimaging research shows changes in cognitive processing in the prefrontal cortex is also associated with changes in emotional regulation in older adults. Understanding the brain's role in emotion requires us to take a closer look at what's really going on inside the prefrontal cortex. The How Do We Know? feature provides insight into that issue and sheds light onto key differences in brain processing of emotion in people with depression.

HOW DO WE KNOW?:

WELL-BEING REFLECTED IN BRAIN FUNCTION IN EMOTION AND DEPRESSION

Who was the investigator, and what was the aim of the study? How emotions get processed in the brain play an important role in determining a person's overall well-being. Although evidence from EEG studies

demonstrated abnormal asymmetries in the frontal cortex in the processing of emotions between people who were and were not depressed, fMRI and PET studies failed to identify specific pathways underlying these differences. Herrington, Heller, Mohanty, Engels, Barich, Webb, and colleagues (2010) set out to discover these underlying paths.

How did the investigators measure the topic of interest? The researchers carefully screened a large

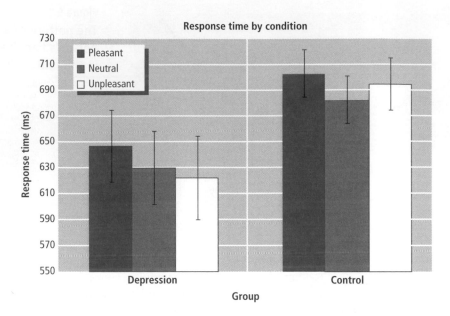

Figure 9.4

Response times for pleasant, neutral, and unpleasant words. Error bars represent 1 standard deviation above and below the mean.

Source: Herrington, J. D., Heller, W., Mohanty, A., Engels, A. S., Barich, M. T., Webb, A. G., et al. (2010). Localization of asymmetric brain function in emotion and depression. Psychophysiology, 47, 442–454. *doi: 10.1111/j.1469-8986.2009.00958.x. Retrieved from http://www.ncbi.nlm.nih.gov/pmc/articles /PMC3086589/. (Figure 1)*

sample to ensure one group had only depression (and no significant levels of anxiety or other mental health problem) and the control group had no significant signs of any mental health problem. This was determined with a series of questionnaires.

While participants were in the fMRI machine, they were given two tasks, the emotion-word Stroop and the color-word Stroop. Both tasks involved participants stating the color of ink in which words were printed. In the emotion-word Stroop, pleasant, unpleasant, and neutral emotion words were printed in one of four color inks. For the color-word task, the words were the four color names printed in the four different colors. The key measure was the speed of response in saying the color of the ink.

Who were the participants in the study? 1688 young adults were screened to create a group of 29, 11 had depression and 18 served as controls.

Were there ethical concerns with the study? All participants were volunteers and provided written consent under a protocol approved by the Institutional Review Board.

What were the results? Reaction times were longer for pleasant and unpleasant words compared to neutral words, and longer for pleasant

than unpleasant words. These findings are shown in Figure 9.4.

Examination of the fMRI data revealed there were significant differences between the groups in how emotional information was processed in the brain. Differences are shown in Figure 9.5. The key finding from frontal lobe and amygdala activation data is participants with depression showed significantly greater lateralization, that is, separate areas of processing for pleasant and unpleasant words, than did participants who did not have depression.

What did the investigators conclude? Herrington and colleagues concluded there is structural brain evidence for abnormal asymmetric processing in the frontal brain region and in the amygdala for emotional information in individuals with depression. This indicates that attentional processing (that heavily involves the frontal region) likely plays a role in depression and the processing of emotional material. These findings open possibilities for understanding the connections between emotional processing and well-being, as well as potential approaches to treating depression through focusing on specific neural pathways.

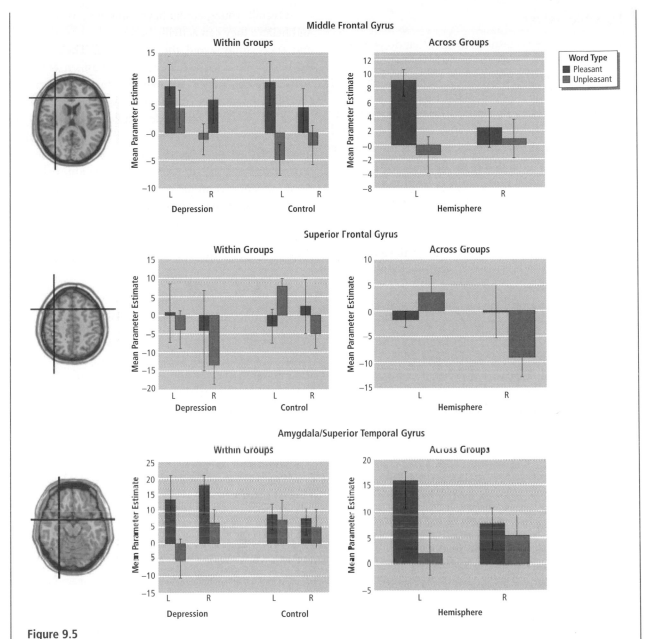

Figure 9.5

Areas yielding a Significant Valence × Hemisphere interactions in middle (top) and superior (bottom) frontal gyri, and peri-amygdala. The left-hand column displays the clusters. Activation is arbitrarily overlaid on left-hemisphere anatomy, as hemisphere was included as a factor in the analysis. The red crosshairs are placed over the center of effect size for each cluster. The right column plots mean parameter estimates (i.e., the average of all voxel values within the cluster) for each level of valence and hemisphere averaged across both groups. Although these regions did not show a three-way interaction involving Group, the middle column contains plots of the average parameter estimates for each level of Group separately. Error bars represent 1 standard error above and below the mean.

Source: Herrington, J. D., Heller, W., Mohanty, A., Engels, A. S., Barich, M. T., Webb, A. G., et al. (2010). Localization of asymmetric brain function in emotion and depression. Psychophysiology, 47, 442–454. doi: 10.1111/j.1469-8986.2009.00958.x. Retrieved from http://www.ncbi.nlm.nih.gov/pmc/articles/PMC3086589/. (Figure 2)

Possible Selves

When we are asked questions like, "What do you think you'll be like a few years from now?" it requires us to imagine ourselves in the future. When we speculate like this, we create a possible self (Markus & Nurius, 1986). **Possible selves** *represent what we could become, what we would like to become, and what we are afraid of becoming.* What we could or would like to become often reflects personal goals; we may see ourselves as leaders, as rich and famous, or in great physical shape. What we are afraid of becoming may show up in our fear of being alone, or overweight, or unsuccessful. Our possible selves are powerful motivators; indeed, how we behave is largely an effort to achieve or avoid these various possible selves and protect the current view of self (Baumeister, 2010).

Researchers examined age differences in the construction of possible selves (Bardach et al., 2010; Cotter & Gonzalez, 2009). In a rare set of similar studies conducted across time and research teams by Cross and Markus (1991) and Hooker and colleagues (Frazier et al., 2000, 2002; Hooker, 1999; Hooker et al., 1996; Morfei et al., 2001), people across the adult life span were asked to describe their hoped-for and feared–possible selves. The responses were grouped into categories (e.g., family, personal, material, relationships, and occupation).

Several interesting age differences emerged. In terms of hoped-for selves, young adults listed family concerns—for instance, marrying the right person—as most important. In contrast, adults in their 30s listed family concerns last; their main issues involved personal concerns, such as being a more loving and caring person. By ages 40 to 59, family issues again became most common—such as being a parent who can "let go" of the children. Reaching and maintaining satisfactory performance in one's occupational career as well as accepting and adjusting to the physiological changes of middle age were important to this age group.

For adults over 60, researchers find personal issues are most prominent—like being active and healthy for at least another decade. The greatest amount of change occurred in the health domain, which predominated the hoped-for and feared-for selves. The health domain is the most sensitive and central to the self in the context of aging and people's possible self with regard to health is quite resilient in the face of health challenges in later life.

Overall, young adults have multiple possible selves and believe they can actually become the hoped-for self and successfully avoid the feared–self. Their outlook tends to be quite positive (Remedios, Chasteen, & Packer, 2010). Life experience may dampen this outlook. By old age, both the number of possible selves and the strength of belief have decreased. Older adults are more likely to believe neither the hoped-for nor the feared-for self is under their personal control. These findings may reflect differences with age in personal motivation, beliefs in personal control, and the need to explore new options.

The emergence of online social media has created new opportunities for young adults to create possible selves (Lefkowitz, Vukman, & Loken, 2012). Such media present different ways for them to speculate about themselves to others.

Religiosity and Spiritual Support

When faced with the daily problems of living, how do older adults cope? Older adults in many countries use their religious faith and spirituality, more often than they use family or friends (Ai, Wink, & Ardelt, 2010). For some older adults, especially African Americans, a strong attachment to God is what they believe helps them deal with the challenges of life (Dilworth-Anderson, Boswell, & Cohen, 2007).

There is considerable evidence linking spirituality and health (Krause, 2006; Park, 2007). In general, older adults who are more involved with and committed to their faith have better physical and mental health than older adults who are not religious (Ai et al., 2010). For example, older Mexican Americans who pray to the saints and the Virgin Mary on a regular basis tend to have greater optimism and better health (Krause & Bastida, 2011).

When asked to describe ways of dealing with problems in life that affect physical and mental health, many people list coping strategies associated with spirituality (Ai et al., 2010; White, Peters, & Schim, 2011). Of these, the most frequently used were placing trust in God, praying, and getting strength and help from God.

Researchers have increasingly focused on **spiritual support**—*meaning they seek pastoral care, participate in organized and nonorganized religious activities, and express faith in a God who cares for people—as a key factor in understanding how older adults cope.* Even when under high levels of stress people who rely on spiritual support report greater personal well-being (Ai et al., 2010; White et al., 2011). Krause (2006) reports feelings of self-worth are lowest in older adults who have very little religious commitment, a finding supported by cross-cultural research with Muslims, Hindus, and Sikhs (Mehta, 1997).

When people rely on spirituality to cope, how do they do it? Krause and colleagues (2000) found older adults reported turning problems over to God really was a three-step process: (1) differentiating between things that can and cannot be changed; (2) focusing one's own efforts on the parts of the problem that can be changed; and (3) emotionally disconnecting from those aspects of the problem that cannot be changed by focusing on the belief that God provides the best outcome possible for those. These findings show reliance on spiritual beliefs acts to help people focus their attention on parts of the problem that may be under their control.

Reliance on religion in times of stress appears to be especially important for many African Americans, who as a group are more intensely involved in religious activities (Taylor, Chatters, & Levin, 2004; Troutman et al., 2011). They also are more likely to rely on God for support than are European Americans (Lee & Sharpe, 2007). Churches have historically offered considerable social support for the African American community, served an important function in advocating social justice, and ministers play a major role in providing support in times of personal need (Chatters et al., 2011).

Similar effects of spirituality are observed in Asian and Asian American groups. The risk of dying in a given year among the old-old in China was found to be 21% lower among frequent religious participants compared to nonparticipants, after initial health condition was equated (Zeng, Gu, & George, 2011). Asian caregivers of dementia patients who are more religious report being able to handle the stresses and burden of caregiving better than nonreligious caregivers (Chan, 2010).

And neuroscience research shows there is a connection between certain practices and brain activity. There is evidence that people who practice meditation show more organized attention systems and less activity in areas of the brain that focus on the self (Davidson, 2010; Lutz et al., 2009). Thus, neurological evidence indicates there may be changes in brain activity associated with spiritual practices that help people cope.

Health care and social service providers would be well advised to keep in mind the self-reported importance of spirituality in the lives of many older adults when designing interventions to help them adapt to life stressors. For example, older adults may be more willing to talk with their minister or rabbi about a personal problem than they would be to talk with a psychotherapist. Overall, many churches offer a wide range of programs to assist poor or homebound older adults in the community. Such programs may be more palatable to the people served than programs based in social service agencies. To be successful, service providers should try to view life as their clients see it.

Spiritual practice in all forms is evident throughout the latter half of the life span.

Pablo Corral Vega/CORBIS

Conclusions about Narratives, Identity, and the Self

We have seen to fully understand a person, we must consider how the individual integrates his or her life into a coherent structure. The life-narrative approach provides a way to learn how people accomplish this integration. The theoretical frameworks developed by McAdams and by Whitbourne offer excellent avenues for research. One of the most promising new areas of inquiry, possible selves, is already providing major insights into how people construct future elements of their life stories.

When combined with the data from the dispositional trait and personal concerns literatures, research findings on identity and the self, provide the capstone knowledge needed to understand what people are like. The complexity of personality is clear from this discussion; perhaps that is why it takes a lifetime to complete.

ADULT DEVELOPMENT IN ACTION

If you were part of a multidisciplinary support team, how would you include spirituality as part of an overall plan to help your clients cope with life issues?

SOCIAL POLICY IMPLICATIONS

Throughout this chapter, we emphasized that all aspects of personality interact in complex ways, and are inextricably linked to other aspects of development (e.g., cognitive development). What we have not examined is the extent to which external forces, such as public policy decisions at the societal level, can affect aspects of personality.

An intriguing analysis of this issue was done in Beijing by Sun and Xiao (2012). They examined the effects perceived fairness of certain social policies on social security and income distribution had on participants' well-being. Based on a survey of over 2100 residents of Beijing, they found perceived fairness of these policies were positively associated with well-being.

Similarly, Raju (2011) points out social policy in developing countries has a profound effect on the well-being of the rapidly increasing aging populations there. In the case of India, Raju argues health care policy in

particular will be an important need in order to maximize the odds that people age successfully.

These studies highlight an increasingly important consideration—that government policies can affect how people's experience of aging actually occurs. Positive government policies that provide the support and services necessary can improve well-being and the likelihood people age successfully. The reverse also appears to be true—that failure to enact such policies has a deleterious effect on people as they age.

We will see in Chapter 14 the United States faces its own challenges with respect to ensuring the needed financial and health supports will be available through Social Security and Medicare. However, the low degree baby boomers are actually prepared for late life (e.g., because of lack of retirement savings) may mean their experience will not live up to their expectations. If that's true, then their well-being may suffer.

SUMMARY

9.1 Dispositional Traits across Adulthood

What is the five-factor model of dispositional traits?

- The five-factor model posits five dimensions of personality: neuroticism, extraversion, openness to experience, agreeableness, and conscientiousness. Each of these dimensions has several descriptors.
- Several longitudinal studies indicate personality traits show long-term stability.

What happens to dispositional traits across adulthood?

- Studies find evidence for change in Big Five factors such as neuroticism, agreeableness, conscientiousness, and extraversion. These are related to two dimensions of personality: adjustment and growth.
- Both stability and change characterize personality development in advanced old age.
- Several criticisms of the five-factor model have been made: The research may have methodological problems; dispositional traits do not describe

the core aspects of human nature and do not provide good predictors of behavior; and dispositional traits do not consider the contextual aspects of development.

■ An intraindividual perspective challenges stability by examining personality at the level of the individual.

What conclusions can we draw about dispositional traits?

■ The bulk of the evidence suggests dispositional traits are relatively stable across adulthood, but there may be a few exceptions. Criticisms of the research point to the need for better statistical analyses and a determination of the role of life experiences.

■ Stability in personality traits may be more evident later in the life span.

9.2 Personal Concerns and Qualitative Stages in Adulthood

What's different about personal concerns?

■ Personal concerns take into account a person's developmental context and distinguish between "having" traits and "doing" everyday behaviors. Personal concerns entail descriptions of what people are trying to accomplish and the goals they create.

What are the main elements of Jung's theory?

■ Jung emphasized various dimensions of personality (masculinity–femininity; extraversion–introversion). Jung argues people move toward integrating these dimensions as they age, with midlife being an especially important period.

What are the stages in Erikson's theory?

■ The sequence of Erikson's stages is trust versus mistrust, autonomy versus shame and doubt, initiative versus guilt, industry versus inferiority, identity versus identity confusion, intimacy versus isolation, generativity versus stagnation, and ego integrity versus despair. Erikson's theory can be seen as a trust-achievement-wholeness cycle repeating twice, although the exact transition mechanisms have not been clearly defined.

■ Generativity has received more attention than other adult stages. Research indicates generative concern and generative action can be found in all age groups of adults, but they are particularly apparent among middle-aged adults.

What are the main points and problems with theories based on life transitions?

■ In general, life transition theories postulate periods of transition that alternate with periods of stability. These theories tend to overestimate the commonality of age-linked transitions.

■ Research evidence suggests crises tied to age 30 or the midlife crisis do not occur for most people. However, most middle-aged people do point to both gains and losses that could be viewed as change.

■ A midlife correction may better characterize this transition for women.

What can we conclude about personal concerns?

■ Theory and research both provide support for change in the personal concerns people report at various times in adulthood.

9.3 Life Narratives, Identity, and the Self

What are the main aspects of McAdams's life-story model?

■ McAdams argues that people create a life story as an internalized narrative with a beginning, middle, and anticipated ending. An adult reformulates that life story throughout adulthood. The life story reflects emotions, motivations, beliefs, values, and goals to set the context for his or her behavior.

What are the main points of Whitbourne's identity theory?

■ Whitbourne believes people have a life-span construct: a unified sense of their past, present, and future. The components of the life-span construct are the scenario (expectations of the future) and the life story (a personal narrative history). She integrates the concepts of assimilation and accommodation from Piaget's theory to explain how people's identity changes over time. Family and work are two major sources of identity.

What is self-concept and how does it develop in adulthood?

■ Self-concept is the organized, coherent, integrated pattern of self-perception. The events people experience help shape their self-concept. Self-presentation across adulthood is related to cognitive-developmental level. Self-concept tends to stay stable at the group mean level.

What are possible selves and how do they show differences during adulthood?

■ People create possible selves by projecting themselves into the future and thinking about what they would like to become, what they could become, and what they are afraid of becoming.

- Age differences in these projections depend on the dimension examined. In hoped-for selves, young adults and middle-aged adults report family issues as most important, whereas 25- to 39-year-olds and older adults consider personal issues to be most important. However, all groups include physical aspects as part of their most feared possible selves.

- Although younger and middle-aged adults view themselves as improving, older adults view themselves as declining. The standards by which people judge themselves change over time.

What role does religion or spiritual support play in adult life?

- Older adults use religion and spiritual support more often than any other strategy to help them cope with problems in life. This provides a strong influence on identity. This is especially true for African American women, who are more active in their church groups and attend services more frequently. Other ethnic groups also gain important aspects of identity from religion.

What conclusions can we draw about narratives, identity, and the self?

- The life-narrative approach provides a way to learn how people integrate the various aspects of their personality. Possible selves, religiosity, and gender-role identity are important areas in need of additional research.

REVIEW QUESTIONS

9.1 Dispositional Traits across Adulthood

- What is a dispositional trait?

- Describe Costa and McCrae's five-factor model of personality. What are the descriptors in each dimension? How do these dimensions change across adulthood?

- What evidence is there in other longitudinal research for change in personality traits in adulthood? Under what conditions is there stability or change?

- What are the specific criticisms raised concerning the five-factor model?

- What does most of the evidence say about the stability of dispositional traits across adulthood?

9.2 Personal Concerns and Qualitative Stages in Adulthood

- What is meant by a personal concern? How does it differ from a dispositional trait?

- Describe Jung's theory. What important developmental changes did he describe?

- Describe Erikson's eight stages of psychosocial development. What cycles have been identified? How has his theory been clarified and expanded? What types of generativity have been proposed? What evidence is there for generativity? What modifications to Erikson's theory has this research suggested?

- What are the major assumptions of theories based on life transitions? What evidence is there a midlife crisis really exists? How can midlife be viewed from a gain–loss perspective?

- Overall, what evidence is there for change in personal concerns across adulthood?

9.3 Life Narratives, Identity, and the Self

- What are the basic tenets of McAdams's life-story theory? What are the seven elements of a life story?

- What is Whitbourne's life-span construct? How does it relate to a scenario and a life story? How did Whitbourne incorporate Piagetian concepts into her theory of identity?

- What is self-concept? What shapes it?

- What are possible selves? What developmental trends have been found in possible selves?

- How are religiosity and spiritual support important aspects of identity in older adults?

INTEGRATING CONCEPTS IN DEVELOPMENT

- What relations can be found among dispositional traits, personal concerns, and life narratives?

- How does personality development reflect the four basic forces of development discussed in Chapter 1?

- How does cognitive development relate to personality change?

- How does personality change relate to stages in occupational transition?

KEY TERMS

cognitive processes A structural component of personality that acts jointly with life narratives to create natural interactions between a storyteller and listener, processes central in organizing life stories.

dispositional trait A relatively stable, enduring aspect of personality.

ego development The fundamental changes in the ways our thoughts, values, morals, and goals are organized. Transitions from one stage to another depend on both internal biological changes and external social changes to which the person must adapt.

epigenetic principle In Erikson's theory, the notion that development is guided by an underlying plan in which certain issues have their own particular times of importance.

five-factor model A model of dispositional traits with the dimensions of neuroticism, extraversion, openness to experience, agreeableness–antagonism, and conscientiousness–undirectedness.

life narrative The aspects of personality that pull everything together, those integrative aspects that give a person an identity or sense of self.

life-span construct In Whitbourne's theory of identity, the way people build a view of who they are.

midlife correction Reevaluating one's roles and dreams and making the necessary corrections.

personal concerns Things that are important to people, their goals, and their major concerns in life.

personality adjustment Involves developmental changes in terms of their adaptive value and functionality such as functioning effectively within society and how personality contributes to everyday life running smoothly.

personality growth Refers to ideal end states such as increased self-transcendence, wisdom, and integrity.

possible selves Aspects of the self-concept involving oneself in the future in both positive and negative ways.

self-concept The organized, coherent, integrated pattern of self-perceptions.

spiritual support Includes seeking pastoral care, participating in organized and nonorganized religious activities, and expressing faith in a God who cares for people as a key factor in understanding how older adults cope.

state processes A structural component of personality that acts with dispositional traits to create transient, short-term changes in emotion, mood, hunger, anxiety, etc.

subjective well-being An evaluation of one's life that is associated with positive feelings.

trait Any distinguishable, relatively enduring way in which one individual differs from others.

trait theories Theories of personality that assume little change occurs across adulthood.

RESOURCES

Access quizzes, glossaries, flashcards, and more at www.cengagebrain.com.

CHAPTER 10

CLINICAL ASSESSMENT, MENTAL HEALTH, AND MENTAL DISORDERS

10.1 MENTAL HEALTH AND THE ADULT LIFE COURSE
Defining Mental Health and Psychopathology • A Multidimensional Life-Span Approach to Psychopathology • Ethnicity, Gender, Aging, and Mental Health

10.2 DEVELOPMENTAL ISSUES IN ASSESSMENT AND THERAPY
Areas of Multidimensional Assessment • Factors Influencing Assessment • Assessment Methods • Developmental Issues in Therapy

10.3 THE BIG THREE: DEPRESSION, DELIRIUM, AND DEMENTIA
Depression • Delirium • Dementia • *Current Controversies: New Diagnostic Criteria for Alzheimer's Disease* • *How Do We Know?: Training Persons with Dementia to Be Group Activity Leaders*

10.4 OTHER MENTAL DISORDERS AND CONCERNS
Anxiety Disorders • Psychotic Disorders • Substance Abuse • *Discovering Development: What Substance Abuse Treatment Options Are Available in Your Area?*

SOCIAL POLICY IMPLICATIONS
Summary • Review Questions • Integrating Concepts in Development • Key Terms • Resources

ALTHOUGH THE INCIDENCE OF MANY DISEASES OFTEN VARIES ACROSS SOCIOECONOMIC CLASS, DEMENTIA does not.

It does not care whether you are rich and famous. As evidence, Rosa Parks, Ronald Reagan, and Margaret Thatcher are three major historical figures to have been diagnosed with dementia. As the person who started the modern civil rights movement by refusing to give up her seat on a bus in Montgomery, Alabama, in 1955, Rosa Parks (1913–2005) became a major national figure and her action launched the career of Rev. Martin Luther King, Jr. For the rest of her life she championed the cause of equal rights.

Ronald Reagan (1911–2004) was the oldest man elected as president of the United States, winning election to his first term at age 69 and to his second term at age 73. He served as the 40th president from 1981 to 1989. As a well-known actor and two-term governor of California, Reagan had broad experience in the limelight. Enormously popular during his tenure, Reagan presided over the United States at a time of major global change. He is still remembered and respected by millions of people for his actions during his presidency. Shortly after he left office, however, Reagan began to experience serious memory difficulties along with other health problems. Eventually he was diagnosed with Alzheimer's disease and his condition slowly deteriorated as the disease progressed.

Margaret Thatcher (1925–2013) was the first woman to serve as Prime Minister of Great Britain, holding that office from 1979 to 1990. A political conservative who was closely aligned with President Reagan, Prime Minister Thatcher was well known for instituting many economic changes in Britain and for her staunchly anti-communist stance. She built strong relations with the United States, particularly on issues related to the Soviet Union. Lady Thatcher's cognitive problems were revealed by her daughter in 2008, and were an important part of the biographical film *The Iron Lady*.

In this chapter, we consider situations such as those of Rosa Parks, Ronald Reagan, and Margaret Thatcher in which the aging process goes wrong. Such problems happen to families every day across all demographic categories. Certainly, Alzheimer's disease is not part of normal aging, nor are the other problems we consider.

This chapter is about the people who do not make it through adulthood to old age by only experiencing normative physiological changes (see Chapters 3 and 4). A minority of adults develop mental health difficulties that cause them problems in their daily lives and robs them of their dignity. We define mental health and how mental problems are assessed and treated. We focus on several specific problems, including depression, delirium, dementia, anxiety disorders, psychotic disorders, and substance abuse. As we consider different types of mental disorders, we note how each is diagnosed, the known causes, and effective treatments that are available.

Former president of the United States, Ronald Reagan, died from Alzheimer's disease.

Bob Daemmrich/The Image Works

Baroness and former prime minister of the United Kingdom Margaret Thatcher developed Alzheimer's disease in later life.

POOL/Tim Graham/Getty Images

Rosa Parks, the black seamstress who pioneered the struggle for civil rights in America in the 1950s by refusing to give up her seat on a bus to a white man, developed Alzheimer's disease late in her life.

Reuters/Corbis

Mental Health and the Adult Life Course

LEARNING OBJECTIVES

- How are mental health and psychopathology defined?
- What are the key dimensions used for categorizing psychopathology?
- Why are ethnicity and aging important variables to consider in understanding mental health?

Janet lives alone in a small apartment. Lately, some of her neighbors have noticed she doesn't come to church services as regularly as she used to. Betty, her friend and neighbor, noticed Janet cries a lot when she's asked whether anything is wrong and at times seems confused. Betty knows several of Janet's friends died recently but still wonders whether something more serious is wrong with her.

Situations like Janet's are common. Like Betty, we might think Janet is trying to deal with the loss of friends and is simply experiencing grief, but there may be something more serious; could Janet's confusion indicate a physical or mental health problem? Janet's situation points out the difficulty in knowing exactly where good mental health ends and mental illness or mental disorder begins. What distinguishes the study of mental disorders, or psychopathology, in adulthood and aging is not so much the content of the behavior as its context, that is, whether it interferes with daily functioning. To understand psychopathology as manifested in adults of different ages, we must see how it fits into the life-span developmental perspective outlined in Chapter 1.

Defining Mental Health and Psychopathology

The precise difference between mental health and mental disorder has never been clear (Segal, Qualls, & Smyer, 2011). Most scholars avoid the issue entirely or simply try to explain what mental health or psychopathology is not. How to tell the difference between normal or abnormal behavior is hard to define precisely because expectations and standards for behavior change over time, situations, and across age groups (Zarit & Zarit, 2006). Researchers and practitioners refer to Birren and Renner's (1980) classic argument

that mentally healthy people have the following characteristics: a positive attitude toward self, an accurate perception of reality, a mastery of the environment, autonomy, personality balance, and growth and self-actualization. Thus, all these characteristics must be evaluated when determining the mental health status of an individual.

One could argue to the extent these characteristics are absent, mental disorder or psychopathology becomes more likely. In that case, we would consider behaviors that are harmful to individuals or others, lowers well-being, and perceived as distressing, disrupting, abnormal, or maladaptive. Although this approach is used frequently with younger or middle-aged adults, it presents problems when applied to older adults (Segal et al., 2011; Zarit & Zarit, 2006). Some behaviors considered abnormal under this definition may actually be adaptive under some circumstances for many older people (such as isolation, passivity, or aggressiveness).

Consequently, an approach to defining abnormal behavior that emphasizes considering behaviors in isolation and from the perspective of younger or middle-aged adults is inadequate for defining abnormal behaviors in older adults. Because of physical, financial, social, health, or other reasons, older adults do not always have the opportunity to master their environment. Depression or hostility may be an appropriate and justified response to such limitations. Moreover, such responses may help them deal with their situation more effectively and adaptively.

Statistics on the prevalence of various mental disorders as a function of age are difficult to obtain due to these definitional issues. Figure 10.1 compares common forms of mental disorder as a function of age from one of the few good investigations of this issue (Kessler, Berglund, Demler, Jin, Merakangas, & Walters, 2005). Further analyses of data from national surveys reveals older European Americans and Caribbean Blacks have a higher lifetime prevalence of major depressive disorder than do African Americans (Woodward, Taylor, Abelson, & Matusko, 2013).

The important point in differentiating mental health from psychopathology is that behaviors must be interpreted in context. We must consider what else is happening and how the behavior fits the situation in addition to such factors as age and other personal characteristics.

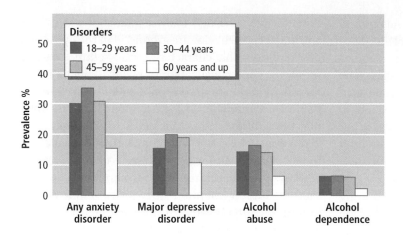

Figure 10.1

Lifetime prevalence of age-of-onset distribution of DSM-IV disorders in the National Comorbidity Survey Replication

Source: Kessler, Ronald C., Berglund, Patricia, Demler, Olga, Jin, Robert, Merakangas, Kathleen, & Walters, Ellen. (2005). Arch Gen Psychiatry, 62, 593–602. Copyright © 2005 by American Medical Association. All rights reserved.

A Multidimensional Life-Span Approach to Psychopathology

Suppose two people, one young and one old, came into your clinic, each complaining about a lack of sleep, changes in appetite, a lack of energy, and feeling down. What would you say to them?

If you evaluate them in identical ways, you might be headed for trouble. As we saw in other chapters, older and younger adults may think or view themselves differently, so the meaning of their symptoms and complaints may also differ, even though they appear to be the same. This point is often overlooked (Segal et al., 2011). Some models of psychopathology assume the same underlying cause is responsible for maladaptive behavior regardless of age and symptoms of the mental disease are fairly constant across age. Although such models often are used in clinical diagnosis, they are inadequate for understanding psychopathology in old age. Viewing adults' behavior from a life-span developmental forces perspective makes a big difference in how we understand psychopathology. Let's see why.

Biological Forces. Various neurological changes, chronic diseases, functional limitations, and other ailments can change behavior. Changes in the structure and functioning of the brain can have important effects on behavior (Chapter 2). Because health problems increase with age (see Chapters 3 and 4) we must be more sensitive to them when dealing with older adults. In addition, genetic factors often underlie important problems in old age. Some forms of Alzheimer's disease have a clear genetic component.

Physical problems may provide clues about underlying psychological difficulties; for example, marked changes in appetite may be a symptom of depression. Moreover, physical problems may present themselves as psychological ones. Extreme irritability can be caused by thyroid problems, and memory loss can result from certain vitamin deficiencies. In any case, physical health and genetic factors are important dimensions to take into account in diagnosing psychopathology in adults and should be among the first avenues explored.

Psychological Forces. Psychological forces across adulthood are key to understanding psychopathology. As we saw in Chapters 6, 7, 8, and 9, several important changes in memory, intelligence, social cognition, and personality must be considered carefully in interpreting behavior. Normative changes with age in these arenas can mimic certain mental disorders; likewise, these changes make it more difficult to tell when an older adult has a given type of psychopathology.

In addition, the nature of a person's relationships with other people, especially family members and friends, is a basic dimension in understanding how psychopathology is manifested in adults of different ages. Important developmental differences occur in the interpersonal realm; younger adults are more likely to be expanding their network of friends, whereas older adults are more likely to be experiencing losses. Chapter 11 summarizes developmental changes in key relationships that may influence adults' interpretation of symptoms.

Sociocultural Forces. The social norms and cultural factors we all experience also play a key role in helping define psychopathology. They influence people's behaviors and affect our interpretation of them. An older woman who lives alone in a high-crime area may be highly suspicious of other people. To label her behavior "paranoid" may be inappropriate because her well-being may depend on maintaining a certain level of suspicion of others' motives toward her. Because customs differ across cultures, behaviors that may be normative in one culture may be viewed as indicating problems in another. In short, we must ask whether the behavior we see is appropriate for a person in a particular setting.

Life-Cycle Factors. How people behave at any point in adulthood is strongly affected by their past experiences and the issues they face. These life-cycle factors must be taken into account in evaluating adults' behaviors. A middle-aged woman who wants to go back to school may not have an adjustment disorder; she may simply want to develop a new aspect of herself. Some might interpret her behavior as an inability to cope with her current life situation when that is not the case at all; rather, she has a rational evaluation of her life and realizes she needs a degree to advance in her profession.

Likewise, an older man who provides vague answers to personal questions may not be resistant; he may simply be reflecting his generation's reluctance to disclose the inner self to a stranger. Most important, the meaning of particular symptoms change with age. Problems with early morning awakenings may indicate depression in a young adult but may simply be a result of normal aging in an older adult (see Chapter 3).

Ethnicity, Gender, Aging, and Mental Health

In neither the general nor the ethnic populations do most people have mental disorders (Muntaner, Ng, Vanroelen, Christ, & Eaton, 2013; Segal et al., 2011). However, social disparities such as differential access to health care can result in apparently different prevalence of mental disorders. Poverty and social class are primary influences (Muntaner et al., 2013).

Neither positive mental health nor psychopathology has been adequately defined in any group in a way that takes social context into account so as to be sensitive to contextual differences in ethnic communities.

For example, although many explanations of deviant and antisocial behavior are grounded in the oppressive life conditions that characterize many ethnic communities, the conceptualization of positive mental health for older ethnic groups does not take into account the lifetime accumulation of such effects (Jackson, Antonucci, & Gibson, 1995; Morrell, Echt, & Caramagno, 2008) nor the effects of a lifetime of inadequate access to health care (Miranda, McGuire, Williams, & Wang, 2008). However, such sensitivity to conditions does not preclude finding commonalities across ethnic groups; indeed, identifying such commonalities would be an excellent place to start.

What little data we have suggest both similarities and differences in the incidence of specific types of psychopathology across different ethnic groups at a general level. However, there are some differences within subgroups of ethnic groups. As noted earlier, Caribbean blacks differ from African Americans in their prevalence of depression (Woodward et al., 2013).

People in different ethnic groups have different ways of describing how they feel, so they may describe symptoms of mental disorders differently. Such differences are amplified by ethnic and cultural differences in what they are supposed to reveal to strangers about their inner self. Placed in a context of important differences in social stressors, physical health, and age, assessing mental health in older ethnic adults is a daunting task (Yancura & Aldwin, 2010).

What can be done to determine the ways ethnicity influences mental health? Jackson et al. (1995) were among the first to argue researchers should adopt an ethnic research matrix that takes as its defining elements ethnicity, national origin, racial group membership, gender, social and economic statuses, age, acculturation, coping reactions, and mental health outcomes (e.g., psychopathology, positive adjustment). Only by adopting this comprehensive approach can we understand what, how, and when aspects of race, ethnicity, age, and the life course influence mental health.

Gender differences in prevalence of various mental disorders are well known and documented (Rosenfield & Mouzon, 2013). A community study in Korea and a study of records in a day hospital in Italy found being female increased the risk of depressive symptoms (Luca, Prossimo, Messina, Luca, Romeo, & Calandra,

2013; Oh, Kim, Lee, Seo, Choi, & Nam, 2013). Males who are depressed are more likely to commit suicide than are women (Hawton, Casañas i Comabella, Haw, & Saunders, 2013).

Just as in the case of ethnicity, though, biases regarding gender and symptom interpretation may influence reported prevalence rates (Rosenfield & Mouzon, 2013). Thus, interpreting data regarding how many people of a specific background have a mental disorder must be done quite carefully, taking into account all of the aspects of the biopsychosocial model.

ADULT DEVELOPMENT IN ACTION

As an elected official, how would you put the data about mental health and aging into social policy?

10.2 Developmental Issues in Assessment and Therapy

LEARNING OBJECTIVES

- What key areas are included in a multidimensional approach to assessment?
- What factors influence the assessment of adults?
- How are mental health issues assessed?
- What are some major considerations for therapy across adulthood?

Juan is a 76 year old World War II veteran living in California. Over the past year, his wife, Rocio, noticed Juan's memory isn't quite as sharp as it used to be; Juan also has less energy, stays home more, and does not show as much interest in playing dominos, a game at which he excels. Rocio wonders what might be wrong with Juan.

Many adults can relate to Rocio because they are concerned about someone they know. Whether the person is 25 or 85, it is important to be able to determine whether memory problems, energy loss, social withdrawal, or other areas of concern really indicate an underlying problem. As you might suspect, health care professionals should not use identical approaches to assess and treat adults of widely different ages. In this section, we consider how assessment methods and therapies must take developmental differences into account.

Areas of Multidimensional Assessment

What does it mean to assess someone? Assessment makes it possible to describe the behavior or other characteristics of people in meaningful ways (Gould, Edelstein, & Gerolimatos, 2012; Stoner, O'Riley, & Edelstein, 2010). Assessment is a formal process of measuring, understanding, and predicting behavior. It involves gathering medical, psychological, and sociocultural information about people through various means, such as interviews, observation, tests, and clinical examinations.

As noted in Chapter 1, two central aspects of any assessment approach are reliability and validity. Without these psychometric properties, we cannot rely on the assessment method to provide good information. In addition, any assessment method must be of practical use in determining the nature of the problem and choosing the appropriate treatment.

A multidimensional assessment approach is most effective (Gould et al., 2012; Stoner et al., 2010). Multidimensional assessment is often done by a team of professionals; a physician may examine the medication regimen; a psychologist, the cognitive functioning; a nurse, the daily living skills; and a social worker, the economic and environmental resources. Let's consider Juan's situation as an example.

A thorough assessment of Juan's physical health is essential, as it is for adults of all ages, especially for older adults. Many physical conditions can create (or hide) mental health problems, so it is important to identify any underlying issues. Laboratory tests can also be ordered provide additional clues to the presence or even the cause of the problem.

Establishing Juan's cognitive ability is also key. Complaints of cognitive problems increase across adulthood, so it is important to determine the extent abnormal changes in older people discriminate from normative change. Adults of all ages can be given intelligence tests, neuropsychological examinations, and mental status examinations. **Mental status exams** *are especially useful as quick screening measures of mental competence used to screen for cognitive impairment;* one commonly used instrument, the Mini Mental Status Exam (MMSE), is shown in Table 10.1. If Juan's score on these brief measures indicated potential problems, more complete follow-up assessments would be used.

Table 10.1

A SAMPLING OF QUESTIONS FROM THE MINI MENTAL STATUS EXAM

Cognitive Area	Activity
Orientation to time	"What is the date?"
Registration stop	"Listen carefully. I am going to say three words. You say them back after I say them. Ready? Here they are … APPLE [pause], PENNY [pause], TABLE [pause]. Now repeat those words back to me." [Repeat up to 5 times, but score only the first trial.]
Naming	"What is this?" [Point to a pencil or pen.]
Reading stimulus form	"Please read this and do what it says." [Show examinee the words on the form.] **CLOSE YOUR EYES**

Source: Reproduced by special permission of the Publisher, Psychological Assessment Resources, Inc., 16204 North Florida Avenue, Lutz, Florida 33549, from the Mini Mental Status Examination, by Marshal Folstein and Susan Folstein. Copyright 1975, 1998, 2001 by Mini Mental LLC, Inc. Published 2001 by Psychological Assessment Resources, Inc. Further reproduction is prohibited without permission of PAR, Inc. The MMSE can be purchased from PAR, Inc., by calling (813) 968–3003.

It is important to remember that scales such as the MMSE are only used for general screening and not for final diagnosis.

Psychological functioning is typically assessed through interviews, observation, and tests or questionnaires. Usually a clinician begins with an interview of Juan and brief screening instruments and follows up, if necessary, with more thorough personality inventories, tests, or more detailed interviews.

How well Juan functions in his daily life is also assessed carefully. Usually this entails determining whether he has difficulty with activities of daily living and instrumental activities of daily living (see Chapter 4). Also assessed is the person's decision-making capacity; each state has legal standards guiding the competency assessment.

In general, it is important to assess the broad array of support resources available to older adults (Randall, Martin, Bishop, Johnson, & Poon, 2012). This includes social networks as well as other community resources.

Factors Influencing Assessment

Health care professionals' preconceived ideas about the people they assess may have negative effects on the assessment process (Gould et al., 2012; Stoner et al., 2010). Two areas of concern are biases (negative or positive) and environmental conditions (where the assessment occurs, sensory or mobility problems, and health of the client).

Many types of bias have been documented as affecting the assessment process (Gould et al., 2012; Stoner et al., 2010). Negative biases about people are widespread and include racial, ethnic, and age stereotypes. Clinicians may hold negative biases against younger adults of ethnic minorities and more readily "diagnose" problems that do not truly exist. Likewise, because of ageism, older adults may be "diagnosed" with untreatable problems such as Alzheimer's disease rather than treatable problems such as depression (see Chapter 1). In contrast, positive biases about certain people also work against accurate assessment. A belief that women do not abuse alcohol may result in a misdiagnosis; beliefs older adults are "cute" may mitigate against accurate assessment of abilities. Clearly, the best defense against bias is for clinicians to be fully educated about their prospective clients.

The environmental conditions where the assessment occurs can also work against accurate outcomes. Clinicians do not always have the option of selecting an ideal environment; rather, assessments sometimes occur in hallways, with a bedridden patient, or in a noisy emergency room. People with sensory or motor difficulties must be accommodated with alternative assessment formats. The patient's physical health may

A thorough assessment of physical health is an essential part of a comprehensive assessment for depression or any mental health problem.

also complicate assessment; in many cases with older adults, health issues can also create a negative bias so mental health issues may be overlooked when a health problem is discovered (Karel, Gatz, & Smyer, 2012; Qualls & Benight, 2007).

Taken together, clinical assessment is an excellent example of how the forces of development come together. Only when all four forces are considered can mental health problems be assessed accurately.

Assessment Methods

How are adults assessed? In terms of cognitive, psychological, and social assessments, there are six primary methods (Edelstein & Kalish, 1999): interview, self-report, report by others, psychophysiological assessment, direct observation, and performance-based assessment.

Clinical interviews are the most widely used assessment method (Gould et al., 2012; Stoner et al., 2010). They are useful because they provide both direct information in response to the questions and nonverbal information such as emotions. Interviews can be used to obtain historical information, determine appropriate follow-up procedures, build rapport with the client, obtain the client's informed consent to participate in the assessment, and evaluate the effects of treatment. All these tasks are important with adults of all ages. When interviewing older adults, though, it may be necessary to use somewhat shorter sessions, and be aware of sensory deficits and cognitive and medical conditions that may interfere with the interview.

Many commonly used assessment measures are presented in a self-report format. As noted in Chapter 1, a major concern is the reliability and validity of these measures with older adults.

Family members and friends are an important source of information. In some cases, such as Alzheimer's disease, discrepancies between the client's and others' description of the problem can be diagnostic. Such sources also are valuable if the client is unlikely or unable to tell the whole story. Such information can be obtained through interviews or self-report.

Psychophysiological assessment examines the relation between physical and psychological functioning. One common psychophysiological measure is the electroencephalogram (EEG), which measures brain wave activity. Other measures include heart rate,

muscle activity, and skin temperature. Such measures provide a way to measure the body's reaction to certain stimuli, especially when the client gets anxious or fearful in response to them.

In some cases it is possible to observe the client through systematic or naturalistic observation (see Chapter 1). Direct observation is especially useful when the problem involves specific behaviors, as in eating disorders. A variety of techniques exist for structuring observations, and they can be used in a wide array of settings, from homes to nursing homes.

Finally, performance-based assessment involves giving clients a specific task to perform. This approach underlies much cognitive and neuropsychological assessment. A person's memory is assessed by giving him or her a list of items to remember and then testing retention. Some neuropsychological tests involve drawing or copying pictures.

Developmental Issues in Therapy

Assuming Juan is assessed properly and found to have a mental disorder, what next? How can he be helped? Therapy for mental disorders generally involves two approaches (Segal et al., 2011): medical treatment and psychotherapy. Medical treatment most often involves the use of various medications based on the underlying physiological causes of the disorders. Psychotherapy usually involves talking to a clinician or participating in a group. In either case, it is essential to take into account developmental differences in people as they age.

As we saw in Chapter 3, the ways medications work change with age. The effective dosage of a specific medication may be different for younger, middle-aged, and older adults. In some cases, medications that work in one age group do not work for others.

In terms of psychotherapy, clinicians must adapt techniques to the unique needs of older adults (Zarit & Zarit, 2006). This has led some to propose a new, positive approach to geriatric psychiatry and geropsychology be adopted (Jeste & Palmer, 2013). This positive approach focuses "on recovery, promotion of successful ageing, neuroplasticity, prevention, and interventions to enhance positive psychological traits such as resilience, social engagement and wisdom" (p. 81).

Another major issue in psychotherapy is establishing whether a particular therapeutic approach is effective, based on research and clinical evidence. Major professional associations provide guidelines in their respective fields; the American Medical Association provides evidence-based approaches to medical therapy (American Medical Association, 2009), and the American Psychological Association developed a set of criteria for evidence-based psychotherapy (American Psychological Association, 2005). The therapeutic approaches that meet the standard for adult therapy appear to be effective for a wide range of ages and are generally the therapies of choice. As we consider specific disorders, we focus on evidence-based approaches to therapy.

ADULT DEVELOPMENT IN ACTION

What factors must be considered in conducting a thorough clinical assessment for mental disorders?

10.3 The Big Three: Depression, Delirium, and Dementia

LEARNING OBJECTIVES

- What are the most common characteristics of people with depression? How is depression diagnosed? What causes depression? What is the relation between suicide and age? How is depression treated?
- What is delirium? How is it assessed and treated?
- What is dementia? What are the major symptoms of Alzheimer's disease? How is it diagnosed? What causes it? What intervention options are there? What are some other major forms of dementia? What do family members caring for patients with dementia experience?

Ling has lived in the same neighborhood in New York for all of her 74 years. Her son, who visits her every week, started noticing Ling's memory problems have gotten much worse, her freezer is empty and her refrigerator has lots of moldy food. When he investigated further, he found her bank accounts were in disarray. Ling's son wonders what could be wrong with her.

Ling's behaviors certainly do not appear to be typical of older adults. Unfortunately, Ling is not alone in experiencing difficulties; many older adults have

similar problems. In this section, we consider three of the most common difficulties: depression, delirium, and dementia. As we will see, both depression and delirium are treatable; the most common form of dementia, Alzheimer's disease, is not. The three conditions are connected by overlapping symptoms and the possibility that they may coexist. Let's consider each in detail.

Depression

Most people feel down or sad from time to time, perhaps in reaction to a problem at work or in one's relationships. But does this mean that most people are depressed? How is depression diagnosed? Are there age-related differences in the symptoms examined in diagnosis? How is depression treated?

First of all, let's dispense with a myth. Contrary to the popular belief most older adults are depressed, the rate of severe depression *declines* from young adulthood to old age for healthy people as shown in Figure 10.2 (National Institute of Mental Health, 2013). However,

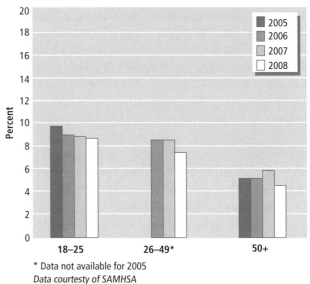

Figure 10.2

12-month prevalence of depression among all U.S. residents by age.

Source: National Institute of Mental Health (2013). Major depressive disorder among adults. Retrieved from http://www.nimh.nih.gov/statistics/1MDD_ADULT.shtml.

this downward age trend does not hold in all cultures; depressive symptoms among Chinese older adults rose over a 24-year period (1987–2010, inclusive) (Shao, Li, Zhang, Zhang, Zhang, & Qi, 2013).

In the United States, the average age at diagnosis for depression is 32 (National Institute of Mental Health, 2013). Being female, unmarried, widowed, or recently bereaved; experiencing stressful life events; and lacking an adequate social support network are more common among older adults with depression than younger adults (Segal et al., 2010). Less than 5% of older adults living in the community show signs of depression, but the percentage rises to over 13% among those who require home health care (National Institute of Mental Health, 2008). Subgroups of older adults who are at greater risk include those with chronic illnesses (of whom up to half may have major depression), nursing home residents, and family care providers (who commonly report feeling depressed; DeFries & Andresen, 2010).

Rates of clinical depression vary across ethnic groups, although correct diagnosis is frequently a problem with minorities due to inadequate access to physical and mental health care (Alegría et al., 2008). These issues also apply to immigrants (Ladin & Reinhold, 2013), who have higher rates of depression, and to treatment disparities relating to minorities (Zurlo & Beach, 2013). Rates for depression tend to be higher in Latino older adults than for other groups of older adults (National Institute of Mental Health, 2012). Latinos who speak primarily Spanish or are foreign-born are especially likely to show depression (Mercado Crespo et al., 2008). Older African Americans have lower rates of depression than European Americans (NIMH, 2013). Clearly, the pattern of ethnic differences indicates the reasons for them are complex and not well understood.

Finally, depression commonly accompanies other chronic conditions. Some common chronic conditions such as coronary heart disease (Tully & Cosh, 2013), diabetes (Kaur, Kumar, & Navis, 2013), and asthma and arthritis (Peltzer & Phaswana-Mafuya, 2013). For those people who do experience depression, let's examine its diagnosis and treatment.

General Symptoms and Characteristics of People with Depression. *The most prominent feature of clinical depression is* dysphoria, *that is, feeling down or blue.*

There are important developmental differences in how dysphoria is expressed (Segal et al., 2010). Older adults may not talk about their feelings at all, have feelings that flow from life events such as bereavement that mimic depression, or label their down feelings as depression but rather as pessimism or helplessness (NIHSeniorHealth, 2011; Zarit & Zarit, 2006). In addition, older adults are more likely to show signs of apathy, subdued self-deprecation, expressionlessness, and changes in arousal than are younger people (Segal et al., 2010). It is common for depressed older adults to withdraw, not speak to anyone, confine themselves to bed, and not take care of bodily functions. Younger adults may engage in some of these behaviors but do so to a much lesser extent. Thoughts about suicide are common, and may reflect a shutdown of a person's basic survival instinct.

The second major component of clinical depression is the accompanying physical symptoms (NIHSeniorHealth, 2011). These include insomnia, changes in appetite, diffuse pain, troubled breathing, headaches, fatigue, and sensory loss. The presence of these physical symptoms in older adults must be evaluated carefully, though. As noted in Chapter 3, some sleep disturbances may reflect normative changes unrelated to depression; however, certain types of sleep disturbance, such as regular early morning awakening, are related to depression, even in older adults (Wiebe, Cassoff, & Gruber, 2012). There is evidence that changes in the prefrontal cortex may be responsible for the link between sleep disturbance and depression; given that such changes occur with age, it may be one reason for the difficulty in understanding whether sleep disturbances are related to clinical depression in older adults.

Alternatively, physical symptoms may reflect an underlying physical disease that is manifested as depression. Indeed, many older adults admitted to the hospital with depressive symptoms turn out to have previously undiagnosed medical problems that are uncovered only after thorough examinations and evaluations (Mulley, 2008). These underlying health problems that appear as depression include vitamin deficiencies (e.g., B12), thyroid disease, certain viruses, and medication interactions and side effects (NIHSeniorHealth, 2011).

The third primary diagnostic characteristic is the symptoms must last at least 2 weeks. This criterion is used to rule out the transient symptoms common to all adults, especially after a negative experience such as receiving a rejection letter from a potential employer or getting a speeding ticket.

Fourth, other causes for the observed symptoms must be ruled out (Mulley, 2008). Other health problems, neurological disorders, medications, metabolic conditions, alcoholism, or other forms of psychopathology can cause depressive symptoms. These causes influence appropriate treatment decisions.

Finally, the clinician must determine how patients' symptoms affecting their daily life. Can they carry out responsibilities at home? How well do they interact with other people? What about effects on work or school? Clinical depression involves significant impairment in daily living.

Assessment Scales. Numerous scales are used to assess depression, but because most were developed on younger and middle-aged adults, they are most appropriate for these age groups. The most important difficulty in using these scales with older adults is they all include several items assessing physical symptoms. The Beck Depression Inventory (Beck, 1967) contains items that focus on feelings and physical symptoms. Although the presence of such symptoms usually is indicative of depression in younger adults, as we noted earlier, such symptoms may not be related to depression at all in older adults.

Scales such as the Geriatric Depression Scale (Yesavage et al., 1983) aimed specifically at older adults have been developed. Physical symptoms are omitted, and the response format is easier for older adults to follow. This approach reduces the age-related symptom bias and scale response problems with other self-report scales measuring depressive symptoms. A third screening inventory, the Center for Epidemiologic Studies-Depression Scale (CES-D; Radloff, 1977) is also frequently used in research.

An important point to keep in mind about these scales is that the diagnosis of depression should never be made on the basis of a single scale. As we have seen, the symptoms observed in clinical depression could be indicative of other problems, and symptom patterns are complex. Only by assessing many aspects of physical and psychological functioning can a clinician make an accurate assessment.

Causes of Depression. Several biological and psychosocial theories about the causes of depression have been proposed (Segal et al., 2010). Biological theories focus most on genetic predisposition, brain changes, and changes in neurotransmitters (McKinney & Sibille, 2013). The genetic evidence is based two sets of data: (a) on several studies that show higher rates of depression in relatives of depressed people than would be expected given base rates in the population; and (b) genetically-driven age-related changes in brain structures. The first type of genetic link is stronger in early-onset depression than in late-onset depression, whereas the second type of evidence is thought to underlie much of late-life onset.

There is substantial research evidence that severe depression is linked to imbalance in neurotransmitters such as low levels of serotonin and the action of brain-derived neurotrophic factor (Hashimoto, 2013). Low levels of serotonin are a likely result from high levels of stress experienced over a long period. The usual signs of low serotonin levels include waking up in the early morning (often around 4:00 A.M.), difficulty in concentrating and paying attention, feeling tired and listless, losing interest in activities such as sex or visiting friends, and racing of the mind with strong feelings of guilt and of reliving bad past experiences and creating negative thoughts. These effects of low serotonin are similar to those that characterize depression, which is why researchers believe that one possible cause is low serotonin.

Brain-derived neurotrophic factor (BDNF) is a compound found in blood serum, and its level is negatively correlated with the severity of depression (i.e., lower levels of BDNF are correlated with higher levels of depression). Research shows the use of antidepressant medication raises the level of BDNF.

Low levels of another neurotransmitter, norepinephrine, that regulates arousal and alertness, may be responsible for the feelings of fatigue associated with depression. These neurochemical links are the basis for the medications developed to treat depression we will consider a bit later.

The psychological effects of loss is the most common basis for psychosocial theories of depression (Segal et al., 2010). Bereavement or other ways of losing a relationship is the type of loss that has received the most attention, but the loss of anything considered personally important could also be a trigger. More-over, these losses may be real and irrevocable, threatened and potential, or imaginary and fantasized. The likelihood these losses will occur varies with age. Middle-aged adults are more likely to experience the loss of physical attractiveness, for example, whereas older adults are more likely to experience the loss of a loved one.

Cognitive-behavioral theories of depression adopt a different approach that emphasizes internal belief systems and focus on how people interpret uncontrollable events (Beck, 1967). The idea underlying this approach is experiencing unpredictable and uncontrollable events instills a feeling of helplessness resulting in depression. In addition, perceiving the cause of negative events as some inherent aspect of the self that is permanent and pervasive also plays an important role in causing feelings of helplessness and hopelessness, as well as feelings of personal responsibility for the "fact" their life is in shambles. Importantly, people tend to ruminate on these negative ideas, often losing sleep doing so. Baddeley (2013) argues such negative self-thoughts and rumination are due to an inappropriate setting of the pleasurable experience detector in the brain, thus linking cognitive-behavior theory with biological theories of depression.

Treatment of Depression.

As we have seen, depression is a complex problem that can result from a wide variety of causes. However, an extremely crucial point is most forms of depression benefit from intervention (Segal et al., 2010). Treatment of depression falls roughly into two categories: medical treatments and psychotherapy.

Medical treatments are typically used in cases of severe depression and involve mainly medication, but in some cases of long-term severe depression, these treatments include electroconvulsive therapy. For less severe forms of depression, and usually in conjunction with medication for severe depression, there are various forms of psychotherapy. A summary of the various treatment options is presented in Table 10.2.

Three families of medications are used to combat severe depression. Increasingly, these medications target specific neurotransmitter receptors rather than work by general action in the brain (Jainer, Kamatchi, Marzanski, and Somashekar, 2013). Each has

Table 10.2

PHYSICAL ILLNESS THAT CAUSES DEPRESSION IN OLDER ADULTS
Coronary artery disease
Hypertension, myocardial infarction, coronary artery bypass surgery, congestive heart failure
Neurological disorders
Cerebrovascular accidents, Alzheimer's disease, Parkinson's disease, amyotrophic lateral sclerosis, multiple sclerosis, Binswanger's disease
Metabolic disturbances
Diabetes mellitus, hypothyroidism or hyperthyroidism, hypercortisolism, hyperparathyroidism, Addison's disease, autoimmune thyroiditis
Cancer
Pancreatic, breast, lung, colonic, and ovarian carcinoma; lymphoma; and undetected cerebral metastasis
Other conditions
Chronic obstructive pulmonary disease, rheumatoid arthritis, deafness, chronic pain, sexual dysfunction, renal dialysis, chronic constipation

Source: Sunderland, T., Lawlor, B. A., Molchan, S. E., & Martinez, R. A. (1988). Depressive syndromes in the elderly: Special concerns. Psychopharmacology Bulletin, 24, 567–576.

potentially serious side effects (for a summary, see the Mayo Clinic's website on side effects of antidepressant medications where you can find up to-date information).

The most common first-line medication used to treat depression is selective serotonin reuptake inhibitors (SSRIs; Jainer et al., 2013) SSRIs have the lowest overall rate of side effects of all antidepressants, although some side effects can be serious in some patients. SSRIs work by boosting the level of serotonin, a neurotransmitter involved in regulating moods that was discussed earlier.

Other types of first-line medications are serotonin and norepinephrine reuptake inhibitors (SNRIs), norepinephrine and dopamine reuptake inhibitors (NDRIs), combined reuptake inhibitors and receptor blockers, and tetracyclic antidepressants.

If the first-line medications do not work, the next most popular medications are the tricyclic antidepressants. These medications are most effective with younger and middle-aged people; in those age groups they work about 70% of the time. The main problem with tricyclic antidepressants in older adults is that they are more likely to have other medical conditions or to be taking other medications that preclude their use. People who are taking antihypertensive medications or who have any of a number of metabolic problems should not take the tricyclic antidepressants. Moreover, the risk of side effects beyond dry mouth, some of which can be severe, is much greater in older adults, although some of the newer tricyclics have significantly lower risk.

If none of these medications are effective, a third group of drugs that relieve depression is the monoamine oxidase (MAO) inhibitors, so named because they inhibit MAO, a substance that interferes with the transmission of signals between neurons. MAO inhibitors generally are less effective than the tricyclics and can produce deadly side effects. Specifically, they interact with foods that contain tyramine or dopamine—mainly cheddar cheese but also others, such as wine and chicken liver—to create dangerously and sometimes fatally high blood pressure. MAO inhibitors are used with extreme caution, usually only after SSRIs and HCAs have proved ineffective.

If periods of depression alternate with periods of mania or extremely high levels of activity, a diagnosis of bipolar disorder is made (American Psychiatric Association, 1994). Bipolar disorder is characterized by unpredictable, often explosive mood swings as the person cycles between extreme depression and extreme activity. The drug therapy of choice for bipolar disorder is lithium (Malhi, Tanious, Das, Coulston, & Berk, 2013). Lithium is effective in controlling the mood swings, although researchers do not completely understand why it works. The use of lithium must be monitored closely because the difference between an effective dosage and a toxic dosage is small. Because lithium is a salt, it raises blood pressure, making it dangerous for people who have hypertension or kidney disease. The effective dosage for lithium decreases with age; physicians unaware of this change run the risk of inducing an overdose, especially in older adults. Compliance is also a problem, because no improvement is seen for 4 to 10 days after the initial dose and because many people with bipolar disorder do not like having their moods controlled by medication.

Electroconvulsive therapy (ECT) is an effective treatment for severe depression, especially in people whose depression has lasted a long time, who are suicidal, who have serious physical problems caused by their depression, and who do not respond to medications (National Institute of Mental Health, 2011). Unlike antidepressant medications, ECT has immediate effects. Usually only a few treatments are needed, in contrast to long-term maintenance schedules for drugs. But ECT may have some side effects that affect cognitive functioning (Gardner & O'Connor, 2008). Memory of the ECT treatment itself is lost. Memory of other recent events is temporarily disrupted, but it usually returns within a week or two.

In addition to ECT, there are other brain stimulation therapies for severe depression. These newer approaches include vagus nerve stimulation (VNS) and repetitive transcranial magnetic stimulation (rTMS). Although these methods are not yet commonly used, research has suggested they show promise.

Psychotherapy is a treatment approach based on the idea that talking to a therapist about one's problems can help. Often psychotherapy can be effective by itself in treating depression. In cases of severe depression, psychotherapy may be combined with drug therapy or ECT. *Two general approaches seem to work best for depression:* behavior therapy, *which focuses on attempts to alter current behavior without necessarily addressing underlying causes, and* cognitive behavior therapy, *which attempts to alter the ways people think.*

The fundamental idea in behavior therapy is that depressed people receive too few rewards or reinforcements from their environment (Lewinsohn, 1975). Thus the goal of behavior therapy is to get them to increase the good things that happen to them. Often this can be accomplished by having people increase their activities; if they do more, the likelihood is more good things will happen. In addition, behavior therapy seeks to get people to decrease the number of negative thoughts they have because depressed people tend to look at the world pessimistically. They get little pleasure out of activities that nondepressed people enjoy a great deal: seeing a funny movie, playing a friendly game of volleyball, or being with a lover.

To get activity levels up and negative thoughts down, behavior therapists usually assign tasks that force clients to practice the principles they are learning during the therapy sessions. This may involve going out more to meet people, joining new clubs, or just learning how to enjoy life. Family members are instructed to ignore negative statements made by the depressed person and to reward positive self-statements with attention, praise, or even money.

Cognitive behavior therapy for depression is based on the idea that depression results from maladaptive beliefs or cognitions about oneself. From this perspective, a depressed person views the self as inadequate and unworthy, the world as insensitive and ungratifying, and the future as bleak and unpromising (Beck et al., 1979). In cognitive behavior therapy the person is taught how to recognize the thoughts that become so automatic and ingrained that other perspectives are not seen. Once this awareness has been achieved, the person learns how to evaluate the self, world, and future more realistically. These goals may be accomplished through homework assignments similar to those used in behavior therapy. These often involve reattributing the causes of events, examining the evidence before drawing conclusions, listing the pros and cons of maintaining an idea, and examining the consequences of that idea. Finally, people are taught to change the basic beliefs responsible for their negative thoughts. People who believe they have been failures all their lives or they are unlovable are taught how to use their newfound knowledge to achieve more realistic appraisals of themselves.

Cognitive behavior therapy is especially effective for older adults (Jeste & Palmer, 2013). This is good news, because medications may not be as effective or as tolerated by older adults because of age-related changes in metabolism.

▌ Delirium

Delirium is characterized by a disturbance of consciousness and a change in cognition that develop over a short period of time (American Psychiatric Association, 1994). The changes in cognition can include difficulties with attention, memory, orientation, and language. Delirium can also affect perception, the sleep–wake cycle, personality, and mood. Although the onset of delirium usually is rapid, its course can vary a great deal over the course of a day, with cognitive symptoms in older adults generally more severe than in younger or middle-aged adults (Leentjens et al., 2008).

Delirium can be caused by any of a number of medical conditions (such as stroke, cardiovascular disease, and metabolic condition), medication side effects, substance intoxication or withdrawal, exposure to toxins, or any combination of factors (Leentjens et al., 2008; Segal et al., 2010). Because they take more medications on average than other age groups, older adults are particularly susceptible to delirium. However, delirium is often undiagnosed or misdiagnosed and symptoms are ascribed to other causes (Anand & MacLullich, 2013).

Assessment and treatment of delirium focus on the physiological causes. In general, the most important aspect of diagnosis is differentiating delirium from depression and dementia. The key features of each are shown in Table 10.3. The severity of delirium is related to the level of the underlying physiological problem. In many cases, delirium is accompanied by severe misinterpretations of the environment and confusion that is best alleviated by having one reliable family member or friend provide reassurance to the patient (Anand & MacLullich, 2013; Leentjens et al., 2008).

About one-third of cases of delirium are preventable (Anand & MacLullich, 2013). If the cause of nonpreventable delirium can be identified and addressed, most cases of delirium can be cured. In some cases, however, delirium can be fatal or result in permanent brain damage (Leentjens et al., 2008).

▌ Dementia

Probably no other condition associated with aging is more feared than the family of disorders known as dementia. In dementia individuals can literally lose their mind, being reduced from a complex, thinking, feeling human being to a confused, vegetative victim unable even to recognize one's spouse and children. Dementias serious enough to impair independent functioning affect nearly 37 million people globally, but predictions of how those numbers will change over the next few decades are mixed (Christensen, Thinggaard, Oksuzyan, Steenstrup, Andersen-Ranberg, Jeune et al., in press; Matthews, Arthur, Barnes, Bond, Jagger, & Brayne, in press; Prince, Bryce, Albanese, Wimo, Ribeiro, & Ferri, 2013). Some research (e.g., Christensen et al., in press; Matthews et al., in press) predicts declining rates of dementia as a result of healthier adults in more recent birth cohorts reaching old age, whereas

Table 10.3

SUMMARY OF DEPRESSION TREATMENT OPTIONS		
Antidepressant medications	Several options, including selective serotonin uptake inhibitors (SSRIs), tricyclics, MAO inhibitors, and others that have been shown to be effective in clinical trials research.	Adequate dosages, plasma levels, and treatment duration are essential to minimize response. Response may take 6–12 weeks, somewhat longer than in younger patients. Side effects may limit use.
Augmentation of antidepressants with lithium, thyroid medications, carbamazepine	Patients nonresponsive to several weeks of treatment with standard antidepressant medications may respond rapidly after these medications are added. Evidence is based on case series and reports.	May be useful in patients who are not responding or only partially responding to standard antidepressant medications. Constitutes acceptable clinical practice.
Electroconvulsive therapy	Clearly effective in severe depression, depression with melancholia, and depression with delusions, and when antidepressants are not fully effective. Sometimes combined with antidepressants.	In medication-resistant patients, acute response rate is approximately 50%. Relapse rate is high, necessitating attention to maintenance antidepressant treatment. Effects are more favorable with increasing age.
Psychotherapy	More effective treatment than waiting list, no treatment, or placebo; equivalent to antidepressant medications in geriatric outpatient populations generally, with major or minor depression. About half of studies are group interventions. Therapy orientations were cognitive, interpersonal, reminiscence, psychodynamic, and eclectic.	Studies have been in older outpatients who were not significantly suicidal and for whom hospitalization was not indicated. There is no evidence of efficacy in severe depression. Distribution of responses may be different from the response to medication.
Combined antidepressant medication and psychotherapy	Effective in outpatients using manual-based therapies; the relative contributions of each component are not well understood.	Combined therapy has not been adequately studied in older adults.
Source: U.S. Public Health Service (1993).		

other research (e.g., Prince et al., 2013) predicts increased rates. Part of the difference in predictions could be because of the specific criteria used to measure cognitive impairment, and part of it may be the composition of the samples. More work is needed to sort through these differing predictions.

Despite the different predictions about the future rate of dementia, it is the case that most older adults are not demented. For many people, the fear of dementia is the most serious problem, leading them to consider every lapse of memory a symptom. It is hard to know how many older adults have unstated fears about no longer being able to remember things in the same ways they did when they were younger; but as noted in Chapter 6, memory abilities show some normative changes with age. Consequently, what many people believe are signs they are becoming demented are actually quite normal.

The Family of Dementias. Dementia *is not a specific disease but rather a family of diseases characterized by cognitive and behavioral deficits involving some form of permanent damage to the brain.* About a dozen forms of dementia have been identified. Dementia involves severe cognitive and behavioral decline and is not caused by a rapid onset of a toxic substance or by infection (Prince et al., 2013). For example, if delirium is present, dementia cannot be diagnosed.

We focus on several types of dementias that are irreversible and degenerative. The most common and widely known of these is Alzheimer's disease, but others are important as well: vascular dementia, Parkinson's disease, Huntington's disease, alcoholic dementia, and AIDS dementia complex.

Alzheimer's Disease.

Alzheimer's disease *is the most common form of progressive, degenerative, and fatal dementia, accounting for perhaps as many as 70% of all cases of dementia* (National Institute on Aging, 2013a). New knowledge about Alzheimer's disease is discovered all the time, so it is important to monitor the research literature. However, because it is such a terrible disease, news of potential breakthroughs too often do not pan out.

Alzheimer's disease has several characteristics we will consider, both in terms of specific changes in the brain and behavioral symptoms.

Neurological Changes in Alzheimer's Disease.

The changes in the brain that characterize Alzheimer's disease are microscopic. Although great progress has

The nature of Alzheimer's disease is that it is difficult to tell just by looking at a person whether it is present.

Angela Hampton/Alamy

been made in diagnosing the disease, it is still the case definitive diagnosis of the disease can be done only at autopsy (National Institute on Aging, 2013b). These progressive changes eventually cause so much brain destruction the person dies. The microscopic changes that define Alzheimer's disease are rapid cell death, neurofibrillary tangles, and neuritic plaques. Several changes in neurotransmitter levels also are observed. Rapid cell death occurs most in the hippocampus (a structure in the brain most closely involved in memory), the cortex (the outer layer of the brain where our higher-level cognitive abilities reside), and the basal forebrain (the lower portion of the front of the brain). This cell death occurs at a rate much greater than normal.

Neurofibrillary tangles (see Chapter 2) are accumulations of pairs of filaments in the neuron that become wrapped around each other; when examined under a microscope, these paired filaments look like intertwined spirals. Neurofibrillary tangles occur in several areas of the brain, and the number of tangles is directly related to the severity of symptoms, specifically the severity of memory impairment (Scuderi & Steardo, 2013).

Neuritic or amyloid plaques (see Chapter3) are spherical structures consisting of a core of **beta-amyloid**, *a protein, surrounded by degenerated fragments of dying or dead neurons.* The plaques are found in various parts of the brain, with the amount of beta-amyloid moderately related to the severity of the disease (Krut, Zetterberg, Blennow, Cinque, Hagberg, & Price, 2013). Degeneration of neurons in some areas of the brain results in the formation of vacuoles, or spaces that become filled with fluid and granular material.

Considerable recent research has focused on beta-amyloid as a major factor in Alzheimer's disease, both in terms of the cause and possible avenues for treatment. The role of beta-amyloid is controversial, though. Some researchers view concentration of beta-amyloid as a biomarker of Alzheimer's disease (Jack, Knopman, Jagust, Petersen, Weiner, Aisen et al., 2013; Krut et al., 2013). Others consider it an early warning of potential cognitive decline, even in the absence of any behavioral symptoms (Gandy & DeKosky, 2013). We will consider the controversy surrounding diagnostic categories related to Alzheimer's disease a bit later.

Another protein involved in Alzheimer's disease that has been the focus of much research is tau protein (Gandy & DeKosky, 2013; Krut et al., 2013). Unlike

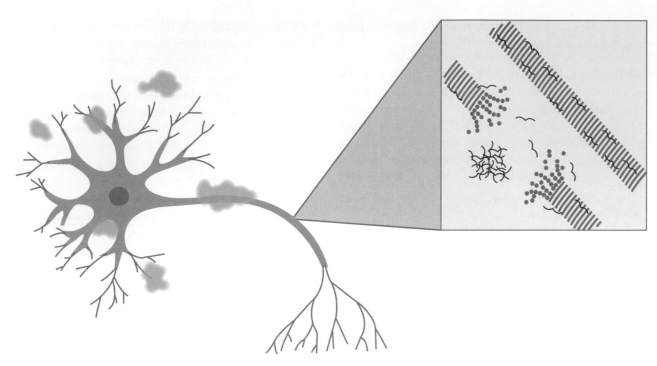

Figure 10.3

Action of beta-amyloid and tau proteins in relation to neurons. Each disrupts neurons, but in different ways.

Source: http://www.nytimes.com/interactive/2012/02/02/science/in-alzheimers-a-tangled-protein.html

beta-amyloid protein, tau protein acts within a neuron (see Figure 10.3). Tau protein spreads across neurons and may provide a key to understanding how neurons die (Liu, Drouet, Wu, Witter, Small, Clelland et al., 2012). More research needs to be done to fully understand the role of tau protein in Alzheimer's disease, but this is a promising avenue.

Although the structural changes occurring in the brains of people with Alzheimer's disease are substantial, we must use caution in assuming they represent qualitative differences from normal aging. They may not. As we saw in Chapter 3, all the changes seen in Alzheimer's disease, including the structural and neurotransmitter changes are also found in normal older adults. To be sure, the changes in Alzheimer's disease are much greater. But the important point is Alzheimer's disease may be merely an exaggeration of normal aging and not something qualitatively different from it.

Recent research also implicated certain neurochemicals as other possible causes of Alzheimer's disease. Increased levels of plasma homocysteine have been associated with the level of cognitive impairment

observed in Alzheimer's disease (Blasko et al., 2008; Bleich et al., 2003). Screening for these increased levels may improve diagnostic accuracy, and these levels are directly addressed by medication with memantine (discussed later).

Symptoms and Diagnosis. The major symptoms of Alzheimer's disease are gradual changes in cognitive functioning: declines in memory beginning with loss of recent memory and progressing to loss of remote memory, learning, attention, and judgment; disorientation in time and space; difficulties in word finding and communication; declines in personal hygiene and self-care skills; inappropriate social behavior; and changes in personality (American Psychiatric Association, 2000).

These symptoms tend to be vague in the beginning, and mimic other psychological problems such as depression or stress reactions. An executive may not be managing as well as she once did and may be missing deadlines more often. Slowly, the symptoms get worse. This executive, who could easily handle millions of dollars, can no longer add two small numbers.

Alzheimer's disease is a degenerative brain disorder that is, at present, incurable.

© Mark Richards/PhotoEdit

A homemaker cannot set the table. A person who was previously outgoing is now quiet and withdrawn; a gentle person is now hostile and aggressive. Emotional problems become increasingly apparent, including depression, paranoia, and agitation. Wandering becomes a serious problem, especially because the person may have no idea where he or she is or how to get home, thus posing a genuine safety concern. Neuroscience research indicates wandering likely results from damage to the specific parts of the brain that help us navigate through the world (the entorhinal cortex), an area usually damaged in the early stages of Alzheimer's disease (Jacobs, Weidemann, Miller, Solway, Burke, Wei et al., in press).

As the disease progresses, the patient becomes incontinent and more and more dependent on others for care, eventually becoming completely incapable of such simple tasks as dressing and eating. *In general, the symptoms associated with Alzheimer's disease are worse in the evening than in the morning, a phenomenon care providers call* sundowning.

The rate of deterioration in Alzheimer's disease varies widely from one patient to the next, although progression usually is faster when onset occurs earlier in life (Gandy & DeKosky, 2013). Alzheimer's disease has an average duration of 9 years (but can range anywhere from 1 to over 15 years) from the onset of noticeable symptoms through death (Zerr, 2013). The early stage is marked especially by memory loss,

disorientation to time and space, poor judgment, and personality changes. The middle stage is characterized by increased memory problems, increased difficulties with speech, restlessness, irritability, and loss of impulse control. People in the late stage of Alzheimer's disease experience incontinence of urine and feces, lose motor skills, have decreased appetite, have great difficulty with speech and language, may not recognize family members or oneself in a mirror, lose most if not all self-care abilities, and decreased ability to fight off infections.

Although a definitive diagnosis of Alzheimer's disease depends on an autopsy, the number and severity of neurological and behavioral changes allow clinicians to make increasingly accurate early diagnoses (Feldman et al., 2008). For an earlier diagnosis to be accurate, however, it must be comprehensive and broad. Figure 10.4 provides an overview of the process used to differentiate Alzheimer's disease from other conditions. Note a great deal of the diagnostic effort goes into ruling out other possible causes for the observed cognitive deficits: All possible treatable causes for the symptoms must be eliminated before a diagnosis of Alzheimer's disease can be made. Unfortunately, many clinicians do not conduct such thorough diagnoses; general practice physicians fail to accurately diagnose a significant number of cases of Alzheimer's disease (Bradford, Kunik, Schulz, Williams, & Singh, 2009). A common reason is the attitude on the part of some physicians that early diagnosis does more harm than good based on the mistaken belief patients and their families would prefer not to know or could not adequately deal with it; both are untrue.

As noted in Figure 10.4, the clinical diagnosis of Alzheimer's disease consists of carefully noting the history of the symptoms, documenting the cognitive impairments, conducting a general physical exam and neurological exam, performing laboratory tests to rule out other diseases, obtaining a psychiatric evaluation, performing neuropsychological tests, and assessing functional abilities.

As noted in the Current Controversies feature, there is considerable debate over the criteria that should be used to diagnose Alzheimer's disease, and whether there should be a diagnosis even before there are any measurable behavioral symptoms.

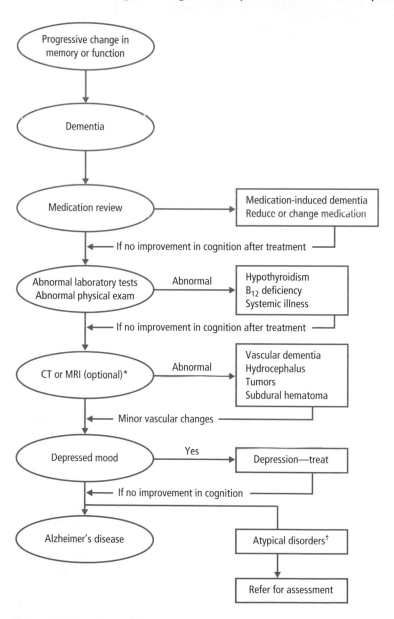

Figure 10.4

Process of differentially diagnosing Alzheimer's disease from other possible conditions.

Source: Alzheimer's Association online document, http://www.alz.org/medical/rtalgrthm.htm Developed and endorsed by the TriAD Advisory Board. Copyright 1996 Pfizer Inc. and Esai Inc. with special thanks to J. L. Cummings. Algorithm reprinted from TriAD, Three for the Management of Alzheimer's Disease, with permission.

*It is required in patients with focal signs, rapid progression, and headache.
†This category contains rare dementias (e.g., frontotemporal degenerations, Jakob–Creutzfeldt disease, Parkinson's disease, and other movement disorders that present with dementias) that should be considered when unusual clinical features are present or a rapidly progressive course is noted.

CURRENT CONTROVERSIES:

NEW DIAGNOSTIC CRITERIA FOR ALZHEIMER'S DISEASE

The diagnostic criteria for Alzheimer's disease currently in use were established in 1984. They are outdated because of the tremendous amount of research done since then has greatly expanded our knowledge of what Alzheimer's disease is, what causes it, and how it develops and progresses. As a result of pressure from clinicians and researchers for revised criteria, in 2011 a draft of new criteria developed jointly by the National Institute on Aging and the Alzheimer's Association were released (Jack, Albert, Knopman, McKhann, Sperling, Carrillo et al., 2011).

The draft criteria created a firestorm. Research indicated that Alzheimer's disease progresses through a series of stages, from a "preclinical" phase when no symptoms can be detected, through mild cognitive impairment, to the various stages of Alzheimer's disease (Albert, DeKosky, Dickson, Dubois, Feldman, Fox et al., 2011; Jack et al., 2011; McKhann, Knopman, Chertkow, Hyman, Jack, Kawas et al., 2011; Sperling, Aisen, Beckett, Dennett, Craft, Fagan et al., 2011). Additionally, the draft called for biomarkers to be associated with each of the various categories. How these elements fit together is shown in Figure 10.5.

What set off the controversy was whether people should be diagnosed with a "preclinical" form of Alzheimer's disease. Many clinicians objected to labeling individuals who had not shown any behavioral symptoms with a form of an incurable disease when many, perhaps most of them would not subsequently develop full-blown Alzheimer's disease (Chiu & Brodaty, 2013).

Research clearly shows a number of potential biomarkers can be associated with Alzheimer's disease (Chong & Lee, 2013). However, many who show high levels of beta-amyloid protein do not go on to develop Alzheimer's disease. This complicates the issue of whether to intervene during this preclinical stage in order to potentially "prevent" a disease that may never develop, or whether to run the risk of not intervening and the person in fact subsequently develops a devastating disease.

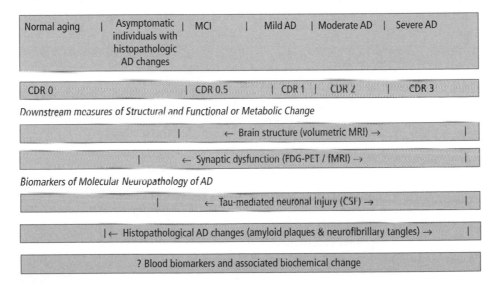

Figure 10.5

Clinical continuum of Alzheimer's disease showing types of changes over time. Blood biomarkers and associated biochemical changes are the focus of current research. AD = Alzheimer's disease; MCI = Mild Cognitive Impairment; CDR = Clinical Dementia Rating (a measure of severity of symptoms); FDG-PET = Positron Emission Tomography scan using 18-FDG as the tracer molecule; fMRI = Functional Magnetic Resonance Imaging; CSF = cerebrospinal fluid.

Source: Chong, S., & Lee, T.-S. (2013). Predicting cognitive decline in Alzheimer's disease (AD): The role of clinical, cognitive characteristics and biomarkers. In I. Zerr (Ed.), Understanding Alzheimer's disease (pp. 375–408). Retrieved from http://www.intechopen.com/books/understanding-alzheimer-s-disease. doi: 10.5772/54289. Figure 1, p. 376.

Until we have definitive evidence of a specific set or pattern of biomarkers that inevitably result in the full clinical manifestation of Alzheimer's disease, though, whether we should identify those who may be "at risk" with a label of a disease will remain highly controversial.

Searching for a Cause. We do not know for certain what causes Alzheimer's disease. What we do know is that certain forms of Alzheimer's disease are caused by autosomal dominant genes related to beta-amyloid protein production (Gandy & DeKosky, 2013). *Autosomal dominant inheritance patterns are those that involve only one gene from either one's mother or father in order to cause a trait or condition to develop.* Autosomal dominant forms of Alzheimer's disease usually involve mutations in the presenillin 1 (PSEN1) and amyloid beta (A4) precursor protein (APP) genes. The strong possibility at least some forms of Alzheimer's disease are inherited is a major concern of patients' families.

Other genetic causes involve the complex interaction of several genes, processes that are not yet well documented or understood. Several sites on various chromosomes have been tentatively identified as being involved in the transmission of Alzheimer's disease, including chromosomes 12, 14, 19, and 21. The most promising work noted links between the genetic markers and the production of amyloid protein, the major component of neuritic plaques (Liu, Kanekiyo, Xu, & Bu, 2013). Much of this research focuses on apolipoprotein E4 (apo E4), associated with chromosome 19, that may play a central role in creating neuritic plaques. People with the apo E4 trait are more likely to get Alzheimer's disease than those with the more common apo E3 trait. Additionally, a related mutation (TREM2) may be involved with apo E4 as well by interfering with the brain's ability to contain inflammation (Jonsson, Stefansson, Steinberg, Jonsdottir, Jonsson, Snaedal et al., 2013).

Interestingly, another version, apo E2, seems to have the reverse effect from apo E4: It decreases the risk of Alzheimer's disease (Liu et al., 2013). Despite the relation between apo E4 and neuritic plaques, and between apo E4 and beta-amyloid buildup, researchers have yet to establish strong relations directly between apolipoprotein E and general cognitive functioning (Liu et al., 2013).

Much of the genetics and related biomarker research focused on beta-amyloid and its proposed relation to Alzheimer's disease reviewed earlier. When viewed as a cause of Alzheimer's disease, researchers refer to the beta-amyloid cascade hypothesis as the process by which this occurs (Reitz, 2012). *The beta-amyloid cascade hypothesis refers to the process by which beta-amyloid deposits create neuritic plaques, that in turn lead to neurofibrillary tangles, that cause neuronal death and, when this occurs severely enough, Alzheimer's disease.* As noted earlier, there is considerable evidence beta-amyloid is involved in Alzheimer's disease. However, there is insufficient evidence at this point to conclude it is the main cause (Reitz, 2012).

Other research regarding the cause(s) of Alzheimer's disease is focusing on the role of changes in the vascular system in the brain. Beason-Held and colleagues (e.g., Beason-Held, Thambisetty, Deib, Sojkova, Landman, Zonderman et al., 2012; Codispoti, Beason-Held, Kraut, O'Brien, Rudow, Pletnikova et al., 2012; Thambisetty, Beason-Held, An, Kraut, Nalls, Hernandez et al., 2012) discovered increased blood flow in the frontal cortex, combined with decreased blood flow in the parietal and temporal lobes, resulted in significant cognitive impairment. Interestingly, the changes in blood flow occurred prior to measurable changes in cognitive functioning. Alternatively, de la Monte (2012) argues Alzheimer's disease is caused at least in part by impairment in the brain's ability to use glucose and produce energy. De la Monte found processed foods containing nitrites and high fat may exacerbate cognitive decline. Support for this idea comes from research showing that high blood sugar (glucose) levels are correlated with increased risk of Alzheimer's disease even in people without diabetes (Crane, Walker, Hubbard, Li, Nathan, Zheng et al., 2013). These results go further than previous findings showing that diabetes is a risk factor for Alzheimer's disease (Vagelatos & Eslick, 2013).

Because researchers can identify definite biomarkers responsible for certain forms of early-onset Alzheimer's disease, they have been able to develop genetic screening tests to see whether people have the inheritance pattern (McQueen & Blacker, 2008). Although research shows no significant negative consequences to people when they know they have the marker for Alzheimer's disease (Marteau et al., 2005), difficult choices may remain. Individuals who know they have the genes responsible for the disease may be faced with difficult decisions about having children and how to live out their lives. Genetic counseling programs that currently focus mostly on diseases of childhood would need to be expanded to help individuals face decisions about diseases occurring later in life. As research advances continue to improve our understanding of the causes of Alzheimer's disease, additional tests may be forthcoming. Helping people understand the true risks of developing (or, equally important, not developing) Alzheimer's disease will be an increasingly important focus of genetic counseling programs.

Intervention Strategies: Medications. Alzheimer's disease is incurable. However, much research has been done to find medications to alleviate the cognitive deficits and behavioral problems that characterize the disease. The flurry of research on biomarkers, especially beta-amyloid and tau proteins, has led to research on potential medication treatments based on blocking their effects on the brain (Lane, Dacks, Shineman, & Fillit, 2013). No medications that prevent the buildup of either beta-amyloid or tau proteins are available yet, but there is expectation a breakthrough will occur in the next several years.

In the meantime, research also continues on various drugs that improve memory and alleviate the declines that occur in Alzheimer's disease, especially in the early and middle stages. Currently, there are two groups of medications approved by the Food and Drug Administration for use with Alzheimer's disease patients: cholinesterase inhibitors that affect the levels of the neurotransmitter acetylcholine (such as donepezil [Aricept®], galantamine [Razadyne®], and rivastigmine [Exelon®]), and memantine (Namenda®) that works on other neurotransmitters and sets of neurons. Unfortunately, none of the drugs is highly effective, especially in later stages of the disease.

Intervention Strategies: Behavioral. To date, the most effective interventions for Alzheimer's disease are behavioral strategies; these approaches are recommended over medications because they give better and more effective outcomes (Gitlin, Kales, & Lyketsos, 2012). These strategies can be used from the time of initial diagnosis throughout the duration of the disease.

Key steps to be taken once a diagnosis is made include:

- obtaining accurate information about the disease,
- involving the patient as much as possible in decisions about his or her care,
- identifying the primary care provider,
- assessing the patient's living situation,
- setting realistic goals,
- making realistic financial plans,
- identifying a source of regular medical care,
- maximizing the patient's opportunity to function at his or her optimal level,
- making realistic demands of the patient, and
- using outside services as needed.

The goal of these early steps is to build a broad support network of relatives, medical personnel, and service providers that may be needed later. The new responsibilities of family members require changes in daily routines; people adjust to these roles at different rates.

When they find themselves caring for a person with Alzheimer's disease, care providers must rethink many behaviors and situations they otherwise take for granted. Dressing, bathing, and grooming become more difficult or even aversive to the affected person. Use of Velcro fasteners, joining the person during a bath or shower, and other such changes may be necessary. Nutritional needs must be monitored, because people with dementia may forget they have just eaten or may forget to eat.

Medications must be used with caution, since patients may forget to taken them or forget they have taken them and take another dose. Changes in personality and sexual behavior must be viewed as part of the disease. Sleeplessness can be addressed by establishing consistent bedtimes, giving warm milk or tryptophan before bedtime, and limiting caffeine intake. Wandering is especially troublesome because it is difficult to

The WanderGuard® device on the woman's wrist keeps people like her who have dementia from wandering away and potentially getting lost or injured without using medication.

control; making sure the affected person has an identification bracelet with the nature of the problem on it and making the house accident-proof are two preventive steps. In severe cases of wandering it may be necessary to use restraints under the direction of a health care professional.

Incontinence, that usually occurs late in the disease, is a troubling and embarrassing issue for the person with dementia; use of special undergarments or medications to treat the problem are two options. Incontinence is not necessarily related to Alzheimer's disease; stress incontinence, that is fairly common among older women, is unrelated to dementia.

Many care providers need to learn how to accomplish these tasks. Programs providing basic care information are available in multiple formats, including onsite face-to-face and online. A comparison of in-person and online formats in Hong Kong showed no differences in effectiveness (Lai, Wong, Liu, Lui, Chan, & Yap, 2013). Burgio and colleagues (2003) showed such skills training is effective for European American and African American care providers, and reduces

the number of problem behaviors the care providers must face from care recipients. Similarly, European American and Latino care providers both reported significant reductions in depressive symptoms, increased use of adaptive coping, and decreased use of negative coping strategies after training and practice in the use of specific cognitive and behavioral skills (Gallagher-Thompson et al., 2003). Additionally, home intervention strategies can result in care providers having more time to themselves and a decrease in the amount of assistance they need from external sources (Nichols et al., 2008).

One of the most difficult issues care providers face concerns taking things away from the affected person and restricting activity. For example, in many cases the person experiences problems handling finances. It is not uncommon for them to spend hundreds or even thousands of dollars on strange items, to leave the checkbook unbalanced and bills unpaid, and to lose money. Although they can be given some money to keep, someone else must handle the day-to-day accounts. That transition may be traumatic, and the caregiver may be accused of trying to steal money.

Traveling alone is another difficult issue. Families of people with dementia often do not recognize their loved one's deteriorating condition until a calamity occurs during travel. Families should limit solo excursions to places within walking distance; all other trips should be made with at least one family member along. Related to this, driving is often a contentious issue, especially if the person does not recognize his or her limitations. Once it is clear the patient cannot drive, the family must take whatever steps are necessary. In some cases this entails simply taking the car keys, but in others it becomes necessary to disable the car. Suggesting the patient could be chauffeured is another alternative. In any case, care providers may be subjected to various sorts of accusations related to these issues.

How can family members and health care professionals deal with the behavioral and cognitive problems experienced by people with Alzheimer's disease? One successful approach for dealing with difficult behavior is a technique called differential reinforcement of incompatible behavior (DRI) (Fisher et al., 2008). In DRI, care providers reduce the incidence of difficult behavior by rewarding the person with Alzheimer's disease for engaging in appropriate behaviors that cannot be done at the same time as the problem behaviors. For example, a person who throws food during dinner could be rewarded for sitting quietly and eating. One major advantage of DRI for care providers is the technique can be used in the home, and provides a good way to deal with troublesome behaviors (Fisher et al., 2008). Most important, the DRI technique is easily learned, has no side effects, and can be as effective as or more effective than medical treatments (Spira & Edelstein, 2006).

Numerous effective behavioral and educational interventions have been developed to address the memory problems in early and middle-stage dementia. *One behavioral intervention involves using an implicit-internal memory intervention called* spaced retrieval. Developed by Camp and colleagues (e.g., Camp, 2001), spaced retrieval involves teaching persons with Alzheimer's disease to remember new information by gradually increasing the time between retrieval attempts (see Chapter 6 for more details). This easy, almost magical technique has been used to teach names of staff members and other information;

it holds considerable potential for broad application at home and in any residential care setting. It is easily taught to any care provider (Hunter et al., 2012). Research also shows combining spaced retrieval with additional memory encoding aids helps even more (Kinsella et al., 2007). Spaced retrieval also works in training non-memory behaviors; spaced retrieval can be used with residents with dementia who have trouble swallowing to help them relearn how to swallow (Camp, Antenucci, Brush, & Slominski, 2012).

In designing interventions for persons with Alzheimer's disease, the guiding principle should be optimizing the person's functioning. Regardless of the level of impairment, attempts should be made to help the person cope as well as possible with the symptoms. The key is helping all persons maintain their dignity as human beings. This can be achieved in creative ways, such as adapting the principles of Montessori methods of education to bring older adults with Alzheimer's disease together with preschool children so they perform tasks together (Malone & Camp, 2007). One example of this approach is discussed in the How Do We Know? feature.

HOW DO WE KNOW?:

TRAINING PERSONS WITH DEMENTIA TO BE GROUP ACTIVITY LEADERS

Who were the investigators, and what was the aim of the study? Dementia is marked by progressive and severe cognitive decline. But despite these losses, can people with dementia be trained to be group leaders? Most people might think the answer is "no," but Cameron Camp and Michael Skrajner (2005) decided to find out by using a training technique based on the Montessori method.

How did the investigators measure the topic of interest? The Montessori method is based on self-paced learning and developmentally appropriate activities. As Camp and Skrajner point out, many techniques used in rehabilitation (e.g., task breakdown, guided repetition, moving from simple to complex and concrete to abstract) and in intervention programs with people who have dementia (e.g., use of external cues and implicit memory) are consistent with the Montessori method.

For this study, a program was developed to train group leaders for Memory Bingo (see Camp, 1999a and 1999b, for details about this game). Group leaders learned what cards to pick for the game, where the answers were located on the card, where to "discard"

the used (but not the winning) cards, and where to put the winning cards. Success in the program was measured by research staff raters, who made ratings of the type and quality of engagement in the task shown by the group leader.

Who were the participants in the study? Camp and Skrajner tested four people who had been diagnosed as probably having dementia who were also residents of a special care unit of a nursing home.

What was the design of the study? The study used a longitudinal design so Camp and Skrajner could track participants' performance over several weeks.

Were there ethical concerns with the study? Having persons with dementia as research participants raises important issues with informed consent. Because of their serious cognitive impairments, these individuals may not fully understand the procedures. Thus, family members such as a spouse or adult child caregiver are also asked to give informed consent. Additionally, researchers must pay careful attention to participants' emotions; if participants become agitated or frustrated, the training or testing session must be stopped. Camp and Skrajner took all these precautions.

What were the results? Results showed at least partial adherence to the established game protocols was achieved at a high rate. Indeed, staff assistance was not required at all for most of the game sessions for any leader. All of the leaders said they enjoyed their role, and one recruited another resident to become a leader in the next phase of the project.

What did the investigators conclude? It appears persons with dementia can be taught to be group activity leaders through a procedure based on the Montessori Method. This is important since it provides a way for such individuals to become engaged in an activity and to be productive.

Although more work is needed to continue refining the technique, applications of the Montessori method offer a promising intervention approach for people with cognitive impairments.

The key conclusion is behavioral intervention strategies are powerful tools to assist care providers in helping people deal with Alzheimer's disease. Having essentially no side effects and easy to learn how to administer, these strategies should be the first option tried.

Caring for Patients with Dementia at Home.

Watching a loved one struggle with Alzheimer's disease can be both heartrending and uplifting for family members (O'Dell, 2007). Watching a spouse, parent, or sibling go from being an independent, mature adult to not remembering the names of family members is extremely difficult. But the unconditional love shown by family care providers and the opportunity for family members to develop closer relationships can be quite positive. In this section, we consider some of the key issues regarding caregiving for persons with dementia; we consider caregiving more generally in Chapter 11.

Most people with dementia (as well as other impairments) are cared for by their family members at home (MetLife Mature Market Institute, 2012). Over 10 million adults over age 50 provide more than 20 hours per week on average in unpaid care for relatives; this is estimated to be worth well over $300 billion annually. Most care providers are over age 50 and are working, mostly full time. Care providers lose about $3 trillion in wages, pensions, and Social Security payments when they take time off work to care for a loved one (MetLife Mature Market Institute, National Alliance for Caregiving, and Center for Long-Term Care Research, 2011). Women average about $324,000 and men average about $290,000 in losses; women's losses are greater even though they generally earn less because they take more time off. Care providers tend to be of moderate financial means, with many being poor.

One useful way to conceptualize family caregiving is as an unexpected career (Aneshensel et al., 1995). The caregiving career begins with the onset of the illness and moves through a number of separate steps. Note the process does not end with the placement of the affected family member in a nursing home, or even with that person's death. Rather, the career continues through the bereavement and social readjustment period, at which point one may continue with life. Observe the kind of caregiving changes, from the comprehensive caregiving that covers all aspects of the process, to sustained caregiving in the home and foreshortened caregiving in the nursing home, to withdrawal from caregiving.

Research documented care providers are at risk for depression (Blom, Bosmans, Cuijpers, Zarit, & Pot, 2013; Cox, 2013). It is important care providers who show depressive symptoms receive appropriate treatment for it. Whether this support is provided in a traditional face-to-face setting or online does not appear to matter, as demonstrated in a study in the Netherlands (Blom et al., 2013).

Taking care of a person with dementia is usually stressful for families. As you can imagine, family members who care for a parent with dementia while also holding down a job and raising children puts incredible demands on time. Two options available to provide some relief for care providers are respite care and adult day care.

Respite care is designed to allow family members to get away from the caregiving situation for a time. It can consist of in-home care provided by professionals or temporary placement in a residential facility. In-home care is typically used to allow care providers to do errands or have a few hours free, whereas temporary residential placement is usually reserved for a more extended respite, such as a weekend. Research documents using respite care is a help to care providers (Roberto & Jarrott, 2008; Zarit & Femia, 2008).

Adult day care provides placement and programing for frail older adults during the day. The goal of adult day care is to delay institutionalization, enhance self-esteem, and encourage socialization (Administration on Aging, 2012). Adult day care typically provides more intensive intervention than respite care. This option is used most often by adult children who are employed. In general, adult day care is an effective approach for care providers (Roberto & Jarrott, 2008).

The demand for respite and adult day care far exceeds their availability, making them limited options. An additional problem is many insurance programs do not pay for these services, making them too expensive for care providers with limited finances. Clearly, with the increase in numbers of people who have dementia, ways to provide support for assistance to family care providers must be found.

Other Forms of Dementia. As we noted, dementia is a family of different diseases. We consider several of them briefly.

Vascular Dementia. Until it was discovered that Alzheimer's disease was not rare, most physicians and researchers believed most cases of dementia resulted from cerebral atherosclerosis and its consequent restriction of oxygen to the brain. As described in Chapter 3, atherosclerosis is a family of diseases that, if untreated, may result in heart attacks or strokes. For the present discussion it is the stroke, or cerebrovascular accident (CVA), that concerns us. CVAs (see Chapter 3) result from a disruption of the blood flow, called an infarct that may be caused by a blockage or hemorrhage.

A large CVA usually produces rapid, severe cognitive decline, but this loss is almost always limited to specific abilities. This pattern differs from the classic, global, more gradual deterioration seen in Alzheimer's disease. *If a person experiences numerous small cerebral vascular accidents, a disease termed* **vascular dementia** *may result.* Vascular dementia may have a sudden onset after a CVA, and its progression is described as stepwise and highly variable across people, especially early in the disease. Again, this is in contrast to the similar cluster of cognitive problems shown by people

with Alzheimer's disease. Most people who have vascular dementia have a history of cerebrovascular or cardiovascular disease, and typical symptoms include hypertension, specific and extensive alterations on an MRI, and differential impairment on neuropsychological tests (a pattern of scores showing some functions intact and others significantly below average; Paul, Lane, & Jefferson, 2013). Individuals' specific symptom patterns may vary a great deal, depending on which specific areas of the brain are damaged. In some cases, vascular dementia has a much faster course than Alzheimer's disease, resulting in death an average of 2 to 3 years after onset; in others, the disease may progress much more slowly with idiosyncratic symptom patterns.

Parkinson's Disease. Parkinson's disease is known primarily for its characteristic motor symptoms that are easily seen: very slow walking, difficulty getting into and out of chairs, and a slow hand tremor. Research indicates these problems are caused by a deterioration of neurons that produce the neurotransmitter dopamine. Dopamine is involved in transmitting messages between the brain structure called the substantia nigra and other parts of the brain to enable us to have smooth body movements. When roughly 60 to 80% of the dopamine-producing cells are damaged, and do not produce enough dopamine, the motor symptoms of Parkinson's disease appear.

However, motor system changes may not be the most important diagnostically. One prominent theory is the earliest indications of Parkinson's are found in a different part of the brain, the medulla and the olfactory bulb, which controls the sense of smell. According to this theory, Parkinson's only progresses to the substantia nigra and cortex over many years. In fact, there is evidence non-motor symptoms such as a loss of sense of smell, sleep disorders, and constipation may precede the motor features of the disease by several years (Hoyles & Sharma, in press; National Parkinson's Foundation, 2012).

Former boxing champion Muhammad Ali and actor Michael J. Fox are some of the more famous individuals who have Parkinson's disease. Parkinson's disease is diagnosed in 40,000 to 50,000 people each year (National Parkinson's Foundation, 2012).

Symptoms are treated effectively with several medications (Parkinson's Disease Foundation, 2013); the most popular are levodopa, which raises the functional level of dopamine in the brain; Sinemet® (a combination of levodopa and carbidopa), that gets more levodopa to the brain; and Stalevo® (a combination of Sinemet® and entacapone), that extends the effective dosage time of Sinemet®. Research indicates a device called a neurostimulator, that acts like a brain pacemaker by regulating brain activity when implanted deep inside the brain, may prove effective in significantly reducing the tremors, shaking, rigidity, stiffness, and walking problems when medications fail (Schuepbach, Rau, Knudsen, Volkman, Krack, Timmerman et al., 2013).

For reasons we do not yet understand, some people with Parkinson's disease also develop severe cognitive impairment and eventually dementia (Zheng, Shemmassian, Wijekoon, Kim, Bookheimer, & Pouratian, in press). As with Alzheimer's disease, attention is focused on beta-amyloid protein levels as a possible cause, but much work remains to be done (Beyer, Alves, Hwang, Babakchanian, Bronnick, Chou et al., 2013).

Huntington's Disease.

Huntington's disease is an autosomal dominant disorder that usually begins between ages 30 and 45 (Sharon et al., 2007). The disease generally manifests itself through involuntary flicking movements of the arms and legs; the inability to sustain a motor act such as sticking out one's tongue; prominent psychiatric disturbances such as hallucinations, paranoia, and depression; and clear personality changes, such as swings from apathy to manic behavior.

Cognitive impairments typically do not appear until late in the disease. The onset of these symptoms is gradual. The course of Huntington's disease is progressive; patients ultimately lose the ability to care for themselves physically and mentally. Walking becomes impossible, swallowing is difficult, and cognitive loss becomes profound. Changes in the brain thought to underlie the behavioral losses include degeneration of the caudate nucleus and the small-cell population, as well as substantial decreases in the neurotransmitters g-aminobutyric acid (GABA) and substance P. A test is available to determine whether someone has the marker for the Huntington's disease gene.

Alcohol-Related Dementia.

Chronic alcohol abuse or dependence may result in cognitive decline, ranging from limited forms of amnesia or mild cognitive impairment to dementia (Ridley, Draper, & Withall, 2013). The causes of these memory problems include deficiency of nutritional factors (such as B-complex vitamins) that cause Wernicke-Korsakoff's syndrome, and/or other problems such as cerebrovascular disease. However, progressive cognitive impairment can occur in the absence of syndromes such as Wernicke-Korsakoff's, and has been attributed to the direct toxic effect of ethanol on the brain.

One key symptom of alcohol-related dementia is confabulation, when the person makes up what sounds believable, but completely fictitious, stories that cover the gaps in memory. Other symptoms include personality changes (e.g., frustration, anger, suspicion, and jealousy), loss of problem-solving skills, communication problems (e.g., word-finding difficulty), and disorientation to time and place. Early in the course of the disease, the memory problems may be reduced or reversed if the person stops drinking alcohol, eats a well-balanced diet, and is given vitamin replacements (especially thiamine and vitamin B1). Thiamine, that limits some of the toxic effects of alcohol, is an important supplement for heavy drinkers.

AIDS Dementia Complex.

AIDS dementia complex (ADC), or HIV-associated encephalopathy, occurs primarily in persons with more advanced HIV infection (Manji, Jäger, & Winston, in press). The virus does not appear to directly invade nerve cells, but it jeopardizes their health and function. The resulting inflammation may damage the brain and spinal cord and cause symptoms such as confusion and forgetfulness, behavioral changes (e.g., apathy, loss of spontaneity, depression, social withdrawal, and personality changes), severe headaches, progressive weakness, loss of sensation in the arms and legs, and stroke. Cognitive motor impairment or damage to the peripheral nerves is also common.

Research shows the HIV infection can significantly alter the size of certain brain structures involved in learning and information processing. Symptoms include encephalitis (inflammation of the brain), behavioral changes, and a gradual decline in cognitive function, including trouble with concentration, memory, and attention. Persons with ADC also show progressive slowing of motor function and loss of dexterity and coordination. When left untreated, ADC can be fatal. In the terminal phase of ADC, patients are bedridden, stare vacantly, and have minimal social and cognitive interaction.

Because HIV infection is largely preventable, ADC can be reduced through the practice of safe sex. Additionally, research shows aggressive treatment of HIV with antiretroviral medications can also dramatically reduce the risk of subsequently developing ADC (Manji et al., in press).

ADULT DEVELOPMENT IN ACTION

How are the key distinguishing features of depression, delirium, and dementia important to social workers?

10.4 Other Mental Disorders and Concerns

LEARNING OBJECTIVES

- What are the symptoms of anxiety disorders? How are they treated?
- What are the characteristics of people with psychotic disorders?
- What are the major issues involved with substance abuse?

Daisy forces herself to do her daily routine. She is shaky all the time because she just doesn't feel safe. Her neighborhood is deteriorating and she is afraid of what the teenagers will do to her. She imagines all sorts of horrible things. Her worst fear is no one would know if she was attacked or fell ill. Her heart races when she thinks about it. She rarely goes out now and has convinced her son to bring her groceries and other supplies.

Daisy's feelings indicate people have difficulties for many reasons. She is clearly afraid, that could reflect a realistic assessment of her neighborhood. But her feelings also make her heart race, which is unusual. In this section, we examine three disorders receiving increased attention: anxiety disorders, psychotic disorders, and substance abuse.

Anxiety Disorders

Imagine you are about to give a speech before an audience of 500 people. In the last few minutes before your address, you begin to feel nervous, your heart starts to pound, and your palms get sweaty. (You now have something in common with Daisy's reactions.) These feelings, common even to veteran speakers, are similar to those experienced by people with anxiety disorders: a group of conditions based on fear or uneasiness.

Anxiety disorders include problems such as feelings of severe anxiety for no apparent reason, phobias with regard to specific things or places, and obsessive–compulsive disorders, when thoughts or actions are repeatedly performed (Segal et al., 2010). Although anxiety disorders occur in adults of all ages, they are particularly common in older adults because of loss of health, relocation stress, isolation, fear of losing independence, and many other reasons. Anxiety disorders are diagnosed in approximately 17% of older men and 21% of older women making them relatively common (Fitzwater, 2008). The reasons for this gender difference are unknown.

Symptoms and Diagnosis of Anxiety Disorders. Common to all the anxiety disorders are physical changes that interfere with social functioning, personal relationships, or work. These physical changes include dry mouth, sweating, dizziness, upset stomach, diarrhea, insomnia, hyperventilation, chest pain, choking, frequent urination, headaches, and a sensation of a lump in the throat (Segal et al., 2010). These symptoms occur in adults of all ages, but they are particularly common in older adults because of loss of health, relocation stress, isolation, fear of losing control over their lives, or guilt resulting from feelings of hostility toward family and friends.

An important issue concerning anxiety disorders in older adults is anxiety may be an appropriate response to the situation. Helplessness anxiety such as Daisy experiences is generated by a potential or actual loss of control or mastery (Varkal, Yalvac, Tufan, Turan, Cengiz, & Emul, 2013). A study in Turkey showed older adults are anxious about their memory, reflecting at least in part a realistic assessment of normative, age-related decline.

In addition, a series of severe negative life experiences may result in a person's reaching the breaking point and appearing highly anxious. Many older adults who show symptoms of anxiety disorder have underlying health problems that may be responsible for the symptoms. In all cases the anxious behavior should be investigated first as an appropriate response that may not warrant medical intervention. The important point is to evaluate the older adult's behavior in context.

These issues make it difficult to diagnose anxiety disorders, especially in older adults (Fitzwater, 2008; Segal et al., 2010). The problem is there usually is nothing specific a person can point to as the specific trigger or cause. In addition, anxiety in older adults often accompanies an underlying physical disorder or illness.

These secondary causes of anxiety must be disentangled from the anxiety symptoms so each may be dealt with appropriately. In short, the trick is to distinguish between the "worried" and the well. Zarit and Zarit (2007) report the key features of late-life anxiety disorder are distress and impairment, frequency and uncontrolled worry, muscle tension, and sleep disturbance.

Treating Anxiety Disorders. Anxiety disorders can be treated with medication and psychotherapy (Hendriks, Keijsers, Kampman, Hoogduin, & Voshaar, 2012; Segal et al., 2010). The most commonly used medications are benzodiazepine (e.g., Valium® and Librium®), paroxetine (an SSRI, e.g.., Paxil®), buspirone, and beta-blockers. Though moderately effective, these drugs must be monitored carefully in older adults because the amount needed to treat the disorder is low and the potential for side effects is great.

For older adults, the clear treatment of choice is psychotherapy, specifically cognitive behavioral or relaxation therapy, especially when anxiety disorders first occur in later life (Hendriks et al., 2012). Relaxation therapy is exceptionally effective, easily learned, and presents a technique that is useful in many situations (e.g., falling asleep at night; Segal et al., 2012). The advantage of these psychotherapeutic techniques is they usually involve only a few sessions, have high rates of success, and offer clients procedures they can take with them.

Psychotic Disorders

Some forms of psychopathology, called psychoses, involve losing touch with reality and the disintegration of personality. Two behaviors that occur in these disorders are delusions, belief systems not based on reality, and hallucinations, distortions in perception.

It is rare older adults develop new cases of psychotic disorders (Salai, 2013). The behaviors present in psychotic disorders are commonly manifested as

Psychotherapy is the treatment of choice for older adults who have anxiety disorders.

Karen Preuss/The Image Works

secondary problems caused by other disorders, especially in dementia, or as side effects from medications. Thus, psychotic symptoms are an important aspect of the diagnosis of other disorders and can be managed in the same way.

Schizophrenia. Schizophrenia is characterized by the severe impairment of thought processes, including the content and style of thinking, distorted perceptions, loss of touch with reality, a distorted sense of self, and abnormal motor behavior (American Psychiatric Association, 1994). People with schizophrenia may show these abnormal behaviors in several ways: loose associations (such as saying that they have a secret meeting with the president of the United States in the local bowling alley), hearing voices that tell them what to do, believing they can read other people's minds, believing their body is changing into something else, or sometimes having bizarre delusions (e.g., that they are Jesus or they are being spied on). In addition, schizophrenic people tend to show little or highly inappropriate emotionality (laughing hysterically at the news of a major tragedy, for instance). They are often confused about their own identity, have difficulty working toward a goal, and tend to withdraw from social contact.

The second hallmark symptom of schizophrenia is delusions, or well-formed beliefs not based in reality. Most often, these delusions involve persecution ("People are out to get me"). The distinction between paranoid disorders and schizophrenia is fuzzy; indeed, one type of schizophrenia is called paranoid-type schizophrenia. In general, hallucinations, loose associations, and absent or inappropriate emotions do not occur in paranoid disorders (American Psychiatric Association, 1994).

The beliefs underlying delusions can result in anger, resentment, or even violent acts. Because people with psychoses are extremely suspicious and rarely seek help on their own, such people tend to come to the attention of authorities after having repeated run-ins with the police or neighbors, starting legal proceedings against others on mysterious grounds, or registering complaints about fictitious or distorted events.

The onset of schizophrenia occurs most often between ages 16 and 30, and much less often after age 40 (Clare & Giblin, 2008). The symptoms of schizophrenia also differ by age; older adults show less thought disorder and less flattening of their emotions than do younger adults. Some researchers disagree, however, maintaining there are few differences with age in the numbers of people who experience schizophrenic symptoms and no differences in the nature of the symptoms. In any case, there is agreement that new cases of schizophrenia are rare in late life.

Longitudinal research indicates the natural course of schizophrenia is improvement over the adult life span (Salai, 2013; Segal et al., 2012). Studies show the first 10 years of the disorder are marked by cycles of remission and worsening, but symptoms generally lessen in more than half of people with schizophrenia in later life. This may be caused by a rebalancing of the neurotransmitters dopamine and acetylcholine that are heavily weighted toward dopamine in younger adults with schizophrenia. Additional rebalancing of other neurotransmitters may also play a role.

Treating Schizophrenia. Traditionally, treatment of schizophrenia has emphasized medication. Drug therapy consists of antipsychotics; medications believed to work on the dopamine system (see Chapter 2). Some of the more commonly used antipsychotics are haloperidol (Haldol®), chlorpromazine HCl (Thorazine®), and thioridazine HCl (Mellaril®). These medications must be used with extreme caution in adults of all ages because of the risk of serious toxic side effects, especially the loss of motor control. Despite these risks, antipsychotics often are used in nursing homes and other institutions as tranquilizing agents to control difficult patients.

In general, people with schizophrenia are difficult to treat with psychotherapy. The severe thought disturbances characteristic of schizophrenia make it difficult for therapists to work with such clients. Because of their extreme suspiciousness, paranoid people may be reluctant to cooperate in psychotherapy. However, there is evidence a comprehensive and integrated social rehabilitation program combined with health care management intervention can be effective (Pratt, Bartels, Mueser, & Forester, 2008). The goals of therapy for such people tend to be adaptive rather than curative, helping these people adapt to daily living.

Substance Abuse

Although you might think substance abuse is primarily a problem of adolescents and young adults, it's not—older adults also have the problem (National Institute on Alcohol Abuse and Alcoholism, 2012). Because of the differences in the types of substances abused by younger and older adults (younger adults are more likely to abuse illegal drugs than are older adults), alcohol provides the best common basis for comparison.

What constitutes alcoholism? Alcoholism, also known as alcohol dependence, is a disease that includes alcohol craving and continued drinking despite repeated alcohol-related problems, such as losing a job or getting into trouble with the law. Alcoholism includes four symptoms: craving, impaired control, physical dependence, and tolerance.

As you can see in Figure 10.6, the prevalence of alcohol dependency drops significantly with age (National Institute on Alcohol Abuse and Alcoholism, 2008). However, when data are examined more closely, there are gender and ethnic group differences in alcohol abuse. The percentage of men who abuse alcohol ranges from about 2 times (ages 18–29) to 6 times (ages 65 and over) higher than those for women. Native Americans have the highest rate of abuse, followed by European Americans, Latinos, African Americans, and Asian Americans (Grant et al., 2004).

Two patterns of onset are evident with older people with alcohol dependency: early-onset in young adulthood or middle-age lifelong problem drinking, and late-onset problem drinking (Segal et al., 2010). Left untreated, alcohol dependency does not improve over time.

Taking a life-span view of alcohol dependence provides insights into important differences in drinking patterns and outcomes (National Institute on Alcohol Abuse and Alcoholism, 2012). Young adults are more likely to binge drink, and consequently more likely to experience problems such as alcohol poisoning, drunk-driving offenses, and assaults. The earlier drinking begins, especially if it starts in adolescence, the more likely brain damage occurs and alcohol dependence develops. Young adult drinkers are less likely to feel the effects of alcohol, such as getting sleepy or losing motor coordination, that may result in their drinking more at one time ("binging"). However, young adults' cognitive performance is more impaired. Taken together, these effects create a dangerous situation—they do not feel the effects as easily, so tend to underestimate the degree they are impaired, and are worse at performing complex tasks such as driving, providing an explanation of why drunk driving is more prevalent among young adults.

Middle age is when the effects of continued alcohol dependence that began in young adulthood become evident. Diseases of the liver, pancreas, and various types of cancer and cardiovascular disease may occur. In part due to these health problems, middle-aged

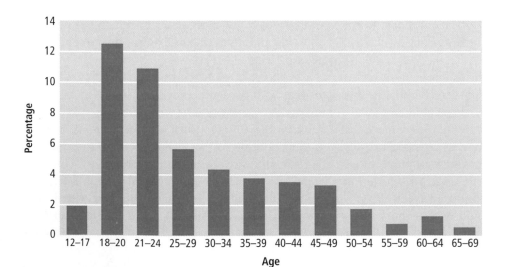

Figure 10.6

Prevalence of past-year alcohol dependence by age in the United States based on DSM-IV criteria.

Source: NIAAA 2001–2002 National Epidemiological Survey on Alcohol and Related Conditions (NESARC) data (18–60+ years of age) and Substance Abuse and Mental Administration (SAMHSA) 2003 National Survey on Drug Use and Health (NSDUH) (12–17 years of age).

adults are the most likely group to seek treatment for their problem.

Drinking among older adults presents a more complicated picture. Even older adults who drink only modest amounts may experience dangerous interactions with medications they may be taking. Additionally, they metabolize alcohol much more slowly, meaning it remains in the bloodstream longer. As a result, older adults are at higher risk for abusing alcohol if they simply continue habits of drinking from earlier points in their lives, even if their consumption when they were younger was only moderate. Diagnosing alcohol dependence in older women can be especially difficult given the higher likelihood that they live alone.

Treatment for substance abuse in all age groups focuses on three goals (Segal et al., 2010): stabilization and reduction of substance consumption, treatment of coexisting problems, and arrangement of appropriate social interventions. Which treatment approach works best depends on the age of the person in question (National Institute on Alcohol Abuse and Alcoholism, 2012). Younger adults respond best to short-term programs tailored specifically to them; traditional programs such as Alcoholics Anonymous are less effective. On college campuses, these programs target high-risk groups (e.g., fraternities, sororities, athletes) and focus on DUI prevention. Middle-aged adults respond to a variety of approaches, but individual differences are quite large, meaning it may be necessary to try several different treatments. Older adults often respond better to education programs rather than direct confrontation to reduce their denial of their problem and to make sure they understand the age-related changes in alcohol metabolism.

What substance abuse treatment options are available in your area? Complete the Discovering Development feature to find out.

DISCOVERING DEVELOPMENT:

WHAT SUBSTANCE ABUSE TREATMENT OPTIONS ARE AVAILABLE IN YOUR AREA?

One of the most controversial topics regarding substance abuse is how to deal with people who have the problem. If they use illicit drugs, should they be treated or jailed? If treatment is the choice, should they be placed in inpatient facilities or in outpatient programs? These decisions have become both political and sensitive. Many politicians built their careers on being perceived as "tough on drugs" and vote to curtail or eliminate treatment options for drug offenders. The rise of health management organizations resulted in the near elimination of inpatient treatment facilities in favor of the less expensive outpatient programs and community treatment centers.

An enlightening exercise is to find out what treatment options are available in your area for people who have substance abuse problems. Find out whether there are any inpatient programs, which outpatient programs and community treatment centers are available, and how long one has to wait to receive treatment. Also, find out the costs of the various programs and whether health insurance policies cover the treatments.

Gather the information from several geographic regions, and compare program availability. Think about what you would do if you were poor and needed help in your area. What do you think should be done to address the problem?

ADULT DEVELOPMENT IN ACTION

Find out which treatment options for anxiety disorders, psychoses, and substance abuse are available in your region.

SOCIAL POLICY IMPLICATIONS

As we have seen, dementia, especially Alzheimer's disease, takes a devastating toll on the people who have a form of it as well as their family and friends. A significant problem facing the United States (as well as many other countries) is the prospect of a dramatic increase in the number of people with dementia over the next few decades. The problem has many facets: the cost of caring for the individuals with dementia, the lost income and productivity of family care providers, and the lack of prospects for effective treatment or cure in the near future.

Estimates are that 4.7 million people in the United States had Alzheimer's disease in 2010 (Hebert, Weuve, Scherr, & Evans, 2013). This number is expected to nearly triple by 2050 to about

14 million, in large part to the aging of the baby boomers. The cost of care for these individuals will be staggering. The current model of funding cannot sustain this level of increase cost (discussed in Chapter 14).

Expecting family members to care for loved ones with dementia is not a good option either. Most adult child care providers and many spouse/partner care providers are still employed, and may not have employers that will provide flexible schedules or paid leave. Lost productivity to organizations due to parent/spouse/partner care is equivalent to billions of dollars each year. Many insurance plans do not cover behavioral or in-home care options.

The social policy implications of the coming wave of people who will develop dementia are clear. First, research funding aimed at finding an effective way to prevent or cure dementia is essential. Second, redesigning health care plans and service delivery to include behavioral and in-home care along with other more cost-effective alternatives needs to be undertaken. Third, ways for employers to provide support for parent/spouse/partner care need to be found.

The increase in the number of people with dementia is only one major aspect of the coming health care crisis resulting from the aging of the baby boomers. We revisit this issue in more detail in Chapter 14.

SUMMARY

10.1 Mental Health and the Adult Life Course

How are mental health and psychopathology defined?

- Definitions of mental health must reflect appropriate age-related criteria.
- Behaviors must be interpreted in context. Mentally healthy people have positive attitudes, accurate perceptions, environmental mastery, autonomy, personality balance, and personal growth.

What key areas are included in a multidimensional approach to assessment?

- Considering key biological, psychological, sociocultural, and life-cycle factors is essential for accurate diagnosis of mental disorders.
- Diagnostic criteria must reflect age differences in symptomatology.

Why are ethnicity and aging important variables to consider in understanding mental health?

- Little research has been done to examine ethnic differences in the definition of mental health and psychopathology in older adults.
- There is some evidence of different incidence rates across groups.

10.2 Developmental Issues in Assessment and Therapy

What are the key dimensions used for categorizing psychopathology?

- Accurate assessment depends on measuring functioning across a spectrum of areas, including medical, psychological, and social.

What factors influence the assessment of adults?

- Negative and positive biases can influence the accuracy of assessment.
- The environmental conditions that the assessment is made can influence its accuracy.

How are mental health issues assessed?

- Six assessment techniques are used most: interview, self-report, report by others, psychophysiological assessment, direct observation, and performance-based assessment.

What are some major considerations for therapy across adulthood?

- The two main approaches are medical therapy (usually involving drugs) and psychotherapy.
- With psychotherapy, clinicians must be sensitive to changes in the primary developmental issues faced by adults of different ages.
- Clear criteria have been established for determining "well established" and "probably efficacious" psychotherapies.

10.3 The Big Three: Depression, Delirium, and Dementia

What are the most common characteristics of people with depression? How is depression diagnosed? What causes depression? What is the relation between suicide and age? How is depression treated?

- The prevalence of depression declines with age. Gender and ethnic differences in rates have been noted.
- Common features of depression include dysphoria, apathy, self-deprecation, expressionlessness,

changes in arousal, withdrawal, and several physical symptoms. In addition, the problems must last at least 2 weeks, not be caused by another disease, and negatively affect daily living. Clear age differences exist in the reporting of symptoms. Some assessment scales are not sensitive to age differences in symptoms.

■ Possible biological causes of severe depression are neurotransmitter imbalance, abnormal brain functioning, or physical illness. Loss is the main psychosocial cause of depression. Internal belief systems also are important.

■ Three families of drugs (SSRIs, HCAs, and MAO inhibitors), electroconvulsive therapy, and various forms of psychotherapy are all used to treat depression. Older adults benefit most from behavior and cognitive therapies.

What is delirium? How is it assessed and treated?

■ Delirium is characterized by a disturbance of consciousness and a change in cognition that develop over a short period of time.

■ Delirium can be caused by a number of medical conditions, medication side effects, substance intoxication or withdrawal, exposure to toxins, or any combination of factors. Older adults are especially susceptible to delirium.

■ Most cases of delirium are cured, but some may be fatal.

What is dementia? What are the major symptoms of Alzheimer's disease? How is it diagnosed? What causes it? What intervention options are there? What are some other major forms of dementia? What do family members caring for patients with dementia experience?

■ Dementia is a family of disorders. Most older adults do not have dementia, but rates increase significantly with age.

■ Alzheimer's disease is a progressive, fatal disease diagnosed at autopsy through neurological changes that include neurofibrillary tangles and neuritic plaques.

■ Major symptoms of Alzheimer's disease include gradual and eventually pervasive memory loss, emotional changes, and eventual loss of motor functions.

■ Diagnosis of Alzheimer's disease consists of ruling out all other possible causes of the symptoms. This involves thorough physical, neurological, and neuropsychological exams.

■ Current research suggests Alzheimer's disease may be genetic, perhaps with an autosomal dominant inheritance pattern, although other hypotheses have been proposed. Much research focuses on beta-amyloid and tau proteins.

■ Although no cure for Alzheimer's disease is available, interventions to relieve symptoms are advisable and possible, including various drug and behavioral interventions. Dealing with declining functioning is especially difficult. Respite and adult day care are two options for care providers.

■ Vascular dementia is caused by several small strokes. Changes in behavior depend on where in the brain the strokes occur.

■ Characteristic symptoms of Parkinson's disease include tremor and problems with walking, along with decreases in the ability to smell. Treatment is done with drugs. Some people with Parkinson's disease develop dementia.

■ Huntington's disease is a genetic disorder that usually begins in middle age with motor and behavioral problems.

■ Alcoholic dementia (Wernicke-Korsakoff syndrome) is caused by a thiamine deficiency.

■ AIDS dementia complex results from a by-product of HIV. Symptoms include a range of cognitive and motor impairments.

10.4 Other Mental Disorders and Concerns

What are the symptoms of anxiety disorders? How are they treated?

■ Anxiety disorders include panic, phobia, and obsessive–compulsive problems. Symptoms include a variety of physical changes that interfere with normal functioning. Context is important in understanding symptoms. Both drugs and psychotherapy are used to treat anxiety disorders.

What are the characteristics of people with psychotic disorders?

■ Psychotic disorders involve personality disintegration and loss of touch with reality. One major form is schizophrenia; hallucinations and delusions are the primary symptoms.

■ Schizophrenia is a severe thought disorder with an onset usually before age 45, but it can begin in late life. People with early-onset schizophrenia often improve over time as neurotransmitters become more balanced. Treatment usually consists of drugs; psychotherapy alone is not often effective.

What are the major issues involved with substance abuse?

- With the exception of alcohol, the substances most likely to be abused vary with age; younger adults are more likely to abuse illicit substances, whereas older adults are more likely to abuse prescription and over-the-counter medications.
- Alcohol dependency declines with age from its highest rates in young adulthood. Older adults take longer to withdraw, but similar therapies are effective in all age groups.

REVIEW QUESTIONS

10.1 Mental Health and the Adult Life Course

- How do definitions of mental health vary with age?
- What are the implications of adopting a multidimensional model for interpreting and diagnosing mental disorders?
- Why are ethnicity and gender important considerations in understanding mental health?

10.2 Developmental Issues in Assessment and Therapy

- What is multidimensional assessment? How is it done?
- What major factors affect the accuracy of clinical assessment?
- How do the developmental forces influence assessment?
- What are the main developmental issues clinicians must consider in selecting therapy?

10.3 The Big Three: Depression, Delirium, and Dementia

- How does the rate of depression vary with age, gender, and ethnicity?
- What symptoms are associated with depression? How do they vary with age?
- What biological causes of depression have been proposed? How are they related to therapy?
- How is loss associated with depression?
- What treatments for depression have been developed? How well do they work with older adults?

- What is delirium? What causes it? Why are older adults more susceptible?
- What is Alzheimer's disease? How is it diagnosed?
- What causes Alzheimer's disease? What interventions are available?
- What other types of dementia have been identified? What are their characteristics?

10.4 Other Mental Disorders and Concerns

- What symptoms are associated with anxiety disorders? How are anxiety disorders treated?
- What are psychoses? What are their major symptoms? What treatments are most effective for schizophrenia?
- What developmental differences have been noted regarding substance abuse? How is alcohol dependency defined

INTEGRATING CONCEPTS IN DEVELOPMENT

- Why is it so difficult to diagnose mental disorders in older adults? What concepts from Chapters 3 and 4 provide major reasons?
- Why do you think people with Alzheimer's disease might experience hallucinations and delusions?
- Why is there a connection between depression and dementia?
- What would studying people with Alzheimer's disease tell us about normal memory changes with age?

KEY TERMS

Alzheimer's disease An irreversible form of dementia characterized by progressive declines in cognitive and bodily functions, eventually resulting in death; it accounts for about 70% of all cases of dementia.

Autosomal dominant inheritance patterns A genetic inheritance pattern that requires only one gene from either one's mother or father in order to cause a trait or condition to develop.

behavior therapy A type of psychotherapy that focuses on and attempts to alter current behavior. Underlying causes of the problem may not be addressed.

beta-amyloid A type of protein involved in the formation of neuritic plaques both in normal aging and in Alzheimer's disease.

beta-amyloid cascade hypothesis The process that beta-amyloid deposits create neuritic plaques, that in turn lead to neurofibrillary tangles, that cause neuronal death and, when this occurs severely enough, Alzheimer's disease.

cognitive behavior therapy A type of psychotherapy aimed at altering the way people think as a cure for some forms of psychopathology, especially depression.

delirium A disorder characterized by a disturbance of consciousness and a change in cognition that develop over a short period of time.

dementia A family of diseases characterized by cognitive decline. Alzheimer's disease is the most common form.

dysphoria Feeling down or blue, marked by extreme sadness; the major symptom of depression.

mental status exam A short screening test that assesses mental competence, usually used as a brief indicator of dementia or other serious cognitive impairment.

spaced retrieval A behavioral, implicit-internal memory intervention used in early- and middle-stage dementia.

sundowning The phenomenon when people with Alzheimer's disease show an increase in symptoms later in the day.

vascular dementia A form of dementia caused by a series of small strokes.

RESOURCES

Access quizzes, glossaries, flashcards, and more at www.cengagebrain.com.

CHAPTER 11

RELATIONSHIPS

11.1 RELATIONSHIP TYPES AND ISSUES
Friendships • Love Relationships • *How Do We Know?: Patterns and Universals of Romantic Attachment Around the World* • Violence in Relationships

11.2 LIFESTYLES AND LOVE RELATIONSHIPS
Singlehood • Cohabitation • Gay and Lesbian Couples • Marriage • Divorce • *Current Controversies: Do Marriage Education Programs Work?* • Remarriage • Widowhood

11.3 FAMILY DYNAMICS AND THE LIFE COURSE
The Parental Role • Midlife Issues: Adult Children and Caring for Aging Parents • *Discovering Development: Caring for Aging Parents* • Grandparenthood

SOCIAL POLICY IMPLICATIONS
Summary • Review Questions • Integrating Concepts in Development • Key Terms • Resources

BARACK AND MICHELLE OBAMA ARE, BY NEARLY EVERY MEASURE, A SUCCESSFUL COUPLE.

Elected president at age 47, Barack Obama is supported by his wife, Michelle, who herself is a successful professional. Their relationship provides them the grounding necessary to support each other. Neither of them could have achieved what they have without the help of many friends.

Barack's and Michelle's experiences reflect some of the key aspects of relationships we examine in this chapter. First, we consider friendships and love relationships and how they change across adulthood. Because love relationships usually involve a couple, we will explore how two people find each other and marry and how marriages develop. We also consider singlehood, divorce, remarriage, and widowhood. Finally, we take up some of the important roles associated with personal relationships, including parenting, family roles, and grandparenting.

Ron Sachs-Pool/Getty Images

President Barack and Michelle Obama

11.1 Relationship Types and Issues

LEARNING OBJECTIVES

- What role do friends play across adulthood?
- What characterizes love relationships? How do they vary across cultures?
- What are abusive relationships? What characterizes elder abuse, neglect, and exploitation?

Jamal and Kahlid have known each other all their lives. They grew up together in New York, attended the same schools, and even married sisters. Their business careers took them in different directions, but they and their families always got together on major holidays. Now as older men, they feel a special bond; many of their other friends have died.

Having other people in our lives we can count on is essential to our well-being. Just imagine how difficult life would be if you were totally alone, without even a Facebook "friend" to communicate with. In this section, we consider the different types of relationships we have with other people, and learn how these relationships help—and sometimes hurt us.

Friendships

Jamal and Kahlid remind us some of the most important people in our lives are our friends. They are often the people to whom we are closest, and are there when we need someone to lean on.

What is an adult friend? Someone who is there when you need to share? Someone that's not afraid to tell you the truth? Someone you have fun with? Friends, of course, are all of these and more. Researchers define friendship as a mutual relationship in which those involved influence one another's behaviors and beliefs, and define friendship quality as the satisfaction derived from the relationship (Blieszner & Roberto, 2012; Flynn, 2007).

Friends are a source of support throughout adulthood (Arnett, 2007). Friendships are predominantly based on feelings and grounded in reciprocity and choice. Friendships are different from love relationships mainly because friendships are less emotionally intense and usually do not involve sex (Blieszner & Roberto, 2012). Having good friendships boosts self-esteem (Bagwell et al., 2005) and happiness (Demir, 2010). Friendships also help us become socialized into new roles throughout adulthood.

Friendship in Adulthood. From a developmental perspective, adult friendships can be viewed as having identifiable stages (Levinger, 1980, 1983): Acquaintanceship, Buildup, Continuation, Deterioration, and Ending. This ABCDE model describes the stages of friendships and how they change. Whether a friendship develops from Acquaintanceship to Buildup depends on where the individuals fall on several dimensions, such as the basis of the attraction, what each person knows about the other, how good the communication is between the partners, the perceived importance of the friendship, and so on. Although many friendships reach the Deterioration stage, whether a friendship ultimately ends depends heavily on the availability of alternative relationships. If potential friends appear, old friendships may end; if not, they may continue even though they are no longer considered important by either person.

Longitudinal research shows how friendships change across adulthood, some in ways that are predictable and others not. As you probably have experienced, life transitions (e.g., going away to college, getting married) usually result in fewer friends and less contact with the friends you keep (Blieszner & Roberto, 2012). People tend to have more friends and acquaintances during young adulthood than at any subsequent period (Sherman, de Vrics, & Lansford, 2000). Friendships are important throughout adulthood, in part because a person's life satisfaction is strongly related to the quantity and quality of contacts with friends. College students with strong friendship networks adjust better to stressful life events whether those networks are face-to-face (e.g., Brissette, Scheier, & Carver, 2002) or through online social networks (DeAndrea, Ellison, LaRose, Steinfield, & Fiore, 2012).

The importance of maintaining contacts with friends cuts across ethnic lines as well. People who have friendships that cross ethnic groups have more positive attitudes toward people with different backgrounds (Aberson, Shoemaker, & Tomolillo, 2004). Thus, regardless of one's background, friendships play a major role in determining how much we enjoy life.

The quality and purpose of late-life friendships are particularly important (Bromell & Cagney, in press; Schulz & Morycz, 2013). Having friends provides a buffer against the losses of roles and status that accompany old age, such as retirement or the death of a loved one, and can increase people's happiness and self-esteem (Schulz & Morycz, 2013). People who live alone especially benefit from friends in the neighborhood (Bromell & Cagney, in press).

Why does friendship have such positive benefits for us? Although scientists do not know for certain, they are gaining insights through neuroscience research. Coan and colleagues (Beckes & Coan, 2013a; Beckes, Coan, & Hasselmo, in press; Coan, 2008) have found being faced with threatening situations results in different brain processing if faced alone or with a close friend. Specifically, neuroimaging showed definitively the parts of the brain that respond to threat operate when facing threat alone but do not when facing the same threat with a close friend. It is becoming clear a close friendship literally changes the way the brain functions, resulting in our perception of feeling safer and the trials we face are more manageable with friends than without them.

Patterns of friendship among older adults tend to mirror those in young adulthood (Rawlins, 2004). Older women have more numerous and intimate friendships than older men do. Men's friendships, like women's, evolve over time and become important sources of support in late life (Adams & Ueno, 2006).

Three broad themes characterize both traditional (e.g., face-to-face) and new forms (e.g., online) of adult friendships (de Vries, 1996; Ridings & Gefen, 2004):

- The affective or emotional basis of friendship refers to self-disclosure and expressions of intimacy, appreciation, affection, and support, and all are based on trust, loyalty, and commitment.

- The shared or communal nature of friendship reflects how friends participate in or support activities of mutual interest.

- The sociability and compatibility dimension represents how our friends keep us entertained and are sources of amusement, fun, and recreation.

In the case of online friendships (e.g., through social media), trust develops on the basis of four sources: (1) reputation; (2) performance, or what users do online; (3) precommitment, through personal self-disclosure; and (4) situational factors, especially the premium placed on intimacy and the relationship (Henderson & Gilding, 2004). Not surprisingly, online social network friendships develop much like face-to-face ones in that the more time people spend online with friends the more likely they are to self-disclose (Chang & Hsiao, in press). Online environments are more conducive to people who are lonely (e.g., live alone), which makes them potentially important for older adults (Cotton, Anderson, & McCullough, 2013).

A special type of friendship exists with one's siblings, who are the friends people typically have the longest and that share the closest bonds; the importance of these relationships varies with age (Carr & Moorman, 2011; Moorman & Greenfield, 2010). The centrality of siblings in later life depends on several things, such as proximity, health, and degree of relatedness (full, step-, or half-siblings). No clear pattern of emotional closeness emerges when viewing sibling relationships on the basis of gender.

Developmental Aspects of Friendships and Socioemotional Selectivity.

Why are friends important to older adults? Some researchers believe one reason may be older adults' not wanting to become burdens to their families (Blieszner & Roberto, 2012; Moorman & Greenfield, 2010). As a result, friends help each other foster independence.

Older adults tend to have fewer relationships with people in general and develop fewer new relationships than people do in midlife and particularly in young adulthood (Carr & Moorman, 2011). Carstensen and colleagues (Carstensen, 2006; Charles & Carstensen, 2010; Reed & Carstensen, 2012) have shown the changes in social behavior seen in late life reflect a more complicated and important process. *They propose a life-span theory of socioemotional selectivity, that argues social contact is motivated by a variety of goals, including information seeking, self-concept, and emotional regulation.*

Each of these goals is differentially salient at different points of the adult life span and results in different social behaviors. When information seeking is the goal, such as when a person is exploring the world trying to figure out how he or she fits, what others are like, and so forth, meeting many new people is an essential part of the process. However, when emotional regulation is the goal, people become highly selective in their choice of social partners and nearly always prefer people who are familiar to them.

Carstensen and colleagues believe information seeking is the predominant goal for young adults, emotional regulation is the major goal for older people, and both goals are in balance in midlife. Their research supports this view; people become increasingly selective in whom they choose to have contact with. Additionally, Magai (2008) summarizes several approaches to emotional development across adulthood and concludes people orient more toward emotional aspects of life and personal relationships as they grow older and emotional expression and experience become more complex and nuanced. Carstensen's theory provides a complete explanation of why older adults tend not to replace, to any great extent, the relationships they lose: Older adults are more selective and have fewer opportunities to make new friends, especially in view of the emotional bonds involved in friendships.

Men's, Women's, and Cross-Sex Friendships.

Men's and women's friendships tend to differ in adulthood, reflecting continuity in the learned behaviors from childhood (Levine, 2009). Women base their friendships on more intimate and emotional sharing and use friendship as a means to confide in others. For women, getting together with friends often takes the form of getting together to discuss personal matters. Confiding in others is a basis of women's friendships. In contrast, men base friendships on shared activities or interests.

What about friendships between men and women? These friendships have a beneficial effect, especially for men (Piquet, 2007). Cross-sex friendships help men have lower levels of dating anxiety and higher capacity for intimacy. These patterns hold across ethnic groups, too. Cross-sex friendships can also prove troublesome because of misperceptions. Some research shows men overestimate and women underestimate their friends' sexual interest in them (Koenig, Kirkpatrick, & Ketelaar, 2007). Maintaining cross-sex friendships once individuals enter into exclusive dating relationships, marriage, or committed relationships is difficult, and often results in one partner feeling jealous (Williams, 2005).

Love Relationships

Love is one of those things everybody feels but nobody can define completely. (Test yourself: Can you explain fully what you mean when you look at someone special and say, "I love you"?) One way researchers try to understand love is to think about what components are essential. In an interesting series of studies, Sternberg (2006) found love has three basic components: (1) *passion*, an intense physiological desire for someone; (2) *intimacy*, the feeling that you can share all your thoughts and actions with another; and (3) *commitment*, the willingness to stay with a person through good and bad times. Ideally, a true love relationship has all three components; when couples have equivalent amounts of love and types of love, they tend to be happier; the balance among these components often shifts as time passes.

Love Through Adulthood. The different combinations of love help us understand how relationships develop (Sternberg, 2006). Research shows the development of romantic relationships is a complex process influenced by relationships in childhood and adolescence (Collins & van Dulmen, 2006). Early in a romantic relationship, passion is usually high whereas intimacy and commitment tend to be low. This is infatuation: an intense, physically based relationship when the two people have a high risk of misunderstanding and jealousy. Indeed, it is sometimes difficult to establish the boundaries between casual sex and hook-ups and dating in young adulthood (Giordano et al., 2012).

Infatuation is short-lived. As passion fades, either a relationship acquires emotional intimacy or it is likely to end. Trust, honesty, openness, and acceptance must be a part of any strong relationship; when they are present, romantic love develops.

This pattern is a good thing. Research shows people who select a partner for a more permanent relationship (e.g., marriage) during the height of infatuation are more likely to divorce (Hansen, 2006). If the couple spends more time and works at their relationship, they may become committed to each other.

Lemieux and Hale (2002) demonstrated these developmental trends hold in romantically involved couples between 17 and 75 years of age. As the length of the relationship increases, intimacy and passion decrease but commitment increases.

Falling in Love. In his book *The Prophet*, Kahlil Gibran points out love is two-sided: Just as it can give you great ecstasy, so can it cause you great pain. Yet most of us are willing to take the risk. As you may have experienced, taking the risk is fun (at times) and difficult (at other times).

The best explanation of the process is the theory of **assortative mating,** *that states people find partners based on their similarity to each other.* Assortative mating occurs along many dimensions, including education, religious beliefs, physical traits, age, socioeconomic status, intelligence, and political ideology, among others (Blossfeld, 2009). Such nonrandom mating occurs most often in Western societies that allow people to have more control over their own dating and pairing behaviors. Common activities are one basis for identifying potential mates, except, that is, in speed dating situations. In that case, it comes down to physical attractiveness (Luo & Zhang, 2009).

People meet people in all sorts of places. Does the location where people meet influence the likelihood they will "click" on particular dimensions and form a couple? Kalmijn and Flap (2001) found that it does. Using data from more than 1,500 couples, they found meeting at school was most likely to result in the most forms of *homogamy*—the degree to which people are similar. Not surprisingly, the pool of available people to meet is strongly shaped by the opportunities available, that in turn constrain the type of people one is likely to meet.

Speed dating provides a way to meet several people in a short period of time. Speed dating is practiced most by young adults (Fein & Schneider, 2013; Whitty & Buchanan, 2009). The rules governing

Speed dating is becoming a popular way to meet people and find something out about them quickly.

Chris Hondros/Getty Images

partner selection during a speed dating session seem quite similar to traditional dating: physically attractive people, outgoing and self-assured people, and moderately self-focused people are selected more often and their dates are rated as smoother (Eastwick, Saigal, & Finkel, 2010).

The popularity of online dating means an increasing number of people meet this way (Fein & Schneider, 2013; Whitty & Buchanan, 2009). Surveys indicate nearly 1 in every 5 couples in the United States meet online (compared with 1 in 10 in Australia, and 1 in 20 in Spain and the United Kingdom; Dutton et al., 2009). Emerging research indicates virtual dating sites offer both problems and possibilities, especially in terms of the accuracy of personal descriptions. Like in the offline world, physical attractiveness strongly influences initial selections online (Sritharan et al., 2010). Many couples have met and formed committed relationships via online sites (Mazzarella, 2007).

One increasing trend among emerging adults is the hookup culture of casual sex, often without even knowing the name of one's sexual partner (Garcia, Reiber, Massey, & Merriwether, 2013). Research indicates both men and women are interested in having hookup sex, but also prefer a more romantic relationship over the long run. However, the perception there are no strings attached to hookup sex appear wrong, as nearly three-fourths of both men and women eventually expressed some level of regret at having hookup sex.

How does couple-forming behavior compare cross-culturally? As described in the Spotlight on Research feature, Schmitt and his team of colleagues (2004) studied 62 cultural regions. They showed secure romantic attachment was the norm in nearly 80% of cultures and "preoccupied" romantic attachment was particularly common in East Asian cultures. In general, multicultural studies show there are global patterns in mate selection and romantic relationships. The romantic attachment profiles of individual nations were correlated with sociocultural indicators in ways that supported evolutionary theories of romantic attachment and basic human mating strategies.

HOW DO WE KNOW?:

PATTERNS AND UNIVERSALS OF ROMANTIC ATTACHMENT AROUND THE WORLD

Who were the investigators and what was the aim of the study? One's attachment style may have a major influence on how one forms romantic relationships. In order to test this hypothesis, David Schmitt (2004) assembled a large international team of researchers.

How did the investigators measure the topic of interest? Great care was taken to ensure equivalent translation of the survey across the 62 cultural regions included. The survey was a two-dimension four-category measure of adult romantic attachment (the Relationship Questionnaire) that measured models of self and others relative to each other: secure romantic attachment (high scores indicate positive models of self and others), dismissing romantic attachment (high scores indicate a positive model of self and a negative model of others), preoccupied romantic attachment (high scores indicate a negative model of self and a positive model of others), and fearful romantic attachment (high scores indicate negative models of self and others). An overall score of model of self is computed by adding together the secure and dismissing scores and subtracting the combination of preoccupied and fearful scores. The overall model of others score is computed by adding together the secure and preoccupied scores and subtracting the combination of dismissing and fearful scores.

Additionally, there were measures of self-esteem, personality traits, and sociocultural correlates of romantic attachment (e.g., fertility rate, national profiles of individualism versus collectivism).

Who were the participants in the study? A total of 17,804 people (7,432 men and 10,372 women) from 62 cultural regions around the world took part in the study. Such large and diverse samples are unusual in developmental research.

What was the design of the study? Data for this cross-sectional, nonexperimental study were gathered by research teams in each country. The principal researchers asked the research collaborators to administer a nine-page survey to the participants that took 20 minutes to complete.

Were there ethical concerns with the study? Because the study involved volunteers, there were no ethical concerns. However, ensuring all participants' rights were protected was a challenge because of the number of countries and cultures involved.

What were the results? The researchers first demonstrated the model of self and others measures were valid across cultural regions, that provided general support for the independence of measures (i.e., they measure different things). Specific analyses showed 79% of the cultural groups studied demonstrated secure romantic attachments, but North American cultures tended to be dismissive and East Asian cultures tended to be high on preoccupied romantic attachment. These patterns are shown in Figure 11.1. Note all the cultural regions except East Asia showed the pattern of model of self scores higher than model of others scores.

What did the investigators conclude? Overall, Schmitt and colleagues concluded although the same attachment pattern holds across most cultures, no one pattern holds across all of them. East Asian cultures in particular tend to fit a pattern in which people report others do not get as emotionally close as the respondent would like, and respondents find it difficult to trust others or to depend on them.

Figure 11.1

In research across 10 global regions, note that only in East Asian cultures were the "model of others" scores higher than the "model of self" scores.

Source: Data from Schmitt et al. (2004).

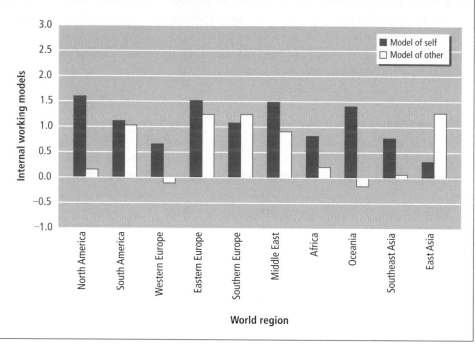

Culture is a powerful force in shaping mate selection choices. Specifically, across 48 different cultures globally, people from cultures that have good health care, education, and resources, and permit young adults to choose their own mates tend to develop more secure romantic attachments than do people from cultures without these characteristics (Schmitt et al., 2009).

Cultural norms are sometimes highly resistant to change. Loyalty of the individual to the family is an important value in India, so despite many changes in mate selection, about 95% of marriages in India are carefully arranged to ensure an appropriate mate is selected (Dommaraju, 2010). Similarly, Islamic societies use matchmaking as a way to preserve family consistency and continuity and ensure couples follow the prohibition on premarital relationships between men and women (Adler, 2001). Matchmaking in these societies occurs both through family connections and

personal advertisements in newspapers. To keep up with the Internet age, Muslim matchmaking has gone online too (Lo & Aziz, 2009).

Violence in Relationships

Up to this point, we have been considering relationships that are healthy and positive. Sadly, this is not always the case. *Sometimes relationships become violent; one person becomes aggressive toward the partner, creating an* **abusive relationship**. Such relationships have received increasing attention since the early 1980s, when the U.S. criminal justice system ruled that, under some circumstances, abusive relationships can be used as an explanation for one's behavior (Walker, 1984). *For example,* **battered woman syndrome** *occurs when a woman believes she cannot leave the abusive situation and may even go so far as to kill her abuser.*

Being female, Latina, African American, having an atypical family structure (something other than two biological parents), having more romantic partners, early onset of sexual activity, and being a victim of child abuse predicts victimization. Although overall national rates of sexual assault have declined more than 60% since the early 1990s, acquaintance rape or date rape is still a major problem; college women are 4 times more likely to be the victim of sexual assault than are women in other age groups (Rape, Abuse, and Incest National Network, 2013), with 40% experiencing abuse in a dating relationship (DatingAbuseStopsHere.com, 2013).

What range of aggressive behaviors occurs in abusive relationships? What causes such abuse? Based on considerable research on abusive partners, O'Leary (1993) argues there is a continuum of aggressive behaviors toward a partner, and progresses as follows: verbally aggressive behaviors, physically aggressive behaviors, severe physically aggressive behaviors, and murder (see Table 11.1). The causes of the abuse also vary with the type of abusive behavior being expressed.

Two points about the continuum should be noted. First, there may be fundamental differences in the types of aggression independent of level of severity. Overall, each year about 5 million women and 3 million men experience partner-related physical assaults and rape in the United States (Centers for Disease Control and Prevention, 2012h); worldwide, between 10% and 69% of women report being physically assaulted or raped (World Health Organization, 2002).

The second point, depicted in the table, is the suspected underlying causes of aggressive behaviors differ as the type of aggressive behaviors change (O'Leary, 1993). Although anger and hostility in the perpetrator are associated with various forms of physical abuse, the exact nature of this relationship remains elusive (Norlander & Eckhardt, 2005).

Men are also the victims of violence from intimate partners, though at a rate about one-third that of women (Conradi & Geffner, 2009). Studies in

Table 11.1

CONTINUUM OF PROGRESSIVE BEHAVIORS IN ABUSIVE RELATIONSHIPS

Verbal aggression → Physical aggression → Severe aggression → Murder

Insults	Pushing	Beating
Yelling	Slapping	Punching
Name-calling	Shoving	Hitting with object

Causes
Need to control*
Misuse of power*
Jealousy*
Marital discord

Accept violence as a means of control
Modeling of physical aggression
Abused as a child
Aggressive personality styles
Alcohol abuse

Personality disorders
Emotional lability
Poor self-esteem

Contributing factors: job stresses and unemployment

Note: Need to control and other variables on the left are associated with all forms of aggression; acceptance of violence and other variables in the middle are associated with physical aggression, severe aggression, and murder. Personality disorders and the variables on the right are associated with severe aggression and murder.

* More relevant for males than for females.

Source: O'Leary, K. D. (1993). Through a psychological lens: Personality traits, personality disorders, and levels of violence. In R. J. Gelles & D. R. Loseke (Eds.), Current Controversies on Family Violence (pp. 7–30). Copyright © 1993 by Sage Publications. Reprinted by permission of the publisher.

New Zealand and the United States revealed both men and women showed similar patterns of holding traditional gendered beliefs, and lacking communication and anger management skills; however, intervention programs tend to focus on male perpetrators (Hines & Douglas, 2009; Robertson & Murachver, 2007). Research in Canada showed heterosexual couples reported more instances of violence than did gay or lesbian couples (Barrett & St. Pierre, 2013).

Culture is also an important contextual factor in understanding partner abuse. In particular, violence against women worldwide reflects cultural traditions, beliefs, and values of patriarchal societies; this can be seen in the commonplace violent practices against women that include sexual slavery, female genital cutting, intimate partner violence, and honor killing (Parrot & Cummings, 2006).

Additionally, international data indicate rates of abuse are higher in cultures that emphasize female purity, male status, and family honor. A common cause of women's murders in Arab countries is brothers or other male relatives killing the victim because she violated the family's honor (Kulwicki, 2002). Intimate partner violence is prevalent in China (43% lifetime risk in one study) and has strong associations with male patriarchal values and conflict resolutions (Xu et al., 2005).

Alarmed by the seriousness of abuse, many communities established shelters for battered women and their children as well as programs that treat abusive men. However, the legal system in many localities is still not set up to deal with domestic violence; women in some locations cannot sue their husbands for assault, and restraining orders all too often offer little real protection from additional violence. Much remains to be done to protect women and their children from the fear and the reality of continued abuse.

Elder Abuse, Neglect, and Exploitation. Although elder abuse, neglect, and exploitation are difficult to define precisely, several categories are commonly used (National Center on Elder Abuse, 2013):

- *Physical abuse:* the use of physical force that may result in bodily injury, physical pain, or impairment

- *Sexual abuse:* nonconsensual sexual contact of any kind

- *Emotional or psychological abuse:* infliction of anguish, pain, or distress

- *Financial or material exploitation:* the illegal or improper use of an older adult's funds, property, or assets

- *Abandonment:* the desertion of an older adult by an individual who had physical custody or otherwise assumed responsibility for providing care for the older adult

- *Neglect:* refusal or failure to fulfill any part of a person's obligation or duties to an older adult

- *Self-neglect:* the behaviors of an older person that threaten his or her own health or safety, excluding those conscious and voluntary decisions by a mentally competent and healthy adult

Researchers estimate perhaps 1 in 4 vulnerable older adults are at risk for some type of abuse, neglect, or exploitation (Cooper, Selwood, & Livingston, 2008; Nerenberg, 2010). Unfortunately, only a small proportion of these cases are actually reported to authorities; of the ones that are, neglect is the most common type. If you suspect an older adult is a victim of elder abuse, neglect, or exploitation, the best thing to do is to contact your local adult protective services office and report it.

ADULT DEVELOPMENT IN ACTION

As a couples therapist, what do you need to know about global friendship and mating patterns?

11.2 Lifestyles and Love Relationships

LEARNING OBJECTIVES

- What are the challenges and advantages of being single?
- Why do people cohabit?
- What are gay male and lesbian relationships like?
- What is marriage like across adulthood?
- Why do people divorce?
- Why do people remarry?
- What are the experiences of widows and widowers?

Bobbie and Jack were high school sweethearts who married a few years after World War II. Despite many trials in their relationship, they have remained firmly committed to each other for more than 60 years. Not only are they still in love, but they are best friends. In looking back, they note that once their children moved away they grew closer again. Bobbie and Jack wonder whether this is typical.

Bobbie and Jack show us forging relationships is only part of the picture in understanding how adults live their lives with other people. For most, one relationship becomes special and results in commitment, typically through marriage. Putting relationships in context is the goal of this section as we explore the major lifestyles of adults. First, we consider people who never get married. Next, we look at those who cohabit and those who are in same-sex relationships. We also consider couples who get married and those who divorce and remarry. Finally, we discuss people who are widowed.

Singlehood

Many men and women are single—defined as not living with an intimate partner—at more than one point in adulthood. In this section, we focus most on young adult singles; elsewhere we return to singlehood in the context of divorce or the death of a spouse/partner.

What's it like to be a single young adult in the United States? It's tougher than you might think. DePaulo (2006) points out numerous stereotypes and biases against single people. Her research found young adults characterized married people as caring, kind, and giving about 50% of the time compared with only 2% for single people. DePaulo also found rental agents preferred married couples 60% of the time (Morris, Sinclair, & DePaulo, 2007).

Many women and men remain single as young adults to focus on establishing their careers rather than marriage or relationships that most do later. Others report they simply did not meet "the right person" or prefer singlehood (Ibrahim & Hassan, 2009). However, the pressure to marry is especially strong for women.

Men remain single longer in young adulthood because they marry at a later age than women (U.S. Census Bureau, 2010a). Fewer men than women remain unmarried throughout adulthood, though, mainly because men find partners more easily as they select from a larger age range of unmarried women.

Ethnic differences in singlehood reflect differences in age at marriage as well as social factors. Nearly twice as many African Americans are single during young adulthood as European Americans, and more are choosing to remain so (U.S. Census Bureau, 2010b). Singlehood is also increasing among Latinos, in part because the average age of Latinos in the United States is lower than other ethnic groups and in part because of poor economic opportunities for many Latinos (Lamanna & Riedmann, 2003).

Globally, the meanings and implications of remaining single are often tied to strongly held cultural and religious beliefs. Muslim women who remain single in Malaysia speak in terms of *jodoh* (the soul mate one finds through fate at a time appointed by God) as a reason; they believe God simply has not decided to have them meet their mate at this time (Ibrahim & Hassan, 2009). But because the role of Malaysian women is to marry, they also understand their marginalized position in society through their singlehood. In Southeast Asia, the number of single adults has increased steadily as education levels rose over the past several decades (Hull, 2009). However, family systems in these cultures have not yet adapted to these changing lifestyle patterns (Jones, 2010).

An important distinction is between adults who are temporarily single (i.e., those who are single only until they find a suitable marriage partner) and those who choose to remain single. For most singles, the decision to never marry is a gradual one. This transition is represented by a change in self-attributed status that occurs over time and is associated with a cultural timetable for marriage. It marks the experience of "becoming single" that occurs when an individual identifies more with singlehood than with marriage (Davies, 2003).

Cohabitation

Being unmarried does not necessarily mean living alone. *People in committed, intimate, sexual relationships but who are not married may decide living together, or* **cohabitation,** *provides a way to share daily life.* Cohabitation is becoming an increasingly popular lifestyle choice in the United States as well as in Canada, Europe, Australia, and elsewhere. Cohabitation in the United States has increased 10-fold over the past three decades: from 523,000 in 1970 to 5.5 million in 2002, the most recent year extensive data were collected (Goodwin, Mosher, & Chandra, 2010). People with lower educational levels cohabit more, and do so in more relationships, than individuals with higher educational levels. European American, African American, and Latino men and women cohabit at about the same rates, other factors being equal.

Couples cohabit for three main reasons, most often in connection with testing their relationship in the context of potential marriage, but also for convenience and as an alternative to marriage (Rhoades, Stanley, & Markman, 2009).

The global picture differs by culture (Popenoe, 2009; Therborn, 2010). In most European, South American, and Caribbean countries, cohabitation is a common alternative to marriage for young adults. Cohabitation is extremely common in the Netherlands, Norway, and Sweden, where this lifestyle is part of the culture; 99% of married couples in Sweden lived together before they married and nearly one in four couples are not legally married. Decisions to marry in these countries are typically made to legalize the relationship after children are born—in contrast to Americans, who marry to confirm their love and commitment to each other.

Interestingly, having cohabitated does not seem to make marriages any better; in fact, it may do more harm than good, resulting in lower quality marriages (Tach & Halpern-Meekin, 2009). These findings reflect two underlying issues: couples who have children while cohabiting, especially for European American women (as compared with African American and Latina women; Tach & Halpern-Meekin, 2009), and couples who are using cohabitation to test their relationship (Rhoades et al., 2009) are most likely to report subsequent problems.

Longitudinal studies find few differences in couples' behavior after living together for many years regardless of whether they married without cohabiting, cohabited then married, or simply cohabited (Stafford, Kline, & Rankin, 2004). Additionally, many countries extend the same rights and benefits to cohabiting couples as they do to married couples, and have done so for many years. Argentina provides pension rights to cohabiting partners, Canada extends insurance benefits, and Australia has laws governing the disposition of property when cohabiting couples sever their relationship (Neft & Levine, 1997).

Gay and Lesbian Couples

Less is known about the developmental course of gay and lesbian relationships than heterosexual relationships (Rothblum, 2009). What is it like to be in a gay or lesbian relationship?

For the most part, the relationships of gay and lesbian couples have many similarities to those of heterosexual couples (Kurdek, 2004). Most gay and lesbian couples are in dual-earner relationships, much like the majority of married heterosexual couples, and are likely to share household chores. However, gay and lesbian couples differ from heterosexual couples in the degree to which both partners are similar on demographic characteristics such as race, age, and education; gay and lesbian couples tend to be more dissimilar (Schwartz & Graf, 2009).

Research indicates committed gay and lesbian couples have most of the same characteristics as committed heterosexual couples.

© Andrew Lever/Shutterstock.com

Gay men, like heterosexual men, separate love and sex and have more short-term relationships (Missildine et al., 2005); both lesbian and heterosexual women are more likely to connect sex and emotional intimacy in fewer, longer-lasting relationships. Lesbians tend to make a commitment and cohabit faster than heterosexual couples (Ganiron, 2007).

Gay and lesbian couples report receiving less support from family members than either married or cohabiting couples (Rothblum, 2009). At a societal level, marriage or civil unions between same-sex couples remains highly controversial in America, with several states passing constitutional amendments or statutes defining marriage as between a man and a woman. The lack of legal recognition for gay and lesbian relationships in the United States also means certain rights and privileges, such as marriage, certain insurance benefits, and hospital visitation rights, are not always granted. Although the legal status of gay and lesbian couples is changing in more countries (most notably in Scandinavia), and a few states in the United States (including New York), most countries and states in the United States do not provide them with the same legal rights as married couples.

Marriage

Most adults want their love relationships to result in marriage. However, U.S. residents are in less of a hurry to achieve this goal; the median age at first marriage for adults in the United States has been rising for several decades. As shown in Figure 11.2, between 1970 and 2010, the median age for first marriage rose roughly 4 years for both men and women (U.S. Census Bureau, 2013a).

What Is a Successful Marriage and What Predicts It? You undoubtedly know couples who appear to have a successful marriage. But what does that mean, really? *Minnotte (2010) differentiates* **marital success,** *an umbrella term referring to any marital outcome (such as divorce rate),* **marital quality,** *a subjective evaluation of the couple's relationship on a number of different dimensions,* **marital adjustment,** *the degree spouses accommodate each other over a certain period of time,* *and* **marital satisfaction,** *a global assessment of one's marriage.* Each of these provides a unique insight into the workings of a marriage.

Marriages, like other relationships, differ from one another, but some important predictors of future success can be identified. One key factor is age. In general, the younger the partners are, the lower the odds the marriage will last—especially when the people are in their teens or early 20s (U.S. Census Bureau, 2013b). Other reasons that increase or decrease the likelihood a marriage will last include financial security and pregnancy at the time of the marriage.

A second important predictor of successful marriage is **homogamy,** *or the similarity of values and interests a couple shares.* As we saw in relation to choosing a mate,

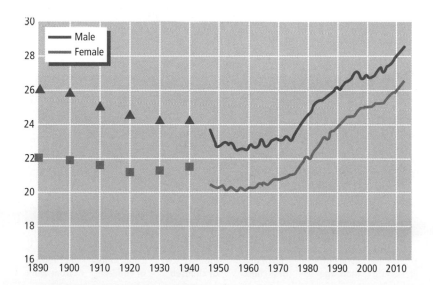

Figure 11.2

Note the median age at first marriage has been increasing for many years during the 20th and early 21st centuries.

Source: U.S Census Bureau, Current Population Survey, Annual Social and Economic Supplements, 1947–2012. Data for years prior to 1947 are from decennial censuses. http://www.census.gov/hhes /families/data/marital.html

the extent the partners share similar age, values, goals, attitudes (especially the desire for children), socioeconomic status, certain behaviors (such as drinking alcohol), and ethnic background increases the likelihood their relationship will succeed (Kippen, Chapman, & Yu, 2009).

A third factor in predicting marital success is a feeling the relationship is equal. *According to exchange theory, marriage is based on each partner contributing something to the relationship the other would be hard-pressed to provide.* Satisfying and happy marriages result when both partners perceive there is a fair exchange, or equity, in all the dimensions of the relationship. Problems achieving equity arise because of the competing demands of work and family, an issue we take up again in Chapter 12.

Cross-cultural research supports these factors. Couples in the United States and Iran (Asoodeh et al., 2010; Hall, 2006; McKenzie, 2003) say trust, consulting each other, honesty, making joint decisions, and commitment make the difference between a successful marriage and an unsuccessful marriage. Couples for whom religion is important also point to commonly held faith.

Do Married Couples Stay Happy? Few sights are happier than a couple on their wedding day. Newlyweds, like Kevin and Beth in the vignette, are at the peak of marital bliss. The beliefs people bring into a marriage influence how satisfied they will be as the marriage develops. But as you may have experienced, feelings change over time, sometimes getting better and stronger, sometimes not.

Research shows for most couples, overall marital satisfaction is highest at the beginning of the marriage, falls until the children begin leaving home, and rises again in later life; this pattern holds for both married and never-married cohabiting couples with children (see Figure 11.3; Hansen, Moum, & Shapiro, 2007). However, for some couples, satisfaction never rebounds and remains low; in essence, they have become emotionally divorced.

The pattern of a particular marriage over the years is determined by the nature of the dependence of each spouse on the other. When dependence is mutual and about equal and both people hold similar values that form the basis for their commitment to each other, the marriage is strong and close (Givertz, Segrin, & Hanzal, 2009). When the dependence of one partner is much higher than that of the other, however, the marriage is likely to be characterized by stress and conflict. Learning how to deal with these changes is the secret to long and happy marriages.

The fact marital satisfaction has a general downward trend but varies widely across couples led Karney and Bradbury (1995) to propose a vulnerability–stress–adaptation model of marriage, depicted in Figure 11.4. *The* **vulnerability–stress–adaptation model** *sees marital quality as a dynamic process resulting from the couple's ability to handle stressful events in the context of their particular vulnerabilities and resources.* As a couple's ability to adapt to stressful situations gets better over time, the quality of the marriage will probably improve. How well couples adapt to various stresses on the relationship determines whether

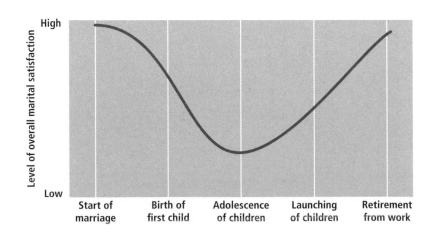

Figure 11.3

Marital satisfaction is highest early on and in later life, dropping during the child-raising years.

Source: Kail, R., & Cavanaugh, J.C. (2010). Human Development: A Life-Span View (5th ed., p. 412). Belmont, CA: Wadsworth.

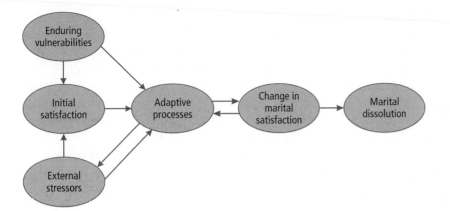

Figure 11.4
The vulnerability-stress-adaptation model shows how adapting to vulnerabilities and stress can result in either adaptation or dissolution of the marriage.

Source: From "Keeping marriages healthy, and why it's so difficult," by B. R. Karney.

the marriage continues or they get divorced. Let's see how this works over time.

Setting the Stage: The Early Years of Marriage.

Marriages are most intense in their early days. Discussing financial matters honestly is key since many newly married couples experience their first serious marital stresses around money issues (Parkman, 2007). How tough issues early in the marriage are handled sets the stage for the years ahead.

Early in a marriage, the couple must learn to adjust to the different perceptions and expectations each person has for the other. Research indicates men and women both recognize and admit when problems occur in their marriage (Moynehan & Adams, 2007). The couple must also learn to handle confrontation and resolve conflicts.

Early in a marriage, couples have global adoration for their spouse regarding the spouse's qualities (Karney, 2010; Neff & Karney, 2005). For wives, but not for husbands, more accurate specific perceptions of what their spouses are really like were associated with more supportive behaviors, feelings of control in the marriage, and a decreased risk of divorce. Couples who are happiest in the early stage of their marriage focus on the good aspects, not the annoyances; nit-picking and nagging do not bode well for long-term wedded bliss (Karney, 2010).

As time goes on and stresses increase, marital satisfaction declines (Lamanna & Riedmann, 2003). For most couples, the primary reason for this drop is having children (Jokela et al., 2009). It's not just a matter of having a child. The temperament of the child matters, with fussier babies creating more marital problems

(Greving, 2007; Meijer & van den Wittenboer, 2007). Parenthood also means having substantially less time to devote to the marriage. Both African American and European American couples report an increase in conflict after the birth of their first child (Crohan, 1996).

However, using the birth of a child as the explanation for the drop in marital satisfaction is much too simplistic, because child-free couples also experience a decline in marital satisfaction (Hansen et al., 2007). Longitudinal research indicates disillusionment—as demonstrated by a decline in feeling in love, in demonstrations of affection, and in the feeling that one's spouse is responsive, as well as an increase in feelings of ambivalence—is a key predictor of marital dissatisfaction (Huston et al., 2001).

During the early years of their marriage, many couples may spend significant amounts of time apart, especially in the military (Fincham & Beach, 2010). Spouses that serve in combat areas on active duty assignment who suffer from post-traumatic stress disorder (PTSD) are particularly vulnerable, since they are at greater risk for other spouse-directed aggression.

What the non-deployed spouse believes turns out to be important. If the non-deployed spouse believes the deployment will have negative effects on the marriage, then problems are much more likely. In contrast, if the non-deployed spouse believes such challenges make the relationship stronger, then they typically can do so (Renshaw, Rodrigues, & Jones, 2008). Research indicates the effects of deployment may be greater on wives than husbands; divorce rates for women service members who are deployed is higher than for their male counterparts (Karney & Crown, 2007).

Marriage at Midlife. For most couples marital satisfaction improves after the children leave, a state called the empty nest. Midlife brings both challenges and opportunities for marriages (Karasu & Karasu, 2005). Some use the launching of children to rediscover each other, and marital satisfaction rebounds.

For some middle-aged couples, however, marital satisfaction continues to be low. *They may have grown apart but continue to live together, a situation sometimes referred to as* **married singles** (Lamanna & Riedmann, 2011). In essence, they become emotionally divorced and live more as housemates than as a married couple; for these couples, spending more time together is not a welcome change. Research shows marital dissatisfaction in midlife is a process that develops over a long period of time and is not spontaneous (Rokach, Cohen, & Dreman, 2004). Later in this chapter we explore the squeeze many midlife couples feel as they continue to provide support for (grown) children and assume more support and care providing responsibility for aging parents (Igarashi, Hooker, Coehlo, & Manoogian, 2013).

Older Couples. Marital satisfaction is fairly high in older couples, who describe their partner in more positive terms than do middle-aged married partners (Henry, Berg, Smith, & Florsheim, 2007). However, satisfaction in long-term marriages—that is, marriages of 40 years or more—is a complex issue. In general, marital satisfaction among older couples increases shortly after retirement but then decreases with health problems and advancing age, and is directly related to the level of perceived support each partner receives (Landis, Peter-Wright, Martin, & Bodenmann, 2013). The level of satisfaction in these marriages appears to be unrelated to the amount of past or present sexual interest or sexual activity, but it is positively related to the degree of social engagement such as interaction with friends (Bennett, 2005). In keeping with the married-singles concept, many older couples have simply developed detached, contented styles (Connidis, 2001; Lamanna & Riedmann, 2003).

Older married couples show several specific characteristics (O'Rourke & Cappeliez, 2005). Many older couples show a selective memory regarding the occurrence of negative events and perceptions of their partner. Older couples have a reduced potential for marital conflict and greater potential for pleasure, are more likely to be similar in terms of mental and physical health, and show fewer gender differences in sources of pleasure. In short, older married couples developed adaptive ways to avoid conflict and grown more alike. In general, marital satisfaction among older couples remains high until health problems begin to interfere with the relationship (Connidis, 2001).

Being married in late life has several benefits. A study of 9,333 European Americans, African Americans, and Latino Americans showed marriage helps people deal better with chronic illness, functional problems, and disabilities (Pienta, Hayward, & Jenkins, 2000). Although the division of household chores becomes more egalitarian after the husband retires than it was when the husband was employed, irrespective of whether the wife was working outside the home, women still do more than half of the work (Kulik, 2011).

Caring for a Spouse/Partner. When couples pledge their love to each other "in sickness and in health," most envision the sickness part to be no worse than an illness lasting a few weeks. That may be the case for many couples, but for some the illness they experience severely tests their pledge.

Francine and Ron is one such couple. After 42 years of mainly good times together, Ron was diagnosed as having Alzheimer's disease. When first contacted by staff at the local chapter of a caregiver support organization, Francine had cared for Ron for 6 years. "At times it's very hard, especially when he looks at me and doesn't have any idea who I am. Imagine, after all these years, not to recognize me. But I love him, and I know that he would do the same for me. But, to be perfectly honest, we're not the same couple we once were. We're just not as close; I guess we really can't be."

Francine and Ron are typical of couples in which one partner cares for the other. Caring for a chronically ill partner presents different challenges than caring for a chronically ill parent. The partner caregiver assumes the new role after decades of shared responsibilities. Often without warning, the division of labor that worked for years must be readjusted. Such change inevitably puts stress on the relationship (Haley, 2013). This is especially true when one's spouse/partner has a debilitating chronic disease.

Studies of spousal caregivers of persons with Alzheimer's disease show marital satisfaction is much lower than for healthy couples (Cavanaugh & Kinney, 1994; Cohen, 2013; Haley, 2013). Spousal caregivers report a loss of companionship and intimacy over the course of caregiving, but also more rewards than adult child caregivers (Raschick & Ingersoll-Dayton, 2004). Marital satisfaction is an important predictor of spousal caregivers' reports of depressive symptoms; the better the perceived quality of the marriage, the fewer symptoms caregivers report (Kinney et al., 1993), a finding that holds across European American and African American spousal caregivers (Parker, 2008).

Most partner caregivers adopt the caregiver role out of necessity. Although evidence about the mediating role of caregivers' appraisal of stressors is unclear, interventions that improve the functional level of the ill partner generally improve the caregiving partner's situation (Van Den Wijngaart, Vernooij-Dassen, & Felling, 2007).

The importance of feeling competent as a partner caregiver fits with the docility component of the competence–environmental press model presented in Chapter 5. Caregivers attempt to balance their perceived competence with the environmental demands of caregiving. Perceived competence allows them to be proactive rather than merely reactive (and docile), that gives them a better chance to optimize their situation.

Even in the best of committed relationships, providing full-time care for a partner is both stressful and rewarding in terms of the marital relationship (Baek, 2005; Chen, 2013; Haley, 2013). Coping with a wife who may not remember her husband's name, acts strangely, and has a chronic and fatal disease presents serious challenges even to the happiest of couples. Yet even in that situation, the caregiving husband may experience no change in marital happiness despite the changes in his wife due to the disease.

Divorce

Despite what couples pledge on their wedding day, many marriages do not last until death parts them; instead, marriages are dissolved through divorce. Most couples enter marriage with the idea their relationship will be permanent. Rather than growing together, though, many couples grow apart.

Who Gets Divorced and Why? Divorce in the United States is common, and the divorce rate is substantially higher than in many other countries around the world; as you can see in Figure 11.5, couples have roughly a 50–50 chance of remaining married for life (National Center for Health Statistics, 2013a). In contrast, the ratio of divorces to marriages in Japan, Italy, and Spain are substantially lower as are rates in Africa and Asia (United Nations, 2008). However, divorce rates in nearly every developed country increased over the past several decades.

Of those marriages ending in divorce, African American and Asian American couples tended to be married longer at the time of divorce than European American couples, and ethnically mixed marriages are at greater risk (National Center for Health Statistics,

Figure 11.5

The United States has one of the highest divorce rates in the world.

Source: U.S. Bureau of Labor Statistics, updated and revised from "Families and Work in Transition in 12 Countries, 1980–2001," Monthly Labor Review, September 2003, with unpublished data. http://www.bls.gov/opub/mlr/2003/09/art1full.pdf

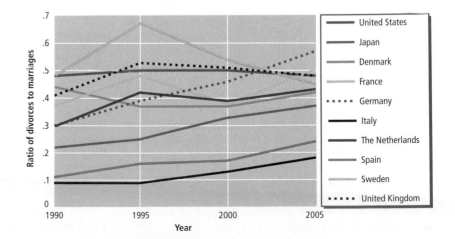

2013a). People with higher levels of education tend to have lower rates of divorce (Cherlin, 2013).

Why people divorce has been the focus of much research. Although how couples manage conflict is important, there is more to it than that (Fincham, 2003).

Gottman and Levenson (2004) developed two models that predicted divorce early (within the first 7 years of marriage) and later (when the first child reaches age 14) with 93% accuracy over the 14-year period of their study. Negative emotions displayed during conflict between the couple predicted early divorce, but not later divorce. In general, this reflects a pattern of wife-demand–husband-withdraw (Christensen, 1990) in which, during conflict, the wife places a demand on her husband, who then withdraws either emotionally or physically. In contrast, the lack of positive emotions in a discussion of events-of-the-day and during conflict predicted later divorce, but not early divorce. An example would be a wife talking excitedly about a project she had just been given at work and her husband showing disinterest. Such "unrequited" interest and excitement in discussions likely carries over to the rest of the relationship.

Gottman's research is important because it clearly shows how couples show emotion is critical to marital success. Couples who divorce earlier typically do so because of high levels of negative feelings such as contempt, criticism, defensiveness, and stonewalling experienced as a result of intense marital conflict. But for many couples, such intense conflict is generally absent. Although this makes it easier to stay in a marriage longer, the absence of positive emotions eventually takes its toll and results in later divorce. For a marriage to last, people need to be told they are loved and what they do and feel really matters to their partner.

But we must be cautious about applying Gottman's model to all married couples. Kim, Capaldi, and Crosby (2007) reported in lower-income high-risk couples, the variables Gottman says predict early divorce did not hold for that sample. For older, long-term married couples, the perception of the spouse's support is the most important predictor of remaining married (Landis et al., 2013).

The high divorce rate in the United States and the reasons typically cited for getting divorced have sparked a controversial approach to keeping couples together, termed *covenant marriage*, that makes divorce much harder to obtain. Other proposals, such as the Healthy Marriage Initiative supported by the Heritage Foundation, raise similar issues. Will they work? That remains to be seen, as discussed in the Current Controversies feature.

CURRENT CONTROVERSIES:

DO MARRIAGE EDUCATION PROGRAMS WORK?

As a way to combat high divorce rates, the U.S. government created the Healthy Marriage Initiative in the Department of Health and Human Services for promotion of healthy marriages and fatherhood. These in turn resulted in the National Healthy Marriage Center and the National Center for Family and Marriage Research. Research related to these initiatives focused on the positive aspects of marriage and on the need to do a better job with marriage education (Fincham & Beach, 2010).

The Healthy Marriage Initiative is an example of marriage education, *an approach based on the idea that the more couples are prepared for marriage, the better the relationship will survive over the long run.* More than 40 states have initiated some type of education program. Do they work?

Most marriage education programs focus on communication between the couple. In addition to government or other publicly sponsored programs, several religious denominations have marriage education programs; the Catholic's Pre-Cana program is one example.

There are numerous challenges to more extensive community-based marriage education programs. In some cases the education programs were originally developed to address poverty (Administration for Children and Families, 2010). Many couples cohabit and are less likely to attend marriage education programs, even though there is little evidence that cohabitation improves communication skills between the couple (Fincham & Beach, 2010). As a result, versions of marriage education programs are being adapted for these situations. Additionally, programs timed at key transition points (e.g., engagement) have also been developed (Halford et al., 2008).

Research to date shows these skills-based education programs have modest but consistently positive effects on marital quality and communication (Cowan, Cowan, & Knox, 2010; Fincham & Beach, 2010), and helps maintain relationship satisfaction during marriage (Halford & Bodenmann, 2013).

These positive outcomes are resulting in a broadening of the approaches used by marriage educators to topics beyond communication. How these programs develop, and whether more couples will participate, remains to be seen. What does appear to be the case is if couples agree to participate in a marriage education program, they may well lower their risk for problems later on.

Effects of Divorce on the Couple. Divorce takes a high toll on the couple. Unlike the situation when one's spouse dies, divorce often means the person's ex-spouse is present to provide a reminder of the failure. As a result, divorced people are typically unhappy in general, at least for a while. Especially because of the financial effects of divorce, the effects can even be traced to future generations due to long-term negative consequences on education (Amato & Cheadle, 2005). Divorced people suffer negative health consequences as well (Lamela, Figueiredo, & Bastos, in press).

Divorced people sometimes find the transition difficult; researchers refer to these problems as "divorce hangover" (Walther, 1991). Divorce hangover reflects divorced partners' inability to let go, develop new friendships, or reorient themselves as single parents. Forgiving the ex-spouse is also important for eventual adjustment postdivorce (Rye et al., 2004). Both low preoccupation and forgiveness may be indicators ex-spouses are able to move on with their lives.

Divorce in middle age or late life has some special characteristics. If women initiate the divorce, they report self-focused growth and optimism; if they did not initiate the divorce, they tend to ruminate and feel vulnerable. Many middle-aged women who divorce also face significant financial challenges if their primary source of income was the ex-husband's earnings (Sakraida, 2005).

Remarriage

The trauma of divorce does not deter people from beginning new relationships that often lead to another marriage. Typically, men and women both wait about 3.5 years before they remarry (National Center for Health Statistics, 2013a). However, remarriage rates vary somewhat across ethnic groups. African Americans remarry a bit more slowly than other ethnic groups.

Although women are more likely to initiate a divorce, they are less likely to remarry unless they are

Remarriage is common for both men and women.

Digital Vision/Getty Images

poor (National Center for, 2013a). However, women in general benefit more from remarriage than do men, particularly if they have children (Ozawa & Yoon, 2002). Although many people believe divorced individuals should wait before remarrying to avoid the so-called "rebound effect," there is no evidence those who remarry sooner have less success in remarriage than those who wait longer (Wolfinger, 2007).

Remarriage options for older adults after either divorce or the death of a spouse are often more constrained. In some cases, widows may lose financial benefits from pensions or other retirement plans if they remarry. This problem exists for widows across cultures; in Namibia widows are constrained in their options and typically must depend on others (Thomas, 2008). Adult children may voice strong opposition to their parent remarrying that can put sufficient pressure on the parent that they remain single.

Adapting to new relationships in remarriage is stressful. Partners may have unresolved issues from the previous marriage that may interfere with satisfaction with the new marriage (Faber, 2004). The effects of remarriage on children is positive, at least for young adult children who report a positive effect on their own intimate relationships as an effect of their parent(s) remarrying happily (Yu & Adler-Baeder, 2007).

Widowhood

Alma still feels the loss of her husband, Chuck. "There are lots of times when I feel him around. We were together for so long that you take it for granted that your husband is just there. And there are times when I just don't want to go on without him. But I suppose I'll get through it."

Like Alma and Chuck, virtually all older married couples see their marriages end because one partner dies. For most people, the death of a partner is one of the most traumatic events they experience, causing an increased risk of death among older European Americans (but not African Americans), an effect that lasts several years (Moorman & Greenfield, 2010). An extensive study of widowed adults in Scotland showed the increased likelihood of dying lasted for at least 10 years (Boyle, Feng, & Raab, 2011). Despite the stress of losing one's partner, most widowed older adults manage to cope reasonably well (Moorman & Greenfield, 2010).

Women are much more likely to be widowed than are men. More than half of all women over age 65 are widows, but only 15% of men the same age are widowers. Women have longer life expectancies and typically marry men older than themselves. Consequently, the average married woman can expect to live at least 10 years as a widow.

The impact of widowhood goes well beyond the ending of a long-term partnership (Boyle et al., 2011; Guiaux, 2010). Loneliness is a major problem. Widowed people may be left alone by family and friends who do not know how to deal with a bereaved person. As a result, widows and widowers may lose not only a partner, but also those friends and family who feel uncomfortable with including a single person rather than a couple in social functions (Guiaux, 2010). Feelings of loss do not dissipate quickly, as the case of Alma shows clearly. Men and women react differently to widowhood. In general, those who were most dependent on their partners during the marriage report the highest increase in self-esteem in widowhood because they learned to do the tasks formerly done by their partners (Carr, 2004). Widowers may recover more slowly unless they have strong social support systems (Bennett, 2010). Widows often suffer more financially because survivor's benefits are usually only half of their husband's pensions (Weaver, 2010). For many women, widowhood results in difficult financial circumstances, particularly regarding medical expenses (McGarry & Schoeni, 2005).

For many reasons, including the need for companionship and financial security, some widowed people cohabit or remarry. A newer variation on re-partnering is "living alone together," an arrangement where two older adults form a romantic relationship but maintain separate living arrangements (Moorman & Greenfield, 2010). Re-partnering in widowhood can be difficult because of family objections (e.g., resistance from children), objective limitations (decreased mobility, poorer health, poorer finances), absence of incentives common to younger ages (desire for children), and social pressures to protect one's estate (Moorman & Greenfield, 2010).

ADULT DEVELOPMENT IN ACTION

As a marital therapist, how would you use data on factors that predict divorce?

11.3 Family Dynamics and the Life Course

LEARNING OBJECTIVES

- What is it like to be a parent? What are the key issues across ethnic groups? What forms of parenting are there? How does parenting develop across adulthood?
- How do middle-aged adults interact with their children? How do they deal with the possibility of providing care to aging parents?
- How do grandparents interact with their grandchildren? What key issues are involved?

*Susan is a 42-year-old married woman with two preadolescent children. **She is an only child.** Her mother, Esther, is a 67-year-old widow and has been showing signs of dementia. Esther has little money and Susan's family is* *barely making ends meet. Susan knows her mother cannot live alone much longer, and she feels she should have her move in with their family. Susan feels she has an obligation to provide care but also feels torn between her mother and her family and job. Susan wonders what to do.*

Increasingly, families face the dilemma confronting Susan. As more people live long lives, the need for families to deal with health problems in their older members is on the rise.

In this section, we consider the dynamics of families, from deciding whether to have children through caring for aging parents and grandparenthood. As we do so, we must recognize the concept of "family" is undergoing change.

The Parental Role

For one thing, the birth of a child transforms a couple (or a single parent) into a family. *The most common form of family in Western societies is the* nuclear family, *consisting only of parent(s) and child(ren). The most common family form around the world is the* extended family, *in which grandparents and other relatives live with parents and children.*

Deciding Whether to Have Children. One of the biggest decisions couples (and many singles) make is whether to have children. This decision appears complicated. You would think potential parents must weigh the many benefits of child rearing with the many

drawbacks. But apparently, this is not what most people actually do.

Rijken (2009) reports potential parents actually don't think deliberately or deeply about when to have a child, and those who are career oriented or like their freedom do not often deliberately postpone parenthood because of those factors. Rather, thoughts about having children do not cross their minds until they are ready to begin thinking about having children. Whether the pregnancy is planned or not (and more than half of all U.S. pregnancies are unplanned), a couple's first pregnancy is a milestone event in a relationship, with both benefits and costs (Greving, 2007; Meijer & van den Wittenboer, 2007). Parents largely agree children add affection, improve family ties, and give parents a feeling of immortality and sense of accomplishment. Most parents willingly sacrifice a great deal for their children and hope they grow up to be happy and successful. In this way, children bring happiness to their parents (Angeles, 2010).

Nevertheless, finances are of great concern to most parents because children are expensive. How expensive? According to Lido (2012), a typical family who had a child in 2011 would spend about $206,000 for food, shelter, and other necessities by the time the child turns 17. College expenses would be an additional expense. These costs do not differ significantly between two-parent and single-parent households but clearly are a bigger financial burden for single parents. Take a look at Figure 11.6 and see where the money goes.

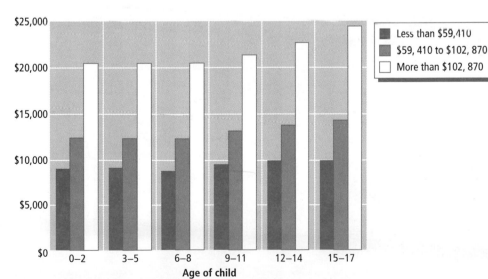

¹U.S. average for the younger child in husband-wife families with two children.

Figure 11.6

Family expenditures on a child, by income level and age of child, 2011.

USDA Expenditures on Children by Families, 2011, United States Department of Agriculture, Center for Nutrition Policy and Promotion, Miscellaneous Publication Number 1528–2011, p. 10, Figure 1

For many reasons that include personal choice, financial instability, and infertility, an increasing number of couples are child-free. Social attitudes in many countries (Austria, Germany, Great Britain, Ireland, Netherlands, and United States) are improving toward child-free couples (Gubernskaya, 2010). Couples without children also have some advantages: higher marital satisfaction, more freedom, and higher standards of living.

Today, couples in the United States typically have fewer children and have their first child later than in the past. The average age at the time of the birth of a woman's first child is nearly 25.5 (National Center for Health Statistics, 2013b). This average age has been increasing steadily since 1970 as a result of two major trends: Many women postpone children because they are marrying later, they want to establish careers, or they make a choice to delay childbearing. Nearly 41% of mothers are unmarried.

Being older at the birth of one's first child is advantageous. Older mothers are more at ease being parents, spend more time with their babies, and are more affectionate, sensitive, and supportive to them (Berlin, Brady-Smith, and Brooks-Gunn, 2002). The age of the father also makes a difference in how he interacts with children (Palkovitz & Palm, 2009). Compared to men who become fathers in their 20s, men who become fathers in their 30s are generally more invested in their paternal role and spend up to 3 times as much time caring for their preschool children as younger fathers do. Father involvement has increased significantly, due in part to social attitudes that support it (Fogarty & Evans, 2010).

Ethnic Diversity and Parenting. Ethnic background matters a great deal in terms of family structure and the parent–child relationship. African American husbands are more likely than their European American counterparts to help with household chores, regardless of their wives' employment status (Dixon, 2009). Overall, most African American parents provide a cohesive, loving environment that often exists within a context of strong religious beliefs (Anderson, 2007; Dixon, 2009), pride in cultural heritage, self-respect, and cooperation with the family (Brissett-Chapman & Issacs-Shockley, 1997).

As a result of several generations of oppression, many Native American parents have lost traditional cultural parenting skills: Children were valued, women were considered sacred and honored, and men cared for and provided for their families (Witko, 2006).

Nearly 25% of all children under 18 in the United States are Latino, and most are at least second generation (National Center for Health Statistics, 2013b).

Family ties are important in many cultures, with some placing more emphasis on the family than on individuals.

Among two-parent families, Mexican American mothers and fathers both tend to adopt similar authoritative behaviors toward their preschool children (Gamble, Ramakumar, & Diaz, 2007).

Latino families demonstrate two key values: familism and the extended family. Familism *refers to the idea the well-being of the family takes precedence over the concerns of individual family members.* This value is a defining characteristic of Latino families; Brazilian and Mexican families consider familism a cultural strength (Carlo et al., 2007; Lucero-Liu, 2007). Indeed, familism account for the significantly higher trend for Latino college students to live at home (Desmond & López Turley, 2009). The extended family is also strong among Latino families and serves as the venue for a wide range of exchanges of goods and services, such as child care and financial support (Almeida et al., 2009).

Asian Americans also value familism (Meyer, 2007) and place an even higher value on extended family. Other key values include obtaining good grades in school, maintaining discipline, being concerned about what others think, and conformity. Asian American adolescents report high feelings of obligation to their families compared with European American adolescents (Kiang & Fuligni, 2009). In general, males enjoy higher status in traditional Asian families (Tsuno & Homma, 2009).

Raising multi-ethnic children presents challenges not experienced by parents of same-race children. Parents of biracial children report feeling discrimination and they are targets of prejudicial behavior from others (Hubbard, 2010; Kilson & Ladd, 2009). These parents also worry their children may be rejected by members of both racial communities.

Single Parents. The proportion of births to unwed mothers in the United States is at an all-time high, now nearly 41% (National Center for Health Statistics, 2013b). Rates vary by ethnic group. More than 70% of births to African American mothers, more than 50% of births to Latina mothers, and nearly 30% of births to European American mothers are to unmarried women.

Many divorced single parents report complex feelings such as frustration, failure, guilt, and a need to be overindulgent. Loneliness can be especially difficult to deal with (Anderson et al., 2004). Separation anxiety is a common and strong feeling among military parents who are about to be deployed (Roper, 2007).

Single parents, regardless of gender, face considerable obstacles. Financially, they are usually much less well-off than their married counterparts. Integrating the roles of work and parenthood are more difficult. Single mothers are hardest hit, mainly because women typically are paid less than men.

One particular concern for many divorced single parents is dating. Single parents often feel insecure about sexuality and how they should behave around their children in terms of having partners stay overnight (Lampkin-Hunter, 2010).

Step-, Foster-, Adoptive, and Same-Sex Couple Parenting. Roughly one third of North American couples become stepparents or foster or adoptive parents some time during their lives. In general, there are few differences among parents who have their own biological children or who become parents in some other way, but there are some unique challenges (McKay & Ross, 2010).

A big issue for foster parents, adoptive parents, and stepparents is how strongly the child will bond with them. Although infants less than 1 year old probably bond well, children who are old enough to have formed attachments with their biological parents may have competing loyalties. As a result, the dynamics in blended families can best be understood as a complex system (Dupuis, 2010). These problems are a major reason second marriages are at high risk for dissolution, as discussed later in this chapter. They are also a major reason why behavioral and emotional problems are more common among stepchildren (Crohn, 2006).

Still, many stepparents and stepchildren ultimately develop good relationships with each other. Allowing stepchildren to develop a relationship with the stepparent at their own pace also helps. What style of stepparenting ultimately develops is influenced by the expectations of the stepparent, stepchild, spouse, and nonresidential parent (Crohn, 2006).

Adoptive parents also contend with attachment to birth parents, but in different ways. Adopted children may wish to locate and meet their birth parents. Such searches can strain the relationships between these children and their adoptive parents who may interpret these actions as a form of rejection (Curtis & Pearson, 2010).

Families with children adopted from another culture pose challenges of how to establish and maintain connection with the child's culture of origin (Yngvesson, 2010). For mothers of transracially adopted Chinese and Korean children, becoming connected to the appropriate Asian American community is a way to accomplish this (Johnston et al., 2007). Research in the Netherlands found children adopted from Columbia, Sri Lanka, and Korea into Dutch homes struggled with looking different, and many expressed desires to be white (Juffer, 2006).

Foster parents have the most tenuous relationship with their children because the bond can be broken for any of a number of reasons having nothing to do with the quality of the care being provided. Dealing with attachment is difficult; foster parents want to provide secure homes, but they may not have the children long enough to establish continuity. Furthermore, because many children in foster care have been unable to form attachments at all, they are less likely to form ones will inevitably be broken. Despite the challenges, placement in good foster care results in the development of attachment between foster parents and children who were placed out of institutional settings (Smyke et al., 2010).

Finally, many gay men and lesbian women also want to be parents. Some have biological children themselves, whereas others choose adoption or foster parenting (Braun, 2007; Goldberg, 2009). Although gay men and lesbian women make good parents, they often experience resistance to their having children (Clifford, Hertz, & Doskow, 2010); Some states in the United States have laws preventing gay and lesbian couples from adopting. Actually, research indicates children reared by gay or lesbian parents do not experience any more problems than children reared by heterosexual parents and are as psychologically healthy as children of heterosexual parents (Biblarz & Savci, 2010). Evidence shows gay parents have more egalitarian sharing of child rearing than do fathers in heterosexual households (Biblarz & Savci, 2010).

Midlife Issues: Adult Children and Caring for Aging Parents

Middle-aged family members, such as the current generation of baby boomers, serve as the links between their aging parents and their own maturing children (Fingerman, Pillemer, Silverstein, & Suitor, 2012; Hareven, 2001). *Middle-aged mothers (more than fathers) tend to take on this role of* kinkeeper, *the person who gathers family members together for celebrations and keeps them in touch with each other.*

Think about the major issues confronting a typical middle-aged couple: maintaining a good marriage, parenting responsibilities, dealing with children who are becoming adults themselves, handling job pressures, and worrying about aging parents, just to name a few. Middle-aged adults truly have a lot to deal with every day in balancing their responsibilities to their children and their aging parents (Riley & Bowen, 2005). *Indeed, middle aged adults are sometimes referred to as the* sandwich generation *because they are caught between the competing demands of two generations: their parents and their children.*

Letting Go: Middle-Aged Adults and Their Children.
Sometime during middle age, most parents experience two positive developments with regard to their children (Buhl, 2008). Suddenly their children see them in a new light, and the children leave home.

The extent parents foster and approve of their children's attempts at being independent matters. Most parents manage the transition successfully (Owen, 2005). That's not to say parents are heartless. As depicted in the cartoon, when children leave home, emotional bonds are disrupted. Mothers in all ethnic groups report feeling sad at the time children leave, but have more positive feelings about the potential for growth in their relationships with their children (Feldman, 2010).

Still, parents provide considerable emotional support (by staying in touch) and financial help (such as paying college tuition, providing a free place to live until the child finds employment) when possible (Mitchell, 2006; Warner, Henderson-Wilson, & Andrew, 2010).

A positive experience with launching children is strongly influenced by the extent the parents perceive a job well done and their children have turned out well

Adult children often move back home when they have financial difficulties, such as was common in the Great Recession.

Ariel Skelley/Age Fotostock

(Mitchell, 2010). Children are regarded as successes when they meet parents' culturally based developmental expectations, and they are seen as "good kids" when there is agreement between parents and children in basic values.

Parents' satisfaction with the empty nest is sometimes short-lived. Roughly half of young adults in the United States return to their parents' home at least once after moving out (Osgood et al., 2005). There is evidence these young adults, called "boomerang kids" (Mitchell, 2006), reflect a less permanent, more mobile contemporary society.

Why do children move back? A major impetus is the increased costs of living on their own when saddled with college debt, especially if the societal economic situation is bad and jobs are not available. This was especially true during the Great Recession of the late 2000s and early 2010s.

Giving Back: Middle-Aged Adults and Their Aging Parents.
Most middle-aged adults have parents who are in reasonably good health. But for nearly a quarter of adults, being a child of aging parents involves providing some level of care (Feinberg, Reinhard, Houser, & Choula, 2011). How adult children become care providers varies a great deal from person to person,

but the job of caring for older parents usually falls to a daughter or a daughter-in-law (Barnett, 2013), and daughters also tend to coordinate care provided by multiple siblings (Friedman & Seltzer, 2010). In Japan, even though the oldest son is responsible for parental care, it is his wife who actually does the day-to-day caregiving for her own parents and her in-laws (Lee, 2010).

Most adult children feel a sense of responsibility, termed filial obligation, *to care for their parents if necessary.* Adult child care providers sometimes express the feeling they "owe it to Mom or Dad" to care for them; after all, their parents provided for them for many years, and now the shoe is on the other foot (Gans, 2007). Adult children often provide the majority of care when needed to their parents in all Western and non-Western cultures studied, but especially in Asian cultures (Barnett, 2013; Haley, 2013; Lai, 2010).

Roughly 50 million Americans provide unpaid care for older parents, in-laws, grandparents, and other older loved ones (National Alliance for Caregiving & AARP, 2010). The typical care provider is a 48-year-old woman who is employed outside the home and provides more than 20 hours per week of unpaid care. These family care providers spend an average of

$7,000 per year in support of their loved one (National Endowment for Financial Education, 2010).

Stresses and Rewards of Providing Care.

Providing care is a major source of both stress and reward. On the stress side, adult children and other family caregivers are especially vulnerable from two main sources (Pearlin et al., 1990):

- Adult children may have trouble coping with declines in their parents' functioning, especially those involving cognitive abilities and problematic behavior, and with work overload, burnout, and loss of the previous relationship with a parent.

- If the care situation is perceived as confining or seriously infringes on the adult child's other responsibilities (spouse, parent, employee, etc.), then the situation is likely to be perceived negatively, and that may lead to family or job conflicts, economic problems, loss of self-identity, and decreased competence.

When caring for an aging parent, even the most devoted adult child caregiver will at times feel depressed, resentful, angry, or guilty (Cavanaugh, 1999; Cohen, 2013; Haley, 2013). Many middle-aged care providers are hard pressed financially: They may still be paying child care or college tuition expenses, perhaps trying to save adequately for their own retirement, and having to work more than one job to do it. Financial pressures are especially serious for those caring for parents with chronic conditions, such as Alzheimer's disease, that require services, such as adult day care, not adequately covered by medical insurance even if the older parent has supplemental coverage. In some cases, adult children may need to quit their jobs to provide care if adequate alternatives, such as adult day care, are unavailable or unaffordable, usually creating even more financial stress.

The stresses of caring for a parent mean the caregiver needs to carefully monitor his or her own health. Indeed, many professionals point out caring for the care provider is an important consideration to avoid care provider burnout (Tamayo et al., 2010).

On the plus side, caring for an aging parent also has rewards. Caring for aging parents can bring parents and their adult children closer together and provide a way for adult children to feel they are giving back to their parents (Miller et al., 2008). Cross-cultural research examining Taiwanese (Lee, 2007) and Chinese (Zhan, 2006) participants confirms adults caring for aging parents can find the experience rewarding.

Cultural values enter into the care providing relationship in an indirect way (Knight & Sayegh, 2010). Care providers in all cultures studied to date show a common set of outcomes: Care providers' stressors are appraised as burdensome, that creates negative health consequences for the care provider. However, cultural values influence the kinds of social support available to the care provider.

Things aren't always rosy from the parents' perspective, either. Independence and autonomy are important traditional values in some ethnic groups, and their loss is not taken lightly. Older adults in these groups are more likely to express the desire to pay a professional for assistance rather than ask a family member for help; they may find it demeaning to live with their children and express strong feelings about "not wanting to burden them" (Cahill et al., 2009). Most move in only as a last resort. Many adults who receive help with daily activities feel negatively about the situation, although cultural norms supporting the acceptance of help, such as in Japanese culture, significantly lessen those feelings (Park, Kitayama, Karasawa, Curhan, Markus, Kawakami et al., 2013).

Determining whether older parents are satisfied with the help their children provide is a complex issue (Cahill et al., 2009; Park et al., 2013). Based on a critical review of the research, Newsom (1999) proposes a model of how certain aspects of care can produce negative perceptions of care directly or by affecting the interactions between care provider and care recipient (see Figure 11.7). The important thing to conclude from the model is even under the best circumstances, there is no guarantee the help adult children provide their parents will be well received. Misunderstandings can occur, and the frustration caregivers feel may be translated directly into negative interactions.

Understanding what resources are available to assist adult children who provide care for their parents is important. Take time and complete the Discovering Development feature to find out what is available in your local area.

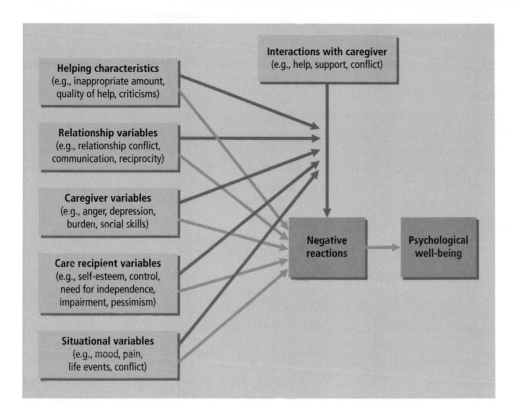

Figure 11.7
Whether a care recipient perceives care to be good depends on interactions with the care provider and whether those interactions are perceived negatively.

Source: From Newsom, J. T. (1999). Another side to caregiving: Negative reactions to being helped. Current Directions in Psychological Science, 8, 185. Reprinted by permission of Blackwell Publishing, Ltd.

DISCOVERING DEVELOPMENT:

CARING FOR AGING PARENTS

As we have seen, caring for aging parents can be both stressful and uplifting. On the stress side, adult child care providers can experience significant health effects from long-term stress. Such stress is sometimes a factor in elder abuse, neglect, or exploitation. Thus, doing what is necessary to help deal with the stressful aspects of providing care is critical.

Communities typically have several sources of help for adult children who are caring for their aging parents. Find out what is available in your area. Check with local social service agencies, organizations dedicated to serving older adults, hospitals, colleges and universities, and churches and synagogues. You may be quite surprised to learn of the many options and opportunities there are for adults to get assistance. These may range from workshops and classes to support groups to formal and informal outings.

Make a list of the programs you discover, and discuss them in class. If possible, talk with individuals who run the programs and with people who take advantage of them to learn from all of their experiences.

Grandparenthood

Becoming a grandparent takes some help. Being a parent yourself, of course, is a prerequisite. But it is your children's decisions and actions that determine whether you experience the transition to grandparenthood, making this role different from most others we experience throughout life. Most people become grandparents in their 40s and 50s, though some are older, or perhaps as young as their late 20s or early 30s. For many middle-aged adults, becoming a grandparent is a peak experience (Gonyea, 2013; Hoffman, Kaneshiro, & Compton, 2012). Although most research on grandparenting has been conducted with respect to heterosexual grandparents, attention to lesbian, gay, and transsexual grandparents is increasing as these family forms increase in society (Orel & Fruhauf, 2013).

How Do Grandparents Interact with Grandchildren? Grandparents have many different ways of interacting with their grandchildren. Categorizing these styles has been attempted over many decades (e.g., Neugarten & Weinstein, 1964), but none of these attempts has been particularly successful because grandparents use different styles with different grandchildren and styles change as grandparents and grandchildren age (Gonyea, 2013; Hoffman et al., 2012).

An alternative approach involves considering the many functions grandparents serve and the changing nature of families (Hills, 2010). The social dimension includes societal needs and expectations of what grandparents are to do, such as passing on family history to grandchildren. The personal dimension includes the personal satisfaction and individual needs fulfilled by being a grandparent. Many grandparents pass on skills—as well as religious, social, and vocational values (social dimension)—through storytelling and advice, and they may feel great pride and satisfaction (personal dimension) from working with grandchildren on joint projects.

Grandchildren give grandparents a great deal in return. Grandchildren keep grandparents in touch with youth and the latest trends. Sharing the excitement of surfing the web in school may be one way grandchildren keep grandparents on the technological forefront.

Being a Grandparent Is Meaningful. Being a grandparent really matters. Most grandparents derive multiple meanings, and they are linked with generativity (Gonyea, 2013; Thiele & Whelan, 2010). For some, grandparenting is the most important thing in their lives. For others, meaning comes from being seen as wise, from spoiling grandchildren, from recalling the relationship they had with their own grandparents, or from taking pride in the fact they will be followed by not one but two generations.

Grandchildren also highly value their relationships with grandparents, even when they are young adults (Alley, 2004). Grandparents are valued as role models as well as for their personalities, the activities they share, and the attention they show to grandchildren. Young adult grandchildren (ages 21–29) derive both stress and rewards from caring for grandparents, much the same way middle-aged adults do when they care for their aging parents (Fruhauf, 2007).

Ethnic Differences. How grandparents and grandchildren interact varies in different ethnic groups. Intergenerational relationships are especially important and historically have been a source of strength in African American families (Waites, 2009) and Latino families (Gladding, 2002). African American grandparents play an important role in many aspects of their grandchildren's lives, such as religious education (King et al., 2006). African American grandfathers, in particular, tend to perceive grandparenthood as a central role to a greater degree than do European American grandfathers (Kivett, 1991). Latino American grandparents are more likely to participate in child rearing owing to a cultural core value of family (Burnette, 1999).

Native American grandparents appear to have some interactive styles that differ from those of other groups (Weibel-Orlando, 1990). These grandparents provide grandchildren with a way to connect with their cultural heritage, and they are also likely to provide a great deal of care for their grandchildren (Mutchler, Baker, & Lee, 2007). Research also indicates Native American grandparents also use their own experiences of cultural disruption to reinvest in their

How grandparents and grandchildren interact varies across cultures.

Catherine Karnow/Corbis

grandchildren to ensure the continuity of culture (Thompson, Cameron, & Fuller-Thompson, 2013). In general, Native American grandmothers take a more active role than do grandfathers, and are more likely to pass on traditional rituals (Woodbridge, 2008).

Asian American grandparents, particularly if they are immigrants, serve as a primary source of traditional culture for their grandchildren (Yoon, 2005). When these grandparents become heavily involved in caring for their grandchildren, they especially want and need services that are culturally and linguistically appropriate.

When Grandparents Care for Grandchildren.
Grandparenthood today is tougher than it used to be. Families are more mobile, and means grandparents are more often separated from their grandchildren by geographical distance. Grandparents are more likely to have independent lives apart from their children and grandchildren. What being a grandparent entails in the 21st century is more ambiguous than it once was (Fuller-Thompson, Hayslip, & Patrick, 2005).

Perhaps the biggest change worldwide for grandparents is the increasing number serving as custodial parents or primary caregivers for their grandchildren (Moorman & Greenfield, 2010). Estimates are about 7 million U.S. grandparents have grandchildren living with them, and 2.7 million of these grandparents provide basic needs (food, shelter, clothing) for one or more of their grandchildren (U.S. Census Bureau, 2012c). These situations result most often when both parents are employed outside the home (Uhlenberg & Cheuk, 2010); when the parents are deceased, addicted, incarcerated, or unable to raise their children for some other reason (Backhouse, 2006; Moorman & Greenfield, 2010); or when discipline or behavior problems have been exhibited by the grandchild (Giarusso

et al., 2000). Lack of legal recognition stemming from the grandparents' lack of legal guardianship also poses problems and challenges such as dealing with schools and obtaining records. Typically, social service workers must assist grandparents in navigating the many unresponsive policies and systems they encounter when trying to provide the best possible assistance to their grandchildren (Cox, 2007). Clearly, public policy changes are needed to address these issues, especially regarding grandparents' rights regarding schools and health care for their grandchildren (Ellis, 2010).

Raising grandchildren is not easy. Financial stress, cramped living space, and social isolation are only some of the issues facing custodial grandmothers (Bullock, 2004). The grandchildren's routines, activities, and school-related issues also cause stress (Musil & Standing, 2005). All of these stresses are also reported cross-culturally; full-time custodial grandmothers in Kenya reported higher levels of stress than part-time caregivers (Oburu & Palmérus, 2005).

Even custodial grandparents raising grandchildren without these problems report more stress and role disruption than noncustodial grandparents, though most grandparents are resilient and manage to cope (Hayslip, Davis, Neumann, Goodman, Smith, Maiden et al., 2013). Most custodial grandparents consider their situation better for their grandchild than any other alternative and report surprisingly few negative effects on their marriages.

ADULT DEVELOPMENT IN ACTION

As a human resources director, what supports might you create to assist middle-aged adults handle family issues?

SOCIAL POLICY IMPLICATIONS

As we saw earlier in this chapter, elder abuse and neglect is a major, underreported global problem. To help protect vulnerable older adults, the U.S. Congress passed and President Obama signed into law the Elder Justice Act in 2010 as part of the Patient Protection and Affordable Care Act. It provides federal resources to

"prevent, protect, treat, understand, intervene in and, where appropriate, prosecute elder abuse, neglect and exploitation."

In brief, the law requires the Department of Health and Human Services to oversee the management of federal programs and resources for protecting older adults from abuse and neglect. Among the most important action steps in the law are:

- Establish the Elder Justice Coordinating Council
- Establish an Advisory Board on Elder Abuse
- Establish Elder Abuse, Neglect, and Exploitation Forensic Centers
- Enhance long-term care
- Fund state and local adult protective service offices
- Provide grants for long-term care ombudsmen programs and for evaluating programs
- Provide training
- Provide grants to state agencies to perform surveys of care and nursing facilities
- Require the U.S. Department of Justice to act to prevent elder abuse by creating elder justice programs, studying state laws and practices relating to elder abuse, neglect, and exploitation,

train personnel, and ensure enough resources are available for investigation and prosecution of perpetrators.

Unfortunately, Congress has not appropriately funded this law as of 2013 (Blancato, 2013). Although the Violence Against Women Act that was reauthorized in 2013 provides $9 million per year to assist older women, that is a far cry from the nearly $200 million per year authorized in the Elder Justice Act, and even more inadequate given that victims of financial exploitation alone lose roughly $3 billion per year.

Numerous national advocacy agencies, such as the Elder Justice Coalition, the National Adult Protective Services Association, and others, are dedicated to ensuring the Elder Justice Act gets the funding it deserves. Child abuse prevention has been funded for years. It is time to help older adults be equally protected.

SUMMARY

11.1 Relationship Types and Issues

What role do friends play across adulthood?

- People tend to have more friendships during young adulthood than during any other period. Friendships in old age are especially important for maintaining life satisfaction.
- Men have fewer close friends and base them on shared activities. Women have more close friends and base them on emotional sharing. Cross-gender friendships are difficult.

What characterizes love relationships? How do they vary across culture?

- Passion, intimacy, and commitment are the key components of love.
- The theory that does the best job explaining the process of forming love relationships is the theory of assortative mating.
- Selecting a mate works best when there are shared values, goals, and interests. There are cross-cultural differences in which specific aspects of these are most important.

What are abusive relationships? What characterizes elder abuse, neglect, or exploitation?

- Levels of aggressive behavior range from verbal aggression to physical aggression to murdering

one's partner. People remain in abusive relationships for many reasons, including low self-esteem and the belief they cannot leave.

- Abuse, neglect, or exploitation of older adults is an increasing problem. Most perpetrators are spouses/partners or adult children. The causes are complex.

11.2 Lifestyles and Love Relationships

What are the challenges of being single?

- Most adults in their 20s are single. People remain single for many reasons; gender differences exist. Ethnic differences reflect differences in age at marriage and social factors.
- Singles recognize the pluses and minuses in the lifestyle. There are health and longevity consequences from remaining single for men but not for women.

Why do people cohabit?

- Cohabitation is on the increase globally.
- Three primary reasons for cohabiting are convenience (e.g., to share expenses), trial marriage, or substitute marriage.

What are gay and lesbian relationships like?

- Gay and lesbian couples are similar to married heterosexual couples in terms of relationship issues. Lesbian couples tend to be more egalitarian.

What is marriage like across adulthood?

- The most important factors in creating stable marriages are maturity, similarity (called homogamy), and conflict resolution skills. Exchange theory is an important explanation of how people contribute to their relationships.

- For couples with children, marital satisfaction tends to decline until the children leave home, although individual differences are apparent, especially in long-term marriages.

- Most long-term marriages tend to be happy, and partners in them express fewer negative emotions.

- Caring for a spouse presents challenges. How well it works depends on the quality of the marriage. Most caregiving spouses provide care based on love.

Why do couples divorce?

- Currently, half of all new marriages end in divorce. Reasons for divorce include a lack of the qualities that make a strong marriage. Also, societal attitudes against divorce have eased and expectations about marriage have increased.

- Recovery from divorce is different for men and women. Men tend to have a tougher time in the short run. Women clearly have a harder time in the long run, often for financial reasons. Difficulties between divorced partners usually involve visitation and child support.

Why do people remarry?

- Most divorced couples remarry. Second marriages are especially vulnerable to stress if stepchildren are involved. Remarriage in later life tends to be happy, but may be resisted by adult children.

What are the experiences of widows and widowers?

- Widowhood is more common among women because they tend to marry men older than they are. Widowed men typically are older.

- Reactions to widowhood depend on the quality of the marriage. Men generally have problems in social relationships and in household tasks; women tend to have more financial problems.

11.3 Family Dynamics and the Life Course

What is it like to be a parent? What are the key issues across ethnic groups? What forms of parenting are there? How does parenting evolve across adulthood?

- Most couples choose to have children, although for many different reasons. The timing of parenthood determines in part how involved parents are in their families as opposed to their careers.

- Instilling cultural values in children is important for parents. In some cultures, familism changes the unit of analysis from the individual to the family.

- Single parents face many problems, especially if they are women and are divorced. The main problem is reduced financial resources. A major issue for adoptive parents, foster parents, and stepparents is how strongly the child will bond with them. Each of these relationships has special characteristics. Gay and lesbian parents also face numerous obstacles, but they usually are good parents.

How do middle-aged adults get along with their children? How do they deal with the possibility of providing care to aging parents?

- Most parents do not report severe negative emotions when their children leave. Difficulties emerge to the extent that children were a major source of a parent's identity. However, parents typically report distress if adult children move back.

- Middle-aged women often assume the role of kinkeeper to the family. Middle-aged parents may be squeezed by competing demands of their children, who want to gain independence, and their parents, who want to maintain independence; therefore, they are often called the sandwich generation.

- Most caregiving by adult children is done by daughters and daughters-in-law. Filial obligation, the sense of responsibility to care for older parents, is a major factor.

- Caring for aging parents can be highly stressful. Symptoms of depression, anxiety, and other problems are widespread. Financial pressures also are felt by most. Parents often have a difficult time in accepting the care. However, many caregivers also report feeling rewarded or uplifted for their efforts.

How do grandparents interact with their grandchildren? What key issues are involved?

- Being a grandparent is a meaningful role. Individual differences in interactive style are large.

- Ethnic differences in grandparenting are evident. Ethnic groups with strong family ties differ in style from groups who value individuality.

- Grandparents are increasingly being put in the position of raising their grandchildren. Reasons include incarceration and substance abuse by the parents.

- Great-grandparenthood is a role enjoyed by more people and reflects a sense of family renewal.

REVIEW QUESTIONS

11.1 Relationship Types and Issues

- How does the number and importance of friendships vary across adulthood?
- What gender differences are there in the number and type of friends?
- What are the components of love?
- What characteristics make the best matches between adults? How do these characteristics differ across cultures?
- What is elder abuse, neglect, or exploitation? Why is it underreported?

11.2 Lifestyles and Love Relationships

- How do adults who never marry deal with the need to have relationships?
- What are the relationship characteristics of gay and lesbian couples?
- What are the most important factors in creating stable marriages?
- What developmental trends are occurring in marital satisfaction? How do these trends relate to having children?
- What factors are responsible for the success of long-term marriages?
- What are the major reasons people get divorced? How are these reasons related to societal expectations about marriage and attitudes about divorce?
- What characteristics about remarriage make it similar to and different from first marriage? How does satisfaction in remarriage vary as a function of age?
- What are the characteristics of widowed people? How do men and women differ in their experience of widowhood?

11.3 Family Dynamics and the Life Course

- What ethnic differences are there in parenting? What is familism and how does it relate to parenting?
- What are the important issues in being an adoptive parent, foster parent, or stepparent? What special challenges are there for gay and lesbian parents?
- What impact do children leaving home have on parents? Why do adult children return?
- What are the important issues facing middle-aged adults who care for their parents?
- How do grandparents and grandchildren relate? How do these relationships change with the age of the grandchild?
- What ethnic differences have been noted in grandparenting?
- What are the important issues and meanings of being a great-grandparent?

INTEGRATING CONCEPTS IN DEVELOPMENT

- What components would a theory of adult relationships need to have?
- What are some examples of each of the four developmental forces as they influence adult relationships?
- What role do the changes in sexual functioning discussed in Chapter 3 have on love relationships?
- What key public policy issues are involved in the different types of adult relationships?

KEY TERMS

abusive relationship A relationship that one partner displays aggressive behavior toward the other partner.

assortative mating A theory that people find partners based on their similarity to each other.

battered woman syndrome A situation where a woman believes she cannot leave an abusive relationship and that she may even go so far as to kill her abuser.

cohabitation Living with another person as part of a committed, intimate, sexual relationship.

exchange theory A theory of relationships based on the idea each partner contributes something to the relationship the other would be hard-pressed to provide.

familism Refers to the idea the well-being of the family takes precedence over the concerns of individual family members.

filial obligation The feeling that, as an adult child, one must care for one's parents.

homogamy The notion similar interests and values are important in forming strong, lasting interpersonal relationships.

kinkeeper The person who gathers family members together for celebrations and keeps them in touch with each other.

marital adjustment The degree spouses accommodate each other over a certain period of time.

marital quality The subjective evaluation of the couple's relationship on a number of different dimensions.

marital satisfaction A global assessment of one's marriage.

marital success An umbrella term referring to any marital outcome.

marriage education An approach based on the idea the more couples are prepared for marriage, the better the relationship will survive over the long run.

married singles Married couples who have grown apart but continue to live together.

sandwich generation Middle-aged adults caught between the competing demands of two generations: their parents and their children.

socioemotional selectivity A theory of relationships that argues social contact is motivated by a variety of goals, including information seeking, self-concept, and emotional regulation.

vulnerability-stress-adaptation model A model that sees marital quality as a dynamic process resulting from the couple's ability to handle stressful events in the context of their particular vulnerabilities and resources.

RESOURCES

Access quizzes, glossaries, flashcards, and more at www.cengagebrain.com.

CHAPTER 12

WORK, LEISURE, AND RETIREMENT

12.1 OCCUPATIONAL SELECTION AND DEVELOPMENT
The Meaning of Work • Occupational Choice Revisited • Occupational Development • Job Satisfaction • *How Do We Know?: Cross-Cultural Aspects of Teachers' Job Satisfaction*

12.2 GENDER, ETHNICITY, AND DISCRIMINATION ISSUES
Gender Differences in Occupational Selection • Women and Occupational Development • Ethnicity and Occupational Development • Bias and Discrimination • *Current Controversies: Do Women Lean Out When They Should Lean In?*

12.3 OCCUPATIONAL TRANSITIONS
Retraining Workers • Occupational Insecurity • Coping with Unemployment • *Discovering Development: What Unemployment Resources Are Available in Your Area?*

12.4 WORK AND FAMILY
The Dependent Care Dilemma • Juggling Multiple Roles

12.5 LEISURE ACTIVITIES
Types of Leisure Activities • Developmental Changes in Leisure • Consequences of Leisure Activities

12.6 RETIREMENT AND WORK IN LATE LIFE
What Does Being Retired Mean? • Why Do People Retire? • Adjustment to Retirement • Employment and Volunteering

SOCIAL POLICY IMPLICATIONS
Summary • Review Questions • Integrating Concepts In Development • Key Terms • Resources

FOR AS LONG AS WE CAN REMEMBER, people ask, "What do you want to be when you grow up?" When we are "grown up," we simply change that question to "… and what do you do?" We are socialized throughout the life span that work is a central aspect of life and a defining characteristic of who we are. For some, work *is* life; for all, our jobs are at least a source of identity.

The world of work has changed dramatically over the past decade in large part to the experiences of the baby boomers who are redefining what it means to age, be engaged in meaningful activity, and ensure they have sufficient income to support the life style to which they have become accustomed. The Great Recession of the late 2000s and early 2010s also affected the workplace by forcing people who lost a significant part of their retirement savings to continue working, forcing middle-aged adults to find new employment following loss of their job through layoff, and making it more difficult for younger adults to enter the workforce.

As a result, all issues regarding occupational preparation and selection now affect adults of all ages, from emerging adults to those in late life. We consider the complexities of the world of work throughout this chapter as we confront the reality of rapidly changing occupational conditions and opportunities, and how those are shaping adult development and aging, and raising issues about basic assumptions people have about retirement.

12.1 Occupational Selection and Development

LEARNING OBJECTIVES

- How do people view work? How do occupational priorities vary with age?
- How do people choose their occupations?
- What factors influence occupational development?
- What is the relationship between job satisfaction and age?

Monique, a 28-year-old senior communications major, wonders about careers. Should she enter the broadcast field as a behind-the-scenes producer, or would she be better suited as a public relations spokesperson? She thinks her outgoing personality is a factor she should consider in making this decision.

Choosing one's work is serious business. Like Monique, we try to select a field in which we are trained and is also appealing. Work influences much of what we do in life. You may be taking this course as part of your preparation for a career in human development,

We are socialized from childhood to think about careers.

Daniel Bendjy/E+/Getty Images

social services, psychology, nursing, allied, health, or other field. Work is a source for friends and often for spouses/partners. People arrange personal activities around work schedules. Parents often choose child-care centers on the basis of proximity to where they work. People often choose where they live in terms of where they work.

The Meaning of Work

Studs Terkel, author of the fascinating classic book *Working* (1974), writes work is "a search for daily meaning as well as daily bread, for recognition as well as cash, for astonishment rather than torpor; in short, for a sort of life rather than a Monday through Friday sort of dying" (xiii). Kahlil Gibran (1923), in his mystical book *The Prophet*, put it this way: "Work is love made visible."

The meaning most of us derive from working includes both the money that can be exchanged for life's necessities (and perhaps a few luxuries) and the possibility of personal growth (Rosso, Dekas, & Wrzesniewski, 2010).

What specific occupation a person holds appears to have no effect on his or her need to derive meaning from work. Finding meaning in one's work can mean the difference between feeling work is the source of one's life problems or a source of fulfillment and contentment (Grawitch, Barber, & Justice, 2010).

Researchers and career coaches write about four common meanings that describe work: developing self, union with others, expressing self, and serving others (Hyson, 2013; Lips-Wiersma, 2003). To the extent these meanings can all be achieved, people experience the workplace as an area of personal fulfillment, sometimes describing it as a spiritual experience (Hyson, 2013). This provides a framework for understanding occupational selection and transition as a means to find better balance among the four.

Contemporary business theory supports the idea that meaning matters. *The concept called* meaning-mission fit *explains how corporate executives with a better alignment between their personal intentions and their firm's mission care more about their employees' happiness, job satisfaction, and emotional well-being* (Abbott, Gilbert, & Rosinski, 2013; French, 2007).

Because work plays such a key role in providing meaning for people, an important question is how people select an occupation. Let's turn our attention to two theories explaining how and why people choose the occupations they do.

Occupational Choice Revisited

Decisions about what people want to do in the world of work do not initially happen in adulthood. Even by adolescence, there is evidence occupational preferences are related to their personalities. But what are people preparing for? Certainly, much has been written about the rapidly changing nature of work and how people cannot prepare for a stable career where a person works for the same organization throughout his or her working life (Savickas, 2013).

Currently, it is more appropriate to consider careers as something people construct themselves rather than enter (Savickas, 2013). Career construction theory *posits people build careers through their own actions that result from the interface of their own personal characteristics and the social context.* What people "do" in the world of work, then, results from how they adapt to their environment, that in turn is a result of biopsychosocial processes grounded in the collection of experiences they have during their life.

In this regard, two specific theories about how people adapt themselves to their environment have influenced research. First, Holland's (1997) personality-type theory proposes people choose occupations to optimize the fit between their individual traits (such as personality, intelligence, skills, and abilities) and their occupational interests. Second, social cognitive career theory (SCCT) *proposes career choice is a result of the application of Bandura's social cognitive theory, especially the concept of self-efficacy.*

Holland categorizes occupations by the interpersonal settings that people must function and their associated lifestyles. He identifies six personality types that combine these factors: investigative, social, realistic, artistic, conventional, and enterprising, that he believes are optimally related to occupations.

How does Holland's theory help us understand the continued development of occupational interests in adulthood? Monique, the college senior in the vignette, found a good match between her outgoing nature and her major, communications. Indeed, college students of all ages prefer courses and majors that fit well with their own personalities. You are likely to be one of

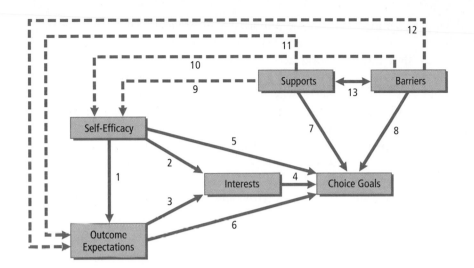

Figure 12.1

The four-variable (paths 1–6) and six-variable (paths 1–13) versions of the SCCT interest and choice models.

© 2015 Cengage Learning

them. Later on, that translates into the tendency of people to choose occupations and careers they like.

Complementarily, social cognitive career theory proposes people's career choices are heavily influenced by their interests (Lent, 2013; Sheu et al., 2010). As depicted in Figure 12.1, SCCT has two versions. The simplest includes four main factors: Self-Efficacy (your belief in your ability), Outcome Expectations (what you think will happen in a specific situation), Interests (what you like), and Choice Goals (what you want to achieve). The more complex version also includes Supports (environmental things that help you) and Barriers (environmental things that block or frustrate you). Several studies show support for the six-variable version of the model (Sheu et al., 2010).

How well do these theories work in actual practice, particularly in the rapidly changing world in which we live and where people's careers are no longer stable? Certainly, the relations among occupation, personality, and demographic variables are complex (Clark, 2007). However, even given the lack of stable careers and the real need to change jobs frequently, there is still a strong tendency on people's part to find occupations in which they feel comfortable and they like (Lent, 2013). As we will see later, loss of self-efficacy through job loss and long-term unemployment provides support for the role the self-statements underlying self-efficacy and SCCT are key.

SCCT has also been used as a framework for career counselors and coaches to help people identify and select both initial occupations and navigate later occupational changes. The goal is to have people understand the work world changes rapidly and they need to develop coping and compensatory strategies to deal with that fact.

Although people may have underlying tendencies relating to certain types of occupations, unless they believe they could be successful in those occupations and careers they are unlikely to choose them. These beliefs can be influenced by external factors. Occupational prestige and gender-related factors need to be taken into account (Deng, Armstrong, & Rounds, 2007).

Occupational Development

How a person advances in a career depends on the socialization that occurs when people learn the unwritten rules of an organization.

Occupational Expectations. Especially in adolescence, people begin to form opinions about what work in a particular occupation will be like, based on what they learn in school and from their parents, peers, other adults, and the media. These expectations influence what they want to become and when they hope to get there.

In adulthood, personal experiences affect people's opinions of themselves as they continue to refine and update their occupational expectations and development (Fouad, 2007). This usually involves trying to achieve their occupational goal, monitoring progress toward it, and changing or even abandoning it as necessary. Modifying the goal happens for many reasons, such as realizing interests have changed, the occupation was not a good fit for them, they never got the chance to pursue the level of education necessary to achieve the goal, or because they lack certain essential skills and cannot acquire them. Still other people modify their goals because of age, race, or sex discrimination, a point we consider later in this chapter.

Research shows most people who know they have both the talent and the opportunity to achieve their occupational and career goals often attain them. When high school students identified as academically talented were asked about their career expectations and outcomes, it turned out that 10 and even 20 years later they had been surprisingly accurate (Perrone et al., 2010). What is also clear from research is the biggest change has been in women's occupational and career expectations (Jacob & Wilder, 2010).

In general, research shows young adults modify their expectations at least once, usually on the basis of new information, especially about their academic ability. The connection between adolescent expectations and adult reality reinforces the developmental aspects of occupations and careers.

Many writers believe occupational expectations also vary by generation. Nowhere has this belief been stronger than in the supposed differences between the baby boom generation (born between 1946 and 1964) and the current millennial generation (born since 1983). What people in these generations, on average, expect in occupations appears to be different (Hershatter & Epstein, 2010). Millennials are more likely to change jobs more often than the older generations did, and are likely to view traditional organizations with more distrust and cynicism.

Contrary to most stereotypes, millennials are no more egotistical, and are just as happy and satisfied as young adults in every generation since the 1970s (Trzesniewski & Donnellan, 2010). However, millennials tend to have an inherent mistrust in organizations, prefer a culture focused on employee development, create information through interactive social media, are more globally aware and comfortable working with people from diverse socio-ethnic backgrounds, and do best in situations that value innovation through teamwork (Dannar, 2013).

The importance of occupational expectations can be seen clearly in the transition from school to the workplace (Moen & Roehling, 2005). The 21st-century workplace is not one where hard work and long hours necessarily lead to a stable career. *It can also be a place where you experience reality shock, a situation that what you learn in the classroom does not always transfer directly into the "real world" and does not represent all you need to know.* When reality shock sets in, things never seem to happen the way we expect. Reality shock befalls everyone. You can imagine how a new teacher feels when her long hours preparing a lesson result in students who act bored and unappreciative of her efforts.

Many professions, such as nursing and teaching, have gone to great lengths to alleviate reality shock (Alhija & Fresko, 2010; Hinton & Chirgwin, 2010). This problem is one best addressed through internship and practicum experiences for students under the careful guidance of experienced people in the field.

The Role of Mentors and Coaches. Entering an occupation involves more than the relatively short formal training a person receives. Instead, most people are oriented by a more experienced person who makes a specific effort to do this, taking on the role of a *mentor* or *coach.*

A mentor or developmental coach is part teacher, sponsor, model, and counselor who facilitates on-the-job learning to help the new hire do the work required in his or her present role and to prepare for future roles (Hunt & Weintraub, 2006). Mentoring and coaching are viewed as primary ways that organizations invest in developing their talent and future leadership (Smits & Bowden, 2013).

The mentor helps a young worker avoid trouble and also provides invaluable information about the unwritten rules governing day-to-day activities in the workplace, and being sensitive to the employment situation (Smith, Howard, & Harrington, 2005). As part of the relationship, a mentor makes sure the protégé is noticed and receives credit from supervisors for good work. Thus, occupational success often depends on the quality of the mentor–protégé relationship and the protégé's perceptions of its importance (Eddleston, Baldridge, & Veiga, 2004). In times of economic downturns, mentors can provide invaluable advice on finding another job (Froman, 2010).

What do mentors get from the relationship? Helping a younger employee learn the job is one way to fulfill aspects of Erikson's phase of generativity. As we saw in Chapter 9, generativity reflects middle-aged adults' need to ensure the continuity of society through activities such as socialization or having children. Mentoring is an important way generativity can be achieved (Marcia & Josselson, in press). Additionally, leaders may need to serve as mentors to activate transformational leadership (leadership that changes the direction of an organization) and promote positive work attitudes and career expectations of followers, enabling the mentor to rise to a higher level in his or her own career (Scandura & Williams, 2004).

Women and minorities have an especially important need for mentors (Ortiz-Walters & Gilson, 2013; Pratt, 2010). When paired with mentors, women benefit by having higher expectations; mentored women also have better perceived career development (Enslin, 2007). Latina nurses in the U.S. Army benefitted from mentors in terms of staying in the military and getting better assignments (Aponte, 2007). It is also critical to adopt a culturally conscious model of mentoring in order to enhance the advantages of developing minority mentees (Campinha-Bacote, 2010). Culturally conscious mentoring involves understanding how an organization's culture affects employees and building those assumptions and behaviors into the mentoring situation. Culturally conscious mentoring can also involve addressing the cultural background of an employee and incorporating that into the mentoring relationship.

Despite the evidence that having a mentor has many positive effects on one's occupational development, there is an important caveat; the quality of the mentor really matters (Tong & Kram, 2013). Having a poor mentor is worse than having no mentor at all. Consequently, prospective protégés must be carefully matched with a mentor and mentorship programs need to select motivated and skilled individuals who are provided with extensive training. It is in the best interest of the organization to get the mentor-protégé match correct.

How can prospective mentors and protégés meet more effectively? Some organizations have taken a page from dating and created speed mentoring as a way to create better matches (Berk, 2010; Cook, Bahn, & Menaker, 2010).

Job Satisfaction

What does it mean to be satisfied with one's job or occupation? Job satisfaction *is the positive feeling that results from an appraisal of one's work.* Research indicates job satisfaction is a multifaceted concept but certain characteristics—including hope, resilience, optimism, and self-efficacy—predict both job performance and job satisfaction (Luthans et al., 2007).

Satisfaction with some aspects of one's job increases gradually with age, and successful aging includes a workplace component (Robson et al., 2006). Why is this? Is it because people sort themselves out and end up in occupations they like? Is it they simply learn to like the occupation they are in? What other factors matter?

For starters, the factors that predict job satisfaction differ somewhat across cultures (Klassen, Usher, & Bong, 2010). This is explored in more detail in the Spotlight on Research feature.

Steve Raymer/Corbis

Mentor-protégé relationships cut across all ages.

HOW DO WE KNOW?:

CROSS-CULTURAL ASPECTS OF TEACHERS' JOB SATISFACTION

Who were the investigators and what was the aim of the study? Robert Klassen, Ellen Usher, and Mimi Bong wondered about the similarities and differences in teachers' job satisfaction, self-efficacy, and job stress. To find out, they studied teachers in the United States, Korea, and Canada. Their main question was whether teachers' cultural values, self-efficacy, and job stress would predict job satisfaction across the three countries.

How did the investigators measure the topic of interest? The researchers measured self-efficacy by assessing teachers' individual perceptions about their school's collective capabilities to influence student achievement. Job satisfaction was measured through four rating scales: (1) "I am satisfied with my job," (2) "I am happy with the way my colleagues and superiors treat me," (3) "I am satisfied with what I achieve at work," and (4) "I feel good at work." Job stress was measured using a single item ("I find teaching to be very stressful"). Collectivism, a cultural value, was measured with a 6-item scale where the first part of the question was, "In your opinion, how important is it that you and your family … ," with the conclusion of the items including the following: (1) "take responsibility for caring for older family members?" (2) "turn to each other in times of trouble?" (3) "raise each other's children whenever there is a need?" (4) "do everything you can to help each other move ahead in life?" (5) "take responsibility for caring for older family members?" and (6) "call, write, or see each other often?". The Korean version of the scales was created using a translation–back-translation process to ensure the meaning of the items was preserved.

Who were the participants in the study? A total of 500 elementary and middle school teachers from the United States (n = 137), Canada (n = 210), and Korea (n = 153) participated. The sample from the United States was included to connect this study to other research on teachers' job satisfaction. Canadian teachers were included to determine the degree findings from the United States could be generalized to a country holding similar (but not identical) cultural values. The Korean teachers represented a group with a different geographic and demographic profile (East Asian, Confucian, Collectivist). Careful analyses showed no significant differences in age, teaching experience, job satisfaction, collective efficacy, job stress, or cultural values across the three countries.

What was the design of the study? The study used a cross-sectional design.

Were there ethical concerns with the study? Because the study involved voluntary completion of a survey, there were no ethical concerns.

What were the results? The analyses revealed North American teachers scored higher on all the variables than the Korean teachers. However, there were no differences across countries regarding the efficacy of the teachers and either the strength or direction of its relation to job satisfaction. In contrast, analyses also revealed job stress had a bigger impact for North American teachers whereas the cultural value of collectivism was more important for Korean teachers.

What did the investigators conclude? The most important finding from the study is the similarity across countries in the connection between the efficacy teachers believe they have and their job satisfaction—the less efficacy, the lower a teacher's satisfaction is likely to be. Second, the higher importance of the cultural value of collectivism for Korean teachers probably reflects a cultural norm of avoiding conflict and working for the betterment of the group. Finally, the finding that job stress was a negative predictor of job satisfaction for North American teachers (the higher the stress, the lower the satisfaction) but a positive predictor for Korean teachers (higher job stress predicted higher satisfaction) indicates job stress may have different components as a function of culture. For Korean teachers, feeling stressed by the presence of more competent teachers may create an urge to improve, rather than a feeling of defeat. In summary, some predictors of job satisfaction transcend countries; others do not.

So how does job satisfaction evolve over young and middle adulthood? You may be pleased to learn research shows, given sufficient time, most people eventually find a job where they are reasonably happy (Hom & Kinicki, 2001). Optimistically, this indicates there is a job out there, somewhere, where you will be happy. That's good, because research grounded in positive psychology theory indicates happiness fuels success (Achor, 2010).

It's also true job satisfaction does not increase in all areas and job types with age. White-collar professionals show an increase in job satisfaction with age, whereas those in blue-collar positions generally do not, and these findings hold with both men and women (Aasland, Rosta, & Nylenna, 2010). This is also true across cultures. A study of Filipino and Taiwanese workers in the long-term health care industry in Taiwan showed workers with 4 or 5 years' experience had lower job satisfaction than workers with less experience, but job satisfaction among older physicians in Norway increases over time (Aasland et al., 2010; Tu, 2007).

However, the changes in the labor market in terms of lower prospects of having a long career with one organization have begun to change the notion of job satisfaction (Bidwell, 2012; Böckerman, Ilmakunnas, Jokisaari, & Yuori, 2013). Specifically, the fact that companies may eliminate jobs and workers not based on performance, making it more difficult for employees to develop a sense of organizational commitment, has made the relationship between worker age and job satisfaction more complicated.

Also complicating traditional relations between job satisfaction and age is the fact that the type of job one has and the kinds of family responsibilities one has at different career stages—as well as the flexibility of work options such as telecommuting and family leave benefits to accommodate those responsibilities—influence the relationship between age and job satisfaction (Marsh & Musson, 2008). This suggests the accumulation of experience, changing context, and the stage of one's career development may contribute to the increase in job satisfaction over time, as does the availability of options such as telecommuting.

Alienation and Burnout.

All jobs create a certain level of stress. For most workers, such negatives are merely annoyances. But for others, extremely stressful situations on the job may result in alienation and burnout.

When workers feel what they are doing is meaningless and their efforts are devalued, or when they do not see the connection between what they do and the final product, a sense of alienation is likely to result. Terkel (1974) reported employees are most likely to feel alienated when they perform routine, repetitive actions. Other workers can become alienated, too. The Great Recession that began in 2008 and resulted in record levels of job loss is only the most recent example of even high-level managerial employees feeling abandoned by their employers.

It is essential for companies to provide positive work environments to ensure the workforce remains stable and committed (Griffin et al., 2010). How can employers avoid alienating workers and improve organizational commitment? Research indicates trust is key (Chen, Aryee, & Lee, 2005; Sousa-Lima, Michel, & Caetano, 2013), as is a perception among employees the employer deals with people fairly and impartially (Howard & Cordes, 2010). It is also helpful to involve employees in the decision-making process, create flexible work schedules, and institute employee development and enhancement programs. Employees in organizations that foster trust are also more likely to want to stay (Sousa-Lima et al., 2013).

Sometimes the pace and pressure of the occupation becomes more than a person can bear, resulting in burnout, *a depletion of a person's energy and motivation, the loss of occupational idealism, and the feeling that one is being exploited.* Burnout is a state of physical, emotional, and mental exhaustion as a result of job stress (Malach-Pines, 2005). Burnout is most common among people in the helping professions—such as police (McCarty & Skogan, 2013), teaching, social work, health care (Bozikas et al., 2000), and occupational therapy (Bird, 2001)—and for those in the military (Harrington et al., 2001). The tendency of companies to keep employee numbers smaller during times of economic uncertainty adds to the workload for people on the job, increasing the risk of burnout (Bosco, di Masi, & Manuti, 2013).

People in these professions and situations must constantly deal with other people's complex problems, usually under difficult time constraints. Dealing with these pressures every day, along with bureaucratic paperwork, may become too much for the worker to bear. Frustration builds, and disillusionment and exhaustion set in—burnout. Burnout negatively affects the people who are supposed to receive services from the burned-out employee (Rowe & Sherlock, 2005).

We know burnout does not affect everyone in a particular profession. Why? Vallerand (2008; Carbonneau & Vallerand, 2012) proposes the difference relates to people feeling different types of passion (obsessive and harmonious) toward their jobs. *A passion is a strong inclination toward an activity individuals like (or even love), they value (and thus find important), and where they invest time and energy* (Vallerand et al., 2010).

Figure 12.2

Model of the relations among passion, satisfaction at work, conflict, and burnout. Harmonious passion predicts higher levels of satisfaction at work that predict lower levels of burnout. In contrast, obsessive passion predicts higher levels of conflict, predicting higher levels of burnout. ***p < .001.

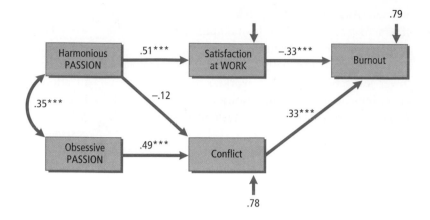

Source: From "On the role of passion for work in burnout: A process model," by R. J. Vallerand, Y. Paquet, F. L. Philippe, and J. Charest, in Journal of Personality, *Vol. 78.*

Vallerand's (2008) Passion Model proposes people develop a passion toward enjoyable activities that are incorporated into identity.

Vallerand's model differentiates between two kinds of passion: obsessive and harmonious. A critical aspect of obsessive passion is the internal urge to engage in the passionate activity makes it difficult for the person to fully disengage from thoughts about the activity, leading to conflict with other activities in the person's life (Vallerand et al., 2010).

In contrast, harmonious passion results when individuals do not feel compelled to engage in the enjoyable activity; rather, they freely choose to do so and it is in harmony with other aspects of the person's life (Vallerand et al., 2010).

Research in France and Canada indicate the Passion Model accurately predicts employees' feelings of burnout (Vallerand, 2008; Vallerand et al., 2010). As shown in Figure 12.2, obsessive passion predicts higher levels of conflict that in turn predicts higher levels of burnout. In contrast, harmonious passion predicts higher levels of satisfaction at work, and predicts lower levels of burnout.

The best ways to lower burnout are intervention programs that focus on both the organization and the employee (Awa, Plaumann, & Walter, 2010) and foster passion (Vallerand, 2012). At the organizational level, job restructuring and employee-provided programs are important. For employees, stress-reduction techniques, lowering other people's expectations, cognitive restructuring of the work situation, and finding alternative ways to enhance personal growth and identity are most effective (van Dierendonck, Garssen, & Visser, 2005).

ADULT DEVELOPMENT IN ACTION

What would be the key aspects of creating an organization that fosters employee commitment and low levels of burnout?

12.2 Gender, Ethnicity, and Discrimination Issues

LEARNING OBJECTIVES

- How do women's and men's occupational expectations differ? How are people viewed when they enter occupations not traditional for their gender?
- What factors are related to women's occupational development?
- What factors affect ethnic minority workers' occupational experiences and occupational development?
- What types of bias and discrimination hinder the occupational development of women and ethnic minority workers?

Janice, a 35-year-old African American manager at a business consulting firm, is concerned because her career is not progressing as rapidly as she hoped. Janice works hard and received excellent performance ratings every year. She noticed there are few women in upper management positions in her company. Janice wonders whether she will ever be promoted.

Occupational choice and development are not equally available to all, as Janice is experiencing.

Gender, ethnicity, and age may create barriers to achieving one's occupational goals. Men and women in similar occupations may nonetheless have different life experiences and probably received different socialization as children and adolescents that made it easier or difficult for them to set their sights on a career. Bias and discrimination also create barriers to occupational success.

Gender Differences in Occupational Selection

About 58% of all women over age 16 in the United States participate in the labor force (down from its peak of 60% in 1999), and they represent roughly 47% of the total workforce (Bureau of Labor Statistics, 2013a).

Across ethnic groups, African American women participate the most (about 59%) and Latina women the least (about 56%). Compared to other countries, women in the United States tend to be employed at a higher rate (see Figure 12.3). Still, structural barriers remain for women in the United States. Let's take a look at both traditional and nontraditional occupations for women.

In the past, women employed outside the home entered traditional, female-dominated occupations such as secretarial, teaching, and social work jobs. This was mainly because of their socialization into these occupational tracks. However, as more women enter the workforce and new opportunities are opened, a growing number of women work in occupations that have been traditionally male-dominated, such

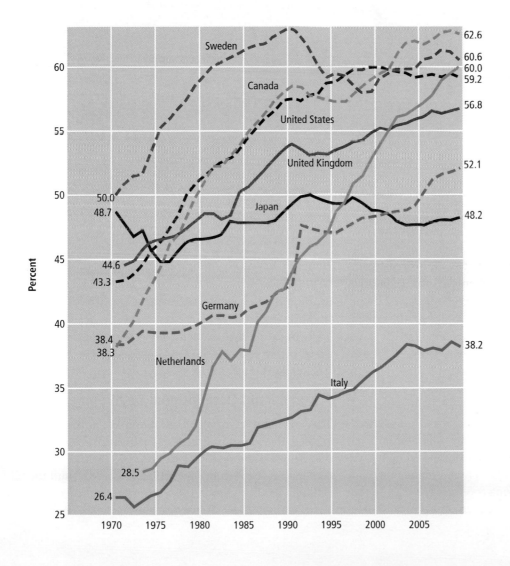

Figure 12.3

Women's labor force participation rates in selected countries, 1970–2010.

Source: From "Women at work," by U.S. Bureau of Labor Statistics, p. 13, 2011.

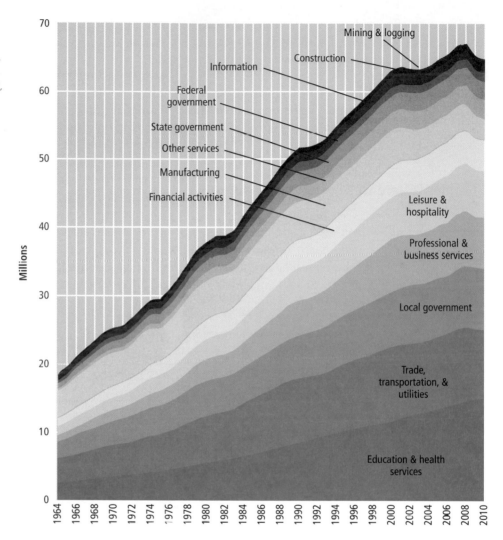

Figure 12.4

Employment of women by industry, 1964–2010.

Source: From "Women at work," by U.S. Bureau of Labor Statistics, p. 11, 2011.

as construction and engineering. The U.S. Department of Labor (2013a) categorizes women's nontraditional occupations as those where women constitute 25% or less of the total number of people employed; the skilled trades (electricians, plumbers, carpenters) still have among the lowest participation rates of women. Trends can be seen in Figure 12.4.

Despite the efforts to counteract gender stereotyping of occupations, women who choose nontraditional occupations and are successful in them are viewed negatively as compared with similarly successful men.

In patriarchal societies, both women and men gave higher "respectability" ratings to males than females in the same occupation (Sharma & Sharma, 2012). In the United States, research shows men still prefer to date

women who are in traditional careers (Kapoor et al., 2010). Additionally, compared to women who work in traditional occupations, women who work in nontraditional occupations are less likely to believe they are being sexually harassed when confronted with the same behavior (Bouldin & Grayson, 2010; Maeder, Wiener, & Winter, 2007).

Women and Occupational Development

The characteristics and aspirations of women who entered the workforce in the 1950s and those from the Baby Boomers (born between 1946 and 1964), Generation X (born between 1965 and 1982), and the Millennials (born since 1983) are significantly different (Dannar, 2013; Strauss & Howe, 2007). Women in previous generations had fewer opportunities for employment choice and had to overcome more barriers.

In the 21st century, women entrepreneurs are starting small businesses at a faster rate than men and are finding a home-based business can solve many of the challenges they face in balancing employment and a home life. As the millennial generation heads into the workforce, it will be interesting to see whether their high degree of technological sophistication will provide more occupational and career options. Technologically mediated workplaces may provide solutions to many traditional issues, such as work–family conflict. When millennial generation women choose nontraditional occupations, their attitudes toward them are more similar to previous generations' attitudes (Real, Mitnick, & Maloney, 2010).

In the corporate world, unsupportive or insensitive work environments, organizational politics, and the lack of occupational development opportunities are most important for women working full-time (Yamini-Benjamin, 2007). Female professionals leave their jobs for two main reasons. First, the organizations where women work are felt to idealize and reward masculine values of working—individuality, self-sufficiency, and individual contributions—while emphasizing tangible outputs, competitiveness, and rationality. Most women prefer organizations that highly value relationships, interdependence, and collaboration.

Second, women may feel disconnected from the workplace. By midcareer, women may conclude they must leave these unsupportive organizations in order to achieve satisfaction, growth, and development at work and rewarded for the relational skills they consider essential for success. As we see a bit later, whether women leave their careers or plateau before reaching their maximum potential level in the organization because of lack of support, discrimination, or personal choice is controversial.

Ethnicity and Occupational Development

Unfortunately, little research has been conducted from a developmental perspective related to occupational selection and development for people from ethnic minorities. Rather, most researchers focused on the limited opportunities ethnic minorities have

and on the structural barriers, such as discrimination, they face.

Women do not differ significantly in terms of participation in nontraditional occupations across ethnic groups (Bureau of Labor Statistics, 2013a). However, African American women who choose nontraditional occupations tend to plan for more formal education than necessary to achieve their goal. This may actually make them overqualified for the jobs they get; a woman with a college degree may be working in a job that does not require that level of education.

Latino Americans are similar to European Americans in occupational development and work values.

Whether an organization is responsive to the needs of ethnic minorities makes a big difference for employees. Ethnic minority employees of a diverse organization in the Netherlands reported more positive feelings about their workplace when they perceived their organizations as responsive and communicative in supportive ways (Dinsbach, Fiej, & de Vries, 2007).

Bias and Discrimination

Since the 1960s, organizations in the United States have been sensitized to the issues of bias and discrimination in the workplace.

Gender Bias and the Glass Ceiling. By the end of the first decade of the 21st century, women accounted for more than half of all people employed in management, professional, and related occupations (Bureau of Labor Statistics, 2013b). However, women are still underrepresented at the top. Janice's observation in the vignette that few women serve in the highest ranks of major corporations is accurate.

Why are there so few women in such positions? *The most important reason is* gender discrimination: *denying a job to someone solely on the basis of whether the person is a man or a woman.* Gender discrimination is still pervasive in too many aspects of the workplace (Purcell, MacArthur, & Samblanet, 2010).

Research in the United States and Britain also confirms women are forced to work harder than men (Gorman & Kmec, 2007). Neither differences in job characteristics nor family obligations account for this difference; the results clearly point to stricter job performance standards being applied to women.

Women like Hillary Clinton who make it to the highest ranks of their profession have had to contend with both the glass ceiling and the glass cliff.

Women themselves refer to a glass ceiling, the level they may rise within an organization but beyond which they may not go. The glass ceiling is a major barrier for women (Johns, 2013; Purcell et al., 2010), and the greatest barrier facing them is at the boundary between lower-tier and upper-tier grades. Men are largely blind to the existence of the glass ceiling (Heppner, 2007).

The glass ceiling is pervasive across higher management and professional workplace settings (Heppner, 2007; Johns, 2013). Despite decades of attention to the issue, little overall progress is being made in the number of women who lead major corporations or serve on their boards of directors (Cundiff & Stockdale, 2013). The glass ceiling has also been used to account for African Americans' and Asian Americans' lack of advancement in their careers as opposed to European American men (Cundiff & Stockdale, 2013; Hwang, 2007). It also provides a framework for understanding limitations to women's careers in many countries around the world such as South Africa (Kiaye & Singh, 2013).

Interestingly, a different trend emerges if one examines who is appointed to critical positions in organizations in times of crisis. Research shows at such times, women are more likely put in leadership positions. *Consequently, women often confront a* **glass cliff** *where their leadership position is precarious.* Evidence shows companies are more likely to appoint a woman to their board of directors if their financial performance had been poor in the recent past, and women are more likely to be political candidates if the seat is a highly contested one (Ryan, Haslam, & Kulich, 2010).

What can be done to eliminate the glass ceiling and the glass cliff? Kolb, Williams, and Frohlinger (2010) argue women can and must be assertive in getting their rightful place at the table by focusing on five key things: drilling deep into the organization so you can make informed decisions, getting critical support, getting the necessary resources, getting buy-in, and making a difference.

Much debate has erupted over the issue of women rising to the top. There is no doubt the glass ceiling and glass cliff exist. The controversy surrounds the extent women decide not to pursue or reluctance to pursue the top positions. As discussed in the Current Controversies feature, this debate is likely to rage for years.

CURRENT CONTROVERSIES:

DO WOMEN LEAN OUT WHEN THEY SHOULD LEAN IN?

Sheryl Sandberg is unquestionably successful. She has held the most important, powerful positions in the most recognizable technology companies in the world. When she published her book *Lean In: Women, Work, and the Will to Lead* in 2013, she set off a fierce debate. Sandberg claimed there is discrimination against women in the corporate word. She also argued an important reason women do not rise to the top more often is because of their own unintentional behavior that holds them back. She claimed women do not speak up enough, need to abandon the myth of "having it all," set boundaries, get a mentor, and not to "check out of work" when thinking about starting a family.

The national debate around these issues raised many issues: Sandberg's ability to afford to pay for support may make her points irrelevant for women who do not have those resources; her husband's ability and willingness to share in child rearing and household chores may make her arguments irrelevant for single parents; she was "blaming the victim"; no one ever puts men in these situations of having to choose; and so on.

Does Sheryl Sandberg have a valid point to make? Do men and women differ in how they approach careers? Are the differences she notes inherent in men and women or are they more learned? What support systems that need to be in place are currently missing? What do you think?

Equal Pay for Equal Work. In addition to discrimination in hiring and promotion, women are also subject to salary discrimination. According to the Bureau of Labor Statistics (2013a), women's median income overall is about 81% of men's. As you can see in Figure 12.5, the wage gap depends on ethnicity and has been narrowing since the 1980s.

The Social Policy Implications feature at the end of the chapter discusses equal pay for equal work in more detail. In general, although few people disagree with the principle, eliminating the salary disparity between men and women has proven more difficult than many originally believed.

Sexual Harassment. Suppose you have been working hard on a paper for a course and think you've done a good job. When you receive an "A" for the paper, you are elated. When you discuss your paper (and your

excitement) with your instructor, you receive a big hug. How do you feel? What if this situation involved a major project at work and the hug came from your boss? Your co-worker? What if it were a kiss on your lips instead of a hug?

Whether such behavior is acceptable, or whether it constitutes sexual harassment, depends on many situational factors, including the setting, people involved, and the relationship between them.

How many people have been sexually harassed? That's a hard question to answer for several reasons: there is no universal definition of harassment, men and women have different perceptions, and many victims do not report it (The Advocates for Human Rights, 2010). Even given these difficulties, global research indicates between 40% and 50% of women in the European Union, and 30–40% of women in Asia-Pacific countries experience workplace sexual harassment (International

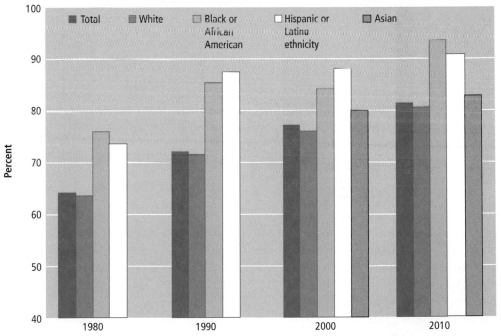

Figure 12.5

Women's earnings as a percent of men's in 2010.

Source: U.S. Bureau of Labor Statistics.
Note: Data for Asians were note tabulated prior to 2000.
© 2015 Cengage Learning

Labour Organization, 2013). Victims are most often single or divorced young adult women (Zippel, 2006), but about 16% of workplace cases that result in formal legal charges involve male victims (Equal Employment Opportunity Commission, 2010). Although the number of formal complaints in the United States is declining, it is unclear whether this is because of increased sensitivity and training by employers, reluctance of victims to report for fear of losing their jobs during economically difficult times, or both.

What are the effects of being sexually harassed? As you might expect, research evidence clearly shows negative job-related, psychological, and physical health outcomes (Lim & Cortina, 2005).

Cultural differences in labeling behaviors as sexually harassing are also important. Research comparing countries in the European Union reveals differences across these countries in terms of definitions and corrective action (Zippel, 2006). Unfortunately, little research has been done to identify what aspects of organizations foster harassment or to determine the impact of educational programs aimed at addressing the problem.

In 1998, the U.S. Supreme Court (in *Oncale v. Sundowner Offshore Services*) ruled the relevant laws also protect men. Thus, the standard by which sexual harassment is judged could now be said to be a "reasonable person" standard.

What can be done to provide people with safe work and learning environments, free from sexual harassment? Training in gender awareness is a common approach that often works, especially given gender differences exist in perceptions of behavior (Lindgren, 2007).

Age Discrimination. *Another structural barrier to occupational development is age discrimination, that involves denying a job or promotion to someone solely on the basis of age.* The U.S. Age Discrimination in Employment Act of 1986 protects workers over age 40. A law that brought together all of the anti-discrimination legislation in the United Kingdom, the Equality Act of 2010, includes a prohibition against age discrimination, and more European countries are protecting middle-aged and older workers (Government Equalities Office, 2013; Lahey, 2010). These laws stipulate people must be hired based on their ability, not their age and cannot segregate or classify workers or otherwise denote their status on the basis of age.

Employment prospects for middle-aged people around the world are lower than for their younger counterparts (Lahey, 2010). Age discrimination toward those over age 45 is common in Hong Kong (Cheung, Kam, & Ngan, 2011), resulting in longer periods of unemployment, early retirement, or negative attitudes.

Age discrimination usually happens prior to or after interaction with human resources staff by other employees making the hiring decisions, and it can be covert (Lahey, 2010; Pillay, Kelly, & Tones, 2006). Employers can make certain types of physical or mental performance a job requirement and argue older workers cannot meet the standard prior to an interview. Or they can attempt to get rid of older workers by using retirement incentives. Supervisors' stereotyped beliefs sometimes factor in performance evaluations for raises or promotions or in decisions about which employees are eligible for additional training (Chiu et al., 2001).

ADULT DEVELOPMENT IN ACTION

What are the key factors that interfere with people's ability to create and manage their own careers?

12.3 Occupational Transitions

LEARNING OBJECTIVES

- Why do people change occupations?
- Is worrying about potential job loss a major source of stress?
- How does job loss affect the amount of stress experienced?

Fred has 32 years of service for an automobile manufacturer. Over the years, more and more assembly-line jobs have been eliminated by new technology (including robots) and the export of manufacturing jobs to other countries. Although Fred has been assured his job is safe, he isn't so sure. He worries he could be laid off at any time.

In the past, people like Fred commonly chose an occupation during young adulthood and stayed in it throughout their working years. Today, however, not many people have that option. Corporations have restructured so often employees now assume occupational changes are part of the career process. Such corporate actions mean people's conceptions of work and career are in flux and losing one's job no longer has only negative meanings (Haworth & Lewis, 2005).

Several factors have been identified as important in determining who will remain in an occupation and who will change. Some factors—such as whether the person likes the occupation—lead to self-initiated occupation changes.

However, other factors—such as obsolete skills and economic trends—may cause forced occupational changes. Continued improvement of robots has caused some auto industry workers to lose their jobs; corporations send jobs overseas to increase profits; and economic recessions usually result in large-scale layoffs and high levels of unemployment.

Retraining Workers

When you are hired into a specific job, you are selected because your employer believes you offer the best fit between the abilities you already have and those needed to perform the job. As most people can attest, though, the skills needed to perform a job usually change over time. Such changes may be based in the introduction of new technology, additional responsibilities, or promotion.

Unless a person's skills are kept up-to-date, the outcome is likely to be either job loss or a career plateau (McCleese & Eby, 2006; Rose & Gordon, 2010). *Career plateauing occurs when there is a lack of challenge in one's job or promotional opportunity in the organization or when a person decides not to seek advancement.* Research in Canada (Foster, Lonial, & Shastri, 2011), Asia (Lee, 2003), and Australia (Rose & Gordon, 2010) shows feeling one's career has plateaued usually results in less organizational commitment, lower job satisfaction, and a greater tendency to leave. But attitudes can remain positive if it is only the lack of challenge and not a lack of promotion opportunity responsible for the plateauing (McCleese & Eby, 2006).

In cases of job loss or a career plateau, retraining may be an appropriate response. Around the world, large numbers of employees participate each year in programs and courses offered by their employer or by a college or university and aimed at improving existing skills or adding new job skills. For midcareer

Mid-career and older workers often engage in retraining or skills updating in order to stay current in their fields.

employees, retraining might focus on how to advance in one's occupation or how to find new career opportunities—for example, through résumé preparation and career counseling. Increasingly, such programs are offered online in order to make them easier and more convenient for people to access (Githens & Sauer, 2010).

Many corporations, as well as community and technical colleges, offer retraining programs in a variety of fields. Organizations that promote employee development typically promote in-house courses to improve employee skills. They may also offer tuition reimbursement programs for individuals who successfully complete courses at colleges or universities.

The retraining of midcareer and older workers highlights the need for lifelong learning (Armstrong-Stassen & Templer, 2005; Sinnott, 1994). If corporations are to meet the challenges of a global economy, it is imperative they include retraining in their employee development programs. Such programs will improve people's chances of advancement in their chosen occupations and also assist people in making successful transitions from one occupation to another.

Occupational Insecurity

Over the past few decades, changing U.S. economic conditions (e.g., the move toward a global economy), changing demographics, and a global recession forced many people out of their jobs. Heavy manufacturing and support businesses (such as the steel, oil, and automotive industries) and farming were the hardest-hit sectors during the 1970s and 1980s. No one is immune. The Great Recession that began in 2008 put many middle- and upper-level corporate executives out of work worldwide.

As a result, many people feel insecure about their jobs. Economic downturns create significant levels of stress, especially when such downturns create massive job loss (Sinclair et al., 2010). Like Fred, the autoworker in the vignette, many worried workers have numerous years of dedicated service to a company. Unfortunately, people who worry about their jobs tend to have poorer physical and psychological well-being (McKee-Ryan et al., 2005). Anxiety about one's job may result in negative attitudes about one's employer or even about work in general, and in turn may result in diminished desire to be successful. Whether there is an actual basis for people's feelings of job insecurity may not matter; sometimes what people *think* is true about their work situation is more important than what is actually the case. Just the possibility of losing one's job can negatively affect physical and psychological health.

So how does the possibility of losing one's job affect employees? Mantler and colleagues (2005) examined coping strategies for comparable samples of laid-off and employed high-technology workers. They found although unemployed participants reported higher levels of stress compared with employed participants, employment uncertainty mediated the association between employment status and perceived stress. That is, people who believe their job is in jeopardy—even if it is not—show levels of stress similar to unemployed participants. This result is due to differences in coping strategies. There are several ways people deal with stress, and two of the more common are emotion-focused coping and problem-focused coping. Some people focus on how the stressful situation makes them feel, so they cope by making themselves feel better about it. Others focus on the problem itself and do something to solve it. People who used emotional avoidance as a strategy reported higher levels of stress, particularly when they were fairly certain of the outcome. Thus, even people whose jobs aren't really in jeopardy can report high levels of stress if they tend to use emotion-focused coping strategies.

Coping with Unemployment

Losing one's job can have enormous personal impact that can last a long time (Gabriel, Gray, & Goregaokar, 2013; Lin & Leung, 2010; McKee-Ryan et al., 2005). When U.S. unemployment rates hit 10.6% in January 2010, millions of people could relate to these feelings.

When unemployment lasts and re-employment does not occur soon, unemployed people commonly experience a wide variety of negative effects (Gabriel et al., 2013; Lin & Leung, 2010) that range from a decline in immune system functioning (Cohen et al., 2007) to decreases in well-being (Gabriel et al., 2013).

Coping with unemployment involves both financial and personal issues. As noted in the Discovering Development feature, the financial support people receive varies across states and situations. Unemployment compensation is typically much lower than one's original salary, resulting in financial hardship and difficult choices for individuals.

DISCOVERING DEVELOPMENT:

WHAT UNEMPLOYMENT BENEFITS ARE AVAILABLE IN YOUR AREA?

When a person loses his or her job, there may be certain benefits available. Some of these are financial, such as weekly or monthly funds. Other benefits may be educational, such as job skills retraining. Find out what the range of benefits are in your area from government and private organization sources. See what programs are available at your local colleges and universities to help people who have lost their jobs. Pay special attention to the length of time benefits last, and whether job retraining programs are free or have tuition attached to them. Then compile the list and discuss it in class.

In a comprehensive study of the effects of unemployment, McKee-Ryan and colleagues (2005) found several specific results from losing one's job. Unemployed workers had significantly lower mental health, life satisfaction, marital or family satisfaction, and subjective physical health (how they perceive their health to be) than their employed counterparts. With reemployment, these negative effects disappear. Figure 12.6 shows physical and psychological health following job displacement is influenced by several factors (McKee-Ryan et al., 2005).

The effects of job loss vary with age, gender, and education. In the United States, middle-aged men are more vulnerable to negative effects than older or younger men—largely because they have greater financial responsibilities than the other two groups—but

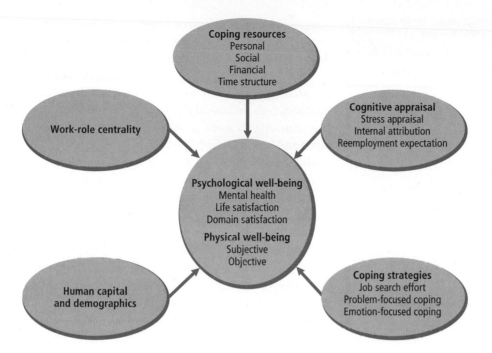

Figure 12.6
Psychological and physical well-being after losing one's job are affected by many variables.

Source: From "Psychological and physical well-being during unemployment: A meta-analytic study," by F. McKee-Ryan, Z. Song, C. R. Wanberg, and A. J. Kinicki, in Journal of Applied Psychology, *Vol. 90.*

women report more negative effects over time (Bambra, 2010). Research in Spain indicates gender differences in responding to job loss are complexly related to family responsibilities and social class (Artazcoz et al., 2004). Specifically, to the extent work is viewed as your expected contribution to the family, losing one's job has a more substantial negative effect. Because this tends to be more the case for men than for women, it helps explain the gender differences. The higher one's education levels, the less stress one typically feels immediately after losing a job, probably because higher education level usually result in faster re-employment (Mandemakers & Monden, 2013).

Because unemployment rates for many ethnic minority groups are substantially higher than for European Americans (Bureau of Labor Statistics, 2013b), the effects of unemployment are experienced by a greater proportion of people in these groups. Cultural differences need to be considered in understanding the effects of unemployment (Grosso & Smith, 2012). Compared to European Americans, however, it usually takes minority workers longer to find another job.

How long you are unemployed also affects how people react. People who are unemployed for at least a year perceive their mental health significantly more negatively than either employed people or those who have removed themselves from the labor force (e.g.,

have stopped looking for work) (Pharr, Moonie, & Bungum, 2012). Those who lost their jobs involuntarily feel a loss of control over their "work" environment and feel less demand placed on them. Importantly, a reasonable amount of "demand" is critical to maintaining good health, whereas too little demand lowers health.

Research also offers some advice for adults who are trying to manage occupational transitions (Ebberwein, 2001):

- Approach job loss with a healthy sense of urgency.

- Consider your next career move and what you must do to achieve it, even if there are no prospects for it in sight.

- Acknowledge and react to change as soon as it is evident.

- Be cautious of stopgap employment.

- Identify a realistic goal and then list the steps you must take to achieve it.

Additionally, the U.S. Department of Labor offers tips for job seekers, as do online services such as LinkedIn that also provides networking groups. These steps may not guarantee you will find a new job quickly, but they will help create a better sense that you are in control.

ADULT DEVELOPMENT IN ACTION

How could the effects of losing a job be reduced?

12.4 Work and Family

LEARNING OBJECTIVES

- What are the issues faced by employed people who care for dependents?
- How do partners view the division of household chores? What is work–family conflict, and how does it affect couples' lives?

Jennifer, a 38-year-old sales clerk at a department store, feels her husband, Bill, doesn't do his share of the housework or child care. Bill says real men don't do housework and he's really tired when he comes home from work. Jennifer thinks this isn't fair, especially because she works as many hours as her husband.

One of the most difficult challenges facing adults like Jennifer is trying to balance the demands of occupation with the demands of family. Over the past few decades, the rapid increase in the number of families where both parents are employed has fundamentally changed how we view the relationship between work and family. This can even mean taking a young child to work as a way to deal with the pushes and pulls of being an employed parent. In roughly 60% of two-parent households today, both adults work outside the home, a rate slightly lower than previous years due to the economic recession (Bureau of Labor Statistics, 2010d). Why? Families need the dual income to pay their bills and maintain a moderate standard of living.

We will see dual-earner couples with children experience both benefits and disadvantages. The stresses of living in this arrangement are substantial, and gender differences are clear—especially in the division of household chores.

The Dependent Care Dilemma

Many employed adults must also provide care for dependent children or parents.

Employed Caregivers. Many mothers have no option but to return to work after the birth of a child. In fact,

nearly two-thirds of married and unmarried mothers with children under the age of 3 years are in the labor force (U.S. Department of Labor, 2013a).

Some women, though, grapple with the decision of whether they want to return to work. Surveys of mothers with preschool children reveal the motivation for returning to work tends to be related to financial need and how attached mothers are to their work. The amount of leave time a woman has matters; the passage of the Family and Medical Leave Act in 1993 entitled workers to take unpaid time off to care for their dependents with the right to return to their jobs. This Act resulted in an increase in the number of women who returned to work at least part time (Schott, 2010). Although working part-time work may seem appealing, what matters more is whether mothers are working hours close to what they consider ideal and are accommodating to their family's needs (Kim, 2000). Perceptions of ideal working hours differ as a function of gender and life-cycle stage regarding children.

A concern for many women is whether stepping out of their occupations following childbirth will negatively affect their career paths. Indeed, evidence clearly indicates it does (Aisenbrey, Evertsson, & Grunow, 2009). Women in the United States are punished, even for short leaves. In women-friendly countries such as Sweden, long leaves typically result in a negative effect on upward career movement.

Often overlooked is the increasing number of workers who must also care for a parent or partner. Of women caring for parents or parents-in-law, more than 80% provide an average of 23 hours per week of care and 70% contribute money (Pierret, 2006). As we saw in Chapter 11, providing this type of care takes a high toll through stress.

Whether assistance is needed for one's children or parents, key factors in selecting an appropriate care site are quality of care, price, and hours of availability (Helpguide.org, 2013; Mitchell & Messner, 2003–2004). Depending on one's economic situation, it may not be possible to find affordable and quality care available when needed. In such cases, there may be no option but to drop out of the workforce or enlist the help of friends and family.

Dependent Care and Effects on Workers. Being responsible for dependent care has significant negative effects on caregivers. Whether responsible for the care of an older parent or a child, women and men report negative effects on their work, higher levels of stress, and problems with coping (Neal & Hammer, 2006). Roxburgh (2002) introduced the notion parents of families dealing with time pressures feel much more stress; indeed, subsequent research clearly shows not only are stress levels higher, but "fast-forward families" also often deal with impacts on career advancement and physical and mental health consequences of this life style (Ochs & Kremer-Sadlik, 2013). Women's careers are usually affected more negatively than men's.

How can these negative effects be lessened? When women's partners provide good support and women have average or high control over their jobs, employed mothers are significantly less distressed than employed nonmothers or mothers without support (Lovejoy & Stone, 2012; Moen & Roehling, 2005). Research focusing on single working mothers also shows those who have support from their families manage to figure out a balance between work and family obligations (Son & Bauer, 2010).

Dependent Care and Employer Responses. Employed parents with small children or dependent spouses/partners or parents are confronted with the difficult prospect of leaving them in the care of others. This is especially problematic when the usual care arrangement is unavailable. *A growing need in the workplace is for backup care, that provides emergency care for dependent children or adults so the employee does not need to lose a day of work.* Does providing a workplace care center or backup care make a difference in terms of an employee's feelings about work, absenteeism, and productivity?

There is no simple answer. Just making a child-care center available to employees does not necessarily reduce parents' work–family conflict or their absenteeism, particularly among younger employees (Connelly, Degraff, & Willis, 2004). A "family-friendly" company must also pay attention to the attitudes of their employees and make sure the company provides broad-based support (Aryee, Chu, Kim, & Ryu, 2013; Moen & Roehling, 2005). The keys are how supervisors act and the number and type of benefits the company provides. Cross-cultural research in Korea confirms having a family-friendly supervisor matters (Aryee et al., 2013).

The most important single thing a company can do is allow the employee to leave work without penalty to tend to family needs (Lawton & Tulkin, 2010).

Research also indicates there may not be differences for either mothers or their infants between work-based and nonwork-based child-care centers in terms of the mothers' ease in transitioning back to work or the infants' ability to settle into day care (Skouteris, McNaught, & Dissanayake, 2007).

It will be interesting to watch how these issues—especially flexible schedules—play out in the United States, where such practices are not yet common. A global study of parental leave, such as granted under the U.S. Family and Medical Leave Act, showed the more generous parental leave policies are, the lower the infant mortality rates, clearly indicating parental leave policies are a good thing (Ferrarini & Norström, 2010).

Juggling Multiple Roles

When both members of a heterosexual couple with dependents are employed, who cleans the house, cooks the meals, and takes care of the children when they are ill? This question goes to the heart of the core dilemma of modern, dual-earner couples: How are household chores divided? How are work and family role conflicts handled?

Dividing Household Chores. Despite much media attention and claims of increased sharing in the duties, women still perform the lion's share of housework, regardless of employment status. As shown in Figure 12.7, this is true globally (Ruppanner, 2010). This unequal division of labor causes the most arguments and the most unhappiness for dual-earner couples. This is the case with Jennifer and Bill, the couple in the vignette; Jennifer does most of the housework.

Although women still do most of the household chores, things are getting a bit better. Women reduced the amount of time they spend on housework (especially when they are employed) and men have increased the amount of time they spend on such tasks (Saginak & Saginak, 2005). The increased participation of men in these tasks is not all that it seems, however. Most of the increase is on weekends, involves specific tasks they agree to perform, and is largely unrelated to women's employment status. In short, the increase in men's

Figure 12.7

Women spend much more time on household chores than men.

Source: Data from "Cross-national reports of housework: An investigation of the gender empowerment measure," by L. E. Ruppanner, in Social Science Research, Vol. 19, *Table 1, p. 968. Copyright © Elsevier 2010.*

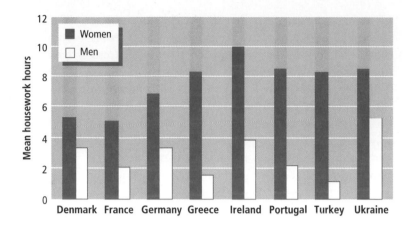

participation has not done much to lower women's burdens around the house.

Men and women view the division of labor differently. Men are often most satisfied with an equitable division of labor based on the number of hours spent, especially if the amount of time needed to perform household tasks is relatively small. Women are often most satisfied when men are willing to perform women's traditional chores (Saginak & Saginak, 2005). When ethnic minorities are studied, much the same is true concerning satisfaction.

Ethnic differences in the division of household labor are also apparent. In Mexican American families with husbands born in Mexico, men help more when family income is lower and their wives contribute a proportionally higher share of the household income (Pinto & Coltrane, 2009). Comparisons of Latino, African American, and European American men consistently show European American men help with the chores less than Latino or African American men (Omori & Smith, 2009).

Work–Family Conflict. When people have both occupations and children, they must figure out how to balance the demands of each. *These competing demands cause* **work–family conflict,** *the feeling of being pulled in multiple directions by incompatible demands from one's job and one's family.*

Dual-earner couples must find a balance between their occupational and family roles. Because nearly 60% of married couples with children consist of dual-earner households (Bureau of Labor Statistics, 2013b), how to divide the household chores and how to care

for the children have become increasingly important questions.

Many people believe in such cases, work and family roles influence each other: When things go badly at work, the family suffers, and when there are troubles at home, work suffers. That's true, but the influence is not the same in each direction (Andreassi, 2007). Whether work influences family or vice versa is a complex function of support resources, type of job, and a host of other issues (Saginak & Saginak, 2005). One key but often overlooked factor is whether the work schedules of both partners allow them to coordinate activities such as child care (van Klaveren, van den Brink, & van Praag, 2013).

Of course, it is important the partners negotiate agreeable arrangements of household and child-care tasks, but we've noted truly equitable divisions of labor are clearly the exception. Most U.S. households with heterosexual dual-worker couples still operate under a gender-segregated system: There are traditional chores for men and women. These important tasks must be performed to keep homes safe, clean, and sanitary, and these tasks also take time. The important point for women is not how much time is spent performing household chores so much as which tasks are performed. What bothers wives the most is when their husbands are unwilling to do "women's work." Men may mow the lawn, wash the car, and even cook, but they are much less likely to vacuum, scrub the toilet, or change the baby's diaper.

So how and when will things change? An important step would be to talk about these issues with your partner. Keep communication lines open all the time, and let your partner know if something is bothering you. Teaching your children men and women are equally responsible for household chores will also help end the problem. Only by creating true gender equality—without differentiating among household tasks—will this unfair division of labor be ended.

Understanding work–family conflict requires taking a life-stage approach to the issue (Blanchard-Fields, Baldi, & Constantin, 2004). Several studies have found the highest conflict between the competing demands of work and family occurs during the peak parenting years, when there are at least two preschool children in the home. Inter-role conflict diminishes in later life stages, especially when the quality of the marriage is high.

A comprehensive review of the research on the experience of employed mothers supports this conclusion (Edwards, 2012). How juggling the demands of housework and child care affect women depends on the complex interplay among the age of the children, the point in career development and advancement the woman is, and her own developmental phase. The combination of challenges that any one of these reflects changes over time. Because all of these factors are dynamic, how they help or hinder a woman in her career changes over time.

In addition to having impacts on each individual, dual-earner couples often have difficulty finding time for each other, especially if both work long hours. The amount of time together is not necessarily the most important issue; as long as the time is spent in shared activities such as eating, playing, and conversing, couples tend to be happy (Ochs & Kremer-Sadlik, 2013). When both partners are employed, getting all of the schedules to work together smoothly can be a major challenge. However, these joint activities are important for creating and sustaining strong relations among family members. Unfortunately, many couples find by the time they have an opportunity to be alone together, they are too tired to make the most of it.

The issues faced by dual-earner couples are global: burnout from the dual demands of work and parenting is more likely to affect women across many cultures (Aryee et al, 2013; van Klaveren et al., Spector et al., 2005). Japanese career women's job satisfaction declines, and turnover becomes more likely, to the extent they have high work–family conflict (Honda-Howard & Homma, 2001). Research comparing sources of work–family conflict in the United States

and China reveals when work demands do not differ, work pressure is a significant source of work–family conflict in both countries (Yang et al., 2000).

So exactly what effects do family matters have on work performance and vice versa? Evidence suggests work–family conflict is a major source of stress in couples' lives. In general, women feel the work-to-family spillover to a greater extent than men, but both men and women feel the pressure (Edwards, 2012; Saginak & Saginak, 2005).

The work-family conflict described here are arguably worst for couples in the United States because Americans work more hours with fewer vacation days than any other developed country (Frase & Gornick, 2013). However, couples can work together to help mitigate the stress. Most important, they can negotiate schedules around work commitments throughout their careers, taking other factors such as child care and additional time demands into account (van Wanrooy, 2013). These negotiations should include discussion of such joint activities as meals and other family activities, too (Ochs and Kremer-Sadlik, 2013).

ADULT DEVELOPMENT IN ACTION

What are the stresses and ways to deal with them facing dual-earner couples?

12.5 Leisure Activities

LEARNING OBJECTIVES

- What activities are leisure activities? How do people choose among them?
- What changes in leisure activities occur with age?
- What do people derive from leisure activities?

Claude is a 55-year-old electrician who has enjoyed outdoor activities his whole life. From the time he was a boy he fished and water-skied in the calm inlets of coastal Florida. Although he doesn't compete in slalom races any more, Claude still skis regularly and participates in fishing competitions every chance he gets.

Adults do not work every waking moment of their lives. As each of us knows, we need to relax sometimes and engage in leisure activities. Intuitively, leisure consists of activities not associated with work. **Leisure** *is discretionary activity that includes simple relaxation, activities for enjoyment, and creative pursuits.* As you might expect, men and women differ in their views of leisure, as do people in different ethnic and age groups (van der Pas & Koopman-Boyden, 2010).

A major issue with leisure is simply finding the time. Young and middle-aged adults must fit leisure into an already busy schedule, so leisure becomes another component in our overall time management problem (Corbett & Hilty, 2006).

Types of Leisure Activities

Leisure can include virtually any activity. To organize the options, researchers classified leisure activities into several categories. Jopp and Hertzog (2010) developed an empirically based set of categories that includes a wide variety of activities: physical (e.g., lifting weights, backpacking, jogging), crafts (e.g., woodworking, household repairs), games (e.g., board/online games, puzzles, card games), watching TV, social-private (e.g., going out with a friend, visiting relatives, going out to dinner), social-public (e.g., attending a club meeting, volunteering), religious (e.g., attending a religious service, praying), travel (e.g., travel abroad, travel out of town), experiential (e.g., collect stamps, read for leisure, gardening, knitting), developmental (e.g., read as part of a job, study a foreign language, attend public lecture), and technology use (e.g., photography, use computer software, play an instrument).

More complete measures of leisure activities not only provide better understanding of how adults spend their time, but can help in clinical settings. Declines in the frequency of leisure activities is associated with depression (Schwerdtfeger & Friedrich-Mei, 2009) and with a later diagnosis of dementia (Hertzog, Kramer, Wilson, & Lindenberger, 2009). Monitoring changes in leisure activity levels during and after intervention programs can provide better outcomes assessments of these interventions.

Given the wide range of options, how do people pick their leisure activities? Apparently, each of us has a leisure repertoire, a personal library of intrinsically motivated activities we do regularly and we take with us into retirement (Nimrod, 2007a,b). The activities in our repertoire are determined by two things: perceived competence (how good we think we are at the activity compared to

Leisure activities may involve creative pursuits.

Jim West/PhotoEdit

other people our age) and psychological comfort (how well we meet our personal goals for performance).

A study of French adults revealed, as for occupations, personality factors are related to one's choice of leisure activities (Gaudron & Vautier, 2007). Other factors are important as well: income, interest, health, abilities, transportation, education, and social characteristics. Some leisure activities, such as downhill skiing, are relatively expensive and require transportation and reasonably good health and physical coordination for maximum enjoyment. In contrast, reading requires minimal finances (if one uses a public library) and is far less physically demanding. Women in all ethnic groups tend to participate less in leisure activities that involve physical activity (Eyler et al., 2002).

The use of computer technology in leisure activities has increased dramatically (Bryce, 2001). Most usage involves e-mail, Facebook, Twitter, or other social networking tools for such activities as keeping in touch with family and friends, pursuing hobbies, and lifelong learning. Computer gaming on the Web has also increased among adult players.

Developmental Changes in Leisure

Cross-sectional studies report age differences in leisure activities. Young adults participate in a greater range of activities than middle-aged adults. Furthermore, young adults prefer intense leisure activities, such as scuba diving and hang gliding. In contrast, middle-aged adults focus more on home- and family-oriented activities. In later middle age, they spend less of their leisure time in strenuous physical activities and more in sedentary activities such as reading and watching television (van der Pas & Koopman-Boyden, 2010).

Longitudinal studies of changes in individuals' leisure activities over time show considerable stability over reasonably long periods, and that level of activity in young adulthood predicts activity level later in life (Hillsdon, Brunner, Guralnik, & Marmot, 2005; Patel et al., 2006). Claude, the 55-year-old in the vignette who likes to fish and ski, is a good example of this overall trend. As Claude demonstrates, frequent participation in particular leisure activities during childhood tends to continue into adulthood. Similar findings hold for the pre- and postretirement years. Apparently, one's preferences for certain types of leisure activities are established early in life; they tend to change over the life span primarily in terms of how physically intense they are.

Consequences of Leisure Activities

What do people gain from participating in leisure activities? Researchers have long known involvement in leisure activities is related to well-being (Warr, Butcher, & Robertson, 2004). This relation holds in other countries, such as China, as well (Dai, Zhang, & Li, 2013). Research shows participating in leisure activities helps promote better mental health in women (Ponde & Santana, 2000), such as when they use family-based leisure as a means to cope during their partner's military deployment (Werner & Shannon, 2013), and buffers the effects of stress and negative life events. It even helps lower the risk of mortality (Talbot et al., 2007).

Studies show leisure activities provide an excellent forum for the interaction of biological, psychological, and sociocultural forces (Kleiber, Hutchinson, & Williams, 2002; Kleiber, 2013). Leisure activities are a good way to deal with stress, which—as we have seen—has significant biological effects. This is especially true for unforeseen negative events (Janoff-Bulman & Berger, 2000). Psychologically, leisure activities have been well documented as one of the primary coping mechanisms people use (Patry, Blanchard, & Mask, 2007). How people cope by using leisure varies across cultures depending on the various types of activities that are permissible and available. Likewise, leisure activities vary across social class; basketball is one activity that cuts across class because it is inexpensive, whereas downhill skiing is more associated with people who can afford to travel to ski resorts and pay the fees.

How do leisure activities provide protection against stress? Kleiber and colleagues (2002; 2013) offer four ways leisure activities serve as a buffer against negative life events:

- Leisure activities distract us from negative life events.

- Leisure activities generate optimism about the future because they are pleasant.

- Leisure activities connect us to our personal past by allowing us to participate in the same activities over much of our lives.

- Leisure activities can be used as vehicles for personal transformation.

Whether the negative life events we experience are personal, such as the loss of a loved one, or societal, such as a terrorist attack, leisure activities are a common and effective way to deal with them. They truly represent the confluence of biopsychosocial forces and are effective at any point in the life cycle.

Participating with others in leisure activities may also strengthen feelings of attachment to one's partner, friends, and family (Carnelley & Ruscher, 2000). Adults use leisure as a way to explore interpersonal relationships or to seek social approval. In fact, research indicates marital satisfaction is linked with leisure time; marital satisfaction is even helped when couples spend some leisure time with others in addition to spending it just as a couple (Zabriskie & Kay, 2013). But there's no doubt couples who play together are happier (Johnson, Zabriskie, & Hill, 2006).

What if leisure activities are pursued seriously? In some cases, people create leisure–family conflict by engaging in leisure activities to extremes (Heo, Lee, McCormick, & Pedersen, 2010). Individuals who are serious about participating in specific leisure activities may experience "flow" or being in the "zone." When things get serious, problems may occur. Only when there is support from others for such extreme involvement are problems avoided. Professional quilters felt much more valued when family members were supportive (Stalp & Conti, 2011). As in most things, moderation in leisure activities is probably best, unless you know you have excellent support.

You have probably heard the saying "no vacation goes unpunished." It appears to be true, and the trouble is not just afterward. Research shows pre-vacation workload is associated with lower health and well-being for both men and women, and pre-vacation homeload (extra work that needs to be done at home) has the same negative effect for women (Nawijn, de Bloom, & Geurts, 2013).

Once on vacation, it matters what you do. If you detach from work, enjoy the activities during vacation, and engage in conversation with your partner, then the vacation can improve health and well-being, even after you return home (de Bloom, Geurts, & Kompier, 2012). However, workers report high postvacation workloads eliminate most of the positive effects of a vacation within about a week (de Bloom, Geurts, Taris, Sonnentag, de Weerth, & Kompier, 2010). Restful vacations do not prevent declines in mood or in sleep due to one's postvacation workload.

One frequently overlooked outcome of leisure activity is social acceptance. For persons with disabilities, this is a particularly important consideration (Choi, Johnson, & Kriewitz, 2013). There is a positive connection between frequency of leisure activities and positive identity, social acceptance, friendship development, and acceptance of differences. These findings highlight the importance of designing inclusive leisure activity programs.

ADULT DEVELOPMENT IN ACTION

What effect does leisure have on adult development and aging?

12.6 Retirement and Work in Late Life

LEARNING OBJECTIVES

- What does being retired mean?
- Why do people retire?
- How satisfied are retired people?
- What employment and volunteer opportunities are there for older adults?

Marcus is a 77-year-old retired construction worker who labored hard all of his life. He managed to save a little money, but he and his wife live primarily off of his monthly Social Security checks. Though not rich, they *have enough to pay the bills. Marcus is largely happy with retirement, and he stays in touch with his friends. He thinks maybe he's a little strange, though, since he has heard retirees are supposed to be isolated and lonely.*

Did you know that until 1934, when a railroad union sponsored a bill promoting mandatory retirement, and 1935, when Social Security was inaugurated, retirement was not even considered a possibility by most Americans like Marcus (McClinton, 2010; Sargent, Lee, Martin, & Zikic, 2013)? Only since World War II has there been a substantial number of retired people in the United States (McClinton, 2010). Although we take retirement for granted, economic downturns have a major disruptive effect on people's retirement decisions and plans—after declining for decades, the number of people over age 65 still in the workforce has increased significantly (Sterns & Chang, 2010). As more people retire and take advantage of longer lives, a significant social challenge is created regarding how to fund retiree benefits and view older adults who are still active (Bengtsson & Scott, 2011; McClinton, 2010; Tsao, 2004).

After having one or several careers across adulthood, many older adults find themselves questioning whether they want to continue in that line of work anymore, or find themselves being forced to go through that questioning because they lost their jobs. This period of questioning and potential exploration enables people to think about their options: retiring, looking for work in the same of a different field, volunteering, or some combination of all of these. With the movement of the baby boom generation into old age, increasing numbers of these adults are redefining what "retirement" and "work" mean in late life. Realizing these generational shifts reflect important changes in how people view the latter part of one's working life, AARP launched the *Life Reimagined* tool that assists people in finding their path, including reawakening long-dormant interests.

As we consider retirement and other options in late life, keep in mind the world is changing, resulting in increased options and the likelihood more older adults will continue in the labor force by choice and necessity.

What Does Being Retired Mean?

Retirement means different things to men and women, and to people in different ethnic groups (Loretto &

Vickerstaff, 2013; Luborsky & LeBlanc, 2003; McClinton, 2010). It has also taken on new and different meanings since the beginning of the Great Recession in 2008 because of the abrupt change in people's planning and expectations as a result of the loss of savings or pensions (Sargent et al., 2013).

Part of the reason it is difficult to define retirement precisely is the decision to retire involves the loss of occupational identity and not what people may add to their lives. What people do for a living is a major part of their identity; we introduce ourselves as postal workers, teachers, builders, or nurses as a way to tell people something about ourselves. Not doing those jobs any more means we either put that aspect of our lives in the past tense—"I used to work as a manager at the Hilton"—or say nothing at all. Loss of this aspect of ourselves can be difficult to face, so some look for a label other than "retired" to describe themselves.

That's why researchers view retirement as another one of many transitions people experience in life (Sargent et al., 2013; Schlossberg, 2004; Sterns & Chang, 2010). This view makes retirement a complex process where people withdraw from full-time participation in an occupation (Sargent et al., 2013), recognizing there are many pathways to this end (Everingham, Warner-Smith, & Byles, 2007; Sargent et al., 2013).

Why Do People Retire?

Provided they have good health, more workers retire by choice than for any other reason (Ekerdt, 2010; McClinton, 2010; Sterns & Chang, 2010), although economic conditions both personally and in society also have powerful effects (Hairault, Langot, & Zylberberg, 2012). Individuals usually retire when they feel financially secure after considering projected income from Social Security, pensions and other structured retirement programs, and personal savings. Of course, some people are forced to retire because of health problems or because they lose their jobs. As corporations downsize during economic downturns or after corporate mergers, some older workers accept buyout packages involving supplemental payments if they retire. Others are permanently furloughed, laid off, or dismissed.

The decision to retire is influenced by one's occupational history and goal expectations (Ekerdt, 2010;

Hairault et al., 2012; McClinton, 2010; Sargent et al., 2013). Whether people perceive they will achieve their personal goals through work or retirement influences the decision to retire and its connection with health and disability.

The rude awakening many people received during the Great Recession was the best made plans are only as good as external factors allow them to be, especially when it comes to financial savings and pensions. Many people lost much, and sometimes all of these financial packages as the value of stocks plummeted and companies eliminated pension plans. Consequently, many people were forced to delay their retirement until they had the financial resources to do so, or to continue working part time when they had not planned to do so to supplement their income. Research shows 44% of people over age 55 in 2013 now think they will retire beyond age 66, compared to 29% in 2003 (Employee Benefits Research Institute, 2013).

Additionally, many people do not have adequate savings for retirement. As you can see in Table 12.1, most people have not saved nearly what they need (Employee Benefits Research Institute, 2013). There has also been a decline in the confidence people have in their savings being adequate.

Table 12.1

REPORTED TOTAL SAVINGS AND INVESTMENTS, AMONG THOSE PROVIDING A RESPONSE					
	All Workers	Ages 25–34	Ages 35–44	Ages 45–54	Ages 55+
Less than $10,000	46%	60%	46%	40%	36%
$10,000–$24,999	11	15	12	11	7
$25,000–$49,999	9	9	11	6	9
$50,000–$99,999	10	8	10	13	8
$100,000–$249,999	12	7	13	14	18
$250,000 or more	12	2	8	16	24

Note: Figures do not include the value of the primary residence or defined benefit plans

Source: Employee Benefits Research Institute. (2013). 2013 Retirement Confidence Survey. (Figure 3).

How much do you need to have in savings to be comfortable in retirement? A decent rule of thumb is to plan for between 65% and 75% of your current income and that usually means having savings equal to about 11 times your final salary in addition to expected income from Social Security (Aon, 2013). This figure takes into account typical medical expenses. The bottom line is longer life expectancies have added to the amount of money you will need in retirement—and that amount is usually much greater than people think.

Gender and Ethnic Differences. Women's experience of retiring can be quite different from men's (Everingham et al., 2007; Frye, 2008; Loretto & Vickerstaff, 2013). Women may enter the workforce after they have stayed home and raised children and in general have more discontinuous work histories; also, having fewer financial resources may affect women's decisions to retire. Women also tend to spend less time planning their retirement (Jacobs-Lawson, Hershey, & Neukam, 2004).

For women who were never employed outside the home, the process of retirement is especially unclear (Gardiner et al., 2007; Loretto & Vickerstaff, 2013). Because they were not paid for all of their work raising children and caring for the home, it is rare for them to have their own pensions or other sources of income in retirement. Additionally, the work they have always done in caring for the home continues, often nearly uninterrupted.

There has not been much research examining the process of retirement as a function of ethnicity. African American older adults are likely to continue working beyond age 65 (Troutman et al., 2011). However, there are no ethnic-based differences in health outcomes between African American women and men following retirement (Curl, 2007).

Adjustment to Retirement

How do people who go through the process of retirement adjust to it? Researchers agree on one point: New patterns of personal involvement must be developed in the context of changing roles and lifestyles in retirement (Potočnik, Tordera, & Peiró, 2013). People's adjustment to retirement evolves over time as a result of complex interrelations involving physical health, financial status, to the degree their retirement was voluntary, and feelings of personal control (Ekerdt, 2010).

Retirement increasingly includes part-time work for extra income.

Jose Luis Pelaez Inc/Blend Images/Alamy

How do most people fare? As long as people have financial security, health, a supportive network of relatives and friends, and an internally driven sense of motivation, they report feeling good about being retired (Ekerdt, 2010; Hershey & Henkens, in press; Potočnik et al., 2013).

One widely held view is being retired has negative effects on health. Research findings show the relation between health and retirement is complex. On the one hand, there is no evidence voluntary retirement has immediate negative effects on health (Hershey & Henkens, in press; Weymouth, 2005). In contrast, there is ample evidence being forced to retire is correlated with significantly poorer physical and mental health (Donahue, 2007; Hershey & Henkens, in press). Health issues are also a major predictor of when a person retires, as a longitudinal study in England showed (Rice et al., 2010).

Employment and Volunteering

Retirement is an important life transition, one best understood through a life-course perspective that takes other aspects of one's life, such as one's marital relationship, into account (Wickrama, O'Neal, & Lorenz, 2013). This life change means retirees must look for ways to adapt to new routines and patterns, while maintaining social integration and being active in various ways (e.g., friendship networks, community engagement).

Working in Late Life. For an increasing number of people, especially for those whose retirement savings either took a significant drop or disappeared during the Great Recession, "retirement" involves working at least part-time. Employment for them is a financial necessity to make ends meet, especially for those whose entire income would consist only of Social Security benefits. For others, the need to stay employed at least part-time represents a way to stay involved and as an income supplement.

As you can see in Figure 12.8, the number of adults age 65 and over who are in the labor force nearly doubled between 2003 and 2013. Note also the trend has been consistently upward, indicating the forces keeping older adults in the labor force have been acting for many years (Bureau of Labor Statistics, 2013c).

Overall, labor force participation of older adults in the United States and other developed countries has been increasing most rapidly among women (Sterns & Chang, 2010). This is due mostly to more women being

in the labor force across adulthood than in decades past and more older women being single and needing the income. Most older adults are employed part-time, and this proportion is increasing because of the loss of full-time jobs in the Great Recession.

Older workers face many challenges, not the least of which are ageism and discrimination (Jackson, 2013). Employers may believe older workers are less capable, and there is some evidence this translates into lower likelihood of getting a job interview compared to younger or middle-aged workers, all other things being equal. Despite the fact age discrimination laws in the United States protect people over age 40, such barriers are still widespread.

The relationship between age and job performance is extremely complex (Sterns & Chang, 2010). This is because it depends a great deal on the kind of job one is considering, such as one that involves a great deal of physical exertion or one involving a great deal of expertise and experience. In general, older workers show more reliability (e.g., showing up on time for work), organizational loyalty, and safety-related behavior.

How have companies adapted to having more older workers? One example is BMW, that changed a number of things in its automobile assembly plants to meet the needs of older workers better (de Pommereau, 2012). BMW provides physical trainers on the factory floor, laid new, softer floors, chairs that rise up and down to make tasks easier, larger print fonts on computer screens, and providing special shoes.

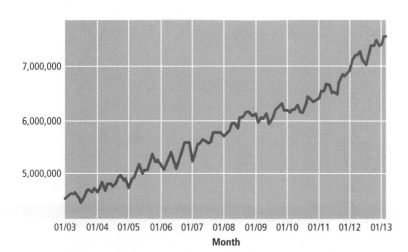

Figure 12.8

Number of adults aged 65 and over in the labor force.

Source: Bureau of Labor Statistics. (2013c). Labor force statistics from the Current Population Survey.

The trend for companies to employ older workers, especially on a part-time basis, is likely to continue because it is a good option of companies (Beck, 2013). Some companies find they need the expertise older workers bring, and the flexibility of older workers in terms of hours and the type of benefits they need (or do not need) often make it less expensive. Consequently, "retirement" is likely to continue to evolve as a concept, and likely to include some aspect of employment well into late life.

Volunteering. The past few decades have witnessed a rapid growth of organizations devoted to offering such opportunities to retirees. Groups at the local community level, including senior centers and clubs, promote the notion of lifelong learning and keep older adults cognitively active. Many also offer travel opportunities specifically designed for active older adults.

Healthy, active retired adults also maintain community ties by volunteering (Kleiber, 2013). Older adults report they volunteer for many reasons that benefit their well-being (Greenfield & Marks, 2005): to provide service to others, to maintain social interactions and improve their communities, and to keep active. Why do so many people volunteer?

Several factors are responsible (Tang, Morrow-Howell, & Choi, 2010): developing a new aspect of the self, finding a personal sense of purpose, desire to share one's skills and expertise, a redefinition of the nature and merits of volunteer work, a more highly educated and healthy population of older adults, and greatly expanded opportunities for people to become involved in volunteer work that they enjoy. Research in New Zealand documents older adults find volunteering enables them to give back to their local communities (Wiles & Jayasinha, 2013). Brown and colleagues (2011) argue volunteerism offers a way for society to tap into the vast resources older adults offer.

There is also evidence the expectations of people who volunteer in retirement are changing. Seaman (2012) notes women in the leading edge of the baby boom generation are interested in volunteering for personal, rather than purely altruistic reasons and do so on their own terms. They are not as willing as were volunteers in previous generations to serve on time consuming boards and engage in fundraising. As a result, organizations that rely on volunteers need to be in touch with the concerns and motivations of their pool of volunteers.

ADULT DEVELOPMENT IN ACTION

What cognitive and physical factors influence the decision to retire?

SOCIAL POLICY IMPLICATIONS

In the United States, the first law regarding pay equity was passed by Congress in 1963. Forty-six years later in 2009, President Obama signed the Lilly Ledbetter Fair Pay Act, showing clearly the problem of pay inequity still exists. In their comprehensive and insightful analysis of the continuing gap between men's and women's paychecks for the same work, Dey and Hill (2007) make a clear case that much needs to be done, and now.

Why? Consider this: Only one year out of college, a woman earns on average about $0.80 for every $1.00 a male college graduate earns. A decade later, she's down to about $0.69. This is even after controlling for such important variables as occupation, hours worked, parenthood, and other factors associated with pay.

What if women choose a college major associated with high-paying jobs, such as those in science, technology, engineering, and mathematics? Will that help reduce the pay differential? No. Choosing a traditionally male-dominated major will not solve the problem alone. Women in mathematics occupations earn only about $0.76 for every $1.00 a male mathematics graduate earns.

A woman is also significantly disadvantaged when it comes to the division of labor at home if she is married to or living with a man. Despite decades of effort in getting men to do more of the housework and child-care tasks, little has changed in terms of the amount of time men actually spend on these tasks. In effect, this means women have two careers, one in the workplace and the other at home. If a college-educated woman stays at home to care for a child or parent, then her return to the workforce will be at a lower salary than it would have been otherwise.

SUMMARY

12.1 Occupational Selection and Development

How do people view work?

- Although most people work for money, other reasons are highly variable.

How do people choose their occupations?

- Holland's theory is based on the idea people choose occupations to optimize the fit between their individual traits and their occupational interests. Six personality types, representing different combinations of these, have been identified. Support for these types has been found in several studies.

- Social cognitive career theory emphasizes how people choose careers is also influenced by what they think they can do and how well they can do it, as well as how motivated they are to pursue a career.

What factors influence occupational development?

- Reality shock is the realization one's expectations about an occupation are different from what one actually experiences. Reality shock is common among young workers.

- Few differences exist across generations in terms of their occupational expectations.

- A mentor or developmental coach is a co-worker who teaches a new employee the unwritten rules and fosters occupational development. Mentor–protégé relationships, like other relationships, develop through stages over time.

What is the relationship between job satisfaction and age?

- Older workers report higher job satisfaction than younger workers, but this may be partly due to self-selection; unhappy workers may quit. Other reasons include intrinsic satisfaction, good fit, lower importance of work, finding nonwork diversions, and life-cycle factors.

- Alienation and burnout are important considerations in understanding job satisfaction. Both involve significant stress for workers.

- Vallerand's Passion Model proposes people develop a passion toward enjoyable activities that are incorporated into identity. Obsessive passion happens when people experience an uncontrollable urge to engage in the activity; harmonious passion results when individuals freely accept the activity as important for them without any contingencies attached to it.

12.2 Gender, Ethnicity, and Discrimination Issues

How do women's and men's occupational expectations differ? How are people viewed when they enter occupations that are not traditional for their gender?

- Boys and girls are socialized differently for work, and their occupational choices are affected as a result. Women choose nontraditional occupations for many reasons, including expectations and personal feelings. Women in such occupations are still viewed more negatively than men in the same occupations.

What factors are related to women's occupational development?

- Women leave well-paid occupations for many reasons, including family obligations and workplace environment. Women who continue to work full-time have adequate child care and look for ways to further their occupational development.

- The glass ceiling, that limits women's occupational attainment, and the glass cliff, that puts women leaders in a precarious position, affect how often women achieve top executive positions and how successful women leaders are.

What factors affect ethnic minority workers' occupational experiences and occupational development?

- Vocational identity and vocational goals vary in different ethnic groups. Whether an organization is sensitive to ethnicity issues is a strong predictor of satisfaction among ethnic minority employees.

What types of bias and discrimination hinder the occupational development of women and ethnic minority workers?

- Gender bias remains the chief barrier to women's occupational development. In many cases, this operates as a glass ceiling. Pay inequity is also a problem; women are often paid less than what men earn in similar jobs.

- Sexual harassment is a problem in the workplace. Current criteria for judging harassment are based on the "reasonable person" standard. Denying employment to anyone over 40 because of age is age discrimination.

12.3 Occupational Transitions

Why do people change occupations?

- Important reasons people change occupations include personality, obsolescence, and economic trends.

- To adapt to the effects of aglobal economy and a gain workforce, many corporations are providing retraining opportunities for workers. Retraining is especially important in cases of outdated skills and career plateauing.

Is worrying about potential job loss a major source of stress?

- Occupational insecurity is a growing problem. Fear that one may lose one's job is a better predictor of anxiety than the actual likelihood of job loss.

How does job loss affect the amount of stress experienced?

- Job loss is a traumatic event that can affect every aspect of a person's life. Degree of financial distress and the extent of attachment to the job are the best predictors of distress.

12.4 Work and Family

What are the issues faced by employed people who care for dependents?

- Caring for children or aging parents creates dilemmas for workers. Whether a woman returns to work after having a child depends largely on how attached she is to her work. Simply providing child care on-site does not always result in higher job satisfaction. A more important factor is the degree that supervisors are sympathetic.

How do partners view the division of household chores? What is work–family conflict? How does it affect couples' lives?

- Although women have reduced the amount of time they spend on household tasks over the past two decades, they still do most of the work. European American men are less likely than either African American or Latino American men to help with traditionally female household tasks.

- Flexible work schedules and the number of children are important factors in role conflict. Recent evidence shows work stress has a much greater impact on family life than family stress has on work performance. Some women pay a high personal price for having careers.

12.5 Leisure Activities

What activities are leisure activities?

- Leisure activities can be simple relaxation, activities for enjoyment, or creative pursuits. Views of leisure activities varies by gender, ethnicity, and age.

What changes in leisure activities occur with age?

- As people grow older, they tend to engage in leisure activities that are less strenuous and more family-oriented. Leisure preferences in adulthood reflect those earlier in life.

What do people derive from leisure activities?

- Leisure activities enhance well-being and can benefit all aspects of people's lives.

12.6 Retirement and Work in Late Life

What does being retired mean?

- Retirement is a complex process by which people withdraw from full-time employment. There is no adequate, single definition for all ethnic groups. People's decisions to retire involve several factors, including eligibility for certain social programs, and personal financial and health resources.

Why do people retire?

- People generally retire because they choose to, but many people are forced to retire because of job loss or serious health problems.

How satisfied are people with retirement?

- Retirement is an important life transition. Most people are satisfied with retirement. Many retired people maintain their health, friendship networks, and activity levels.

What employment and volunteer opportunities are there for older adults?

- Increasingly, people continue some level of participation in the labor force during retirement, usually for financial reasons. Labor force participation among older adults continues to increase. Volunteer work is another way of achieving this.

REVIEW QUESTIONS

12.1 Occupational Selection and Development

- What are occupational priorities and how do they change over time?

- How is work changing as a result of the global economy?
- Briefly describe social cognitive career theory (SCCT).
- How is reality shock a developmental concept?
- What is a mentor? What role does a mentor play in occupational development? How does the mentor–protégé relationship change over time?
- What is the developmental course of job satisfaction? What factors influence job satisfaction?
- What are alienation and burnout? How are they related to job satisfaction?
- Briefly describe Vallerand's Passion Model.

12.2 Gender, Ethnicity, and Discrimination

- What gender differences have been identified relating to occupational choice? How are men and women socialized differently in ways that influence occupational opportunities?
- How are women in nontraditional occupations perceived?
- What are the major barriers to women's occupational development?
- What major barriers to occupational development are related to ethnicity?
- How are sex discrimination and the glass ceiling/glass cliff related?
- What are the structural barriers ethnic minorities face in occupational settings?
- How is sexual harassment defined?
- What is age discrimination and how does it operate?

12.3 Occupational Transitions

- What are the major reasons why people change occupations?
- Why is retraining workers important?
- What effects do people report after losing their jobs?

12.4 Work and Family

- What factors are important in dependent care for employees?
- How do dual-earner couples balance multiple roles and deal with role conflict?

- What important factors contribute to work-family conflict? What other occupational development effects occur?

12.5 Leisure Activities

- What are the major reasons people engage in leisure activities? What benefits occur?
- What kinds of leisure activities do people perform?
- How do leisure activities change over the life span?

12.6 Retirement and Work in Late Life

- In what ways can retirement be viewed? How may the definition of retirement change in the next several years?
- What are the main predictors of the decision to retire?
- How do people adjust to being retired?
- What factors influence decisions to continue working or volunteering in retirement?

INTEGRATING CONCEPTS IN DEVELOPMENT

- What role do personal relationships play in one's work, leisure, and retirement?
- How does cognitive development and personality influence work roles?
- What implications are there for the removal of mandatory retirement in terms of normal cognitive changes with age?

KEY TERMS

age discrimination Denying a job or a promotion to a person solely on the basis of age.

alienation Situation in which workers feel they are doing is meaningless and their efforts are devalued, or when they do not see the connection between what they do and the final product.

backup care Emergency care for dependent children or adults so the employee does not need to lose a day of work.

burnout The depletion of a person's energy and motivation, the loss of occupational idealism, and the feeling of being exploited.

Career construction theory Posits people build careers through their own actions that result from the interface of their own personal characteristics and the social context.

career plateauing Situation occurring when there is a lack of challenge in the job or promotional opportunity in the organization or when a person decides not to seek advancement.

gender discrimination Denying a job to someone solely on the basis of whether the person is a man or a woman.

glass ceiling The level to which a woman may rise in an organization but beyond which they may not go.

glass cliff A situation in which a woman's leadership position in an organization is precarious.

job satisfaction The positive feeling that results from an appraisal of one' work.

leisure A discretionary activity that includes simple relaxation, activities for enjoyment, and creative pursuits.

meaning-mission fit Alignment between people's personal intentions and their company's mission

mentor or developmental coach A person who is part teacher, sponsor, model, and counselor who facilitates on-the-job learning to help a new hire do the work required in his or her present role and to prepare for future roles.

passion A strong inclination toward an activity that individuals like (or even love), that they value (and thus find important), and in which they invest time and energy.

reality shock Situation in which what you learn in the classroom does not always transfer directly into the "real world" and does not represent all you need to know.

social cognitive career theory (SCCT) Proposes career choice is a result of the application of Bandura's social cognitive theory, especially the concept of self-efficacy.

work–family conflict The feeling of being pulled in multiple directions by incompatible demands from job and family.

RESOURCES

Access quizzes, glossaries, flashcards, and more at www.cengagebrain.com.

13.1 DEFINITIONS AND ETHICAL ISSUES
Sociocultural Definitions of Death • Legal and Medical Definitions • Ethical Issues • *Current Controversies: The Terri Schiavo Case* • The Price of Life-Sustaining Care

13.2 THINKING ABOUT DEATH: PERSONAL ASPECTS
Discovering Development: A Self-Reflective Exercise on Death • Life-Course Approach to Dying • Dealing With One's Own Death • Death Anxiety

13.3 END-OF-LIFE ISSUES
Creating a Final Scenario • The Hospice Option • Making Your End-of-Life Intentions Known

13.4 SURVIVING THE LOSS: THE GRIEVING PROCESS
The Grief Process • Normal Grief Reactions • Coping With Grief • *How Do We Know?: Grief Processing and Avoidance in the United States and China* • Complicated or Prolonged Grief Disorder • Adult Developmental Aspects of Grief • Conclusion

SOCIAL POLICY IMPLICATIONS
Summary • Review Questions • Integrating Concepts in Development • Key Terms • Resources

WHEN FAMOUS PEOPLE SUCH AS HEATH LEDGER, MICHAEL JACKSON, WHITNEY HOUSTON, OR AMY WINEHOUSE DIE UNEXPECTEDLY, people are confronted with the reality that death happens to everyone.

We have a paradoxical relationship with death. Sometimes we are fascinated by it. As tourists, we visit places where famous people died or are buried. We watch as television newscasts show scenes of devastation in natural disasters and war. But when it comes to pondering our own death or people close to us, we have many problems. As French writer and reformer La Rochefoucauld wrote over 300 years ago, "looking into the sun is easier than contemplating our death." When death is personal, we become uneasy. Looking at the sun is hard indeed.

In this chapter we delve into thanatology. **Thanatology** *is the study of death, dying, grief,*

Amy Winehouse

Shirlaine Forrest/WireImage/Getty Images

Michael Jackson

Europa Newswire/Alamy

bereavement, and social attitudes toward these issues. We first consider definitional and ethical issues surrounding death. Next, we look specifically at the process of dying. Dealing with grief is important for survivors, so we consider this topic in the third section. Finally, we examine how people view death at different points in the life span.

13.1 Definitions and Ethical Issues

LEARNING OBJECTIVES

- How is death defined?
- What legal and medical criteria are used to determine when death occurs?
- What are the ethical dilemmas surrounding euthanasia?
- What issues surround the costs of life-sustaining care?

Ernesto and Paulina had been married 48 years when Ernesto developed terminal pancreatic cancer. Ernesto was suffering terrible pain and begged Paulina to make it stop. He said she would not let their pet suffer this way, so why let him? Paulina heard about "mercy killing" that involved administering high dosages of certain medications, but she believed this was the same as murder. Yet, she could hardly bear to watch her beloved husband suffer. Paulina wondered what she should do.

When one first thinks about it, death seems a simple concept to define: It is the point when a person is no longer alive. Similarly, dying is simply the process of making the transition from being alive to being dead. It all seems clear enough, doesn't it? But death and dying are actually far more complicated concepts.

As we will see, there are many cultural and religious differences in the definition of death and the customs surrounding it. The meaning of death depends on the observer's perspective as well as the specific medical and biological criteria one uses.

Sociocultural Definitions of Death

What comes to mind when you hear the word *death*? A driver killed in a traffic accident? A transition to an eternal reward? Flags at half-staff? A cemetery? A car battery that doesn't work anymore? Each of these possibilities represents a way death can be considered in Western culture and has its own set of specific rituals (Bustos, 2007; Penson, 2004). All cultures have their own views. Some cultures pull their hair (Lewis, 2013). Melanesians have a term, *mate*, that includes the extremely sick, the very old, and the dead; the term *toa* refers to all other living people (Counts & Counts, 1985). Other South Pacific cultures believe the life force leaves the body during sleep or illness; sleep, illness, and death are considered together. Thus people "die" many times before experiencing "final death."

In Ghana people are said to have a "peaceful" or "good" death if the dying person finished all business and made peace with others before death, and implies being at peace with his or her own death (van der Geest, 2004). A good and peaceful death comes "naturally" after a long and well-spent life. Such a death preferably takes place at home, the epitome of peacefulness, surrounded by children and grandchildren. Finally, a good death is a death accepted by the relatives.

Mourning rituals and states of bereavement also vary in different cultures (Lee, 2010; Norton & Gino, in press). There is great variability across cultures in the meaning of death and whether there are rituals or other behaviors to express grief. Some cultures have formalized periods of time during which certain prayers or rituals are performed. After the death of a close relative, Orthodox Jews recite ritual prayers and cover all the mirrors in the house. The men slash their ties as a symbol of loss. In Papua New Guinea, there are accepted time periods for phases of grief (Herner, 2010). The Muscogee Creek tribe's rituals include digging the grave by hand and giving a "farewell handshake" by throwing a handful of dirt into the grave before covering it (Walker & Balk, 2007). Ancestor worship, a deep respectful feeling toward individuals from whom a family is descended or who are important to them, is an important part of customs of death in many Asian cultures (Roszko, 2010). We must keep in mind the experiences of our culture or particular group may not generalize to other cultures or groups.

Death can be a truly cross-cultural experience. The international outpouring of grief over the death of

The symbols we use when people die, such as these elaborate caskets from Ghana, provide insights into how cultures think about death.

Harry Hook/Stone/Getty Images

world leaders such Nelson Mandela in 2013, the thousands killed in the terrorist attacks against the United States in September 2001, and the hundreds of thousands killed in such natural disasters as the earthquake in Haiti in 2010 drew much attention to the ways the deaths of people we do not know personally can still affect us. It is at these times we realize death happens to us all and death can simultaneously be personal and public.

The many ways of viewing death can be seen in various customs involving funerals. You may have experienced a range of different types of funeral customs, from small, private services to elaborate rituals. Variations in the customs surrounding death are reflected in some of the most iconic structures on earth, such as the pyramids in Egypt, and some of the most beautiful, such as the Taj Mahal in India.

Legal and Medical Definitions

Sociocultural approaches help us understand the different ways people conceptualize and understand death; but they do not address a fundamental question: How do we determine someone has died? The medical and legal communities grappled with this question for centuries and continue to do so today. Let's see what the current answers are.

Determining when death occurs has always been subjective. *For hundreds of years, people accepted and applied the criteria that now define* **clinical death**: *lack of heartbeat and respiration. Today, however, the most widely accepted criteria are those that characterize*

whole-brain death. In 1981, the President's Commission for the Ethical Study of Problems in Medicine and Biomedical and Behavioral Research established several criteria still used today that must be met for the determination of whole-brain death:

- No spontaneous movement in response to any stimuli
- No spontaneous respirations for at least one hour
- Total lack of responsiveness to even the most painful stimuli
- No eye movements, blinking, or pupil responses
- No postural activity, swallowing, yawning, or vocalizing
- No motor reflexes
- A flat electroencephalogram (EEG) for at least 10 minutes
- No change in any of these criteria when they are tested again 24 hours later

For a person to be declared dead, all eight criteria must be met. Moreover, other conditions that mimic death—such as deep coma, hypothermia, or drug overdose—must be ruled out. Finally, according to most hospitals, the lack of brain activity must occur both in the brainstem that involves vegetative functions such as heartbeat and respiration, and in the cortex, involving higher processes such as thinking. In the United States, all 50 states and the District of Columbia use the whole-brain standard to define death.

A major problem facing the medical profession is how brain death is diagnosed in practice (Sung & Greer, 2011). In part this is due to variable intervals taken to make the second assessment (Lustbader et al., 2011). Because patients declared brain dead on first examination do not spontaneously recover brain stem function, and because long delays in second assessments lower the rate that patients' families agree to organ donation, some medical professionals are calling for a single assessment or at least a simpler, more direct process (Sung & Greer, 2011).

Brain death is also controversial from some religious perspectives. For example, some Islamic scholars argue brain death is not complete death; complete death must include the cessation of respiration (Bedir & Aksoy, 2011). Roman Catholics focus on what they term "natural death" (Verheijde, 2010).

It is possible for a person's cortical functioning to cease while brainstem activity continues; this is a **persistent vegetative state,** *from which the person does not recover.* This condition can occur following disruption of the blood flow to the brain, a severe head injury, or a drug overdose. Persistent vegetative state allows for spontaneous heartbeat and respiration but not for consciousness. The whole-brain standard does not permit a declaration of death for someone who is in a persistent vegetative state. Because of conditions like persistent vegetative state, family members sometimes face difficult ethical decisions concerning care for the individual. These issues are the focus of the next section.

Ethical Issues

An ambulance screeches to a halt and emergency personnel rush a woman into the emergency room. As a result of an accident at a swimming pool, she has no pulse and no respiration. Working rapidly, the trauma team reestablishes a heartbeat through electric shock. A respirator is connected. An EEG and other tests reveal extensive and irreversible brain damage—she is in a persistent vegetative state. What should be done?

This is an example of the kinds of problems faced in the field of **bioethics,** *the study of the interface between human values and technological advances in health and life sciences.* Bioethics grew from two bases: respect for individual freedom and the impossibility of establishing any single version of morality by rational argument or common sense. Both of these factors are increasingly based on empirical evidence and cultural contexts (Priaulx, 2013; Sherwin, 2011). In practice, bioethics emphasizes the importance of individual choice and the minimization of harm over the maximization of good. That is, bioethics requires people to weigh how much the patient will benefit from a treatment relative to the amount of suffering he or she will endure as a result of the treatment. Examples of the tough choices required are those facing cancer patients about aggressive treatment for cancer that is quite likely to be fatal in any case and those facing family members about whether to turn off a life-support machine attached to their loved one.

In the arena of death and dying, the most important bioethical issue is euthanasia—the practice of ending life for reasons of mercy. The moral dilemma posed by euthanasia becomes apparent when trying to decide the circumstances a person's life should be ended, that implicitly forces one to place a value on the life of another (Bedir & Aksoy, 2011; Munoz & Fox, 2013; Verheijde, 2010). It also makes us think about the difference between "killing" and "letting die" at the end of life (Dickens, Boyle, & Ganzini, 2008). In our society, this dilemma occurs most often when a person is being kept alive by machines or when someone is suffering from a terminal illness. This is the situation confronting Ernesto and Paulina in the opening vignette.

Euthanasia. Euthanasia can be carried out in two different ways: actively and passively (Moeller, Lewis, & Werth, 2010). *Active euthanasia involves the deliberate ending of someone's life, that may be based on a clear statement of the person's wishes or be a decision made by someone else who has the legal authority to do so.* Usually, this involves situations when people are in a persistent vegetative state or suffer from the end stages of a terminal disease. Examples of active euthanasia would be administering a drug overdose or ending a person's life through so-called mercy killing.

A second form of euthanasia, passive euthanasia, *involves allowing a person to die by withholding available treatment.* A ventilator might be disconnected, chemotherapy might be withheld from a patient with terminal cancer, a surgical procedure might not be performed, or food could be withdrawn.

Some ethicists and medical professionals do not differentiate active and passive euthanasia. The European Association of Palliative Care (EAPC, 2011) established an ethics task force opposing euthanasia, and claims the expression "passive euthanasia" is a contradiction in terms because any ending of a life is by definition active. Despite these concerns, Garrard and Wilkinson (2005) conclude there is really no reason to abandon the category provided it is properly and narrowly understood and "euthanasia reasons" for withdrawing or withholding life-prolonging treatment are carefully distinguished from other reasons, such as family members not wanting to wait to divide the patient's estate. Still, whether there is a difference between active and passive euthanasia remains controversial (Busch & Rodogno, 2011).

Most Americans favor such actions as disconnecting life support in situations involving patients in a persistent vegetative state, withholding treatment if the person agrees or is in the later stages of a terminal illness, and the concept of assisted death. But feelings also run strongly against such actions for religious or other reasons (Bedir & Aksoy, 2011; Meilaender, 2013; Verheijde, 2010). Even political debates incorporate the issue, as demonstrated in the summer of 2009 in the United States when opponents of President Obama's health care reform falsely claimed "death panels" would make decisions about terminating life support if the reform measure passed.

Globally, opinions about euthanasia vary (Bosshard & Materstvedt, 2011). A systematic survey of laypersons and health care professionals in the Netherlands and Belgium found most said they would support euthanasia under specific conditions (Teisseyre, Mullet, & Sorum, 2005). Respondents assigned most importance to patients' specific requests for euthanasia and supported these requests, but they did not view patients' willingness to donate organs—without another compelling reason—as an acceptable reason to request euthanasia.

Greek physicians and nurses oppose euthanasia, but support the legalization of hastening the death of an advanced cancer patient (e.g., not reviving a terminal cancer patient) (Parpa, Mystakidou, Tsilika, Sakkas, Patiraki, Pistevou-Gombaki et al., 2010). Other analyses show opinions are often related to religious or political beliefs (Swinton & Payne, 2009). Western Europeans tend to view active euthanasia more positively based on less influence of religion and more social welfare services than residents of Eastern European and Islamic countries, who are more influenced by religious beliefs arguing against such practices (Baumann et al., 2011; Góra & Mach, 2010; Hains & Hulbert-Williams, in press; Nayernouri, 2011).

Disconnecting a life support system is one thing; withholding nourishment from a terminally ill person is quite another for many people. Indeed, such cases often end up in court. The first high-profile legal case involving passive euthanasia in the United States was brought to the courts in 1990; the U.S. Supreme

Court took up the case of Nancy Cruzan, whose family wanted to end her forced feeding. The court ruled, unless clear and incontrovertible evidence is presented that an individual desires to have nourishment stopped, such as through a health care power of attorney or living will, a third party (such as a parent or partner), cannot decide to end it.

The most widely publicized and politicized case of euthanasia in the United States involved Terri Schiavo, who died in Florida in 2005. This extremely controversial case involving the withdrawal of forced feeding had its origins in a disagreement between Terri's husband Michael, who said Terri would have wanted to die with dignity and therefore the feeding tube should be removed, and her parents who argued the opposite. The debate resulted in the involvement of government officials, state and federal legislators, and the courts. As discussed in the Current Controversies feature, such cases reveal the difficult legal, medical, and ethical issues as well as the high degree of emotion surrounding the topic of euthanasia and death with dignity.

CURRENT CONTROVERSIES:

THE TERRI SCHIAVO CASE

On February 25, 1990, 26-year-old Terri Schiavo collapsed in her home from a possible potassium imbalance caused by an eating disorder, temporarily stopping her heart and cutting off oxygen to her brain. On March 31, 2005, Terri Schiavo died after her feeding tube was removed 13 days earlier. On these two points everyone connected with Terri's case agreed. But on all other essential aspects of it, Terri's husband Michael and Terri's parents deeply disagreed.

The central point of disagreement was Terri's medical condition. Terri's husband and numerous physicians argued she was in a persistent vegetative state. Based on this diagnosis, Michael Schiavo requested Terri's feeding tube be withdrawn and she be allowed to die with dignity in the way he asserted she would have wanted to.

Terri's parents and other physicians said she was not in a persistent vegetative state and was capable of recognizing them and others. Based on this diagnosis, their belief Terri would not want the intervention stopped, and their contention passive euthanasia is morally wrong, they fought Michael's attempts to remove the feeding tube.

What made this case especially difficult was that Terri left no written instructions clearly stating her thoughts and intentions on the issue. The ensuing legal and political debates became based on what various people thought Terri would have wanted and reflected various aspects of people's positions on personal rights regarding life and death.

The legal and political battles began in 1993 when Terri's parents tried unsuccessfully to have Michael removed as Terri's guardian. But the most heated aspects of the case began in 2000 when a circuit court judge ruled Terri's feeding tube could be removed based on his belief she had told Michael she would not have wanted it. In April 2001, the feeding tube was removed after state courts and the U.S. Supreme Court refused to hear the case. However, the tube was reinserted 2 days later upon another judge's order. In November 2002, the original circuit court judge ruled Terri had no hope of recovery and again ordered the tube removed, an order eventually carried out in October 2003. Within a week, however, Florida Governor Jeb Bush signed a bill passed by the Florida legislature requiring the tube be reinserted. This law was ruled unconstitutional by the Florida Supreme Court in September 2004. In February 2005, the original circuit court judge again ordered the tube removed. Between March 16 and March 27, the Florida House introduced and passed a bill that require the tube be reinserted, but the Florida Senate defeated a somewhat different version of the bill. From March 19 to 21, bills that would allow a federal court to review the case passed in the U.S. House of Representatives and the U.S. Senate, but the two versions could not be reconciled. Over the next ten days, the Florida Supreme Court, the U.S. district court, and a U.S. circuit court refused to hear the case, as did the U.S. Supreme Court.

Getty Images

Terri Schiavo and her mother.

The original circuit court judge rejected a final attempt by Terri's parents to have the feeding tube reinserted.

The public debate on the case was as long and complex as the legal and political arguments. The debate had several positive outcomes. The legal and political complexities dramatically illustrated the need for people to reflect on end-of-life issues and make their wishes known to family members and others (e.g., health care providers) in writing. The case also brought to light the high cost of long-term care, the difficulties in actually determining whether someone is in a persistent vegetative state (and what that implies about life), the tough moral and ethical issues surrounding the withdrawal of nutrition, and the individual's personal feelings about death. The legal and medical communities have proposed reforms concerning how these types of cases are heard in the courts and the processes used to resolve them (Berlinger, Jennings, & Wolf, 2013; Moran, 2008).

What do *you* think? Should Terri Schiavo's feeding tube have been removed? Discuss your thoughts in class.

Physician-Assisted Suicide. Taking one's own life through suicide has never been popular in the United States because of religious and other prohibitions. In other cultures, such as Japan, suicide is viewed as an honorable way to die under certain circumstances (Joiner, 2010).

Attitudes regarding suicide in certain situations are changing. *Much of this change concerns the topic of physician-assisted suicide, in which physicians provide dying patients with a fatal dose of medication that the patient self-administers.* A Harris Poll released in 2011 indicated 70% of all adult respondents (and 62% of those over age 65) agreed people who are terminally ill, in great pain and have no chance of recovery should have the right to choose to end their lives. Only 17% of the respondents disagreed. By a margin of 58% to 20%, respondents supported physician-assisted suicide for such patients (Harris Interactive, 2011). A similar poll in 2012 by NPR-Truven Health Analytics showed 55% of Americans favored physician assisted suicide for those with less than six months to live (Hensley, 2012). Clearly, most Americans favor having a choice.

Several countries—including Switzerland, Belgium, and Colombia—tolerate physician-assisted suicide. In 1984, the Dutch Supreme Court eliminated prosecution of physicians who assist in suicide if five criteria are met:

1. The patient's condition is intolerable with no hope for improvement.

2. No relief is available.

3. The patient is competent.

4. The patient makes a request repeatedly over time.

5. Two physicians review the case and agree with the patient's request.

The Dutch Parliament approved the policy in April 2001, making the Netherlands the first country to have an official policy legalizing physician-assisted suicide (Deutsch, 2001).

Voters in Oregon passed the Death With Dignity Act in 1994, the first physician-assisted suicide law in the United States (Initiative-1000, the Death With Dignity Act passed in Washington state in 2008, was modeled after the Oregon law). These laws make it legal for people to request a lethal dose of medication if they have a terminal disease and make the request voluntarily. Although the U.S. Supreme Court ruled in two cases in 1997 (*Vacco v. Quill* and *Washington v. Glucksberg*) there is no right to assisted suicide, the Court decided in 1998 not to overturn the Oregon law.

The Oregon and Washington laws are more restrictive than the law in the Netherlands (Deutsch, 2001). Both laws provide for people to obtain and use prescriptions for self-administered lethal doses of medication. The law requires a physician to inform the person he or she is terminally ill and describe alternative options (e.g., hospice care, pain control). The person must be mentally competent and make two oral and one written request, with at least 15 days between each oral request. Such provisions are included to ensure people making the request fully understand the issues and the request is not made hastily.

Several studies examined the impact of the Oregon law. The numbers of patients who received prescriptions and died between 1998 and 2012 are shown in Figure 13.1. Over the period, a total of 525 patients died under the terms of the law (Oregon Department of Human Services, 2013). Comprehensive reviews

Figure 13.1

Number of Oregon Death with Dignity Act prescription (Rx) recipients and deaths.

Source: http://public.health.oregon.gov/ProviderPartnerResources/EvaluationResearch/DeathwithDignityAct/Pages/arindex.Aspx

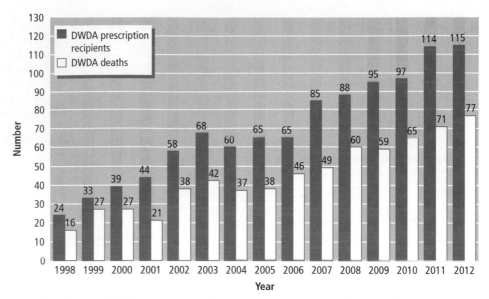

*As of January 14, 2013, prescriptions for lethal medications were written for 115 people during 2012 under the provisions of the DWDA, compared to 114 during 2011 (Figure 1). At the time of this report, there were 77 known DWDA deaths during 2012. This corresponds to 23.5 DWDA deaths per 10,000 total deaths.

of the implementation of the Oregon law soon after its passage concluded all safeguards worked and such things as depression, coercion, and misunderstanding of the law were carefully screened (Orentlicher, 2000). Available data also indicate laws such as Oregon's has psychological benefits for patients, who value having autonomy in death as in life, especially in situations involving unbearable suffering (Hendry, Pasterfield, Lewis, Carter, Hodgson, & Wilkinson, 2013).

There is no question the debate over physician-assisted suicide will continue. As the technology to keep people alive continues to improve, the ethical issues about active euthanasia in general and physician-assisted suicide in particular will continue to become more complex and will likely focus increasingly on quality of life.

The Price of Life-Sustaining Care

A growing debate in the United States, particularly in the aftermath of the Affordable Care Act passed in 2010, concerns the financial, personal, and moral costs of keeping people alive on life-support machines and continuing aggressive care when people have terminal conditions. Debate continues on whether secondary

health conditions in terminally ill people should be treated. The argument is such care is expensive, these people will die soon anyway, and needlessly prolonging life is a burden on society.

However, many others argue all means possible should be used, whether for a premature infant or an older adult, to keep them alive despite the high cost and possible risk of negative side effects of the treatment or intervention. They argue life is precious, and humans should not "play God" and decide when it should end.

There is no question extraordinary interventions are expensive. Health care costs can soar during the last year of a person's life. Data indicate less than 7% of people who receive hospital care die each year, but account for nearly 25% of all Medicare expenditures (Adamy & McGinty, 2012). Expenditures are typically less for those having advance directives (discussed later in this chapter).

The biggest challenge in confronting these differences in approach and cost is the difficulty in deciding when to treat or not treat a disease a person has. There are no easy answers. Witness the loud criticism when research evidence indicated various types of cancer screening (e.g., breast, prostate) should not be provided to everyone as early or as often as initially thought. Despite the lack of evidence to support and the cost of continuing traditional approaches, many patients and physicians do so anyway. Failure to base care on evidence has a price. Whether that is affordable in the long run seems unlikely.

ADULT DEVELOPMENT IN ACTION

How should the biopsychosocial model influence political debates about dying and death?

13.2 Thinking About Death: Personal Aspects

LEARNING OBJECTIVES

- How do feelings about death change over adulthood?
- How do people deal with their own death?
- What is death anxiety, and how do people show it?

Jean is a 49-year-old woman whose parents have both died in the past three years. She now realizes she is the oldest living member of her family (she has two younger siblings). She started thinking about the fact that someday she too will die. Jean gets anxious when she thinks about her death, and tries to block it out of her mind.

Like Jean, most people are uncomfortable thinking about their own death, especially if they think it will be unpleasant. As one research participant put it, "You are nuts if you aren't afraid of death" (Kalish & Reynolds, 1976). Still, death is a paradox, as we noted at the beginning of the chapter. That is, we are afraid of or anxious about death but we are drawn to it, sometimes in public ways. We examine this paradox at the personal level in this section. Specifically, we focus on two questions: How do people's feelings about death differ with age? What is it about death we fear or that makes us anxious?

Before proceeding, however, take a few minutes to complete the exercise in the Discovering Development feature.

DISCOVERING DEVELOPMENT:

A SELF-REFLECTIVE EXERCISE ON DEATH

As we noted, thinking about death, especially one's own, is difficult. One common way to remember people is through an obituary, an experience we may have with hundreds of people we know but never our own. Here's a chance to think about one's own death from that perspective.

- In 200 words or less, write your own obituary. Be sure to include your age and cause of death. List your lifetime accomplishments. Don't forget to list your survivors.
- Think about all the things you will have done that are not listed in your obituary. List some of them.
- Think of all the friends you will have made and how you will have affected them.
- Would you make any changes in your obituary now?

A Life-Course Approach to Dying

Suppose you learned today you had only a few months to live. How would you feel about dying? Do you think people of different ages feel the same way? It probably doesn't surprise you to learn feelings about dying vary across adulthood such as adults of various ages who live with a person with a life-threatening illness. Each comes to terms with death in an individual and a family-based way, and together they co-create ways the patient meets his or her goals (Bergdahl, Benzein, Ternestedt, Elmberger, & Andershed, in press; Carlander, Ternestedt, Sahlberg-Blom, Hellström, & Sandberg, 2011).

Although not specifically addressed in research, the shift from formal operational thinking to post-formal thinking (see Chapter 7) could be important in young adults' contemplation of death. Presumably, this shift in cognitive development is accompanied by a lessening of the feeling of immortality in adolescence to one that integrates personal feelings and emotions with their thinking.

Midlife is the time when most people in developed countries confront the death of their parents. Until that point, people tend not to think much about their own death; the fact their parents are still alive buffers them from reality. After all, in the normal course of events, our parents are supposed to die before we do.

Once their parents die, people realize they are now the oldest generation of their family—the next in line to die. Reading the obituary pages, they are reminded of this, as the ages of many of the people who died get closer and closer to their own.

Probably as a result of this growing realization of their own mortality, middle-aged adults' sense of time undergoes a subtle yet profound change. It changes from an emphasis on how long they have already lived to how long they have left to live, a shift that increases into late life (Cicirelli, 2006; Maxfield, Solomon, Pyszczynski, & Greenberg, 2010). This may lead to occupational change or other redirection such as improving relationships that deteriorated over the years.

In general, older adults are less anxious about death and more accepting of it than any other age group. Still, because the discrepancy between desired and expected number of years left to live is greater for young-old than for mid-old adults, anxiety is higher for young-old adults (Cicirelli, 2006). In part, the greater overall acceptance of death results from the achievement of ego integrity, as described in Chapter 9. For other older adults, the joy of living is diminishing. More than any other group, they experienced loss of family and friends and have come to terms with their own mortality. Older adults have more chronic diseases (see Chapters 3 and 4) that are not likely to go away. They may feel their most important life tasks have been completed (Kastenbaum, 1999).

Understanding how adults deal with death and their consequent feelings of grief is best approached from the perspective of attachment theory (Mercer, 2011; Stroebe, Schut, & Stroebe, 2005). In this view, a person's reactions are a natural consequence of forming attachments and then losing them. We consider adult grief a bit later in the chapter.

Dealing With One's Own Death

Many authors have tried to describe the dying process, often using the metaphor of a trajectory that captures the duration of time between the onset of dying (e.g., from the diagnosis of a fatal disease) as well as death and the course of the dying process (Field & Cassel, 2010; Kheirbek, Alemi, Citron, Afaq, Wu, & Fletcher, 2013). These dying trajectories vary a great deal across diseases, as illustrated in Figure 13.2. Some diseases, such as lung cancer, have a clear and rapid period of decline; this "terminal phase" is often used to determine eligibility for certain services (e.g., hospice, discussed later). Other diseases, such as congestive heart failure, have no clear terminal phase. The two approaches of describing the dying process we consider will try to account for both types of trajectories.

Kübler-Ross's Work. Elisabeth Kübler-Ross changed the way we approach dying. When she began her investigations into the dying process in the 1960s, such research was controversial; her physician colleagues initially were outraged and some even denied their patients were terminally ill. Still, she persisted. More than

Figure 13.2

Some fatal diseases, such as lung cancer, have a clear decline phase, whereas others, such as congestive heart failure, do not.

Source: From Skolnick, A. A. (1998). MediCaring project to demonstrate and evaluate innovative end-of-life program for chronically ill. Journal of the American Medical Association, 279, 1511–1512. Reprinted with permission of the American Medical Association.

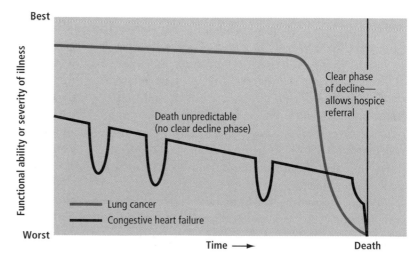

200 interviews with terminally ill people convinced her most people experienced several emotional reactions. Using her experiences, she described five reactions that represented the ways people dealt with death: denial, anger, bargaining, depression, and acceptance (Kübler-Ross, 1969). Although they were first presented as a sequence, it was subsequently realized the emotions can overlap and be experienced in different order.

Although she believed these five stages represent the typical range of emotional development in the dying, Kübler-Ross (1974) cautioned not everyone experiences all of them or progresses through them at the same rate or in the same order. Research supports the view her "stages" should not be viewed as a sequence (Charlton & Verghese, 2010; Parkes, 2013). In fact, we could actually harm dying people by considering these stages as fixed and universal. Individual differences are great. Emotional responses may vary in intensity throughout the dying process. Thus, the goal in applying Kübler-Ross's ideas to real-world settings would be to help people achieve an appropriate death: one that meets the needs of the dying person, allowing him or her to work out each problem as it comes.

A Contextual Theory of Dying. Describing the process of dying is difficult. One reason for these problems is the realization there is no one right way to die, although there may be better or worse ways of coping (Corr, 2010a,b; Corr & Corr, 2013; Corr, Corr, & Nabe, 2008). Corr identified four dimensions of the issues or tasks a dying person faces from their perspective: bodily needs, psychological security, interpersonal attachments, and spiritual energy and hope. This holistic approach acknowledges individual differences and rejects broad generalizations. Corr's task work approach also recognizes the importance of the coping efforts of family members, friends, and caregivers as well as those of the dying person.

Kastenbaum and Thuell (1995) argue what is needed is an even broader contextual approach that takes a more inclusive view of the dying process. They point out theories must be able to handle people who have a wide variety of terminal illnesses and be sensitive to dying people's own perspectives and values related to death. The socio-environmental context where dying occurs often changes over time and must

be recognized. A person may begin the dying process living independently but end up in a long-term care facility. Such moves may have profound implications for how the person copes with dying. A contextual approach provides guidance for health care professionals and families for discussing how to protect the quality of life, provide better care, and prepare caregivers for dealing with the end of life. Such an approach would also provide research questions such as how does one's acceptance of dying change across various stages?

Although we do not yet have a comprehensive theory of dying, we examine people's experiences as a narrative that can be written from many points of view (e.g., the patient, family members, caregivers). What emerges would be a rich description of a dynamically changing process.

Death Anxiety

We have seen how people view death varies with age. In the process, we encountered the notion of feeling anxious about death. **Death anxiety** *refers to people's anxiety or even fear of death and dying.* Death anxiety is tough to pin down; indeed, it is the ethereal nature of death rather than something about it in particular, that makes us feel so uncomfortable. We cannot put our finger on something specific about death causes us to feel uneasy. Because of this, we must look for indirect behavioral evidence to document death anxiety. Research findings suggest death anxiety is a complex, multidimensional construct.

For nearly three decades, researchers have applied terror management theory as a framework to study death anxiety (Burke, Martens, & Faucher, 2010; Tam, 2013). **Terror management theory** *addresses the issue of why people engage in certain behaviors to achieve particular psychological states based on their deeply rooted concerns about mortality* (Arndt & Vess, 2008). The theory proposes ensuring the continuation of one's life is the primary motive underlying behavior and all other motives can be traced to this basic one.

Additionally, some suggest older adults present an existential threat for the younger and middle-aged adults because they remind us all that death is inescapable, the body is fallible, and the bases that we may secure self-esteem (and manage death anxiety) are transitory (Martens, Goldenberg, & Greenberg, 2005). That may be why some people seek cosmetic surgery as a way to deal with their death anxiety (Tam, 2013). Thus, death anxiety is a reflection of one's concern over dying, an outcome that would violate the prime motive.

Neuroimaging research shows terror management theory provides a useful framework for studying brain activity related to death anxiety. Quirin, Loktyushin, Arndt, Küstermann, Lo, Kuhl, and colleagues (2012) found brain activity in the right amygdala, left rostral anterior cingulate cortex, and right caudate nucleus was greater when male participants were answering questions about fear of death and dying than when they were answering questions about dental pain. Similarly, electrical activity in the brain indicates people defend themselves against emotions related to death (Klackl, Jonas, & Kronbichler, 2013). There is neurophysiological evidence that shows Jean's attempts to block thoughts of her own death in the opening vignette are common across people.

On the basis of several diverse studies using many different measures, researchers now conclude death anxiety consists of several components. Each of these components is most easily described with terms that resemble examples of great concern (anxiety) but cannot be tied to any one specific focus. Some research on U.S. and Atlantic Canadian adults indicates components of death anxiety included pain, body malfunction, humiliation, rejection, nonbeing, punishment, interruption of goals, being destroyed, and negative impact on survivors (Power & Smith, 2008). To complicate matters further, each of these components can be assessed at any of three levels: public, private, and nonconscious. What we admit feeling about death in public may differ greatly from what we feel when we are alone with our own thoughts. In short, the measurement of death anxiety is complex and researchers need to specify what aspects they are assessing.

Much research has been conducted to learn what demographic and personality variables are related to death anxiety. Although the results often are ambiguous, some patterns have emerged. Older adults tend to have lower death anxiety than younger adults, perhaps because of their tendency to engage in life review, have a different perspective about time, and their higher level of religious motivation (Henrie, 2010). Men show greater fear of the unknown than women, but women report more specific fear of the dying process (Cicirelli, 2001). In Taiwan, higher death anxiety among patients with cancer is associated with not having a purpose in life and level of fear of disease relapse (Tang, Chiou, Lin, Wang, & Liand, 2011).

Strange as it may seem, death anxiety may have a beneficial side. For one thing, being afraid to die means we often go to great lengths to make sure we stay alive, as argued by terror management theory (Burke, Martens, & Faucher, 2010). Because staying alive ensures the continuation and socialization of the species, fear of death serves as a motivation to have children and raise them properly.

Learning to Deal With Death Anxiety. Although some degree of death anxiety may be appropriate, we must guard against letting it become powerful enough to interfere with normal daily routines. Several ways exist to help us in this endeavor. Perhaps the one most often used is to live life to the fullest. Kalish (1984, 1987) argues people who do this enjoy what they have; although they may still fear death and feel cheated, they have few regrets. Adolescents are particularly likely to do this; research shows teenagers, especially males, engage in risky behavior that is correlated with low death anxiety (Ben-Zur & Zeidner, 2009; Cotter, 2003).

Koestenbaum (1976) proposes several exercises and questions to increase one's death awareness. Some of these are to write your own obituary (like you did earlier in this chapter) and to plan your own death and funeral services. You can also ask yourself: "What circumstances would help make my death acceptable?" "Is death the sort of thing that could happen to me right now?"

These questions serve as a basis for an increasingly popular way to reduce anxiety: death education. Most death education programs combine factual information about death with issues aimed at reducing anxiety and fear to increase sensitivity to others' feelings. These programs vary widely in orientation; they include such topics as philosophy, ethics, psychology, drama, religion, medicine, art, and many others. Additionally, they focus on death, the process of dying, grief and bereavement, or any combination of those. In general, death education programs help primarily by increasing our awareness of the complex emotions felt and expressed by dying people and their families. It is important to make education programs reflect the diverse backgrounds of the participants (Fowler, 2008).

Facing death regularly, such as firefighters do, often forces people to confront their death anxiety.

Research shows participating in experiential workshops about death significantly lowers death anxiety in younger, middle-aged, and older adults and raises awareness about the importance of advance directives (Moeller, Lewis, & Werth, 2010).

ADULT DEVELOPMENT IN ACTION

How might different approaches to lowering death anxiety be useful to you as a health care worker?

13.3 End-of-Life Issues

LEARNING OBJECTIVES

- What are end-of-life issues? What is a final scenario?
- What is hospice? How does hospice relate to end-of-life issues?
- How does one make end-of-life desires and decisions known?

Jean is a 72-year-old woman recently diagnosed with advanced colon cancer. She has vivid memories of her father dying a long, protracted death in great pain. Jean is afraid she will suffer the same fate. She heard the hospice in town emphasizes pain management and provides a lot of support for families. Jean wonders whether that is something she should explore in the time has left.

When people think about how they would like to die, no one chooses a slow, painful process where medical intervention continues well beyond the point of increasing quality of life over quantity of life. However, medical intervention such as life support or cardiopulmonary resuscitation (CPR), are common even in situations that people would prefer them not to be used. How can people make their wishes about how they want to experience the end of their life known?

Creating a Final Scenario

When given the chance, many adults would like to discuss a variety of issues, collectively called **end-of-life issues:** *management of the final phase of life, after-death disposition of their body, memorial services, and distribution of assets* (Moeller et al., 2010). How these issues are confronted represents a significant generational shift (Green, 2008). Parents and grandparents of the baby boom generation spoke respectfully about those who had "passed away," and very rarely planned ahead for or made their wishes known about medical care they did or did not want. Baby boomers are far more likely to plan and be more matter-of-fact. People want to manage the final part of their lives by thinking through the choices between traditional care (e.g., provided by hospitals and nursing homes) and alternatives (such as hospices, that we discuss in the next section), completing advance directives (e.g., health care power of attorney, living will), resolving key personal relationships, and perhaps choosing the alternative of ending one's life prematurely through euthanasia.

What happens to one's body and how one is memorialized is important to most people. Is a traditional burial preferred over cremation? A traditional funeral over a memorial service? Such choices often are based in people's religious beliefs and their desire for privacy for their families after they have died.

Making sure one's estate and personal effects are passed on appropriately often is overlooked. Making a will is especially important to ensure one's wishes are carried out. Providing for the informal distribution of personal effects also helps prevent disputes between family members.

Whether people choose to address these issues formally or informally, it is important they be given the opportunity to do so. In many cases, family members are reluctant to discuss these matters with the dying relative because of their own anxiety about death. *Making such choices known about how they do and do not want their lives to end constitutes a* **final scenario.**

One of the most difficult and important parts of a final scenario for most people is the process of separation from family and friends (Corr et al., 2008; Corr & Corr, 2013; Wanzer & Glenmullen, 2007). The final days, weeks, and months of life provide opportunities to affirm love, resolve conflicts, and provide peace to dying people. The failure to complete this process often leaves survivors feeling they did not achieve closure in the relationship, and can result in bitterness toward the deceased.

Health care workers realize the importance of giving dying patients the chance to create a final scenario and recognize the uniqueness of each person's final passage. A key part of their role is to ease this process (Wanzer & Glenmullen, 2007). Any given final scenario reflects the individual's personal past, that is the unique combination of the development forces the person experienced. Primary attention is paid to how people's total life experiences prepared them to face end-of-life issues (Moeller et al., 2010).

One's final scenario helps family and friends interpret one's death, especially when the scenario is constructed jointly, such as between spouses, and when communication is open and honest (Byock, 1997; Green, 2008). The different perspectives of everyone involved are unlikely to converge without clear communication and discussion. Respecting each person's perspective is basic and greatly helps in creating a good final scenario.

Encouraging people to decide for themselves how the end of their lives should be handled helps people take control of their dying (Hains & Hulbert-Williams, in press). Taking personal control over one's dying process is a trend occurring even in cultures like Japan that traditionally defer to physician's opinions (Alden, Merz, & Akashi, 2012). The emergence of final scenarios as an important consideration fits well with the emphasis on addressing pain through palliative care, an approach underlying hospice.

The Hospice Option

As we have seen, most people would like to die at home among family and friends. An important barrier to this choice is the availability of support systems when the person has a terminal disease. Most people believe they have no choice but to go to a hospital or nursing home. However, another alternative exists. **Hospice** *is an approach to assist dying people emphasizing pain management, or palliative care, and death with dignity* (Knee, 2010; Winslow & Meldrum, 2013). The emphasis in a hospice is on the dying person's quality of life. This approach grows out of an important distinction between the prolongation of life and the prolongation of death, a distinction important to Jean, the woman we met in the vignette. In a hospice the concern is to make the person as peaceful and comfortable as possible, not to delay an inevitable death. Although medical care is available at a hospice, it is aimed primarily at controlling pain and restoring normal functioning. *The approach to care in hospice is called* **palliative care** *and is focused on providing relief from pain and other symptoms of disease at any point during the disease process* (Reville, 2011).

Modern hospices are modeled after St. Christopher's Hospice in England, founded in 1967 by Dr. Cicely Saunders. Hospice services are requested only after the person or physician believes no treatment or cure is possible, making the hospice program markedly different from hospital or home care. The differences are evident in the principles that underlie hospice care:

- Clients and their families are viewed as a unit, clients should be kept free of pain, emotional and social impoverishment must be minimal;

- Clients must be encouraged to maintain competencies, conflict resolution and fulfillment of realistic desires must be assisted; and

- Clients must be free to begin or end relationships, an interdisciplinary team approach is used, and staff members must seek to alleviate pain and fear. (Knee, 2010).

Two types of hospices exist: inpatient and outpatient. Inpatient hospices provide all care for clients;

outpatient hospices provide services to clients who remain in their own homes. The outpatient variation, when a hospice nurse visits clients in their home, is becoming increasingly popular, largely because more clients can be served at a lower cost. Having hospice services available to people at home is a viable option for many people, especially in helping home-based caregivers cope with loss, but should be provided by specially-trained professionals (Newman, Thompson, & Chandler, 2013).

Hospices do not follow a hospital model of care. The role of the staff in a hospice is not so much to treat the client as it is just to be with the client. A client's dignity is always maintained; often more attention is paid to appearance and personal grooming than to medical tests. Hospice staff members also provide a great deal of support to the client's family.

Hospice and hospital patients differ in important ways (Knee, 2010). Hospice clients are more mobile, less anxious, and less depressed; spouses visit hospice clients more often and participate more in their care; and hospice staff members are perceived as more accessible. Research consistently shows significant improvements in clients' quality of life occur after hospice placement or beginning palliative care (Rocque & Cleary, 2013).

Although the hospice is a valuable alternative for many people, it may not be appropriate for everyone. Those who trust their physician regarding medical care options are more likely to select hospice than those who do not trust their physician, especially among African Americans (Ludke & Smucker, 2007). Most people who select hospice suffer from cancer, AIDS, cardiovascular disease, pulmonary disease, or a progressive neurological condition such as dementia; two-thirds are over age 65; and most are in the last six months of life (Hospice Foundation of America, 2013a).

Needs expressed by staff, family, and clients differ (Hiatt et al., 2007). Staff and family members tend to emphasize pain management, whereas many clients want more attention paid to personal issues, such as spirituality and the process of dying. This difference means the staff and family members may need to ask clients more often what they need instead of making assumptions about what they need.

How do people decide to explore the hospice option? Families need to consider several things (Hospice Foundation of America, 2013b; Karp & Wood, 2012; Knee, 2010):

- *Is the person completely informed about the nature and prognosis of his or her condition?* Full knowledge and the ability to communicate with health care personnel are essential to understanding what hospice has to offer.

- *What options are available at this point in the progress of the person's disease?* Knowing about all available treatment options is critical. Exploring treatment options also requires health care professionals to be aware of the latest approaches and be willing to disclose them.

- *What are the person's expectations, fears, and hopes?* Some older adults, like Jean, remember or have heard stories about people who suffered greatly at the end of their lives. This can produce anxiety about one's own death. Similarly, fears of becoming dependent play an important role in a person's decision making. Discovering and discussing these anxieties helps clarify options.

- *How well do people in the person's social network communicate with each other?* Talking about death is taboo in many families. In others, intergenerational communication is difficult or impossible. Even in families with good communication, the pending death of a loved relative is difficult. As a result, the dying person may have difficulty expressing his or her wishes. The decision to explore the hospice option is best made when it is discussed openly.

- *Are family members available to participate actively in terminal care?* Hospice relies on family members to provide much of the care that is supplemented by professionals and volunteers. We saw in Chapter 11 being a primary caregiver can be highly stressful. Having a family member who is willing to accept this responsibility is essential for the hospice option to work.

- *Is a high-quality hospice care program available?* Hospice programs are not uniformly good. As with any health care provider, patients and family members must investigate the quality of local hospice programs before making a choice. The

Hospice Foundation of America provides excellent material for evaluating a hospice.

- *Is hospice covered by insurance?* Hospice services are reimbursable under Medicare in most cases, but any additional expenses may or may not be covered under other forms of insurance.

Hospice provides an important end-of-life option for many terminally ill people and their families. Moreover, the supportive follow-up services they provide are often used by surviving family and friends. Most important, the success of the hospice option has had important influences on traditional health care. For example, the American Academy of Pain Medicine (2009) published an official position paper advocating the use of medical and behavioral interventions to provide pain management.

Despite the importance of the hospice option for end-of-life decisions, terminally ill persons face the barriers of family reluctance to face the reality of terminal illness and participate in the decision-making process and health care providers hindering access to hospice care (Karp & Wood, 2012; Knee, 2010; Melhado & Byers, 2011; Reville, 2011).

As the end of life approaches, the most important thing to keep in mind is that the dying person has the right to state-of-the-art approaches to treatment and pain management. Irrespective of the choice of traditional health care or hospice, the wishes of the dying person should be honored, and family members must participate.

Making Your End-of-Life Intentions Known

As has been clearly shown, euthanasia raises complex legal, political, and ethical issues. In most jurisdictions, euthanasia is legal only when a person has made known his or her wishes concerning medical intervention. Unfortunately, many people fail to take this step, perhaps because it is difficult to think about such situations or because they do not know the options available to them. Without clear directions, medical personnel may be unable to take a patient's preferences into account.

There are two ways to make one's intentions known. *In a* **living will**, *a person simply states his or her wishes about life support and other treatments. In a* **health care power of attorney**, *an individual appoints someone to act as his or her agent for health care decisions*

(see Figure 13.3). A major purpose of both is to make one's wishes known about the use of life support interventions in the event the person is unconscious or otherwise incapable of expressing them, along with other related end-of-life issues such as organ transplantation and other health care options (Baumann et al., 2011; Castillo et al., 2011). A durable power of attorney for health care has an additional advantage: It names an individual who has the legal authority to speak for the person if necessary.

Although there is considerable support for both mechanisms, there are several problems as well (Castillo, Williams, Hooper, Sabatino, Weithorn, & Sudore, 2011; Moorman & Inoue, 2013). States vary in their laws relating to advance directives. Many people fail to inform their relatives and physicians about their health care decisions. Others do not tell the person named in a durable power of attorney where the document is kept. Obviously, this puts relatives at a serious disadvantage if decisions concerning the use of life-support systems need to be made.

A living will or a durable power of attorney for health care can be the basis for a "Do Not Resuscitate" medical order. *A* **Do Not Resuscitate (DNR) order** *means cardiopulmonary resuscitation (CPR) is not started should one's heart and breathing stop*. In the normal course of events, a medical team will immediately try to restore normal heartbeat and respiration. With a DNR order, this treatment is not done. As with living wills and health care power of attorney, it is extremely important to let all appropriate medical personnel know a DNR order is in effect.

Patient Self-Determination and Competency Evaluation. A key factor in making your decisions about health care known, concern your ability to make those decisions for yourself. The Patient Self-Determination Act, passed in 1990, requires most health care facilities to provide information to patients in writing that they have several rights to:

- Make their own health care decisions.
- Accept or refuse medical treatment.
- Make an advance health care directive.

Patients must be asked if they have an advance directive, and, if so, include it in the medical record. Staff

3. General statement of authority granted.

Except as indicated in section 4 below, I hereby grant to my health care agent named above full power and authority to make health care decisions on my behalf, including, but not limited to, the following:

A. To request, review, and receive any information, verbal or written, regarding my physical or mental health, including, but not limited to, medical and hospital records, and to consent to the disclosure of this information;

B. To employ or discharge my health care providers;

C. To consent to and authorize my admission to and discharge from a hospital, nursing or convalescent home, or other institution;

D. To give consent for, to withdraw consent for, or to withhold consent for, X ray, anesthesia, medication, surgery, and all other diagnostic and treatment procedures ordered by or under the authorization of a licensed physician, dentist, or podiatrist. This authorization specifically includes the power to consent to measures for relief of pain.

E. To authorize the withholding or withdrawal of life-sustaining procedures when and if my physician determines that I am terminally ill, permanently in a coma, suffer severe dementia, or am in a persistent vegetative state. Lifesustaining procedures are those forms of medical care that only serve to artificially prolong the dying process and may include mechanical ventilation, dialysis, antibiotics, artificial nutrition and hydration, and other forms of medical treatment which sustain, restore or supplant vital bodily functions. Life-sustaining procedures do not include care necessary to provide comfort or alleviate pain.

> I DESIRE THAT MY LIFE NOT BE PROLONGED BY LIFE-SUSTAINING PROCEDURES IF I AM TERMINALLY ILL, PERMANENTLY IN A COMA, SUFFER SEVERE DEMENTIA, OR AM IN A PERSISTENT VEGETATIVE STATE.

F. To exercise any right I may have to make a disposition of any part or all of my body for medical purposes, to donate my organs, to authorize an autopsy, and to direct the disposition of my remains.

G. To take any lawful actions that may be necessary to carry out these decisions, including the granting of releases of liability to medical providers.

4. Special provisions and limitations.

(Notice: The above grant of power is intended to be as broad as possible so that your health care agent will have authority to make any decisions you could make to obtain or terminate any type of health care. If you wish to limit the scope of your health care agent's powers, you may do so in this section.)

In exercising the authority to make health care decisions on my behalf, the authority of my health care agent is subject to the following special provisions and limitations *(Here you may include any specific limitations you deem appropriate such as: your own definition of when life-sustaining treatment should be withheld or discontinued, or instructions to refuse any specific types of treatment that are inconsistent with your religious beliefs, or unacceptable to you for any other reason.):*

_____

_____

_____

_____

5. Guardianship provision.

If it becomes necessary for a court to appoint a guardian of my person, I nominate my health care agent acting under this document to be the guardian of my person, to serve without bond or security.

6. Reliance of third parties on health care agent.

A. No person who relies in good faith upon the authority of or any representations by my health care agent shall be liable to me, my estate, my heirs, successors, assigns, or personal representatives, for actions or omissions by my health care agent.

Figure 13.3
Example of a durable power of attorney document for health care decisions.

Source: North Carolina State University, A&T State University Cooperative Extension.

at the health care facility must receive training about advance directives, and cannot make admissions or treatment decisions based on whether those directives exist.

Although this legal requirement for health care facilities has been in effect for decades, its extension to individual physicians that would have included financial reimbursement for their discussions with patients about these issues was not included in the Affordable Care Act of 2010 due to opposition such discussions would create the equivalent of "death panels" (Pear, 2011). As a result, the opportunity to encourage people to think about what kind of medical care and intervention they desire before such situations arise was essentially lost.

One major concern regarding end-of-life decisions is whether the person is cognitively or legally able to make them (Moye, Sabatino, & Brendel, 2013). There are two types of determination: the *capacity* to make decisions, that is a clinical determination, and a *competency* decision, made legally by the court (Wettstein, 2013). With capacity determinations, the issue is whether the individual is able to make a decision about specific tasks, and the abilities necessary are subject to measurement. With competency determinations, the individual is being judged either with respect to a specific task or in general, and the determination can be made subjectively by the court.

At this point, the case law is limited regarding whether a person who lacks the capacity to make health care decisions can still designate a surrogate to make them on their behalf. This situation is rather common, though, given the tendency for families to not discuss these issues, individual's reluctance to face the potential need, and the politicization of the conversation in the health care arena. Guidelines for professionals regarding the assessment of competence are available, and they should be aware of the legal issues (Moye et al., 2013; Wettstein, 2013).

Research indicates family members and other surrogate decision-makers are often wrong about what patients really want (Moorman & Inoue, 2013). This further emphasizes the critical need to discuss end-of-life issues ahead of time and ensure the appropriate advance directives are in place and key individuals are aware of them.

ADULT DEVELOPMENT IN ACTION

What steps are necessary to ensure that your advance directives about health care are followed?

13.4 Surviving The Loss: The Grieving Process

LEARNING OBJECTIVES

- How do people experience the grief process?
- What feelings do grieving people have?
- How do people cope with grief?
- What is the difference between normal and complicated or prolonged grief disorder?
- What developmental aspects are important in understanding grief?

After 67 years of marriage, Bertha recently lost her husband. At 90, Bertha knew neither she nor her husband was likely to live much longer, but the death was a shock just the same. Bertha thinks about him much of the time and often finds herself making decisions on the basis of "what John would have done" in the same situation.

Each of us suffers many losses over a lifetime. Whenever we lose someone close to us through death or other separation, like Bertha we experience bereavement, grief, and mourning. **Bereavement** *is the state or condition caused by loss through death.* **Grief** *is the sorrow, hurt, anger, guilt, confusion, and other feelings that arise after suffering a loss.* **Mourning** *concerns the ways we express our grief.* You can tell people in some cultures are bereaved and in mourning because of the clothing they wear. Mourning is highly influenced by culture. For some, mourning may involve wearing black, attending funerals, and observing an official period of grief; for others, it means drinking, wearing white, and marrying the deceased spouse's sibling. Grief corresponds to the emotional reactions following loss, whereas mourning is the culturally approved behavioral manifestations of those feelings. Even though mourning rituals may be fairly standard within a culture, how people grieve varies, as we see next. We will also see how Bertha's reactions are fairly typical of most people.

The Grief Process

How do people grieve? What do they experience? Perhaps you already have a good idea about the answers to these questions from your own experience. If so, you already know the process of grieving is a complicated and personal one. Just as there is no right way to die, there is no right way to grieve. Recognizing there are plenty of individual differences, we consider these patterns in this section.

The grieving process is often described as reflecting many themes and issues people confront that may be expressed through rituals (Norton & Gino, in press). Like the process of dying, grieving does not have clearly demarcated stages through which we pass in a neat sequence, although there are certain issues people must face similar to those faced by dying people. When someone close to us dies, we must reorganize our lives, establish new patterns of behavior, and redefine relationships with family and friends. Indeed, Attig (1996) provided one of the best descriptions of grief when he wrote grief is the process by which we relearn the world.

Customs regarding how bereaved persons should behave or dress vary around the world.

Unlike bereavement, over which we have no control, grief is a process that involves choices in coping, from confronting the reality and emotions to using religion to ease one's pain (Ivancovich & Wong, 2008; Norton & Gino, in press). From this perspective, grief is an active process when a person must do several things (Worden, 1991):

- *Acknowledge the reality of the loss.* We must overcome the temptation to deny the reality of our loss; we must fully and openly acknowledge it and realize it affects every aspect of our life.

- *Work through the emotional turmoil.* We must find effective ways to confront and express the complete range of emotions we feel after the loss and must not avoid or repress them.

- *Adjust to the environment where the deceased is absent.* We must define new patterns of living that adjust appropriately and meaningfully to the fact the deceased is not present.

- *Loosen ties to the deceased.* We must free ourselves from the bonds of the deceased in order to reengage with our social network. This means finding effective ways to say good-bye.

The notion that grief is an active coping process emphasizes survivors must come to terms with the physical world of things, places, and events as well as our spiritual place in the world; the interpersonal world of interactions with family and friends, the dead, and, in some cases, God; and aspects of our inner selves and our personal experiences (Ivancovich & Wong, 2008; Papa & Litz, 2011). Bertha, the woman in the vignette, is in the middle of this process. Even the matter of deciding what to do with the deceased's personal effects can be part of this active coping process (Attig, 1996).

In considering the grief process, we must avoid making several mistakes. First, grieving is a highly individual experience (Mallon, 2008; Papa & Litz, 2011). A process that works well for one person may not be the best for someone else. Second, we must not underestimate the amount of time people need to deal with the various issues. To a casual observer, it may appear a survivor is "back to normal" after a few weeks. Actually, it takes much longer to resolve the complex emotional issues faced during bereavement. Researchers and therapists alike agree a person needs at least a year following the loss to begin recovery, and two years is not uncommon.

Finally, "recovery" may be a misleading term. It is probably more accurate to say we learn to live with our loss rather than we recover from it (Attig, 1996). The impact of the loss of a loved one lasts a long time, perhaps for the rest of one's life. Still, most people reach a point of moving on with their lives in a reasonable timeframe (Bonanno, 2009; Bonnano, Westphal, & Mancini, 2011).

Recognizing these aspects of grief makes it easier to know what to say and do for bereaved people. Among the most useful things are to simply let the person know you are sorry for his or her loss, you are there for support, and mean what you say.

Risk Factors in Grief. Bereavement is a life experience most people have many times, and most people eventually handle it, often better than we might suspect (Bonanno, 2009; Bonanno et al., 2011). However, there are some risk factors that make bereavement more difficult. Several of the more important are the mode of death, personal factors (e.g., personality, religiosity, age, gender), income, and interpersonal context (social support, kinship relationship; Kersting, Brähler, Glaesmer, & Wagner, 2011; Thieleman & Cacciatore, in press).

Most people believe the circumstances or mode of death affects the grief process. A person whose family member was killed in an automobile accident has a different situation to deal with than a person whose family member died after a long period of suffering with Alzheimer's disease. *It is believed when death is anticipated, people go through a period of* **anticipatory grief** *before the death that supposedly serves to buffer the impact of the loss when it does come and to facilitate recovery* (Haley, 2013; Lane, 2007). However, the research evidence for this is mixed. Anticipating the loss of a loved one from cancer or other terminal disease can provide a framework for understanding family members' reactions (Coombs, 2010). Not all family members actually experience it, though. However, people who do, tend to disengage from the dying person (Haley, 2013; Lane, 2007).

The strength of attachment to the deceased person does make a difference in dealing with a sudden as opposed to an unexpected death. Attachment theory provides a framework for understanding different reactions (Stroebe & Archer, 2013; Stroebe, Schut, & Boerner, 2010). When the deceased person was one whom the survivor had a strong and close attachment and the loss was sudden, greater grief is experienced (Wayment & Vierthaler, 2002). However, such secure attachment styles tend to result in less depression after the loss because of less guilt over unresolved issues (because there are fewer of them), things not provided (because more were likely provided), and so on.

Few studies of personal risk factors have been done, and few firm conclusions can be drawn. To date there are no consistent findings regarding personality traits that either help buffer people from the effects of bereavement or exacerbate them (Haley, 2013; Stroebe & Archer, 2013; Stroebe et al., 2010). There is some evidence to suggest church attendance or spirituality in general helps people deal with bereavement and subsequent grief through the post-grief period (Bratkovich, 2010; Gordon, 2013). There are, however, consistent findings regarding gender. Men have higher mortality rates following bereavement than women, who have higher rates of depression and complicated grief (discussed later in this section) than men, but the reasons

for these differences are unclear (Kersting et al., 2011). Research also consistently shows older adults suffer the least health consequences following bereavement, with the impact perhaps being strongest for middle-aged adults, but strong social support networks lessen these effects to varying degrees (Papa & Litz, 2011).

Two interpersonal risk factors have been examined: lack of social support and kinship. Studies indicate social support and mastery help buffer the effects of bereavement more for older adults than for middle-aged adults (Haley, 2013; Papa & Litz, 2011). This may change as more support begins to come from online social networks, a medium used more widely by younger and middle-aged adults (Massimi, 2013).

Normal Grief Reactions

The feelings experienced during grieving are intense, that not only makes it difficult to cope but can also make a person question her or his own reactions. The feelings involved usually include sadness, denial, anger, loneliness, and guilt.

Many authors refer to the psychological side of coming to terms with bereavement as **grief work**. Whether the loss is ambiguous and lacking closure (e.g., waiting to learn the fate of a missing loved one) or certain (e.g., verification of death through a dead body), people need space and time to grieve (Berns, 2011; Rosenblatt, 2013). Even without personal experience of the death of close family members, people recognize the need to give survivors time to deal with their many feelings. However, American society does not support long periods of grieving, and pressures bereaved individuals to come to "closure" as quickly as possible. That is not how people really feel or want to deal with their grief.

Muller and Thompson (2003) examined people's experience of grief in a detailed interview study and found five themes. *Coping* concerns what people do to deal with their loss in terms of what helps them. *Affect* refers to people's emotional reactions to the death of their loved one; such as certain topics that serve as emotional triggers for memories of their loved one. *Change* involves the ways survivors' lives change as a result of the loss; personal growth (e.g., "I didn't think I could deal with something that painful, but I did") is a common experience. *Narrative* relates to the stories survivors tell about their deceased loved one, that sometimes includes details about the process of the death. Finally, *relationship* reflects who the deceased person was and the nature of the ties between that person and the survivor. Collectively, these themes indicate the experience of grief is complex and involves dealing with one's feelings as a survivor as well as memories of the deceased person.

How people show their feelings of grief varies across ethnic groups (Papa & Litz, 2011). Latino American men show more of their grief behaviorally than do European American men (Sera, 2001). Such differences are also found across cultures. Families in KwaZulu-Natal, South Africa, have a strong desire for closure and need for dealing with the "loneliness of grief" (Brysiewicz, 2008). In many cultures the bereaved construct a relationship with the person who died, but how this happens differs widely, from "ghosts" to appearances in dreams to connection through prayer (Rosenblatt, 2001).

In addition to psychological grief reactions, there are also physiological ones (McKissock & McKissock, 2012). Physical health may decline, illness may result, and use of health care services may increase. In some cases it is necessary to treat severe depression following bereavement; we consider complicated grief reactions a bit later. Widows report sleep disturbances as well as neurological and circulatory problems (Kowalski & Bondmass, 2008). Widowers in general report major disruptions in their daily routines (Naef, Ward, Mahrer Imhof, & Grande, 2013).

In the time following the death of a loved one, dates having personal significance may reintroduce feelings of grief. Holidays such as Thanksgiving or birthdays that were spent with the deceased person may be difficult times. The actual anniversary of the death can be especially troublesome. *The term anniversary reaction refers to changes in behavior related to feelings of sadness on this date.* Personal experience and research show recurring feelings of sadness or other examples of the anniversary reaction are common in normal grief (Holland & Neimeyer, 2010). Such feelings also accompany remembrances of major catastrophes across cultures, such as Thais remembering the victims of a major flood (Assanangkornchai et al., 2007).

Most research on how people react to the death of a loved one is cross-sectional. This work shows grief tends to peak within the first six months following the death of a loved one (Maciejewski, Zhang, Block, & Prigerson, 2007). However, some work has been done to examine how people continue grieving many years after the loss. Some widows show no sign of lessening of grief after five years (Kowalski & Bondmass, 2008). Rosenblatt (1996) reported people still felt the effects of the deaths of family members 50 years after the event. The depth of the emotions over the loss of loved ones never totally went away, as people still cried and felt sad when discussing the loss despite the length of time that had passed. In general, though, people move on with their lives within a relatively short period of time and deal with their feelings reasonably well (Bonanno, 2009; Bonanno et al., 2011).

Coping With Grief

Thus far, we considered the behaviors people show when they are dealing with grief. We have also seen these behaviors change over time. How does this happen? How can we explain the grieving process?

Numerous theories have been proposed to account for the grieving process, such as general life-event theories, psychodynamic, attachment, and cognitive process theories (Stroebe & Archer, 2013; Stroebe et al., 2010). All of these approaches to grief are based on more general theories that results in none of them providing an adequate explanation of the grieving process. Two integrative approaches have been proposed specific to the grief process: the four-component model and the dual-process model of coping with bereavement.

The Four-Component Model. *The* four-component model *proposes understanding grief is based on four things:* (1) *the context of the loss,* referring to the risk factors such as whether the death was expected; (2) *continuation of subjective meaning associated with loss,* ranging from evaluations of everyday concerns to major questions about the meaning of life; (3) *changing representations of the lost relationship over time*; and (4) *the role of coping and emotion regulation processes* that cover all coping strategies used to deal with grief (Bonanno et al., 2011; Bonanno, 2009). The four-component model relies heavily on emotion theory, has much in common with the transactional model of stress, and has empirical support. According to the four-component model, dealing with grief is a complicated process only understood as a complex outcome that unfolds over time.

There are several important implications of this integrative approach. One of the most important is helping a grieving person involves helping them make meaning from the loss (Bratkovich, 2010; Wong, 2008). Second, this model implies encouraging people to express their grief may actually not be helpful. *An alternative view, called the* **grief work as rumination hypothesis**, *not only rejects the necessity of grief processing for recovery from loss but views extensive grief processing as a form of rumination that may actually increase distress* (Bonanno, Papa, & O'Neill, 2001). Although it may seem people who think obsessively about their loss or who ruminate about it are confronting the loss, rumination is actually considered a form of avoidance because the person is not dealing with his or her real feelings and moving on (Robinaugh & McNally, 2013; Stroebe et al., 2007).

One prospective study shows, for instance, bereaved individuals who were not depressed prior to their spouse's death but then evidenced chronically elevated depression through the first year and a half of bereavement (i.e., a chronic grief pattern) also tended to report more frequently thinking about and talking about their recent loss at the six-month point in bereavement (Bonanno, Wortman, & Neese, 2004). Thus, some bereaved individuals engage in minimal grief processing whereas others are predisposed toward more extensive grief processing. Furthermore, the individuals who engage in minimal grief processing will show a relatively favorable grief outcome, whereas those who are predisposed to more extensive grief processing tend toward ruminative preoccupation and, consequently, to a more prolonged grief course (Bonanno, 2009; Bonanno et al., 2011).

As noted earlier, the grief work as rumination hypothesis also views grief avoidance as an independent but maladaptive form of coping with loss (Stroebe et al., 2007). In contrast to the traditional perspective, that equates the absence of grief processing with grief avoidance, the grief work as rumination framework assumes resilient individuals are able to minimize processing of a loss through relatively automated processes, such as distraction or shifting attention toward more positive emotional experiences (Bonanno, 2009; Bonanno et al., 2011). The grief work as rumination framework argues the deliberate avoidance or suppression of grief represents a less effective form of coping (Wegner & Gold, 1995) that exacerbates rather than minimizes the experience of grief (Bonanno, 2009; Bonanno et al., 2011).

The Spotlight on Research feature explores grief work regarding the loss of a spouse and the loss of a child in two cultures, the United States and China. As you read it, pay special attention to the question of whether encouraging people to express and deal with their grief is necessarily a good idea.

HOW DO WE KNOW?:

GRIEF PROCESSING AND AVOIDANCE IN THE UNITED STATES AND CHINA

Who were the investigators and what was the aim of the study? Bonanno and colleagues (2005) noted grief following the loss of a loved one often tends to be denied. However, research evidence related to positive benefits of resolving grief is largely lacking. Thus, whether unresolved grief is "bad" remains an open issue. Likewise, cross-cultural evidence is also lacking.

How did the investigators measure the topic of interest? Collaborative meetings between U.S. and Chinese researchers resulted in a 13-item grief processing scale and a 7-item grief avoidance scale, with both English and Mandarin Chinese versions. Self-reported psychological symptoms and physical health were also collected.

Who were the participants in the study? Adults under age 66 who had experienced the loss of either a spouse or child approximately four months prior to the start of data collection were asked to participate through solicitation letters. Participants were from either the metropolitan areas of Washington, D.C., or Nanjing, Jiangsu Province in China.

What was the design of the study? Two sets of measures were collected at approximately 4 months and 18 months after the loss.

Were there ethical concerns in the study? Because participation was voluntary, there were no ethical concerns.

What were the results? Consistent with the grief work as rumination view, scores on the two grief measures were uncorrelated. Overall, women tended to show more grief processing than men, and grief processing decreased over time. As you can see in

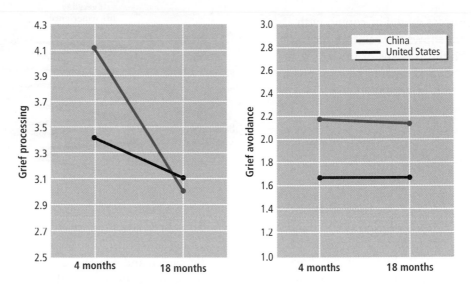

Figure 13.4

Grief processing and deliberate grief avoidance across time in China and the United States.

Source: From Bonanno et al. (2005), p. 92.

Figure 13.4, Chinese participants reported more grief processing and grief avoidance than U.S. participants at the first time of measurement, but differences disappeared by the second measurement for grief processing.

What did the investigators conclude? Based on converging results from the United States and China, the researchers concluded the data supported the grief work as rumination view. The results support the notion excessive processing of grief may actually increase a bereaved person's stress and feelings of discomfort rather than being helpful. These findings contradict the idea people should be encouraged to work through their grief and doing so will always be helpful.

The Dual Process Model. *The dual process model (DPM) of coping with bereavement integrates existing ideas regarding stressors* (Stroebe & Archer, 2013; Stroebe et al., 2010). As shown in Figure 13.5, the DPM defines two broad types of stressors. *Loss-oriented stressors* concern the loss itself, such as the grief work that needs to be done. *Restoration-oriented stressors* are those that involve adapting to the survivor's new life situation, such as building new relationships and finding new activities. The DPM proposes dealing with these stressors is a dynamic process, as indicated by the lines connecting them in the figure. This is a distinguishing feature of DPM. It shows how bereaved people cycle back and forth between dealing mostly with grief and trying to move on with life. At times the emphasis will be on grief; at other times on moving forward.

The DPM captures well the process bereaved people themselves report—at times they are nearly overcome with grief, while at other times they handle life well. The DPM also helps us understand how, over time, people come to a balance between the long-term effects of bereavement and the need to live life. Understanding how people handle grief requires understanding of the various context that people live and interact with others (Sandler, Wolchik, & Ayers, 2008).

Complicated or Prolonged Grief Disorder

Not everyone is able to cope with grief well and begin rebuilding a life. Sometimes the feelings of hurt, loneliness, and guilt are so overwhelming they become the focus of the survivor's life to such an extent there is never any closure and the grief

Figure 13.5

The dual process model of coping with bereavement shows the relation between dealing with the stresses of the loss itself (loss-oriented) and moving on with one's life (restoration-oriented).

Source: M. Stroebe & Schut (2001).

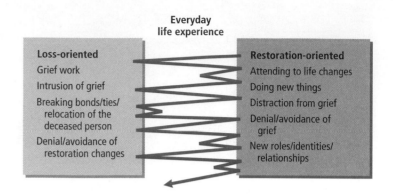

continues to interfere indefinitely with one's ability to function. *When this occurs, individuals are viewed as having* **complicated or prolonged grief disorder,** *and is distinguished from depression and normal grief in terms of separation distress and traumatic distress* (Stroebe, Schut, van den Bout, 2012). *Symptoms of* **separation distress** *include preoccupation with the deceased to the point it interferes with everyday functioning, upsetting memories of the deceased, longing and searching for the deceased, and isolation following the loss. Symptoms of* **traumatic distress** *include feeling disbelief about the death, mistrust, anger, and detachment from others as a result of the death, feeling shocked by the death, and the experience of physical presence of the deceased.*

Complicated grief forms a separate set of symptoms from depression (Stroebe et al., 2012). Individuals experiencing complicated grief report high levels of separation distress (such as yearning, pining, or longing for the deceased person), along with specific cognitive, emotional, or behavioral indicators (such as avoiding reminders of the deceased, diminished sense of self, difficulty in accepting the loss, feeling bitter or angry), as well as increased morbidity, increased smoking and substance abuse, and difficulties with family and other social relationships. Similar distinctions have been made between complicated or prolonged grief disorder and anxiety disorders.

Adult Developmental Aspects of Grief

Dealing with the loss of a loved one is never easy. How we deal with such losses as adults depends somewhat on the nature of the loss and our age and experience with death.

Special Challenges in Young Adulthood. Because young adults are just beginning to pursue the family, career, and personal goals they have set, they tend to be more intense in their feelings toward death. When asked how they feel about death, young adults report a strong sense those who die at this point in their lives would be cheated out of their future (Attig, 1996). Complicated grief is relatively common (Mash, Fullerton, & Ursano, in press)

Wrenn (1999) relates one of the challenges faced by bereaved college students is learning "how to respond to people who ignore their grief, or who tell them they need to get on with life and it's not good for them to continue to grieve" (134). College students have a need to express their grief like other bereaved people do, so providing them the opportunity to do so is crucial (Fajgenbaum, Chesson, & Lanzl, 2012; Servaty-Seib & Taub, 2010).

Experiencing the loss of one's partner in young adulthood can be traumatic, not only because of the loss itself but also because such loss is unexpected. As Trish Straine, a 32-year-old widow whose husband was killed in the World Trade Center attack put it: "I suddenly thought, 'I'm a widow.' Then I said to myself, 'A widow? That's an older woman, who's dressed in black. It's certainly not a 32-year-old like me'" (Lieber, 2001). One of the most difficult aspects for young widows and widowers is they must deal with both their own and their young children's grief and provide the support their children need and that can be extremely difficult. "Every time I look at my children, I'm reminded of Mark," said Stacey, a 35-year-old widow whose husband died of bone cancer. "And people don't want to hear you say you don't feel like moving on, even though there is great pressure from them to do that."

Becoming a widow as a young adult can be especially traumatic.

© iStockphoto.com/Nancy Honeycutt

Stacey is a good example of what research shows: Young adult widows report their level of grief does not typically diminish significantly until five to ten years after the loss, and they maintain strong attachments to their deceased husbands for at least that long (Derman, 2000). Young Canadian widows also report intense feelings and a desire to stay connected through memories (Lowe & McClement, 2010–2011).

Death of One's Child. The death of one's child, for most parents, brings unimaginable grief (Stroebe, Finkenauer, Wijngaards-de Meij, Schut, van den Bout, & Stroebe, 2013). Because children are not supposed to die before their parents, it is as if the natural order of things has been violated, shaking parents to their core (Rubin & Malkinson, 2001). Mourning is always intense; some parents never recover or reconcile themselves to the death of their child and may terminate their relationship with each other (Rosenbaum, Smith, & Zollfrank, 2011). The intensity of feelings is due to the strong parent–child bond that begins before birth and lasts a lifetime (Maple, Edwards, Plummer, & Minichiello, 2010; Rosenbaum et al., 2011).

Young parents who lose a child unexpectedly report high anxiety, a more negative view of the world, and much guilt, that results in a devastating experience (Seyda & Fitzsimons, 2010). The most overlooked losses of a child are those that happen through stillbirth, miscarriage, abortion, or neonatal death (Earle, Komaromy, & Layne, 2012; Rosenbaum, Smith, & Zollfrank 2011). Attachment to the child begins before birth, especially for mothers, so the loss hurts deeply. For this reason, ritual is extremely important to

acknowledge the death and validate parents' feelings of grief (Kobler, Limbo, & Kavanaugh, 2007).

Yet parents who experience this type of loss are expected to recover quickly. The lived experience of parents tells a different story (Seyda & Fitzsimons, 2010). These parents talk about a life-changing event, and report a deep sense of loss and hurt, especially when others do not understand their feelings. Worst of all, if societal expectations for quick recovery are not met the parents may be subjected to unfeeling comments. As one mother notes, parents often just wish somebody would acknowledge the loss (Okonski, 1996).

The loss of a young adult child for a middle-aged parent is experienced differently but is equally devastating (Maple, Edwards, Minichiello, & Plummer, 2013; Schneider, 2013). Parents who lost sons in wars (Rubin, Malkinson, & Witztum, 2012) and in traffic accidents (Shalev, 1999) still report strong feelings of anxiety, problems in functioning, and difficulties in relationships with both surviving siblings and the deceased as long as 13 years after the loss.

Death of One's Parent. Most parents die after their children are grown. But whenever parental death occurs, it hurts. Losing a parent in adulthood is a rite of passage as one is transformed from being a "son" or "daughter" to being "without parents" (Abrams, 2013; Edwards, 2006). We, the children, are now next in line.

The loss of a parent is a significant one. For young adult women transitioning to motherhood, losing their own mother during adolescence raises many feelings, such as deep loss at not being able to share their pregnancies with their mothers and fear of dying young themselves (Franceschi, 2005). Middle-aged women who lose a parent report feeling a complex set of emotions (Westbrook, 2002): they have intense emotional feelings of both loss and freedom, they remember both positive and negative aspects of their parent, and they experience shifts in their own sense of self.

The feelings accompanying the loss of an older parent reflect a sense of letting go, loss of a buffer against death, better acceptance of one's own eventual death, and a sense of relief the parent's suffering is over (Abrams, 2013; Igarashi et al., 2013). Yet, if the parent died from a cause, such as Alzheimer's disease, that involves the loss of the parent–child relationship along the way, then bodily death can feel like the second time the parent died (Shaw, 2007). Whether the adult child now tries to separate from the deceased parent's expectations or finds comfort in the memories, the impact of the loss is great.

Conclusion

Death is not as pleasant a topic as children's play or occupational development. It's not something we can go to college to master. What it represents to many people is the end of their existence, and that is a scary prospect. But because we all share in this fear at some level, each of us is equipped to provide support and comfort for grieving survivors.

Death is the last life-cycle force we encounter, the ultimate triumph of biological forces limit the length of life. Yet the same psychological and social forces so influential throughout life help us deal with death, either our own or someone else's. As we come to the end of our life journey, we understand death through an interaction of psychological forces—such as coping skills and intellectual and emotional understanding of death—and the sociocultural forces expressed in a particular society's traditions and rituals.

Learning about and dealing with death is clearly a developmental process across the life span that fits well in the biopsychosocial framework. Most apparent is that biological forces are essential to understanding death. The definition of death is based on whether certain biological functions are present; these same definitions create numerous ethical dilemmas that must be dealt with psychologically and socioculturally. Life-cycle forces also play a key role. We have seen, depending on a person's age, the concept of death has varied meanings beyond the mere cessation of life.

How a person's understanding of death develops is also the result of psychological forces. As the ability to think and reflect undergoes fundamental change, the view of death changes from a mostly magical approach to one that can be transcendent and transforming. As we have seen, people who face their own imminent death experience certain feelings. Having gained experience through the deaths of friends and relatives, a person's level of comfort with his or her own death may increase. Such personal experience may also come about by sharing the rituals defined through sociocultural forces. People observe how others deal with death and how the culture sets the tone and prescribes behavior for survivors. The combined action of forces also determines how they cope with the grief that accompanies the loss of someone close. Psychologically, confronting grief depends on many things, including the quality of the support system we have.

Thus, just as the beginning of life represents a complex interaction of biological, psychological, sociocultural, and life-cycle factors, so does death. What people believe about what follows after death is also an interaction of these factors. So, as we bring our study of human development to a close, we end where we began: What we experience in our lives cannot be understood from only a single perspective.

ADULT DEVELOPMENT IN ACTION

How is grief a product of the biopsychosocial model? How would you use the biopsychosocial model to create a support group for bereaved people?

SOCIAL POLICY IMPLICATIONS

As you probably surmised from the text, issues surrounding death and health care can be extremely controversial. Although the use of life-sustaining technologies (such as life support machines) is widespread, and the courts ensured individuals and designated others can make decisions about the extent and types of care received, the emotion attached to these events and decisions is high. Because most people do not spend time thinking about what they truly want and then making others, including their health care professional, aware of those decisions, most are left trying to make them in the midst of a health care crisis. To make matters worse, if a person has not made any plans known, and is not in a condition to make them (e.g., is unconscious), steps may be taken that would not have been welcomed had those decisions been made an made known.

Discussions in the chapter referenced two key events that brought end-of-life decisions to the forefront of public discourse. The first was the Terri Schiavo case in 2005 that raised the issue of when intervention is allowed to end and who can make that decision when the patient had no advance directive, and the second was the debate in 2009 in the midst of Congressional consideration of the Affordable Care Act that raised the specter of "death panels."

The core social policy issue facing us is the extent individuals have the right to make their own decisions about care, even when that decision is contrary to medical advice; how to know whether that decision is made freely by a capable, competent person; whether physicians' declarations of brain death are accurate; and the extent a government has an interest in the decision, especially if public funds are used in the care being provided or contemplated. These are quite complex issues that also extend into people's private belief structures, particularly religious/spiritual beliefs in matters of life and death.

Medically, the issues are complicated, too. To maximize the success of organ transplants, individuals may need to be kept on life support until the organs are ready to be taken. Is that ethical? Does that violate religious beliefs? Does the potential organ recipient have anything to say about the decision?

The current situation in the United States is that physicians are not provided reimbursement under certain medical insurance plans (e.g., Medicare) for taking the time to discuss end-of-life issues with their patients. This means these critical decisions and discussions often remain unmade and not held. The consequences are serious—individuals and families are then put in the situation of having to make them in crisis, when the time to reflect on the various options is unlikely to be available.

Clearly, more open discussion about end-of-life issues need to be held and policies more reflective of the reality of the complexity of the issues need to be created. With the aging of the baby boom generation, more families than ever will be faced with the inevitable: having to decide whether they themselves, or a close family member, dies with dignity or has his or her life needlessly prolonged.

SUMMARY

13.1 Definitions and Ethical Issues

How is death defined?

- Death is a difficult concept to define precisely. Different cultures have different meanings for death. Among the meanings in Western culture are images, statistics, events, state of being, analogy, mystery, boundary, basis for anxiety, and reward or punishment.

What legal and medical criteria are used to determine when death occurs?

- For many centuries, a clinical definition of death was used: the absence of a heartbeat and respiration. Currently, whole-brain death is the most widely used definition. It is based on several highly specific criteria, including brain activity and responses to specific stimuli.

What are the ethical dilemmas surrounding euthanasia?

- Two types of euthanasia are distinguished. Active euthanasia consists of deliberately ending someone's life, such as turning off a life-support system. Physician-assisted suicide is a controversial issue and a form of active euthanasia. Passive euthanasia is ending someone's life by withholding some type of intervention or treatment (e.g.,

by stopping nutrition). It is essential people make their wishes known through either a health care power of attorney or a living will.

What issues surround the costs of life-sustaining care?

- The personal and financial costs of prolonging life when the patient would have preferred another option are significant.

13.2 Thinking About Death: Personal Aspects

How do feelings about death change over adulthood?

- Young adults report a sense of being cheated by death. Cognitive developmental level is important for understanding how young adults view death.

- Middle-aged adults begin to confront their own mortality and undergo a change in their sense of time lived and time until death.

- Older adults are more accepting of death.

How do people deal with their own death?

- Kübler-Ross's approach includes five stages: denial, anger, bargaining, depression, and acceptance. People may be in more than one stage at a time and do not necessarily go through them in order.

- A contextual theory of dying emphasizes the tasks a dying person must face. Four dimensions of these tasks have been identified: bodily needs, psychological security, interpersonal attachments, and spiritual energy and hope. A contextual theory incorporates differences in reasons people die and the places people die.

What is death anxiety, and how do people show it?

- Most people exhibit some degree of anxiety about death, even though it is difficult to define and measure. Individual difference variables include gender, religiosity, age, ethnicity, and occupation. Death anxiety may have some benefits.

- The main ways death anxiety is shown are by avoiding death (e.g., refusing to go to funerals) and deliberately challenging it (e.g., engaging in dangerous sports).

- Several ways to deal with anxiety exist: living life to the fullest, personal reflection, and education. Death education has been shown to be extremely effective.

13.3 End-of-Life Issues

How do people deal with end-of-life issues and create a final scenario?

- Managing the final aspects of life, after-death disposition of the body, memorial services, and distribution of assets are important end-of-life issues. Making choices about what people want and do not want done constitute making a final scenario.

What is hospice?

- The goal of a hospice is to maintain the quality of life and manage the pain of terminally ill patients. Hospice clients typically have cancer, AIDS, or a progressive neurological disorder. Family members tend to stay involved in the care of hospice clients.

How does one make one's end-of-life desires and decisions known?

- End-of-life decisions are made know most often through a living will, health care power of attorney, or a Do Not Resuscitate order. It is important family and health care professionals are aware of these decisions. The Patient Self-Determination Act requires health care facilities to inform patients of these rights.

13.4 Surviving the Loss: The Grieving Process

How do people experience the grief process?

- Grief is an active process of coping with loss. Four aspects of grieving must be confronted: the reality of the loss, the emotional turmoil, adjusting to the environment, and loosening the ties with the deceased. When death is expected, survivors go through anticipatory grief; unexpected death is usually more difficult for people to handle.

What feelings do grieving people have?

- Dealing with grief, called *grief work*, usually takes at least one to two years. Grief is equally intense for both expected and unexpected death, but it may begin before the actual death when the patient has a terminal illness. Normal grief reactions include sorrow, sadness, denial, disbelief, guilt, and anniversary reactions.

How do people cope with grief?

- In terms of dealing with normal grief, middle-aged adults have the most difficult time. Poor copers tend to have low self-esteem before losing a loved one.

What is the difference between normal and complicated or prolonged grief?

- The four-component model proposes the grief process is described by context of the loss, continuation of subjective meaning associated with the loss, changing representations of the lost relationship over time, and the role of coping and emotion-regulation processes.

- The dual process model of coping with bereavement focuses on loss-oriented and restoration-oriented stressors.

- Prolonged grief involves symptoms of separation distress and traumatic distress. Excessive guilt and self-blame are common manifestations of traumatic grief.

What developmental aspects are important in understanding grief?

- Young and middle-aged adults usually have intense feelings about death. Attachment theory provides a useful framework for understanding these feelings.

- Midlife is a time when people usually deal with the death of their parents and confront their own mortality.

- The death of one's child is especially difficult to cope with.

- The death of one's parent deprives an adult of many important things, and the feelings accompanying it are often complex.

REVIEW QUESTIONS

13.1 Definitions and Ethical Issues

- What are the three legal criteria for death?
- What are the criteria necessary for brain death?
- What is bioethics, and what kinds of issues does it deal with?
- What are the types of euthanasia? How do they differ?
- How do the personal and financial costs of life-sustaining treatment affect health care decisions?

13.2 Thinking about Death: Personal Aspects

- How do cognitive development and issues at midlife influence feelings about death?
- Describe Kübler-Ross's concepts of dying. How do people progress through the different feelings?
- What is necessary for creating a contextual theory of dying?
- What is death anxiety? What factors influence death anxiety? How does it relate to terror management theory?
- How do people demonstrate death anxiety?
- How do people learn to deal with death anxiety?

13.3 End-of-Life Issues

- What are end-of-life issues?
- How do people create a final scenario?
- What is a hospice? How does hospice care differ from hospital care?
- What are the major ways that people inform others of their end-of-life decisions?

13.4 Survivors: The Grieving Process

- What is meant by grief, bereavement, and mourning?
- What is the process of grief? What are the risk factors associated with grief?
- What are normal grief reactions and grief work?
- How does grief change over time?
- What is the four component model of grief?
- What is the dual process model of grief?
- What is the grief-work-as-rumination hypothesis?
- What are complicated or prolonged grief reactions?
- How do adults of different ages deal with different types of loss?

INTEGRATING CONCEPTS IN DEVELOPMENT

- What effect do you think being at different levels of cognitive development has on people's thinking about death?
- What parallels are there between the stages of dying and the experience of grief? Why do you think they may be similar?
- How can we use the study of death, dying, bereavement, and grief to provide insights into the psychological development of people across adulthood?

KEY TERMS

active euthanasia The deliberate ending of someone's life.

anniversary reaction Changes in behavior related to feelings of sadness on the anniversary date of a loss.

anticipatory grief Grief experienced during the period before an expected death occurs that supposedly serves to buffer the impact of the loss when it does come and to facilitate recovery.

bereavement The state or condition caused by loss through death.

bioethics Study of the interface between human values and technological advances in health and life sciences.

clinical death Lack of heartbeat and respiration.

complicated or prolonged grief disorder Expression of grief that is distinguished from depression and from normal grief in terms of separation distress and traumatic distress.

death anxiety People's anxiety or even fear of death and dying.

Do Not Resuscitate (DNR) order A medical order that means cardiopulmonary resuscitation (CPR) is not started should one's heart and breathing stop.

dual-process model (DPM) View of coping with bereavement that integrates loss-oriented stressors and restoration-oriented stressors.

end-of-life issues Issues pertaining to the management of the final phase of life, after-death disposition of their body, memorial services, and distribution of assets.

euthanasia The practice of ending life for reasons of mercy.

final scenario Making one's choices known about how they do and do not want their lives to end.

four-component model Model of grief that understanding grief is based on (1) the context of the loss; (2) continuation of subjective meaning associated with loss; (3) changing representations of the lost relationship over time; and (4) the role of coping and emotion regulation processes.

grief The sorrow, hurt, anger, guilt, confusion, and other feelings that arise after suffering a loss.

grief work The psychological side of coming to terms with bereavement.

grief work as rumination hypothesis An approach that not only rejects the necessity of grief processing for recovery from loss but views extensive grief processing as a form of rumination that may actually increase distress.

health care power of attorney A document in which an individual appoints someone to act as his or her agent for health care decisions.

hospice An approach to assisting dying people that emphasizes pain management, or palliative care, and death with dignity.

living will A document in which a person states his or her wishes about life support and other treatments.

mourning The ways in which we express our grief.

palliative care Care that is focused on providing relief from pain and other symptoms of disease at any point during the disease process.

passive euthanasia Allowing a person to die by withholding available treatment.

persistent vegetative state Situation in which a person's cortical functioning ceases while brainstem activity continues.

physician-assisted suicide Process in which physicians provide dying patients with a fatal dose of medication the patient self-administers.

separation distress Expression of complicated or prolonged grief disorder that includes preoccupation with the deceased to the point it interferes with everyday functioning, upsetting memories of the deceased, longing and searching for the deceased, and isolation following the loss.

terror management theory Addresses the issue of why people engage in certain behaviors to achieve particular psychological states based on their deeply rooted concerns about mortality.

thanatology The study of death, dying, grief, bereavement, and social attitudes toward these issues.

traumatic distress Expression of complicated or prolonged grief disorder that includes feeling disbelief about the death, mistrust, anger, and detachment from others as a result of the death, feeling shocked by the death, and the experience of physical presence of the deceased.

whole-brain death Death that is declared only when the deceased meets eight criteria established in 1981.

RESOURCES

Access quizzes, glossaries, flashcards, and more at www.cengagebrain.com.

CHAPTER 14

SUCCESSFUL AGING

WELCOME TO YOUR FUTURE. IN THIS EPILOGUE, WE TAKE A

different perspective on aging. Based on what we know now about older adults and the process of aging, we look to our own future. We consider what society must do to keep the social programs we have come to rely on. We consider what each of us can do to keep ourselves in the best health possible in order to delay or even prevent some of the negative aspects of aging. We take a look at how the baby boomers will change everything from how older adults are viewed to the coming enormous pressure on governmental resources. We also look around the corner and ahead a few decades to preview what may be in store for current young adults when they reach late life.

Aging today and in the future is not what it was even a few years ago. Technical advances have and will continue to make commonplace what is only science fiction today. For example, it is likely we will get our annual physical examination remotely, be in classes or meetings led by someone's interactive holographic projection when they are in another place, and may meet many of our friends through only Skype or FaceTime. Medicine will make advances such as offering genetic interventions that cure dementia and cancer, offering the possibility of much longer average life spans. It is a future with many more support structures and systems for older adults. It will be an interesting experience, to say the least.

For now, though, we must be content with working with what we do and do not know. Throughout this book we made predictions about this future and guessed how older people may fare. Some of these predictions are not so happy; as many people live to an old age, there will be greater need for long-term care. Whether we will be able to afford to provide the care for them is much in doubt. Other aspects of the future may be more positive; for instance, as many people live to older ages there will be a larger pool of older workers to balance the labor force. These predictions represent our best guess about what life will be like in the next few decades, based on what we know now and what is likely to happen if we continue down our current path.

We cannot always predict the path our lives will take.

John C. Cavanaugh

The purpose of this epilogue is to pull together several crucial issues facing gerontologists as we move through the 21st century and to illustrate how we can set the best stage for our own aging. This survey will not be exhaustive; rather, we focus on two things: points singled out for special concern and areas where major advances may have a dramatic impact on our own development.

14.1 Demographic Trends and Social Policy

LEARNING OBJECTIVES

- What key demographic changes will occur by 2030?
- What are the challenges facing Social Security and Medicare?

Nancy, a 35-year-old new employee at a marketing and public relations firm, was flipping through the company's benefits package. When it came to the retirement plan, she commented to the human resources person, "I guess I better pay attention. I don't think Social Security and Medicare will be there for me when the time comes."

Nancy isn't alone. Many younger adults in the United States do not believe Social Security, Medicare, or other government programs will be in existence by the time they get old enough to qualify for them. Demographic and financial trends support this pessimistic view. As we will show, the baby-boom generation, coupled with structural problems in Social Security and Medicare, give young adults good reasons to be concerned.

Demographic Trends: 2030

In Chapter 1, we noted several trends in the population of the United States and the rest of the world during the upcoming century. These trends are not likely to change in the foreseeable future. Changes in the composition of the older adult population contribute to potentially critical issues that will emerge over the next few decades. Keep in mind the baby boomers represent the largest generation ever to reach older adulthood. Generation X, the group right behind them, is much smaller. Although larger than Gen-X, the Millennials will still feel the brunt of the effects of aging boomers. One especially important area concerns the potential for intergenerational conflict.

Because the resources and roles in a society are never divided equally among different age groups, the potential for conflict always exists. One well-known intergenerational conflict is between adolescents and their parents. Less well known is the potential for conflict between young/middle-aged adults and older adults. This type of conflict has not traditionally been a source of serious problems in society, for several reasons: Older adults made up a small proportion of the population, family ties between adult children and their parents worked against conflict, and middle-aged people were hesitant to withdraw support from programs for older adults. Despite these potent forces protecting against conflict, the situation is changing. The controversy over the rate of growth of Medicare and Social Security and the proportion they represent of the federal budget would have been unthinkable just a few years earlier.

To see more clearly how these changing demographics will have an enormous effect on society at large and on the programs that target older adults, let us project forward to the year 2030, when the last of the baby boomers reach age 65. Between now and 2030, the following changes will have set in:

- The proportion of older adults in the United States will nearly double.

- Older adults will be more educated, politically sophisticated, and organized than past generations. They will be familiar with life in a highly complex society where one must learn to deal with (and have little tolerance for) bureaucracies and they will be proficient users of the Internet and technology in general.

- Older adults will expect to keep their affluent lifestyle, Social Security benefits, Medicare/health care benefits, and other benefits accrued throughout their adult life. A comfortable retirement will be viewed as a right, not a privilege. However, they will not, on average, have the financial savings necessary to support those expectations.

- The dependency ratio will change. *The **dependency ratio** reflects the number of people under age 15 and over age 64 in a country.* The dependency ratio provides insight into the relative number of people who have to provide the financial support for others not as able to do so. The lower the number, the more workers are needed to pay taxes to provide the revenue for social support programs.

As shown in Figure 14.1, the dependency ratio for developed countries is about to shift dramatically compared to what happened while the baby boomers were growing up and working. For the United States, this plays out most visibly in funding for Social Security and Medicare.

For example, the ratio of workers to retirees will fall from its current level of roughly 3:1 to 2:1. This means to maintain the level of benefits in programs such as Social Security, the working members of society will have to pay significantly higher taxes than workers do now. This is because Social Security is a pay-as-you-go system so the money collected from workers today is used to pay current retirees. Contrary to popular belief, Social Security is not a savings plan. Whether policymakers will make the

Demographic cliff

Change in total dependency ratio*, 1960–2010 and 2010–2060, respectively (in %)

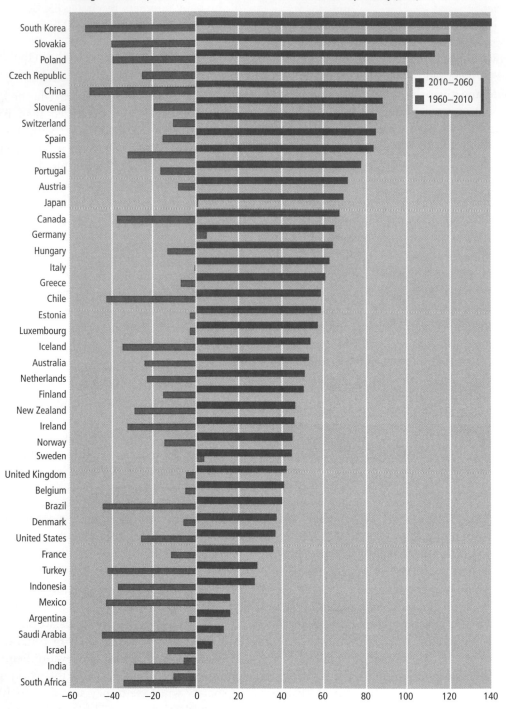

*Persons aged <15 & 65+ per person aged 15–64

Figure 14.1
Projected change in dependency ratio 1960–2060.

Source: United Nations Population Division, World Population Prospects: The 2010 Revision.

necessary changes to maintain benefits that citizens came to view as entitlements remains to be seen. We take a closer look at both Social Security and Medicare later.

- The increase in divorce that has occurred over the past few decades may result in a lowered sense of obligation on the part of middle-aged adults toward parents or step parents who were not involved in their upbringing or who the adult child feels disrespected the other parent. Should this lowered sensc of obligation result it is likely fewer older adults will have family members available to care for them, placing a significantly greater burden on society for care.

- The rapid increase in the number of ethnic minority oldcr adults compared to European American older adults will force a reconsideration of issues such as discrimination and access to health care, goods, and services, as well as provide a much richer and broader understanding of the aging process.

No one knows for certain what society will be like by 2030. However, the changes we noted in demographic trends suggest a need for taking action now. Two areas facing the most challenge are Social Security and Medicare. Let's take a look at these to understand why they face trouble.

Social Security and Medicare

Without doubt, the 20th and the beginning of the 21st centuries saw a dramatic improvement in the everyday lives of older adults in industrialized countries. The increase in the number of older adults and their gain in political power, coupled with increased numbers of social programs addressing issues specifically involving older adults, created unprecedented gains for the average older person and changed the way they are viewed in society (Giele, 2013).

As you can see in Figure 14.2, the economic well-being of the majority of older adults has never been better than it is currently. In 1959, 35% of older adults were below the federal poverty line compared to only 9% in 2010 (AgingStats.gov, 2012a).

Whether this downward trend in poverty rates will continue remains to be seen. The baby boomers complicate things (National Academy of Social Insurancc, 2012). They will be the first generation since the inception of Social Security in the mid-1930s to face a long average life span without the reality of corporate-provided pensions, relatively modest Social Security payments, little personal savings on average, and high projected health care costs during their late life. Those with the financial resources may well prosper; others will drive the costs of social support programs much higher, forcing difficult social policy decisions about

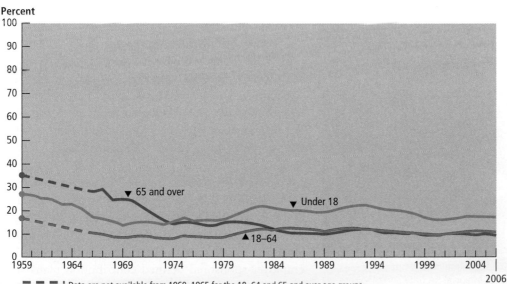

Figure 14.2

Poverty rates in the United States by age group, 1959–2010.

Source: U.S. Census Bureau, Current Population Survey, Annual Society and Economic Supplement, 1960 2007.

Data are not available from 1960–1965 for the 18–64 and 65 and over age groups.
Reference population: These data refer to the civilian noninstitutionalized population.

how much base financial support is necessary and affordable.

The Political Landscape. Beginning in the 1970s, older adults began to be portrayed as scapegoats in the political debates concerning government resources. Part of the reason was due to the tremendous growth in the amount and proportion of federal dollars expended on benefits to them, such as through the increase of benefits paid from Social Security during the 1970s (Crown, 2001). At that time in history, older adults were also portrayed as highly politically active, fiscally conservative, and selfish (Fairlie, 1988; Gibbs, 1988; Smith, 1992). The health care reform debate of the early 1990s focused attention on the spiraling costs of care for older adults that were projected to bankrupt the federal budget if left uncontrolled (Binstock, 1999). This theme would echo for decades.

It was in this context the U.S. Congress began making substantive changes in the benefits for older adults on the grounds of intergenerational fairness. Beginning in 1983, Congress has made several changes in Social Security, Medicare, the Older Americans Act, and other programs and policies. Some of these changes reduced benefits to wealthy older adults, changed eligibility rules (e.g., age at which one is eligible for full benefits), whereas others provided targeted benefits for poor older adults, all of which had an effect on how older adults are viewed (Binstock, 1999; Polivka, 2010).

The aging of the baby boomers presents difficult and expensive problems (Office of Management and Budget, 2013). In fiscal year 2014, President Obama proposed federal spending on Social Security and Medicare alone at over $1.38 trillion, just over a third of the total budget. In terms of actual spending, in fiscal year 2011, they accounted for 36% of all federal spending. Considering baby boomers have only begun to collect these benefits, you get the sense of urgency felt by elected officials.

If spending patterns do not change, by 2030 (when most of the baby boomers have reached old age) expenditures for Social Security and Medicare alone are projected to consume roughly 12% of the entire gross domestic product (GDP) of the United States (Congressional Budget Office, 2012a). Without major reforms in these programs, that will increase to over 14% by 2050. Such growth will force extremely difficult choices regarding how to pay for them.

Clearly, the political and social issues concerning benefits to older adults are quite complex. Driven by the eligibility of the first baby boomers for reduced Social Security benefits in 2008 and their eligibility for Medicare in 2011, the next decade will see the impact of previous inaction, and likely increased urgency to confront the issues. There are no easy solutions, and it will be essential to discuss all aspects of the problem. Let's look more closely at Social Security and Medicare.

Social Security. Social Security had its beginnings in 1935 as an initiative by President Franklin Roosevelt to "frame a law which will give some measure of protection to the average citizen and to his family against the loss of a job and against poverty-ridden old age." Thus Social Security was originally intended to provide a supplement to savings and other means of financial support.

Two key things have changed since then. First, the proportion of people who reach age 65 has increased significantly. In 1940, about 54% of men and 61% of women reached age 65. Today, that's changed to about 75% of men and 85% of women. Since 1940, men collect payments about 3 years longer, and women collect about 5 years longer. Both trends increase the cost of the program.

Second, revisions to the original law have changed Social Security so it now represents the primary source of financial support after retirement for most U.S. citizens, and the only source for many (Polivka, 2010). Since the 1970s, more workers have been included in employer-sponsored defined contribution plans such as 401(k), 403(b), 457 plans, and mutual funds, as well

The aging of the baby boom generation will put severe strain on the federal budget in Social Security and Medicare.

© Bikeriderlondon/Shutterstock.com

as various types of individual retirement accounts (IRAs), but fewer defined benefit traditional pension plans (Polivka, 2010). A key difference in these plans is defined contribution plans rely a great deal on employee participation (i.e., workers saving money for retirement) whereas traditional pension programs did not require employee participation as they provided a monthly income for life paid completely by the company.

On the face of it, this inclusion of various retirement plans, especially savings options, may permit more future retirees to use Social Security as the supplemental financial source it was intended to be, thereby shifting retirement financial planning responsibility to the individual (Henrikson, 2007). But it may also be an increasing number of older adults rely on Social Security as their primary income source because of a lack of personal savings (Polivka, 2010).

The primary challenge facing Social Security is the aging of the baby boomers and the much smaller generation that follows (National Academy of Social Insurance, 2012). That's why Nancy, the woman we met in the vignette, and other young adults are concerned. Because Social Security is funded by payroll taxes, the amount of money each worker must pay depends to a large extent on the ratio of the number of people paying Social Security taxes to the number of people collecting benefits. By 2030, this ratio will drop nearly in half; that is, by the time baby boomers have

largely retired, there will be nearly twice as many people collecting Social Security per worker paying into the system as there is today (Social Security Administration, 2012b).

Various plans have been proposed since the early 1970s to address this issue, and it has been a major agenda item in several presidential campaigns (e.g., 2004 and 2012). The 2012 election campaign focused attention on both Social Security and Medicare costs through proposals offered first by the Romney/Ryan ticket. Additionally, spending was a focus of the numerous debates on the federal budget in 2012 and 2013, especially in confronting the mandatory reductions brought by the sequestration cuts that went into effect in 2013.

President Obama tackled the structure of Social Security in his FY2014 budget proposal by suggesting the calculation underlying the annual cost-of-living increases be redone to provide lower increases (Montgomery, 2913). Although the proposal would only lower increases by 0.3% per year, the cumulative savings would be substantial—amounting to about 20% of the projected 75-year deficit. Such discussions and proposals will need to be considered and acted on before the baby boomers all reach maximum eligibility for the savings programs to have maximum effect.

How much of one's wages are actually provided by Social Security depends on how much you made on average during your employment career. Figure 14.3 shows

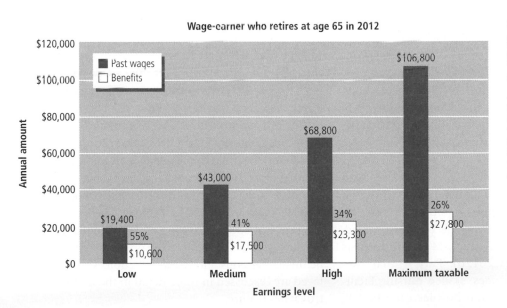

Figure 14.3

Social Security benefits compared to average annual wages.

Source: Social Security Administration. (2012). The 2012 Annual Report of the Board of Trustees of the Federal Old-Age and Survivors Insurance and Federal Disability Insurance Trust Funds. *Retrieved from http://www.ssa.gov/oact /tr/2012/index.html. Table V.C7*

this relation for a worker retiring in 2012 at age 65 who earned various wages on average while employed. As you can see, this ranges quite a bit depending on whether previous wages were low or the maximum taxable.

One point that confuses many people is the benefits received do not come from an "account" that reflects what you actually contributed over your employed career. Because Social Security is a revenue-in/payments-out model, people do not build up Social Security "savings." Rather, the money they pay in taxes goes out as payments to those who are collecting benefits. So the payments current workers receive in the future will actually be from the taxes paid by workers in the labor force at that future time. That's why the payee/recipient ratio matters—Social Security tax rates must inevitably go up or the benefits received must go down if there are fewer people paying to support an increasing number of recipients.

Over most of the life of Social Security, revenues were greater than payments. But that's changed, as now payments exceed revenues. As a result, the interest from those saved revenues in the Social Security Trust Fund is now being spent to make up the difference, and will keep the gap closed until 2021. If there are no changes in the law, and the moderate cost scenario occurs, by 2021 the Trust Fund itself will need to be liquidated by redeeming Treasury bonds. To get the money to redeem these bonds, the federal government will need to increase taxes, reduce spending in other government programs, or borrow money (thereby increasing the national debt). By 2033, all of the Trust Fund assets will be gone. Revenue from Social Security taxes would only cover about 75% of the benefits promised.

Despite knowing the fiscal realities for decades, Congress has not yet taken the actions necessary to ensure the long-term financial stability of Social Security (Social Security Administration, 2012a,b).

Medicare. Over 52 million U.S. citizens depend on Medicare for their medical insurance (CMS.gov, 2012a). To be eligible, a person must meet one of the following criteria: be over age 65, be disabled, or have permanent kidney failure. Medicare consists of three parts (CMS.gov, 2012b): Part A, that covers inpatient hospital services, skilled nursing facilities, home health services, and hospice care; Part B, that

covers the cost of physician services, outpatient hospital services, medical equipment and supplies, and other health services and supplies; and Part D, that provides some coverage for prescription medications. Expenses relating to most long-term care needs are funded by Medicaid, another major health care program funded by the U.S. government and aimed at people who are poor. Out-of-pocket expenses associated with co-payments and other charges are often paid by supplemental insurance policies, sometimes referred to as "Medigap" policies (Medicare.gov, 2013).

Like Social Security, Medicare is funded by a payroll tax. But unlike Social Security, where the income on which the tax is based has a cap, the tax supporting Medicare is paid on all of one's earnings. Still, the funding problems facing Medicare are arguably worse than those facing Social Security and are grounded in the aging of the baby-boom generation. In addition, Medicare costs have increased dramatically because of more rapid cost increases in health care. Expenditures will increase rapidly as the baby boomers increase the ranks of those covered.

Because of these rapid increases expected with the baby-boom generation, cost containment remains a major concern. The presidential elections of 2008 and 2012 included numerous debates about rapidly rising health care costs as a major economic problem facing the United States. Certainly, the debate around the Patient Protection and Affordable Care Act of 2010 heightened awareness of the issues.

Unlike Social Security, though, Medicare has been subjected to significant cuts in expenditures, typically through reduced payouts to health care providers. Projected Medicare costs over the next 75 years are much lower than they would have been prior to the passage of the Patient Protection and Affordable Care Act in 2010 (Social Security Administration, 2012a).

Taken together, the challenges facing society concerning older adults' financial security and health will continue to be major political issues throughout the first few decades of the 21st century. There are no easy answers, but open discussion of the various arguments will be essential for creating the optimal solution. Public misperceptions and the tough choices that must be faced are discussed in more detail in the Current Controversies feature.

CURRENT CONTROVERSIES:

WHAT TO DO ABOUT SOCIAL SECURITY AND MEDICARE

As pointed out earlier in the chapter, the amount of money people collect in Social Security and Medicare is not directly connected to the amount they paid in taxes over their working careers. That's a point many people misunderstand—they think they get out what they have put in. This misperception makes it difficult to make changes in the benefits structure (the cost) of these programs, especially Medicare.

The fact is in 2012, the average person collected about $3.00 in Medicare benefits for each dollar they paid in taxes on their earnings, premiums, and medical co-payments. This imbalance (and misperception) is a major reason why restructuring the benefits or raising co-payments to control costs is so difficult to

do, and why the current benefit structure is unsustainable for the baby boomers (Calmes, 2013).

On average, older Americans pay about 25% of the cost of Medicare Part B and Part D through premiums, deductibles, and co-insurance (higher income people pay a larger share, up to 80%). General revenue in the national budget pays for the rest, and is why an increasing percentage of the federal budget is going to Medicare.

Similar analyses can be done for Social Security, but with a different outcome. Whereas nearly all Medicare recipients get much more out of the program than they paid in taxes, that's not true for many people regarding Social Security.

Figure 14.4 shows comparisons between what a people earning various amounts of money on average during their employment careers and what they could expect to receive from Social Security and Medicare. Note, for example, a low-earning couple would receive

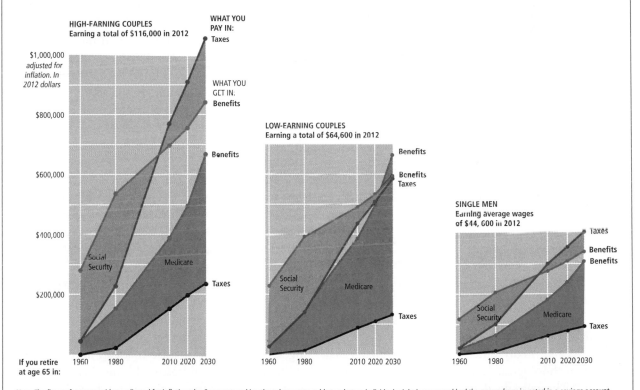

Note: The figures for taxes paid are adjusted for inflation plus 2 percent, making the values comparable to what an individual might have earned had the money been invested in a savings account. The payroll tax calculations assume both the individual and employer contribution (most economists assume that individuals effectively bear the total expense through lower wages than employers might pay absent the tax). Figures for Medicare benefits are reduced to account for premiums that beneficiaries have paid. For example, a single male with average wages who retired at age 65 in 2010 would have paid about as much in Social Security taxes in his lifetime as he will receive in benefits. He receives more in Medicare benefits than he paid in taxes.

Figure 14.4

Average lifetime taxes paid and benefits received from Social Security and Medicare.

about what they paid in taxes in Social Security benefits, and much more from Medicare. What's especially obvious is everyone receives far more in Medicare benefits than they paid.

The challenge is the costs of Medicare must be controlled given the imminent arrival of most of the baby boomers. But explaining to those who are already receiving or are about to receive the benefit is a daunting task. That's why most proposals target individuals who are about 10 years away from receiving Medicare benefits.

The political debates around Social Security and Medicare will not end soon. What is clear, though, is the current financial model is unsustainable in the long run, and action, especially with respect to Medicare, is needed now.

ADULT DEVELOPMENT IN ACTION

How are demographics affecting social policy in the United States?

14.2 Health Issues And Quality Of Life

LEARNING OBJECTIVES

- What are the key issues in health promotion and quality of life?
- What are the major strategies for maintaining and enhancing competence?
- What are the primary considerations in designing health promotion and disease prevention programs?
- What are the principal lifestyle factors that influence competence?

Jack heard about all the things available on the Web, and that he was missing a great deal. So, after he purchased his first home computer at age 68, he began surfing. He never stopped. Now at age 73, he's a veteran with a wide array of bookmarked sites, especially those relating to health issues. He also communicates by e-mail, and designed the community newsletter using his word-processing program. He recently created his Facebook page so he can keep up with his grandsons.

Jack is like many older adults—better educated and more technologically sophisticated than their predecessors. The coming demographic changes in the United States and the rest of the world in the aging baby boom generation present a challenge for improving the kind of lives older adults live. For this reason, promoting healthy lifestyles is seen as one of the top health care priorities of the 21st century (Lunenfeld, 2008). Remaining healthy is important for decelerating the rate of aging (Aldwin & Gilmer, 2013). Promoting healthy lifestyles is important in all settings, including long-term care facilities (Thompson & Oliver, 2008).

Health Promotion and Quality of Life

Even though changing unhealthy habits such as smoking and poor diet are difficult, chronic diseases such as arthritis make exercise challenging, and terminal disease makes it tough to see the benefits of changing one's habits, the fact remains such changes typically increase functional capability. Current models of behavioral change are complex and include not only behavioral, but also motivational, cognitive, and social components (Aldwin & Gilmer, 2013). The two that are the focus of most research are the self-efficacy model that emphasizes the role of goal setting and personal beliefs in the degree one influences the outcome, and the self-regulation model, that focuses on the person's motivation for change.

There is insufficient research on health promotion programs designed specifically for older adults (Aldwin & Gilmer, 2013). However, a few trends are apparent. First, although exercise is basic for good health, because older adults are more prone to injury, exercise programs for them need to take such issues into account and focus more on low impact aerobic approaches. Second, health education programs are effective in minimizing the effects of emotional stress. Third, health screening programs effectively identifying serious chronic disease that can limit the quality of life, and can be addressed through behavioral interventions. Each of these areas within health promotion is most successful when ethnic differences are taken into account in designing the programs (Westmaas, Gil-Rivas, & Silver, 2011).

*People's state of health influences their **quality of life**, that is, their well-being and life satisfaction.* Quality of life includes interpersonal relationships and social support, physical and mental health, environmental comfort, and many psychological constructs such as locus of control, emotions, usefulness, personality, and meaning in life (Aldwin & Gilmer, 2013). Quality of life is usually divided into environmental, physical, social, and psychological domains of well-being. Personal evaluation of these dimensions is critical to understanding how people view their situations. Although half of the people in Strawbridge, Wallhagen, and Cohen's (2002) study did not meet certain objective criteria for successful aging, they nevertheless defined themselves as successful and as having a good quality of life.

In short, quality of life is a person's subjective assessment or value judgment of his or her own life (Aldwin & Gilmer, 2013). This subjective judgment may or may not correspond to the evaluation of others. And even though self- and other-perceived quality of life may diminish in late life, it may not seem like a loss for the older person. An older woman who has difficulty walking may feel happy to simply be alive, whereas another who is in objective good health may feel useless. Quality of life is best studied from the point of view of the person.

Still, when the level of medical intervention increases as people grow more frail, medical professionals must be concerned about the trade-off between extending life at all costs and the quality of that life, as discussed in chapter 13 (Michel, Newton, & Kirkwood, 2008). A longitudinal study in England showed clearly good health care makes a major difference in people's quality of life and their average longevity (Steel, Melzer, & Richards (2013).

A Framework for Maintaining and Enhancing Competence

Although most older adults are not as computer literate as Jack, the man introduced in the vignette, increasing numbers of older adults are discovering computers can be a major asset. Many take advantage of the growing resources available on the Web, including sites dedicated specifically to older adults. E-mail and social networking enable people of all ages to stay in touch with friends and family, and the growing success of e-commerce makes it easier for people with limited time or mobility to purchase goods and services. Computers are already used in many health devices and likely to become ubiquitous in the home environment

Older adults are increasingly using technology to stay in touch with family.

Phil Masturzo/MCT/Newscom

of older adults in the relatively near future (Lesnoff-Caravaglia, 2010).

The use of technology is one way that technology can be used to enhance the competence of older adults. In this section, we consider the general topic of how to maintain and enhance competence through a variety of interventions. How to grow old successfully is a topic of increasing concern in view of the demographic changes we considered earlier.

The life span perspective we considered in Chapter 1 is an excellent starting point for understanding how to maintain and enhance people's competence. In this perspective, the changes that occur with age result from multiple biological, psychological, sociocultural, and life-cycle forces. Mastering tasks of daily living and more complex tasks (such as personal finances) contributes to a person's overall sense of competence even if the person has dementia (Mayo, 2008). How can this sense be optimized for successful aging?

The answer lies in applying three key adaptive mechanisms for aging: selection, optimization, and compensation (SOC) (Baltes et al., 2006). This framework addresses what Bieman-Copland, Ryan, and Cassano (2002) call the "social facilitation of the nonuse of competence": the phenomenon of older people intentionally or unintentionally failing to perform up to their true level of ability because of social stereotypes that operate to limit what older adults are expected to do. Instead of behaving at their true ability level, older adults behave in ways they believe typical or characteristic of their age group (Lang, 2004).

This phenomenon is the basis for the communication patterns we considered earlier in this chapter.

A key issue in the powerful role of stereotypes is to differentiate usual or typical aging from successful aging (Aldwin & Gilmer, 2013; Guralnik, 2008). Successful aging involves avoiding disease, being engaged with life, and maintaining high cognitive and physical functioning. Successful aging is subjective. It is reached when a person achieves his or her desired goals with dignity and as independently as possible.

The life-span perspective can be used to create a formal model for successful aging. Heckhausen, Wrosch, & Schulz (2010) developed a theory of life-span development based on motivation and control by applying core assumptions that recognize aging as a complex process that involves increasing specialization and is influenced by factors unrelated to age. The basic premises of successful aging include keeping a balance between the various gains and losses that occur over time and minimizing the influence of factors unrelated to aging. In short, these premises involve paying attention to both internal and external factors impinging on the person. The antecedents include all the changes that happen to a person. The mechanisms in the model are the selection, optimization, and compensation processes that shape the course of development. Finally, the outcomes of the model denote that enhanced competence, quality of life, and future adaptation are the visible signs of successful aging.

Using the SOC model, enhanced by Heckhausen et al.'s (2010) notions of control and motivation, various types of interventions can be created to help people age successfully. In general, such interventions focus on the individual or on aspects of tasks and the physical and social environment that emphasize competence (Aldwin & Gilmer, 2013; Allaire & Willis, 2006; Bieman-Copland et al., 2002; Thornton, Paterson, & Yeung, 2013). When designing interventions aimed primarily at the person, it is important to understand the target person's goals (rather than the goals of the researcher). For example, in teaching older adults how to use technology, it is essential to understand the kinds of concerns and fears older adults have and ensure the training program addresses them (Lesnoff-Caravaglia, 2010).

Performance on tests of everyday competence predicts longer term outcomes (Allaire & Willis, 2006).

Careful monitoring of competence can be an early indicator of problems, and appropriate interventions should be undertaken as soon as possible.

Health Promotion and Disease Prevention

By now you're probably wondering how to promote successful aging. You may not be surprised to learn there is no set of steps or magic potion you can take to guarantee you will age optimally. But research using traditional methods as well as cutting-edge neuroimaging is showing there are some steps you can take to quality of life and the odds of aging well (Aldwin & Gilmer, 2013; Guralnik, 2008; Reuter-Lorenz, 2013).

As you can see in Table 14.1, most of the methods are not complex, but they do capture the results of applying the model for maintaining and enhancing competence we examined at the beginning of the section. The key strategies are sound health habits; good habits of thought, including an optimistic outlook and interest in things; a social network; and sound economic habits.

These simple steps are difficult in practice, of course. Nevertheless, they will maximize the chances of aging successfully. Setting up this favorable outcome is important. Because of the demographic shifts in the population, health care costs for older adults in most developed countries are expected to skyrocket during the first half of the 21st century, as we noted earlier. Minimizing this increase is key; following these principles can make that happen.

To support these changes, the U.S. Department of Health and Human Services created a national initiative to improve the health of all Americans through a coordinated and comprehensive emphasis on prevention. Updated every 10 years, the current version of

Table 14.1

PREVENTIVE STRATEGIES FOR MAXIMIZING SUCCESSFUL AGING
Adopt a healthy lifestyle. Make it part of your daily routine.
Stay active cognitively. Keep an optimistic outlook and maintain your interest in things.
Maintain a social network and stay engaged with others.
Maintain good economic habits to avoid financial dependency.

this effort, the *Healthy People 2020* initiative, sets targets for a healthier population based on three broad goals: increase the length of healthy life, reduce health disparities among Americans, and achieve access to preventive services for all.

Although significant gains have been made in earlier versions of the initiative, they were not universal. Many members of ethnic minority groups and the poor still have not seen significant improvements in their lives. With this in mind, there has been a shift from a focus that included only prevention to one that also includes optimum health practices.

The U.S. government allocates funds appropriated by the Older Americans Act through the Administration on Aging (AoA) to provide programs specifically aimed at improving the health of older adults. These funds support a wide variety of programs, including health risk assessments and screenings, nutrition screening and education, physical fitness, health promotion programs on chronic disabling conditions, home injury control services, counseling regarding social services, and follow-up health services.

One goal of these low-cost programs is to address the lack of awareness many people have about their own chronic health problems; the AoA estimates half of those with diabetes mellitus, more than half with hypertension, and 70% of those with high cholesterol levels are unaware they have serious conditions. Health promotion and disease prevention programs such as those sponsored by the AoA could reduce the cost of treating the diseases through earlier diagnosis and better prevention education. Getting people to participate and then engage in healthy behavior, though, remains elusive.

Issues in Prevention. In Chapter 4, we saw Verbrugge and Jette's (1994) theoretical model offers a comprehensive account of disability resulting from chronic conditions and provides much guidance for research. Another benefit of the model is it also provides insight into ways to intervene so disability can be prevented or its progress slowed. Prevention efforts can be implemented in many ways, from providing flu vaccines to furnishing transportation to cultural events so otherwise homebound people can enjoy these activities.

Traditionally, three types of prevention have been discussed that can be applied to aging: primary, secondary, and tertiary (Haber, 2013). More recently, the concept of quaternary prevention has begun to be used (Scally, Imtiaz, Bethune, Young, Ward, Herzig et al., 2012). A brief summary is presented in Table 14.2. **Primary prevention** *is any intervention that prevents a disease or condition from occurring.* Examples of primary prevention include immunizing against illnesses such as polio and influenza or controlling risk factors such as serum cholesterol levels and cigarette smoking in healthy people.

Secondary prevention *is instituted early after a condition has begun (but may not yet have been diagnosed) and before significant impairments have occurred.* Examples of secondary intervention include cancer and cardiovascular disease screening and routine

Table 14.2

TYPES OF PREVENTION INTERVENTIONS

Type of Prevention	Description	Examples
Primary	Any intervention that prevents a disease or condition from occurring	Immunizations against diseases, healthy diet
Secondary	Program instituted early after a condition has begun (but may not have been diagnosed) and before significant impairment has occurred	Cancer screening, other medical tests
Tertiary	Efforts to avoid the development of complications or secondary chronic conditions, manage the panic associated with the primary chronic condition, and sustain life	Moving a bedridden person to avoid sores, getting medical intervention, getting a patient out of bed to improve mobility after surgery
Quaternary	Effort specifically aimed at improving the functional capacities of people who have chronic conditions	Cognitive interventions for people with Alzheimer's disease, rehabilitation programs after surgery

medical testing for other conditions. These steps help reduce the severity of the condition and may even reduce mortality from it. In terms of the main pathway in Verbrugge and Jette's (1994) model, secondary prevention occurs between pathology and impairments.

Tertiary prevention *involves efforts to avoid the development of complications or secondary chronic conditions, manage the pain associated with the primary chronic condition, and sustain life through medical intervention.* Some chronic conditions have a high risk of creating additional medical problems; for example, being bedridden as a result of a chronic disease often is associated with getting pneumonia. Tertiary prevention involves taking steps such as sitting the person up in bed to lower the risk of contracting additional diseases. In terms of the model, tertiary interventions are aimed at minimizing functional limitations and disability.

Tertiary prevention efforts do not usually focus on functioning but rather on avoiding additional medical problems and sustaining life (Haber, 2013). Consequently, the notion of quaternary prevention has been developed to address functional issues (Scally et al., 2012). **Quaternary prevention** *efforts are specifically aimed at improving the functional capacities of people who have chronic conditions.* Quaternary prevention strategies help health care professionals avoid unnecessary or excessive medical interventions, especially invasive ones. Some examples of quaternary prevention are cognitive interventions to help people with Alzheimer's disease remember things and occupational therapy to help people maintain their independence.

Although most efforts with older adults to date have focused on primary prevention, increasing attention is being paid to secondary prevention through screening for early diagnosis of diseases such as cancer and cardiovascular disease (see Chapters 2 and 3). Few systematic studies of the benefits and outcomes of tertiary and quaternary prevention efforts have been done with older adult participants, though. However, the number of such programs being conducted in local senior centers, health care facilities, and other settings is increasing steadily, with the focus of many of them on nutrition and exercise, as well as other behaviorally based strategies (Rippe, 2013).

The stakes are high. Because tertiary and quaternary prevention programs are aimed at maintaining functional abilities and minimizing disability, they can be effective, lower-cost alternatives for addressing the needs of older adults with chronic conditions. Lifestyle factors are the basis for these behavioral approaches that are clearly gaining favor in the health care professional community (Rippe, 2013). Comprehensive health care reform will likely adopt many more of these approaches; especially given they are grounded in research, making them evidence-based. Let's take a closer look.

Lifestyle Factors

Most attention in health promotion and disease prevention programs is on tackling a handful of behaviors that have tremendous payoff, such as keeping fit and eating properly. In turn, these programs educate adults about good health care practices and identify conditions such as hypertension, high cholesterol levels, and elevated blood sugar levels, which, if left untreated, can cause atherosclerosis, heart disease, strokes, diabetes mellitus, and other serious conditions.

Exercise. Since the ancient Greeks, physicians and researchers have known exercise significantly slows the aging process. Indeed, evidence suggests a program of regular exercise, in conjunction with a healthy lifestyle, can slow the physiological aging process (Aldwin & Gilmer, 2013). Being sedentary is absolutely hazardous to your health.

Adults benefit from **aerobic exercise,** *that places moderate stress on the heart by maintaining a pulse rate between 60% and 90% of the person's maximum heart rate.* You can calculate your maximum heart rate by subtracting your age from 220. Thus, if you are 40 years old, your target range would be 108–162 beats per minute. The minimum time necessary for aerobic exercise to be of benefit depends on its intensity; at low heart rates, sessions may need to last an hour, whereas at high heart rates, 15 minutes may suffice. Examples of aerobic exercise include jogging, step aerobics, swimming, and cross-country skiing.

What happens when a person exercises aerobically (besides becoming tired and sweaty)? Physiologically, adults of all ages show improved cardiovascular functioning and maximum oxygen consumption;

Exercise is a major way to help delay or prevent chronic disease and promote a healthy late life.

lower blood pressure; and better strength, endurance, flexibility, and coordination (Mayo Clinic, 2011). Psychologically, people who exercise aerobically report lower levels of stress, better moods, and better cognitive functioning.

The best way to gain the benefits of aerobic exercise is to maintain physical fitness throughout the life span, beginning at least in middle age. The benefits of various forms of exercise are numerous, and include lowering the risk of cardiovascular disease, osteoporosis (if the exercise is weight bearing), and a host of other conditions. The Mayo Clinic's Fitness Center provides an excellent place to start. In planning an exercise program, three points should be remembered. First, check with a physician before beginning an aerobic exercise program. Second, bear in mind that moderation is important. Third, just because you intend to exercise doesn't mean you will; you must take the necessary steps to turn your intention into action (Schwarzer, 2008). If you do, and stick with it, you may feel much younger (Joyner & Barnes, 2013).

Without question, regular exercise is one of the two most important behaviors you can do to promote healthy living and good aging (not smoking is the other). In addition to the wide variety of positive effects on health (e.g., lower risk of cardiovascular disease, diabetes, hypertension), there is also substantial evidence exercise is also connected to less cortical atrophy, better brain function, and enhanced cognitive performance (Erickson, Gildengers, & Butters, 2013). Specifically, exercise has a positive effect on the prefrontal and hippocampal areas of the brain, and as we have seen, is closely associated with

memory and other cognitive functions. Whether exercise can delay or prevent diseases associated with these brain structures, such as Alzheimer's disease, remains to be seen. But the evidence to date points to reason to promote exercise as a way to a healthy, better functioning brain in later life. A better functioning brain may well be related to the mood improvements seen as another positive benefit of exercise, as shown in Figure 14.5.

In summary, if you want to maximize the odds of aging well, exercise. Guidelines state about 150 minutes of moderate aerobic exercise weekly with additional whole-body strength training and balance work is sufficient to produce positive effects (Batt, Tanji, & Börjesson, 2013). When you are done your routine for the day, watch what you eat, as discussed next.

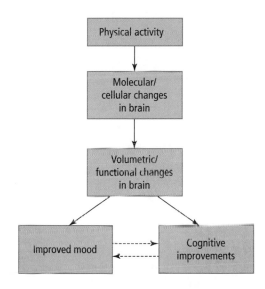

Figure 14.5

A schematic representation of the general path by which cognitive function and mood are improved by physical activity, it could be hypothesized that improvements in cognitive function mediate the improvements in mood or that improvements in mood mediate some of the improvements in cognitive function. The dotted lines represent these hypothesized paths.

Source: Erickson, K. I., Gildengers, A. G., & Butters, M. A. (2013). Physical activity and brain plasticity in late adulthood. Dialogues in Clinical Neuroscience, 15, *99–108. Open source, retrieved from http:// www.ncbi.nlm.nih.gov/pmc/articles/PMC3622473/. Image retrieved from http://www.ncbi.nlm.nih.gov/pmc/articles/PMC3622473/figure /DialoguesClinNeurosci-15-99-g001/.*

Nutrition. How many times did your parents tell you to eat your vegetables? Or perhaps they said, "You are what you eat." Most people have disagreements with parents about food while growing up, but as adults they realize those lima beans and other despised foods their parents urged them to eat really are healthy.

Experts agree nutrition directly affects one's mental, emotional, and physical functioning (Hammar & Östgren, 2013). Diet has been linked to cancer, cardiovascular disease, diabetes, anemia, and digestive disorders. Nutritional requirements and eating habits change across the life span. *This change is due mainly to differences in, or how much energy the body needs, termed* metabolism. Body metabolism and the digestive process slow down with age (Janssen, 2005).

The U.S. Department of Agriculture publishes dietary guidelines based on current research. In its *Dietary Guidelines for Americans 2010* (U.S. Department of Agriculture, 2010), the USDA recommends we eat a variety of nutrient-dense foods and beverages across the basic food groups. The general guidelines for older adults can be seen in Figure 14.6. These guidelines are based on the general guidelines for younger and middle-aged adults. As you can see, the USDA approaches nutrition from the perspective of ensuring people eat a healthy plate of food at each meal, and the contents of that plate be appropriately balanced. Most important, we should choose foods that limit the intake of saturated and *trans* fats, cholesterol, added sugars, salt, and alcohol. And we need to keep our target calorie intake in mind.

Of course, most people do not eat perfectly all the time. Did you ever worry as you were eating a triple-dip cone of premium ice cream you really should be eating fat-free frozen yogurt instead? If so, you are among the people who have taken to heart (literally) the link between diet and cardiovascular disease. The American Heart Association (2013) makes it clear foods high in saturated fat (such as our beloved ice cream) should be replaced with foods low in fat (such as fat-free frozen yogurt). Check out their website for the latest in advice on eating a heart-healthy diet.

Figure 14.6
Dietary guidelines for older adults

Copyright 2011 Tufts University. For details about MyPlate for Older Adults, please see http://www.nutrition.tufts.edu/documents/MyPlateforOlderAdults.pdf

MyPlate for Older Adults

The main goal of these recommendations is to lower your level of cholesterol because high cholesterol is one risk factor for cardiovascular disease. There is an important difference between two different types of cholesterol, that are defined by their effect on blood flow. Lipoproteins are fatty chemicals attached to proteins carried in the blood. **Low-density lipoproteins (LDLs)** *cause fatty deposits to accumulate in arteries, impeding blood flow, whereas* **high-density lipoproteins (HDLs)** *help keep arteries clear and break down LDLs.* It is not so much the overall cholesterol number but the ratio of LDLs to HDLs that matters most in cholesterol screening. High levels of LDLs are a risk factor in cardiovascular disease, and high levels of HDLs are considered a protective factor. Reducing LDL levels is effective in diminishing the risk of cardiovascular disease in adults of all ages; in healthy adults, a high level of LDL (over 160 mg/dL) is associated with higher risk for cardiovascular disease (Mayo Clinic, 2012c). In contrast, higher levels of HDL are good (in healthy adults, levels at least above 40 mg/dL for men and 50 mg/dL for women). LDL levels can be lowered and HDL levels can be raised through various interventions such as exercise and a high-fiber diet. Weight control is also an important component.

If diet and exercise are not effective in lowering cholesterol, numerous medications exist for treating cholesterol problems. The most popular of these drugs are from a family of medications called *statins* (e.g., Lipitor, Crestor). These medications lower LDL and moderately increase HDL. Because of potential side effects on liver functioning, patients taking cholesterol-lowering medications should be monitored on a regular basis.

Obesity is a growing health problem related to diet. One good way to assess your own status is to compute your body mass index. **Body mass index (BMI)** *is a ratio of body weight and height and is related to total body fat.* You can compute BMI as follows:

$$BMI = w/h^2$$

where w = weight in kilograms (or weight in pounds divided by 2.2), and h = height in meters (or inches divided by 39.37).

The Centers for Disease Control and Prevention (2011) defines healthy weight as having a BMI of less than 25. However, this calculation may overestimate body fat in muscular people and underestimate body fat in those who appear of normal weight but have little muscle mass.

BMI is related to the risk of serious medical conditions and mortality: the higher one's BMI, the higher one's risk (Centers for Disease Control and Prevention, 2011). Figure 14.7 shows the increased risk for several diseases and mortality associated with increased BMI. Based on these estimates, you may want to lower your BMI if it's above 25. But be careful—lowering your BMI too much may not be healthy either. Very low BMIs may indicate malnutrition, which is also related to increased mortality.

	BMI (Kg/m²)	Obesity class	Disease risk * Relative to normal weight and waist circumference	
			Men 102 cm (40 in) or less Women 88 cm (35 in) or less	Men > 102 cm (40 in) Women > 88 cm (35 in)
Underweight	<18.5		–	–
Normal	18.5–24.9		–	–
Overweight	25.0–29.9		Increased	High
Obesity	30.0–34.9	I	High	High
	35.9–39.9	II	Very high	Very high
Extreme obesity	40.0	III	Extremely high	Extremely high

Figure 14.7

Classification of overweight and obesity by BMI, waist circumference, and associate disease risks.

Source: Centers for Disease Control and prevention (2007b).

ADULT DEVELOPMENT IN ACTION

How could the information about exercise and nutrition in this section be combined with the health information in Chapters 3 and 4 to create an education program for adults?

14.3 Successful Aging

LEARNING OBJECTIVES

- What is successful aging? What theoretical models have been proposed?
- What criticisms have been raised about the successful aging framework?

Marie Chen just celebrated her 100th birthday. During the daylong festivities, many people asked her whether she believed she had a good life and had, in a sense, aged successfully. She answered everyone the same way, telling them she had her health, enough money to live on, and her family. What more could she want?

Marie gives every sign of having aged well. She's 100 years old, with a loving family, good enough health to live in the community, and enough income to pay her bills. But is there more to it than that? Before you read what researchers have to say about aging successfully, complete the exercise in the Discovering Development feature.

DISCOVERING DEVELOPMENT:

WHAT IS SUCCESSFUL AGING?

What does it mean to age successfully? Take some time to think about this question for yourself. Develop a thorough list of everything it would take for you to say you will have aged successfully when the time comes. Then ask this question to several people of different ages and backgrounds. Compare their answers. Do the criteria differ as a function of age or background characteristics? Discuss your findings with others in your class to see whether your results were typical.

Approaches to Successful Aging

Everyone hopes his or her later years are ones filled with good health, continued high cognitive and physical competence, and engagement with life. As common sense as this view seems, it did not significantly influence research on aging until the latter part of the twentieth century. Rowe and Kahn (1998) changed that. They considered these views to be the foundation on which successful aging is built:

> The absence of disease and disability makes it easier to maintain mental and physical function. Maintenance of mental and physical function in turn enables (but does not guarantee) active engagement with life. It is the combination of all three—avoidance of disease and disability, maintenance of cognitive and physical function, and sustained engagement with life—that represents the concept of successful aging most fully (39).

Research participants agree. An extensive study of people's own definitions of successful aging conducted in Canada showed substantial agreement between participants' definitions and Rowe and Kahn's three dimensions (Tate, Lah, & Cuddy, 2003).

This three-part view of successful aging has become the central theoretical paradigm in gerontology and geriatrics. Numerous calls for a rethinking of research, clinical and application approaches to aging have been made that are grounded in this work (e.g., Aldwin & Gilmer, 2013; Jeste & Palmer, 2013; Reuter-Lorenz, 2013).

Vaillant (2002) proposed a similar model of successful aging that has six criteria rather than three. He proposes three criteria related to health:

- No physical disability at age 75 as rated by a physician
- Good subjective physical health (i.e., no problems with instrumental activities of daily living)
- Length of undisabled life

Vaillant's other three criteria relate to social engagement and productive activity:

- Good mental health

- Objective social support
- Self-rated life satisfaction in eight domains: marriage, income-producing work, children, friendships and social contacts, hobbies, community service activities, religion, and recreation/sports

What is important in Vaillant's model is not only what predicts long life but also what does not. Interestingly, having had long-lived ancestors was important only up to age 60 but not beyond. Stress-related diseases before age 50 were not predictive. Childhood factors that were important predictors of health at midlife did not predict health in late life. Thus Vaillant's research emphasizes late life has many unique aspects and may not relate to variables that predict health at earlier points in life.

A related view of successful aging is one we encountered several times throughout the book: the selection, optimization, and compensation (SOC) model (Baltes et al., 2006). Recall in this model *selection* refers to developing and choosing goals, *optimization* to the application and refinement of goal-relevant means or actions, and *compensation* to substitution of means when previous ones are no longer available.

The SOC model can be applied to the proactive strategies of life management. From this perspective, it is adaptive (i.e., a sign of successful aging) to set clear goals, to acquire and invest means into pursuing these goals, and persist despite setbacks or losses. So the point here, in contrast to a coping strategy, that would emphasize a more passive approach, is taking positive action to find substitute ways of doing things is adaptive (Freund & Baltes, 2002).

Critiques of the Successful Aging Framework

Taking a broad view to defining successful aging permits researchers to establish what is associated with it. But there's a fundamental problem. Unlike the case with diseases, in which labels have specific meanings, the term "successful aging" lack that consensus, making it difficult to specify exactly what the criteria are for achieving it (Cosco, Stephan, & Brayne, 2013). The lack of consensus makes it hard to know whether the outcome is something specific, or simply the result of a certain confluence of other factors.

Studies indicate aging successfully is more likely when people have higher levels of education, household income, and personal income. We saw earlier that income is related to health, because of better access to health care and greater knowledge of healthy behaviors and ability to engage in them. Additionally, unfavorable conditions in childhood lower the odds of people aging successfully according to research in Europe (Brandt, Deindl, & Hank, 2012). This is sobering news given the numbers of children globally that live in poverty; that experience follows them for life.

The increased emphasis on successful aging regardless of definition raises important questions about the quality of life for older adults. Researchers have not focused much attention on the issue of whether one can outlive one's *expected* longevity, that is, how long you *think* you will live, and if so, what psychological effects that can have. If you think you will not live past age 75, perhaps because no one in your family ever has, you may map out your life based on this assumption. But what do you do when you celebrate your 76th birthday? The birthday wasn't planned, and you may feel confused as to what you should be doing with yourself. Do you feel fortunate you have more life to live? Or not?

Rowe and Kahn's view of successful aging, along with similar models, make several key assumptions that may not be universally true: (a) people have the resources to live a healthy life, (b) access to health care, (c) live in a safe environment, (d) have life experiences that support individual decision making, and so forth (de Lange, 2013; Holstein & Minkler, 2003). Not

Aging well is a subjective experience each person decides individually.

Marcia Keegan

all older adults' lives meet these assumptions (Liang & Luo, 2012). Poverty, widowhood, and differential social expectations based on gender influence whether a person will be able to exert individual control and decisions over health (Cruikshank, 2013).

There is another, more serious concern with Rowe and Kahn's model. By equating health and successful aging, they imply older people who have health problems have not aged successfully (Holstein & Minkler, 2003; Liang & Luo, 2012). By suggesting people who have disabilities or health limitations signify failure, or at best "usual" aging, the message that only the fit and vigorous are successful is a negative one. It can also inadvertently reinforce the antiaging stereotype for physical beauty as well as a stereotype for the "active older adult."

Holstein and Minkler (2003) point out we should return to an ancient question: What is the good life—for the whole of life—and what does it take to live a good old age? When she was in her late 60s, the late poet May Sarton (1997) wrote this about the imminence of death: "[P]reparing to die we shed our leaves, without regret, so that the essential person may be alive and well at the end" (230).

Sarton's view may remind you of another, related perspective. Erikson (1982) talked about successful aging as ego integrity, a point made by some researchers as well (Chang et al., 2008). Successful aging may be the ability to pull one's life together from many perspectives into a coherent whole and to be satisfied with it. From this perspective, successful aging is assessed more from the older adult's vantage point than from any other (Bowling, 2007). In this sense, older adults may say they are aging successfully while others, especially those who adopt a medical model, would not say that about them. But who is to say which perspective is "correct"?

Perhaps the middle ground is to aim for harmonious aging (Liang & Luo, 2012) that aims for balance, not uniformity. In this view, "good aging" is grounded in one's culture, and reflects the fact there is no one right way to age well. And it just may come down to what you think about your own situation. If you are happy with the way your life is, then perhaps that's all that's necessary.

Epilogue

In this book, you have seen a snapshot of what adult development and aging are like today. You learned about their complexities, myths, and realities. But more

than anything else, you have seen what we really know about the pioneers who blazed the trail ahead of us.

In a short time, it will be your turn to lead the journey. The decisions you make will have an enormous impact on those who will be old: your parents, grandparents, and the people who taught you. The decisions will not be easy ones, but you have an advantage that the pioneers did not. You have the collected knowledge of gerontologists to help. With a continued concerted effort, you will be able to address the problems and meet the challenges that lie ahead. Then, when you yourself are old, you will be able to look back on your life and say, "I lived long—and I prospered."

SUMMARY

14.1 Demographic Trends and Social Policy

What key demographic changes will occur by 2030?

- The rapid increase in the number of older adults between now and 2030 means social policy must take the aging of the population into account. Changing demographics will affect every aspect of life in the United States and in most other countries, including health care and all social service programs.

What are the challenges facing Social Security and Medicare?

- Although designed as an income supplement, Social Security has become the primary source of retirement income for most U.S. citizens. The aging of the baby boom generation will place considerable stress on the financing of the system.

- Medicare is the principal health insurance program for adults in the United States over age 65. Cost containment is a major concern, resulting in emphases on program redesign for long-term sustainability.

14.2 Health Issues and Quality of Life

What are the key issues in health promotion and quality of life?

- Health promotion will become an increasingly important aspect of health care for older adults. Two models of behavioral change currently drive research: the self-efficacy model and the self-regulation model.

- Quality of life, a person's well-being and life satisfaction is best studied from the perspective of the individual.

What are the major strategies for maintaining and enhancing competence?

- A useful framework for enhancing and maintaining competence is the selection, optimization, and compensation (SOC) model.
- The life-span approach provides a guide for designing competency-enhancing interventions.

What are the primary considerations in designing health promotion and disease prevention programs?

- Effective strategies for health promotion and disease prevention are adopting a healthy lifestyle, staying active cognitively, maintaining a social network, and preserving good economic habits.
- Four levels of prevention are: primary (preventing a disease or condition from occurring), secondary (intervening after a condition has occurred but before it causes impairment), tertiary (avoiding the development of complications), and quaternary (improving functional capacities in people with chronic conditions).

What are the principal lifestyle factors that influence competence?

- Maintaining a good exercise program and getting good nutrition are essential for delaying or preventing many negative aspects of physiological aging, especially chronic diseases.

14.3 Successful Aging

What is successful aging? What theoretical models have been proposed?

- Successful aging is a commonly used, but ill-defined framework. Models of successful aging include this notion: Rowe and Kahn's, Vaillant's, and variations on the selection, optimization, and compensation (SOC) model.

What criticisms have been raised about the successful aging framework?

- The successful aging framework has been criticized because of its reliance on good health, adequate income, and other variables that heavily influence outcomes in late life. Advocating a balance in one's life may be a better approach.

REVIEW QUESTIONS

14.1 Demographic Trends and Social Policy

- What will the population of the United States look like in 2030?

- What social policy impact will these changes have?
- What pressures are there on Social Security and Medicare?

14.2 Health Issues and Quality of Life

- Why is health promotion likely to become increasingly important?
- What is meant by the term *quality of life?*
- What theoretical framework provides the best approach for enhancing competency?
- What are four effective strategies for health promotion and disease prevention?
- What are the four types of prevention strategies?
- Why are exercise and nutrition important for health promotion and disease prevention?

14.3 Successful Aging

- What is successful aging, and how is it best studied?
- What are the similarities and differences among the Rowe and Kahn, Vaillant, and SOC models?
- What criticisms have been raised regarding the successful aging framework?

INTEGRATING CONCEPTS IN DEVELOPMENT

- Suppose you were brought in as a consultant on aging policy issues to your national government. Based on the demographic information in Chapter 1 and this chapter, what recommendations would you make?
- What trends in health care do you think will emerge based on information in this chapter and in Chapters 3, 4, and 10?
- How do you think older adults will define successful aging in the future?

KEY TERMS

aerobic exercise Exercise that places moderate stress on the heart by maintaining a pulse rate between 60% and 90% of the person's maximum heart rate.

body mass index (BMI) A ratio of body weight and height that is related to total body fat.

dependency ratio The ratio of the number of people under age 15 and over age 64 in a country to the number of people between 15 and 64.

high-density lipoproteins (HDLs) Help keep arteries clear and break down LDLs.

low-density lipoproteins (LDLs) Cause fatty deposits to accumulate in arteries, impeding blood flow.

metabolism How much energy the body needs.

primary prevention Any intervention that prevents a disease or condition from occurring.

quality of life A person's well-being and life satisfaction.

quaternary prevention Efforts specifically aimed at improving the functional capacities of people who have chronic conditions.

secondary prevention Instituted early after a condition has begun (but may not yet have been diagnosed) and before significant impairments have occurred.

tertiary prevention Involves efforts to avoid the development of complications or secondary chronic conditions, manage the pain associated with the primary chronic condition, and sustain life through medical intervention.

RESOURCES

Access quizzes, glossaries, flashcards, and more at www.cengagebrain.com.

REFERENCES

AARP. (1999). *AARP/Modern maturity sexuality survey.* Retrieved from http://assets.aarp.org/rgcenter/health/mmsexsurvey.pdf.

AARP. (2005). *Sexuality at midlife and beyond: 2004 update of attitudes and behaviors.* Retrieved from http://assets.aarp.org/rgcenter/general/2004_sexuality.pdf.

AARP. (2010). *Sex, romance, and relationships: AARP survey of midlife and older adults.* Retrieved from http://assets.aarp.org/rgcenter/general/srr_09.pdf.

Aasland, O. G., Rosta, J., & Nylenna, M. (2010). Healthcare reforms and job satisfaction among doctors in Norway. *Scandinavian Journal of Public Health, 38,* 253–258. doi:10.1177/1403494810364559.

Abbott, G., Gilbert, K., & Rosinski, P. (2013). Cross-cultural working in coaching and mentoring. In J. Passmore, D. B. Peterson, & T. Freire (Eds.), *The Wiley-Blackwell handbook of coaching and mentoring* (pp. 483–500). Oxford, UK: Wiley-Blackwell.

Aberson, C. L., Shoemaker, C., & Tomolillo, C. (2004). Implicit bias and contact: The role of interethnic friendships. *Journal of Social Psychology, 144,* 335–347. doi:10.3200/SOCP.144.3.335–347

Abraham, A., Beudt, S., Ott, D. V. M., & von Cramon, D. Y. (2012). Creative cognition and the brain: Dissociations between frontal, parietal-temporal and basal ganglia groups. *Brain Research, 1482,* 55–70. doi:10.1016/j.bbr.2011.03.031.

Abrams, R. (2013). *When parents die: Learning to live with the loss of a parent* (3rd ed.). New York: Routledge.

Achor, S. (2010). *The happiness advantage: The seven principles of positive psychology that fuel success and performance at work.* New York: Random House.

Adams, C., Smith, M. C., Pasupathi, M., & Vitolo, L. (2002). Social context effects on story recall in older and younger women: Does the listener make a difference? *Journals of Gerontology: Psychological Sciences, 57B,* P28–P40. doi:10.1093/geronb/57.1.P28.

Adams, R. B., Jr., Nelson, A. J., Soto, J. A., Hess, U., & Kleck, R. E. (2012). Emotion in the neutral face: A mechanism for impression formation? *Cognition and Emotion, 26,* 431–441. doi:10.1080/02699931.2012.666502

Adams, R. G., & Ueno, K. (2006). Middle-aged and older adult men's friendships. In V. H. Bedford & B. Formaniak Turner (Eds.), *Men in relationships: A new look from a life course perspective* (pp. 103–124). New York: Springer.

Adamy, J., & McGinty, T. (2012). *The crushing cost of care.* Retrieved from http://online.wsj.com/article/SB10001424052702304441404577483050976766184.html.

Adler, L. L. (2001). Women and gender roles. In L. L. Adler & U. P. Gielen (Eds.), *Cross-cultural topics on psychology* (2nd ed., pp. 103–114). Westport, CT: Praeger/Greenwood.

Administration for Children and Families. (2010). *Administration for children and families healthy marriage initiative, 2002–2009.* Retrieved from http://www.healthymarriageinfo.org/resource-detail/index.aspx?rid=3298.

Administration on Aging. (2012). *Adult day care.* Retrieved from http://www.eldercare.gov/Eldercare.NET/Public/Resources/Factsheets/Adult_Day_Care.aspx.

Administration on Aging. (2012). *Older adults and HIV/AIDS.* Retrieved from http://www.aoa.gov/AoARoot/Press_Room/Products_Materials/fact/pdf/Seniors_and_HIV_AIDS.pdf.

Administration on Aging. (2012a). *Disability and activity limitations.* Retrieved from http://www.aoa.gov/AoARoot/Aging_Statistics/Profile/2011/16.aspx.

AgingStats.gov. (2012a). *Older Americans 2012: Key indicators of well-being.* Retrieved from http://agingstats.gov/agingstatsdotnet/Main_Site/Data/2012_Documents/Docs/EntireChartbook.pdf.

AgingStats.gov. (2012b). *Older Americans 2012: Key indicators of well-being.* Retrieved from http://agingstats.gov/agingstatsdotnet/Main_Site/Data/2012_Documents/Docs/EntireChartbook.pdf.

Agrawal, Y., Platz, E. A., & Niparko, J. K. (2008). Prevalence of hearing loss and differences by demographic characteristics among US adults: Data from the National Health and Nutrition Examination Survey, 1999–2004. *Archives of Internal Medicine, 168,* 1522–1530. doi:10.1001/archinte.168.14.1522.

Ai, A. L., Wink, P., & Ardelt, M. (2010). Spirituality and aging: A journey for meaning through deep interconnection in humanity. In J. C. Cavanaugh & C. K. Cavanaugh (Eds.), *Aging in America: Vol. 3: Societal issues* (pp. 222–246). Santa Barbara, CA: Praeger Perspectives.

Aisenbrey, S., Evertsson, M., & Grunow, D. (2009). Is there a career penalty for mothers' time out? A comparison of Germany, Sweden, and the United States. *Social Forces, 88,* 573–605. doi:10.1353/sof.0.0252.

Ajrouch, K. (2008). Introduction to a special issue of *Research in Human Development:* Aging families in global context. *Research in Human Development, 5,* 1–5. doi:10.1080/15427600701853806.

Alam, S., Patel, J., & Giordano, J. (2012). Working towards a new psychiatry—Neuroscience, technology and the DSM-5. *Philosophy, Ethics, and Humanities in Medicine, 7(1).* Retrieved from http://www.biomedcentral.com/content/pdf/1747-5341-7-1.pdf.

Albert, M. S., DeKosky, S. T., Dickson, D., Dubois, B., Feldman, H. A., Fox, N. C. et al. (2011). The diagnosis of mild cognitive impairment due to Alzheimer's disease: Recommendations from the National Institute on Aging—Alzheimer's Association workgroups on diagnostic guidelines for Alzheimer's disease. *Alzheimer's and Dementia: Journal of the Alzheimer's Assocation, 7,* 270–279. doi:10.1016/jalz.2011.03.008.

Alden, D. L., Merz, M. Y., & Akashi, J. (2012). Young adult preference for physician decision-making style in Japan and the United States. *Asia-Pacific Journal of Public Health, 24,* 173–184. doi:10.1177/1010539510365098.

Aldwin, C. M., & Gilmer, D. F. (2013). *Health, illness, and optimal aging: Biological and psychosocial perspectives* (2nd ed.). New York: Springer.

Aldwin, C., & Igarashi, H. (2012). An ecological model of resilience in late life. *Annual Review of Gerontology and Geriatrics, 32,* 115–130. doi:10.1891/0198-8794.32.115.

Alegría, M., Chatterji, P., Wells, K., Cao, Z., Chen, C.-N., Takeuchi, D., Jackson, J., & Meng, X.-L. (2008). Disparity in depression treatment among racial and ethnic minority populations in the United States. *Psychiatric Services, 59,* 1264–1272. doi:10.1176/appi.ps.59.11.1264.

Alexander, B. H., Ryan, L., Bowers, D., Foster, T. C., Bizon, J. L., Geldmacher, D. S. et al. (2012). Characterizing cognitive aging in humans with links to animal models. *Frontiers in Aging Neuroscience, 4(21).* doi:10.3389/fnagi.2012.00021. Retrieved from http://www.ncbi.nlm.nih.gov/pmc/articles/PMC3439638/.

Alexander, G. T. (2012). Bioenergetics theory of aging. In K. Clark (Ed.), *Bioenergetics.* Retrieved from http://www.intechopen.com/books/bioenergetics/bioenergetics-theoryof-aging.

Alhija, F. N.-A., & Fresko, B. (2010). Socialization of new teachers: Does induction matter? *Teaching and Teacher Education, 26,* 1592–1597. doi:10.1016/j.tate.2010.06.010.

Allaire, J. C. (2012). Everyday cognition. In S. K. Whitbourne & M. J. Sliwinski (Eds.), *The Wiley-Blackwell handbook of adulthood and aging* (pp. 190–207). Oxford, UK: Wiley-Blackwell. doi:10.1002/9781118392966.ch10.

Allaire, J. C., & Marsiske, M. (1999). Everyday cognition: Age and intellectual ability correlates. *Psychology and Aging, 14,* 627–644. doi:10.1037/0882-7974.14.4.627.

Allaire, J. C., & Marsiske, M. (2002). Well- and ill-defined measures of everyday cognition: Relationship to older adults' intellectual ability and functional status. *Psychology and Aging, 17,* 101–115. doi:10.1037/0882 7974.17.1.101.

Allaire, J. C., & Willis, S. L. (2006). Competence in everyday activities as a predictor of cognitive risk and morbidity. *Aging, Neuropsychology, and Cognition, 13,* 207–224. doi:10.1080/13825580490904228.

Allemand, M., Zimprich, D., & Hendriks, A. A. J. (2008). Age differences in five personality domains across the life span. *Developmental Psychology, 44(3),* 758–770. doi:10.1037/0012-1649.44.3.758.

Allen, J. E. (2011). *Nursing home administration* (6th ed.). New York: Springer.

Allen, R. S., & Shuster, J. L. (2002). The role of proxies in treatment decisions: Evaluating functional capacity to consent to end-of-life treatments within a family context. *Behavioral Sciences and the Law, 20,* 235 252. doi:10.1002/bsl.484.

Allen, R. S., DeLaine, S. R., Chaplin, W. F., Marson, D. C., Bourgeois, M. S., Kijkstra, K., & Burgio, L. D. (2003). Advance care planning in nursing homes: Correlates of capacity and possession of advance directives. *The Gerontologist, 43,* 309 317. doi:10.1093/geront/43.3.309.

Alley, J. L. (2004). The potential meaning of the grandparent-grandchild relationship as perceived by young adults An exploratory study. *Dissertation Abstracts International. Section B. Sciences and Engineering, 65(3-B),* 1536.

Almeida, J., Molnar, B. E., Kawachi, I., & Subramanian, S. V. (2009). Ethnicity and nativity status as determinants of perceived social support: Testing the concept of familism. *Social Science and Medicine, 68,* 1852–1858. doi:10.1016/j.socscimed.2009.02.029.

Almendarez, B. L. (2008). Mexican American elders and nursing home transition. *Dissertation Abstracts International: Section B: The Sciences and Engineering, 68(7-B),* 4384.

Alzheimer's Association. (2004). Research consent for cognitively impaired adults: Recommendations for institutional review boards and investigators. *Alzheimer's Disease and Associated Disorders, 8,* 171–175. Retrieved from https://www.alz.org/national/documents/research_consent_for_irbs_article_reprint.pdf.

Amato, P. R., & Cheadle, J. (2005). The long reach of divorce: Divorce and child well-being across three generations. *Journal of Marriage & Family, 67,* 191–206. doi:10.1111/j.0022-2445.2005.00014.x.

Ambati, J., & Fowler, B. J. (2012). Mechanisms of age-related macular degeneration. *Neuron, 75,* 26–39. doi:10.1016/j.neuron.2012.08.018.

American Academy of Pain Medicine. (2009). Pain medicine position paper. *Pain Medicine, 10,* 972–1000. Retrieved from http://onlinelibrary.wiley.com/doi/10.1111/j.1526-4637.2009.00696.x/pdf.

American Bar Association/American Psychological Association. (2005). *Assessment of older adults with diminished capacity: A handbook for lawyers.* Retrieved from http://www.apa.org/pi/aging/resources/guides/diminished-capacity.pdf.

American Bar Association/American Psychological Association. (2006). *Judicial determination of capacity of older adults in guardianship proceedings.* Retrieved from http://www.apa.org/pi/aging/resources/guides/judges-diminished.pdf.

American Bar Association/American Psychological Association. (2008). *Assessment of older adults with diminished capacity: A handbook for psychologists.* Retrieved from http://www.apa.org/pi/aging/programs/assessment/capacity-psychologist-handbook.pdf.

American Cancer Society. (2012a). *Prostate cancer.* Retrieved from http://www.cancer.org/cancer/prostatecancer/index.

American Cancer Society. (2012b). *Cancer facts and figures 2012.* Retrieved from http://www.cancer.org/acs/groups/content/@epidemiologysurveillance/documents/document/acspc-031941.pdf.

American Cancer Society. (2012c). *Cancer screening guidelines.* Retrieved from http://www.cancer.org/healthy/findcancerearly/cancerscreeningguidelines/index.

American Diabetes Association. (2012). *Diabetes basics.* Retrieved from http://www.diabetes.org/diabetes-basics/.

American Geriatrics Society Ethics Committee. (1996). Making treatment decisions for incapacitated older adults without advance directives. *Journal of the American Geriatrics Society, 44,* 986–987.

American Geriatrics Society Ethics Committee. (1998). Position statement: Informed consent for research on human subjects with dementia. *Journal of the American Geriatrics Society, 46,* 1308–1310.

American Heart Association. (2011). *Sodium (salt or sodium chloride).* Retrieved from http://www.heart.org/HEARTORG/GettingHealthy/NutritionCenter/HealthyDietGoals/Sodium-Salt-or-Sodium-Chloride_UCM_303290_Article.jsp.

American Heart Association. (2013). *Meet the fats.* Retrieved from http://www.heart.org/HEARTORG/GettingHealthy/FatsAndoils/Fats-Oils_UCM_001084_SubHomePage.jsp.

American Lung Association. (2012). *Understanding COPD.* Retrieved from http://www.lung.org/lung-disease/copd/about-copd/understanding-copd.html.

American Medical Association. (2013). *PCPI™ Physician Consortium for Performance Improvement®.* Retrieved from http://www.ama-assn.org/resources/doc/cqi/pcpi-overview-flyer.pdf.

American Psychiatric Association. (1994). *Diagnostic and statistical manual of mental disorders* (4th ed. [DSM-IV]). Washington, DC: Author.

American Psychiatric Association. (2000). *Diagnostic and statistical manual-IV-TR.* Washington, DC: Author.

Amoyal, N., & Fallon, E. (2012). Physical exercise and cognitive training clinical interventions used in slowing degeneration associated with mild cognitive impairment: A review of the recent literature. *Topics in Geriatric Rehabilitation, 28,* 208–216. doi:10.1097/TGR.0b013e31825fc8d3.

Anand, A., & MacLullich, A. M. J. (2013). Delirium in hospitalized older adults. *Medicine, 41,* 39–42. doi:10.1016/j.mpmed.2012.10.011.

Andel, R., Crowe, M., Pedersen, N. L., Fratiglioni, L., Johansson, B., & Gatz, M. (2008). Physical exercise at midlife and risk of dementia three decades later: A population-based study of Swedish twins. *Journals of Gerontology: Medical Sciences, 63A,* M62–M66. doi:10.1093/gerona/63.1.62.

Andersen, G. J. (2012). Aging and vision: Changes in function and performance from optics to perception. *Wiley Interdisciplinary Reviews: Cognitive Science, 3,* 403–410. doi:10.1002/wcs.1167.

Andersen, S. L., Sebastiani, P., Dworkis, D. A., Feldman, L., & Perls, T. T. (2012). Health span approximates life span among many supercentenarians: Compression of morbidity at the approximate limit of life span. *Journal of Gerontology: Biological Sciences, 67A,* 395–405. doi:10.1093/gerona/glr223.

Anderson, E. R., Greene, S. M., Walker, L., Malerba, C., Forgatch, M. S., & DeGarmo, D. S. (2004). Ready to take a chance again: Transitions into dating among divorced parents. *Journal of Divorce & Remarriage, 40,* 61–75. doi:10.1300/J087v40n03_04.

Anderson, V. D. (2007). Religiosity as it shapes parenting processes in preadolescence: A contextualized process model. *Dissertation Abstracts International. Section B. Sciences and Engineering, 67(9-B),* 5439.

Ando, S. (2012). Neuronal dysfunction with aging and its amelioration. *Proceedings of the Japan Academy, Series B: Physical and Biological Sciences, 88,* 266–282. doi:10.2183/pjab.88.266.

Andreassi, J. K. (2007). The role of personality and coping in work-family conflict: New directions. *Dissertation Abstracts International. Section A. Humanities and Social Sciences, 67(8-A),* 3053.

Andrews-Hanna, J. R. (2012). The brain's default network and its adaptive role in internal mentation. *The Neuroscientist, 18,* 251–270. doi:10.1177/1073858411403316.

Aneshensel, C. S., Pearlin, L. I., Mullan, J. T., Zarit, S. H., & Whitlach, C. J. (1995). *Profiles in caregiving: The unexpected career.* San Diego: Academic Press.

Angeles, L. (2010). Children and life satisfaction. *Journal of Happiness Studies, 11,* 523–538. doi:10.1007/s10902-009-9168-z.

Anticevic, A., Repovs, G., & Barch, D. M. (2012). Emotion effects on attention, amygdala activation, and functional capacity in schizophrenia. *Schizophrenia Bulletin, 38,* 967–980.

Aon. (2013). *Addressing the employee retirement savings gap.* Retrieved from http://www.aon.com/human-capital-consulting/thought-leadership/retirement/article_retirement_gap.jsp.

Aponte, M. (2007). Mentoring: Career advancement of Hispanic army nurses. *Dissertation Abstracts International. Section A. Humanities and Social Sciences, 68(4-A),* 1609.

Apperly, I. A. (2012). What is "theory of mind"? Concepts, cognitive processes and individual differences. *Quarterly Journal of Experimental Psychology, 65,* 825–839. doi:10.1080/17470218.2012.676055,

Araujo, A. B., Mohr, B. A., & McKinlay, J. B. (2004). Changes in sexual function in middle-aged and older men: Longitudinal data from the Massachusetts Aging Study. *Journal of the American Geriatrics Society, 52,* 1502–1509. doi:10.1111/j.0002-8614.2004.52413.x.

Ardelt, M. (2010). Age, experience, and the beginning of wisdom. In D. Dannefer & C. Phillipson (Eds.), *The SAGE handbook of social gerontology* (pp. 306–316). Thousand Oaks, CA: Sage Publications.

Armstrong-Stassen, M., & Templer, A. (2005). Adapting training for older employees: The Canadian response to an aging workforce. *Journal of Management Development, 24,* 57–67. doi:10.1108/02621710510572353.

Arndt, J., & Vess, M. (2008). Tales from existential oceans: Terror management theory and how the awareness of our mortality affects us all. *Social and Personality Psychology Compass, 2,* 909–928. doi:10.1111/j.1751-9004.2008.00079.x.

Arnett, J. J. (2007). Socialization in emerging adulthood: From the family to the wider world, from socialization to self-socialization. In J. E. Grusec & P. D. Hastings (Eds.), *Handbook of socialization: Theory and research* (pp. 208–231). New York: Guilford Press.

Arnett, J. J. (2012). New horizons in research on emerging and young adulthood. In A. Booth, S. L. Brown, N. S. Landale, W. D. Manning, & S. M. McHale (Eds.), *Early adulthood in family context* (Vol. 2, Part 5, pp. 231–244). New York: Springer.

Arnett, J. J., & Tanner, J. L. (2009). Toward a cultural-developmental stage theory of life course. In K. McCartney & R. A. Weinberg (Eds.), *Experience and development: A festschrift in honor of Sandra Wood Scarr* (pp. 17–38). New York: Psychology Press.

Arnold, M. (2008). Polypharmacy and older adults: A role for psychology and psychologists. *Professional Psychology: Research and Practice, 38,* 283–289. doi:10.1037/0735-7028.39.3.283.

Artistico, D., Cervone, D., & Pezzuti, L. (2003). Perceived self-efficacy and everyday problem solving among young and older adults. *Psychology and Aging, 18,* 68–79. doi:10.1037/0882-7974.18.1.68.

Aryee, S., Chu, C. W. L., Kim, T.-Y., & Ryu, S. (2013). Family-supportive work environment and employee work behaviors: An investigation of mediating mechanisms. *Journal of Management, 39,* 792–813. doi:10.1177/0149206311435103.

Aslan, A., & Bäuml, K.-H. T. (2012). Retrieval-induced forgetting in old and very old age. *Psychology and Aging, 27,* 1027–1032. doi:10.1037/a0028379.

Asoodeh, M. H., Khalili, S., Daneshpour, N., & Lavasani, M. G. (2010). Factors of successful marriage: Accounts from self-described happy couples. *Procedia Social and Behavioral Sciences, 5,* 2042–2046. doi:10.1016/j.sbspro.2010.07.410.

Asp, E., Manzel, K., Koestner, B., Cole, C. A., Denburg, N. L., & Tranel, D. (2012). A neuropsychological test of belief and doubt: Damage to ventromedial prefrontal cortex increases credulity for misleading advertising. *Frontiers in Neuroscience, 6.* doi:10.3389/fnins.2012.00100.

Assanangkornchai, S., Tangboonngam, S., Samangsri, N., & Edwards, J. G. (2007). A Thai community's anniversary reaction to a major catastrophe. *Stress and Health, 23,* 43–50. doi:10.1002/smi.1118.

Attig, T. (1996). *How we grieve: Relearning the world.* New York: Oxford University Press.

Awa, W. L., Plaumann, M., & Walter, U. (2010). Burnout prevention: A review of intervention programs. *Patient Education and Counseling, 78,* 184–190. doi:10.1016/j.pec.2009.04.008.

Bach, P. B. (2010). Postmenopausal hormone therapy and breast cancer: An uncertain trade-off. *JAMA, 304,* 1719–1720. doi:10.1001/jama.2010.1528.

Backhouse, J. (2006). *Grandparents-as-parents: Social change and its impact on grandparents who are raising their grandchildren.* In: *Social Change in the 21st Century Conference,* Carseldine QUT, Brisbane, Australia. Retrieved from http://eprints.qut.edu.au/6072/1/6072.pdf.

Bäckman, L. Nyberg, L., Lindenberger, U., Li, S-C., & Farde, L. (2006). The correlative triad among aging, dopamine, and cognition: Current status and future prospects. *Neuroscience and Behavioral Reviews, 30,* 791–807. doi:10.1016/j.neubiorev.2006.06.005.

Baddeley, A. (2012). Working memory: Theories, models, and controversies. *Annual Review of Psychology, 63,* 1–29. doi:10.1146/annurev-psych-120710-100422.

Baddeley, A. (2013). Working memory and emotion: Rumination on a theory of depression. *Review of General Psychology, 17*, 20–27. doi:10.1037/a0030029.

Bade, M. K. (2012). *Personal growth in the midst of negative life experiences: The role of religious coping strategies and appraisals.* Dissertation submitted to Texas Tech University. Retrieved from http://repositories.tdl.org/tdl-ir/handle/2346/10475?show=full.

Badham, S. P., Estes, Z., & Maylor, E. A. (2012). Integrative and semantic relations equally alleviate age-related associative memory deficits. *Psychology and Aging, 27*, 141–152. doi:10.1037/a0023924.

Baek, J. (2005). Individual variations in family caregiving over the caregiving career. *Dissertation Abstracts International: Section B: The Sciences and Engineering, 65(B)*, 3769.

Bagwell, C. L., Bender, S. E., Andreassi, C. L., Kinoshita, T. L., Montarello, S. A., & Muller, J. G. (2005). Friendship quality and perceived relationship changes predict psychosocial adjustment in early adulthood. *Journal of Social & Personal Relationships, 22*, 235–254. doi:10.1177/0265407505050945.

Baillargeon, A., Lassonde, M., Leclerc, S., and Ellemberg, D. (2012). Neuropsychological and neurophysiological assessment of sports concussion in children, adolescents, and adults. *Brain Injury, 26*, 211–220. doi:10.3109/02699052.2012.654590.

Balistreri, C. R., Candore, G., Accardi, G., Bova, M., Buffa, S., Bulati, M., et al. (2012). Genetics of longevity. Data from the studies on Sicilian centenarians. *Immunity and Ageing, 9*. Retrieved from http://www.biomedcentral.com/content/pdf/1742-4933-9-8.pdf.

Ball, K., Berch, D. B., Helmers, K. F., Jobe, J. B., Leveck, M. D., Marsiske, M., et al. (2002). Effects of cognitive training interventions with older adults: A randomized controlled trial. *JAMA, 288*, 2271–2281. doi:10.1001/jama.288.18.2271.

Baltes, B. B., & Rudolph, C. W. (2012). Selective optimization with compensation. In M. Wang (Ed.), *The Oxford handbook of retirement* (pp. 88–101). New York: Oxford University Press.

Baltes, P. B. (1987). Theoretical propositions of life-span developmental psychology: On the dynamics between growth and decline. *Developmental Psychology, 23*, 611–626. doi:10.1037/0012-1649.23.5.611.

Baltes, P. B. (1993). The aging mind: Potential and limits. *The Gerontologist, 33*, 580–594. doi:10.1093/geront/33.5.580.

Baltes, P. B., & Kliegl, R. (1992). Further testing of limits of cognitive plasticity: Negative age differences in mnemonic skill are robust. *Developmental Psychology, 28*, 121–125. doi:10.1037/0012-1649.28.1.121.

Baltes, P. B., & Schaie, K. W. (1974). Aging and IQ: The myth of the twilight years. *Psychology Today, 7*, 35–40.

Baltes, P. B., & Staudinger, U. M. (2000). Wisdom: A metaheuristic (pragmatic) to orchestrate mind and virtue toward excellence.

American Psychologist, 55, 122–136. doi:10.1037/0003-066X.55.1.122.

Baltes, P. B., Lindenberger, U., & Staudinger, U. M. (1998). Life-span theory in developmental psychology. In R. M. Lerner (Ed.), *Handbook of child psychology: Vol. 1. Theoretical models of human development* (5th ed., pp. 1029–1143). New York: Wiley.

Baltes, P. B., Lindenberger, U., & Staudinger, U. M. (2006). Life-span theory in developmental psychology. In R. M. Lerner & W. Damon (Eds.), *Handbook of child psychology: Vol. 1. Theoretical models of human development* (6th ed., pp. 569–664). Hoboken, NJ: Wiley.

Baltes, P. B., Staudinger, U. M., & Lindenberger, U. (1999). Life-span psychology: Theory and application to intellectual functioning. *Annual Review of Psychology, 50*, 471–507. doi:10.1146/annurev.psych.50.1.471.

Banerjee, A. V., & Duflo, E. (2007). Aging and death under a dollar a day. In D. A. Wise (Ed.), *Research findings in the economics of aging* (pp. 169–203). Chicago: University of Chicago Press.

Baracchini, C., Tonello, S., Farina, F., Viaro, F., Atzori, M., Ballotta, E. et al. (2012). Jugular veins in transient global amnesia: Innocent bystanders. *Stroke, 43*, 2289–2292. doi:10.1161/STROKEAHA.112.654087.

Bardach, S. H., Gayer, C. C., Clinkinbeard, T., Zanjani, F., & Watkins, J. F. (2010). The malleability of possible selves and expectations regarding aging. *Educational Gerontology, 36*, 407–424. doi:10.1080/03601270903212393.

Bargh, J. A., Chen, M., & Burrows, L. (1996). Automaticity of social behavior: Direct effects of trait construct and stereotype activation on action. *Journal of Personality and Social Psychology, 71*, 230–244. doi:10.1037/0022-3514.71.2.230.

Barja, G. (2008). The gene cluster hypothesis of aging and longevity. *Biogerontology, 9*, 57–66. doi:10.1007/s10522-007-9115-5.

Barnett, A. E. (2013). Pathways of adult children providing care to older parents. *Journal of Marriage and the Family, 75*, 178–190. doi:10.1111/j.1741-3737.2012.01022.x

Barrett, B. J., & St. Pierre, M. (2013). Intimate partner violence reported by lesbian-, gay-, and bisexual-identified individuals living in Canada: An exploration of within-group variations. *Journal of Gay and Lesbian Social Services, 25*, 1–23. Doi: 10.1080/10538720.2013.751887.

Bar-Tal, Y., Shrira, A., & Keinan, G. (2013). The effect of stress on cognitive structuring: A cognitive motivational model. *Personality and social Psychology Review, 17*, 87–99. doi:10.1177/1088868312461309.

Barzilai, N., Huffman, D. M., Muzumdar, R. H., & Bartke, A. (2012). The critical role of metabolic pathways in aging. *Diabetes, 61*, 1315–1322. doi:10.2337/db11-1300.

Basak, C., Boot, W. R., Voss, M. W., & Kramer, A. F. (2008). Can training in a real-time strategy video game attenuate cognitive decline in older

adults? *Psychology and Aging, 23*, 765–777. doi:10.1037/a0013494.

Batt, M. E., Tanji, J., & Börjesson, M. (2013). Exercise at 65 and beyond. *Sports Medicine, 43*, 525–530. doi:10.1007/s40279-013-0033-1.

Battista, R. N., Blancquaert, I., Laberge, A.-M., van Schendel, N., & Leduc, N. (2012). Genetics in health care: An overview of current and emerging models. *Public Health Genomics, 15*, 34–45. doi:10.1159/000328846.

Batty, G. D., Wennerstad, K. M., Smith, G. D., Gunnell, D., Deary, I. J., Tynelius, P., & Rasmussen, F. (2009). IQ in early adulthood and mortality in middle age: Cohort study of 1 million Swedish men. *Epidemiology, 20*, 100–109. doi:10.10907/EDE.0b013e31818ba076.

Baumann, A., Claudot, F., Audibert, G., Mertes, P.-M., & Puybasset, M. (2011). The ethical and legal aspects of palliative sedation in severely brain-injured patients: A French perspective. *Philosophy, Ethics, and Humanities in Medicine, 6*. Retrieved from http://preview.peh-med.com/content/pdf/1747-5341-6-4.pdf.

Baumeister, R.F. (2010). The self. In R. F. Baumeister & E. J. Finkel (Eds.), *Advanced social psychology: The state of the science* (pp. 139–175). New York: Oxford University Press.

Beason-Held, L. L., Thambisetty, M., Deib, G., Sojkova, J., Landman, B. A., Zonderman, A. B. et al. (2012). Baseline cardiovascular risk predicts subsequent changes in resting brain function. *Stroke, 43*, 1542–1547. doi:10.1161/STROKEAHA.111.638437.

Beaulieu, E. (2012). *A guide for nursing home social workers* (2nd ed.). New York: Springer.

Beck, A. T. (1967). *Depression: Clinical, experimental and theoretical aspects.* New York: Harper & Row.

Beck, A. T., Rush, J., Shaw, B., & Emery, G. (1979). *Cognitive therapy of depression.* New York: Guilford.

Beck, J. G., & Averill, P. M. (2004). Older adults. In R. G. Heimberg, C. L. Turk, & D. S. Mennin (Eds.), *Generalized anxiety disorder: Advances in research and practice* (pp. 409–433). New York: Guilford Press.

Beck, V. (2013). Employers' use of older workers in the recession. *Employee Relations, 35*, 257–271. doi:10.1108/01425451311320468.

Beckes, L., & Coan, J. A. (2013a). Voodoo versus me-you correlations in relationship neuroscience. *Journal of Social and Personal Relationships, 30*, 189–197. doi:10.1177/0265407512454768.

Beckes, L., Coan, J. A., & Hasselmo, K. (in press). Familiarity promotes the blurring of self and other in the neural perception of threat. *Social Cognitive and Affective Neuroscience.*

Bedir, A., & Aksoy, S. (2011). Brain death revisited: It is not 'complete death' according to Islamic sources. *Journal of Medical Ethics, 37*, 290–294. doi:10.1136/jme.2010.040238.

Bengtsson, T., & Scott, K. (2011). Population aging and the future of the welfare state: The example of Sweden. *Population and Review, 37 (Supplement S1)*,

158–170. doi:10.1111/j.1728-4457.2011.00382.x.

Benjamin, A. S. (2001). On the dual effects of repetition on false recognition. *Journal of Experimental Psychology: Learning, Memory, and Cognition, 27*, 941–947. doi:10.1037/0278-7393.4.941.

Benjamin, A. S. (2010). Representational explanations of "process" dissociations in recognition: The DRYAD theory of aging and memory judgments. *Psychological Review, 177*, 1055–1079. doi:10.1037/a0020810.

Benjamin, A. S., Diaz, M., Matzen, L. E., & Johnson, B. (2012). Tests of the DRYAD theory of the age-related deficit in memory for context: Not about context, and not about aging. *Psychology and Aging, 27*, 418–428. doi:10.1037/a0024786.

Benjamins, M. R., Hirschman, J., Hirschtick, J., & Whitman, S. (2012). Exploring differences in self-rated health among Blacks, Whites, Mexicans, and Puerto Ricans. *Ethnicity and Health, 17*, 463–476. doi:10.1080/13557858.2012.654769.

Bennett, K. M. (2005). Psychological wellbeing in later life: The longitudinal effects of marriage, widowhood and marital status change. *International Journal of Geriatric Psychiatry, 20*, 280–284. doi:10.1002/gps.1280.

Bennett, K. M. (2010). How to achieve resilience as an older widower: Turning points or gradual change? *Ageing and Society, 30*, 369–382. doi:10.1017/S0144686X09990572.

Ben-Zur, H., & Zeidner, M. (2009). Threat to life and risk-taking behaviors: A review of empirical findings and explanatory models. *Personality and Social Psychology Review, 13*, 109–128. doi:10.1177/1088868308330104.

Berg, C. A. (2008). Everyday problem solving in context. In S. M. Hofer & D. F. Alwin (Eds.), *Handbook of cognitive aging: Interdisciplinary perspectives* (pp. 207–223). Greenwich, CT: Sage.

Berg, C. A., & Sternberg, R. J. (1992). Adults' conceptions of intelligence across the adult life span. *Psychology and Aging, 7*, 221–231. doi:10.1037/0882-7974.7.2.221.

Berg, C. A., Strough, J., Calderone, K. S., Sansone, C., & Weir, C. (1998). The role of problem definitions in understanding age and context effects on strategies for solving every day problems. *Psychology and Aging, 13*, 29–44. doi:10.1037/0882-7974.13.1.29.

Bergdahl, E., Benzein, E., Ternestedt, B.-M., Elmberger, E., & Andershed, B. (in press). Co-creating possibilities for patients in palliative care to reach vital goals—A multiple case study of home-care nursing encounters. *Nursing Inquiry.* doi:10.1111/nin.12022.

Berger, R. G., Lunkenbein, S., Ströhle, A., & Hahn, A. (2012). Antioxidants in food: Mere myth or magic medicine? *Critical Reviews in Food Science and Nutrition, 52*, 162–171. doi:10.1080/10408398.2010.499481.

Bergman-Evans, B. (2004). Beyond the basics: Effects of the Eden Alternative model on quality of life issues. *Journal of Gerontological Nursing, 30,* 27–34.

Bergsma, A., & Ardelt, M. (2012). Self-reported wisdom and happiness: An empirical investigation. *Journal of Happiness Studies, 13,* 481–499. doi:10.1007/s10902-011-9275-5.

Berk, R. A. (2010). Where's the chemistry in mentor-mentee academic relationships? Try spend mentoring. *The International Journal of Mentoring and Coaching, 8,* 85–92. Retrieved from http://www.ronberk.com/articles/2010_mentor.pdf.

Berlin, L. J., Brady-Smith, C., & Brooks-Gunn, J. (2002). Links between childbearing age and observed maternal behaviors with 14-month-olds in the Early Head Start Research and Evaluation Project. *Infant Mental Health Journal, 23,* 104–129. doi:10.1002/imhj.10007.

Berlinger, N., Jennings, B., & Wolf, S. M. (2013). *The Hastings Center guidelines for decisions on life-sustaining treatment and care near the end of life* (revised and expanded 2nd ed.). New York: Oxford University Press.

Berns, N. (2011). *Closure: The rush to end grief and what it costs.* Philadelphia, PA: Temple University Press.

Berry, J. M. (1989). Cognitive efficacy across the life span: Introduction to the special series. *Developmental Psychology, 25,* 683–686.

Berry, J. M., West, R. L., & Cavanaugh, J. C. (2013). *Roots of successful aging: Bandura's self-efficacy construct.* Unpublished manuscript.

Besedeš, T., Deck, C., Sarangi, S., & Shor, M. (2012). Age effects and heuristics in decision making. *The Review of Economics and Statistics, 94,* 580–595. doi:10.1162/REST_a_00174.

Beyer, M. K., Alves, G., Hwang, K. S., Babakchanian, S., Bronnick, K. S., Chou, Y.-Y. et al. (2013). Cerebrospinal fluid Aβ levels correlate with structural brain changes in Parkinson's disease. *Movement Disorders, 28,* 302–310. doi:10.1002/mds.25282.

Bialystok, E., Craik, F. I. M., & Luk, G. (2012). Bilingualism: Consequences for mind and brain. *Trends in Cognitive Sciences, 16,* 240–250. doi:10.1016/j.tics.2012.03.001.

Biblarz, T. J., & Savci, E. (2010). Lesbian, gay, bisexual, and transgender families. *Journal of Marriage and Family, 72,* 480–497. doi:10.1111/j.1741-3737.2010.00714.x.

Bidwell, M. (2012). *What happened to long term employment? The role of worker power and environmental turbulence in explaining declines in worker tenure.* Retrieved from http://www.uc3m.es/portal/page/portal/inst_desarr_empres_carmen_vidal_ballester/investigacion/workshops/workshops_2012/madrid_work_and_organizations_symposium/Bidwell2012a.pdf.

Bieman-Copland, S., Ryan, E. B., & Cassano, J. (2002). Responding to the challenges of late life. In D. Pushkar, W. M. Bukowski, A. E. Schwartzman, D. M. Stack, & D. R. White (Eds.), *Improving competence across the lifespan* (pp. 141–157). New York: Springer.

Bigby, C. (2008). Beset by obstacles: A review of Australian policy development to support ageing in place for people with intellectual disability. *Journal of Intellectual and Developmental Disability, 33,* 76–86. doi:10.1080/13668250701852433.

Binstock, R. H. (1999). Public policy issues. In J. C. Cavanaugh & S. K. Whitbourne (Eds.), *Gerontology: Interdisciplinary perspectives* (pp. 414–447). New York: Oxford University Press.

Bird, D. J. (2001). The influences and impact of burnout on occupational therapists. *Dissertation Abstracts International. Section B. Sciences and Engineering, 62(1-B),* 204.

Birditt, K. S., Tighe, L. A., Fingerman, K. L. & Zarit, S. H. (2012). Intergenerational relationship quality across three generations. *Journal of Gerontology: Psychological Sciences, 67,* 627–638. doi:10.1093/geronb/gbs050.

Birren, J. E., & Cunningham, W. (1985). Research on the psychology of aging: Principles, concepts, and theory. In J. E. Birren & K. W. Schaie (Eds.), *Handbook of the psychology of aging* (2nd ed., pp. 3–34). New York: Van Nostrand Reinhold.

Birren, J. E., & Renner, V. J. (1980). Concepts and issues of mental health and aging. In J. E. Birren & R. B. Sloane (Eds.), *Handbook of mental health and aging* (pp. 3–33). Englewood Cliffs, NJ: Prentice Hall.

Bitnes, J., Martens, H., Ueland, Ø., & Martens, M. (2007). Longitudinal study of taste identification of sensory panellists: Effects of ageing, experience and exposure. *Food Quality and Preference, 18,* 230–241. doi:10.1016/j.foodqual.2005.11.003.

Blancato, R. B. (2013). *Violence against older women and the Elder Justice Act.* Retrieved from http://www.huffingtonpost.com/robert-b-blancato/elder-justice-act_b_2789814.html.

Blanchard-Fields, F. (1996). Causal attributions across the adult life span: The influence of social schemas, life context, and domain specificity. *Applied Cognitive Psychology, 10* (Special Issue), S137–S146. doi:10.1002/(SICI)1099-0720(199611)10.7<137:: AID-ACP431>3.0.CO;2-Z.

Blanchard-Fields, F. (1999). Social schematicity and causal attributions. In T. M. Hess & F. Blanchard-Fields (Eds.), *Social cognition and aging* (pp. 219–236). San Diego: Academic Press.

Blanchard-Fields, F. (2009). Flexible and adaptive socio-emotional problem solving in adult development and aging. *Restorative Neurology and Neuroscience, 27,* 539–550. doi:10.3233/RNN-2009-0516.

Blanchard-Fields, F. (2010). Neuroscience and aging. In J. C. Cavanaugh & C. K. Cavanaugh (Eds.), *Aging in America: Vol. 1: Psychological aspects* (pp. 1–25). Santa Barbara, CA: Praeger Perspectives.

Blanchard-Fields, F., & Beatty, C. (2005). Age differences in blame attributions: The role of relationship outcome ambiguity and personal identification. *Journals of Gerontology: Psychological Sciences, 60,* P19–P26. doi:10.1093/geronb/60.1.P19.

Blanchard-Fields, F., & Hertzog, C. (2000). Age differences in schematicity. In U. von Hecker, S. Dutke, & G. Sedek (Eds.), *Processes of generative mental representation and psychological adaptation* (pp. 175–198). Dordrecht, The Netherlands: Kluwer.

Blanchard-Fields, F., & Horhota, M. (2006). How can the study of aging inform research on social cognition? *Social Cognition, 24,* 207–217.

Blanchard-Fields, F., Baldi, R. A., & Constantin, L. P. (2004). *Interrole conflict across the adult lifespan: The role of parenting stage, career stages and quality of experiences.* Unpublished manuscript, School of Psychology, Georgia Institute of Technology.

Blanchard-Fields, F., Chen, Y., & Herbert, C. E. (1997). Interrole conflict as a function of life stage, gender, and gender-related personality attributes. *Sex Roles, 37,* 155–174. doi:10.1023/A:1025691626240.

Blanchard-Fields, F., Hertzog, C., & Horhota, M. (2012). Violate my beliefs? Then you're to blame! Belief content as an explanation for causal attribution biases. *Psychology and Aging, 27,* 324–337. doi:10.1037/a0024423.

Blanchard-Fields, F., Horhota, M., & Mienaltowski, A. (2008). Social context and cognition. In S. M. Hofer & D. F. Alwin (Eds.), *Handbook of cognitive aging: Interdisciplinary perspectives* (pp. 614–628). Greenwich, CT: Sage.

Blanchard-Fields, F., Mienaltowski, A., & Seay, R. (2007). Age differences in everyday problem-solving effectiveness: Older adults select more effective strategies for interpersonal problems. *Journals of Gerontology: Psychological Sciences, 62,* P61–P64. doi:10.1093/geronb/62.1.P61.

Blasko, I., Jellinger, K., Kemmler, G., Krampla, W., Jungwirth, S., Wichart, I., Tragl, K., & Fischer, P. (2008). Conversion from cognitive health to mild cognitive impairment and Alzheimer's disease: Prediction by plasma amyloid beta 42, medial temporal lobe atrophy and homocysteine. *Neurobiology of Aging, 29,* 1–11. doi:10.1016/j.neurobiolaging.2006.09.002.

Blatteis, C. M. (2012). Age-dependent changes in temperature regulation—A mini review. *Gerontology, 58,* 289–295. doi:10.1159/000333148.

Blatt-Eisengart, I., & Lachman, M. E. (2004). Attributions for memory performance in adulthood: Age differences and mediation effects. *Aging, Neuropsychology, and Cognition, 11,* 68–79. doi:10.1076/anec.11.1.68.29364.

Blazer, D. G. (2008). How do you feel about…? Health outcomes in late life and self-perceptions of health and well-being. *The Gerontologist, 48,* 415–422. doi:10.1093/geront/48.4.415.

Bleich, S., Wiltfang, J., & Kornhuber, J. (2003). Memantine in moderate-to-severe Alzheimer's disease. *New England Journal of Medicine, 349,* 609–610. doi:10.1056/NEJM200308073490616.

Blieszner, R., & Roberto, K. A. (2012). Partners and friends in adulthood.

In S. K. Whitbourne & M. J. Sliwinski (Eds.), *The Wiley-Blackwell handbook of adulthood and aging* (pp. 381–398). Oxford, UK: Wiley-Blackwell.

Blom, M. M., Bosmans, J. E., Cuijpers, P., Zarit, S. H., & Pot, A. M. (2013). Effectiveness and cost-effectiveness of an internet intervention for family caregivers of people with dementia: Design of a randomized controlled trial. *BMC Psychiatry, 13.* doi:10.1186/1471-244X-13-17. Retrieved from http://www.biomedcentral.com/1471-244X/13/17/.

Blossfeld, H.-P. (2009). Educational assortative marriage in comparative perspective. *Annual Review of Sociology, 35,* 513–530. doi:10.1146/annurev-soc-070308-115913.

Blümel, J. E., Chedraui, P., Baron, G., Belzares, E., Bencosme, A., Calle, A. et al. (2012). Menopausal symptoms appear before the menopause and persist 5 years beyond: A detailed analysis of a multinational study. *Climacteric, 15,* 542–551. doi:10.3109/13697137.2012.658462.

Boccardi, V., & Herbig, U. (2012). Telomerase gene therapy: A novel approach to combat aging. *EMBO Molecular Medicine, 4,* 685–687. doi:10.1002/emmm.201200246.

Böckerman, P., Ilmakunnas, P. Jokisaari, M., & Vuori, J. (2013). Who stays unwillingly in a job? A study based on a representative random sample of employees. *Economic and Industrial Democracy, 34,* 25–43. doi:10.1177/0143831X11429374.

Bolkan, C., & Hooker, K. (2012). Self-regulation and social cognition in adulthood. In S. K. Whitbourne & M. J. Sliwinski (Eds.), *The Wiley-Blackwell handbook of adulthood and aging* (pp. 355–380). Oxford, UK: Wiley-Blackwell.

Bonanno, G. A. (2009). *The other side of sadness: What the new science of bereavement tells us about life after loss.* New York, NY: Basic Books.

Bonanno, G. A., Papa, A., & O'Neill, K. (2001). Loss and human resilience. *Applied and Preventive Psychology, 10,* 193–206. doi:10.1016/S0962-1849(01)80014-7.

Bonanno, G. A., Papa, A., Lalande, K., Zhang, N., & Noll, J. G. (2005). Grief processing and deliberate grief avoidance: A prospective comparison of bereaved spouses and parents in the United States and the People's Republic of China. *Journal of Consulting and Clinical Psychology, 73,* 86–98. doi:10.1037/0022-006X.73.1.86.

Bonanno, G. A., Westphal, M., & Mancini, A. D. (2011). Resilience to loss and trauma. *Annual Review of Clinical Psychology, 7,* 511–535. doi:10.1146/annurev-clinpsy-032210-104526

Bonanno, G. A., Wortman, C. B., & Neese, R. M. (2004). Prospective patterns of resilience and maladjustment during widowhood. *Psychology and Aging, 19,* 260–271. doi:10.1037/0882-7974.19.2.260.

Boom, J. (2012). A new model for strategy development combining categorical data analysis with growth modeling. *Journal of Adult Development*. Retrieved from http://adultdevelopment.org/Boom2012.pdf.

Booth, A. L., & Carroll, N. (2008). Economic status and the indigenous/non-indigenous health gap. *Economic Letters, 99*, 604–606. doi:10.1016/j.econlet.2007.10.005.

Bosco, A., di Masi, M. N., & Manuti, A. (2013). Burnout internal factors—self-esteem and negative affectivity in the workplace: The mediation role of organizational identification in times of job uncertainty. In S. Bährer-Kohler (Ed.), *Burnout for experts* (pp. 145–158). New York: Springer.

Bosma, H., van Boxtel, M. P. J., Ponds, R. W. H. M., Houx, P. J. H., & Jolles, J. (2003). Education and age-related cognitive decline: The contribution of mental workload. *Educational Gerontology, 29*, 165–173. doi:10.1080/1071576980300191.

Bosshard, G., & Materstvedt, L. J. (2011). Medical and societal issues in euthanasia and assisted suicide. In R. Chadwick, H. Ten Have, & E. M. Meslin (Eds.), *The SAGE handbook of health care ethics* (pp. 202–218). Thousand Oaks, CA: Sage Publications.

Botwinick, J. (1977). Intellectual abilities. In J. E. Birren & K. W. Schaie (Eds.), *Handbook of the psychology of aging* (pp. 580–605). New York: Van Nostrand Reinhold.

Bouldin, P. L., & Grayson, A. M. (2010). *Perceptions of sexual harassment and sexual assault: A study of gender differences among U.S. Navy officers*. Master's thesis completed at the Naval Postgraduate School, Monterey, CA. Retrieved from http://edocs.nps.edu/npspubs/scholarly/theses/2010/Mar/10Mar_Bouldin.pdf.

Bourgeois, M. S., Camp, C., Rose, P., White, B., Malone, M., Carr, J., & Rovine, M. (2003). A comparison of training strategies to enhance use of external aids by persons with dementia. *Journal of Communication Disorders, 36*, 361–378. doi:10.1016/S0021-9924(03)00051-0.

Bowling, A. (2007). Aspirations for older age in the 21st century: What is successful aging? *International Journal of Aging and Human Development, 64*, 263–297. doi:10.2190/L0K1-8/W4-9R01-7127.

Bowman, G. L., Silbert, L. C., Howieson, D., Dodge, H. H., Traber, M. G., Frei, B., et al. (2012). Nutrient biomarker patterns, cognitive function, and MRI measures of brain aging. *Neurology, 78*, 241–249. doi:10.1212/WNL.0b013e3182436598.

Boyle, P. J., Feng, Z., & Raab, G. M. (2011). Does widowhood increase mortality risk? Testing for selection effects by comparing causes of spousal death. *Epidemiology, 22*, 1–5. doi:10.1097/EDE.0b013e3181fdcc0b.

Boywitt, C. D., Kuhlmann, B. G., & Meiser, T. (2012). The role of source memory in older adults' recollective experience. *Psychology and Aging, 27*, 484–497. doi:10.1037/a0024729.

Bozikas, V., Kioseoglou, V., Palialia, M., Nimatoudis, I., Iakovides, A., Karavatos, A., & Kaprinis, G. (2000). Burnout among hospital workers and community-based mental health staff. *Psychiatriki, 11*, 204–211. doi:

Bradford, A., Kunik, M. E., Schulz, P., Williams, S. P., & Singh, H. (2009). Missed and delayed diagnosis of dementia in primary care: Prevalence and contributing factors. *Alzheimer's Disease and Associated Disorders, 23*, 306–314. doi:10.1097/WAD.0b013e3181a6bebc.

Brancucci, A. (2012). Neural correlates of cognitive ability. *Journal of Neuroscience Research, 90*, 1299–1309. doi:10.1002/jnr.23045.

Brandburg, G. L., Symes, L., Mastel-Smith, B., Hersch, G., & Walsh, T. (2013). Resident strategies for making a life in a nursing home: A qualitative study. *Journal of Advanced Nursing, 69*, 862–874. doi:10.1111/j.1365-2648.2012.06075.x.

Brandt, M., Deindl, C., & Hank, K. (2012). Tracing the origins of successful aging: The role of childhood conditions and social inequality in explaining later life health. *Social Science and Medicine, 74*, 1418–1425. doi:10.1016/j.socscimed.2012.01.004.

Brandtstädter, J. (1997). Action culture and development: Points of convergence. *Culture and Psychology, 3*, 335–352. doi:10.1177/1354067X9733007.

Brandtstädter, J. (1999). Sources of resilience in the aging self. In T. M. Hess & F. Blanchard-Fields (Eds.), *Social cognition and aging* (pp. 123–141). San Diego: Academic Press.

Bratkovich, K. L. (2010). *The relationship of attachment and spirituality with posttraumatic growth following a death for college students*. Doctoral dissertation submitted to the Department of Psychology at Oklahoma State University.

Braun, S. D. (2007). Gay fathers with children adopted from foster care: Understanding their experiences and predicting adoption outcomes. *Dissertation Abstracts International. Section B. Sciences and Engineering, 68(2-B)*, 1296.

Brett, C. E., Gow, A. J., Corley, J., Pattie, A., Starr, J. M., & Deary, I. J. (2012). Psychosocial factors and health as determinants of quality of life in community-dwelling older adults. *Quality of Life Research, 21*, 505–516. doi:10.1007/s11136-011-9951-2.

Bribiescas, R. G. (2010). An evolutionary and life history perspective on human male reproductive senescence. *Annals of the New York Academy of Sciences, 1204*, 54–64. doi:10.1111/j.1749-6632.2010.05524.x.

Brissett-Chapman, S., & Isaacs-Shockley, M. (1997). *Children in social peril: A community vision for preserving family care of African American children and youth*. Washington, DC: Child Welfare League of America.

Brissette, I., Scheier, M. F., & Carver, C. S. (2002). The role of optimism in social network development, coping, and psychological adjustment during a life transition. *Journal of Personality and Social Psychology, 82*, 102–111. doi:10.1037//0022-3514.82.1.102.

Bromell, L., & Cagney, K. A. (in press). Companionship in the neighborhood context: Older adults' living arrangements and perceptions of social cohesion. *Research on Aging*. doi:10.1177/0164027512475096.

Bronson-Castain, K. W., Bearse, M. A., Jr., Neuville, J., Jonasdottir, S., King-Hoope, B., Barez, S., et al. (2012). Early neural and vascular changes in the adolescent Type 1 and Type 2 diabetic retina. *Retina, 32*, 92–102. doi:10.1097/IAE.0b013e318219deac.

Brown, A. S. (2012). *The tip of the tongue state*. New York: Psychology Press.

Brown, J. W., Chen, S-I., Mefford, L., Brown, A., Callen, B., & McArthur, P. (2011). Becoming an older volunteer: A grounded theory study. *Nursing Research and Practice, 2011*. doi:10.1155/2011/361250. Retrieved from http://www.hindawi.com/journals/nrp/2011/361250.html.

Bryce, J. (2001). The technological transformation of leisure. *Social Science Computer Review, 19*, 7–16. doi:10.1177/089443930101900102.

Brysiewicz, P. (2008). The lived experience of losing a loved one to a sudden death in KwaZulu-Natal, South Africa. *Journal of Clinical Nursing, 17*, 224–231. doi:10.1111/j.1365-2702.2007.01972.x.

Buhl, H. (2008). Development of a model describing individuated adult child-parent relationships. *International Journal of Behavioral Development, 32*, 381–389. doi:10.1177/0165025408093656.

Bull, M. J., & McShane, R. E. (2008). Seeking what's best during the transition to adult day health services. *Qualitative Health Research, 18*, 597–605. doi:10.1177/1049732308315174.

Bullock, K. (2004). Family social support. In P. J. Bomar (Ed.), *Promoting health in families: Applying family research and theory to nursing practice* (3rd ed., pp. 142–161). Philadelphia: W.B. Saunders.

Bureau of Labor Statistics. (2010). *Employment Characteristics of Families survey*. Retrieved from http://www.bls.gov/news.release/famee.nr0.htm.

Bureau of Labor Statistics. (2013a). *Women in the labor force: A databook*. Retrieved from http://www.bls.gov/cps/wlf-databook-2012.pdf.

Bureau of Labor Statistics. (2013b). *Occupational employment statistics*. Retrieved from http://www.bls.gov/oes/home.htm.

Bureau of Labor Statistics. (2013c). *Labor force statistics from the Current Population Survey*. Retrieved from http://data.bls.gov/timeseries/LNU02000097.

Burgio, J., Stevens, A. Guy, D., Roth, D. L., & Haley, W. E. (2003). Impact of two psychosocial interventions on white and African American family caregivers of individuals with dementia. *The Gerontologist, 43*, 568–579. doi:10.1093/geront/43.4.568.

Burke, B. L., Martens, A., & Faucher, E. H. (2010). Two decades of terror management theory: A meta-analysis of mortality salience research. *Personality and Social Psychology Review, 14*, 155–195. doi:10.1177/1088868309352321.

Burnette, D. (1999). Social relationships of Latino grandparent caregivers:

A role theory perspective. *The Gerontologist, 39*, 49–58. doi:10.1093/geront/39.1.49.

Busch, J., & Rodogno, R. (2011). Life support and euthanasia, a perspective on Shaw's new perspective. *Journal of Medical Ethics, 37*, 81–83. doi:10.1136/jme.2010.037275.

Bustos, M. L. C. (2007). La muerte en la cultura occidental: Antropología de la muerte [Death in Western culture: Anthropology of death]. *Revista Colombiana de Psiquiatría, 36*, 332–339. Retrieved from http://www.scielo.org.co/scielo.php?pid=S0034-74502007000200012&script=sci_arttext.

Byock, I. (1997). *Dying well*. New York: Riverhead.

Cabeza, R. (2002). Hemispheric asymmetry reduction in older adults: The HAROLD model. *Psychology and Aging, 17*, 85–100. doi:10.1037/0882-7974.17.1.85.

Cabeza, R. (2004). Neuroscience frontiers in cognitive aging. In R. A. Dixon & L. G. Nilsson (Eds.), *New frontiers in cognitive aging* (pp.179–196). New York: Oxford University Press.

Cabeza R., & Dennis N. A. (2013). Frontal lobes and aging: Deterioration and compensation. In D. T. Stuss & R. T. Knight (Eds.), *Principles of frontal lobe function* (2nd ed., pp. 628–652). New York: Oxford University Press. Retrieved from http://canlab.psych.psu.edu/compensationchapter_stussknight book_cabezadennis_final.pdf.

Cacioppo, J. T., Berntson, G. G., Bechara, A., Tranel, D., & Hawkley, H. C. (2011). Could an aging brain contribute to subjective well-being? The value added by a social neuroscience perspective. In A. Todorov, S. Fiske, & D. Prentice (Eds.), *Social neuroscience: toward understanding the underpinnings of the social mind* (pp. 249–262). New York: Oxford University Press.

Cadigan, R. O., Grabowski, D. C., Givens, J. L., & Mitchell, S. L. (2012). The quality of advanced dementia care in the nursing home: The role of special care units. *Medical Care, 50*, 856–862. doi:10.1097/MLR.0b013e31825dd713.

Cahill, E., Lewis, L. M., Barg, F. K., & Rogner, H. R. (2009). "You don't want to burden them": Older adults' views on family involvement in care. *Journal of Family Nursing, 27*, 295–317. doi:10.1177/1074840709337247.

Cairney, J., & Krause, N. (2008). Negative life events and age-related decline in mastery: Are older adults more vulnerable to the control-eroding effect of stress? *The Journals of Gerontology: Social Sciences, 63*, S162–S170.

Calmes, J. (2013). *Misperceptions of benefits make trimming them harder*. Retrieved from http://www.nytimes.com/2013/04/04/us/politics/misperception-of-government-benefits-makes-trimming-them-harder.html?pagewanted=all&_r=0.

Camp, C. J. (1999a). Memory interventions for normal and pathological older adults. In R. Schulz, M. P. Lawton, & G. Maddox (Eds.), *Annual review of gerontology and geriatrics* (Vol. 18, pp. 155–189). New York: Springer.

Camp, C. J. (Ed.). (1999b). *Montessori-based activities for persons with dementia* (Vol. 1). Beachwood, OH: Menorah Park Center for Senior Living.

Camp, C. J. (2001). From efficacy to effectiveness to diffusion: Making transitions in dementia intervention research. *Neuropsychological Rehabilitation, 11,* 495–517. doi:10.1080/09602010042000079.

Camp, C. J. (2005). Spaced retrieval: A model for dissemination of a cognitive intervention for persons with dementia. In D. K. Attix & K. A. Velsh-Bohmer (Eds.), *Geriatric neuropsychology: Assessment and intervention* (pp. 275–292). New York: Guilford Press.

Camp, C. J., Antenucci, V., Brush, J., & Slominski, T. (2012). Using spaced retrieval to effectively treat dysphagia in clients with dementia. *Perspectives on Swallowing and Swallowing Disorders (Dysphagia), 21,* 96–104. doi:10.1044/sasd21.3.96.

Camp, C. J., Foss, J. W., Stevens, A. B., Reichard, C. C., McKitrick, L. A., & O'Hanlon, A. M. (1993). Memory training in normal and demented elderly populations: The E-I-E-I-O model. *Experimental Aging Research, 19,* 277–290. doi: 10.1080/03610739308253938.

Camp, C. J., Skrajner, M. J., & Kelly, M. (2005). Early stage dementia client as group leader. *Clinical Gerontologist, 28,* 81–85. doi: 10.1300/J018v28n04_06.

Campbell, A. (2008). Attachment, aggression, and affiliation: The role of oxytocin in female social behavior. *Biological Psychology, 77,* 1–10. doi: 10.1016/j.biopsycho.2007.09.001.

Campbell, J., & Ehlert, U. (2012). Acute psychosocial stress: Does the emotional stress response correspond with physiological responses? *Psychoneuroendocrinology, 37,* 1111–1134. doi: 10.1016/j.psyneuen.2011.12.010.

Campinha-Bacote, J. (2010). A culturally conscious model of mentoring. *Nurse Educator, 35,* 130–135. doi: 10.1097/NNE.0b013e3181d950bf.

Cansino, S., Estrada-Manilla, C., Hernández-Ramos, E., Martinez-Galindo, J. G., Torres-Trejo, F., Gómez-Fernández, T., et al. (2013). The rate of source memory decline across the adult life span. *Developmental Psychology, 49,* 973–985. doi: 10.1037/a0028894.

Cantor, N. (1990). From thought to behavior: "Having" and "doing" in the study of personality and cognition. *American Psychologist, 45,* 735–750. doi: 10.1037/0003-066X.45.6.735.

Carbonneau, N., & Vallerand, R. J. (2012). Toward a tripartite model of intrinsic motivation. *Journal of Personality, 80,* 1147–1178. doi: 10.1111/j.1467-6494.2011.00757.x.

Carlander, I., Ternestedt, B.-M., Sahlberg-Blom, E., Hellström, I., & Sandberg, J. (2011). Being me and being us in a family living close to death at home. *Qualitative Health Research, 5,* 683–695. doi: 10.1177/1049732310396102.

Carlo, G., Koller, S., Raffaelli, M., & de Guzman, M. R. T. (2007). Culture-related strengths among Latin American families: A case study of Brazil. *Marriage & Family Review, 41,* 335–360. doi: 10.1300/J002v41n03_06.

Carnelley, K., & Ruscher, J. B. (2000). Adult attachment and exploratory behavior in leisure. *Journal of Social Behavior and Personality, 15,* 153–165.

Caron, C. D., Ducharme, F., & Griffith, J. (2006). Deciding on institutionalization for a relative with dementia: The most difficult decision for caregivers. *Canadian Journal on Aging, 25,* 193–205. doi: 10.1353/cja.2006.0033.

Carr, D. (2004). Gender, preloss marital dependence, and older adults' adjustment to widowhood. *Journal of Marriage and Family, 66,* 220–235. doi: 10.1111/j.0022-2445.2004.00016.x.

Carr, D., & Moorman, S. M. (2011). Social relations and aging. In R. A. Settersten & J. L. Angel (Eds.), *Handbook of sociology of aging* (pp. 145–160). New York: Springer.

Carstensen, L. L. (2006). The influence of a sense of time on human development. *Science, 312,* 1913–1915. doi: 10.1126/science.1127488.

Carstensen, L. L., & Freund, A. M. (1994). The resilience of the aging self. *Developmental Review, 14,* 81–92. doi: 10.1006/drev.1994.1004.

Carstensen, L. L., & Fried, L. P. (2012). The meaning of old age. In J. Beard, S. Biggs, D. Bloom, L. Fried, P. Hogan, A., Kalache et al. (Eds.), *Global population ageing: Peril or promise?* Harvard University Program on the Global Demography of Aging. Retrieved from http://e.hsph.harvard.edu/pgda/WorkingPapers/2012/PGDA_WP_89.pdf#page=18.

Carstensen, L. L., & Mikels, J. A. (2005). At the intersection of emotion and cognition: Aging and the positivity effect. *Current Directions in Psychological Science, 14,* 117–121. doi: 10.1111/j.0963-7214.2005.00348.x.

Carstensen, L. L., Mikels, J. A., & Mather, M. (2006). Aging and the intersection of cognition, motivation, and emotion. In J. E. Birren & K. W. Schaie (Eds.), *Handbook of the psychology of aging* (6th ed., pp. 343–362). Amsterdam: Elsevier.

Casey, V. A., Dwyer, J. T., Coleman, K. A., Krall, E. A., Gardner, J., & Valadian, I. (1991). Accuracy of recall by middle-aged participants in a longitudinal study of their body size and indices of maturation earlier in life. *Annals of Human Biology, 18,* 155–166. doi: 10.1080/03014469100001492.

Caspi, A., Roberts, B. W., & Shiner, R. (2005). Personality development. *Annual Review of Psychology, 56,* 453–484. doi:10.1146/annurev.psych.55.090902.141913.

Castel, A. D., McGillivray, S., & Friedman, M. C. (2012). Metamemory and memory efficiency in older adults: Learning about the benefits of priority processing and value-directed remembering. In

Naveh-Benjamin & N. Ohta (Eds.), *Memory and aging: Current issues and future directions* (pp. 245–268). New York: Psychology Press.

Castillo, L. S., Williams, B. A., Hooper, S. M., Sabatino, C. P., Weithorn, L. A., & Sudore, R. L. (2011). Lost in translation: the unintended consequences of advance directive law on clinical care. *Annals of Internal Medicine, 154,* 121–128. doi:10.7326/0003-4819-154-2-201101180-00012.

Cavallini, E., Bottiroli, S., Fastame, M. C., & Hertzog, C. (2013). Age and subcultural differences on personal and general beliefs about memory. *Journal of Aging Studies, 27,* 71–81. doi: 1-1016/j.jaging.2012.11.002.

Cavanaugh, J. C. (1996). Memory self-efficacy as a key to understanding memory change. In F. Blanchard-Fields & T. M. Hess (Eds.), *Perspectives on cognitive changes in adulthood and aging* (pp. 488–507). New York: McGraw-Hill.

Cavanaugh, J. C. (1999a). Caregiving to adults: A life event challenge. In I, H. Nordhus, G. R. VandenBos, S. Berg, & P. Fromholt (Eds.), *Clinical geropsychology* (pp. 131–135). Washington, DC: American Psychological Association.

Cavanaugh, J. C. (1999b). Theories of aging in the biological, behavioral, and social sciences. In J. C. Cavanaugh & S. K. Whitbourne (Eds.), *Gerontology: Interdisciplinary perspectives* (pp. 1–32). New York: Oxford University Press.

Cavanaugh, J. C., & Green, E. E. (1990). I believe, therefore I can: Self-efficacy beliefs in memory aging. In E. A. Lovelace (Ed.), *Aging and cognition: Mental processes, self-awareness, and interventions* (pp. 189–230). Amsterdam: North-Holland.

Cavanaugh, J. C., & Kinney, J. M. (1994, July). *Marital satisfaction as an important contextual factor in spousal caregiving.* Paper presented at the 7th International Conference on Personal Relationships, Groningen, The Netherlands.

Cavanaugh, J. C., & Whitbourne, S. K. (2003). Research methods in adult development. In J. Demick & C. Andreoletti (Eds.), *Handbook of adult development* (pp. 85–100). New York: Kluwer Academic/Plenum.

Centers for Disease Control and Prevention. (2011a). *Body mass index.* Retrieved from http://www.cdc.gov/healthyweight/assessing/bmi/index.html.

Centers for Disease Control and Prevention. (2011b). *National diabetes fact sheet, 2011.* Retrieved from http://www.cdc.gov/diabetes/pubs/pdf/ndfs_2011.pdf.

Centers for Disease Control and Prevention. (2012a). *Health, United States, 2011.* Retrieved from http://www.cdc.gov/nchs/data/hus/hus11.pdf.

Centers for Disease control and Prevention. (2012b). *Stroke fact sheet.* Retrieved from http://www.cdc.gov/dhdsp/data_statistics/fact_sheets/fs_stroke.htm.

Centers for Disease control and Prevention. (2012c). *Observances—February African American history month.* Retrieved from

http://www.cdc.gov/minorityhealth/observances/BAA.html.

Centers for Disease Control and Prevention. (2012d). *Focus on preventing falls.* Retrieved from http://www.cdc.gov/Features/OlderAmericans/.

Centers for Disease Control and Prevention. (2012e). *National Health Interview Survey.* Retrieved from http://www.cdc.gov/nchs/nhis.htm.

Centers for Disease Control and Prevention. (2012f). *Chronic diseases and health promotion.* Retrieved from http://www.cdc.gov/chronicdisease/overview/index.htm.

Centers for Disease Control and Prevention. (2012g). *Deaths: Leading causes for 2009.* Retrieved from http://www.cdc.gov/nchs/data/nvsr/nvsr61/nvsr61_07.pdf.

Centers for Disease Control and Prevention. (2012h). *Intimate partner violence.* Retrieved from http://www.cdc.gov/violenceprevention/intimatepartnerviolence/index.html.

Centers for Medicare and Medicaid Services. (2012). *National health expenditure projections 2011-2021.* Retrieved from http://www.cms.gov/Research-Statistics-Data-and-Systems/Statistics-Trends-and-Reports/NationalHealthExpendData/Downloads/Proj2011PDF.pdf.

Chan, S. W-C. (2010). Family caregiving in dementia: The Asian perspective of a global problem. *Dementia and Geriatric Cognitive Disorders, 30,* 469–478. doi:10.1159/000322086.

Chang, S., Kim, J., Kong, E., Kim, C., Ahn, S., & Cho, N. (2008). Exploring ego-integrity in old adults: A Q-methodology study. *International Journal of Nursing Studies, 45,* 246–256. doi:10.1016/j.ijnurstu.2006.07.020.

Chang, T.-S., & Hsiao, W.-H. (in press). Time spent on social networking sites: Understanding user behavior and social capital. *Systems Research and Behavioral Science.* doi:10.1002/sres.2169.

Charles, S. T., & Carstensen, L. L. (2010). Social and emotional aging. *Annual Review of Psychology, 61,* 383–409. doi:10.1146/annurev.psych.093008.100448.

Charlton, B., & Verghese, A. (2010). Caring for Ivan Ilyich. *Journal of General Internal Medicine, 25,* 93–95. doi:10.1007/s11606-009-1177-4.

Charman, W. N. (2008). The eye in focus: accommodation and presbyopia. *Clinical and Experimental Optometry, 91,* 207–225. doi:10.1111/j.1444-0938.2008.00256.x.

Charness, N., & Bosman, E. A. (1990). Expertise and aging: Life in the lab. In T. M. Hess (Ed.), *Aging and cognition: Knowledge organization and utilization* (pp. 343–385). Amsterdam: North-Holland.

Chatters, L. M., Mattis, J. S., Woodward, A. T., Taylor, R. J., Neighbors, H. J., & Grayman, N. A. (2011). Use of ministers for a serious personal problem among African Americans: Findings from the National Survey of American Life. *American Journal of Orthopsychiatry, 81,* 118–127. doi:10.1111/j.1939-0025.2010.01079.x.

Chee, F. Y. T. (2011). *Elderspeak in Singapore: A case study.* Retrieved from http://dr.ntu.edu.sg/bitstream /handle/10220/7795/Felicia%20Chee .pdf?sequence=1.

Chen, J., & Wu, Z. (2008). Gender differences in the effects of self-rated health status on mortality among the oldest old in China. In Z. Yi, D. L. Poston, Jr., D. Asbaugh Vlosky, & D. Gu (Eds.), *Healthy longevity in China* (pp. 397–418). New York: Springer.

Chen, Y. (2002). Unwanted beliefs: Age differences in beliefs of false information. *Aging, Neuropsychology, and Cognition, 9,* 217–228. doi:10.1076 /anec.9.3.217.9613.

Chen, Z. X., Aryee, S., & Lee, C. (2005). Test of a mediation model of perceived organizational support. *Journal of Vocational Behavior, 66,* 457–470. doi:10.1016/j. jvb.2004.01.001.

Cheng, C. (2009). Dialectical thinking and coping flexibility: A multimethod approach. *Journal of Personality, 77,* 471–494. doi:10.1111 /j.1467-6494.2008.00555.x.

Cherlin, A. J. (2013). Health, marriage, and same-sex partnerships. *Journal of Health and Social Behavior, 54,* 64–66. doi:10.1177/0022146512474430.

Cherry, K. E., Brigman, S., Reese-Melancon, C., Burton-Chase, A., & Holland, K. (2013). Memory aging knowledge and memory self-appraisal in younger and older adults. *Educational Gerontology, 39,* 168–178. doi:10.1080/03601277.20 12.699838.

Cheung, C. K., Kam, P. K., & Ngan, R. M. H. (2011). Age discrimination in the labour market from the perspectives of employers and older workers. *International Social Work, 54,* 118–136. doi:10.1177/0020872810372368.

Chi, M. T. H. (2006). Laboratory methods for assessing experts' and novices' knowledge. In K. A. Ericsson, N. Charness, P. J. Feltovich, & R. R. Hoffman (Eds.), *The Cambridge handbook of expertise and expert performance* (pp. 167–184). New York: Cambridge University Press.

Chidgey, A. (2008). Effects of growth hormone in enhancing thymic regrowth and T-cell reconstitution. *Expert Review of Clinical Immunology, 4,* 433–439. doi:10.1586/1744666X.4.4.433.

Chin, L., & Quine, S. (2012). Common factors that enhance the quality of life for women living in their own homes or in aged care facilities. *Journal of Women and Aging, 24,* 269–279. doi: 10.1080/08952841.2012.650605.

Chiu, H. F. K., & Brodaty, H. (2013). Arguments against the biomarker-driven diagnosis of AD. *International Psychogeriatrics, 25,* 177–181. Doi: 10.1017/S1041610212002104.

Chiu, W. C. K., Chan, A. W., Snape, E., & Redman, T. (2001). Age stereotypes and discriminatory attitudes towards older workers: An East–West comparison. *Human Relations, 54,* 629–661. doi:10.1177/0018726701545004.

Choi, H. S., Johnson, B., & Kriewitz, K. (2013). Benefits of inclusion and segregation for individuals with disabilities in leisure. *International Journal on Disability and Human Development, 12,* 15–23. doi:10.1515/ ijdhd-2012-0120.

Chong, S., & Lee, T.-S. (2013). Predicting cognitive decline in Alzheimer's disease (AD): The role of clinical, cognitive characteristics and biomarkers. In I. Zerr (Ed.), *Understanding Alzheimer's disease* (pp. 375–408). Retrieved from http://www.intechopen.com/books /understanding-alzheimer-s-disease. doi:10.5772/54289.

Chou, S.-C., Boldy, D. P., & Lee, A. H. (2003). Factors influencing residents' satisfaction in residential aged care. *The Gerontologist, 43,* 459–472. doi:10.1093/geront/43.4.459.

Christensen, A. (1990). Gender and social structure in the demand/ withdrawal pattern of marital conflict. *Journal of Personality and Social Psychology, 59,* 73–81. doi:10.1037/0022-3514.59.1.73.

Christensen, A. J., & Johnson, J. A. (2002). Patient adherence with medical treatment regimens: An interactive approach. *Current Directions in Psychological Science, 11,* 94–97. doi:10.1111/1467-8721.00176.

Cicirelli, V. G. (2001). Personal meaning of death in older adults and young adults in relation to their fears of death. *Death Studies, 25,* 663–683. doi:10.1080/713769896.

Cicirelli, V. G. (2006). Fear of death in mid-old age. *Journals of Gerontology: Psychological Sciences, 61B,* P75–P81.

Cirelli, C. (2012). Brain plasticity, sleep and aging. *Gerontology, 58,* 441–445. doi:10.1159/000336149.

Clare, L., & Giblin, S. (2008). Late onset psychosis. In R. Woods & L. Clare (Eds.), *Handbook of the clinical psychology of ageing* (2nd ed., pp. 133–144). New York: Wiley.

Clarke, L. H., & Griffin, M. (2008). Visible and invisible ageing: Beauty work as a response to ageism. *Ageing and Society, 28,* 653–674. doi:10.1017/S0144686X07007003.

Clifford, D., Hertz, F., & Doskow, E. (2010). *A legal guide for lesbian and gay couples* (15th ed.). Berkeley, CA: Nolo.

CMS.gov. (2012a). *CMS Fast Facts overview.* Retrieved from http:// cms.gov/Research-Statistics-Data -and-Systems/Statistics-Trends-and -Reports/CMS-Fast-Facts/index.html.

CMS.gov. (2012b). *Medicare program—General information.* Retrieved from http://cms.gov/Medicare /Medicare-General-Information /MedicareGenInfo/index.html.

Coan, J. A. (2008). Toward a neuroscience of attachment. In J. Cassidy & P. R. Shaver (Eds.), *Handbook of attachment: Theory, research, and clinical implications* (2nd ed., pp. 241–265). New York: Guilford.

Codispoti, K.-E. T., Beason-Held, L. L., Kraut, M. A., O'Brien, R. J., Rudow, G., Pletnikova, O. et al. (2012). Longitudinal brain activity in asymptomatic Alzheimer disease. *Brain and Behavior, 2,* 221–230. doi:10.1002/brb3.47.

Cohen, D. (2013). End-of-life issues for caregivers of individuals with Alzheimer's disease and related dementias. In S.H. Zarit & R. C. Talley (Eds.), *End-of-life issues for caregivers of individuals with Alzheimer's disease and related dementias* (pp. 121–135). New York: Springer.

Cohen, F., Kemeny, M. E., Zegans, L., Johnson, P., Kearney, K. A., & Sites, D. P. (2007). Immune function declines with unemployment and recovers after stressor termination. *Psychosomatic Medicine, 69,* 225–234. doi: doi:10.1097 /PSY.0b013e31803139a6.

Cohen, S., & Janicki-Deverts, D. (2012). Who's stressed? Distributions of psychological stress in the United States in probability samples from 1983, 2006, and 2009. *Journal of Applied Social Psychology, 42,* 1320–1334. doi:10.1111/j.1559-1816.2012.00900.x.

Cohen, S., Janicki-Deverts, D., Doyle, W. J., Miller, G. E., Frank, E., Rabin, B. S., et al. (2012). Chronic stress, glucocorticoid receptor resistance, inflammation, and disease risk. *Proceedings of the National Academy of Sciences, 109,* 5995–5999. doi:10.1073/pnas.1118355109.

Colcombe, S., & Kramer, A. F. (2003). Fitness effects on the cognitive function of older adults: A meta-analytic study. *Psychological Science, 14,* 125–130. doi:10.1111/1467-9280. t01-1-01430.

Collins, K., & Mohr, C. (2013). Performance of younger and older adults in lateralized right and left hemisphere asymmetry tasks supports the HAROLD model. *Laterality, 18,* 491–512 doi:10.1080/1 357650X.2012.724072.

Collins, W. A., & van Dulmen, M. (2006). "The course of true love(s)…": Origins and pathways in the development of romantic relationships. In A. C. Crouter & A. Booth (Eds.), *Romance and sex in adolescence and emerging adulthood: Risks and opportunities* (pp. 63–86). Mahwah, NJ: Erlbaum.

Coman, A., & Hirst, W. (2012). Cognition through a social network: The propagation of induced forgetting and practice effects. *Journal of Experimental Psychology: General, 141,* 321–336. doi:10.1037 /a0024747.

Congressional Budget Office. (2012a) *The 2012 long-term budget outlook.* Retrieved from http://www.cbo.gov /publication/43288.

Connelly, R., Degraff, D. S., & Willis, R. A. (2004). The value of employer-sponsored child care to employees. *Industrial Relations: A Journal of Economy & Society, 43,* 759–792. doi:10.1111/j.0019-8676.2004.00361.x.

Connidis, I. A. (2001). *Family ties and aging.* Thousand Oaks, CA: Sage.

Connolly, A., Sampson, E. L., & Purandare, N. (2012). End-of-life care for people with dementia form ethnic minority groups: A systematic review. *Journal of the American Geriatrics Society, 60,* 351–360. doi:10.1111/j.1532-5415.2011.03754.x.

Conradi, L., & Geffner, R. (2009). Introduction to Part I of the special issue on female offenders of intimate partner violence. *Journal of Aggression, Maltreatment and Trauma, 18,* 547–551. doi:10.1080/10926770903120143.

Constantinidou, F., Christodoulou, M., & Prokopiou, J. (2012). The effects of age and education on executive functioning and oral naming performance in Greek Cypriot adults: The neurocognitive study for the aging. *Folia Phoniatrica et Logopaedica, 64,* 187–198. doi:10.1159/000340015.

Conway, M. A., & Holmes, A. (2004). Psychosocial stages and the accessibility of autobiographical memories across the life cycle. *Journal of Personality, 72,* 461–480. doi:10.1111/ j.0022.3506.2004.00269.x.

Cook, D. A., Bahn, R. S., & Menaker, R. (2010). Speed mentoring: An innovative method to facilitate mentoring relationships. *Medical Teacher, 32,* 692–694. doi:10.3109/01421591003686278.

Coombs, M. A. (2010). The mourning that comes before: Can anticipatory grief theory inform family care in adult intensive care? *International Journal of Palliative Nursing, 16,* 580–584.

Cooper, C., Selwood, A., & Livingston, G. (2008). Prevalence of elder abuse and neglect: A systematic review. *Age and Ageing, 37,* 151–160. doi:10.1093/ageing/afm194.

Corbett, B. A., & Hilty, D. M. (2006). Managing your time. In L. W. Roberts & D. M. Hilty (Eds.), *Handbook of career development in academic psychiatry and behavioral sciences* (pp. 83–91). Washington, DC: American Psychiatric Publishing.

Corr, C. A. (2010a). Children, development, and encounters with death, bereavement, and coping. In C. A. Corr & D. E. Balk (Eds.), *Children's encounters with death, bereavement, and coping* (pp. 3–19). New York: Springer

Corr, C. A. (2010b). Children's emerging awareness and understandings of loss and death. In C. A. Corr & D. E. Balk (Eds.), *Children's encounters with death, bereavement, and coping* (pp. 21–37). New York: Springer.

Corr, C. A., & Corr, D. M. (2013). *Death and dying: Life and living* (7th ed.). Belmont, CA: Wadsworth.

Corr, C. A., Corr, D. M., & Nabe, C. M. (2008). *Death and dying: Life and living.* Belmont, CA: Wadsworth.

Cosco, T. D., Stephan, B. C. M., & Brayne, C. (2013). Letter to the editor: On the success of the successful aging paradigm. *Journal of Applied Gerontology, 32,* 275–276. doi:10.1177/0733464813481562.

Costa, P. T., & McCrae, R. R. (1988). Personality in adulthood: A six-year longitudinal study of self-reports and spouse ratings on the NEO Personality Inventory. *Journal of Personality and Social Psychology, 54,* 853–863. doi:10.1037/0022-3514.54.5.853.

Costa, P. T., & McCrae, R. R. (1994). Set like plaster? Evidence for the stability of adult personality. In T. F. Heatherton & J. L. Weinberger

(Eds.), *Can personality change?* (pp. 21–40). Washington, DC: Academic Psychological Association.

Costa, P. T., & McCrae, R. R. (1997). Longitudinal stability of adult personality. In R. Hogan, J. Johnson, & S. Briggs (Eds.), *Handbook of personality psychology* (pp. 269–292). San Diego: Academic Press.

Costa, P. T., & McCrae, R. R. (1998). Six approaches to the explication of facet-level traits examples from conscientiousness. *European Journal of Personality, 12*, 117–134. doi:10.1002/(SICI)1099-0984(199803/04)12:2<117::AIDPER295>3.0.CO;2-C.

Costa, P. T., Jr., & McCrae, R. R. (2011). Five-factor theory, and interpersonal psychology. In L. M. Horowitz & S. Strack (Eds.), *Handbook of interpersonal psychology: Theory, research, assessment, and therapeutic interventions* (pp. 91–104). Hoboken, NJ: Wiley.

Cotter, R, P. (2003). High risk behaviors in adolescence and their relationship to death anxiety and death personifications. *Omega—Journal of Death and Dying, 47*, 119–137. doi:10.2190/38CT-ESMB-12NG-YXAR.

Cotter, V. T., & Gonzalez, E. W. (2009). Self-concept in older adults: An integrative review of empirical literature. *Holistic Nursing Practice, 23*, 335–348. doi:10.1097/HNP.0b013e3181bf37ea.

Cotton, S. R., Anderson, W. A., & McCullough, B. M. (2013). Impact of Internet use on loneliness and contact with others among older adults: Cross-sectional analysis. *Journal of Medical Internet Research, 15*, e 39. doi:10.2196/jmir.2306.

Counts, D., & Counts, D. (Eds.). (1985). *Aging and its transformations: Moving toward death in Pacific societies*. Lanham, MD: University Press of America.

Cowan, P. A., Cowan, C. P., & Knox, V. (2010). Marriage and fatherhood programs. *Fragile Families, 20*, 205–230. doi:10.1353/foc.2010.0000. Retrieved from https://www.future ofchildren.org/futureofchildren/ publications/docs/20_02_10.pdf.

Cox, C. (2013). Factors associated with the health and well-being of dementia caregivers. *Current Translational Geriatrics and Experimental Gerontology, 2*, 31–36. doi:10.1007 /s13670-012-0033-2.

Cox, C. B. (2007). Grandparent-headed families: Needs and implications for social work interventions and advocacy. *Families in Society, 88*, 561–566.

Cox, K., & McAdams, D. P. (2012). The transforming self: Service narratives and identity change in emerging adulthood. *Journal of Adolescent Research, 27*, 18–43. Doi: 10.1177/074355841038732.

Coyle, C. E., & Dugan, E. (2012). Social isolation, loneliness, and health among older adults. *Journal of Aging and Health, 24*, 1346–1363. doi:10.1177/0898264312460275.

Craik, F. I. M., & Rose, N. S. (2012). Memory encoding and aging: A neurocognitive approach. *Neuroscience and Biobehavioral Reviews, 36*,

1729–1739. doi:10.1016/j.neubio-rev.2011.11.007.

Crisp, R. J., & Turner, R. N. (2012). The imagined contact hypothesis. *Advances in Experimental Social Psychology, 46*, 125–182. doi:10.1016 /B978-0-12-394281-4.00003-0.

Crohan, S. E. (1996). Marital quality and conflict across the transition to parenthood in African American and white couples. *Journal of Marriage and Family, 58*, 933–944. doi:10.2307/353981.

Crohn, H. M. (2006). Five styles of positive stepmothering from the perspective of young adult stepdaughters. *Journal of Divorce & Remarriage, 46*, 119–134. doi:10.1300/ J087v46n01_07.

Cross, S., & Markus, H. (1991). Possible selves across the lifespan. *Human Development, 34*, 230–255. doi:10.1159/000277058.

Crown, W. (2001). Economic status of the elderly. In R. H. Binstock & L. K. George (Eds.), *Handbook of aging and the social sciences* (5th ed., pp. 352–368). San Diego. Academic Press.

Cruikshank, M. (2013). *Learning to be old: Gender, culture, and aging*. Lanham, MD: Rowman & Littlefield.

Cundiff, N. L., & Stockdale, M. S. (2013). Social psychological perspectives on discrimination against women leaders. In M. A. Paludi (Ed.), *Women and management: Global issues and promising solutions* (pp. 155–174). Santa Barbara, CA: ABC-CLIO.

Cunnane, S. C., Chouinard-Watkins, R., Castellano, C. A., & Barberger-Gateau, P. (2013). Docosahexaenoic acid homeostasis, brain aging and Alzheimer's disease: Can we reconcile the evidence? *Prostaglandins, Leukotrienes, and Essential Fatty Acids, 88*, 61–70. doi:10.1016/j. plefa.2012.04.006.

Cunningham, W. R. (1987). Intellectual abilities and age. In K. W. Schaie (Ed.), *Annual review of gerontology and geriatrics* (Vol. 7, pp. 117–134). New York: Springer.

Curl, A. L. (2007). The impact of retirement on trajectories of physical health of married couples. *Dissertation Abstracts International. Section A. Humanities and Social Sciences, 68(4-A)*, 1606.

Curtin, N., & Stewart, A. J. (2012). Linking personal and social histories with collective identity narratives. In S. Wiley, R. Philogène, & T. A. Revenson (Eds.), *Social categories in everyday experience* (pp. 83–102). Washington, DC: American Psychological Association.

Curtis, R., & Pearson, F. (2010). Contact with birth parents: Differential psychological adjustment for adults adopted as infants. *Journal of Social Work, 10*, 347–367. doi:10.1177/1468017310369273.

Dabelko-Shoeny, H. & King, S. (2010). In their own words: Participants' perceptions of the impact of adult day services. *Journal of Gerontological Social Work, 53*, 176–192. doi:10.1080/01634370903475936.

Dahlin, E., Stigsdotter Neely, A., Larsson, A., Bäckman, L., & Nyberg,

L. (2008). Transfer of learning after updating training mediated by the striatum. *Science, 320* (5882), 1510–1512. Doi: 10.1126/science .1155466.

Dahlin, E., Stigsdotter Neely, A., Larsson, A., Bäckman, L., & Nyberg, L. (2008). Transfer of learning after updating training mediated by the striatum. *Science, 320*, 1510–1512. doi:10.1126/science.1155466.

Dai, B., Zhang, B., & Li, J. (2013). Protective factors for subjective well-being in Chinese older adults: the roles of resources and activity. *Journal of Happiness Studies, 14*, 1225–1239. doi:10.1007/s10902-012-9378-7.

Dalton, C., & Harrison, J. D. (2012). Conceptualisation of an intelligent salutogenic room environment. In P. Breedon (Ed.), *Smart design* (pp. 87–95). New York: Springer.

Dalton, D. S., Cruickshanks, K. J., Klein, B. E. K., Klein, R., Wiley, T. L., & Nondahl, D. M. (2003). The impact of hearing loss on quality of life in older adults. *The Gerontologist, 43*, 661–668. doi:10.1093/ geront/43.5.661.

Dannar, P. R. (2013). Millennials: What they offer our organizations and how leaders can make sure they deliver. *Journal of Values-Based Leadership, 6*, Article 3. Retrieved from http:// scholar.valpo.edu/cgi/viewcontent .cgi?article=1073&context=jvbl.

DatingAbuseStopsHere.com. (2013). *Facts*. Retrieved from http://www .datingabusestopshere.com/facts/.

Davidson, R. J. (2010). Empirical explorations of mindfulness: Conceptual and methodological conundrums. *Emotion, 10*, 8–11. doi:10.1037/ a0018480.

Davies, L. (2003). Singlehood: Transitions within a gendered world. *Canadian Journal on Aging, 22*, 343–352. doi:10.1017 /S071498080000-4219.

Davies, P. G. (2007). Between health and illness. *Perspectives in Biology and Medicine, 50*, 444–452. doi:10.1353 /pbm.2007.0026.

Davis, B. W. (1985). *Visits to remember: A handbook for visitors of nursing home residents*. University Park, PA: Pennsylvania State University Cooperative Extension Service.

De Andrade, C. E. (2000). Becoming the wise woman: A study of women's journeys through midlife transformation. *Dissertation Abstracts International. Section B. Sciences and Engineering, 61(2-B)*, 1109.

de Bloom, J., Geurts, S. A. E., & Kompier, M. A. J. (2012). Effects of short vacations, vacation activities and experiences on employee health and well-being. *Stress and Health, 28*, 305–318. doi:10.1002/smi.1434.

de Bloom, J., Geurts, S. A. E., Taris, T. W., Sonnentag, S., de Weerth, C., & Kompier, M. A. J. (2010). Effects of vacation from work on health and well-being: Lots of fun, quickly gone. *Work and Stress, 24*, 196–216. doi:10. 1080/02678373.2010.493385.

de Frias, C. M., Dixon, R. A., & Bäckman, L. (2003). Use of memory compensation strategies is related to psychosocial and health indicators. *Journals of Gerontology: Psychological*

Sciences, 58B, P12–P22. doi:10.1093/ geronb/58.1.P12.

De Grip, A., Bosma, H., Willems, D., & van Boxtel, M. (2008). Job-worker mismatch and cognitive decline. *Oxford Economic Papers, 60*, 237–253. doi:10.1093/oep/gpm023.

De Jager, C. A. (2012). Vitamins and brain health. *Vitamin Trace Element, 1*, 3103. doi:10.4172/vte.100003103. Retrieved from http://omicsgroup. org/journals/VTE/VTE-1-e103.php.

De Jong, P., Rouwendal, J., van Hattum, P., & Brouwer, A. (2012). *Housing preferences of an ageing population: Investigation in the diversity among Dutch older adults*. Retrieved from http://arno.uvt.nl/show .cgi?fid=123055.

De la Monte, S. (2012). Brain insulin resistance and deficiency as therapeutic targets in Alzheimer's disease. *Current Alzheimer's Research, 9*, 35–66. doi:10.2174/156720512799015037.

de Lange, F. (2013). Imaging good aging. In M. Schermer & W. Pinxten (Eds.), *Ethics, health policy and (anti-) aging: Mixed blessings* (pp. 135–146). New York: Springer.

De Paula Couto, M. C. P., & Koller, S. H. (2012). Warmth and competence: Stereotypes of the elderly among young adults and older persons in Brazil. *International Perspectives in Psychology: Research, Practice, Consultation, 1*, 52–62. Doi: 10.1037 /a0027118.

de Pommereau, I. (2012). *How BMW reinvents the factory for older workers*. Retrieved from http://www .csmonitor.com/World /Europe/2012/0902/How-BMW -reinvents-the-factory-for-older -workers.

de Vries, B. (1996). The understanding of friendship: An adult life course perspective. In C. Magai & S. H. McFadden (Eds.), *Handbook of emotion, adult development, and aging* (pp. 249–268). San Diego: Academic Press.

DeAndrea, D. C., Ellison, N. B., LaRose, R., Steinfield, C., & Fiore, A. (2012). Serious social media: On the use of social media for improving students' adjustment to college. *The Internet and Higher Education, 15*, 15–23. doi:10.1016/j.iheduc.2011.05.009.

DeCarli, C., Kawas, C., Morrison, J. H., Reuter-Lorenz, P., Sperling, R. A., & Wright, C. B. (2012). Session II: Mechanisms of age-related cognitive change and targets for intervention: Neural circuits, networks, and plasticity. *The Journal of Gerontology: Biological Sciences and Medical Sciences, 67*, 747–753. doi:10.1093 /Gerona/gls111.

DeFries, E., & Andresen, E. (2010). Caregiving and health. In J. C. Cavanaugh & C. K. Cavanaugh (Eds.), *Aging in America: Volume 2: Physical and mental health* (pp. 81–99). Santa Barbara, CA: ABC-CLIO.

DeGroot, D. W., & Kenney, W. L. (2007) Impaired defense of core temperature in aged humans during mild cold stress. *American Journal of Physiology—Regulatory, Integrative, and Comparative Physiology, 292*,

R103–R108. doi:10.1152/ajp-regu.00074.2006.

del Zoppo, G. J. (2013). Plasminogen activators and ischemic stroke: Conditions for acute delivery. *Seminars in Thrombosis and Hemostasis, 39*, 406–25. doi:10.1055/s-0033-1338126.

Dellefield, M. E. (2008). Best practices in nursing homes: Clinical supervision, management, and human resources practices. *Research in Gerontological Nursing, 1*, 197–207. doi:10.3928/00220124-20091301-04.

Demir, M. (2010). Close relationships and happiness among emerging adults. *Journal of Happiness Studies, 11*, 293–313. doi:10.1007/s10902-009-9141-x.

Denney, N. W. (1984). A model of cognitive development across the life span. *Developmental Review, 4*, 171–191. doi:10.1016/0273-2287(84)90006-6.

Denney, N. W., Pearce, K. A., & Palmer, A. M. (1982). A developmental study of adults' performance on traditional and practical problem-solving tasks. *Experimental Aging Research, 8*, 115–118. doi:10.1080/03610738208258407.

DePaulo, B. M. (2006). *Singled out: How singles are stereotyped, stigmatized, and ignored, and still live happily ever after.* New York: St Martin's Press.

Derman, D. S. (2000). Grief and attachment in young widowhood. *Dissertation Abstracts International Section A: Humanities and Social Sciences, 60(7-A)*, 2383.

Desmond, N., & López Turley, R. N. (2009). The role of familism in explaining the Hispanic-white college application gap. *Social Problems, 56*, 311–334. doi:10.1525/sp.2009.56.2.311.

Deutsch, A. (2001, April 11). Dutch parliament OKs strict euthanasia bill. *Wilmington (NC) Morning Star.*

Dey, J. G., & Hill, C. (2007). *Behind the pay gap.* Washington, DC: American Association of University Women Educational Foundation.

Dickens, B. M., Boyle, J. M., Jr., & Ganzini, L. (2008). Euthanasia and assisted suicide. In P. A. Singer & A. M. Viens (Eds.), *The Cambridge textbook of bioethics* (pp. 72–77). New York: Cambridge University Press.

Diehl, M., Hay, E. L., & Chui, H. (2012). Personal risk and resilience factors in the context of daily stress. *Annual Review of Gerontology and Geriatrics, 32*, 251–274. doi:10.1891/0198-8794.32.251.

Diehl, M., Marsiske, M., Horgas, A. L., Rosenberg, A., Saczynski, J. S., & Willis, S. L. (2005). The Revised Observed Tasks of Daily Living: A performance-based assessment of everyday problem solving in older adults. *Journal of Applied Gerontology, 24*, 211–230. doi:10.1177/0733464804273772.

Diehl, M., Willis, S. L., & Schaie, K. W. (1995). Everyday problem solving in older adults: Observational assessment and cognitive correlates. *Psychology and Aging, 10*, 478–491. doi:10.1037/0882-7974.10.3.478.

Diersch, N., Cross, E. S., Stadler, W., Schütz-Bosbach, S., & Rieger, M.

(2012). Representing others' actions: The role of expertise in the aging mind. *Psychological Research, 76*, 525–541. doi:10.1007/s00426-011-0404-x.

Dillaway, H., Byrnes, M., Miller, S., & Rehnan, S. (2008). Talking "among us": How women from different racial-ethnic groups define and discuss menopause. *Health Care for Women International, 29*, 766–781. doi:10.1080/07399330802179247.

Dilworth-Anderson, P., Boswell, G., & Cohen, M. D. (2007). Spiritual and religious coping values and beliefs among African American caregivers: A qualitative study. *Journal of Applied Gerontology, 26*, 355–369. doi:10.1177/0733464807302669.

Dinsbach, A. A., Fiej, J. A., & de Vries, R. E. (2007). The role of communication content in an ethnically diverse organization. *International Journal of Intercultural Relations, 31*, 725–745. doi:10.1016/j.ijintrel.2007.08.001.

Dirk, J., & Schmiedek, F. (2012). Processing speed. In S. K. Whitbourne & M. J. Sliwinski (Eds.), *The Wiley-Blackwell handbook of adulthood and aging* (pp. 133–153). Oxford, U.K.: Wiley-Blackwell.

Disability Policy Research Working Group. (2011). *National stocktake of future planning initiatives for families of people with disability.* Retrieved from http://www.dprwg.gov.au/sites/default/files/attachments/national_stocktake_of_future_planning_initiatives.pdf.

Dismukes, R. K. (2012). Prospective memory in workplace and everyday situations. *Current Directions in Psychological Science, 21*, 215–220. doi:10.1177/0963721412447621.

Dixon, P. (2009). Marriage among African Americans: What does the research reveal? *Journal of African American Studies, 13*, 29–46. doi:10.1007/s12111-008-9062-5.

Dixon, R. A. (2011). Evaluating everyday competence in older adult couples: Epidemiological considerations. *Gerontology, 57*, 173–179. doi:10.1159/000320325.

Dixon, R. A., & Hultsch, D. F. (1999). Intelligence and cognitive potential in late life. In J. C. Cavanaugh & S. K. Whitbourne (Eds.), *Gerontology: An interdisciplinary perspective* (pp. 213–237). New York: Oxford University Press.

Dobbs, D., Eckert, J. K., Rubinstein, B., Keimig, L., Clark, L., Frankowski, A. C., & Zimmerman, S. (2008). An ethnographic study of stigma and ageism in residential care or assisted living. *The Gerontologist, 48*, 517–526. doi:10.1093/geront/48.4.517.

Dommaraju, P. (2010). *The changing demography of marriage in India.* Podcast retrieved from http://www.ari.nus.edu.sg/events_categorydetails.asp?categoryid=8&eventid=1030.

Donahue, P. J. (2007). Retirement reconceptualized: Forced retirement and its relationship to health. *Dissertation Abstracts International. Section A. Humanities and Social Sciences, 67(7-A)*, 2750.

Donnellan, M. B., & Lucas, R. E. (2008). Age differences in the Big Five across the life span: Evidence from two national samples. *Psychology and*

Aging, 23, 558–566. doi:10.1037/a0012897.

Doubeni, C. A., Schootman, M., Major, J. M., Torres Stone, R. A., Laiyemo, A. O., Park, Y., et al. (2012). Health status, neighborhood socioeconomic context, and premature mortality in the United States: The National Institutes of Health—AARP Diet and Health Study. *American Journal of Public Health, 102*, 680–688. doi:10.2105/AJPH.2011.300158.

Doyle, K. O., Jr. (1974). Theory and practice of ability testing in ancient Greece. *Journal of the History of the Behavioral Sciences, 10*, 202–212. doi:10.1002/1520-6696(197404)10:2<202: AID-JHBS2300100208>3.0.CO;2-Q.

DuBois, P. H. (1968). A test-dominated society: China 1115 B.C.–1905 A.D. In J. L. Barnette (Ed.), *Readings in psychological tests and measurements* (pp. 249–255). Homewood, IL: Dorsey Press.

Dugdale, D. C. (2012). *Aging changes in the male reproductive system.* Retrieved from http://www.nlm.nih.gov/medlineplus/ency/article/004017.htm.

Dulas, M. R., & Duarte, A. (2012). The effects of aging on material-independent and material-dependent neural correlates of source memory retrieval. *Cerebral Cortex, 22*, 37–50. doi:10.1093/cercor/bhr056.

Dumas, J. A., McDonald, B. C., Saykin, A. J., McAllister, T. W., Hynes, M. L., West, J. D., et al. (2010). Cholinergic modulation of hippocampal memory during episodic memory encoding in postmenopausal women: A pilot study. *Menopause, 17*, 852–859. doi:10.1097/gme.0b013e3181e04db9.

Dunlosky, J., Bailey, H., & Hertzog, C. (2011). Memory enhancement strategies: What works best for obtaining memory goals? In P. E. Hartman-Stein & A. La Rue (Eds.), *Enhancing cognitive fitness in adults* (pp. 3–23). New York: Springer.

Dunn, T. R., & Merriam, S. B. (1995). Levinson's age thirty transition: Does it exist? *Journal of Adult Development, 2*, 113–124. doi:10.1007/BF02251259.

Dupuis, S. (2010). Examining the blended family: The application of systems theory toward an understanding of the blended family system. *Journal of Couple and Relationship Therapy, 9*, 239–251. doi:10.1080/15332691.2010.491784.

Dutta, D., Calvani, R., Bernabei, R., Leeuwenburgh, C., & Marzetti, E. (2012). Contribution of impaired mitochondrial autophagy to cardiac aging: Mechanisms and therapeutic opportunities. *Circulation Research, 110*, 1125–1138. doi:10.1161/CIRCRESAHA.111.246108.

Dutton, W. H., Helsper, E. J., Whitty, M. T., Li, N., Buckwalter, J. G., & Lee, E. (2009). The role of the Internet in reconfiguring marriages: A cross-national study. *Interpersona: An International Journal on Personal Relationships, 3*(Suppl. 2). Retrieved from http://abpri.files.wordpress.com/2010/12/interpersona-3-suppl-2_1.pdf.

Dwivedi, Y., Rizavi, H. S., Conley, R. R., Roberts, R. C., Tamminga,

C. A., & Pandey, G. N. (2003). Altered gene expression of brain-derived neurotrophic factor and receptor tyrosine kinase B in post-mortem brain of suicide subjects. *JAMA Psychiatry, 60*, 804–815. doi:10.1001/archpsyc.60.8.804.

Earle, S., Komaromy, C., & Layne, L. (Eds.). (2012). *Understanding reproductive loss: Perspectives on life, death and fertility.* Farnham, UK: Ashgate.

Eastwick, P. W., Saigal, S. D., & Finkel, E. J. (2010). Smooth operating: A structural analysis of social behavior (SASB) perspective on initial romantic encounters. Retrieved from http://faculty.wcas.northwestern.edu/eli-finkel/documents/55_Eastwick SaigalFinkelInPress_SPPS.pdf.

Eaton, J., & Salari, S. (2005). Environments for lifelong learning in senior centers. *Educational Gerontology, 31*, 461–480. doi:10.1080/03601270590928189.

Ebner, N. C., Freund, A. M., & Baltes, P. B. (2006). Developmental changes in personal goal orientation from young to late adulthood: From striving for gains to maintenance and prevention of losses. *Psychology and Aging, 21*, 664–678. doi:10.1037/0882-7974.21.4.664.

Eddleston, K. A., Baldridge, D. C., & Veiga, J. F. (2004). Toward modeling the predictors of managerial career success: Does gender matter? *Journal of Managerial Psychology, 19*, 360–385. doi:10.1108/02683940410537936.

Edelstein, B., & Kalish, K. (1999). Clinical assessment of older adults. In J. C. Cavanaugh & S. K. Whitbourne (Eds.), *Gerontology: An interdisciplinary perspective* (pp. 269–304). New York: Oxford University Press.

Edwards, M. B. (2006). The relationship between the internal working model of attachment and patterns of grief experienced by college students after the death of a parent. *Dissertation Abstracts International Section A: Humanities and Social Sciences, 66(11-A)*, 4197.

Edwards, M. R. (2012). A temporal multifaceted adaptation approach to the experiences of employed mothers. *Marriage and Family Review, 48*, 732–760. doi:10.1080/01494929.2012.700911.

Effros, R. B. (2012). Stress and immune system aging. In S. Segerstrom (Ed.), *The Oxford handbook of psychoneuroimmunology* (pp. 63–76). New York: Oxford University Press.

Eichenbaum, H. *The cognitive neuroscience of memory: An introduction* (2nd ed.). New York: Oxford University Press.

Einstein, G. O., & McDaniel, M. A. (1990). Normal aging and prospective memory. *Journal of Experimental Psychology: Learning, Memory, and Cognition, 16*, 717–726. doi:10.1037/0278-7394.16.4.717.

Einstein, G. O., Earles, J. L., & Collins, H. M. (2002). Gaze aversion: Spared inhibition for visual distraction in older adults. *Journals of Gerontology: Psychological Sciences, 57B*, P65–P73. doi:10.1093/geronb/57.1.P65.

Ekerdt, D. J. (2010). Frontiers of research on work and retirement. *Journal of Gerontology:*

Social Sciences, 65(B), S69–S80. doi:10.1093/geronb/gbp109.

El Haber, N., Erbas, B., Hill, K. D., & Wark, J. D. (2008). Relationship between age and measures of balance, strength, and gait: Linear and non-linear analyses. *Clinical Science, 114*, 719–727. doi:10.1042/CS20070301.

Eldercare.gov. (2012). *Assisted living*. Retrieved from http://www.eldercare.gov/ELDERCARE.NET/Public/Resources/Factsheets/Assisted_Living.aspx.

Ellis, J. W. (2010). Yours, mine, ours? Why the Texas legislature should simplify caretaker consent capabilities for minor children and the implications of the addition of Chapter 34 to the Texas Family Code. *Texas Tech Law Review, 42*, 987. Retrieved from http://papers.ssrn.com/sol3/papers.cfm?abstract_id=1811045.

Emanuel, L. L. (2008). Advance directives. *Annual Review of Medicine, 59*, 187–198. doi:10.1146/annurev.med.58.072905.062804.

Employee Benefits Research Institute. (2013). *2013 Retirement Confidence Survey*. Retrieved from http://www.ebri.org/files/Final-FS.RCS-13.FS_4.Age.FINAL.pdf.

Enslin, C. (2007). Women in organizations: A phenomenological study of female executives mentoring junior women in organizations. *Dissertation Abstracts International. Section A. Humanities and Social Sciences, 68(4-A)*, 1692.

Epel, E. (2012). How "reversible" is telomeric aging? *Cancer Prevention Research, 5*, 1163–1168. doi:10.1158/1940-6207.CAPR-12-0370.

Equal Employment Opportunity Commission. (2010). *Sexual harassment charges: EEOC and FEPAs combined: FY1997-FY2009*. Retrieved from http://www.eeoc.gov/eeoc/statistics/enforcement/sexual_harassment.cfm.

Erber, J. T., & Long, B. A. (2006). Perceptions of forgetful and slow employees: Does age matter? *Journal of Gerontology: Psychological Sciences, 61*, P333–P339.

Erber, J. T., & Prager, I. G. (1999). Perceptions of forgetful young and older adults. In T. M. Hess & F. Blanchard-Fields (Eds.), *Social cognition and aging* (pp. 197–217). San Diego: Academic Press.

Erber, J. T., & Szuchman, L. T. (2002). Age and capability: The role of forgetting and personal traits. *International Journal of Aging and Human Development, 54(3)*, 173–189. doi:10.2190/H5KN-N1PF-RLCY-V6A6.

Erber, J. T., Szuchman, L. T., & Rothberg, S. T. (1990). Everyday memory failure: Age differences in appraisal and attribution. *Psychology and Aging, 5*, 236–241. doi:10.1037/0882-7974.5.2.236.

Erickson, K. I., Gildengers, A. G., & Butters, M. A. (2013). Physical activity and brain plasticity in late adulthood. *Dialogues in Clinical Neuroscience, 15*, 99–108. Open source, retrieved from http://www.ncbi.nlm.nih.gov/pmc/articles/PMC3622473/.

Erickson, K. I., Prakash, R. S., Voss, M. W., Chaddock, L., Hu, L., Morris, K. S., et al. (2009). Aerobic fitness is associated with hippocampal volume in elderly humans. *Hippocampus, 19*, 1030–1039. doi:10.1002/hipo.20547.

Erikson, E. H. (1968). *Identity: Youth and crisis*. New York: Norton.

Erikson, E. H. (1982). *The life cycle completed: Review*. New York: Norton.

Etezadi, S., & Pushkar, D. (2013). Why are wise people happier? An explanatory model of wisdom and emotional well-being in older adults. *Journal of Happiness Studies, 14*, 929–950. doi:10.1007/s10902-012-9362-2.

European Association for Palliative Care. (2011). *The EAPC ethics task force on palliative care and euthanasia*. Retrieved from http://www.eapcnet.eu/Themes/Ethics/PCeuthanasiataskforce/tabid/232/Default.aspx.

Everingham, C., Warner-Smith, P., & Byles, J. (2007). Transforming retirement: Re-thinking models of retirement to accommodate the experiences of women. *Women's Studies International Forum, 30*, 512–522. doi:10.1016/j.wsif.2007.09.006.

Eyler, A. E., Wilcox, S., Matson-Koffman, D., Evenson, K. R., Sanderson, B., Thompson, J., et al. (2002). Correlates of physical activity among women from diverse racial/ethnic groups. *Journal of Women's Health and Gender Based Medicine, 11*, 239–253. doi:10.1089/152460902753668448.

Faber, A. J. (2004). Examining remarried couples through a Bowenian family systems lens. *Journal of Divorce & Remarriage, 40*, 121–133. doi:10.1300/J087v40n03_08.

Facal, D., Juncos-Rabadán, O., Rodríguez, M. S., & Pereiro, A. X. (2012). Tip-of-the-tongue in aging: Influence of vocabulary, working memory and processing speed. *Aging Clinical Experimental Research, 24*, 647–656. doi:10.3275/8586.

Fairlie, H. (1988). Talkin' bout my generation. *New Republic, 198*, 19–22.

Fajgenbaum, D., Chesson, B., & Lanzl, R. G. (2012). Building a network of grief support on college campuses: A national grassroots initiative. *Journal of College Student Psychotherapy, 26*, 99–120. doi:10.1080/87568225.2012.659159.

Fauth, E. B., Zarit, S. H., & Malmberg, B. (2008). Mediating relationships within the Disablement Process model: A cross-sectional study of the oldest-old. *European Journal of Aging, 5*, 161–179. doi:10.1007/s10433-008-0092-6.

Fein, E., & Schneider, S. (2013). *Not your mother's rules: the new secrets for dating*. New York: Grand Central Publishing.

Feinberg, L., Reinhard, S. C., Houser, A., & Choula, R. (2011). *Valuing the invaluable: The growing contributions and costs of family caregiving*. Retrieved from http://assets.aarp.org/rgcenter/ppi/ltc/i51-caregiving.pdf.

Feldman, H. H., Jacova, C., Robillard, A., Garcia, A., Chow, T., Borrie, M., Schipper, H. M., Blair, M., Kertesz, A., & Chertkow, H. (2008). Diagnosis and treatment of dementia: 2. Diagnosis. *Canadian Medical Association Journal, 178*, 825–836. doi:10.1503/cmaj.070798. Retrieved from http://www.canadianmedicaljournal.ca/content/178/7/825.full.

Feldman, K. (2010). *Post parenthood redefined: Race, class, and family structure differences in the experience of launching children*. Doctoral dissertation completed at Case Western Reserve University. Retrieved from http://etd.ohiolink.edu/send-pdf.cgi/Feldman%20Karie%20Ellen.pdf?case1267730564.

Feltz, A., & Samayoa, S. (2012). Heuristics and life-sustaining treatments. *Journal of Bioethical Inquiry, 9*, 443–455. doi:10.1007/s11673-012-9396-5.

Femia, E. E., Zarit, S. H., & Johansson, B. (2001). The disablement process in very late life: A study of the oldest-old in Sweden. *Journals of Gerontology: Psychological Sciences, 56B*, P12–P23. doi:10.1093/geronb/56.1.P12.

Feng, Z., Fennell, M. L., Tyler, D. A. Clark, M., & Mor, V. (2011). Growth of racial and ethnic minorities in US nursing homes driven by demographics and possible disparities in options. *Health Affairs, 30*, 1358–1365. doi:10.1377/hithaff.2011.0126.

Ferrarini, T., & Norström, T. (2010). Family policy, economic development, and infant mortality: A longitudinal comparative analysis. *International Journal of Social Welfare, 19*, S89–S102. doi:10.1111/j.1468-2397.2010.00736.x.

Field, M. J., & Cassel, C. K. (2010). Approaching death: Improving care at the end of life. In D. Meier, S. L. Isaacs, & R. G. Hughes (Eds.), *Palliative care: Transforming the care of serious illness* (pp. 79–91). San Francisco: Jossey-Bass.

Fincham, F. D. (2003). Marital conflict: Correlates, structure, and context. *Current Directions in Psychological Science, 12*, 23–27. doi:10.1111/1467-8721.01215.

Fincham, F. D., & Beach, S. R. H. (2010). Marriage in the new millennium: A decade in review. *Journal of Marriage and Family, 72*, 630–649. doi:10.1111/j.1741-3737.2010.00722.x.

Fingerman, K. L., Pillemer, K. A., Silverstein, M., & Suitor, J. J. (2012). The baby boomers' intergenerational relationships. *The Gerontologist, 52*, 199–209. doi:10.1093/geront/gnr139.

Fischer-Shofty, M., Levkovitz, Y., & Shamay-Tsoory, S. G. (2013). Oxytocin facilitates accurate perception of competition in men and kinship in women. *Social Cognitive and Affective Neuroscience*. doi:10.1093/scan/nsr100.

Fisher, G., Plassman, B., Heeringa, S., Langa, K. (2008). Assessing the relationship of cognitive aging and processes of dementia. In S. M. Hofer & D. F. Alwin (Eds.), *Handbook of cognitive aging: Interdisciplinary perspectives* (pp. 340–351). Greenwich, CT: Sage.

Fisher, J. E., Drossel, C., Ferguson, K., Cherup, S., & Sylvester, M. (2008). Treating persons with dementia in context. In D. Gallagher-Thompson, A. M. Steffen, & L. W. Thompson (Eds.), *Handbook of behavioral and cognitive therapies with older adults* (pp. 200–218). New York: Springer.

Fisher, L. L. (2010). Sex, romance, and relationships: AARP survey of midlife and older adults. Retrieved from http://assets.aarp.org/rgcenter/general/srr_09.pdf.

Fitzgerald, J. M. (1999) Autobiographical memory and social cognition: Development of the remembered self in adulthood. In T. M. Hess & F. Blanchard-Fields, *Social cognition in aging* (pp. 147–171). San Diego: Academic Press.

Fitzwater, E. L. (2008). *Older adults and mental health: Part 2: Anxiety disorder*. Retrieved from http://www.netwellness.org/healthtopics/aging/anxietydisorder.cfm.

Flynn, E., Pine, K., & Lewis, C. (2006). The microgenetic method: Time for change? *The Psychologist, 19*, 152–155. Retrieved from http://www.thepsychologist.org.uk/archive/archive_home.cfm/volumeID_19-editionID_133-ArticleID_997-getfile_getPDF/thepsychologist/0306flyn.pdf.

Flynn, H. K. (2007). Friendship: A longitudinal study of friendship characteristics, life transitions, and social factors that influence friendship quality. *Dissertation Abstracts International. Section A. Humanities and Social Sciences, 67(9-A)*, 3608.

Fogarty, K., & Evans, G. D. (2010). Being an involved father: What does it mean? Retrieved from http://edis.ifas.ufl.edu/he141.

Fossati, P. (2012). Neural correlates of emotion processing: From emotional to social brain. *European Neuropsychopharmacology, 22 (Suppl. 3)*, S487–S491. doi:10.1016/j.euroneuro.2012.07.008.

Foster, B. P., Lonial, S., & Shastri, T. (2011). Mentoring, career plateau tendencies, turnover intentions and implications for narrowing pay and position gaps due to gender—Structural equations modeling. *Journal of Applied Business Research, 27*. Retrieved from http://www.journals.cluteonline.com/index.php/JABR/article/view/6467/6545.

Foubert-Samier, A., Catheline, G., Amieva, H., Dilharreguy, B., Helmer, C., Allard, M. et al., (2012). Education, occupation, leisure activities, and brain reserve: A population-based study. *Neurobiology of Aging, 33*, 423.e15-423.e25. doi:10.1016/j.neurobiolaging.2010.09.023.

Fowler, K. L. (2008). "The wholeness of things": Infusing diversity and social justice into death education. *Omega: Journal of Death and Dying, 57*, 53–91. doi:10.2190/OM.57.1.d.

Franceschi, K. A. (2005). The experience of the transition to motherhood in women who have suffered maternal loss in adolescence. *Dissertation Abstracts International: Section B: The Sciences and Engineering, 65(8-B)*, 4282.

Frase, P., & Gornick, J. C. (2013). The time divide in cross-national perspective: The work week, education and institutions that matter. *Social*

Forces, *91*, 697–724. doi:10.1093/sf/sos189.

Frazier, L. D., Hooker, K., Johnson, P. M., & Kaus, C. R. (2000). Continuity and change in possible selves in later life: A 5-year longitudinal study. *Basic and Applied Social Psychology, 22*, 237–243. doi:10.1207/S15324834BASP2203_10.

Frazier, L. D., Johnson, P. M., Gonzalez, G. K., & Kafka, C. L. (2002) Psychosocial influences on possible selves: A comparison of three cohorts of older adults. *International Journal of Behavioral Development, 26*, 308–317. doi:10.1080/01650250143000184.

Freitas, A. A., & de Magalhães, J. P. (2011). A review and appraisal of the DNA damage theory of aging. *Mutation Research/Reviews in Mutation Research, 728*, 12–22. doi:10.1016/j.mrrev.2011.06.01.

Fretz, B. R. (2001). Coping with licensing, credentialing, and lifelong learning. In S. Walfish & A. K. Hess (Eds.), *Succeeding in graduate school: The career guide for psychology students* (pp. 353–367). Mahwah, NJ: Erlbaum.

Freund, A. M., & Baltes, P. B. (2002). The adaptiveness of selection, optimization, and compensation as strategies of life management: Evidence from a preference study on proverbs. *Journals of Gerontology: Psychological Sciences, 57B*, P426–P434. doi:10.1093/geronb/57.5.P426.

Freund, A. M., & Ritter, J. O. (2009). Midlife crisis: A debate. *Gerontology, 55*, 582–591. doi:10.1159/000227322.

Friedman, E. M., & Seltzer, J. A. (2010). *Providing for older parents: Is it a family affair?* California Center for Population Research paper #PWP-CCPR-2010-12. Retrieved from http://www.n4a.org/pdf/PWP-CCPR-2010-012.pdf.

Frith, C. D., & Frith, U. (2012). Mechanisms of social cognition. *Annual Review of Social Cognition, 63*, 287–313. doi:10.1146/annurev-psych-120710-100449.

Froman, L. (2010). Positive psychology in the workplace. *Journal of Adult Development, 17*, 59–69. doi:10.1007/s10804-009-9080-0.

Fruhauf, C. A. (2007). Grandchildren's perceptions of caring for grandparents. *Dissertation Abstracts International. Section A. Humanities and Social Sciences, 68(3-A)*, 1120.

Frye, K. L. (2008). Perceptions of retirement and aging as experienced by self-identified lesbians ages 51 through 60. *Dissertation Abstracts International. Section B. Sciences and Engineering, 68(7-B)*, 4886.

Fuentealba, L. C., Obernier, K., & Alvarez-Buylla, A. (2012). Adult neural stem cells bridge their niche. *Cell Stem Cell, 10*, 698–708. doi:10.1016/j.stem.2012.05.012.

Fuentes, A., & Desrocher, M. (2012). Autobiographical memory in emerging adulthood: Relationship with self-concept clarity. *Journal of Adult Development, 19*, 28–39. doi:10.1007/s10804-011-9131-1.

Fuller-Thompson, E., Hayslip, B., Jr., & Patrick, J. H. (2005). Introduction to the special issue: Diversity among grandparent caregivers.

International Journal of Aging & Human Development, 60, 269–272. doi:10.2190/J6UE-PKMP-UDWL-YBT1.

Gabriel, Y., Gray, D. E., & Goregaokar, H. (2013). Job loss and its aftermath among managers and professionals: Wounded, fragmented and flexible. *Work, Employment and Society, 27*, 56–72. doi:10.1177/0950017012460326.

Galenkamp, H., Deeg, D. J. H., Braam, A. W., & Huisman, M. (2013). "How was your health 3 years ago?" Predicting mortality in older adults using a retrospective change measure of self-rated health. *Geriatrics and Gerontology International, 13*, 678–686. doi:10.1111/j.1447-0594.2012.00963.x

Gallagher-Thompson, D., Coon, D. W., Solano, N., Ambler, C., Rabinowitz, Y., & Thompson, L. W. (2003). Change in indices of distress among Latino and Anglo female caregivers of elderly relatives with dementia: Site-specific results from the REACH national collaborative study. *The Gerontologist, 43*, 580–591. doi:10.1093/geront/43.4.580.

Gamble, W. C., Ramakumar, S., & Diaz, A. (2007). Maternal and paternal similarities and differences in parenting: An examination of Mexican-American parents of young children. *Early Childhood Research Quarterly, 22*, 72–88. doi:10.1016/j.ecresq.2006.11.004.

Gandy, S., & DeKosky, S. T. (2013). Toward the treatment and prevention of Alzheimer's disease: Rational strategies and recent progress. *Annual Review of Medicine, 64*, 367–383. doi:10.1146/annurev-med-092611-084441.

Ganiron, E. E. (2007). Mutuality and relationship satisfaction in the formation of lesbian relationships across the life cycle: Unpacking the U-Haul myth. *Dissertation Abstracts International. Section B. Sciences and Engineering, 68(3-B)*, 1924.

Gans, D. (2007). Normative obligations and parental care in social context. *Dissertation Abstracts International. Section A. Humanities and Social Sciences, 68(5-A)*, 2115.

Garcia, J. R., Reiber, C., Massey, S. G., & Merriwether, A. M. (2013). Sexual hook-up culture. *Monitor on Psychology, 44*, 60–67.

Gardiner, J., Stuart, M., Forde, C., Greenwood, I., MacKenzie, R., & Perrett, R. (2007). Work-life balance and older workers: Employees' perspectives on retirement transitions following redundancy. *International Journal of Human Resource Management, 18*, 476–489. doi:10.1080/09585190601167904.

Gardner, B. K., & O'Connor, D. W. (2008). A review of the cognitive effects of electroconvulsive therapy in older adults. *Journal of ECT, 24*, 68–80. doi:10.1097/YCT.0b013e318165c7b0.

Garrard, J., & Wilkinson, S. (2005). Passive euthanasia. *Journal of Medical Ethics, 31*, 64–68. doi:10.1136/jme.2003.005777.

Gaudron, J.-P., & Vautier, S. (2007). Analyzing individual differences in vocational, leisure, and family interests: A multitrait-multimethod

approach. *Journal of Vocational Behavior, 70*, 561–573. doi:10.1016/j.jvb.2007.01.004.

Gaugler, J. E., Kane, R. L., & Newcomer, R. (2007). Resilience and transitions from dementia caregiving. *Journal of Gerontology: Psychological Sciences, 62*, P38–P44.

Gay Men's Health Crisis. (2010). *Growing older with the epidemic: HIV and aging.* Retrieved from http://www.gmhc.org/files/editor/file/a_pa_aging10_emb2.pdf.

Georgia Health Care Association. (2012). *Choosing a nursing home.* Retrieved from http://www.ghca.info/index.php?option=com_content&view=article&id=19&Item id=10.

Gerontological Society of America. (2012). *Communicating with older adults: An evidence-based review of what really works.* Washington, DC: Author.

Giarrusso, R., Feng, D., Silverstein, M., & Marenco, A. (2000). Primary and secondary stressors of grandparents raising grandchildren: Evidence from a national survey. *Journal of Mental Health and Aging, 6*, 291–310.

Gibbs, N. R. (1988). Grays on the go. *Time, 131*(8), 66–75.

Giele, J. Z. (2013). *Family policy and the American safety net.* Thousand Oaks, CA: Sage Publications.

Gilbert, D. T., & Malone, P. S. (1995). The correspondence bias. *Psychological Bulletin, 117*, 21–38. doi:10.1037/0033-2909.117.1.21.

Gillick, M. R. (2012). Doing the right thing: A geriatrician's perspective on medical care for the person with advanced dementia. *The Journal of Law, Medicine and Ethics, 40*, 51–56. doi:10.1111/j.1748-720X.2012.00645.x.

Gilliver, M., Carter, L., Macoun, D., Rosen, J., & Williams, W. (2012). Music to whose ears? The effect of social norms on young people's risk perceptions of hearing damage resulting from their music listening behavior. *Noise and Health, 14*, 47–51. Retrieved from http://www.noiseandhealth.org/article.asp?issn=1463-1741;year=2012;volume=14;issue=57;spage=47;epage=51;aulast=Gilliver.

Giovanello, K. S., & Schacter, D. L. (2012). Reduced specificity of hippocampal and posterior ventrolateral prefrontal activity during relational retrieval in normal aging. *Journal of Cognitive Neuroscience, 24*, 159–170. doi:10.1162/jocn_a_00013.

Githens, R., & Sauer, T. (2010). Going green online: Distance learning prepares students for success in green-collar job markets. *Community College Journal, 80*, 32–35.

Gitlin, L. N., Kales, H. C., & Lyketsos, C. G. (2012). Nonpharmacological management of behavioral symptoms in dementia. *JAMA, 308*, 2020–2029. doi:10.1001/jama.2012.36918.

Givertz, M., Segrin, C., & Hansal, A. (2009). The association between satisfaction and commitment differs across marital couple types. *Communication Research, 36*, 561–584. doi:10.1177/0093650209333035.

Gladding, S. T. (2002). *Family therapy: History, theory, and practice* (3rd

ed.). Upper Saddle River, NJ: Merrill Prentice Hall.

Goh, J. O., & Park, D. C. (2009). Neuroplasticity and cognitive aging: The scaffolding theory of aging and cognition. *Restorative and Neurological Neuroscience, 27*, 391–403. doi:10.3233/RNN-2009-0493. Retrieved from http://www.ncbi.nlm.nih.gov/pmc/articles/PMC3355602/.

Golant, S. M. (2008a). The future of assisted living residences: A response to uncertainty. In S. M. Golant & J. Hyde (Eds.), *The assisted living residence: A vision for the future* (pp. 3–45). Baltimore: The Johns Hopkins University Press.

Golant, S. M. (2008b). Affordable clustered housing-care: A category of long-term care options for the elderly poor. *Journal of Housing for the Elderly, 22*, 3–44. doi:10.1080/027638908802096906.

Golant, S. M. (2011). The quest for residential normalcy by older adults: Relocation but one pathway. *Journal of Aging Studies, 25*, 193–205. doi:10.1016/j.jaging.2011.03.003.

Golant, S. M. (2012). Out of their residential comfort and mastery zones: toward a more relevant environmental gerontology. *Journal of Housing for the Elderly, 26*, 26–43. doi:10.1080/02766389.2012.655654.

Gold, D. A. (2012). An examination of instrumental activities of daily living assessment in older adults and mild cognitive impairment. *Journal of Clinical and Experimental Neuropsychology, 34*, 1–34. doi:10.1080/13803395.2011.614598.

Goldberg, A. E. (2009). *Lesbian and gay parents and their children: Research on the family life cycle.* Washington, DC: American Psychological Association.

Goldstein, D. (2012). Role of aging on innate responses to viral infections. *Journal of Gerontology. Biological Sciences, 67A*, 242–246. doi:10.1093/gerona/glr194.

Goldstein, E. G. (2005). *When the bubble bursts: Clinical perspectives on midlife issues.* New York: Routledge.

Gonyea, J. G. (2013). Midlife, multigenerational bonds, and caregiving. In R. C. Talley & R. J. V. Montgomery (Eds.), *Caregiving across the lifespan* (pp. 105–130). New York: Springer.

Goodwin, P.Y., Mosher, W. D., & Chandra, A. (2010). *Marriage and cohabitation in the United States: A statistical portrait based on Cycle 6 (2002) of the National Survey of Family Growth.* Retrieved from http://www.cdc.gov/nchs/data/series/sr_23/sr23_028.pdf.

Góra, M., & Mach, Z. (2010). Between old fears and new challenges: The Polish debate on Europe. In J. Lacroix & K. Nicholaïdis. *European stories: Intellectual debates on Europe in national contexts.* (pp. 221–240). Oxford, UK: Oxford University Press.

Gordon, T. A. (2013). Good grief: Exploring the dimensionality of grief experiences and social work support. *Journal of Social Work in End-of-Life and*

Palliative Care, 9, 27–42. doi: 10.1080/15524256.2012.758607.

Gorman, E. H., & Kmec, J. A. (2007). We (have to) try harder: Gender and required work effort in Britain and the United States. *Gender & Society, 21,* 828–856. doi: 10.1177/0891243207309900.

Goronzy, J. J., & Weyand, C. M. (2012). Immune aging and autoimmunity. *Cellular and Molecular Life Sciences, 69,* 1615–1623. doi: 10.1007/s00018-012-0970-0.

Gottman, J. M., & Levenson, R. W. (2004). The timing of divorce: Predicting when a couple will divorce over a 14-year period. *Journal of Marriage and the Family, 62,* 737–745. doi: 10.1111/j.1741-3737.2000.00737.x

Gouin, J.-P., Glaser, R., Malarkey, W. B., Beversdorf, D., & Kiecolt-Glaser, J. (2012). Chronic stress, daily stressors, and circulating inflammatory markers. *Health Psychology, 31,* 264–268. doi: 10.1037/a0025536.

Gould, C. E., Edelstein, B. A., & Gerolimatos, L. A. (2012). Assessment of older adults. In S. K. Whitbourne & M. J. Sliwinski (Eds.), *The Wiley-Blackwell handbook of adulthood and aging* (pp. 331–354). Oxford, UK: Wiley-Blackwell. doi: 10.1002/9781118392966.ch17.

Gould, S. J. (1999). A critique of Heckhausen and Schulz's (1995) life-span theory of control from a cross-cultural perspective. *Psychological Review, 106,* 597–604. doi: 10.1037/033-295X.106.3.597.

Government Equalities Office. (2013). *Equality Act 2010: Guidance.* Retrieved from https://www.gov.uk /equality-act-2010-guidance.

Grady, C. (2012). The cognitive neuroscience of ageing. *Nature Reviews Neuroscience, 13,* 491–505. doi: 10.1038/nrn3256.

Graham, E. K., & Lachman, M. E. (2012). Personality and aging. In S. K. Whitbourne & M. J. Sliwinski (Eds.), *The Wiley-Blackwell handbook of adulthood and aging* (pp. 254–272). Oxford, UK: Wiley-Blackwell.

Granacher, U., Muehlbauer, T., & Gruber, M. (2012). A qualitative review of balance and strength performance in healthy older adults: Impact for testing and training. *Journal of Aging Research, 2012.* doi:10.1155/2012/708905. Retrieved from http://www.hindawi.com /journals/jar/2012/708905/.

Grant, B. F., Dawson, D. A., Stinson, F. S., Chou, S. P., Dufour, M. C., & Pickering, R. P. (2004). The 12-month prevalence and trends in DSM-IV alcohol abuse and dependence: United States, 1991–1992 and 2001–2002. *Drug and Alcohol Dependence, 74,* 223–234. doi:10.1016/j.drugalcdep.2004.02.004.

Green, J. S. (2008). *Beyond the good death: An anthropology of modern dying.* Baltimore, MD: University of Pennsylvania Press.

Greenberg, D. L. (2004). President Bush's false [flashbulb] memory of 9/11/01. *Applied Cognitive Psychology, 18,* 363–370. doi:10.1002/acp.1016.

Greenfield, E. A., & Marks, N. F. (2005). Formal volunteering as a protective factor for older adults' psychological well-being. *Journals of Gerontology: Social Sciences, 59,* S258–S264. doi:10.1093/ geronb/59.5.S258.

Gretebeck, R. J., Ferraro, K. F., Black, D. R., Holland, K., & Gretebeck, K. A. (2012). Longitudinal change in physical activity and disability in adults. *American Journal of Health Behavior, 36,* 385–394. doi:10.5993 /AJHB.36.3.9.

Greving, K. A. (2007). Examining parents' marital satisfaction trajectories: Relations with children's temperament and family demographics. *Dissertation Abstracts International. Section A. Humanities and Social Sciences, 68(4-A),* 1676.

Grey, R. (1756). *Memoria technica* (4th ed.). London: Hinton.

Groger, L. (1995). A nursing home can be a home. *Journal of Aging Studies, 9,* 137–153. doi:10.1016/0890-4065(95)90008-X.

Groger, L. (2002). Coming to terms: African-Americans' complex ways of coping with life in a nursing home. *The International Journal of Aging and Human Development, 55,* 183–205. doi:10.2190/MDLP-UDE7-P376-QXE3.

Gross, A. L., Parisi, J. M., Spira, A. P., Kueider, A. M., Ko, J. Y., Saczynski, J. S. et al. (2012). Memory training interventions for older adults: A meta-analysis. *Aging and Mental Health, 16,* 722–734. doi:10.1080/136 07863.2012.667783.

Grossman, I., Karasawa, M., Izumi, S., Na, J., Varnum, M. E. W., Kitayama, S. et al. (2012). Aging and wisdom: Culture matters. *Psychological Science, 23,* 1059–1066. doi:10.1177/0956797612446025.

Gruenewald, T. L., Liao, D. H., & Seeman, T. E. (2012). Contributing to others, contributing to oneself: Perceptions of generativity and health in later life. *Journal of Gerontology: Psychological Sciences, 67,* 660–665. doi:10.1093/geronb /gbs034.

Grühn, D., Lumley, M. A., Diehl, M., Labouvie-Vief, G. (2013). Time-based indicators of emotional complexity: Interrelations and correlates. *Emotion, 13,* 226–237. doi:10.1037 /a0030363.

Grühn, D., Smith, J., & Baltes, P. B. (2005). No aging bias favoring memory for positive material: Evidence from a heterogeneity-homogeneity list paradigm using emotionally toned words. *Psychology and Aging, 20,* 579–588. doi:10.1037/0882-7974.20.4.579.

Gruneir, A., Lapane, K. L., Miller, S. C., & Mor, V. (2008a). Is dementia special care really special? A new look at an old question. *Journal of the American Geriatrics Society, 56,* 199–205. doi:10.1111/j.1532-5415.2007.01559.x.

Gruneir, A., Lapane, K. L., Miller, S. C., & Mor, V. (2008b). Does the presence of a dementia special care unit improve nursing home quality? *Journal of Aging and Health, 20,* 837–854. doi:10.1177/0898264308324632.

Gu, X., Liu, X., Van Dam, N. T., Hof, P. R., & Fan, J. (2013). Cognition-emotion integration in the anterior insular cortex. *Cerebral Cortex, 23,* 20–27. doi:10.1093/cercor/bhr367.

Gubernskaya, Z. (2010). Changing attitudes toward marriage and children in six countries. *Sociological Perspectives, 53,* 179–200. doi:10.1525/sop.2010.53.2.179.

Guergova, S., & Dufour, A. (2011). Thermal sensitivity in the elderly: A review. *Ageing Research Reviews, 10,* 80–92. doi:10.1016/j.arr.2010.04.009.

Guiaux, M. (2010). *Social adjustment to widowhood: Changes in personal relationships and loneliness before and after partner loss.* Doctoral dissertation completed at Vrije Universiteit Amsterdam. Retrieved from http://dspace.ubvu.vu.nl /bitstream/1871/17427/2/2010%20 PhD%20Dissertation%20 Guiaux.pdf.

Guidotti Breting, L. M., Tuminello, E. R., & Han, S. D. (2012). Functional neuroimaging studies in normal aging. In M.-C. Pardon & M. W. Bondi (Eds.), *Current topics in behavioral neurosciences: Vol. 10. Behavioral neurobiology of aging* (pp. 91–111). New York: Springer.

Guilford, J. P. (1959). *Personality.* New York: McGraw-Hill.

Guralnik, J. M. (2008). Successful aging: Is it in our future? *Archives of Internal Medicine, 168,* 131–132. doi:10.1001/archinternmed.2007.11.

Haber, D. (2013). *Health promotion and aging: Practical applications for health professionals* (6th ed.). New York: Springer.

Hacker, N., Messer, W. S., & Bachmann, K. A. (2009). *Pharmacology: Principles and practice.* New York: Elsevier.

Haier, R. J., Schroeder, D. H., Tang, C., Head, K., & Colom, R. (2010). Gray matter correlates of cognitive ability tests used for vocational guidance. *BMC Research Notes, 3.* Retrieved from http://www.biomedcentral .com/1756-0500/3/206.

Hains, C.-A. M., & Hulbert-Williams, N. J. (in press). Attitudes toward euthanasia and physician-assisted suicide: A study of the multivariate effects of healthcare training, patient characteristics, religion and locus of control. *Journal of Medical Ethics.* doi:10.1136/medethics-2012-100729.

Hainselin, M., Quinette, P., Desgranges, B., Martinaud, O., De La Sayette, V., Hannequin, D. et al. (2012). Awareness of disease state without explicit knowledge of memory failure in transient global amnesia. *Cortex, 48,* 1079–1084. doi:10.1016/j.cortex.2012.02.003.

Hairault, J.-O., Langot, F., & Zylberberg, A. (2012). Equilibrium unemployment and retirement. IZA Discussion Paper No. 6511. Retrieved from http://papers.ssrn.com/sol3/papers .cfm?abstract_id=2051354.

Haley, W. E. (2013). Family caregiving at the end-of-life: Current status and future directions. In R. C. Talley & R. J. V Montgomery (Eds.), *Caregiving across the lifespan* (pp. 157–175). New York: Springer.

Halford, W. K., & Bodenmann, G. (2013). Effects of relationship education on maintenance of couple relationship satisfaction. *Clinical Psychology Review, 33,* 512–525. doi:10.1016/j.cpr.2013.02.001.

Halford, W. K., Markman, H. J., & Stanley, S. (2008). Strengthening couples' relationships with education: Social policy and public health perspectives. *Journal of Family Psychology, 22,* 497–505. doi:10.1037 /a0012789.

Hall, S. S. (2006). Marital meaning: exploring young adult's belief systems about marriage. *Journal of Family Issues, 27,* 1437–1458. doi:10.1177/0192513X06290036.

Hammar, M., & Östgren, C. J. (2013). Healthy aging and age-adjusted nutrition and physical fitness. *Best Practices and Research Clinical Obstetrics and Gynaecology, 27,* 741–752. doi:10.1016/j.bpobgyn.2013.01.004.

Hansen, S. R. (2006). Courtship duration as a correlate of marital satisfaction and stability. *Dissertation Abstracts International: Section B: The Sciences and Engineering, 67(4-B),* 2279.

Hansen, T., Moum, T., & Shapiro, A. (2007). Relational and individual well-being among cohabitors and married individuals in midlife: Recent trends from Norway. *Journal of Family Issues, 28,* 910–933. doi:10.1177/0192513X07299610.

Hareven, T. K. (2001). Historical perspectives on aging and family relations. In R. H. Binstock & L. K. George (Eds.), *Handbook of aging and the social sciences* (5th ed., pp. 141–159). San Diego, CA: Academic Press.

Harley, C. B. (2008). Telomerase and cancer therapeutics. *Nature Reviews: Cancer, 8,* 167–179. doi:10.1038/ nrc.2275.

Harrington, D., Bean, N., Pintello, D., & Mathews, D. (2001). Job satisfaction and burnout: Predictors of intentions to leave a job in a military setting. *Administration in Social Work, 25,* 1–16. doi:10.1300/J147v25n03_01.

Harris Interactive. (2011). *Large majorities support doctor assisted suicide for terminally ill patients in great pain.* Retrieved from http://www .harrisinteractive.com/NewsRoom /HarrisPolls/tabid/447/mid/1508 /articleId/677/ctl/ReadCustom%20 Default/Default.aspx.

Harris, R. L., Ellicott, A. M., & Holmes, D. S. (1986). The timing of psychosocial transitions and changes in women's lives: An examination of women aged 45 to 60. *Journal of Personality and Social Psychology, 51,* 409–416. doi:10.1037/0022-3514.51.2.409.

Hartman, P. S. (2001). Women developing wisdom: Antecedents and correlates in a longitudinal sample. *Dissertation Abstracts International. Section B. Sciences and Engineering, 62(1-B),* 591.

Hashimoto, K. (2013). Understanding depression: Linking brain-derived neurotrophic factor, transglutaminase 2 and serotonin. *Expert Review of Neurotherapeutics, 13,* 5–7.

Haslam, C., Hodder, K. I., & Yates, P. J. (2011). Errorless learning and spaced retrieval: How do these methods fare in healthy and clinical populations? *Journal of Clinical and Experimental Neuropsychology, 33,* 1–16. doi:10.10 80/13803395.2010.533155.

Havaldar, R., Pilli, S. C., & Putti, B. B. (2012). Effects of ageing on bone mineral composition and bone strength. *IOSR Journal of Dental and Medical Sciences, 1,* 12–16. Retrieved from http://iosrjournals. org/iosr-jdms/papers/vol1-issue3 /C0131216.pdf.

Haworth, J., & Lewis, S. (2005). Work, leisure and well-being. *British Journal of Guidance & Counselling, 33,* 67–78. doi:10.1080/03069880412 331335902.

Hawton, K., Casañas i Comabella, C., Haw, C., & Saunders, K. (2013). Risk factors for suicide in individuals with depression: A systematic review. *Journal of Affective Disorders, 147,* 17–28. doi:10.1016/j.jad.2013.01.004.

Hayflick, L. (1996). *How and why we age* (2nd ed.). New York: Ballantine.

Hayflick, L. (1998). How and why we age. *Experimental Gerontology, 33,* 639–653. doi:10.1016/jS0531-5565(98)00023-0.

Hayslip, B., & Cooper, A. M. (2012). Subjective and objective intellectual change in older adults. *Educational Gerontology, 38,* 190–200. doi:10.108 0/03601277.2010.532069.

Hayslip, B., Jr., Caballero, D., Ward-Pinson, M., & riddle, R. R. (2013). Sensitizing young adults to their biases about middle-aged and older persons: A pedagogical approach. *Educational Gerontology, 39,* 37–44.

Hayslip, B., Jr., Davis, S. R., Neumann, C. S., Goodman, C., Smith, G. C., Maiden, R. J. et al. (2013). The role of resilience in mediating stressor-outcome relationships among grand-parents raising their grandchildren. In B. Hayslip, Jr., & G. C. Smith (Eds.), *Resilient grandparent caregiv-ers: A strengths-based perspective* (pp. 48–69). New York: Routledge.

Hebert, L. E., Weuve, J., Scherr, P. A., & Evans, D. A. (2013). Alzheimer disease in the United States (2010–2050) estimated using the 2010 census. *Neurology, 80,* 1778–1783. doi:10.1212 /WNL.0b013e31828726f5.

Heckhausen, J., Wrosch, C., & Schulz, R. (2010). A motivational theory of life-span development. *Psychological Review, 117,* 32–60. doi:10.1037 /a0017668.

Hehman, J. A., Corpuz, R., & Bugental, D. (2012). Patronizing speech to older adults. *Journal of Nonverbal Behavior, 36,* 249–261. doi:10.1007 /s10919-012-0135-8.

HelpGuide.org. (2013). *Finding good childcare.* Retrieved from http:// helpguide.org/life/finding_caregiver _child.htm.

Helson, R., & Kwan, V. S.V. (2000). Personality change in adulthood: The big picture and processes in one longitudinal study. In S. E. Hampton (ed.), *Advances in personality psy-chology* (Vol. 1, pp. 77–106). Hove, England: Psychology Press.

Hemer, S. R. (2010). Grief as social experience: Death and bereave-ment in Lahir, Papua New Guinea. *TAJA: The Australian Journal of Anthropology, 21,*

281–297. doi:10.1111/j.1757-6547.2010.00097.x.

Henderson, S., & Gilding, M. (2004). "I've never clicked this much with anyone in my life": Trust and hyperpersonal communica-tion in online friendships. *New Media & Society, 6,* 487–506. doi:10.1177/146144804044331.

Hendriks, G.-J., Keijsers, G. P. J., Kampman, M., Hoogduin, C. A. L., & Voshaar, R. C. O. (2012). Predictors of outcome of pharma-cological and psychological treat-ment of late-life panic disorder with agoraphobia. *International Journal of Geriatric Psychiatry, 27,* 146–150. doi:10.1002/gps.2700.

Hendry, M., Pasterfield, D., Lewis, R., Carter, B., Hodgson, D., & Wilkinson, C. (2013). Why do we want the right to die? A systematic review of the international literature on the views of patients, carers and the public on assisted dying. *Palliative Medicine, 27,* 13–26. doi:10.1177/0269216313489909.

Henkin, R. I. (2008). Taste and appetite loss in the aged. *Perspectives on Gerontology, 13,* 20–32. doi:10.1044 /gero13.1.20.

Henrie, J. A. (2010). *Religiousness, future time perspective, and death anxiety among adults.* Dissertation submitted to West Virginia University.

Henrikson, C. R. (2007). Longevity's impact on retirement security. In M. Robinson, W. Novelli, C. Pearson, & L. Norris (Eds.), *Global health and global aging* (pp. 323–336). San Francisco: Jossey-Bass.

Henry, N. J. M., Berg, C. A., Smith, T. W., & Florsheim, P. (2007). Positive and negative characteristics of marital interaction and their asso-ciation with marital satisfaction in middle-aged and older couples. *Psychology and Aging, 22,* 428–441. doi:10.1037/0882-7974.22.3.428.

Hensley, S. (2012). *Americans support physician-assisted suicide for terminally ill.* Retrieved from http://www.npr.org/blogs /health/2012/12/27/168150886 /mericans-support-physician assisted-suicide-for-terminally-ill.

Heo, J., Lee, Y., McCormick, B. P., & Pedersen, P. M. (2010). Daily experi-ence of serious leisure, flow and subjective well-being of older adults. *Leisure Studies, 29,* 207–225. Doi: 10.1080/02614360903434092.

Heppner, R. S. (2007). A paradox of diversity: Billions invested, but women still leave. *Dissertation Abstracts International. Section A. Humanities and Social Sciences, 68*(4-A), 1527.

Herrington, J. D., Heller, W., Mohanty, A., Engels, A. S., Barich, M. T., Webb, A. G., et al. (2010). Localization of asym-metric brain function in emotion and depression. *Psychophysiology, 47,* 442–454. doi:10.1111/j.1469-8986.2009.00958.x.

Hershatter, A., & Epstein, M. (2010). Millennials and the world of work: An organization and management perspective. *Journal of Business and Psychology, 25,* 211–223. doi:10.1007 /s10869-010-9160-y.

Hershey, D. A., & Henkens, K. (in press). Impact of different types of retirement transitions on per-ceived retirement satisfaction with life. *The Gerontologist.* doi: 10/1093/geront /gnt006.

Hershey, D. A., Jacobs-Lawson, J. M., & Austin, J. T. (2013). Effective finan-cial planning for retirement. In M. Wang (Ed.), *The Oxford handbook of retirement* (pp. 402–430). New York: Oxford University Press.

Hertzog, C. (2008). Theoretical approaches to the study of cogni-tive aging: An individual differences perspective. In S. M. Hofer & D. F. Alwin (Eds.), *Handbook of cognitive aging: Interdisciplinary perspectives* (pp. 34–49). Greenwich, CT: Sage.

Hertzog, C., & Dixon, R. A. (1996). Methodological issues in research on cognition and aging. In F. Blanchard-Fields & T. Hess (Eds.), *Perspectives on cognitive change in adulthood and aging* (pp. 66–121). New York: McGraw-Hill.

Hertzog, C., & Dunlosky, J. (2011). Metacognition in later adult-hood: Spared monitoring can benefit older adults' self regulation. *Current Directions in Psychological Science, 20,* 167–173. doi:10.1177/0963721411409026.

Hertzog, C., & Dunlosky, J. (2012). Metacognitive approaches can pro-mote transfer of training: Comment on McDaniel and Bugg. *Journal of Applied Research in Memory and Cognition, 1,* 61–63. doi:10.1016/j. jarmac.2012.01.003.

Hertzog, C., Dixon, R. A., Hultsch, D. F., & MacDonald, S. W. S. (2003). Latent change models of adult cognition: Are changes in process-ing speed and working memory associated with changes in episodic memory? *Psychology and Aging, 18,* 755–769. doi:10.1037/0882-7974.18.4.755.

Hertzog, C., Fulton, E. K., Mandviwala, L., & Dunlosky, J. (2013). Older adults show deficits in retrieving and decoding associative mediators generated at study. *Developmental Psychology, 49,* 1127–1131. doi:10.1037/a0029414.

Hertzog, C., Kramer, A. F., Wilson, R. S., & Lindenberger, U. (2009). Fit body, fit mind? *Scientific American Mind, 20,* 24–31. doi:10.1038/scienti-ficamericanmind0709-24.

Hertzog, C., Kramer, A. F., Wilson, R. S., & Lindenberger, U. (2008). Enrichment effects on adult cognitive development: Can the functional capacity of older adults be preserved and enhanced? *Psychological Science in the Public Interest, 9,* 1–65. doi:10.1111/j.1539-6053.2009.01034.x.

Hertzog, C., Price, J., & Dunlosky, J. (2012). Age differences in the effects of experimenter-instructed versus self-generated strategy use. *Experimental Aging Research, 38,* 42–62. doi:10.1080/036107 3X.2012.637005.

Hess, T. M. (2005). Memory and aging in context. *Psychological Bulletin, 131,* 383–406. doi:10.1037/0033-2909.131.3.383.

Hess, T. M. (2006). Adaptive aspects of social cognitive functioning

in adulthood: Age-related goal and knowledge influences. *Social Cognition, 24,* 279–309. doi:10.1521 /soco.2006.24.3.279.

Hess, T. M., & Emery, L. (2012). Memory in context: The impact of age-related goals on performance. In M. Naveh-Benjamin & N. Ohta (Eds.), *Memory and aging: Current issues and future directions* (pp. 183–214). New York: Psychology Press.

Hess, T. M., & Pullen, S. M. (1994). Adult age differences in impression change processes. *Psychology and Aging, 9,* 237–250. doi:10.1037/0882-7974.9.2.237.

Hess, T. M., Auman, C., Colcombe, S. J., & Rahhal, T. A. (2003). The impact of stereotype threat on age differences in memory. *Journals of Gerontology: Psychological Sciences, 58B,* P3–P11. doi:10.1093 /geronb/58.1.P3.

Hess, T. M., Germain, C. M., Rosenberg, D. C., Leclerc, C. M., & Hodges, E. A. (2005). Aging-related selectivity and susceptibility to irrelevant affec-tive information in the construction of attitudes. *Aging, Neuropsychology, and Cognition, 12,* 149–174. doi:10.1080/13825580590925170.

Hess, T. M., Queen, T. L., & Ennis, G. E. (2013). Age and self-relevance effects on information search dur-ing decision making. *Journal of Gerontology: Psychological Sciences, 68,* 703–711. doi:10.1093/geronb /gbs108.

Heyl, V., & Wahl, H.-W. (2012). Managing daily life with age-related sensory loss: Cognitive resources gain in importance. *Psychology and Aging, 27,* 510–521. doi:10.1037 /a0025471.

Heyl, V., & Wahl, H. W. (2012). Managing daily life with age-related sensory loss: Cognitive resources gain in importance. *Psychology and Aging, 27,* 510–521. doi:10.1037 /a0025471.

Hiatt, K., Stelle, C., Mulsow, M., & Scott, J. P. (2007). The importance of perspective: Evaluation of hospice care from multiple stakeholders. *American Journal of Hospice & Palliative Medicine, 24,* 376–382. doi:10.1177/1049909107300760.

Hill, P. L., Turiano, N. A., Mroczek, D. K., & Roberts, B. W. (2012). Examining concurrent and longi-tudinal relations between personal-ity traits and social well-being in adulthood. *Social Psychological and Personality Science, 3,* 698–705. doi:10.1177/1948550611433888.

Hills, L. (2013). Why legacy mat-ters more in midlife. *Lasting female educational leadership: Leadership legacies of women leaders* (pp. 15–26). New York: Springer.

Hills, W. E. (2010). Grandparenting roles in the evolving American family. In D. Wiseman (Ed.), *The American family: Understanding its changing dynamics and place in society* (pp. 65–78.) Springfield, IL: Charles C. Thomas.

Hillsdon, M., Brunner, E., Guralnik, J., & Marmot, M. (2005). Prospective study of physical activity and physical function in early old age. *American Journal of Preventive*

Medicine, 28, 245–250. doi:10.1016/j.amepre.2004.12.008.

Hines, D. A., & Douglas, E. M. (2009). Women's use of intimate partner violence against men: Prevalence, implications, and consequences. *Journal of Aggression, Maltreatment and Trauma, 18,* 572–586. doi:10.1080/10926770903103099.

Hinton, A., & Chirgwin, S. (2010). Nursing education: Reducing reality shock for graduate indigenous nurses—It's all about time. *Australian Journal of Advanced Nursing, 28,* 60–66. Retrieved from http://www.ajan.com.au/Vol28/28-1.pdf#page=61.

Hirve, S., Juvekar, S., Sambhudas, S., Lele, P., Blomstedt, Y., Wall, S. et al. (2012). Does self-rated health predict death in adults aged 50 years and above in India? Evidence from a rural population under health and demographic surveillance. *International Journal of Epidemiology, 41,* 1719–1727. doi:10.1093/ije/dys163.

Holland, J. M., & Neimeyer, R. A. (2010). An examination of stage theory of grief among individuals bereaved by natural and violent causes: A meaning-oriented contribution. *OMEGA: Journal of Death and Dying, 61,* 103–120. doi:10.2190/OM.61.2.b.

Holstein, M. B., & Minkler, M. (2003). Self, society, and the "new gerontology." *The Gerontologist, 43,* 787–796. doi:10.1093/geront/43.6.787.

Hom, P. W., & Kinicki, A. J. (2001). Toward a greater understanding of how dissatisfaction drives employee turnover. *Academy of Management Journal, 44,* 975–987. doi:10.2307/3069441.

Honda-Howard, M., & Homma, M. (2001). Job satisfaction of Japanese career women and its influence on turnover intention. *Asian Journal of Social Psychology, 4,* 23–38. doi:10.1111/1467-839X.00073.

Hooker, K. (1999). Possible selves in adulthood. In T. M. Hess & F. Blanchard-Fields (Eds.), *Social cognition and aging* (pp. 97–122). San Diego, CA: Academic Press.

Hooker, K., & McAdams, D. P. (2003). Personality reconsidered: A new agenda for aging research. *Journal of Gerontology: Psychological Sciences, 58,* P296-P304. doi:10.1093/geronb/58.6.P296.

Hooker, K., Fiese, B. H., Jenkins, L., Morfei, M. Z., & Schwagler, J. (1996). Possible selves among parents of infants and preschoolers. *Developmental Psychology, 32,* 542–550. doi:10.1037/0012-1649.32.3.542.

Hoppmann, C., & Gerstorf, D. (2009). Spousal interrelations in old age—A mini-review. *Gerontology, 55,* 449–459. doi:10.1159/000211948.

Horhota, M., Lineweaver, T., Ositelu, M., Summers, K., & Hertzog, C. (2012). Young and older adults' beliefs about effective ways to mitigate age-related memory decline. *Psychology and Aging, 27,* 293–304. 10.1037/a0026088.

Horn, J. L. (1982). The aging of human abilities. In B. B. Wolman (Ed.), *Handbook of developmental psychology* (pp. 847–870). Englewood Cliffs, NJ: Prentice Hall.

Horn, J. L., & Hofer, S. M. (1992). Major abilities and development in the adult period. In R. J. Sternberg & C. A. Berg (Eds.), *Intellectual development* (pp. 44–99). Cambridge, UK: Cambridge University Press.

Hospice Foundation of America. (2013a). *Hospice patients and staff.* Retrieved from http://www.hospicefoundation.org/patientsandstaff.

Hospice Foundation of America. (2013b). *Choosing hospice: Questions to ask.* Retrieved from http://www.hospicefoundation.org/pages/page.asp?page_id=171093.

Howard, D. V., & Howard, J. H., Jr. (2012). Dissociable forms of implicit learning in aging. In M. Naveh-Benjamin & N. Ohta (Eds.). *Memory and aging: Current issues and future directions* (pp. 125–151). New York: Psychology Press.

Howard, L. W., & Cordes, C. L. (2010). Flight from unfairness: Effects of perceived injustice on emotional exhaustion and employee withdrawal. *Journal of Business and Psychology, 25,* 409–428. doi:10.1007/s10869-010-9158-5.

Howe, A. L., Jones, A. E., & Tilse, C. (2013). What's in a name? Similarities and differences in international terms and meanings for older peoples' housing with services. *Ageing and Society, 33,* 547–578. doi:10.1017/S0144686X12000086.

Hoyles, K., & Sharma, J. C. (in press). Olfactory loss as a supporting feature in the diagnosis of Parkinson's disease: A pragmatic approach. *Journal of Neurology.* doi:10.1007/s00415-013-6848-8.

Hsu, H.-C. (2005). Gender disparity of successful aging in Taiwan. *Women and Health, 42,* 1–21. doi:10.1300/J013v42n01_01.

Hubbard, R. R. (2010). *Afro-German biracial identity development.* Retrieved from http://digarchive.library.vcu.edu/bitstream/10156/2804/1/Afro-German%20HEMBAGI%20%28F3%29.pdf.

Hull, T. H. (2009). *Fertility prospects in south-eastern Asia: Report of the United Nations Expert Group Meeting on Recent and Future Trends in Fertility.* Retrieved from http://www.un.org/esa/population/meetings/EGM-Fertility2009/P14_Hull.pdf.

Hummert, M. L., Garstka, T. A., O'Brien, L. T., Greenwald, A. G., & Mellott, D. S. (2002). Using the implicit association test to measure age differences in implicit social cognitions. *Psychology and Aging, 17,* 482–495. doi:10.1037/0882-7974.17.3.482.

Hunt, J. M., & Weintraub, J. R. (2006). *The coaching organization: A strategy for developing leaders.* Thousand Oaks, CA: Sage.

Hunter, C. E. A., Ward, L., & Camp, C. J. (2012). Transitioning spaced retrieval training to care staff in an Australian residential aged care setting for older adults with dementia: A case study approach. *Clinical Gerontologist, 35,* 1–14. doi:10.1080/0731717115.2011.626513.

Hunter, C. E. A., Ward, L., & Camp, C. J. (2012). Transitioning spaced retrieval training to care staff in an Australian residential aged care setting for older adults with dementia: A case study approach. *Clinical Gerontologist, 35,* 1–14. doi:10.1080/0731715.2011.626513.

Huston, T. L., Caughlin, J. P., Houts, R. M., Smith, S. E., & George, L. J. (2001). The connubial crucible: Newlywed years as a predictor of marital delight, distress, and divorce. *Journal of Personality and Social Psychology, 80,* 237–252. doi:10.1037/0022-3514.80.2.237.

Hwang, M. J. (2007). Asian social workers' perceptions of glass ceiling, organizational fairness and career prospects. *Journal of Social Service Research, 33,* 13–24. doi:10.1300/J079v33n04_02.

Hyson, P. (2013). *Coaching with meaning and spirituality.* New York: Routledge.

Ibrahim, R., & Hassan, Z. (2009). Understanding singlehood from the experiences of never-married Malay Muslim women in Malaysia: Some preliminary findings. *European Journal of Social Sciences, 8,* 395–405.

Igarashi, H., Hooker, K. Coehlo, D. P., & Manoogian, M. M. (2013). "My nest is full!" Intergenerational relationships at midlife. *Journal of Aging Studies, 27,* 102–112. doi:10.1016/j.jaging.2012.12.004.

Ihle, A., Schnitzspahn, K., Rendell, P. G., Luong, C., & Kliegel, M. (2012). Age benefits in everyday prospective memory: The influence of personal task importance, use of reminders, and everyday stress. *Aging, Neuropsychology, and Cognition, 19,* 84–101. doi:10.1080/13825585.201 1.629288.

Imoscopi, A., Inelmen, E. M., Sergi, G., Miotto, F., & Manzato, E. (2012). Taste loss in the elderly: Epidemiology, causes and consequences. *Aging Clinical and Experimental Research, 24,* 570–579. doi:10.3275/8520.

International Labour Organization. (2013). *When work becomes a sexual battleground.* Retrieved from http://www.ilo.org/global/about-the-ilo/newsroom/features/WCMS_205996/lang--en/index.htm.

Intlekofer, K. A. & Cotman, C. W. 2013. Exercise counteracts declining hippocampal function in aging and Alzheimer's disease. *Neurobiology of Disease, 57,* 47–55. doi:10.1016/j.nbd.2012.06.011.

Irwin, M. R. (2008). Human psychoneuroimmunology: 20 years of discovery. *Brain, Behavior, and Immunity, 22,* 129–139. doi:10.1016/j.bbi.2007.07.013.

Isaacowitz, D. M., & Blanchard-Fields, F. (2012). Linking process and outcome in the study of emotion and aging. *Perspectives on Psychological Science, 7,* 3–16. doi:10.1177/1745691611424750.

Ivancovich, D. A., & Wong, T. P. (2008). The role of existential and spiritual coping in anticipatory grief. In A. Tomer, G. T. Eliason, & P. T. P. Wong (Eds.), *Existential and spiritual issues in death attitudes* (pp. 209–233). Mahwah, NJ: Lawrence Erlbaum.

Iwarsson, S., Slaug, B., & Fänge, A. M. (2012). The Housing Enabler Screening Tool: Feasibility and interrater agreement in a real estate company practice context. *Journal of Applied Gerontology, 31,* 641–660. doi:10.1177/0733464810397354.

Jack, C. R., Jr., Albert, M. A., Knopman, D. S., McKhann, G. M., Sperling, R. A., Carrillo, M. C. et al. (2011). Introduction to the recommendations from the National Institute on Aging—Alzheimer's Association workgroups on diagnositc guidelines for Alzheimer's disease. *Alzheimer's and Dementia: Journal of the Alzheime'rs Assocation, 7,* 257–262. doi:10.1016/jalz.2011.03.004.

Jack, C. R., Jr., Knopman, D. S., Jagust, W. J., Petersen, R. C., Weiner, M. W., Aisen, P. S. et al. (2013). Tracking pathophysiological processes in Alzheimer's disease: An updated hypothetical model of dynamic biomarkers. *The Lancet Neruology, 12,* 207–216. doi:10.1016/s1474-4422(12)70291-0.

Jackson, J. S., Antonucci, T. C., & Gibson, R. C. (1995). Ethnic and cultural factors in research on aging and mental health: A life-course perspective. In D. K. Padgett (Ed.), *Handbook on ethnicity, aging, and mental health* (pp. 22–46). Westport, CT: Greenwood.

Jackson, M. A. (2013). Counseling older workers confronting ageist stereotypes and discrimination. In P. Brownell & J. J. Kelly (Eds.), *Ageism and mistreatment of older workers* (pp. 135–144). New York: Springer.

Jacob, B. A., & Wilder, T. (2010). *Educational expectations and attainment.* National Bureau of Economic Research Working Paper No. 15683. Retrieved from http://www.nber.org/papers/w15683.pdf?new_window=1.

Jacobs-Lawson, J. M., Hershey, D. A., & Neukam, K. A. (2004). Gender differences in factors that influence time spent planning for retirement. *Journal of Women & Aging, 16,* 55–69. doi:10.1300/J074v16n03_05.

Jacoby, L. L., & Rhodes, M. G. (2006). False remembering in the aged. *Current Directions in Psychological Science, 15*(2), 49–53. doi:10.1111/j.0963.7214.2006.00405.x.

Jacoby, L. L., Rogers, C. S., Bishara, A. J., & Shimizu, Y. (2012). Mistaking the recent past for the present: False seeing by older adults. *Psychology and Aging, 27,* 22–32. doi:10.1037/a0025924.

Jagoda, A. (2012). *The fog of concussion: Controversies in diagnosis and prognosis.* Retrieved from http://www.emergemeetings.com/filebin/pdf/Jagoda-Traumatic-Brain-Injury.pdf.

Jain, E., & Labouvie-Vief, G. (2010). Compensatory effects of emotional avoidance in adult development. *Biological Psychology, 84,* 497–513. doi:10.1016/j.biopsycho.2010.03.008.

Jainer, A. K., Kamatchi, R., Marzanski, M., & Somashekar, B. (2013). Current advances in the treatment of major depression: Shift towards receptor specific drugs. In R. Woolfolk & L. Allen (Eds.), *Mental disorders: Theoretical and empirical* perspectives (pp. 269–288). Doi: 10.5772/46217. Retrieved from http://cdn.intechopen.com /pdfs/41703/InTech-Current _advances_in_the_treatment_of _major_depression_shift_towards _receptor_specific_drugs.pdf.

Jak, A. J. (2012). The impact of physical and mental activity on cognitive aging. In M.-C. Pardon & M. W. Bondi (Eds.), Current topics in behavioral neurosciences: Vol. 10. Behavioral neurobiology of aging (pp. 273–291). New York: Springer.

Janoff-Bulman, R., & Berger, A. R. (2000). The other side of trauma: Toward a psychology of appreciation. In J. H. Harvey & E. D. Miller (Eds.), Loss and trauma: General and close relationship perspectives (pp. 29–44). Philadelphia: Brunner-Routledge.

Janssen I, R. R. (2005). Linking age-related changes in skeletal muscle mass and composition with metabolism and disease. Journal of Nutrition, Health and Aging, 9, 408–419.

Janssen, J., Tattersall, C., Waterink, W., van den Berg, B., van Es, R., Bolman, C., & Koper, R. (2007). Self-organising navigational support in lifelong learning: How predecessors can lead the way. Computers & Education, 49, 781–793. doi:10.1016/j.compedu.2005.11.022.

Jaspal, R., & Cinnirella, M. (2012). The construction of ethnic identity: Insights from identity process theory. Ethnicities, 12, 503–530. doi:10.1177/1468796811432689.

Jeste, D. V., & Palmer, B. W. (2013). A call for a new positive psychiatry of ageing. British Journal of Psychiatry, 202, 81–83. doi:10.1192/bjp. bp.112.110643.

Jeste, D. V., & Palmer, B. W. (2013). A call for a new positive psychiatry of ageing. The British Journal of Psychiatry, 202, 81–83. doi:10.1192/ bjp.bp.112.110.643.

Jeste, D. V., Savla, G. N., Thompson, W. K., Vahia, I. V., Glorioso, D. K., Martin, A. S. et al. (2013). Association between older age and more successful aging: Critical role of resilience and depression. American Journal of Psychiatry, 170, 188–196. doi:10.1176/appi ajp.2012.12030386.

Johns, M. L. (2013). Breaking the glass ceiling: Structural, cultural, and organizational barriers preventing women form achieving senior and executive positions. Perspectives in Health Information Management, 10. Published online at http://www .ncbi.nlm.nih.gov/pmc/articles /PMC3544145/.

Johnson, H. A., Zabriskie, R. B., & Hill, B. (2006). The contribution of couple leisure involvement, leisure time, and leisure satisfaction to marital satisfaction. Marriage & Family Review, 40, 69–91. doi:10.1300/ J002v40n01_05.

Johnson, M. K., Raye, C. L., Mitchell, K. J., & Ankudowich, E. (2012). The cognitive neuroscience of true and false memories. Nebraska Symposium on Motivation, 58, 15–52. doi:10.1007/978-1-4614-1195-6_2.

Johnson, M. M., & Rhodes, R. (2007). Institutionalization: A theory of human behavior and the social environment. Advances in Social Work, 8, 219–236. Retrieved from http://journals.iupui.edu/index .php/advancesinsocialwork/article /view/143/144.

Johnston, K. E., Swim, J. K., Saltsman, B. M., Deater-Deckard, K., & Petrill, S. A. (2007). Mothers' racial, ethnic, and cultural socialization of transracially adopted Asian children. Family Relations, 56, 390–402. doi:10.1111/ j.1741-3729.2007.00468.x.

Joiner, T. (2010). Myths about suicide. Cambridge, MA: Harvard University Press.

Jokela, M., Kivimäki, M., Elovainio, M., & Keltikangas-Järvinen, L. (2009). Personality and having children: A two-way relationship. Journal of Personality and Social Psychology, 96, 218–230. doi:10.1037/a0014058.

Jones, B. F. (2010). Age and great invention. Review of Economics and Statistics, 92, 1–14. Retrieved from http://www.mitpressjournals.org/doi /pdfplus/10.1162/rest.2009.11724.

Jones, G. W. (2010). Changing marriage patterns in Asia (Asia Research Institute Working Paper Series No. 131). Retrieved from http://www.ari .nus.edu.sg/docs/wps/wps10_131.pdf.

Jones, R. N., Marsiske, M., Ball, K., Rebok, G., Willis, S. L., Morris, J. N., et al. (in press). The ACTIVE cognitive training interventions and trajectories of performance among older adults. Journal of Aging and Health. doi:10.1177/0898264312461938.

Jonsson, T., Stefansson, H., Steinberg, S., Jonsdottir, I., Jonsson, P. V., Snaedal, J. et al. (2013). Variant of TREM2 associated with the risk of Alzheimer's disease. New England Journal of Medicine, 368, 107–116. doi:10.1056/NEJMoa1211103.

Jopp, D. S., & Hertzog, C. (2010). Assessing adult leisure activities: An extension of a self-report activity questionnaire. Psychological Assessment, 22, 108–120. doi:10.1037/a0017662.

Joyner, M. J., & Barnes, J. N. (2013). I am 90 going on 18: Exercise and the fountain of youth. Journal of Applied Physiology, 114, 1–2. doi:10.1152/ japplphysiol.01313.2012.

Juffer, F. (2006). Children's awareness of adoption and their problem behavior in families with 7-year-old internationally adopted children. Adoption Quarterly, 9, 1–22. doi:10.1300/ J145v09n02_01.

Jung, R. E., & Haier, R. J. (2007). The parieto-frontal integration theory (P-FIT) of intelligence: Converging neuroimaging evidence. Behavioral and Brain Sciences, 30, 135–154. doi:10.1017/S0140525X07001185

Jung, R. E., Segall, J. M., Bockholt, H. J., Flores, R. A., Smith, S. M., Chavez, R. S., et al. (2010). Neuroanatomy of creativity. Human Brain Mapping, 31, 398–409. doi:10.1002/hbm.20874.

Juraska, J. M., & Lowry, N. C. (2012). Neuranatomical changes associated with cognitive aging. Current Topics in Behavioral Neurosciences: Behavioral Neurobiology of Aging, 10, 137–162. doi:10.1007/7854_2011_137.

Kahana, E., & Kahana, B. (2003). Patient proactivity enhancing doctor-patient-family communication in cancer prevention and care among the aged. Patient Education and Counseling, 50, 67–73. doi:10.1016/ S0738-3991(03)00083-1.

Kahana, E., Kahana, B., & Zhang, J. (2005). Motivational antecedents of preventive proactivity in late life: Linking future orientation and exercise. Motivation and Emotion, 29, 438–459 (Figure 1). doi:10.1007/ s11031-006-9012-2. Retrieved from http://www.springerlink.com /content/61304201gm163778 //fulltext.html#Fig1.

Kahana, E., Kelley-Moore, J., & Kahana, B. (2012). Proactive aging: A longitudinal study of stress, resources, and well-being in late life. Aging and Mental Health, 16, 438–451. doi:10.1080/13607863.20 11.644519.

Kalish, R. A. (1984). Death, grief, and caring relationships (2nd ed.). Pacific Grove, CA: Brooks/Cole.

Kalish, R. A. (1987). Death and dying. In P. Silverman (Ed.), The elderly as modern pioneers (pp. 320–334). Bloomington: Indiana University Press.

Kalish, R. A., & Reynolds, D. (1976). Death and ethnicity: A psychocultural study. Los Angeles: University of Southern California Press.

Kallio, E. (2011). Integrative thinking is the key: An evaluation of current research into the development of adult thinking. Theory and Psychology, 21, 785–801.

Kalmijn, M., & Flap, H. (2001). Assortative meeting and mating: Unintended consequences of organized settings for partner choices. Social Forces, 79, 1289–1312. doi:10.1353/sof.2001.0044.

Kalpouzos, G., Persson, J., & Nyberg, L. (2012). Local brain atrophy accounts for functional activity differences in normal aging. Neurobiology of Aging, 33, 623.e1–623.e13. doi:10.1016/j. neurobiolaging.2011.02.021.

Kalpouzos, G., & Nyberg, L. (2012). Multimodal neuroimaging in normal aging: Structure-function interactions. In M. Naveh-Benjamin & N. Ohta (Eds.), Memory and aging: Current issues and future directions (pp. 273–304). New York: Psychology Press.

Kane, R. A., Lum, T. Y., Cutler, L. J., Degenholz, H. B., & Yu, T.-C. (2007). Resident outcomes in small-house nursing homes: A longitudinal evaluation of the initial Green House program. Journal of the American Geriatrics Society, 55, 832–839. doi:10.1111/j.1532-5415.2007 01169.x.

Kanehisa, M., Araki, M., Goto, S., Hattori, M., Hirakawa, M., Itoh, M., Katayama, T., Kawashima, S., Okuda, S., Tokimatsu, T., & Yamanishi, Y. (2008). KEGG for linking genomes to life and the environment. Nucleic Acids Research, 36, D480–D484. doi:10.1093/nar/gkm882.

Kapoor, U., Pfost, K. S., House, A. E., & Pierson, E. (2010). Relation of success and nontraditional career choice to selection for dating and friendship. Psychological Reports, 107, 177–184. doi:10.2466/07.17. PR0.107.4.177-184.

Kapp, M. B. (2008). Legal issues in dementia. International Journal of Risk and Safety in Medicine, 20, 91–103. doi:10.3233/JRS-2008-0429.

Kapp, M. B. (in press). Nursing home culture change: Legal apprehensions and opportunities. The Gerontologist. doi:10.1093/geront/gns131.

Karasu, S. R., & Karasu, T. B. (2005). The art of marriage maintenance. Lanham, MD: Jason Aronson.

Karel, M. J., Gatz, M., & Smyer, M. A. (2012). Aging and mental health in the decade ahead: What psychologists need to know. American Psychologist, 67, 184–198. doi:10.1037/a0025393.

Karim, S. S., Ramanna, G., Petit, T., Doward, L., & Burns, A. (2008). Development of the Dementia Quality of Life questionnaire (D-QOL): UK version. Aging and Mental Health, 12, 144–148. 10.1080/13607860701616341.

Karney, B. R. (2010). Keeping marriages healthy, and why it's so difficult. Retrieved from http://www.apa.org /science/about/psa/2010/02/sci-brief .aspx.

Karney, B. R., & Bradbury, T. N. (1995). The longitudinal course of marital quality and stability: A review of theory, method, and research. Psychological Bulletin, 118, 3–34. doi:10.1037/0033-2909.1881.1.3.

Karney, B. R., & Crown, J. S. (2007). Families under stress: An assessment of data, theory, and research on marriage and divorce in the military (MG-599-OSD). Santa Monica, CA: RAND Corporation.

Karp, J. F., Shega, J. W., Morone, N. E., & Weiner, D. K. (2008). Advances in understanding the mechanisms and management of persistent pain in older adults. British Journal of Anaesthesia, 101, 111–120. doi:10.1093/bja/aen090.

Karp, N., & Wood, E. (2012). Choosing home for someone else: Guardian residential decision making. Utah Law Review, 2012, 1445–1490. Retrieved from http://epubs.utah .edu/index.php/ulr/article /view/837/646.

Karpel, M. E., Hoyer, W. J., & Toglia, M. P. (2001). Accuracy and qualities of real and suggested memories: Nonspecific age differences. Journals of Gerontology: Psychological Sciences, 56, P103–P110. doi:10.1093 /geronb/56.2.P103.

Kastenbaum, R. (1999). Dying and bereavement. In J. C. Cavanaugh & S. K. Whitbourne (Eds.), Gerontology: An interdisciplinary perspective. New York: Oxford University Press.

Kastenbaum, R., & Thuell, S. (1995). Cookies baking, coffee brewing: Toward a contextual theory of dying. Omega: The Journal of Death and Dying, 31, 175–187. doi:10.2190/ LQPX-71DE-V5AA-EPFT.

Kasuya, H., Yoshida, H., Mori, H., & Kido, H. (2008). A longitudinal study of vocal aging: Changes in F0, jitter, shimmer, and glottal noise. Journal of the Acoustical Society of America, 123, 3428-3428. doi:10.1121/1.2934194.

Kasezniak, A. W., & Menchola, M. (2012). Behavioral neuroscience of emotion in aging. *Current Topics in Behavioral Neurosciences: Behavioral Neurobiology of Aging, 10*, 51–66. doi:10.1007/7854_2011_163.

Kaur, A., Kumar, S. L. H., & Navis, S. (2013). Comorbidity of depression in diabetes. *International Journal of Pharmacology and Therapeutics, 3*, 19–33.

Kavé, G., Eyal, N., Shorek, A., Cohen-Mansfield, J. (2008). Multilingualism and cognitive state in the oldest old. *Psychology and Aging, 23*, 70–78. doi:10.1037/0882-7974.23.1.70.

Kazanis, I. (2012). Can adult neural stem cells create new brains? Plasticity in the adult mammalian neurogenic niches: Realities and expectations in the era of regenerative biology. *Neuroscientist, 18*, 15–27. doi:10.1177/1073858410390379.

Kegan, R. (1982). *The evolving self.* Cambridge, MA: Harvard University Press.

Kegan, R. (1994). *In over our heads: The mental demands of modern life.* Cambridge. MA: Harvard University Press.

Kegan, R. (2009). A constructive-developmental approach to transformative learning. In K. Illeris (Ed.), *Contemporary theories of learning: Learning theorists…in their own words* (pp. 35–52). New York: Routledge.

Kelley, K. (1995). Visions: Maya Angelou. *Mother Jones, May/June.* Retrieved from http://www.motherjones.com/media/1995/05/visions-maya-angelou.

Kensinger, E. A. (2012). Emotion-memory interactions in older adulthood. In M. Naveh-Benjamin & N. Ohta (Eds.), *Memory and aging: Current issues and future directions* (pp. 215–244). New York: Psychology Press.

Kensinger, E. A., & Corkin, S. (2004). The effects of emotional content and aging on false memories. *Cognitive, Affective and Behavioral Neuroscience, 4*, 1–9. doi:10.3758/CABN.4.1.1.

Kensinger, E. A., & Corkin, S. (2006). Aging, neural changes in. *Encyclopedia of Cognitive Science.* doi:10.1002/0470018860.s00304.

Kensinger, E. A., Piguet, O., Krendl, A. C., & Corkin, S. (2005). Memory for contextual details: Effects of emotion and aging. *Psychology and Aging, 20*, 241–250. doi:10.1037/0882-7974.20.2.241.

Kersting, A., Brähler, E., Glaesmer, H., & Wagner, B. (2011). Prevalence of complicated grief in a representative population-based sample. *Journal of Affective Disorders, 131*, 339–343. Doi: 10.1016/j.jad.2010.11.032.

Kersting, A., Brähler, E., Glaesmer, H., & Wagner, B. (2011). Prevalence of complicated grief in a representative population-based sample. *Journal of Affective Disorders, 131*, 339–343. doi:10.1016/j.jad.2010.11.032.

Kessler, R. C., Berglund, P., Demler, O., Jin, R., Merakangas, K., & Walters, E. (2005). *JAMA Psychiatry, 62*, 593–602.

Kheirbek, R. E., Alemi, F., Citron, B. A., Afaq, M. A., Wu, H., & Fletcher, R. D. (2013). Trajectory of illness for patients with congestive heart failure. *Journal of Palliative Medicine, 16*, 478–484. doi:10.1089/jpm.2012.0510.

Kiang, L., & Fuligni, A. J. (2009). Ethnic identity and family processes among adolescents from Latin American, Asian, and European backgrounds. *Journal of Youth and Adolescence, 38*, 228–241. doi:10.1007/s10964-008-9353-0.

Kiaye, R. E., & Singh, A. M. (2013). The glass ceiling: A perspective of women working in Durban. *Gender in Management: An International Journal, 28*, 28–42. doi:10.1108/17542411311301556.

Kilson, M., & Ladd, F. (2009). *Is that your child? Mothers talking about rearing biracial children.* Lanham, MD: Lexington Books.

Kim, H. K., Capaldi, D. M., & Crosby, L. (2007). Generalizability of Gottman and Colleagues' affective process models of couples' relationship outcomes. *Journal of Marriage and Family, 69*, 55–72. doi:10.1111/j.1741-3737.2006.00343.x.

Kim, S. S. (2000). Gradual return to work: The antecedents and consequences of switching to part-time work after first childbirth. *Dissertation Abstract International. Section A. Humanities and Social Sciences, 61(3-A)*, 1182.

Kim, S., Hasher, L., & Zacks, R. T. (2007). Aging and a benefit of distractibility. *Psychonomic Bulletin and Review, 14* (2): 301–305. doi:10.3758/BF03194068.

Kim, S., Healey, M. K., Goldstein, D., Hasher, L., & Wiprzycka, U. J. (2008). Age differences in choice satisfaction: A positivity effect in decision making. *Psychology and Aging, 23*, 33–38. doi:10.1037/0882-7974.23.1.33.

Kimbler, K. J., Margrett, J. A., & Johnson, T. L. (2012). The role of supportive messages and distracting thoughts on everyday problem-solving performance. *Experimental Aging Research, 38*, 537–558. doi:10.1080/0361073X.2012.726158.

King, L. M. (2012). Nutrition and cognitive functioning: Multifaceted analysis of physiological and psychological components. *PURE Insights, 1.* Retrieved from http://digitalcommons.wou.edu/pure/vol1/iss1/6/.

King, P. M., & Kitchener, K. S. (2002). The reflective judgment model: Twenty years of research on epistemic cognition. In B. K. Hofer & P. R. Pintrich (Eds.), *Personal epistemology: The psychology of beliefs about knowledge and knowing* (pp. 37–61). Mahwah, NJ: Erlbaum.

King, P. M., & Kitchener, K. S. (2004). Reflective judgment: Theory and research on the development of epistemic assumptions through adulthood. *Educational Psychologist, 39*, 5–18. doi:10.1207/s15326985ep3901_2.

King, S. V., Burgess, E. O., Akinyela, M., Counts-Spriggs, M., & Parker, N. (2006). The religious dimensions of the grandparent role in three-generation African American households. *Journal of Religion, Spirituality & Aging, 19*, 75–96. doi:10.1300/J496v19n01_06.

Kingma, E. M., de Jonge, P., van der Harst, P., Ormel, J., & Rosmalen, J. G. M. (2012). The association between intelligence and telomere length: A longitudinal population based study. *PLoS ONE 7*, e49356. doi:10.1371/journal.pone.0049356. Retrieved from http://www.plosone.org/articleinfo%3Adoi%2F10.1371%2Fjournal.pone.0049356.

Kingston, A., Collerton, J., Davies, K., Bond, J., Robinson, L., & Jagger, C. (2012). Losing the ability in activities of daily living in the oldest old: A Hierarchic disability scale from the Newcastle 85+ study. *PLoS ONE, 7*, e31665. doi:10.1371/journal.pone.0031665.

Kinney, J. M., & Cavanaugh, J. C. (1993 November). *Until death do us part: Striving to find meaning while caring for a spouse with dementia.* Paper presented at the meeting of the Gerontological Society of America, New Orleans.

Kinney, J. M., Ishler, K. J., Pargament, K. I., & Cavanaugh, J. C. (2003). Coping with the uncontrollable: The use of general and religious coping by caregivers to spouses with dementia. *Journal of Religious Gerontology, 14*, 171–188. doi:10.1300/J078v14n02_06.

Kinsella, G. J., Ong, B., Storey, E., Wallace, J., & Hester, R. (2007). Elaborated spaced-retrieval and prospective memory in mild Alzheimer's disease. *Neuropsychological Rehabilitation, 17*, 688–706. doi:10.1080/09602010600892824.

Kinsella, G. J., Ong, B., Storey, E., Wallace, J., & Hester, R. (2007). Elaborated spaced-retrieval and prospective memory in mild Alzheimer's disease. *Neuropsychological Rehabilitation, 17*, 688–706. doi:10.1080/09602010600892824.

Kinsella, G. J., Ong, B., Storey, E., Wallace, J., & Hester, R. (2007). Elaborated spaced-retrieval and prospective memory in mild Alzheimer's disease. *Neuropsychological Rehabilitation, 17*, 688–706. doi:10.1080/09602010600892824.

Kinsella, K., & Phillips, D. R. (2005). Global aging: The challenge of success. *Population Bulletin, 60.* Retrieved from http://www.prb.org/pdf05/60.1GlobalAging.pdf.

Kippen, R., Chapman, B., & Yu, P. (2009). *What's love got to do with it? Homogamy and dyadic approaches to understanding marital instability.* Retrieved from http://www.elbourneinstitute.com/downloads/hilda/Bibliography/HILDA_Conference_Papers/2009_papers/Kippen,%20Rebecca_paper.pdf.

Kitchener, K. S., King, P. M., & DeLuca, S. (2006). Development of reflective judgment in adulthood. In C. Hoare (Ed.), *Handbook of adult development and learning* (pp. 73–98). New York: Oxford University Press.

Kivett, V. R. (1991). Centrality of the grandfather role among older rural black and white men. *Journal of Gerontology: Social Sciences, 46*, S250–S258. doi:10.1093/geronb/46.5.S250.

Klackl, J., Jonas, E., & Kronbichler, M. (2013). Existential neuroscience: Neurophysiological correlates of proximal defenses against death-related thoughts. *Social Cognitive and Affective Neuroscience, 8*, 333–340. doi:10.1093/scan/nss003.

Klaczynski, P. A., & Robinson, B. (2000). Personal theories, intellectual ability, and epistemological beliefs: Adult age differences in everyday reasoning biases. *Psychology and Aging, 15*, 400–416. doi:10.1037/0882-7974.15.3.400.

Klassen, R. M., Usher, E. L., & Bong, M. (2010). Teachers' collective efficacy, job satisfaction, and job stress in cross-cultural context. *Journal of Experimental Education, 78*, 464–486. doi:10.1080/00220970903292975.

Kleiber, D. A. (2013). Redeeming leisure in later life. In T. Freire (Ed.), *Positive leisure science* (pp. 21–38). New York: Springer.

Kleiber, D. A., Hutchinson, S. L., & Williams, R. (2002). Leisure as a resource in transcending negative life events: Self-protection, self-restoration, and personal transformation. *Leisure Sciences, 24*, 219–235. doi:10.1080/01490400252900167.

Klug, M. G., Volkov, B., Muus, K., & Halaas, G. W. (2012). Deciding when to put grandma in the nursing home: Measuring inclinations to place persons with dementia. *American Journal of Alzheimer's Disease and Other Dementias, 27*, 223–227. doi:10.1177/1533317512449729.

Knee, D. O. (2010). Hospice care for the aging population in the United States. In J. C. Cavanaugh & C. K. Cavanaugh (Eds.), *Aging in America: Vol. 3: Societal issues* (pp. 203–221). Santa Barbara, CA: Praeger Perspectives.

Knight, B. G., & Sayegh, P. (2010). Cultural values and caregiving: The updated sociocultural stress and coping model. *Journal of Gerontology: Psychological Sciences and Social Sciences, 65B*, P5–P13. doi:10.1093/geronb/gbp096.

Knowles, M. S., Swanson, R. A., & Holton, E. F. (2005). *The adult learner: The definitive classic in adult education and human resource development.* New York: Elsevier.

Kobler, K., Limbo, R., & Kavanaugh, K. (2007). Meaningful moments: The use of ritual in perinatal and pediatric death. *MCN: The American Journal of Maternal/Child Nursing, 32*, 288–297. doi:10.1097/01.NMC.0000287998.80005.79.

Koenig, B. L., Kirkpatrick, L. A., & Ketelaar, T. (2007). Misperception of sexual and romantic interests in opposite-sex friendships: Four hypotheses. *Personal Relationships, 14*, 411–429. doi:10.1111/j.1475-6811.2007.00163.x.

Koestenbaum, P. (1976). *Is there an answer to death?* Englewood Cliffs, NJ: Prentice Hall.

Kolb, D. M., Williams, J., & Frohlinger, C. (2010). *Her place at the table: A woman's guide to negotiating five key challenges to leadership success.* San Francisco, CA: Jossey-Bass.

Kornadt, A. E., & Rothermund, K. (2012). Internalization of age stereotypes into the self-concept via future self-views: A general model and domain-specific differences. *Psychology and Aging, 27*, 164–172. doi:10.1037/a0025110.

Kotre, J. N. (1999). *Make it count: How to generate a legacy that gives meaning to your life.* New York: Free Press.

Kotre, J. N. (2005). Generativity: Reshaping the past into the future. *Science and Theology News, September,* 42–43. Retrieved from http://www.johnkotre.com/images /generativity_s_t_news_2005.pdf.

Kotter-Grühn, D., & Hess, T. M. (2012). The impact of age stereotypes on self-perceptions of aging across the adult lifespan. *Journal of Gerontology: Psychological Sciences, 67,* 563–571. doi:10.1093/geronb/gbr153.

Kowalski, S. D., & Bondmass, M. D. (2008). Physiological and psychological symptoms of grief in widows. *Research in Nursing & Health, 31,* 23–30. doi:10.1002/nur.20228.

Kozbelt, A., & Durmysheva, Y. (2007). Lifespan creativity in a non-Western artistic tradition: A study of Japanese Ukiyo-e printmakers. *International Journal of Aging & Human Development, 65,* 23–51. doi:10.2190/166N-6470-1325-T341.

Kramer, D. A., Kahlbaugh, P. E., & Goldston, R. B. (1992). A measure of paradigm beliefs about the social world. *Journals of Gerontology: Psychological Sciences, 47,* P180–P189. doi:10.1093/geronj/47.3.P180.

Krampe, R. T., Schaefer, S., Lindenberger, U., & Baltes, P. B. (2011). Lifespan changes in multitasking: Concurrent walking and memory search in children, young, and older adults. *Gait and Posture, 33,* 401–405. doi:10.1016/j.gaitpost.2012.12.012.

Krause, N. (2006). Religion and health in late life. In J. E. Birren & K. W. Schaie (Eds.), *Handbook of the psychology of aging* (6th ed., pp. 499–518). Amsterdam: Elsevier.

Krause, N., & Bastida, E. (2011). Prayer to the saints or the Virgin and health among older Mexican Americans. *Hispanic Journal of Behavioral Sciences, 33,* 71–87. doi:10.1177/0739986310393628.

Krause, N., Morgan, D., Chatters, L., & Meltzer, T. (2000). Using focus groups to explore the nature of prayer in late life. *Journal of Aging Studies, 14,* 191–212. doi:10.1016/S0890-4065(00)80011-0.

Kross, E., & Grossmann, I. (2012). Boosting wisdom: Distance from the self enhances reasoning, attitudes, and behavior. *Journal of Experimental Psychology: General, 141,* 43–48. doi:10.1037/a0024158.

Krueger, D., & Ludwig, A. (2007). On the consequences of demographic change for rates of return on capital, and the distribution of wealth and welfare. *Journal of Monetary Economics, 54,* 49–87. doi:10.1016/j.jmoneco.2006.12.016.

Krut, J. J., Zetterberg, H., Blennow, K., Cinque, P., Hagberg, L., Price, R. W. et al. (2013). Cerebrospinal fluid Alzheimer's biomarker profiles in CNS infections. *Journal of Neurology,* *260,* 620–626. Doi: 10.1007/s00415-012-6688-y.

Kübler-Ross, E. (1969). *On death and dying.* New York: Macmillan.

Kübler-Ross, E. (1974). *Questions and answers on death and dying.* New York: Macmillan.

Kulik, L. (2011). Developments in spousal power relations: Are we moving toward equality? *Marriage and Family Review, 47,* 419–435. doi:10.1080/01494929.2011.619297.

Kulwicki, A. D. (2002). The practice of honor crimes: A glimpse of domestic violence in the Arab world. *Issues in Mental Health Nursing, 23,* 77–87. doi:10.1080/01612840252825491.

Kunda, Z., & Spencer, S. J. (2003). When do stereotypes come to mind and when do they color judgment? A goal-based theoretical framework for stereotype activation and application. *Psychological Bulletin, 129,* 522–544. doi:10.1037/0033-2909.129.4.522.

Kunkle, F. (2012). Pioneering the granny pod: Fairfax County family adapts to high-tech dwelling that could change elder care. *Washington Post.* Retrieved from http://www .washingtonpost.com/local /dc-politics/pioneering-the-granny-po -fairfax-county-family-adapts-to-high -tech-dwelling-that-could-change- elder-care/2012/11/25/4d9ccb44- 1e18-11e2-ba31-3083ca97c314 _story.html?hpid=z3.

Kunz, J. A. (2007). Older adult development. In J. A. Kunz & F. G. Soltys (Eds.), *Transformational reminiscence: Life story work* (pp. 19–39). New York: Springer.

Kurdek, L. A. (2004). Are gay and lesbian cohabiting couples really different from heterosexual married couples? *Journal of Marriage and Family, 66,* 880–900. doi:10.1111/j.0022-2445.2004.00060.x.

Kwon, S., & Tae, Y.-S. (2012). Nursing home placement: The process of decision making and adaptation among adult children caregivers of demented parents in Korea. *Asian Nursing Research, 6,* 143–151. doi:10.1016/j.anr.2012.10.006.

Kyulo, N. L., Knutsen, S. F., Tonstad, S., Fraser, G. E., & Singh, P. N. (2012). Validation of recall of body weight over a 26-year period in cohort members of the Adventist health Study 2. *Annals of Epidemiology, 22,* 744–746. doi:10.1016/j.annepidem.2012.06.106.

Labouvie-Vief, G. (1980). Beyond formal operations: Uses and limits of pure logic in life-span development. *Human Development, 23,* 141–161. doi:10.1159/000272546.

Labouvie-Vief, G. (1997). Cognitive-emotional integration in adulthood. In K. W. Schaie & M. P. Lawton (Eds.), *Annual review of gerontology and geriatrics: Focus on emotion and adult development* (Vol. 17. pp. 206–237). New York: Springer.

Labouvie-Vief, G. (2003). Dynamic integration: Affect, cognition, and the self in adulthood. *Current Directions in Psychological Science, 12,* 201–206. doi:10.1046/j.0963-7214.2003.01262.x.

Labouvie-Vief, G. (2005). Self-with-other representations and the organization of the self. *Journal of* *Research in Personality, 39,* 185–205. doi:10.1016/j.jrp.2004.09.007.

Labouvie-Vief, G. (2006). Emerging structures of adult thought. In J. J. Arnett & J. T. Tanner (Eds.), *Emerging adults in America: Coming of age in the 21st century* (pp. 59–84). Washington, DC: American Psychological Association.

Labouvie-Vief, G. (2008). When differentiation and negative affect lead to integration and growth. *American Psychologist, 63,* 564–565. doi:10.1037/0003-066X.63.6.564.

Labouvie-Vief, G., & Diehl, M. (1999). Self and personality development. In J. C. Cavanaugh & S. K. Whitbourne (Eds.), *Gerontology: An interdisciplinary perspective* (pp. 238–268). New York: Oxford University Press.

Labouvie-Vief, G., Chiodo, L. M., Goguen, L. A., Diehl, M., & Orwoll, L. (1995). Representations of self across the life span. *Psychology and Aging, 10,* 404–415. doi:10.1037/0882-7974.10.3.404.

Labouvie-Vief, G., & Grühn, D., & Mouras, H. (2009). Dynamic emotion–cognition interactions in development: Arousal, stress, and the processing of affect. In H. B. Bosworth & C. Hertzog (Eds.), *Aging and cognition: Research methodologies and empirical advances* (pp. 181–196). Washington, DC: American Psychological Association.

Labouvie-Vief, G., Grühn, D., & Studer, J. (2010). Dynamic integration of emotion and cognition: Equilibrium regulation in development and aging. In M. E. Lamb & A. M. Freund (Eds.), *The handbook of life-span development: Vol. 2. Social and emotional development* (pp. 79–115). Hoboken, NJ: Wiley.

Lachman, M. E. (2004). Development in midlife. *Annual Review of Psychology, 55,* 305–331. doi:10.1146/annurev.psych.55.090902.141521.

Lachman, M. E. (2006). Perceived control over aging-related declines: Adaptive beliefs and behaviors. *Current Directions in Psychological Science, 15* (6) 282–286. doi:10.1111/j.1467-8721.2006.00453.x.

Lachman, M. E., & Agrigoroaei, S. (2012). Low perceived control as a risk factor for episodic memory: The mediational role of anxiety and task interference. *Memory and Cognition, 40,* 287–296. doi:10.3758/s13421-011-0140-x.

Lachman, M. E., & Andreoletti, C. (2006). Strategy use mediates the relationship between control beliefs and memory performance for middle-aged and older adults. *Journals of Gerontology: Psychological Sciences, 61,* P88–P94.

Lachman, M. E., Rosnick, C., & Röcke, C. (2009) The rise and fall of control beliefs in adulthood: Cognitive and biopsychosocial antecedents of stability and change over nine years. In H. Bosworth & C. Hertzog (Eds.), *Aging and cognition: Research methodologies and empirical advances* (pp. 143–160) Washington, DC: American Psychological Association.

Ladin, K., & Reinhold, S. (2013). Mental health of aging immigrants and native-born men across 11 European countries. *Journal of Gerontology:* *Social Sciences, 68,* 298–309. doi:10.1093/geronb/gbs163.

Lahey, J. N. (2010). International comparison of age discrimination laws. *Research on Aging, 32,* 679–697. doi:10.1177/0164027510379348.

Lai, C. K. Y., Wong, L. F., Liu, K.-H., Lui, W., Chan, M. F., & Yap, L. S. Y. (2013). Online and onsite training for family caregivers of people with dementia: Results form a pilot study. *International Journal of Geriatric Psychiatry, 28,* 107–108. doi:10.1002/gps.3798.

Lai, D. W. L. (2010). Filial piety, caregiving appraisal, and caregiving burden. *Research on Aging, 32,* 200–223. doi:10.1177/0164027509351475.

Lamanna, M. A., & Riedmann, A. (2011). *Marriages, families, and relationships* (11th ed.). Belmont, CA: Wadsworth.

Lambert-Pandraud, E., Laurent, G., & Lapersonne (2005). Repeat purchasing of new automobiles by older consumers: Empirical evidence and interpretations. *Journal of Marketing, 69,* 97–113. doi: 1509/jmkg.69.2.97.60757.

Lamela, D., Figueiredo, B., & Bastos, A. (in press). The Portuguese version of the Psychological Adjustment to Separation Test—Part A (PAST—A): A study with recently and non-recently divorced adults. *Journal of Happiness Studies,.* doi:10.1007/s10902-013-9427-x.

Lampkin-Hunter, T. (2010). *Single parenting.* Bloomington, IN: Xlibris.

Landis, M., Peter-Wright, M., Martin, M., & Bodenmann, G. (2013). Dyadic coping and marital satisfaction of older spouses in long-term marriages. *GeroPsych: The Journal of Gerontopsychology and Geriatric Psychiatry, 26,* 39–47. doi:10.1024/1662-9647/a000077.

Lane, B. N. (2007). Understanding anticipatory grief: Relationship to coping style, attachment style, caregiver strain, gender role identification, and spirituality. *Dissertation Abstracts International. Section B. Sciences and Engineering, 67(8-B),* 4714.

Lane, R. D., & Nadel, L. (Eds.). (2000). *Cognitive neuroscience of emotion.* New York: Oxford University Press.

Lane, R. T., Ducks, P. A., Shineman, D. W., & Fillit, H. M. (2013). Diverse therapeutic targets and biomarkers for Alzheimer's disease and related dementias: Report on the Alzheimer's Drug Discovery Foundation 2012 International Conference on Alzheimer's drug discovery. *Alzheimer's Research and Therapy, 5,* Article 5. doi:10.1186/alzrt159.

Lang, F. R. (2004). Social motivation across the life span. In F. R. Lang & K. L. Fingerman (Eds.), *Growing together: Personal relationships across the life span* (pp. 341–367). New York: Cambridge University Press.

Langer, E. J. (1989). *Mindfulness.* Reading, MA: Addison-Wesley.

Langer, E. J., & Rodin, J. (1976). The effects of choice and enhanced personal responsibility for the aged: A field experiment in an institutional setting. *Journal of Personality and Social Psychology, 34,* 191–198.

Lawlor, D., & York, M. (2007). Assessing goal attainment for quality improvement. *Journal of Intellectual Disabilities, 11*, 241–255. doi:10.1177/1744629507080786.

Lawton, L. E., & Tulkin, D. O. (2010). Work-family balance, family structure and family-friendly employer programs. Paper presented at the annual meeting of the Population Association of America, Dallas. Retrieved from http://paa2010.princeton.edu/download.aspx?submissionId=100573.

Lawton, M. P. (1982). Competence, environmental press, and the adaptation of old people. In M. P. Lawton, P. G. Windley, & T. O. Byerts (Eds.), *Aging and the environment: Theoretical approaches* (pp. 33–59). New York: Springer.

Lawton, M. P. (1989). Environmental proactivity in older people. In V. L. Bengtson & K. W. Schaie (Eds.), *The course of later life: Research and reflections* (pp. 15–23). New York: Springer.

Lawton, M. P., & Nahemow, L. (1973). Ecology of the aging process. In C. Eisdorfer & M. P. Lawton (Eds.), *The psychology of adult development and aging* (pp. 619–674). Washington, DC: American Psychological Association.

Lawton, M. P., Moss, M., Hoffman, C., Grant, R., Have, T. T., & Kleban, M. H. (1999). Health, valuation of life, and the wish to live. *The Gerontologist, 39*, 406–416. doi:10.1093/geront/39.4.406.

Lazarus, R. S. (1984). Puzzles in the study of daily hassles. *Journal of Behavioral Medicine, 7*, 375–389. doi:10.1007/BF00845271.

Lazarus, R. S., & Folkman, S. (1984). *Stress, appraisal, and coping.* New York: Springer.

Lazarus, R. S., DeLongis, A., Folkman, S., & Gruen, R. (1985). Stress and adaptational outcomes: The problem of confounded measures. *American Psychologist, 40*, 770–779. 10.1037/0003-066X.40.7.770.

Le Couteur, D. G, McLachlan, A. J., & de Cabo, R. (2012) Aging, drugs, and drug metabolism. *Journal of Gerontology: Medical Sciences, 67A*, 137–139. doi:10.1093/Gerona/glr084.

Lee, E.-K. O., & Sharpe, T. (2007). Understanding religious/spiritual coping and support resources among African American older adults: A mixed-method approach. *Journal of Religion, Spirituality & Aging, 19*, 55–75. doi:10.1300/J496v19n03_05.

Lee, K. H., & Siegle, G. J. (2012). Common and distinct brain networks underlying explicit emotional evaluation: A Meta-analytic study. *Social Cognitive and Affective Neuroscience, 7*, 521–534. doi:10.1093/scan/nsp001.

Lee, K. S. (2010). Gender, care work, and the complexity of family membership in Japan. *Gender & Society, 24*, 647–671. doi:10.1177/0891243210382903.

Lee, M.-D. (2007). Correlates of consequences of intergenerational caregiving in Taiwan. *Journal of Advanced Nursing, 59*, 47–56. doi:10.1111/j.1365-2648.2007.04274.x.

Lee, R. E., Hitchcock, R., & Biesele, M. (2002). Foragers to first peoples: The Kalahari San today. *Cultural Survival Quarterly, 26*, 8.

Lee, T.-Y. (2010). The loss and grief in immigration: Pastoral care for immigrants. *Pastoral Psychology, 59*, 159–169. doi:10.1007/s11089-009-0261-3.

Leentjens, A. F., Schieveld, J. N., Leonard, M., Lousberg, R., Verhey, F. R., & Meagher, D. J. (2008). A comparison of the phenomenology of pediatric, adult, and geriatric delirium. *Psychosomatic Research, 64*, 219–223. doi:10.1016/j.psychores.2007.11.003.

Lemieux, A. (2012). Post-formal thought in gerontagogy or beyond Piaget. *Journal of Behavioral and Brain Science, 2*, 399–406. doi:10.4236/jbbs.2012.23046.

Lemieux, R., & Hale, J. L. (2002). Cross-sectional analysis of intimacy, passion, and commitment: Testing the assumptions of the triangular theory of love. *Psychological Reports, 90*, 1009–1014. doi:10.2466/pr0.2002.90.3.1009.

Lent, R. W. (2013). Career-life preparedness: Revisiting career planning and adjustment in the new workplace. *Career Development Quarterly, 61*, 2–14. doi:10.1002/j.2161-0045.2013.00031.x.

Leon, G. R., Gillum, B., Gillum, R., & Gouze, M. (1979). Personality stability and change over a 30-year period: Middle to old age. *Journal of Consulting and Clinical Psychology, 47*, 517–524. doi:10.1037/0022-006X.47.3.517.

Lerner, R. M. (2001). *Concepts and theories of human development* (3rd ed.). Mahwah, NJ: Lawrence Erlbaum.

LeRoux, H., & Fisher, J. E. (2006). Strategies for enhancing medication adherence in the elderly. In W. T. O'Donohue & E. R. Levensky (Eds). *Promoting treatment adherence: A practical handbook for health care providers* (pp. 353–362). Thousand Oaks, CA: Sage.

Lesnoff-Caravaglia, G. (2010). Technology and aging: The herald of a new age. In J. C. Cavanaugh & C. K. Cavanaugh (Eds.), *Aging in America: Volume 3: Societal issues* (pp. 247–277). Santa Barbara, CA: ABC-CLIO.

Levine, I. S. (2009). *Best friends forever: Surviving a breakup with your best friend.* New York: Penguin.

Levinger, G. (1980). Toward the analysis of close relationships. *Journal of Experimental Social Psychology, 16*, 510–544. doi:10.1016/0022-1031(80)90056-6.

Levinger, G. (1983). Development and change. In H. H. Kelley, E. Berscheid, A. Christensen, J. H. Harvey, T. L. Huston, G. Levinger, et al. (Eds.), Close relationships (pp. 315–359). New York: Freeman.

Levinson, D. J., Darrow, C., Kline, E., Levinson, M., & McKee, B. (1978). *The seasons of a man's life.* New York: Knopf.

Levinson, D., & Levinson, J. D. (1996). *The seasons of a woman's life.* New York: Knopf.

Levy, B. (1996). Improving memory in old age through implicit stereotyping. *Journal of Personality and Social Psychology, 71*, 1092–1107.

Levy, B. R., & Leifheit-Limson, E. (2009). The stereotype-matching effect: Greater influence on functioning when age stereotypes correspond to outcomes. *Psychology and Aging, 24*(1), 230–233. doi:10.1037/a0014563.

Levy, B. R., Hausdorff, J. M., Hencke, R., & Wei, J. Y. (2000). Reducing cardiovascular stress with positive self-stereotypes of aging. *Journals of Gerontology: Psychological Sciences, 55B*, P20–P213. doi:10.1093/geronb/55.4.P205.

Levy, B. R., Slade, M. D., & Kasl, S. V. (2002). Longitudinal benefit of positive self-perceptions of aging on functional health. *Journals of Gerontology: Psychological Sciences, 57B*, P409–P417. doi:10.1093/geronb/57.5.P409.

Levy, B. R., Zonderman, A. B., Slade, M. D., & Ferrucci, L. (2012). Memory shaped by age stereotypes over time. *Journal of Gerontology: Psychological Sciences, 67*, 432–436. doi:10.1093/geronb/gbr120.

Levy, B., & Langer, E. (1994). Aging free from negative stereotypes: Successful memory in China and among the American deaf. *Journal of Personality and Social Psychology, 66*, 989–997. doi:10.1037/0022-3514.66.6.989.

Lewinsohn, P. M. (1975). The behavioral study and treatment of depression. In M. Hersen, R. M. Eisler, & P. M. Miller (Eds.), Progress in behavior modification (Vol. 1, pp. 19–64). New York: Academic Press.

Lewis, J. R. (2013). Hair-pulling, culture, and unmourned death. *International Journal of Psychoanalytic Self Psychology, 8*, 202–217. doi:10.1080/15551024.2013.768749.

Li, F., Harmer, P., Glasgow, R., Mack, K. A., Sleet, D., Fisher, K. J, Kohn, M. A., Millet, L. M., Mead, J., Xu, J., Lin, M.-L., Yang, T., Sutton, B., & Tompkins, Y. (2008). Translation of an effective tai chi intervention into a community-based falls-prevention program. *American Journal of Public Health, 98*, 1195–1198. Retrieved from http://ajph.apha publications.org/doi/pdf/10.2105/AJPH.2007.120402.

Li, K. Z. H., Lindenberger, U., Freund, A. M., & Baltes, P. B. (2001). Walking while memorizing: Age-related differences in compensatory behavior. *Psychological Science, 12*, 230–237. doi:10.1111/1467-9280.00341.

Liang, J., & Luo, B. (2012). Toward a discourse shift in social gerontology: From successful aging to harmonious aging. *Journal of Aging Studies, 26*, 327–334. doi:10.1016/j.jaging.2012.03.001.

Lichtenberg, P. A., MacNeill, S. E., & Mast, B. T. (2000). Environmental press and adaptation to disability in hospitalized live-alone older adults. *The Gerontologist, 40*, 549–556. 10.1093/geront/40.5.549.

Lieber, J. (2001). Widows of tower disaster cope, but with quiet fury. *USA Today*, A1–A2.

Lieberman, M. D., Gaunt, R., Gilbert, D. T., & Trope, Y. (2002). Reflexion and reflection: A social cognitive neuroscience approach to attributional inference. *Advances in Experimental Social Psychology, 34*, 199–249.

doi:10.1016/S0065-2601(02)80006-5.

Light, L. L. (2012). Dual-process theories of memory in old age: An update. In M. Naveh-Benjamin & N. Ohta (Eds.). *Memory and aging: Current issues and future directions* (pp. 97–124). New York: Psychology Press.

Li-Korotky, H.-S. (2012). Age-related hearing loss: Quality of care for quality of life. *The Gerontologist, 52*, 265–271. doi:10.1093/geront/gnr159.

Lilgendahl, J. P., & McAdams, D. P. (2011). Constructing stories of self-growth: How individual differences in patterns of autobiographical reasoning relate to well-being in midlife. *Journal of Personality, 79*, 391–428. doi:10.1111/j.1467-6494.2010.00688.x.

Lilley, L., Rainforth Collins, S., & Snyder, J. (2014). *Pharmacology and the nursing process* (7th ed.). New York: Mosby.

Lim, S., & Cortina, L. M. (2005). Interpersonal mistreatment in the workplace: The interface and impact of general incivility and sexual harassment. *Journal of Applied Psychology, 90*, 483–496. doi:10.1037/0021-9010.90.3.483.

Lin, J., Epel, E., & Blackburn, E. (2012). Telomeres and lifestyle factors: Roles in cellular aging. *Mutation Research/Fundamental and Molecular Mechanisms of Mutagenesis, 730*, 85–89. doi:10.1016/j.mrfmmm.2011.08.003.

Lin, X., & Leung, K. (2010). Differing effects of coping strategies on mental health during prolonged unemployment: A longitudinal analysis. *Human Relations, 63*, 637–665. doi:10.1177/0018726709342930.

Linden, D. E. J. (2012). The challenges and promise of neuroimaging in psychiatry. *Neuron, 73*, 8–22. doi:10.1016/j.neuron.2011.12.014.

Lindgren, K. P. (2007). Sexual intent perceptions: Review and integration of findings, investigation of automatic processes, and development and implementation of a dynamic assessment methodology. *Dissertation Abstracts International. Section B. Sciences and Engineering, 67*(9-B), 5469.

Lindley, R. I. (2012). Drug trials for older people. *Journal of Gerontology: Biological Sciences, 67A*, 152–157. doi:10.1093/gerona/glr065.

Lino, M. (2012). *Expenditures on children by families, 2011.* Retrieved from http://www.cnpp.usda.gov/Publications/CRC/crc2011.pdf.

Lipp, I., Benedek, M., Fink, A., Koschutnig, K., Reishofer, G., Bergner, S. et al. (2012). Investigating neural efficiency in the visuo-spatial Domain: An fMRI Study. *PLoS ONE, 7*, e51316. doi:10.1371/journal.pone.0051316. Retrieved from http://www.plosone.org/article/info%3Adoi%2F10.1371%2Fjournal.pone.0051316.

Liu, C.-C., Kanekiyo, T., Xu, H., & Bu, G. (2013). Apolipoprotein E and Alzheimer's disease: Risk, mechanisms and therapy. *Nature Reviews Neurology, 9*, 106–118. doi:10.1038/nrneurol.2012.263.

Liu, G., Dupre, M. E., Gu, D., Mair, C. A., & Chen, F. (2012). Psychological well-being of the institutionalized and community-residing oldest old in China: The role of children. *Social Science and Medicine, 75*, 1874–1882. doi:10.1016/j.socscimed.2012.07.019.

Liu, L., Drouet, V., Wu, J. W., Witter, M. P., Small, S. A, Clelland, C. et al. (2012). Trans-synaptic spread of tau pathology *in vivo*. PLoS ONE, *7*, e31302. doi:10.1371/journal. pone.0031302.

Lloyd, L. (2012). *Health and care in ageing societies: A new international approach*. Chicago: The Policy Press.

Lo, M., & Aziz, T. (2009). Muslim marriage goes online: The use of Internet matchmaking by American Muslims. *Journal of Religion and Popular Culture, 21*(3). Retrieved from http://www.questia.com /library/1G1-213033176/muslim -marriage-goes-online-the-use-of -internet-matchmaking.

Löckenhoff, C. E., & Carstensen, L. L. (2007). Aging, emotion, and health-related decision strategies: Motivational manipulations can reduce age differences. *Psychology and Aging, 22*, 134–146. doi:10.1037/0882-7974.22.1.134.

Logan, R. D. (1986). A reconceptualization of Erikson's theory: The repetition of existential and instrumental themes. *Human Development, 29*, 125–136. doi:10.1159/000273036.

Londoño-Vallejo, J. A. (2008). Telomere instability and cancer. *Biochimie, 90*, 73–82. doi:10.1016/j.biochi.2007.07.009.

Longest, K. C., & Thoits, P. A. (2012). Gender, the stress approach, and health: A configurational approach. *Society and Mental health, 2*, 187–206. doi:10.1177/2156869312451151.

Longo, B., Camoni, L., Boros, S., & Suligoi, B. (2008). AIDS patient care and STDs. *AIDS Patient Care and STDs, 22*, 365–371. doi:10.1089/apc.2007.0168.

Lorayne, H. (2008). *Ageless memory: The memory expert's prescription for a razor-sharp mind*. New York: Black Dog & Leventhal.

Loretto, W., & Vickerstaff, S. (2013). The domestic and gendered context for retirement. *Human Relations, 66*, 65–86. doi:10.1177/0018726712455832.

Lou, V. W. Q., & Ng, J. W. (2012). Chinese older adults' resilience to the loneliness of living alone: A qualitative study. *Aging and Mental Health, 16*, 1039–1046. doi:10.1080/1360786 3.2012.692764.

Lovejoy, M., & Stone, P. (2012). Opting back in: The influence of time at home on professional women's career redirection after opting out. *Gender, Work and Organization, 19*, 631–653. doi:10.1111/j.1468-0432.2010.00550.x.

Lowe, M. E., & McClement, S. E. (2010–2011). Spousal bereavement: The lived experience of young Canadian widows. *OMEGA: The Journal of Death and Dying, 62*, 127–148. doi:10.2190/OM.62.2.c.

Lu, T., & Finkel, T. (2008). Free radicals and senescence. *Experimental Cell Research, 314*, 1918–1922. doi:10.1016/j.yexcr.2008.01.011.

Luborsky, M. R., & LeBlanc, I. M. (2003). Cross-cultural perspectives on the concept of retirement: An analytic redefinition. *Journal of Cross-Cultural Gerontology, 18*, 251–271. doi:10.1023/B: JCCG.0000004898.24738.7b.

Luca, M., Prossimo, G., Messina, V., Luca, A., Romeo, S., & Calandra, C. (2013). Epidemiology and treatment of mood disorders in a day hospital setting from 1996 to 2007: An Italian study. *Neuropsychiatric Disease and Treatment, 9*, 169–176. doi:10.2147 /NDT.S39227.

Lucero-Liu, A. A. (2007). Exploring intersections in the intimate lives of Mexican origin women. *Dissertation Abstracts International. Section A. Humanities and Social Sciences, 68*(3-A), 1175.

Ludke, R. L., & Smucker, D. R. (2007). Racial differences in the willingness to use hospice services. *Journal of Palliative Medicine, 10*, 1329–1337. doi:10.1089/jpm.2007.0077.

Lunenfeld, B. (2008). An aging world—demographics and challenges. *Gynecological Endocrinology, 24*, 1–3. doi:10.1080/09513590701718364.

Lustbader, N., O'Hara, M. S., Wijdicks, E. F. M., MacLean, L., Tajik, W., Ying, A., et al. (2011). Second brain death examination may negatively affect organ donation. *Neurology, 76*, 119–124. doi:10.1212/ WNL.0b013e3182061b0c.

Luthans, F., Avolio, B. J., Avey, J. B., & Norman, S. M. (2007). Positive psychological capital: Measurement and relationship with performance and satisfaction. *Personnel Psychology, 60*, 541–572. doi:10.1111/j.1744-6570.2007.00083.x.

Lutz, A., Slagter, H. A., Rawlings, N. B., Francis, A. D., Greischar, L. L., & Davidson, R. J. (2009). Mental training enhances attentional stability: Neural and behavioral evidence. *The Journal of Neuroscience, 29*, 13418–13427. doi:10.1523/ JNEUROSCI.1614-09.2009.

MacDonald, S. W. S., Dixon, R. A., Cohen, A., & Hazlitt, J. E. (2004). Biological age and 12-year cognitive change in older adults: Findings from the Victoria Longitudinal Study. *Gerontology, 50*, 64–81, doi:10.1159/0000/5557.

Mace, J. H., & Clevinger, A. M. (2013). Priming voluntary autobiographical memories: Implications for the organization of autobiographical memory and voluntary recall processes. *Memory, 21*, 524–536. doi:10. 1080/09658211.2012.744422.

Maciejewski, P. K., Zhang, B, Block, S. D., & Prigerson, H. G. (2007). An empirical examination of the stage theory of grief. *JAMA, 297*, 716–723. doi:10.1001/jama.297.7.716.

Mackenzie, P. (2012). Normal changes of ageing. *InnovAiT.* doi:10.1093/ innovait/ins099.

Madden, D. J., Bennett, I. J., Burzynska, A., Potter, G. G., Chen, N-K., & Song, A. W. (2012). Diffusion tensor imaging of cerebral white matter integrity in cognitive aging. *Biochemica et Biophysica Acta (BBA)—Molecular Basis of Disease, 1822*, 386–400. doi:10.1016/j.bbadis.2011.08.003.

Madeo, A., Feld, S., & Spencer, B. (2008). Ethical and practical challenges raised by an adult day care program's caregiver satisfaction survey. *American Journal of Alzheimer's Disease and Other Dementias, 23*, 423–429. doi:10.1177/1533317508320891

Maeder, E. M., Wiener R. L., & Winter, R. (2007). Does a truck driver see what a nurse sees? The effects of occupation type on perceptions of sexual harassment. *Sex Roles, 56*, 801–810. doi:10.1007/s11199-007-9244-y.

Magai, C. (2008). Long-lived emotions: A life course perspective on emotional development. In M. Lewis, J. M. Haviland-Jones, & L. F. Barrett (Eds.), *Handbook of emotions* (3rd ed., pp. 376–392). New York: Guilford.

Mahady, G. B., Locklear, T. D., Doyle, B. J., Huang, Y., Perez, A. L. & Caceres, A. (2008). Menopause, a universal female experience: Lessons from Mexico and Central America. *Current Women's Health Reviews, 4*, 3–8. doi:10.2174/157340408783572033.

Mak, T., & Saunders, M. (2014). *Primer to the immune response* (2nd ed.). San Diego: Academic Press.

Malach-Pines, A. (2005). The Burnout Measure, Short Version. *International Journal of Stress Management, 12*, 78–88. doi:10.1037/1072-5245.12.1.78.

Malhi, G. S., Tanious, M., Das, P., Coulston, C. M., & Berk, M. (2013). Potential mechanisms of action of lithium in bipolar disorder. *CNS Drugs, 27*, 135–153.

Malone, M. L., & Camp, C. J. (2007). Montessori Based Dementia Programming®: Providing tools for engagement. *Dementia: The International Journal of Social Research and Practice, 6*, 150–157. doi:10.1177/1471301207079099.

Mandemakers, J. J., & Monden, C. W. S. (2013). Does the effect of job loss on psychological distress differ by educational level? *Work, Employment and Society, 27*, 73–93. doi:10.1177/0950017012460312.

Manji, H., Jäger, H. R., & Winston, A. (in press). HIV, dementia and antiretroviral drugs: 30 years of an epidemic. *Journal of Neurology, Neurosurgery, and Psychiatry with Practical Neurology.* doi:10.1136 /jnnp-2012-304022.

Mantler, J., Matejicek, A., Matheson, K., & Anisman, H. (2005). Coping with employment uncertainty: A comparison of employed and unemployed workers. *Journal of Occupational Health Psychology, 10*, 200–209. doi:10.1037/1076-8998.10.3.200.

Maple, M., Edwards, H. E., Minichiello, V., & Plummer, D. (2013). Still part of the family: The importance of physical, emotional and spiritual memorial places and spaces for parents bereaved through the suicide death of their son or daughter. *Mortality, 18*, 54–71. doi:10.1080/13576275.201 2.755158.

Maple, M., Edwards, H., Plummer, D., & Minichiello, V. (2010). Silenced voices: Hearing the stories of parents bereaved through the suicide death of a young adult child. *Health and Social Care in the Community, 18*, 241–248. doi:10.1111/j.1365-2524.2009.00886.x.

Marcia, J., & Josselson, R. (in press). Eriksonian personality research and its implications for psychotherapy. *Journal of Personality.* doi:10.1111/ jopy.12014.

Markland, A. D., Vaughan, C. P., Johnson, T. M., Burgio, K. L., & Goode, P. S. (2012). Incontinence. *The Medical Clinics of North America, 95*, 539–554. doi:10.1016/j. mcna.2011.02.006.

Markus, H., & Nurius, P. (1986). Possible selves. *American Psychologist, 41*, 954–969. doi:10.1037/0003-066X.41.9.954.

Marques-Aleixo, I., Oliveira, P. J., Moreira, P. I., Magalhães, J., & Ascensão, A. (2012). Physical exercise as a possible strategy for brain protection: Evidence from mitochondrial-mediated mechanisms. *Progress in Neurobiology, 99*, 149–162. doi:10.1016/j.pneurobio.2012.08.002.

Marteau, T. M., Roberts, S., LaRusse, S., & Green, R. C. (2005). Predictive genetic testing for Alzheimer's disease: Impact upon risk perception. *Risk Analysis, 25*, 397–404. doi:10.1111/j.1539-6924.2005.00598.x.

Martens, A., Goldenberg, J. L., & Greenberg, J. (2005). A terror management perspective on ageism. *Journal of Social Issues, 61*, 223–239. doi:10.1111/j.1540-4560.2005.00403.x.

Martin, M., Long, M. V., & Poon, L. W. (2002). Age changes and differences in personality traits and states of the old and very old. *Journals of Gerontology: Psychological Sciences, 57B*, P144–P152. doi:10.1093/ geronb/57.2.P144.

Martin, P., Hagberg, B., & Poon, L. W. (2012). Models for studying centenarians and healthy ageing. *Asian Journal of Gerontology and Geriatrics, 7*, 11–18. Retrieved from http://ajgg.org/AJGG/V7N1 /v7n1_SA2_P%20Martin.pdf.

Martin, P., Kliegel, M., Rott, C., Poon, L. W., & Johnson, M. A. (2008). Age differences and changes of coping behavior in three age groups: Findings from the Georgia Centenarian Study. *International Journal of Aging and Human Development, 66*, 97–114. doi:10.2190/AG.66.2.a.

Mash, H. B. H., Fullerton, C. S., & Ursano, R. J. (in press). Complicated grief and bereavement in young adults following close friend and sibling loss. *Depression and Anxiety.* doi:10.1002/da.22068.

Massimi, M. (2013). Exploring remembrance and social support behavior in an online bereavement support group. *CSCW'13: Proceedings of the 2013 Conference on Computer Supported Cooperative Work*, 1169–1180. doi:10.1145/ 2441776.2441908.

Masunaga, H., & Horn, J. (2001). Expertise and age-related changes in components of intelligence. *Psychology and Aging, 16*, 293–311. doi:10.1037/0882-7974.16.2.293.

Masunari, N., Fujiwara, S., Kasagi, F., Takahashi, I., Yamada, M., & Nakamura, T. (2012). Height loss starting in middle age predicts increased mortality in the elderly. *Journal of Bone and Mineral Research, 27*, 138–145. doi:10.1002/jbmr.513.

Mather, M. (2012). The emotion paradox in the aging brain. *Annals of the New York Academy of Sciences, 1251*, 33-49. doi:10.1111/j.1749-6632.2012.06471.x.

Matsumoto, D., & Juang, L. (2013). *Culture and psychology* (5th ed.). Belmont, CA: Wadsworth.

Maxfield, M., Solomon, S., Pyszczynski, T., & Greenberg, J. (2010). Mortality salience effects on the life expectancy estimates of older adults as a function of neuroticism. *Journal of Aging Research*. Doi: 10.4061/2010/260123. Retrieved from http://www.hindawi.com/journals/jar/2010/260123/.

May, C. P., Rahhal, T., Berry, E. M., & Leighton, E. A. (2005). Aging, source memory, and emotion. *Psychology and Aging, 20*, 571–578. doi:10.1037/0882-7974.20.4.571.

Mayes, A. R. (1995). The assessment of memory disorders. In A. D. Baddeley, B. A. Wilson, & F. N. Watts (Eds.), *Handbook of memory disorders* (pp. 367–391). Chichester, UK: Wiley

Mayo, A. M. (2008). Measuring functional status in older adults with dementia. *Clinical Nurse Specialist, 22*, 212–213.

Mayo Clinic. (2011a). *Fitness basics*. Retrieved from http://www.mayoclinic.com/health/fitness/MY00396.

Mayo Clinic. (2011b). *Angina*. Retrieved from http://www.mayoclinic.com/health/angina/DS00994.

Mayo Clinic. (2012a). *Wrinkles*. Retrieved from http://www.mayoclinic.com/health/wrinkles/DS00890.

Mayo Clinic. (2012b). *Hormone therapy: Is it right for you?* Retrieved from http://www.mayoclinic.com/health/hormone-therapy/WO00046.

Mayo Clinic. (2012c). *Cholesterol levels: What numbers should you aim for?* Retrieved from http://www.mayoclinic.com/health/cholesterol-levels/CL00001.

Mayo Clinic. (2012d). *Urinary incontinence*. Retrieved from http://www.mayoclinic.org/urinary-incontinence/types.html.

Mazerolle, M., Régner, I., Morisset, P., Rigalleau, F., & Huguet, P. (2012). Stereotype threat strengthens automatic recall and undermines controlled processes in older adults. *Psychological Science, 23*, 723–727. doi:10.1177/0956797612437607.

Mazzarella, S. R. (2007). Cyberdating success stories and the mythic narrative of living "Happily-Ever-After with the One." In M.-L. Galician & D. L. Merskin (Eds.), *Critical thinking about sex, love, and romance in the mass media* (pp. 23–37). Mahwah, NJ: Erlbaum

McAdams, D. P. (1999). Personal narratives and the life story. In L. Pervin & O. John (Eds.), *Handbook of personality: Theory and research* (2nd ed., pp. 478–500). New York: Guilford.

McAdams, D. P. (2001). The psychology of life stories. *Review of General Psychology, 5*, 100–122. doi:10.1037/1089-2680.5.2.100.

McAdams, D. P., & Olson, B. D. (2010). Personality development: Continuity and change over the life course. *Annual Review of Psychology, 61*, 517–542. doi:10.1146/annurev.psych.093008.100507.

McCabe, D. P. & Loaiza, V. M. (2012). Working memory. In S. K. Whitbourne & M. J. Sliwinski (Eds.), The Wiley-Blackwell handbook of adulthood and aging (pp. 154–173). Oxford, UK: Wiley-Blackwell.

McCarty, W. P., & Skogan, W. G. (2013). Job-related burnout among civilian and sworn police personnel. *Police Quarterly, 16*, 66–84. doi:10.1177/1098611112457357.

McCleese, C. S., & Eby, L. T. (2006). Reactions to job content plateaus: Examining role ambiguity and hierarchical plateaus as moderators. *Career Development Quarterly, 55*, 64–76. doi:10.1002/j.2161-0045.2006.tb00005.x.

McClinton, B. E. (2010). *Preparing for the third Age: A retirement planning course outline for lifelong learning programs*. Master's thesis from California State University, Long Beach. Retrieved January 30, 2011 from http://gradworks.umi.com/1486345.pdf.

McCrae, R. R., & Costa, P. T. (1994). The stability of personality: Observation and evaluations. *Current Directions in Psychological Sciences, 3*, 173–175. doi:10.1111/1467-8721.ep10770693.

McCrory, P., Meeuwisse, W., Johnston, K., Dvorak, J., Aubry, M., Molloy, M. Et al. (2009). Consensus statement on concussion in sport: The 3rd International Conference on Concussion in Sport held in Zurich, November 2008. *British Journal of Sports Medicine, 43*, i76–i84. Retrieved from http://bjsm.bmj.com/content/43/Suppl_1/i76.full.

McDowd, J. M., & Shaw, R. J. (2000). Attention and aging: A functional perspective. In F. I. M. Craik & T. A. Salthouse (Eds.), *Handbook of aging and cognition* (2nd ed., pp. 221–292). Mahwah, NJ: Erlbaum.

McGarry, K., & Schoeni, R. F. (2005). Widow(er) poverty and out-of-pocket medical expenditures near the end of life. *Journal of Gerontology: Social Sciences, 60*, S160–S168. doi:10.1093/geronb/60.3.S160.

McGee, W. (2007). *Sodium in diet*. Retrieved September 7, 2008, from http://www.nlm.nih.gov/medlineplus/ency/article/002415.htm.

McGuire, L. C., Morian, A., Codding, R., & Smyer, M. A. (2000). Older adults' memory for medical information: Influence of elderspeak and note taking. *International Journal of Rehabilitation and Health, 5*, 117–128. doi:10.1023/A:1012906222395.

McGuire, L. C., Morian, A., Codding, R., & Smyer, M. A.

(2000). Older adults' memory for medical information: Influence of elderspeak and note taking. *International Journal of Rehabilitation and Health, 5*, 117–128. doi:10.1023/A:1012906222395.

McKay, K., & Ross, L. E. (2010). The transition to adoptive parenthood: A pilot study of parents adopting in Ontario, Canada. *Children and Youth Services Review, 32*, 604–610. doi:10.1016/j.childyouth.2009.12.07.

McKee-Ryan, F., Song, Z., Wanberg, C. R., & Kinicki, A. J. (2005). Psychological and physical well-being during unemployment: A meta-analytic study. *Journal of Applied Psychology, 90*, 53–76. doi:10.1037/0021-9010.90.1.53.

McKenzie, P. T. (2003). *Factors of Successful Marriage: Accounts from Self-Described Happy Couples*. In partial fulfillment of the requirements for the degree of doctor of philosophy, Howard University.

McKhann, G. M., Knopman, D. S., Chertkow, H., Hyman, B. T., Jack, C. R., Jr., Kawas, C. H. et al. (2011). The diagnosis of dementia due to Alzheimer's disease: Recommendations from the National Institute on Aging—Alzheimer's Association workgroups on diagnostic guidelines for Alzheimer's disease. *Alzheimer's and Dementia: Journal of the Alzheimer's Association, 7*, 263–269. doi:10.1016/j.jalz.2011.03.005.

McKinney, B. C., & Sibille, E. (2013). The age-by-disease interaction hypothesis of late-life depression. *American Journal of Geriatric Psychiatry, 21*, 418–432. doi:10.1016/j.jagp.2013.01.053.

McKissock, D., & McKissock, M. (2012). *Coping with grief* (4th ed.). Sydney: HarperCollins.

McLean, K. C., & Pasupathi, M. (2012). Processes of identity development: Where I am and how I got there. *Identity, 12*, 8–28. doi:10.1080/15283488.2011.632363.

McQueen, M. B., & Blacker, D. (2008). Genetics of Alzheimer's disease. In J. W. Smoller, B. R. Sheidley, & M. T. Tsuang (Eds.), *Psychiatric genetics: Applications in clinical practice* (pp. 177–193). Arlington, VA: American Psychiatric Publishing

Meade, M. L., Nokes, T. J., & Morrow, D. G. (2009). Expertise promotes facilitation on a collaborative memory task. *Memory, 17*, 39–48. doi:10.1080/09658210802524240.

Medicare.gov. (2013). *What's Medicare supplement (Medigap) insurance?* Retrieved from http://www.medicare.gov/supplement-other-insurance/medigap/whats-medigap.html.

MedlinePlus. (2012a). *Sodium in diet*. Retrieved from http://www.nlm.nih.gov/medlineplus/ency/article/002415.htm.

MedlinePlus. (2012b). *Aging changes in the male reproductive system*. Retrieved from http://www.nlm.nih.gov/medlineplus/ency/article/004017.htm.

Mehta, K. K. (1997). The impact of religious beliefs and practices on aging: A cross-cultural comparison. *Journal of Aging Studies, 11*, 101–114. doi:10.1016/S0890-4065(97)90015-3.

Meijer A. M., & van den Wittenboer, G. L. H. (2007). Contribution of infants' sleep and crying to marital relationship of first-time parent couples in the 1st year after childbirth. *Journal of Family Psychology, 21*, 49–57. doi:10.1037/0893-3200.21.1.49.

Meilaender, G. (2013). *Bioethics: A primer for Christians* (3rd ed.). Grand Rapids, MI: Eerdmans Publishing.

Meléndez, J. C., Mayordomo, T., Sancho, P., & Tomás, J. M. (2012). Coping strategies: Gender differences and development throughout life span. *The Spanish Journal of Psychology, 15*, 1089–1098.

Melhado, L. W., & Byers, J. F. (2011). Patients' and surrogates' decision-making characteristics: Withdrawing, withholding, and continuing life-sustaining treatments. *Journal of Hospice and Palliative Nursing, 13*, 16–28. doi:10.1097/NJH.0b013e3182018f09.

Meng X., & D'Arcy, C. (2012). Education and dementia in the context of the cognitive reserve hypothesis: A systematic review with meta-analyses and qualitative analyses. *PLoS ONE 7*, e38268. doi:10.1371/journal.pone.0038268. Retrieved from http://www.plosone.org/article/info%3Adoi%2F10.1371%2Fjournal.pone.0038268.

Menon, U. (2001). Middle adulthood in cultural perspective: The imagined and the experienced in three cultures. In M. E. Lachman (Ed.), *Handbook of midlife development* (pp. 40–74). New York: Wiley.

Menon, U., & Shweder, R. A. (1998). The return of the "White man's burden": The moral discourse of anthropology and the domestic life of Hindu women. In R. A. Shweder (Ed.), *Welcome to the middle age!: (And other cultural fictions)* (pp. 139–188). Chicago: University of Chicago Press.

Mercado-Crespo, M. C., Arroyo, L. E., Rios-Ellis, B., D'Anna, L. H., Londoño, C., Núñez, L., Salazar, J., D'Oliveira, V., & Millar, C. (2008). *Latinos and depression: Findings from a community-based mental health promotion effort*. Paper presented at the annual meeting of the American Public Health Association, San Diego, CA.

Mercer, J. (2011). Attachment theory and its vicissitudes: Toward an updated theory. *Theory and Psychology, 21*, 25–45. doi:10.1177/0959354309356136.

MetLife. (2010). *The MetLife national study of adult day services: Providing support to individuals and their family caregivers*. Retrieved from https://www.metlife.com/assets/cao/mmi/publications/studies/2010/mmi-adult-day-services.pdf.

MetLife. (2012). *The 2012 MetLife market survey of nursing homes, assisted living, adult day services, and home care costs*. Retrieved from https://www.metlife.com/mmi/research/2012-market-survey-long-term-care-costs.html?WT.ac=PRO_Pro3_PopularContent_5-18491_T4297-MM-mmióid=PRO_Pro3

_PopularContent_5-18491_T4297 -MM-mmi#keyfindings.

MetLife Mature Market Institute. (2012). *Market survey of long-term care costs.* Retrieved from https://www.metlife.com/mmi /research/2012-market-survey-long-term-care-costs.html#keyfindings.

MetLife Mature Market Institute, National Alliance for Caregiving, and Center for Long-Term Care Research. (2011). *The MetLife study of caregiving costs to working caregivers.* Retrieved from https:// www.metlife.com/mmi/research /caregiving-cost-working-caregivers .html#key findings.

Meyer, B. J. F., Talbot, A. P., & Ranalli, C. (2007). Why older adults make more immediate treatment decisions about cancer than younger adults. *Psychology and Aging, 22,* 505–524. doi:10.1037/0882-7974.22.3.505.

Meyer, J. F. (2007). Confucian "familism" in America. In D. S. Browning & D. A. Clairmont (Eds.), *American religions and the family: How faith traditions cope with modernization and democracy* (pp. 168–184). New York: Columbia University Press

Meza-Kubo, V., & Morán, A. L. (in press). UCSA: A design framework for usable cognitive systems for the worried-well. *Personal and Ubiquitous Computing.* doi:10.1007/ s00779-012-0554-x.

Michel, J. P., Newton, J. L., & Kirkwood, T. B. (2008). Medical challenges of improving the quality of a longer life. *JAMA, 299,* 688–690. doi:10.1001/ jama.299.6.688.

Milaszewski, D., Greto, E., Klochkov, T., & Fuller-Thomson, E. (2012). A systematic review of education for the prevention of HIV/AIDS among older adults. *Journal of Evidence-Based Social Work, 9,* 213–230. doi:10.1080/15433714.20 10.494979.

Miller, K. I., Shoemaker, M. M., Willyard, J., & Addison, P. (2008). Providing care for elderly parents: A structurational approach to family caregiver identity. *Journal of Family Communication, 8,* 19–43. doi:10.1080/15267430701389947.

Miller, K. J., Siddarth, P., Gaines, J. M., Parish, J. M., Ercoli, L. M., Marx, K, et al. (2012). The Memory Fitness Program: Cognitive effects of a healthy aging intervention. *American Journal of Geriatric Psychiatry, 20,* 514–523. doi:10.1097/ JGP.0b013e3318227f821.

Minnotte, K. L. (2010). *Methodologies of assessing marital success.* Retrieved from https://workfamily.sas.upenn .edu/wfrn-repo/object/w2yp4p7i f8lm7q4k.

Miranda, J., McGuire, T. G., Williams, D. R., & Wang, P. (2008). Mental health in the context of health disparities. *American Journal of Psychiatry, 165,* 1102–1108. doi:10.1176/appi.ajp.2008.08030333.

Missildine, W., Feldstein, G., Punzalan, J. C., & Parsons, J. T. (2005). S/ he loves me, s/he loves me not: Questioning heterosexist assumptions of gender differences in romantic and sexually motivated behaviors. *Sexual Addiction*

& *Compulsivity, 12,* 65–74. doi:10.1080/10720160590933662.

Mitchell, B. A. (2006). *The boomerang age: Transitions to adulthood in families.* New Brunswick, NJ: AldineTransaction.

Mitchell, B. A. (2010). Happiness in midlife parental roles: A contextual mixed methods analysis. *Family Relations, 59,* 326–339. doi:10.1111/ j.1741-3729.2010.00605.x.

Mitchell, L. M., & Messner, L. (2003–2004). Relative child care: Supporting the providers. *Journal of Research in Childhood Education, 18,* 105–113. doi:10.1080/02568540409595026.

Moeller, J. R., Lewis, M. M., & Werth, J. L., Jr. (2010). End of life issues. In J. C. Cavanaugh & C. K. Cavanaugh (Eds.), Aging in America: Vol. 1: Psychological aspects (pp. 202–231). Santa Barbara, CA: Praeger Perspectives.

Moen, P., & Roehling, P. (2005). *The career mystique: Cracks in the American dream.* Oxford, UK: Rowman & Littlefield.

Mohlman, J., Sirota, K. G., Papp, L. A., Staples, A. M., King, A., & Gorenstein, E. E. (2012). Clinical interviewing with older adults. *Cognitive and Behavioral Practice, 19,* 89–100. doi:10.1016/j. cbpra.2010.10.001.

Mojon-Azzi, S. M., Sousa-Poza, A., & Mojon, D. S. (2008). Impact of low vision on well-being in 10 European countries. *Ophthalmologica, 222,* 205–212. doi:10.1159/000126085.

Molony, S. L., Evans, L. K., Jeon, S., Rabig, J., & Straka, L. A. (2011). Trajectories of at-homeness and health in usual care and small house nursing homes. *The Gerontologist, 51,* 504–515. doi:10.1093/geront/ gnr022.

Molony, S. L., McDonald, D. D., & Palmisano-Mills, C. (2007). Psychometric testing of an instrument to measure the experience of home. *Research in Nursing and Health, 30,* 518–530. doi:10.1002/ nur.20210.

Montgomery, L. (2013). *Republicans embrace Obama's offer to trim Social Security benefits.* Retrieved from http://www.washingtonpost.com /business/economy/republicans -embrace-obamas-offer-to -trim-social-security -benefits/2013/04/15/9de1c594 -a448-11e2-9c03-6952ff305f35_story. html?hpid=z4.

Moore, K. D. (2005). Using place rules and affect to understand environmental fit: A theoretical exploration. *Environment and Behavior, 37,* 330–363. doi:10.1177/0013916504272657.

Moorman, S. M., & Greenfield, E. A. (2010). Personal relationships in later life. In J. C. Cavanaugh & C. K. Cavanaugh (Eds.), *Aging in America: Vol. 3: Societal Issues* (pp. 20–52). Santa Barbara, CA: ABC-CLIO

Moorman, S. M., & Inoue, M. (2013). Persistent problems in end-of-life planning among young- and middle-aged American couples. *Journal of Gerontology: Social Sciences, 68,* 97–106. doi:10.1093 /geronb/gbs103.

Moran, J. D. (2008). Families, courts, and the end of life: Schiavo and its

implications for the family justice system. *Family Court Review, 46,* 297–330. doi:10.1111/j.1744-1617.2008.00202.x.

Morcom, A. M., & Friston, K. J. (2012). Decoding episodic memory in ageing: A Bayesian analysis of activity patterns predicting memory. *Neuroimage, 59,* 1772–1782. doi:10.1016/j.neuroimage.2011.08.071.

Morfei, M. Z., Hooker, K., Fiese, B. H., & Cordeiro, A. M. (2001). Continuity and change in parenting possible selves: A longitudinal follow-up. *Basic and Applied Social Psychology, 23,* 217–223. doi:10.1207/153248301750433777.

Morgan, S., & Yoder, L. H. (2012). A concept analysis of person-centered care. *Journal of Holistic Nursing, 30,* 6–15. doi:10.1177/0898010111412189.

Moriarty, J., Rutter, D., Ross, P. D. S., & Holmes, P. (2012). *End of life care for people with dementia living in care homes.* Retrieved from http://www .scie.org.uk/publications/briefings /files/briefing40.pdf.

Morrell, R. W., Echt, K. V., & Caramagno, J. (2008). *Older adults, race/ethnicity, and mental health disparities: A consumer focused research agenda.* Human Resources Research Organization. Retrieved from http:// www.tapartnership.org/docs /researchAgendaOnAgeAndMHD isparities.pdf.

Morris, W. L., Sinclair, S., & DePaulo, B. M. (2007). No shelter for singles: The perceived legitimacy of marital status discrimination. *Group Processes & Intergroup Relation, 10,* 457–470. doi:10.1177/1368430207081535.

Mossello, E., Caleri, V., Razzi, E., Di Bari, M., Cantini, C., Tonon, E., Lopilato, F., Marini, M., Simoni, D., Cavallini, D. C., Marchionni, N., Biagini, C. A., & Masotti, G. (2008). Day care for older dementia patients: Favorable effects on behavioral and psychological symptoms and caregiver stress. *International Journal of Geriatric Psychiatry, 23,* 1066–1072. doi:10.1002/gps.2034.

Mõttus, R., Johnson, W., & Deary, I. J. (2012). Personality traits in old age: Measurement and rank-order stability and some mean-level change. *Psychology and Aging, 27*(1), 243–249. doi:10.1037/a0023690

Moye, J., Sabatino, C. P., & Brendel, R. W. (2013). Evaluation of the capacity to appoint a health-care proxy. *American Journal of Geriatric Psychiatry, 21,* 326–336. doi:10.1016/j.jagp.2012.09.001.

Moyle, W., & O'Dwyer, S. (2012). Quality of life in people living with dementia in nursing homes. *Current Opinion in Psychiatry, 25,* 480–484. doi:10.1097/ YCO.0b013e32835a1ccf.

Moynehan, J., & Adams, J. (2007). What's the problem? A look at men in marital therapy. *American Journal of Family Therapy, 35,* 41–51. doi:10.1080/01926180600553381.

Mroczek, D. K., & Spiro, A. (2003). Modeling intraindividual change in personality traits: Findings from the normative aging study. *Journals of Gerontology: Psychological Sciences,*

58B, P153–P165. doi:10.1093/ geronb/58.3.P153.

Mühlig-Versen, A., Bowen, C. E., & Staudinger, U. M. (2012). Personality plasticity in later adulthood: Contextual and personal resources are needed to increase openness to new experiences. *Psychology and Aging, 27,* 855–866. doi:10.1037/ a0029357.

Muller, E. D., & Thompson, C. L. (2003). The experience of grief after bereavement: A phenomenological study with implications for mental health counseling. *Journal of Mental Health Counseling, 25,* 183–203.

Mulley, G. (2008). Depression in physically ill older patients. In S. Curran & J. P. Wattis (Eds.), *Practical management of affective disorders in older people* (pp. 126–145). Abingdon, UK: Radcliffe.

Munoz, R. T., & Fox, M. D. (2013). Legal aspects of brain death and organ donorship. In D. Novitzky & D. K. C. Cooper (Eds.), *The brain-dead organ donor* (pp. 21–35). New York: Springer.

Muntaner, C., Ng, E., Vanroelen, C., Christ, S., & Eaton, W. W. (2013). Social stratification, social closure, and social class as determinants of mental health disparities. In C. S. Aneshensel, J. C. Phelan, & A. Bieman (Eds.), *Handbook of the sociology of mental health* (pp. 206–227). New York: Springer.

Murray, C. J. L., & Evans, D. (2003). *Health systems performance assessment.* Geneva, Switzerland: World Health Organization.

Musil, C. M., & Standing, T. (2005). Grandmothers' diaries: A glimpse at daily lives. *International Journal of Aging & Human Development, 60,* 317–329. doi:10.2190/LPTU-JAUX-W7F9-341K.

Mutchler, J. E., Baker, L. A., & Lee, S. A. (2007). Grandparents responsible for grandchildren in Native-American families. *Social Science Quarterly, 88,* 990–1009. doi:10.1111/j.1540-6237.2007.00514.x.

Mwanyangala, M. A., Mayombana, C., Urassa, H., Charles, J., Mahutanga, C., Abdullah, S., et al. (2010). Health status and quality of life among older adults in rural Tanzania. *Global Health Action, 3.* Retrieved from http://journals.sfu.ca/coaction/index .php/gha/article/viewArticle /2142/6055.

Naef, R., Ward, R., Mahrer-Imhof, R., & Grande, G. (2013). Characteristics of the bereavement experience of older persons after spousal loss: An integrative review. *International Journal of Nursing Studies, 50,* 1108–1121. doi:10.1016/j. ijnurstu.2012.11.026.

Nahemow, L. (2000). The ecological theory of aging: Powell Lawton's legacy. In R. L. Rubinstein & M. Moss (Eds.), *The many dimensions of aging* (pp. 22–40). New York: Springer

Nashiro, K., Sakaki, M., Huffman, D., & Mather, M. (2013). Both younger and older adults have difficulty updating emotional memories. *Journal of Gerontology: Psychological Sciences, 68,* 224–227. doi:10.1093/ geronb/gbs039.

Nashiro, K., Sakaki, M., Huffman, D., & Mather, M. (2013). Both younger and older adults have difficulty updating emotional memories. *Journal of Gerontology: Psychological Sciences, 68,* 224–227. doi:10.1093/geronb/gbs039.

National Academy of Social Insurance. (2012). *Social Security benefits, finances, and policy options: A primer.* Retrieved from http://www.nasi.org/sites/default/files/research/Social_Security_Primer_PDF.pdf.

National Adult Day Services Association. (2012). *Adult day services: Overview and facts.* Retrieved from http://www.nadsa.org/consumers/overview-and-facts/.

National Alliance for Caregiving and AARP. (2010). *Caregiving in the U.S.: Executive Summary.* Retrieved from http://assets.aarp.org/rgcenter/il/caregiving_09_es.pdf.

National Cancer Institute. (2012). *Prostate cancer.* Retrieved from http://www.cancer.gov/cancertopics/types/prostate.

National Center for Health Statistics. (2012a). *Health, United States, 2011.* Retrieved from http://www.cdc.gov/nchs/data/hus/hus11.pdf.

National Center for Health Statistics. (2012b). *United States life tables, 2008.* Retrieved from http://www.cdc.gov/nchs/data/nvsr/nvsr61/nvsr61_03.pdf.

National Center for Health Statistics. (2012c). *Summary health statistics for the U.S. population: National Health Interview Survey, 2011.* Retrieved from http://www.cdc.gov/nchs/data/series/sr_10/sr10_255.pdf.

National Center for Health Statistics (2013a). *Marriage and divorce.* Retrieved from http://www.cdc.gov/nchs/fastats/divorce.htm.

National Center for Health statistics. (2013b). *Births and natality.* Retrieved from http://www.cdc.gov/nchs/fastats/births.htm.

National Center on Elder Abuse. (2013). *Types of abuse.* Retrieved from http://www.ncea.aoa.gov/FAQ/Type_Abuse/index.aspx.

National Comprehensive Cancer Network. (2012). *NCCN guidelines for patients: Prostate cancer.* Retrieved from http://www.nccn.org/patients/patient_guidelines/prostate/files/assets/seo/toc.html.

National Endowment for Financial Education. (2010). *Life transitions.* Retrieved from http://www.smartaboutmoney.org/Your-Money/Life-Transitions/Search-Results.aspx?topic=57.

National Heart, Lung and Blood Institute. (2011). *What is atherosclerosis?* Retrieved from http://www.nhlbi.nih.gov/health/health-topics/topics/atherosclerosis/.

National Institute of Arthritis and Musculoskeletal and Skin Diseases. (2010a). *Osteoarthritis.* Retrieved from http://www.niams.nih.gov/Health_Info/Osteoarthritis/default.asp.

National Institute of Arthritis and Musculoskeletal and Skin Diseases. (2009). *Rheumatoid arthritis.* Retrieved from http://www.niams.nih.gov/Health_Info/Rheumatic_Disease/default.asp.

National Institute of Arthritis and Musculoskeletal and Skin Diseases. (2011). *Calcium and vitamin D: Important at every age.* Retrieved from http://www.niams.nih.gov/Health_Info/Bone/Bone_Health/Nutrition/default.asp.

National Institute of Mental Health. (2008). *Major depressive disorder among adults.* Retrieved from http://www.nimh.nih.gov/statistics/1MDD_ADULT.shtml.

National Institute of Mental Health. (2012). *Ethnic disparities persist in depression diagnosis and treatment among older Americans.* Retrieved from http://www.nimh.nih.gov/science-news/2012/ethnic-disparities-persist-in-depression-diagnosis-and-treatment-among-older-americans.shtml.

National Institute of Mental Health. (2013). *Major depressive disorder among adults.* Retrieved from http://www.nimh.nih.gov/statistics/1MDD_ADULT.shtml.

National Institute on Aging. (2012a) *Longer lives and disability.* Retrieved from http://www.nia.nih.gov/research/publication/global-health-and-aging/longer-lives-and-disability.

National Institute on Aging. (2012b). *Aging hearts and arteries: A scientific quest.* Retrieved from http://www.nia.nih.gov/health/publication/aging-hearts-and-arteries-scientific-quest.

National Institute on Aging. (2013a). *About Alzheimer's disease: Alzheimer's basics.* Retrieved from http://www.nia.nih.gov/alzheimers/topics/alzheimers-basics.

National Institute on Aging. (2013b). *About Alzheimer's disease: Diagnosis.* Retrieved from http://www.nia.nih.gov/alzheimers/topics/diagnosis.

National Institute on Alcohol Abuse and Alcoholism. (2008). *Alcohol research: A lifespan perspective.* Retrieved from http://pubs.niaaa.nih.gov/publications/AA74/AA74.pdf.

National Institute on Alcohol Abuse and Alcoholism. (2012). *Alcohol use in older people.* Retrieved from http://www.nia.nih.gov/health/publication/alcohol-use-older-people.

National Institutes of Health. (2011). *Heart attack first aid.* Retrieved from http://www.nlm.nih.gov/medlineplus/ency/article/000063.htm.

National Parkinson's Foundation. (2012). *What is Parkinson's disease?* Retrieved from http://www.parkinson.org/Parkinson-s-Disease/PD-101/What-is-Parkinson-s-disease.

National Parkinson's Foundation. (2013). *Medications for motor symptoms.* Retrieved from http://www.parkinson.org/Parkinson-s-Disease/Treatment.

Naveh-Benjamin, M., & Ohta, N. (Eds.). (2012). *Memory and aging: Current issues and future directions.* New York: Psychology Press.

Naveh-Benjamin, M., Craik, F. I. M., Guez, J., & Kreuger, S. (2005). Divided attention in younger and older adults: Effects of strategy and relatedness on memory performance and secondary task costs. *Journal of Experimental Psychology: Learning, Memory and Cognition, 32,* 520–537. doi:10.1037/0278-7393.31.3.520.

Nawijn, J., De Bloom, J., & Geurts, S. (2013). Pre-vacation time: Blessing or burden? *Leisure Sciences, 35,* 33–44. doi:10.1080/01490400.2013.739875.

Nayernouri, T. (2011). Euthanasia, terminal illness and quality of life. *Archives of Iranian Medicine, 14,* 54–55. Retrieved from http://sid.ir/En/VEWSSID/J_pdf/86920110109.pdf.

Neal, M. B., & Hammer, L. B. (2006). *Working couples caring for children and aging parents: Effects on work and well-being.* Mahwah, NJ: Erlbaum.

Neff, L. A., & Karney, B. R. (2005). To know you is to love you: The implications of global adoration and specific accuracy for marital relationships. *Journal of Personality and Social Psychology, 88,* 480–497. doi:10.1037/0022-3514.88.3.480.

Neft, N., & Levine, A. D. (1997). *Where women stand: An international report on the status of women in over 140 countries, 1997–1998.* New York: Random House.

Neisser, U. (1976). *Cognition and reality.* San Francisco: W. H. Freeman.

Neisser, U. (2012). Flashbulb memories. In S. R. R. Schmidt (Ed.), *Extraordinary memories for exceptional events* (pp. 45–66). New York: Psychology Press.

Nerenberg, L. (2010). Elder abuse prevention: A review of the field. In J. C. Cavanaugh & C. K. Cavanaugh (Eds.), *Aging in America: Vol.3: Societal Issues* (pp. 53–80). Santa Barbara, CA: Praeger Perspectives.

Neugarten, B. L., & Weinstein, K. K. (1964). The changing American grandparent. *Journal of Marriage and Family, 26,* 299–304. doi:10.2307/349727.

Newman, A., Thompson, J., & Chandler, E. M. (2013). Continuous care: A home hospice benefit. *Clinical Journal of Oncology Nursing, 17,* 19–20. doi:10.1188/13.CJON.19-20.

Newsom, J. T. (1999). Another side to caregiving: Negative reactions to being helped. *Current Directions in Psychological Science, 8,* 183–187. doi:10.1111/1467-8721.00043.

Newton, N. J., & Stewart, A. J. (2012). Personality development in adulthood. In S. K. Whitbourne & M. J. Sliwinski (Eds.), *The Wiley-Blackwell handbook of adulthood and aging* (pp. 209–235). Oxford, UK: Wiley-Blackwell.

Nichols, L. O., Chang, C., Lummus, A., Burns, R., Martindale-Adams, J., Graney, M. J., Coon, D. W., & Czaja, S. (2008). The cost-effectiveness of a behavioral intervention with caregivers of patients with Alzheimer's disease. *Journal of the American Geriatrics Society, 56,* 413–420. doi:10.1111/j.1532-5415.2007.01569.x.

Nigro, N., & Christ-Crain, M. (2012). Testosterone treatment in the aging male: Myth or reality? *Swiss Medical Weekly.* doi:10.4414/smw.2012.13539. Retrieved from http://www.smw.ch/content/smw-2012-13539/.

NIHSeniorHealth. (2011). *Depression.* Retrieved from http://nihseniorhealth.gov/depression/aboutdepression/01.html.

NIHSeniorHealth. (2011a). *Osteoporosis: What Is Osteoporosis?.* Retrieved from http://nihseniorhealth.gov/osteoporosis/toc.html.

NIHSeniorHealth. (2011b). *Osteoporosis: Prevention.* Retrieved from http://nihseniorhealth.gov/osteoporosis/prevention/01.html.

Nimrod, G. (2007a). Retirees' leisure: Activities, benefits, and their contribution to life satisfaction. *Leisure Studies, 26,* 65–80. doi:10.1080/02614360500333937.

Nimrod, G. (2007b). Expanding, reducing, concentrating and diffusing: Post retirement leisure behavior and life satisfaction. *Leisure Sciences, 29,* 91–111. doi:10.1080/01490400600983446.

Nisbett, R. E., Aronson, J., Blair, C., Dickens, W., Flynn, J., Halpern, D. F. et al. (2012). Intelligence: New findings and theoretical developments. *American Psychologist, 67,* 130–159. doi:10.1037/a0026699.

Noonan, D. (2005, June 6). *A little bit louder, please.* Retrieved from http://www.thedailybeast.com/newsweek/2005/06/05/a-little-bit-louder-please.html.

Norcross, J. C., Beutler, L. E., & Levant, R. F. (Eds.). (2005). *Evidence-based practices in mental health: Debate and dialogue on the fundamental questions.* Washington, DC: American Psychological Association.

Nordahl, C. W., Ranganath, C., Yonelinas, A. P., DeCarli, C., Fletcher, E., & Jagust, W. J. (2006). White matter changes compromise prefrontal cortex function in healthy elderly individuals. *Journal of Cognitive Neuroscience, 18* (3), 418–429. Retrieved from http://www.mitpressjournals.org/doi/pdf/10.1162/jocn.2006.18.3.418.

Nordin, S. (2012). Olfactory impairment in normal aging and Alzheimer's disease. In G. M. Zucco, R. S. Herz, & I. Schaal (Eds.), *Olfactory cognition: From perception and memory to environmental odours and neurosciences* (pp. 199–217). Philadelphia: John Benjamin.

Norem, J. K. (2012). Motivation and goal pursuit: Integration across the social/personality divide. In K. Deaux & M. Snyder (Eds.), *The Oxford handbook of personality and social psychology* (pp.287–314). New York: Oxford University Press.

Norlander, B., & Eckhardt, C. (2005). Anger, hostility, and male perpetrators of intimate partner violence: A meta-analytic review. *Clinical Psychology Review, 25,* 119–152. doi:10.1016/j.cpr.2004.10.001.

North, M. S., & Fiske, S. T. (2012). An inconvenienced youth? Ageism and its potential intergenerational roots. *Psychological Bulletin, 138,* 982–997. doi:10.1037/a0027843.

Norton, M. I., & Gino, F. (in press). Rituals alleviate grieving for loved ones, lovers, and lotteries. *Journal of Experimental Psychology: General.* doi:10.1037/a0031772.

Nosek, M., Kennedy, H. P., & Gudmundsdottir, M. (2012). Distress during the menopause transition: A rich contextual analysis of midlife women's narratives. *Sage Open, 2.* 10.1177/2158244012455178.

Nyberg, L., Lövdén, M., Riklund, K., Lindenberger, U., & Bäckman, L. (2012). Memory aging and brain maintenance. *Trends in Cognitive Sciences, 16*, 292–306. doi:10.1016/j.tics.2012.04.005.

O'Brien, L. T., & Hummert, M. L. (2006). Memory performance of late middle-aged adults: Contrasting self-stereotyping and stereotype threat accounts of assimilation to age stereotypes. *Social Cognition, 24*, 338–358. doi:10.1521/soco.2006.24.3.338.

O'Dell, C. D. (2007). *Mothering mother: A daughter's humorous and heartbreaking memoir.* Largo, FL: Kunati, Inc.

O'Donovan, A., Tomiyama, A. J., Lin, J., Puterman, E., Adler, N. E., Kemeny, M., et al. (2012). Stress appraisals and cellular aging: A key role for anticipatory threat in the relationship between psychological stress and telomere length. *Brain, Behavior, and Immunity, 26*, 573–579. doi:10.1016/j.bbi.2012.01.007.

O'Leary, K. D. (1993). Through a psychological lens: Personality traits, personality disorders, and levels of violence. In R. J. Gelles & D. R. Loseke (Eds.), *Current controversies on family violence* (pp. 7–30). Newbury Park, CA: Sage.

O'Rourke, N., & Cappeliez, P. (2005). Marital satisfaction and self-deception: Reconstruction of relationship histories among older adults. *Social Behavior and Personality, 33*, 273–282. doi:10.2224/sbp.2005.33.3.273.

Oburu, P. O., & Palmérus, K. (2005). Stress related factors among primary and part-time caregiving grandmothers of Kenyan grandchildren. *International Journal of Aging & Human Development, 60*, 273–282. doi:10.2190/XLQ2-UJEM-TAQR-4944.

Ochs, E., & Kremer-Sadlik, T. (2013). *Fast-forward family: Home, work, and relationships in middle-class America.* Berkeley, CA: University of California Press.

Oedekoven, C. S. H., Jansen, A., Kircher, T. T., & Leube, D. T. (2013). Age-related changes in parietal lobe activation during an episodic memory retrieval task. *Journal of Neural Transmission, 120*, 799–806. doi:10.1007/s00702-012-0904-x.

Office of Management and Budget. (2013). *Fiscal year 2014 budget of the U.S. government.* Retrieved from http://www.whitehouse.gov/sites/default/files/omb/budget/fy2014/assets/budget.pdf.

Ogden, J. (2012). *Health psychology* (5th ed.). New York: McGraw-Hill.

Oh, D. H., Kim, S. A., Lee, H. Y., Seo, J. Y., Choi, B.-Y., & Nam, J. H. (2013). Prevalence and correlates of depressive symptoms in Korean adults: Results of a 2009 Korean community health survey. *Journal of Korean Medical Science, 28*, 128–135. doi:10.3346/jkms.2013.28.1.128.

Okonski, B. (1996, May 6). Just say something. *Newsweek*, 14.

Old, S., & Naveh-Benjamin, M. (2008). Memory for people and their actions: Further evidence for an age-related associative deficit. *Psychology and Aging, 23*, 467–472. doi:10.1037/0882-7974.23.2.467.

Omori, M., & Smith, D. T. (2009). The impact of occupational status on household chore hours among dual earner couples. *Sociation Today, 7.* Retrieved from http://www.ncsociology.org/sociationtoday/v71/chore.htm.

Oosterman, J. M., Morel, S., Meijer, L., Buvens, C., Kessels, R. P. C., & Postma, A. (2011). Differential age effects on spatial and visual working memory. *International Journal of Aging and Human Development, 73*, 195–208. doi:10.2190/AG.73.3.a.

Oregon Department of Human Services. (2013). *Oregon's Death with Dignity Act—2012.* Retrieved from http://public.health.oregon.gov/ProviderPartnerResources/EvaluationResearch/DeathwithDignityAct/Documents/year15.pdf.

Orel, N. A., & Fruhauf, C. A. (2013). Lesbian, gay, bisexual, and transgender grandparents. In A. E. Goldberg & K. R. Allen (Eds.), *LGBT-parent families* (pp. 177–192). New York: Springer.

Orentlicher, D. (2000). The implementation of Oregon's Death with Dignity Act: Reassuring, but more data are needed. *Psychology, Public Policy, and Law, 6*, 489–502. doi:10.1037/1076-8971.6.2.489.

Ortiz-Walters, R., & Gilson, L. L. (2013). Mentoring programs for under-represented groups. In J. Passmore, D. B. Peterson, & T. Freire (Eds.), *The Wiley-Blackwell handbook of coaching and mentoring* (pp. 266–282). Oxford, U.K.: Wiley-Blackwell.

Osgood, D. W., Ruth, G., Eccles, J. S., Jacobs, J. E., & Barber, B. L. (2005). Six paths to adulthood: Fast starters, parents without careers, educated partners, educated singles, working singles, and slow starters. In R. A. Settersten, Jr., F. F. Furstenberg, Jr., & R. G. Rumbaut (Eds.), *On the frontier of adulthood: Theory, research, and public policy* (pp. 320–355). Chicago, IL: University of Chicago Press.

Ossher, L., Flegal, K. E., & Lustig, C. (2013). Everyday memory errors in older adults. *Aging, Neuropsychology, and Cognition, 20*, 220–243. doi:10.1080/13825585.2012.690365.

Oswald, A. J., & Wu, S. (2010). Objective confirmation of subjective measures of human well-being: Evidence from the USA. *Science, 327*, 576–579. doi:10.1126/science.1180606.

Ota, H., McCann, R. M., & Honeycutt, J. M. (2012). Inter-Asian variability in intergenerational communication. *Human Communication Research, 38*, 172–198. doi:10.1111/j.1468-2958.2011.01422.x.

Owen, C. J. (2005). The empty nest transition: The relationship between attachment style and women's use of this period as a time for growth and change. *Dissertation Abstracts International. Section B. Sciences and Engineering, 65(7-B)*, 3747.

Ownby, R. L., Hertzog, C., & Czaja, S. J. (2012). Relations between cognitive status and medication adherence in patients treated for memory disorders. *Ageing Research.* doi:10.4081/ar.2012.e2. Retrieved from http://www.pagepress.org/journals/index.php/ar/article/viewArticle/2729.

Ozawa, M. N., & Yoon, H. S. (2002). The economic benefit of remarriage: Gender and class income. *Journal of Divorce and Remarriage, 36*, 21–39. doi:10.1300/J087v36n03_02.

Palkovitz, R., & Palm, G. (2009). Transitions within fathering. *Fathering, 7*, 3–22. doi:10.3149/fth.0701.3.

Palmore, E. B. (2007). Healthy behaviors or age denials? *Educational Gerontology, 33*, 1087–1097. doi:10.1080/03601270701700706.

Papa, A., & Litz, B. (2011). Grief. In W. T. O'Donohue & C. Draper (Eds.), *Stepped care and e-health: Practical applications to behavioral disorders* (pp. 223–245). New York: Springer.

Paris, D. L. (2008). *Alzheimer's disease special care units.* Retrieved from http://www.caregiver.com/channels/alz/articles/alz_special_care_unit.htm.

Park D. C., & Reuter-Lorenz, P. (2009). The adaptive brain: Aging and neurocognitive scaffolding. *Annual Review of Psychology, 60*, 173–196. doi:10.1146/annurev.psych.59.103006.093656. Retrieved from http://www.ncbi.nlm.nih.gov/pmc/articles/PMC3359129/.

Park, C. L. (2007). Religiousness/spirituality and health: A meaning systems perspective. *Journal of Behavioral Medicine, 30*, 319–328. doi:10.1007/s10865-007-9111-x.

Park, D. C., & Reuter-Lorenz, P. (2009). The adaptive brain: Aging and neurocognitive scaffolding. *Annual Review of Psychology, 60*, 173–196. doi:10.1146/annurev.psych.59.103006.093656.

Park, J., Kitayama, S., Karasawa, M., Curhan, K., Markus, H. R., Kawakami, N. et al. (2013). Clarifying the links between social support and health: Culture, stress, and neuroticism matter. *Journal of Health Psychology, 18*, 226–235. doi:10.1177/1359105312439731.

Park, Y.-H. (2008). Day healthcare services for family caregivers of older people with stroke: Needs and satisfaction. *Journal of Advanced Nursing, 61*, 619–630. doi:10.1111/j.1365-2648.2007.04545.x.

Parker, L. D. (2008). A study about older African American spousal caregivers of persons with Alzheimer's disease. *Dissertation Abstracts International: Section B: The Sciences and Engineering, 68(10-B)*, 6589.

Parkes, C. M. (2013). Elisabeth Kübler-Ross, On death and dying: A reappraisal. *Mortality, 18*, 94–97. doi:10.1080/13576275.2012.758629.

Parkman, A. M. (2007). *Smart marriage: Using your (business) head as well as your heart to find wedded bliss.* Westport, CT: Praeger.

Parpa, E., Mystakidou, K., Tsilika, E., Sakkas, P., Patiraki, E., Pistevou-Gombaki, A. et al. (2010). Attitudes of health care professionals, relatives of advanced cancer patients and public towards euthanasia and physician assisted suicide. *Health Policy, 97*, 160–165. doi:10.1016/j.healthpol.2010.04.008.

Parrot, A., & Cummings, N. (2006). *Forsaken females: The global brutalization of women.* Lanham, MD: Rowman & Littlefield.

Passalacqua, S. A., & Harwood, J. (2012). VIPS communications skill straining for paraprofessional dementia caregivers: an intervention to increase person-centered dementia care. *Clinical Gerontologist, 35*, 425–445. doi:10.1080/07317115.2012.702655.

Passarella, S., & Duong, M-T. (2008). Diagnosis and treatment of insomnia. American *Journal of Health-System Pharmacy, 65*, 927–934. doi:10.2146/ajhp060640.

Pasupathi, M. (2001). The social construction of the personal past and its implications for adult development. *Psychological Bulletin, 127*, 651–672. doi:10.1037/0033-2909.127.5.651.

Pasupathi, M. (2013). Making meaning for the good life: A commentary on the special issue. *Memory, 21*, 143–149. doi:10.1080/09658211.2012.744843.

Pasupathi, M., & Carstensen, L. L. (2003). Age and emotional experience during mutual reminiscing. *Psychology and Aging, 18*, 430–442. doi:10.1037/0882-7974.18.3.430.

Patel, K., Coppin, A., Manini, T., Lauretani, F., Bandinelli, S., Ferrucci, L., & Guralnik, J. (2006). Midlife physical activity and mobility in older age: The InCHIANTI study. *American Journal of Preventive Medicine, 31*, 217–224. doi:10.1016/j.amepre.2006.05.005.

Patry, D. A., Blanchard, C. M., & Mask, L. (2007). Measuring university students' regulatory leisure coping styles: Planned breathers or avoidance? *Leisure Sciences, 29*, 247–265. doi:10.1080/01490400701257963.

Patterson, A. V. (2012). *Emerging adulthood as a unique stage in Erikson's psychosocial development theory: Incarnation v. impudence.* Dissertation submitted to the Graduate School of the University of Texas at Arlington. Retrieved from http://dspace.uta.edu/bitstream/handle/10106/11059/Patterson_uta_2502D_11766.pdf?sequence=1.

Paul, R., Lane, E., & Jefferson, A. (2013). Vascular cognitive impairment. In L. D. Ravdin & H. L. Katzen (Eds.), *Handbook of the neuropsychology of aging and dementia* (pp. 281–294). New York: Springer.

Pear, R. (2011). *U.S. alters rule on paying for end-of-life planning.* Retrieved from http://www.nytimes.com/2011/01/05/health/policy/05health.html?_r=0.

Pearlin, L. I., & Bierman, A. (2013). Current issues and future directions in research into the stress process. In C. S. Aneshensel, J. C. Phelan, & A. Bierman (Eds.), *Handbook of the sociology of mental health* (pp. 325–340). New York: Springer.

Pearlin, L. I., Mullan, J. T., Semple, S. J., & Skaff, M. M. (1990). Caregiving and the stress process: An overview of concepts and their measures. *The Gerontologist, 30*, 583–594. doi:10.1093/geront/30.5.583.

Peltzer, K., & Phaswana-Mafuya, N. (2013). Depression and associated factors in older adults in South Africa. *Global Health Action, 6.* doi:10.3402/gha.v6i0.18871. Available online at http://www.ncbi.nlm.nih.gov/pmc/articles/PMC3549465/.

Penson, R. T. (2004). Bereavement across cultures. In R. J. Moore & D. Spiegel (Eds.), *Cancer, culture, and communication* (pp. 241–279). New York: Kluwer/Plenum.

Perls, T., & Terry, D. (2003). Genetics of exceptional longevity. *Experimental Gerontology, 38*, 725–730. doi:10.1016/S0531-5565(03)00098-6.

Peters, E., Hess, T. M., Vastfjall, D., & Auman, C. (2007). Adult age differences in dual information processes: Implications for the role of affective and deliberative processes in older adults' decision making. *Perspectives on Psychological Science, 2*, 1–23. doi:10.1111/j.1745-6916.2007.00025.x.

Peterson, B. E., & Stewart, A. J. (1996). Antecedents and contexts of generativity motivation at midlife. *Psychology and Aging, 11*, 21–33. doi:10.1037/0882-7974.11.1.21.

Peterson, C. B., Prasad, N. R., & Prasad, R. (2012). Assessing assistive technology outcomes with dementia. *Gerotechnology, 11*. doi:10.4017/gt.2012.11.02.414.00. Open source retrieved from http://vbn.aau.dk /files/66413578/Assessing_ATs _with_dementia_1744_2025_1 _SP_1.pdf.

Pettinato, J. (2013). Financing long-term care. In A. E. McDonnell (Ed.), *Managing geriatric health services* (pp. 147–172). Burlington, MA: Jones & Bartlett Learning.

Pfeiffer, E. (2013). *Winning strategies for successful aging.* New Haven, CT: Yale University Press.

Phillips, D. R., & Siu, O.-l. (2012). Global aging and aging workers. In J. W. Hedge & W. C. Borman (Eds.), *The Oxford handbook of work and aging* (pp. 11–32). New York: Oxford University Press.

Phillips, J., Ajrouch, K., & Hillcoat-Nalletamby, S. (2010). *Key concepts in social gerontology.* Thousand Oaks, CA: Sage Publications.

Piaget, J. (1970). Piaget's theory. In P. H. Mussen (Ed.), *Carmichael's manual of child psychology* (3rd ed., Vol. 1, pp. 703–732). New York: Wiley.

Piaget, J. (1972). Intellectual evolution from adolescence to adulthood. *Human Development, 15*, 1–12. doi:10.1159/0002/1225.

Piaget, J. (1980). *Les formes et les mentaires de la dialectique.* Paris: Gallimard.

Pienta, A. M., Hayward, M. D., & Jenkins, K. R. (2000). Health consequences of marriage for the retirement years. *Journal of Family Issues, 21*, 559–586. doi:10.1177/019251300021005003.

Pierret, C. R. (2006). The "sandwich generation": Women caring for parents and children. *Monthly Labor Review, September.* Retrieved from http://www.bls.gov/opub /mlr/2006/09/art1full.pdf.

Pillai, J. A., McEvoy, L. K., Hagler, D. J., Jr., Holland, D., Dale, A. M., Salmon, D. P. et al. (2012). Higher education is not associated with greater cortical thickness in brain areas related to literacy or intelligence in normal aging or mild cognitive impairment. *Journal of Clinical and Experimental Neuropsychology, 34*, 925–935. doi:10 .1080/13803395.2012.702733.

Pillay, H., Kelly, K., & Tones, M. (2006). Career aspirations of older workers: An Australian study. *International Journal of Training and Development, 10*, 298–305. doi:10.1111/j.1468-2419.2006.00263.x.

Pinto, K. M., & Coltrane, S. (2009). Division of labor in Mexican origin and Anglo families: Structure and culture. *Sex Roles, 60*, 482–495. doi:10.1007/s11199-008-9549-5.

Piquet, B. J. (2007). That's what friends are for. *Dissertation Abstracts International. Section B. Sciences and Engineering, 67(7-B)*, 4114.

Plonsky, L., & Oswald, F. L. (2012). How to do a meta-analysis. In A. Mackey & S. M. Gass (Eds.), *Research methods in second language acquisition: A practical guide* (pp. 275–295). New York: Wiley.

Poldrack, R. A. (2012). The future of fMRI in cognitive neuroscience. *NeuroImage, 62*, 1216–1220. doi:10.1016/j.neuroimage.2011.08.007.

Polivka, L. (2010). Neoliberalism and the new politics of aging and retirement security. In J. C. Cavanaugh & C. K. Cavanaugh (Eds.), *Aging in America: Vol. 3: Societal Issues* (pp. 161–202). Santa Barbara, CA: ABC-CLIO.

Ponde, M. P., & Santana, V. S. (2000). Participation in leisure activities: Is it a protective factor for women's mental health? *Journal of Leisure Research, 32*, 457–472.

Popenoe, D. (2009). Cohabitation, marriage, and child wellbeing: A cross-national perspective. *Society: Social science and Public Policy, 46*, 429–436. doi:10.1007/s12115-009-9242-5.

Potočnik, K., Tordera, N., & Peiró, J. M. (2013). Truly satisfied with your retirement or just resigned? Pathways toward different patterns of retirement satisfaction. *Journal of Applied Gerontology, 32*, 164–187. doi:10.1177/0733464811405988.

Power, T. L., & Smith, S. M. (2008). Predictors of fear of death and self-mortality: An Atlantic Canadian perspective. *Death Studies, 32*, 252–272. doi:10.1080/07481180701880935.

Pratt, H. D. (2010). Perspectives from a non-traditional mentor. In C. A. Rayburn, F. L. Denmark, M. E. Reuder, & A.M. Austria, (Eds.), *A handbook for women mentors: Transcending barriers of stereotype, race, and ethnicity* (pp. 223–232). Santa Barbara, CA: ABC-CLIO.

Pratt, S. I., Bartels, S. J., Mueser, K. T., & Forester, B. (2008). Helping older people experience success: An integrated model of psychosocial rehabilitation and health care management for older adults with serious mental illness. *American Journal of Psychiatric Rehabilitation, 11*, 41–60. doi:10.1080/15487760701853193.

Prebble, S. C., Addis, D. R., & Tippett, L. J. (2013). Autobiographical memory and sense of self. *Psychological Bulletin, 139*, 815–840. doi:10.1037/a0030146.

Priaulx, N. (2013). The troubled identity of the bioethicist. *Health Care Analysis, 21*, 6–19. doi:10.1007/s10728-012-0229-9.

Pride, N. B. (2005). Ageing and changes in lung mechanics. *European Respiratory Journal, 26*, 563–565. doi:10 .1183/09031936.05.00079805.

Prince, M., Bryce, R., Albanese, E., Wimo, A., Ribeiro, W., & Ferri, C. P. (2013). The global prevalence of dementia: A systematic review and meta-analysis. *Alzheimer's & Dementia: The Journal of the Alzheimer's Association, 9*, 63–75. doi:10.1016/j.jalz.2012.11.007.

Ptak, R. (2012). The frontoparietal attention network of the human brain: Action, saliency, and a priority map of the environment. *Neuroscientist, 18*, 502–515. doi:10.1177/1073858411409051.

Punnoose, A. R., Lynm, C., & Golub, R. M. (2012). Adult hearing loss. *JAMA, 307*, 1215. doi:10.1001/jama.2012.185.

Purcell, D., MacArthur, K. R., & Samblanet, S. (2010). Gender and the glass ceiling at work. *Sociology Compass, 4*, 705–717. doi:10.1111 /j.1751-9020.2010.00304.x.

Purser, J. L., Feng, Q., Yi, Z., & Hoenig, H. (2012). A new classification of function and disability in China: Subtypes based on performance-based and self-reported measures. *Journal of Aging and Health, 24*, 779–798. doi:10.1177/0898264312444310.

Pynoos, J. Caraviello, R., & Cicero, C. (2010). Housing in an aging America. In J. C. Cavanaugh & C. K. Cavanaugh (Eds.), *Aging in America: Vol. 3: Societal issues* (pp. 129–159). Santa Barbara, CA: Praeger Perspectives.

Pynoos, J., Steinman, B. A., Do Nguyen, A. Q., & Bressette, M. (2012). Assessing and adapting the home environment to reduce falls and meet the changing capacity of older adults. *Journal of Housing for the Elderly, 26*, 137–155. doi:10.1080/027 63893.2012.673382.

Qualls, S. H., & Benight, C. C. (2007). The role of clinical health geropsychology in the health care of older adults. In C. M. Aldwin, C. L. Park, & A. Spiro (Eds.), *Handbook of health psychology and aging* (pp. 367–389). New York: Guilford.

Quéniart, A., & Charpentier, M. (2013). Initiate, bequeath, and remember: Older women's transmission role within the family. *Journal of Women and Aging, 25*, 45–65. doi:10.1080/08 952841.2012.720181.

Rabig, J., Thomas, W., Kane, R. A., Cutler, L. J., & McAlilly, S. (2006). Radical redesign of nursing homes: Applying the green house concept in Tupelo, MS. *The Gerontologist, 46*, 533–539. doi:10.1093/geront/46.4.533.

Radloff, L.S. (1977). The CES-D scale: A self-report depression scale for research in the general population. *Applied Psychological Measurement, 1*, 385–401. doi:10.1177/014662167700100306.

Rahman, A. N., & Schnelle, J. F. (2008). The nursing home culture-change movement: Recent past, present, and future directions for research. *The Gerontologist, 48*, 142–148. doi:10.1093/geront/48.2.142.

Raju, S. S. (2011). *Studies on ageing in India: A review.* New Delhi: United Nations Population Fund. Retrieved from http://www.isec.ac.in/BKPAI%20 Working%20paper%202.pdf.

Ramos-Zúñiga, R., González-Pérez, O., Macías-Ornelas, A., Capilla-González, V., & Quiñones-Hinojosa, A. (2012). Ethical implications in the use of embryonic and adult neural stem cells. *Stem Cells International, Vol. 2012*, doi:10.1155/2012/470949. doi: 10.1155/2012/470949. Retrieved from http://www.hindawi.com /journals/sci/2012/470949/.

Randall, G. K., Martin, P., Bishop, A. J., Johnson, M. A., & Poon. L. W. (2012). Social resources and change in functional health comparing three age groups. *International Journal of Aging and Human Development, 75*, 1–29. doi:10.2190/AG.75.1.c.

Rando, T. A., & Chang, H. Y. (2012). Aging, rejuvenation, and epigenetic reprogramming: Resetting the aging clock. *Cell, 148*, 46–57. doi:10.1016/j.cell.2012.01.003.

Ranwez, S., Leidig, T., & Crampes, M. (2000). Formalization to improve lifelong learning. *Journal of Interactive Learning Research, 11*, 389–409.

Rape, Abuse, and Incest national Network. (2013). *Statistics.* Retrieved from http://www.rainn.org /statistics.

Raschick, M., & Ingersoll-Dayton, B. (2004). The costs and rewards of caregiving among aging spouses and adult children. *Family Relations: Interdisciplinary Journal of Applied Family Studies, 53*, 317–325. doi:10.1111/j.0022-2445.2004 .0008.x.

Rattan, S. I. S., Kryzch, V., Schnebert, S., Perrier, E., & Nizard, C. (2013). Hormesis-based anti-aging products: A case study of a novel cosmetic. *Dose-Response, 11*, 99-108. doi:10.2203/dose-response.11-054. Rattan. Retrieved from http:// dose-response.metapress.com /media/p3d6qpmvyp7ud5tpulft /contributions/l/4/5/4 /l45443612h506376.pdf.

Rattan, S. I. S. (2012). Biogerontology: From here to where? The Lord Cohen Medal lecture—2011. *Biogerontology, 13*, 83–91. doi:10.1007/s10522-011-9354-3.

Rauers, A., Riediger, M., Schmiedek, F., & Lindenberger, U. (2011). With a little help from my spouse: Does spousal collaboration compensate for the effects of cognitive aging? *Gerontology, 57*, 161–166. doi:10.1159/000317335.

Rawlins, W. K. (2004). Friendships in later life. In J. F. Nussbaum & J. Coupland (Eds.), *Handbook of communication and aging research* (2nd ed., pp. 273–299). Mahwah, NJ: Erlbaum.

Ray, R. D., & Zald, D. H. (2012). Anatomical insights into the interaction of emotion and cognition in the prefrontal cortex. *Neuroscience & Biobehavioral Reviews, 36*, 479–501. doi:10.1016/j.neubio-rev.2011.08.005.

Ready, R. E., Carvalho, J. O., & Åkerstedt, A. M. (2012). Evaluative organization of the self-concept in younger, midlife, and older adults. *Research on Aging, 34*, 56–79. doi:10.1177/0164027511415244.

Real, K., Mitnick, A. D., & Maloney, W. F. (2010). More similar than different: Millennials in the U.S. building trades. *Journal of Business and Psychology, 25*, 303–313. doi:10.1007/s10869-010-9163-8.

Redzanowski, U., & Glück, J. (2013). Who knows who is wise? Self and peer ratings of wisdom. *Journal of Gerontology: Psychological Sciences, 68,* 391–394. doi:10.1093/geronb/gbs079.

Reed, A. E., & Carstensen, L. L. (2012). The theory behind the age-related positivity effect. *Frontiers in Psychology.* doi:10.3389/fpsyg.2012.00339.

Reese, D. (2001, May). Putting the resident first. *Contemporary Long Term Care,* 24–28.

Reid, R. C. (2008). Quality of care and mortality among long-term care residents with dementia. *Canadian Studies in Population, 35,* 49–71. Retrieved from http://www.canpop soc.ca/CanPopSoc/assets/File/publi cations/journal/CSPv35n1p49.pdf.

Reinke, B. J., Holmes, D. S., & Harris, R. L. (1985). The timing of psychosocial change in women's lives: The years 25 to 45. *Journal of Personality and Social Psychology, 48,* 1353–1364. doi:10.1037/0022-3514.48.5.1353.

Reitz, C. (2012) Alzheimer's disease and the amyloid cascade hypothesis: A critical review. *International Journal of Alzheimer's Disease, 2012.* doi:10.1155/2012/369808. Retrieved from http://www.hindawi.com /journals/ijad/2012/369808/.

Remedios, J. D., Chasteen, A. L., & Packer, D. J. (2010). Sunny side up: The reliance on positive age stereotypes in descriptions of future older selves. *Self and Identity, 9,* 257–275. doi:10.1080/15298860903054175.

Rendeiro, C., Guerreiro, J. D. T., Williams, C. M., & Spencer, J. P. E. (2012). Flavonoids as modulators of memory and learning: Molecular interactions resulting in behavioural effects. *Proceedings of the Nutrition Society, 71,* 246–262. doi:10.1017/S0029665112000146.

Renshaw, K. D., Rodrigues, C., & Jones, D. H. (2008). Psychological symptoms and marital satisfaction in spouses of operation Iraqi freedom veterans: Relationships with spouses' perceptions of veterans' experiences and symptoms. *Journal of Family Psychology, 22,* 586–594. doi:10.1037/0893-3200.22.3.586.

Reuter-Lorenz, P. A. (2002). New visions of the aging mind and brain. *Trends in Cognitive Sciences, 6* (9), 394–400. doi:10.1016/S1364-6613(02)01957-5.

Reuter-Lorenz, P. A., & Mikels, J. A. (2006). The aging mind and brain: Implications of enduring plasticity for behavioral and cultural change. In P. B. Baltes, P. A. Reuter-Lorenz, & F. Rösler (Eds.), *Lifespan development and the brain: The perspective of biocultural co-constructivism* (pp. 255–276). New York: Cambridge University Press.

Reville, B. (2011). Utilization of palliative care: providers still hinder access. *Health Policy Newsletter, 24(1).* Retrieved from http://jdc .jefferson.edu/cgi/viewcontent .cgi?article=1714&context=hpn.

Rhoades, G. K., Stanley, S. M., & Markman, H. J. (2009). Couples' reasons for cohabitation: Associations with individual well-being and relationship quality. *Journal of Family Issues, 30,* 233–258. doi:10.1177/0192513X08324388.

Rice, N. E., Lang, I. A., Henley, W., & Melzer, D. (2010). Common health predictors of early retirement: Findings from the English Longitudinal Study of Ageing. *Age and Ageing, 40,* 54–61. doi:10.1093 /ageing/afq153.

Rich, K. L. (2013). Introduction to bioethics and ethical decision making. In J. B. Butts & K. L. Rich (Eds.), *Nursing ethics: Across the curriculum and into practice* (3rd ed., pp. 31–68). Burlington, MA: Jones & Bartlett Learning.

Rickard, A. P., Chatfield, M. D., Powell, J. J., Stephen, A. M., & Richards, M. (2012). Dietary iron is associated with memory in midlife: Longitudinal cohort study. *Journal of Pharmacy and Nutritional Sciences, 2,* 57–62. Retrieved from http://life scienceglobal.com/pms/index.php /jpns/article/view/238/pdf.

Ridings, C., & Gefen, D. (2004). Virtual community attraction: Why people hang out online. *Journal of Computer-Mediated Communication, 10,* http://jcmc.indiana.edu/vol10/ issue1/ridings.gefen.html.

Ridley, N. J., Draper, B., & Withall, A. (2013). Alcohol-related dementia: An update of the evidence. *Alzheimer's Research and Therapy, 5,* Article 3. doi:10.1186/alzrt157.

Riediger, M., Freund, A. M., & Baltes, P. B. (2005). Managing life through personal goals: Intergoal facilitation and intensity of goal pursuit in younger and older adulthood. *Journals of Gerontology: Psychological Sciences, 60B,* P84–P91. doi:10.1093/geronb/60.2.P84.

Rijken, A. J. (2009). *Happy families, high fertility?: Childbearing choices in the context of family and partner relationships.* Dissertation submitted in partial fulfillment of the doctor of philosophy degree, University of Utrecht.

Riley, L. D., & Bowen, C. (2005). The sandwich generation: Challenges and coping strategies of multigenerational family. *Counseling & Therapy for Couples & Families, 13,* 52–58. doi:10.1177/1066480704270099.

Rippe, J. M. (2013). *Lifestyle medicine* (2nd ed.). Boca Raton, FL: CRC Press.

Rizzuto, T. E., Cherry, K. E., & LeDoux, J. A. (2012). The aging process and cognitive capabilities. In J. W. Hedge & W. C. Borman (Eds.), *The Oxford handbook of work and aging* (pp. 236–255). New York: Oxford University Press.

Robert, L., Labat-Robert, J., & Robert, A. A. (2012). Physiology of skin aging. *Clinics in Plastic Surgery, 39,* 1–8. doi:10.1016/j.cps.2011.09.006.

Roberto, K. A., & Jarrott, S. E. (2008). Family caregivers of older adults: A life span perspective. *Family Relations, 57,* 100–111. doi:10.1111/j.1741-3729.2007.00486.x.

Roberts, B. W., & DelVecchio, W. F. (2000). The rank-order consistency of personality traits from childhood to old age: A quantitative review of longitudinal studies. *Psychological Bulletin, 126,* 3–25. doi:10.1037/0033-2909.126.1.3.

Roberts, B. W., Walton, K., Bogg, T., & Caspi, A. (2006). De-investment in work and non-normative personality trait change in young adulthood. *European Journal of Personality, 20,* 461–474. doi:10.1002/per.607.

Roberts, P., & Newton, P. M. (1987). Levinsonian studies of women's adult development. *Psychology and Aging, 2,* 154–163. doi:10.1037/0882-7974.2.2.154.

Robertson, K., & Murachver, T. (2007). It takes two to tangle: Gender symmetry in intimate partner violence. *Basic and Applied Social Psychology, 29,* 109–118. doi:10.1080/01973530701331247.

Robinaugh, D. J., & McNally, R. J (2013). Remembering the past and envisioning the future in bereaved adults with and without complicated grief. *Clinical Psychological Science, 1,* 290–300. doi:10.1177/2167702613476027.

Robinson, A., Lea, E., Hemmings, L., Vosper, G., McCann, D., Weeding, F., et al. (2012). Seeking respite: Issues around the use of day respite care for the carers of people with dementia. *Ageing and Society, 32,* 196–218. doi:10.1017/S0144686X11000195.

Robinson, G. E., & Gallagher, A. (2008). Culture change impacts quality of life for nursing home residents. *Topics in Clinical Nutrition, 23,* 120–130. doi:10.1097/01.TIN.0000318908.08617.49.

Robson, S. M., Hansson, R. O., Abalos, A., & Booth, M. (2006). Successful aging: Criteria for aging well in the workplace. *Journal of Career Development, 33,* 156–177. doi:10.1177/0894845306292533.

Röcke, C., & Lachman, M. E. (2008). Perceived trajectories of life satisfaction across past, present, and future: Profiles and correlates of subjective change in young, middle-aged, and older adults. *Psychology and Aging, 23,* 833–847. doi:10.1037/a0013680.

Rockwell, J. (2012). From person-centered to relational care: Expanding the focus in residential care facilities. *Journal of Gerontological Social Work, 55,* 233–248. doi:10.1080/0163 4372.2011.639438.

Rockwood, K., Howlett, S. E., MacKnight, C., Beattie, B. L., Bergman, H., Hébert, R., et al. (2004). Prevalence, attributes, and outcomes of fitness and frailty in community-dwelling older adults: Report from the Canadian study of health and aging. *Journal of Gerontology: Medical Sciences, 59,* 1310–1317. doi:10.1093/gero na/59.12.1310.

Rocque, G. B., & Cleary, J. F. (2013). Palliative care reduces morbidity and mortality in cancer. *Nature Reviews Clinical Oncology, 10,* 80–89. doi:10.1038/nrclinonc.2012.211.

Rodin, J., & Langer, E. J. (1977). Long-term effects of a control-relevant intervention with the institutionalized aged. *Journal of Personality and Social Psychology, 35,* 897–902.

Rodrigue, K. M., Kennedy, K. M., Devous, M. D., Sr., Rieck, J. R., Hebrank, A. C., Diaz-Arrastia, R. et al. (2012). β-amyloid burden in healthy aging: Regional distribution and cognitive consequences. *Neurology, 78,* 387–395. doi:10.1212/WNL.0b013e318245d295.

Rodriguez, J. J., Noristani, H. N., & Verkhratsky, A. (2012). The serotonergic system in ageing and Alzheimer's disease. *Progress in Neurobiology, 99,* 15–41. doi:10.1016/j.pneurobio.2012.06.010.

Roediger, H. L., III, Wixted, J. H., & DeSoto, K. A. (2012). The curious complexity between confidence and accuracy in reports from memory. In L. Nadel & W. P. Sinnott-Armstrong (Eds.), *Memory and law* (pp. 84–118). New York: Oxford University Press.

Roger, V., Go, A. S., Lloyd-Jones, D. M., Benjamin, E. J., Berry, J. D., Borden, W. B. et al. (2012). Heart disease and stroke statistics—2012 update: A report from the American Heart Association. *Circulation, 125,* e-2-e220. doi:10.1161/CIR.0b013e31823ac046. Retrieved from http://circ.ahajournals.org /content/125/1/e2.full.

Rokach, R., Cohen, O., & Dreman, S. (2004). Triggers and fuses in late divorce: The role of short term crises vs. ongoing frustration on marital break-up. *Journal of Divorce & Remarriage, 40,* 41–60. doi:10.1300/J087v40n03_03.

Romeijn, N., Raymann, R. J. E. M., Most, E., Te Lindert, B., Van Der Meijden, W. P., Fronczek, R., et al., (2012). Sleep, vigilance, and thermosensitivity. *Pflügers Archiv—European Journal of Physiology, 463,* 169–176. doi:10.1007/s00424-011-1042-2.

Rönnlund, M., Nyberg, L., Bäckman, L., & Nilsson, L.G. (2005). Stability, growth, and decline in adult life span development of declarative memory: cross-sectional and longitudinal data from a population-based study. *Psychology and Aging, 20(1),* 3–18. doi:10.1037/0882-7974.20.1.3

Roper, L. L. (2007). Air force single parent mothers and maternal separation anxiety. *Dissertation Abstracts International, Section A: Humanities and Social Sciences, 67(11–A),* 4349.

Rose, D. M., & Gordon, R. (2010). Retention practices for engineering and technical professionals in an Australian public agency. *Australian Journal of Public Administration, 69,* 314–325. doi:10.1111/j.1467-8500.2010.00693.x.

Rosenbaum, J. L., Smith, J. R., & Zollfrank, B. C. C. (2011). Neonatal end-of-life support care. *Perinatal and Neonatal Nursing, 25,* 61–69. doi:10.1097/JPN.0b013e318209e1d2.

Rosenberg, S. D., Rosenberg, H. J., & Farrell, M. P. (1999). Midlife crisis revisited. In S. L. Willis & J. D. Reid (Eds.), *Life in the middle: Psychological and social development in middle age* (pp. 47–70). San Diego: Academic Press.

Rosenblatt, P. C. (1996). Grief that does not end. In D. Klass, P. R. Silverman, & S. L. Nickman (Eds.), *Continuing bonds: New understandings of grief* (pp. 45–58). Washington, DC: Taylor & Francis.

Rosenblatt, P. C. (2001). A social constructivist perspective on cultural differences in grief. In M. S. Stroebe, R. O. Hansson, W. Stroebe, & H. Schut (Eds.), *Handbook of bereavement research: Consequences, coping, and care* (pp. 285–300). Washington, DC: American Psychological Association.

Rosenblatt, P. C. (2013). A review of *Closure in American culture*. *Death Studies, 37,* 589–594. doi:10.1080/07481187.2011.643750.

Rosenfield, S., & Mouzon, D. (2013). Gender and mental health. In C. S. Aneshensel, J. C. Phelan, & A. Bieman (Eds.), *Handbook of the sociology of mental health* (pp. 277–296). New York: Springer.

Ross, N. A., Garner, R., Bernier, J., Feeny, D. H., Kaplan, M. S., McFarland, B., et al. (2012). Trajectories of health-related quality of life by socioeconomic status in a nationally representative Canadian cohort. *Journal of Epidemiology and Community Health, 66,* 593–598. doi:10.1136/jech.2010.115378.

Roszko, E. (2010). Commemoration and the state: Memory and legitimacy in Vietnam. *Sojourn: Journal of Social Issues in Southeast Asia, 25,* 1–28. doi:10.1353/soj.0.0041.

Rothblum, E. D. (2009). An overview of same-sex couples in relationships: A research area still at sea. *Nebraska Symposium on Motivation: Contemporary Perspectives on Lesbian, Gay, and Bisexual Identities, 54,* 113–139. doi:10.1007/978-0-387-09556-1_5

Rowe, G. (2011). *Determinants of working memory performance.* Dissertation presented to the Department of Psychology, University of Toronto. Retrieved from https://tspace.library.utoronto.ca/handle/1807/26515.

Rowe, J. W., & Kahn, R. L. (1998). *Successful aging.* New York: Pantheon.

Rowe, M. M., & Sherlock, H. (2005). Stress and verbal abuse in nursing: Do burned out nurses eat their young? *Journal of Nursing Management, 13,* 242–248. doi:10.1111/j.1365-2834.2004.00533.x.

Rowles, G. D. (2006). Commentary: A house is not a home: But can it become one? In H. W. Wahl et al. (Eds.), *The many faces of health, competence and well-being in old age* (pp. 25–32). New York: Springer.

Rowles, G. D., & Watkins, J. F. (2003). History, habit, heart, and hearth: On making spaces into places. In K. W. Schaie, H.-W. Wahl, H. Mollenkopf, & F. Oswald (Eds.), *Aging independently: Living arrangements and mobility* (pp. 77–96). New York: Springer.

Rowles, G., Oswald, F., & Hunter, E. (2004). Interior living environments in old age. In K. W. Schaie (Series Ed.), H.W. Wahl, R. J. Scheidt, & P. G. Windley (Eds.), *Annual review of gerontology and geriatrics: Vol. 23. Aging in context: Socio-physical environments* (pp. 167–194). New York: Springer.

Roxburgh, S. (2002). Racing through life. The distribution of time pressures by roles and roles resources among full-time workers. *Journal of Family and Economic Issues, 23,* 121–145. doi:10.1023/A:1015734516575.

Roy, A., Punhani, S., & Shi, L. (2012). *Living longer: Why and how it affects us all?* Retrieved from http://tmp-sa.com/pdf/How%20increasing%20longevity%20affects%20us.pdf.

Royal Australian College of General Practitioners. (2013). *Medical care of older persons in residential facilities.* Retrieved from http://www.racgp.org.au/your-practice/guidelines/silverbook/.

Rozin, P., & Royzman, E. B. (2001). Negativity bias, negativity dominance, and contagion. *Personality and Social Psychology Review, 5,* 296–320. doi:10.1207/S15327957PSPR0504_2.

Rubin, S. S., & Malkinson, R. (2001). Parental response to child loss across the life cycle: Clinical and research perspectives. In M. S. Stroebe, R. O. Hansson, W. Stroebe, & H. Schut (Eds.), *Handbook of bereavement research: Consequences, coping, and care* (pp. 169–197). Washington, DC: American Psychological Association.

Rubin, S. S., Malkinson, R., & Witztum, E. (2012). *Working with the bereaved: Multiple lenses on loss and mourning.* New York: Routledge.

Ruckh, J. M., Zhao, J.-W., Shadrach, J. L., van Wijngaarden, P., Nageswara Rao, T., Wagers, A. J., et al. (2012). Rejuvenation of regeneration in the aging central nervous system. *Cell Stem Cell, 10,* 96–103. doi:10.1016/j.stem.2011.11.019.

Rummel, J., Hepp, J., Klein, S. A., & Silberleitner, N. (2012). Affective state and event-based prospective memory. *Cognition and Emotion, 26,* 351–361. doi:10.1080/02699931.2011.574873.

Ruppanner, L. E. (2010). Cross national reports of housework: An investigation of the gender empowerment measure. *Social Science Research, 19,* 963–975. doi:10.1016/j.ssresearch.2010.04.002.

Rutherford, A., Markopoulos, G., Bruno, D., & Brady-Van den Bos, M. (2012). Long-term memory: Encoding to retrieval. In N. Braisby & A. Gellatly (Eds.), *Cognitive psychology* (pp. 229–265). New York: Oxford University Press.

Ryan, E. B., Giles, H., Bartolucci, G., & Henwood, K. (1986). Psycholinguistic and social psychological components of communication by and with the elderly. *Language and Communication, 6,* 1–24. doi:10.1016/0271-5309(86)90002-9.

Ryan, E. B., Meredith, S. D., MacLean, M. J., & Orange, J. B. (1995). Changing the way we talk with elders: Promoting health using the communication enhancement model. *International Journal of Aging and Human Development, 41,* 89–107. doi:10.2190/FP05-FM8V-0Y9F-53FX.

Ryan, M. K., Haslam, S. A., & Kulich, C. (2010). Politics and the glass cliff: Evidence that women are preferentially selected to contest hard-to-win seats. *Psychology of Women Quarterly, 34,* 56–64. doi:10.1111/j.1471-6402.2009.01541.x.

Rye, M. S., Folck, C. D., Heim, T. A., Olszewski, B. T., & Traina, E. (2004). Forgiveness of an ex-spouse: How does it relate to mental health following a divorce? *Journal of Divorce & Remarriage, 41,* 31–51. doi:10.1300/J087v41n03_02.

Saavedra, C., Iglesias, J., & Olivares, E. I. (2012). Event-related potentials elicited by face identity processing in elderly adults with cognitive impairment. *Experimental Aging Research, 38,* 220–245. doi:10.1080/0361073X.2012.660057.

Sabia, S., Guéguen, A., Marmot, M. G., Shipley, M. J., Ankri, J., & Singh-Manoux, A. (2010). Does cognition predict mortality in midlife? Results from the Whitehall II cohort study. *Neurobiology of Aging, 31,* 688–695. doi:10.1016/j.neurobiolaging.2008.05.007.

Saginak, K. A., & Saginak, M. A. (2005). Balancing work and family: Equity, gender, and marital satisfaction. *Family Journal: Counseling & Therapy for Couples & Families, 13,* 162–166. doi:10.1177/1066480704273230.

Sakaki, M., Niki, K., & Mather, M. (2012). Beyond arousal and valence: The importance of the biological versus social relevance of emotional stimuli. *Cognitive, Affective, and Behavioral Neuroscience, 12,* 115–139. doi:10.3758/s13415-011-0062-x.

Sakraida, T. J. (2005). Divorce transition differences of midlife women. *Issues in Mental Health Nursing, 26,* 225–249. doi:10.1080/01612840590901699.

Salai, L. K. (2013). Late-life psychosis. In M. D. Miller & L. K. Salai (Eds.), *Geriatric psychiatry* (pp. 237–251). New York: Oxford University Press.

Salari, P., & Abdollahi, M. (2012). Long term bisphosphonate use in osteoporotic patients: A step forward, two steps back. *Journal of Pharmacy and Pharmaceutical Sciences, 15,* 305–317. Retrieved from http://wigan-ojs.library.ualberta.ca/index.php/JPPS/article/view/12519/13679.

Salthouse, T. A. (1996). The processing speed theory of adult age differences in cognition. *Psychological Review, 103,* 403–428. doi:10.1037/0033-295X.103.3.403.

Samieri, C., Maillard, P., Crivello, F., Proust-Lima, C., Peuchant, E., Helmer, C., et al. (2012). Plasma long-chain omega-3 fatty acids and atrophy of the medial temporal lobe. *Neurology, 79,* 642–650. doi:10.1212/WNL.0b013e318264e394.

Sandler, I. N., Wolchik, S. A., & Ayers, T. S. (2008). Resilience rather than recovery: A contextual framework on adaptation following bereavement. *Death Studies, 32,* 59–73. doi:10.1080/07481180701741343.

Sanfey, A. G., & Hastie, R. (2000). Judgment and decision making across the adult life span: A tutorial review of psychological research. In D. Park & N. Schwartz (Eds.), *Cognitive aging: A primer* (pp. 253–273). Philadelphia: Psychology Press.

Sargent, L. D., Lee, M. D., Martin, B., & Zikic, J. (2013). Reinventing retirement: New Pathways, new arrangements, new meanings. *Human Relations, 66,* 3–21. doi:10.1177/0018726712465658.

Sarton, M. (1997). Toward another dimension. In M. Pearsall (Ed.), *The other within us: Feminist explorations of women and aging* (pp. 229–232). Boulder, CO: Westview Press.

Sasson, E., Doniger, G. M., Pasternak, O., Tarrasch, R., & Assaf, Y. (2012). Structural correlates of cognitive domains in normal aging with diffusion tensor imaging. *Brain Structure and Function, 217,* 503–515. doi:10.1007/s00429-011-0344-7.

Savela, S., Saijonmaa, O., Strandberg, T. E., Koistinen, P., Strandberg, A. Y., Tilvis, R. S., et al. (2013). Physical activity in midlife and telomere length measured in old age. *Experimental Gerontology, 48,* 81–84. doi:10.1016/j.exger.2012.02.003.

Saver, J. L., Fonarow, G. C., Smith, E. E., Reeves, M. J., Grau-Sepulveda, M. V., Pan, W., et al. (2013). Time to treatment with intravenous tissue plasminogen activator and outcome from acute ischemic stroke. *JAMA, 309,* 2480–2488. doi:10.1001/jama.2013.6959.

Savickas, M. L. (2013). Career construction theory and practice. In S. D. Brown & R. W. Lent (Eds.), *Career development and counseling: Putting theory and research to work* (pp. 147–183). New York: Wiley.

Saxon, S. V., & Etten, M. J. (2010). *Physical changes and aging: A guide for the helping professions* (5th ed.). New York: Springer.

Scally, G., Imtiaz, J., Bethune, R., Young, A., Ward, W., Herzig, H. et al. (2012). Helping clinicians improve the health of their communities: The Beddoes Fellows Programme. *Journal of Behavioral Health, 1,* 167–171. doi:10.5455/jbh.20120506123015.

Scandura, T. A., & Williams, E. A. (2004). Mentoring and transformational leadership: The role of supervisory career mentoring. *Journal of Vocational Behavior, 65,* 448–468. doi:10.1016/j.jvb.2003.10.003.

Schaie, K. W. (1977–1978). Toward a stage theory of adult cognitive development. *International Journal of Aging and Human Development, 8,* 129–138. doi:10.2190/1TEA-M6PK-28A0-49HV.

Schaie, K. W. (1994). The course of adult intellectual development. *American Psychologist, 49,* 304–313.

Schaie, K. W. (1996). Intellectual functioning in adulthood. In J. E. Birren & K. W. Schaie (Eds.), *Handbook of the psychology of aging* (4th ed., pp. 266–286). San Diego: Academic Press.

Schaie, K. W. (2005). *Developmental influences on adult intelligence: The Seattle longitudinal study.* New York: Oxford University Press.

Schaie, K. W. (2008). A lifespan developmental perspective of psychological aging. In K. Laidlaw & B. G. Knight (Eds.), *Handbook of emotional disorders in late life: Assessment and treatment* (pp. 3–32). Oxford, UK: Oxford University Press.

Schaie, K. W. (2011). Historical influences on aging and behavior. In K. W. Schaie & S. L. Willis (Eds.). *Handbook of the psychology of aging* (7th ed., pp. 41–55). Burlington, MA: Academic Press.

Schaie, K. W., & Willis, S. L. (1999). Theories of everyday competence and aging. In V. L. Bengtson & K. W. Schaie (Eds.), *Handbook of theories of aging* (pp. 174–195). New York: Springer.

Schaie, K. W., & Zanjani, F. (2006). Intellectual development across adulthood. In C. Hoare (Ed.), *Oxford handbook of adult development and* learning (pp. 99–122). New York: Oxford University Press.

Schaie, K. W., Maitland, S. B., Willis, S. L., & Intrieri, R. L. (1998). Longitudinal invariance of adult psychometric ability factor structures across seven years. Psychology and Aging, 13, 8–20.

Schaie, K. W., Plomin, R., Willis, S. L., Gruber-Baldini, A., & Dutta, R. (1992). Natural cohorts: Family similarity in adult cognition. In T. Sonderegger (Ed.), Psychology and aging: Nebraska symposium on motivation, 1991 (pp. 205–243). Lincoln: University of Nebraska Press.

Scheibe, S., & Carstensen, L. L. (2010). Emotional aging: Current and future trends. Journal of Gerontology: Psychological Sciences, 65B, 133–144. doi:10.1093/geronb/gbp132.

Scheibe, S., Kunzmann, U., & Baltes, P. B. (2007). Wisdom, life longings, and optimal development. In J. A. Blackburn & C. N. Dulmus (Eds.), Handbook of gerontology: Evidence based approaches to theory, practice, and policy (pp. 117–142). Hoboken, NJ: Wiley.

Scheidt, R. J., & Schwarz, B. (2010). Environmental gerontology: A sampler of issues and application. In J. C. Cavanaugh & C. K. Cavanaugh (Eds.), Aging in America: Vol. 1: Psychological aspects (pp. 156–176). Santa Barbara, CA: Praeger Perspectives.

Schlossberg, N. K. (2004). Retire smart, retire happy: Finding your true path in life. Washington, DC: American Psychological Association.

Schmitt, D. P., Alcalay, L., Allensworth, M., Allik, J., Ault, L., Austers, I., et al. (2004). Patterns and universals of adult romantic attachment across 62 cultural regions: Are models of self and of other pancultural constructs? Journal of Cross-Cultural Psychology, 35, 367–402. doi:10.1177/0022022104266105.

Schneider, J. (2013). The death of an adult child: Contemporary psychoanalytic models of mourning. In S. Arbiser & G. Saragnano (Eds.), On Freud's inhibitions, symptoms, and anxiety (pp. 219–230). London, UK: Karnac Books.

Schoeneman, K. (2008). The environmental side of the culture change movement: Identifying barriers and potential solutions to furthering innovation in nursing homes. Retrieved from http://www.pioneernetwork.net/Data/Documents/Creating-Home-Bkgrnd-Paper.pdf.

Schoklitsch, A., & Bauman, U. (2012). Generativity and aging: A promising future research topic? Journal of Aging Studies, 26, 262–272. doi:10.1016/jaging.2012.01.002.

Schooler, K. K. (1982). Response of the elderly to environment: A stress-theoretical perspective. In M. P. Lawton, P. G. Windley, & T. O. Byerts (Eds.), Aging and the environment: Theoretical approaches (pp. 80–96). New York: Springer.

Schott, W. (2010). Going back part-time: Federal leave legislation and women's return to work. Retrieved from http://paa2010.princeton.edu/papers/101198.

Schuepbach, W. M. M., Rau, J., Knudsen, K., Volkman, J., Krack, P., Timmerman, L., et al. (2013). Neurostimulation for Parkinson's disease with early motor complications. New England Journal of Medicine, 368, 610–622. doi:10.1056/NEJMoa1205158. Available online at http://www.nejm.org/doi/full/10.1056/NEJMoa1205158.

Schulz, R., & Morycz, R. (2013). Psychosocial actors, health, and quality of life. In M. D. Miller & L. K. Salai (Eds.), Geriatric psychiatry (pp. 343–371). New York: Oxford University Press.

Schwartz, C. R., & Graf, N. L. (2009). Assortative matching among same-sex and different-sex couples in the United States. Demographic Research, 21, 843–878. Retrieved from http://www.demographic-research.org/volumes/vol21/28/21-28.pdf.

Schwarzer, R. (2008). Modeling health behavior change: How to predict and modify the adoption and maintenance of health behaviors. Applied Psychology, 57, 1–29. doi:10.1111/j.1464-0597.2007.00325.x.

Schwerdtfeger, A., & Friedrich-Mai, P. (2009). Social interaction moderates the relationship between depressive mood and heart rate variability: Evidence from an ambulatory monitoring study. Health Psychology, 28, 501–509. doi:10.1037/a0014664.

Scuderi, C., & Steardo, L. (2013). Neurological roots of neurodegenerative diseases: Therapeutic potential of palmitoylethanolamide in models of Alzheimer's disease. CNS and Neurological Disorders Drug Targets. Retrieved from http://europepmc.org/abstract/MED/23394526/reload=0;jsessionid=5Buc55DVOpdmeC2ngigi.2.

Scullin, M. K., Bugg, J. M., & McDaniel, M. A. (2012). Whoops, I did it again: Commission errors in prospective memory. Psychology and Aging, 27, 46–53. doi:10.1037/a0026112.

Seaman, P. M. (2012). Time for my life now: Early boomer women's anticipation of volunteering in retirement. The Gerontologist, 52, 245–254. doi:10.1093/geront/gns001.

Seene, T., Kaasik, P., & Riso, E.-M. (2012). Review on aging, unloading and reloading: Changes in skeletal muscle quantity and quality. Archives of Gerontology and Geriatrics, 54, 374–380. doi:10.1016/j.archger.2011.05.002.

Segal, D. L., Qualls, S. H., & Smyer, M. A. (2011). Aging and mental health (2nd ed.). Malden, MA: Wiley-Blackwell.

Segerstrom, S. (Ed.), The Oxford handbook of psychoneuroimmunology. New York: Oxford University Press.

Sengupta, M., Decker, S. L., Harris-Kojetin, L., & Jones, A. (2012). Racial differences in dementia care among nursing home residents. Journal of Aging and Health, 24, 711–731. doi:10.1177/0898264311432311.

Sera, E. J. (2001). Men and spousal bereavement: A cross-cultural study of majority-culture and Hispanic men and the role of religiosity and acculturation on grief. Dissertation Abstracts International Section

B: The Sciences and Engineering, 61(11–B), 6149.

Sergeant, J. F., & Ekerdt, D. J. (2008). Motives for residential mobility in later life: Post-move perspectives of elders and family members. International Journal of Aging and Human Development, 66, 131–154. doi:10.2190/AG.66.2.c.

Servaty-Seib, H. L., & Taub, D. J. (2010). Bereavement and college students: the role of counseling psychology. The Counseling Psychologist, 38, 947–975. doi:10.1177/0011000010366485.

Seyda, B. A., & Fitzsimons, A. M. (2010). Infant deaths. In C. A. Corr & D. A. Balk (Eds.), Children's encounters with death, bereavement, and coping (pp. 83–107). New York: Springer.

Shalev, R. (1999). Comparison of war-bereaved and motor vehicle accident-bereaved parents. Unpublished master's thesis, University of Haifa.

Shamliyan T., Wyman J., & Kane, R. L. Nonsurgical treatments for urinary incontinence in adult women: Diagnosis and comparative effectiveness. Retrieved from: http://www.ncbi.nlm.nih.gov/books/NBK92960/.

Shao, J., Li, D., Zhang, D., Zhang, L., Zhang, Q., & Qi, X. (2013). Birth cohort changes in the depressive symptoms of Chinese older adults: a cross-temporal meta-analysis. International Journal of Geriatric Psychiatry, 28, 1101–1108. doi:10.1002/gps.3942.

Sharma, A., & Sharma, V. (2012). The psycho-cultural analysis of sex discrimination. Advances in Asian Social Science, 2, 411–414. Retrieved from http://www.worldsciencepublisher.org/journals/index.php/AASS/article/viewFile/380/362.

Sharon, I., Sharon, R., Wilkens, J. P., & Ersan, T. (2012). Huntington disease dementia. Retrieved from http://emedicine.medscape.com/article/289706-overview.

Shaw, S. S. (2007). Losing a parent twice. American Journal of Alzheimer's Disease and Other Dementias, 21, 389–390. doi:10.1177/1533317506292860.

Shea, S. C. (2006). Improving medication adherence: How to talk to patients about their medications. Philadelphia: Lippincott, Williams & Wilkins.

Sheehy, G. (1976). Passages. New York: Dutton.

Sheehy, G. (1981). Pathfinders. New York: Morrow.

Sheehy, G. (1995). New passages: Mapping your life across time. New York: Random House.

Sheehy, G. (1998). Understanding men's passages. New York: Random House.

Shega, J. W., Dale, W., Andrew, M., Paice, J., Rockwood, K., & Weiner, D. K. (2012). Persistent pain and frailty: A case for homeostenosis. Journal of the American Geriatrics Society, 60, 113–117. doi:10.1111/j.1532-5415.2011.03769.x.

Sherman, A. M., de Vries, B., & Lansford, J. E. (2000). Friendship in childhood and adulthood: Lessons across the life span. International Journal of Aging & Human Development, 51, 31–51. doi:10.2190/4QFV-D52D-TPYP-RLM6.

Sherwin, S. (2011). Looking backwards, looking forward: Hope for Bioethics' next twenty-five years. Bioethics, 25, 75–82. doi:10.1111/j.1467-8519.2010.01866.x.

Shield, R. R. (1988). Uneasy endings: Daily life in an American nursing home. Ithaca, NY: Cornell University Press.

Shih, P. C., & Jung, R. E. (2009). Gray matter correlates of fluid, crystallized, and spatial intelligence: Testing the P-FIT model. Intelligence, 37, 124–135. doi:10.1016/j.intell.2008.07.007.

Shivapour, S. K., Nguyen, C. M., Cole, C. A., & Denburg, N. L. (2012). Effects of age, sex, and neuropsychological performance on financial decision-making. Frontiers in Neuroscience, 6. doi:10.3389/fnins.2012.00082.

Shonkoff, J. P., Garner, A. S., the Committee on Psychosocial Aspects of Child and Family Health, Committee on Early Childhood, Adoption, and Dependent Care, and Section on Developmental and Behavioral Pediatrics, et al., (2012). The lifelong effects of early childhood adversity and toxic stress. Pediatrics, 129, e232–e246. doi:10.1542/peds.2011-2668.

Simonton, D. K. (2012). Creative productivity and aging. In S. K. Whitbourne & M. J. Sliwinski (Eds.), The Wiley-Blackwell handbook of adulthood and aging (pp. 477–496). Oxford, UK: Wiley-Blackwell.

Simpson, T., Camfield, D., Pipingas, A., Macpherson, H., & Stough, C. (2012). Improved processing speed: Online computer-based cognitive training in older adults. Educational Gerontology, 38, 445–458. doi:10.1080/03601277.2011.559858.

Sinclair, R. R., Sears, L. E., Zajack, M., & Probst, T. (2010). A multilevel model of economic stress and employee well-being. In J. Houdmont & S. Leka (Eds.), Contemporary occupational health psychology: Global perspectives on research and practice (Vol. 1, pp. 1–20). Malden, MA: Wiley-Blackwell.

Sinnott, J. D. (1994). New science models for teaching adults: Teaching as a dialogue with reality. In J. D. Sinnott (Ed.), Interdisciplinary handbook of adult lifespan learning (pp. 90–104). Westport, CT: Greenwood Press.

Sinnott, J. D. (1998). The development of logic in adulthood: Postformal thought and its applications. New York: Plenum.

Sinnott, J. D. (2009). Complex thought and construction of the self in the face of aging and death. Journal of Adult Development, 16, 155–165. doi:10.1007/s10804-009-9057-z.

Skevington, S. M., & McCrate, F. M. (2012). Expecting a good quality of life in health: Assessing people with diverse diseases using the WHOQOL-BREF. Health Expectations, 15, 49–62. doi:10.1111/j.1369-7625.2010.00650.x.

Skouteris, H., McNaught, S., & Dissanayake, C. (2007). Mothers' transition back to work and infants' transition to child care: Does work-based child care make a difference? Child Care in Practice, 13, 33–47. doi:10.1080/13575270601103432.

Slater, C. L. (2003). Generativity versus stagnation: An elaboration of Erikson's adult stage of human development. *Journal of Adult Development, 10*, 53–65. doi:10.1023/A:1020790820868.

Small, B. J., Dixon, R. A., McArdle, J. J., & Grimm, K. J. (2012). Do changes in lifestyle engagement moderate cognitive decline in normal aging? Evidence from the Victoria Longitudinal Study. *Neuropsychology, 26*, 144–155. doi:10.1037/a0026579.

Smith, L. (1992). The tyranny of America's old. *Fortune, 125*(1), 68–72.

Smith, S. (2011). *Duerson brain tissue analyzed: Suicide linked to brain disease.* Retrieved from http://www.cnn.com/2011/HEALTH/05/02/duerson.brain.exam.results/index.html.

Smith, W. J., Howard, J. T., & Harrington, K. V. (2005). Essential formal mentor characteristics and functions in governmental and non-governmental organizations from the program administrator's and the mentor's perspective. *Public Personnel Management, 34*, 31–58. Retrieved from http://dspace.library.drexel.edu/bitstream/1860/2629/1/2007005143.pdf.

Smits, S. J., & Bowden, D. E. (2013). Leveraging psychological assets fro the development and maintenance of leadership capabilities. *International Leadership Journal, 5*, 3–26. Retrieved from http://www.tesc.edu/documents/ILJ_Winter_2013.pdf#page=4.

Smyer, M. A., & Allen-Burge, R. (1999). Older adults' decision-making capacity: Institutional settings and individual choices. In J. C. Cavanaugh & S. K. Whitbourne (Eds.), *Gerontology: An interdisciplinary perspective* (pp. 391–413). New York: Oxford University Press.

Smyke, A. T., Zeanah, C. H. Fox, N. A., Nelson, C. A., & Guthrie, D. (2010). Placement in foster care enhances quality of attachment among young institutionalized children. *Child Development, 81*, 212–223. doi:10.1111/j.1467-8624.2009.01390.x.

Sneed, J. R., & Whitbourne, S. K. (2003). Identity processing and self-consciousness in middle and later adulthood. *Journals of Gerontology: Psychological Sciences, 58B*, P313–P319.

Sneed, J. R., & Whitbourne, S. K. (2005). Models of the aging self. *Journal of Social Issues, 61*, 375–388. doi:10.1111/j.1540-4560.2005.00411.x

Social Security Administration. (2012a). *A summary of the 2012 annual reports.* Retrieved from http://www.ssa.gov/oact/trsum/.

Social Security Administration. (2012b). *The 2012 annual report of the Board of Trustees of the Federal Old-Age and Survivors Insurance and Federal Disability Insurance Trust Funds.* Retrieved from http://www.ssa.gov/oact/tr/2012/index.html.

Son, S., & Bauer, J. W. (2010). Employed rural, low income, single mothers' family and work over time. *Journal of Family and Economic Issues, 31*, 107–120. doi:10.1007/s10834-009-9173-8.

Sousa-Lima M., Michel, J. W., & Caetano, A. (2013). Clarifying the importance of trust in organizations as a component of effective work relationships. *Journal of Applied Social Psychology, 43*, 418–427. doi:10.1111/j.1559-1816.2013.01012.x.

Spaniol, J., & Grady, C. (2012). Aging and the neural correlates of source memory: Over-recruitment and functional reorganization. *Neurobiology of Aging, 33*, 425.e3–425.e18. doi:10.1016/j.neurobiolaging.2010.10.005.

Spaniol, J., Madden, D. J., & Voss, A. (2006). A diffusion model analysis of adult age differences in episodic and semantic long-term memory retrieval. *Journal of Experimental Psychology: Learning, Memory, and Cognition, 32*, 101–117. doi:10.1037/0278-7393.32.1.101.

Spector, P. E., Allen, T. D., Poelmans, S., Cooper, C. L., Bernin, P., Hart, P., et al. (2005). An international comparative study of work-family stress and occupational strain. In S. A. Y. Poelmans (Ed.), *Work and family: An international research perspective* (pp. 71–84). Mahwah, NJ: Erlbaum.

Sperling, R. A., Aisen, P. S., Beckett, L. A., Dennett, D. A., Craft, S., Fagan, A. M., et al. (2011). Toward defining the preclinical stages of Alzheimer's disease: Recommendations from the National Institute on Aging—Alzheimer's Association work groups on diagnositc guidelines for Alzheimer's disease. *Alzheimer's and Dementia: Journal of the Alzheimer'rs Assocation, 7*, 280–292. doi:10.1016/jalz.2011.03.003.

Spira, A. P., & Edelstein, B. A. (2006). Behavioral interventions for agitation ni older adults with dementia: An evaluative review. *International Psychogeriatrics, 18*, 195–225. doi:10.1017/S1041610205002747.

Spiro, A., III, & Brady, C. B. (2008). Integrating health into cognitive aging research and theory: Quo vadis? In S. M. Hofer & D. F. Alwin (Eds.), *Handbook of cognitive aging: Interdisciplinary perspectives* (pp. 260–283). Greenwich, CT: Sage.

Sritharan, R., Heilpern, N., Wilbur, C. J., & Gawronski, B. (2010). I think I like you: Spontaneous and deliberate evaluations of potential romantic partners in an online dating context. *European Journal of Social Psychology, 40*, 1062–1077. doi:10.1002/ejsp.703.

Srivastava, S., John, O. P., Gosling, S. D., & Potter, J. (2003). Development of personality in early and middle adulthood: Set like plaster or persistent change? *Journal of Personality and Social Psychology, 84*, 1041–1053. doi:10.1037/0022-3514.84.5.1041.

Stafford, L., Kline, S. L., & Rankin, C. T. (2004). Married individuals, cohabiters, and cohabiters who marry: A longitudinal study of relational and individual well-being. *Journal of Social & Personal Relationships, 21*, 231–248. doi:10.1177/0265407504041385.

Stalp, M. C., & Conti, R. (2011). Serious leisure in the home: Professional quilters negotiate family space. *Gender, Work and Organization, 18*, 399–414. doi:10.1111/j.1468-0432.2009.0044.x.

Stanley, J. T., & Isaacowitz, D. M. (2012). Socioemotional perspectives on adult development. In S. K. Whitbourne & M. J. Sliwinski (Eds.), *The Wiley-Blackwell handbook of adulthood and aging* (pp. 237–253). Oxford, UK: Wiley-Blackwell.

Staudinger, U. M., & Glück, J. (2011). Psychological wisdom research: Commonalities and differences in a growing field. *Annual Review of Psychology, 62*, 215-241. doi:10.1146/annurev.psych.121208.131659.

Staudinger, U. M., & Kunzmann, U. (2005). Positive adult personality development: Adjustment and/or growth? *European Psychologist, 10*, 320–329. doi:10.1027/1016-9040.10.4.320.

Staudinger, U. M., Dörner, J., & Mickler, C. (2005). Wisdom and personality. In R. J. Sternberg & J. Jordan (Eds.), *A handbook of wisdom: Psychological perspectives* (pp. 191–219). New York: Cambridge University Press.

Steel, N., Melzer, D., & Richards, S. (2013). Quality of health care: Approaches and findings from the English Longitudinal Study of Ageing. *Annual Review of Gerontology and Geriatrics, 33*, 61–78. doi:10.1891/0198-8794.33.61.

Steffener, J., & Stern, Y. (2012). Exploring the neural basis of cognitive reserve in aging. *Biochemica et Biophysica Acta (BBA)—Molecular Basis of Disease, 1822*, 467–473. doi:10.1016/j.bbadis.2011.09.012.

Steffens, D. C., & Potter, G. G. (2008). Geriatric depression and cognitive impairment. *Psychological Medicine, 38*, 163–175.

Stein, R., Blanchard-Fields, F., & Hertzog, C. (2002). The effects of age-stereotype priming on the memory performance of older adults. *Experimental Aging Research, 28*, 169–191. doi:10.1080/03610730252800184.

Stein-Morrow, E. L., & Miller, L. M. S. (2009). Aging, self-regulation, and learning from text. *Psychology of Learning and Motivation, 51*, 255–296. doi:10.1016/S0079-7421(09)1008-0.

Sternberg, R. J. (1985). *Beyond IQ: A triarchic theory of human intelligence.* New York: Cambridge University Press.

Sternberg, R. J. (2006). A duplex theory of love. In R. J. Sternberg & K. Weis (Eds.), *The new psychology of love* (pp. 184–199). New Haven, CT: Yale University Press.

Sternberg, R. J., & Lubart, T. I. (2001). Wisdom and creativity. In J. E. Birren & K. W. Schaie (Eds.), *Handbook of the psychology of aging* (5th ed., pp. 500–522). San Diego, CA: Academic Press.

Sternberg, R. J., Jarvin, L., & Grigorenko, E. L. (2010). *Explorations in giftedness.* New York: Cambridge University Press.

Sterns, H. L., & Chang, B. (2010). Workforce issues and retirement. In J. C. Cavanaugh & C. K. Cavanaugh (Eds.), *Aging in America: Vol. 3: Societal issues* (pp. 81–105). Santa Barbara, CA: ABC-CLIO.

Sterns, H. L., & Huyck, M. H. (2001). The role of work in midlife. In M. E. Lachman (Ed.), *Handbook of midlife development* (pp. 447–486). New York: Wiley.

Stevens, J. C. (1992). Aging and spatial acuity of touch. *Journals of Gerontology: Psychological Sciences, 47*, P35–P40. doi:10.1093/geronj/47.1.P35.

Stojnov, D. (2013). Stereotypes that help define who we are. *Journal of Constructivist Psychology, 26*, 21–29. doi:10.1080/10720537.2013.732530.

Stoner, S., O'Riley, A., & Edelstein, B. (2010). Assessment of mental health. In J. C. Cavanaugh & C. K. Cavanaugh (Eds.), *Aging in America: Volume 2: Physical and mental health* (pp. 141–170). Santa Barbara, CA: ABC-CLIO.

Strauss, W., & Howe, N. (2007). *Millennials go to college: Strategies for a new generation on campus* (2nd ed.). Ithaca, NY: Paramount.

Strawbridge, W. J., Shema, S. J., Balfour, J. L., Higby, H. R., & Kaplan, G. A. (1998). Antecedents of frailty over three decades in an older cohort. *Journals of Gerontology: Social Sciences, 53B*, S9–S16. doi:10.1093/geronb/53B.1.S9.

Strawbridge, W. J., Wallhagen, M. I., & Cohen, R. D. (2002). Successful aging and well-being: Self-rated compared with Rowe and Kahn. *The Gerontologist, 42*, 727–733. doi:10.1093/geront/42.6.727.

Street, D., & Burge, S. W. (2012). Residential context, social relationships, and subjective well-being in assisted living. *Research on Aging, 34*, 365–394. doi:10.1177/0164027511423928.

Stroebe, M. S., & Archer, J. (2013). Origins of modern ideas on love and loss: Contrasting forerunners of attachment theory. *Review of General Psychology, 17*, 28–39. doi:10.1037/a0030030.

Stroebe, M., Finkenauer, C., Wijngaards-de Meij, L., Schut, H., van den Bout, J., & Stroebe, W. (2013). Partner-oriented self-regulation among bereaved parents: The costs of holding in grief for the partner's sake. *Psychological Science.* doi:10.1177/0956797612457383.

Stroebe, M., Schut, H., & Boerner, K. (2010). Continuing bonds in adaptation to bereavement: Toward theoretical integration. *Clinical Psychology Review, 30*, 259–268. doi:10.1016/j.cpr.2009.11.007.

Stroebe, M., Schut, H., & Stroebe, W. (2005). Attachment in coping with bereavement: A theoretical integration. *Review of General Psychology, 9*, 48–66. doi:10.1037/1089-2680.9.1.48.

Stroebe, M., Schut, H., & Stroebe, W. (2007). Health outcomes of bereavement. *Lancet, 370*, 1960–1973. doi:10.1016/S0140-6736(07)61816-9.

Stroebe, M., Schut, H., & van den Bout, J. (Eds.). (2012). *Complicated grief: Scientific foundations for health care professionals.* New York: Routledge.

Stroebe, W., Abakoumkin, G., & Stroebe, M. (2010). Beyond depression: Yearning for the loss of a loved one. *OMEGA: Journal of Death and*

Dying, 61, 85–101. doi:10.2190/OM.61.2.a.

Strough, J., & Margrett, J. (2002). Overview of the special section on collaborative cognition in later adulthood. *International Journal of Behavioral Development, 26*, 2–5. doi:10.1080/01650250143000300.

Strough, J., Berg, C. A., & Sansone, C. (1996). Goals for solving everyday problems across the interpersonal concerns. *Developmental Psychology, 32*, 1106–1115. doi:10.1037/0012-1649.32.6.1106.

Stula, S. (2012). *Living in old age in Europe—Current developments and challenges.* Retrieved from http://www.sociopolitical-observatory.eu/fileadmin/user_upload/Dateien/Unterstuetzende_Dienstleistungen/AP_7_EN.pdf.

Sun, F., & Xiao, J. J. (2012). Perceived social policy fairness and subjective well-being: Evidence from China. *Social Indicators Research, 107*, 171–186. doi:10.1007/s11205-011-9834-5.

Sun, J., Tong, S., & Yang, G.-Y. (2012). Reorganization of brain networks in aging and age-related diseases. *Aging and Disease, 3*, 181–193. Retrieved from http://www.ncbi.nlm.nih.gov/pmc/articles/PMC3377830/.

Sung, G., & Greer, D. (2011). The case for simplifying brain death criteria. *Neurology, 76*, 113–114. doi:10.1212/WNL.0b013c318205d534.

Swanson, D. A., & Sanford, D. A. (2012). Socio-economic status and life expectancy in the United States, 1990-2010. *Population Review, 51.* Retrieved from http://muse.jhu.edu/journals/population_review/v051/51.2.swanson.html.

Swindell, R. (2012). Successful ageing and international approaches to later-life learning. In G. Boulton-Lewis & M. Tam (Eds.), *Active ageing, active learning* (pp. 35–63). New York: Springer.

Swinton, J., & Payne, R. (Eds.). (2009). *Living well and dying faithfully: Christian practices for end-of-life care.* Grand Rapids, MI: Eerdmans.

Tach, L., & Halpern-Meekin, S. (2009). How does premarital cohabitation affect trajectories of marital quality? *Journal of Marriage and the Family, 71*, 298–317. doi:10.1111/j.1741-3737.2009.00600.x.

Takeuchi, H., Taki, Y., Sassa, Y., Hashizume, H., Sekiguchi, A., Fukushima, A., et al. (2010). White matter structures associated with creativity: Evidence from diffusion tensor imaging. *Neuroimage, 51*, 11–18. doi:10.1016/j.neuroimage.2010.02.035.

Talamini, L. M., & Gorree, E. (2012). Aging memories: Differential decay of episodic memory components. *Learning and Memory, 19*, 239–246. doi:10.1101/lm.024281.111.

Talbot, L. A., Morrell, C. H., Fleg, J. L., & Metter, E. J. (2007). Changes in leisure time physical activity and risk of all-cause mortality in men and women: The Baltimore longitudinal study of aging. *Preventive Medicine, 45*, 169–176. doi:10.1016/j.ypmed.2007.05.014.

Tam, K.-P. (2013). Existential motive underlying cosmetic surgery: A

terror management analysis. *Journal of Applied Social Psychology, 43*, 947–955. doi:10.1111/jasp.12059.

Tamayo, G. J., Broxson, A., Munsell, M., & Cohen, M. Z. (2010). Caring for the caregiver. *Oncology Nursing Forum, 37*, E50–E57. doi:10.1188/10.ONF.E50-E57.

Tang, F., Morrow-Howell, N., & Choi, E. (2010). Why do older adult volunteers stop volunteering? *Ageing and Society, 30*, 859–878. doi:10.1017/S0144686X10000140.

Tang, P.-L., Chiou, C.-P., Lin, H.-S., Wang, C., & Liand, S.-L. (2011). Correlates of death anxiety among Taiwanese cancer patients. *Cancer Nursing, 34*, 286–292. doi:10.1097/NCC.0b013e31820254c6.

Tangredi, L. A., Danvers, K., Molony, S. L., & Williams, A. (2008). New CDEC recommendations for HIV testing in older adults. *Nurse Practitioner, 33*, 37–44.

Tanner, J. L., & J. J. Arnett (2009). The emergence of emerging adulthood: the new life stage between adolescence and young adulthood. In A. Furlong (Ed.), *Handbook of youth and young adulthood: New perspectives and agendas* (pp. 39–45). London: Routledge.

Tate, R. B., Lah, L., & Cuddy, T. E. (2003). Definition of successful aging by elderly Canadian males: The Manitoba follow-up study. *The Gerontologist, 43*, 735–744. doi:10.1093/geront/43.5.735.

Taylor, J. L., O'Hara, R., Mumenthaler, M. S., Rosen, A. C., & Yesavage, J. A. (2005). Cognitive ability, expertise, and age differences in following air-traffic control instructions. *Psychology and Aging, 20*, 117–133. doi:10.1037/0882-7974.20.1.117.

Taylor, R. J., Chatters, L. M., & Levin, J. (2004). *Religion in the lives of African Americans.* Thousand Oaks, CA: Sage.

Taylor, S. E. (2006). Tend and befriend: Biobehavioral bases of affiliation under stress. *Current Directions in Psychological Science, 15*, 273–277. doi:10.1111/j.1467-8721.2006.00451.x.

Teisseyre, N., Mullet, E., & Sorum, P. C. (2005). Under what conditions is euthanasia acceptable to lay people and health professionals? *Social Science and Medicine, 60*, 357–368. doi:10.1016/j.socscimed.2004.05.016.

Tennstedt, S. L., Link, C. L., Steers, W. D., & McKinlay, J. B. (2008). Prevalence of and risk factors for urine leakage in a racially and ethnically diverse population of adults: The Boston Area Community Health (BACH) Survey. *American Journal of Epidemiology, 167*, 390–399. doi:10.1093/aje/kwm356.

Thambisetty, M., Beason-Held, L. L., An, Y., Kraut, M., Nalls, M., Hernandez, D. G., et al. (2012). Alzheimer risk variant *CLU* and brain function during aging. *Biological Psychiatry, 73*, 399–405. Doi:10.1016/j.biopsych.2012.06.026.

The Advocates for Human Rights. (2010). Prevalence of sexual harassment. Retrieved from http://www.stopvaw.org/prevalence_of_sexual_harassment.html.

Therborn, G. (2010). Families in global perspective. In A. Giddens & P. W. Sutton (Eds.), *Sociology: Introductory readings* (3rd ed., pp. 119–124). Malden, MA: Polity Press.

Thiele, D. M., & Whelan, T. A. (2010). The relationship between grandparent satisfaction, meaning, and generativity. *International Journal of Aging and Human Development, 66*, 21–48. doi:10.2190/AG.66.1.b.

Thieleman, K., & Cacciatore, J. (in press). When a child dies: A critical analysis of grief-related controversies in *DSM-V. Research on Social Work Practice.* doi:10.1177/1049731512474695.

Thomas, A. G., Dennis, A., Bandettini, P. A., & Johansen-Berg, H. (2012). The effects of aerobic activity on brain structure. *Frontier in Psychology, 3.* doi:10.3389/fpsyg.2012.00086. Retrieved from http://www.ncbi.nlm.nih.gov/pmc/articles/PMC3311131/.

Thomas, F. (2008). Remarriage after spousal death: Options facing widows and implications for livelihood security. *Gender and Development, 16*, 73–83. doi:10.1080/13552070701876235.

Thomas, M. D., Guihan, M., & Mambourg, F. (2011). What do potential residents need to know about assisted living facility type? The trade-off between autonomy and help with more complex needs. *Journal of Housing for the elderly, 25*, 109–124. doi:10.1080/02763893.2011.571108.

Thomas, R. C., & Hasher, L. (2006). The influence of emotional valence on age differences in early processing and memory. *Psychology and Aging, 21*, 821–825. doi:10.1037/0882-7974.21.4.821.

Thomas, R. C., & Hasher, L. (2012). Reflections of distraction in memory: Transfer of previous distraction improves recall in younger and older adults. *Journal of Experimental Psychology: Learning, Memory, and Cognition, 38*, 30–39. doi:10.1037/a0024882.

Thompson, G. E., Cameron, R. E., & Fuller-Thompson, E. (2013). Walking the red road: the role of First Nations grandparents in promoting cultural well-being. *International Journal of Aging and Human development, 76*, 55–78. doi:10.2190/AG.76.1.c.

Thompson, M. M., Naccarato, M. E., & Parker, K. (1992). Measuring cognitive needs: The development and validation of the personal need for structure and personal fear of invalidity scales. Unpublished manuscript.

Thompson, P., Koorenhof, L., & Kapur, N. (2012). Memory rehabilitation for people with epilepsy. In A. Zeman, N. Kapur, & M. Jones-Gotman (Eds.). *Epilepsy and memory* (pp. 425–440). Oxford, UK: Oxford University Press.

Thompson, S., & Oliver, D. (2008). A new model for long-term care: Balancing palliative and restorative care delivery. *Journal of Housing for the Elderly, 22*, 169–194. doi:10.1080/02763890802232014.

Thornton, W. J. L., & Dumke, H. A. (2005). Age differences in everyday problem-solving and decision-making effectiveness: A meta-analytic review.

Psychology and Aging, 20, 85–99. doi:10.1037/0882-7974.20.1.85.

Thornton, W. L., Paterson, T. S. E., & Yeung, S. E. (2013). Age differences in everyday problem solving: The role of problem context. *International Journal of Behavioral Development, 37*, 13–20. doi:10.1177/0165025412454028.

Toles, M., & Anderson, R. A. (2011). State of the science: Relationship-oriented management practices in nursing homes. *Nursing Outlook, 59*, 221–227. doi:10.1016/j.outlook.2011.05.001.

Tong, C., & Kram, K. E. (2013). The efficacy of mentoring—the benefits for mentees, mentors, and organizations. In J. Passmore, D. B. Peterson, & T. Freire (Eds.), *The Wiley-Blackwell handbook of coaching and mentoring* (pp. 217–242). Oxford, UK: Wiley-Blackwell.

Tonković, M., & Vranić, A. (2011). Self-evaluation of memory systems: Development of the questionnaire. *Aging and Mental Health, 15*, 830–837. doi:10.1080/13607863.2011.569483.

Torges, C. M., Stewart, A. J., & Duncan, L. E. (2008). Achieving ego integrity: Personality development in late midlife. *Journal of Research in Personality, 42*, 1004–1019. doi:10.1016/j.jrp.2008.02.006.

Troutman, M., Nies, M. A., & Mavellia, H. (2011). Perceptions of successful aging in Black older adults. *Journal of Psychosocial Nursing and Mental Health Services, 49*, 28–34. doi:10.3928/02793695-20101201-01.

Truxillo, D. M., McCune, E. A., Bertolino, M., & Fraccaroli, F. (2012). Perceptions of older versus younger workers in terms of Big Five facets, proactive personality, cognitive ability, and job performance. *Journal of Applied Social psychology, 42*, 2607–2639. doi:10.1111/j.1559-1816.2012.00954.x.

Trzesniewski, K., H., & Donnellan, M. B. (2010). Rethinking "Generation Me": A study of cohort effects from 1976–2006. *Perspective on Psychological Science, 5*, 58–75. doi:10.1177/1745691609356789.

Tsao, T.-C. (2004). New models for future retirement: A study of college/university-linked retirement communities. *Dissertation Abstracts International. Section A. Humanities and Social Sciences, 64(10-A)*, 3511.

Tsuno, N., & Homma, A. (2009). Aging in Asia—The Japan experience. *Ageing International, 34*, 1–14. doi:10.1007/s12126-009-9032-9.

Tully, P. J., & Cosh, S. M. (in press). Generalized anxiety disorder prevalence and comorbidity with depression in coronary heart disease: A meta-analysis. *Journal of Health Psychology.* doi:10.1177/1359105312467390.

Tyers, R., & Shi, Q. (2012). Global demographic change, labor force growth, and economic performance. In E. Ianchovichina & T. L. Valmsley (Eds.), *Dynamic modeling and applications for global economic analysis* (pp. 342–376). New York: Cambridge University Press.

U.S. Census Bureau. (2012a). *The 2012 statistical abstract: The national data book.* Retrieved from http://www.census.gov/compendia/statab/.

U.S. Census Bureau. (2012b). *International data base*. Retrieved from http://www.census.gov/population/international/data/idb/informationGateway.php.

U.S. Census Bureau. (2012c). *Grandparents Day 2012*. Retrieved from http://www.census.gov/newsroom/releases/archives/facts_for_features_special_editions/cb12-ff17.html.

U.S. Census Bureau. (2013a). *Valentine's Day 2013: Feb. 14*. Retrieved from http://www.census.gov/newsroom/releases/archives/facts_for_features_special_editions/cb13-ff06.html.

U.S. Census Bureau. (2013b). *American Community Survey on Marriage and Divorce*. Retrieved from http://www.census.gov/hhes/socdemo/marriage/data/acs/index.html.

U.S. Department of Agriculture. (2010). *Dietary guidelines for Americans 2010*. Retrieved from http://www.cnpp.usda.gov/Publications/DietaryGuidelines/2010/PolicyDoc/PolicyDoc.pdf.

U.S. Department of Health and Human Services. (1991). *Healthy people 2000: National health promotion and disease prevention*. Publication No. PHS 91-50212. Washington, DC: US Government Printing Office.

U.S. Food and Drug Administration. (2012). *Medicines and you: A guide for older adults*. Retrieved from http://www.fda.gov/Drugs/ResourcesForYou/ucm163959.htm.

Uleman, J. S., & Saribay, S. A. (2012). Initial impressions of others. In K. Deaux & M. Snyder (Eds.), *The Oxford handbook of personality and social psychology* (pp. 337–366). New York: Oxford University Press.

United Nations. (2008). *Divorces and crude divorce rates by urban/rural residence: 2002–2006*. Retrieved from http://unstats.un.org/unsd/demographic/products/dyb/dyb2006/Table25.pdf.

Unverzagt, F. W., Smith, D. M., Rebok, G. W., Marsiske, M., Morris, J. N., Jones, R., et al. (2009). The Indiana Alzheimer Disease Center's Symposium on Mild Cognitive Impairment. Cognitive training in older adults: Lessons from the ACTIVE Study. *Current Alzheimer Research, 0,* 375–383. Retrieved from http://www.ncbi.nlm.nih.gov/pmc/articles/PMC2729785/.

Utian, W. H. (2005). Psychosocial and socioeconomic burden of vasomotor symptoms in menopause: A comprehensive review. *Health and Quality of Life Outcomes, 3,* 47. doi:10.1186/1477-7525-3-47. Retrieved from http://www.hqlo.com/content/3/1/47.

Vagelatos, N. T., & Eslick, G. D. (2013). Type 2 diabetes as a risk factor for Alzheimer's disease: The confounders, interactions, and neuropathology associated with this relationship. *Epidemiologic Reviews, 35,* 152–160. doi:10.1093/epirev/mxs012.

Vaillant, G. E. (1977). *Adaptation to life*. Boston: Little, Brown.

Vaillant, G. E. (2002). *Aging well: Surprising guideposts to a happier life*. Boston: Little, Brown.

Vaillant, G. E., & Vaillant, C. O. (1990). Natural history of male psychological health: XII. A 45-year study

of predictors of successful aging. *American Journal of Psychiatry, 147,* 31–37.

Vallerand, R. J. (2008). On the psychology of passion: In search of what makes people's lives most worth living. *Canadian Psychology, 49,* 1–13. doi:10.1037/0708-5591.49.1.1.

Vallerand, R. J. (2012). From motivation to passion: In search of the motivational processes involved in a meaningful life. *Canadian Psychology/Psychologie Canadienne, 53,* 42–52. doi:10.1037/a0026377.

Vallerand, R. J., Paquet, Y., Philippe, F. L., & Charest, J. (2010). On the role of passion for work in burnout: A process model. *Journal of Personality, 78,* 289–312. doi:10.1111/j.1467-6494.2009.00616.x.

van den Wijngaart, M. A. G., Vernooij-Dassen, M. J. F. J., & Felling, A. J. A. (2007). The influence of stressors, appraisal and personal conditions on the burden of spousal caregivers of persons with dementia. *Aging & Mental Health, 11,* 626–636. doi:10.1080/13607860701368463.

van der Geest, S. (2004). Dying peacefully: Considering good death and bad death in Kwahu-Tafo, Ghana. *Social Science and Medicine, 58,* 899–911. doi:10.1016/j.socscimed.2003.10.041.

van der Pas, S., & Koopman-Boyden, P. (2010). Leisure and recreation activities and wellbeing among midlife New Zealanders. In C. Waldegrave & P. Koopman-Boyden (Eds.), *Midlife New Zealanders aged 40-64 in 2008: Enhancing well-being in an aging society* (pp. 111–128). Hamilton, New Zealand: Family Centre Social Policy Research Unit, Lower Hutt, Wellington and the Population Studies Centre, University of Waikato. Retrieved November 24, 2010 from http://www.ewas.net.nz/Publications/filesEWAS/EWAS_M2.pdf#page=126.

van Dierendonck, D., Garssen, B., & Visser, A. (2005). Burnout prevention through personal growth. *International Journal of Stress Management, 12,* 62–77. doi:10.1037/1072-5245.12.1.62.

van Impe, A., Coxon, J. P., Goble, D. J., Doumas, M., & Swinnen, S. P. (2012). White matter fractional anisotropy predicts balance performance in older adults *Neurobiology of Aging, 33,* 1900–1912. doi:10.1016/j/neurobiolaging.2011.06.013.

van Klaveren, C., van den Brink, H. M., & van Praag, B. (2013). Intrahousehold work timing: the effect on joint activities and the demand for child care. *European Sociological Review, 29,* 1–18. doi:10.1093/esr/jcr035.

van Muijden, J., Band, G. P. H., & Hommel, B. (2012). Online games training aging brains: Limited transfer to cognitive control functions. *Frontiers in Human Neuroscience, 6.* doi:10.3389/fnhum.2012.00221. Retrieved from http://www.ncbi.nlm.nih.gov/pmc/articles/PMC3421963/.

van Someren, E. J. W. (2007). Thermoregulation and aging. *American Journal of Physiology—Regulatory, Integrative, and*

Comparative Physiology, 292, R99–R102. doi:10.1152/ajpregu.00557.2006.

van Wanrooy, B. (2013). Couple strategies: Negotiating working time over the life course. In A. Evans, & J. Baxter (Eds.), *Negotiating the life course: Stability and change in life pathways* (pp. 175–190). New York: Springer.

Varkal, M. D., Yalvac, D., Tufan, F., Turan, S., Cengiz, M., & Emul, M. (2013). Metacognitive differences between elderly and adult outpatients with generalized anxiety disorder. *European Geriatric Medicine, 4,* 150–153. doi:10.1016/j.eurger.2012.12.001.

Verbrugge, L. M. (1994). Disability in late life. In R. P. Abeles, H. C. Gift, & M. G. Ory (Eds.), *Aging and quality of life* (pp. 79–98). New York: Springer.

Verbrugge, L. M. (2005). Flies without wings. In J. R. Carey, J.-M. Robine, J. P. Michel, & Y. Christen (Eds.), *Longevity and frailty* (pp. 67–81). New York: Springer.

Verbrugge, L. M., & Jette, A. M. (1994). The disablement process. *Social Science and Medicine, 38,* 1–14. doi: 10.1016/0277-9536(94)90294-1.

Vereeck, L., Wuyts, F., Truijen, S., & Van de Heyning, P. (2008). Clinical assessment of balance: Normative data, and gender and age effects. *International Journal of Audiology, 47,* 67–75. doi:10.1080/14992020701689688.

Verheijde, J. L. (2010). Commentary on the concept of brain death within the Catholic bioethical framework. *Christian Bioethics, 16,* 246–256. doi:10.1093/cb/cbq019.

Viña, J., Borás, C., & Miguel, J. (2007). Theories of aging. *IUBMB Life, 59,* 249–254. doi:10.1080/15216540601178067.

Vintildea, J. C., & Miguel, J. (2007). Theories of ageing. *IUBMB Life, 59,* 249–254.

Voelkle, M. C., Ebner, N. C., Lindenberger, U., & Riediger, M. (2012). Let me guess how old you are: Effects of age, gender, and facial expression on perceptions of age. *Psychology and Aging, 27,* 265–277. doi:10.1037/a0025065.

Von Hippel, W., & Henry, J. D. (2012). Social cognitive aging. In S. T. Fiske & C. N. Macrae (Eds.), *The SAGE handbook of social cognition* (pp. 390–410). Thousand Oaks, CA: Sage Publications.

Vorvick, L. J. (2010). *Aging changes in the female reproductive system*. Retrieved from http://www.nlm.nih.gov/medlineplus/ency/article/004016.htm.

Wahl, H.-W., Fänge, A., Oswald, F., Gitlin, L., & Iwarsson, S. (2009). The home environment and disability-related outcomes in aging individuals: What is the empirical evidence? *The Gerontologist, 49,* 335–367.

Wahl, H.-W., Heyl, V., & Schilling, O. (2012). Robustness of personality and affect relations under chronic conditions: The case of age-related vision and hearing impairment. *Journal of Gerontology: Psychological Sciences, 67,* 687–696. doi:10.1093/geronb/gbs002.

Wahl, H.-W., Iwarsson, S., & Oswald, F. (2012). Aging well and the

environment: Toward an integrative model and research agenda for the future. *The Gerontologist, 52,* 306–316. doi:10.1093/geront/gnr154.

Waites, C. (2009). Building on strengths: Intergenerational practice with African-American families. *Social Work, 54,* 278–287. doi:10.1093/sw/54.3.278.

Walker, A. C., & Balk, D. E. (2007). Bereavement rituals in the Muscogee Creek tribe. *Death Studies, 31,* 633–652. doi:10.1080/07481180701405188.

Walker, L. E. A. (1984). *The battered woman syndrome*. New York: Springer.

Wallace, T., & Morris, J. (2012). *Mobile apps for managing memory impairment after brain injury*. Retrieved from http://www.wirelessrerc.org/sites/default/files/publications/ASHA%202012%20Memory%20Aids%20FINAL.pdf.

Walther, A. N. (1991). *Divorce hangover*. New York: Pocket Books.

Wang, M., & Chen, Y. (2006). Age differences in attitude change: Influence of cognitive resources and motivation on responses to argument quantity. *Psychology and Aging, 21,* 581–589. doi:10.1037/0882-7974.21.3.581.

Wang, T.-J., Chern, H.-L., & Chiou, Y.-E. (2005). A theoretical model for preventing osteoarthritis-related disability. *Rehabilitation Nursing, 30,* 62–67. doi:10.1002/j.2048-7940.2005.tb00361.x.

Wanzer, S. H., & Glenmullen, J. (2007). *To die well: Your right to comfort, calm, and choice in the last days of life*. Cambridge, MA: Da Capo Press.

Waring, J. D., Addis, D. R., & Kensinger, E. A. (2013). Effects of aging on neural connectivity underlying selective memory for emotional scenes. *Neurobiology of Aging, 34,* 451–467. doi:10.1016/j.neurobiolaging.2012.03.011.

Warner, D. F., & Kelley-Moore, J. (2012). The social context of disablement among older adults: Does marital quality matter for loneliness? *Journal of Health and Social Behavior, 53,* 50–66. doi:10.1177/0022146512439540.

Warner, E., Henderson-Wilson, C., & Andrew, F. (2010). Flying the coop: why is the move out of the home proving unsustainable? In B. Randolph, T. Burke, K. Hulse, & V. Milligan, (Eds.). Refereed papers presented at the 4th Australasian Housing Researchers Conference, Sydney, University of New South Wales. Retrieved from http://dro.deakin.edu.au/view/DU:30031216.

Warr, P., Butcher, V., & Robertson, I. (2004). Activity and psychological well-being in older people. *Aging & Mental Health, 8,* 172–183. doi:10.1080/13607860410001649662.

Warren, D. E., Duff, M., Magnotta, V., Capizzano, A. A., Cassell, M. D., & Tranel, D. (2012). Long-term neuropsychological, neuroanatomical, and life outcome in hippocampal amnesia. *The Clinical Neuropsychologist, 26,* 335–369. doi:10.1080/13854046.2012.655781.

Watson, P. W. B., & McKinstry, B. (2009). A systematic review of interventions to improve recall of medical advice in healthcare consultations. *Journal of the Royal Society of Medicine, 102,* 235–243. doi:10.1258/jrsm.2009.090013. Retrieved from http://www.ncbi.nlm.nih.gov/pmc/articles/PMC2697041/.

Wayment, H. A., & Vierthaler, J. (2002). Attachment style and bereavement reactions. *Journal of Loss & Trauma, 7,* 129–149. doi:10.1080/153250202753472291.

Weaver, D. A. (2010). Widows and Social Security. *Social Security Bulletin, 70,* 89–109. Retrieved from http://heinonline.org/HOL/LandingPage?collection=journals&handle=hein.journals/ssbul70&div=20&id=&page=.

WebMD. (2010). *Pain management health center.* Retrieved from http://www.webmd.com/pain-management/guide/cause-treatments.

WebMD. (2011a). *Hypertension /high blood pressure health center.* Retrieved from http://www.webmd.com/hypertension-high-blood-pressure/tc/high-blood-pressure-hypertension-cause.

WebMD. (2011b). *Low blood pressure (hypotension)—Topic overview.* Retrieved from http://www.webmd.com/heart/tc/low-blood-pressure-hypotension-topic-overview.

WebMD. (2012a). *Definition of hypertension.* Retrieved from http://www.webmd.com/hypertension-high-blood-pressure/guide/whypertension-diagnosing-high-blood-pressure.

WebMD. (2012b). *Emphysema directory.* Retrieved from http://www.webmd.com/lung/emphysema-topic-directory.

Webster, D. M., & Kruglanski, A. W. (1994). Individual differences in need for cognitive closure. *Journal of Personality and Social Psychology, 67,* 1049–1062. doi:10.1037/0022-3514.67.6.1049.

Webster, M. J., Knable, M. B., O'Grady, J., Orthman, J., & Weickert, C. S. (2002). Regional specificity of brain glucocorticoid receptor mRNA alterations in subjects with schizophrenia and mood disorders. *Molecular Psychiatry, 7,* 985–994. doi:10.1038/sj.mp.1001139.

Webster-Marketon, J., & Glaser, R. (2008). Stress hormones and immune function. *Cellular Immunology, 252,* 16–26. doi:10.1016/j.cellimm.2007.09.006.

Wechsler, D. (1958). *The measurement and appraisal of adult intelligence* (4th ed.). Baltimore: Williams & Wilkins.

Wegner, D. M., & Gold, D. G. (1995). Fanning old flames: Emotional and cognitive effects of suppressing thoughts of a past relationship. *Journal of Personality and Social Psychology, 68,* 782–792. doi:10.1037/0022-3514.68.5.782.

Weibel-Orlando, J. (1990). Grandparenting styles: Native American perspectives. In J. Sokolovsky (Ed.), *The cultural context of aging* (pp. 109–125). New York: Bergin & Garvey.

Weisberg, R. W., & Reeves, L. M. (2013). *Cognition: From memory to creativity.* New York: Wiley.

Weiss, D., & Freund, A. M. (2012). Young at heart: Negative age-related information motivates distancing from same-aged friends. *Psychology and Aging, 27,* 173–180. doi:10.1037/a0024819.

Weiss, D., & Lang, F. R. (2012). "They" are old but "I" feel younger: Age-group dissociation as a self-protective strategy in old age. *Psychology and Aging, 27,* 153–163. doi:10.1037/a0024887.

Weiss, R. A., Munavalli, G. S., Choudhary, S., Leiva, A., & Nouri, K. (2012). Laser Treatment of leg veins. In K. Nouri (Ed.), *Lasers in dermatology and medicine* (pp. 53–61). New York: Springer.

Wentura, D., & Brandtstädter, J. (2003). Age stereotypes in younger and older women: Analyses of accommodative shifts with a sentence-priming task. *Experimental Psychology, 50,* 16–26. doi:10.1027/1618-3169.50.1.16.

Werner, T. L., & Shannon C. S. (20130. Doing more with less: Women's leisure during their partners' military deployment. *Leisure Sciences, 35,* 63–80. Doi:10.1080/01490400.2013.739897.

Westbrook, L. A. (2002). The experience of mid-life women in the years after the deaths of their parents. *Dissertation Abstracts International Section A: Humanities and Social Sciences, 62(8A),* 2884.

Westmaas, J. L., Gil-Rivas, V., & Silver, R. C. (2011). Designing and conducting interventions to enhance physical and mental health outcomes. In H. S. Friedman (Ed.), *The Oxford handbook of health psychology* (pp. 73–94). New York: Oxford University Press.

Wettstein, R. M. (2013). Legal issues geriatric psychiatrists should understand. In M. D. Miller & L. K. Salai (Eds.), *Geriatric psychiatry* (pp. 55–77). New York: Oxford University Press.

Weymouth, P. L. (2005). A longitudinal look at the predictors of four types of retirement. *Dissertation Abstracts International. Section B. Sciences and Engineering, 65(7-B),* 3760.

Whitbourne, S. K. (1986). The psychological construction of the life span. In J. E. Birren & K. W. Schaie (Eds.), *Handbook of the psychology of aging* (pp. 594–618). New York: Van Nostrand Reinhold.

Whitbourne, S. K. (1987). Personality development in adulthood and old age: Relationships among identity style, health, and well-being. In K. W. Schaie (Ed.), *Annual review of gerontology and geriatrics* (Vol. 7, pp. 189–216). New York: Springer.

Whitbourne, S. K. (1996a). *The aging individual: Physical and psychological perspectives.* New York: Springer.

Whitbourne, S. K. (1996b). *Identity and adaptation to the aging process.* Unpublished paper, Department of Psychology, University of Massachusetts.

Whitbourne, S. K. (2010). *The search for fulfillment: Revolutionary new research that reveals the secret to long-term happiness.* New York: Ballantine Books.

Whitbourne, S. K., Culgin, S., & Cassidy, E. (1995). Evaluation of infantilizing intonation and content of speech directed at the aged. *International Journal of Aging and Human Development, 41,* 109–116. doi:10.2190/J9XE-2GB6-H49G-MR7V.

Whitbourne, S. K., Sneed, J. R., & Skultety, K. M. (2002). Identity processes in adulthood: Theoretical and methodological challenges. *Identity, 2,* 29–45. doi:10.1207/S1532706XID0201_03.

White, M. L., Peters, R., & Schim, S. M. (2011). Spirituality and spiritual self-care: Expanding self-care deficit nursing theory. *Nursing Science Quarterly, 24,* 48–56. doi:10.1177/0894318410389059.

Whitty, M. T., & Buchanan, T. (2009). Looking for love in so many places: Characteristics of online daters and speed daters. *Interpersona: An International Journal on Personal Relationships, 3(Suppl. 2).* Retrieved from https://lra.le.ac.uk/bitstream/2381/9747/1/Looking%20for%20love%20_interpersona-3-suppl-2_4.pdf.

Wickrama, K. A. S., O'Neal, C. W., & Lorenz, F. O. (2013). Marital functioning from middle to later years: A life course-stress process framework. *Journal of Family Theory and Review, 5,* 15–34. doi:10.1111/jftr.12000.

Wiles, J. L., & Jayasinha, R. (2013). Care for place: The contributions older people make to their communities. *Journal of Aging Studies, 27,* 93–101. doi:10.1016/j.jaging.2012.12.001.

Willander, J., & Larsson, M. (2006). Smell your way back to childhood: Autobiographical odor memory. *Psychonomic Bulletin and Review, 13,* 240–244. doi:10.3758/BF03193837.

Williams, A., Giles, H., Ota, H., Pierson, H. D., Gallois, C., Ng, S. H., Lim, T.-S., Ryan, E. B., Somera, L., Maher, J., & Harwood, J. (1997). Young people's beliefs about intergenerational communication: An initial cross-cultural comparison. *Communication Research, 24,* 370–393. doi:10.1177/009365097024004003.

Williams, K. N., Herman, R., Gajewski, B., & Wilson, K. (2008). Elderspeak communication: Impact on dementia care. *American Journal of Alzheimer's Disease and Other Dementias, 24,* 11–20. doi:10.1177/1533317508318472.

Williams, S. A. (2005). Jealousy in the cross-sex friendship. *Journal of Loss & Trauma, 10,* 471–485. doi:10.1080/15325020500193937.

Willis, S. L. (1991). Cognition and everyday competence. In K. W. Schaie (Ed.), *Annual review of gerontology and geriatrics* (Vol. 11, pp. 80–109). New York: Springer.

Willis, S. L., & Boron, J. B. (2008). Midlife cognition: The association of personality with cognition and risk of cognitive impairment. In S. M. Hofer & D. F. Alwin (Eds.), *Handbook of cognitive aging: Interdisciplinary perspectives* (pp. 647–660). Greenwich, CT: Sage.

Willis, S. L., & Schaie, K. W. (2009). Cognitive training and plasticity: Theoretical perspectives and methodological consequences. *Restorative Neurology and Neuroscience, 27,* 375–389. doi:10.3233/RNN-2009-0527.

Willis, S. L., Blieszner, R., & Baltes, P. B. (1981). Intellectual training research in aging: Modification of performance on the fluid ability of figural relations. *Journal of Educational Psychology, 73,* 41–50. doi:10.1016/0193-3973(81)90005-8.

Willis, S. L., Tennstedt, S. L., Marsiske, M., Ball, K., Elias, J., Koepke, K. M. et al. (2006). Long-term effects of cognitive training on everyday functional outcomes in older adults. *JAMA, 296,* 2805–2814. doi:10.1001/jama.296.23.2805.

Wilson, R. S., Arnold, S. E., Schneider, J. A., Kelly, J. F., Tang, Y., & Bennett, D. A. (2006). Chronic psychological distress and risk of Alzheimer's disease in old age. *Neuroepidemiology, 27,* 143–153. doi:10.1159/000095761.

Wilson, R. S., Bennett, D. A., Mendes de Leon, C. F., Bienias, J. L., Morris, M. C., & Evans, D. A. (2005). Distress proneness and cognitive decline in a population of older persons. *Psychoneuroendocrinology, 30,* 11–17. doi:10.1016/j.psyneuen.2004.04.005.

Wilson, R. S., Krueger, K. R., Arnold, S. E., Schneider, J. A., Kelly, J. F., Barnes, L. L., et al. (2007). Loneliness and risk of Alzheimer's disease. *JAMA Psychiatry, 64,* 234–240. doi:10.1001/archpsyc.64.2.234.

Wilt, J., Cox, K. S., & McAdams, D. P. (2010). The Eriksonian life story: Developmental scripts and psychosocial adaptation. *Journal of Adult Development, 17,* 156–161. doi:10.1007/s10804-010-9093-8.

Winecoff, A., LaBar, K. S., Madden, D. J., Cabeza, R., & Huettel, S. A. (2011). Cognitive and neural contributions to emotion regulation in aging. *Social Cognitive and Affective Neuroscience, 6,* 165–176. doi:10.1093/scan/nsq030.

Winslow, M., & Meldrum, M. (2013). A history of hospice and palliative care. In S. Lutz, F. Chow, & P. Hoskin (Eds.), *Radiation oncology in palliative cancer care* (pp. 63–71). New York: Wiley.

Winter, L., & Parks, S. M. (2012). Elders' preferences for life-prolonging treatment and their proxies' substituted judgment: Influence of the elders' current health. *Journal of Aging and Health, 24,* 1157–1178. doi:10.1177/0898264312454572.

Witko, T. M. (2006). A framework for working with American Indian parents. In T. M. Witko (Ed.), *Mental health care for urban Indians: Clinical insights from Native practitioners* (pp. 155–171). Washington, DC: American Psychological Association.

Wolfinger, N. H. (2007). Does the rebound effect exist? Time to remarriage and subsequent union stability. *Journal of Divorce & Remarriage, 46,* 9–20. doi:10.1300/J087v46n03_02.

Wolinsky, F. D., & Tierney, W. M. (1998). Self-rated health and adverse health outcomes: An exploration and refinement of the trajectory hypothesis. *Journals of Gerontology: Social Sciences, 53B,* S336–S340. doi:10.1093/geronb/53B.6.S336.

Wolinsky, F. D., Miller, T. R., Malmstrom, T. K., Miller, J. P., Schootman, M., Andresen, E. M., & Miller, J. C. (2008). Self-rated health: Changes, trajectories, and their antecedents among African Americans. *Journal of Aging and Health, 20,* 143–158. doi:10.1177/0898264307310449.

Wolinsky, F. D., Vander Weg, M. W., Martin, R., Unverzagt, F. D., Willis, S. L., Marsiske, M., et al., (2010). Does cognitive training improve internal locus of control among older adults? *Journal of Gerontology: Social Sciences, 65B*, S591–S598. doi:10.1093/geronb/gbp117.

Wolkove, N., Elkholy, O., Baltzan, M., & Palayew, M. (2007a). Sleep and aging 1: Sleep disorders commonly found in older people. *Canadian Medical Association Journal, 176*, 1299–1304. doi:10.1503/cmaj.060792.

Wolkove, N., Elkholy, O., Baltzan, M., & Palayew, M. (2007b). Sleep and aging 2: Management of sleep disorders in older people. *Canadian Medical Association Journal, 176*, 1449–1454. doi:10.1503/cmaj.070335.

WomensHealth.gov. (2010a). *Menopause basics.* Retrieved from http://www.omenshealth.gov/menopause/menopause-basics/index.html.

WomensHealth.gov. (2010b). *Menopause symptom relief and treatment.* Retrieved from http://www.womenshealth.gov/menopause/symptom-relief-treatment/index.html.

Wong, P. T. P. (2008). Transformation of grief through meaning: Meaning-centered counseling for bereavement. In A. Tomer, G. T. Eliason, & P. T. P. Wong (Eds.), *Existential and spiritual issues in death attitudes* (pp. 375–396). Mahwah, NJ: Erlbaum.

Wood, S., & Kisley, M. A. (2006). The negativity bias is eliminated in older adults: Age-related reduction in event-related brain potentials associated with evaluative categorization. *Psychology and Aging, 21*, 815–820. doi:10.1037/0882-7974.21.4.815.

Woodbridge, S. (2008). Sustaining families in the 21st century: The role of grandparents. *International Journal of Environmental, Cultural, Economic and Social Sustainability.* Retrieved from http:// www98. griffith. edu.au/dspace/ bitstream/10072/27417/1/5 0932_1.pdf.

Woodward, A. T., Taylor, R. J., Abelson, J. M., & Matusko, N. (2013). Major depressive disorder among older African Americans, Caribbean blacks, and non-Hispanic whites: Secondary analysis of the National Survey of American Life. *Depression and Anxiety, 30*, 589–597. doi:10.1002/da.22041.

Worden, W. (1991). *Grief counseling and grief therapy: A handbook for the mental health practitioner* (2nd ed.). New York: Springer.

World Health Organization. (2002). *Worldwide report on violence and health: Chapter 4: Violence by intimate partners.* Retrieved from http://www.who.int/violence_injury_prevention/violence/global_campaign/en/chap4.pdf.

World Health Organization. (2007). *Working for health.* Retrieved from http://www.who.int/about/brochure_en.pdf.

World Health Organization. (2012). *Seniors and disabilities.* Retrieved from http://new.paho.org/hq/index.php?option=com_content&view=article&id=7316%3Aseniors-a-disabilities-april-2012&catid=4684%3Afch-hl-disabilities-and-rehabilitation&Itemid=936&lang=en.

Wrenn, R. L. (1999). The grieving college student. In J. D. Davidson & K. J. Doka (Eds.), *Living with grief: At work, at school, at worship* (pp. 131–141). Levittown, PA: Brunner/Mazel.

Wurtele, S. K., & Maruyama, L. (2013). Changing students' stereotypes of older adults. *Teaching of Psychology, 40*, 59–61. doi:10.1177/0098628312465867.

Xu, X., Zhu, F., O'Campo, P., Koenig, M. A., Mock, V., & Campbell, J. (2005). Prevalence of and risk factors for intimate partner violence in China. *American Journal of Public Health, 95*, 78–85. doi:10.2105/AJPH.2003.023978.

Yamini-Benjamin, Y. I. (2007). Moving toward a better understanding of Black women's work adjustment: The role of perceived discrimination and self-efficacy in predicting job satisfaction and psychological distress in Black women. *Dissertation Abstracts International. Section B. Sciences and Engineering, 67(10-B)*, 6085.

Yan, Q. (2012). The role of psychoneuroimmunology in personalized and systems medicine. *Psychoneuroimmunology: Methods in Molecular Biology, 934*, 3–19. doi:10.1007/978-1-62703-071-7_1.

Yang, N., Chen, C. C., Choi, J., & Zou, Y. (2000). Sources of work-family conflict: A Sino-U.S. comparison of the effects of work and family. *Academy of Management Journal, 43*, 113–123. doi:10.2307/1556390.

Yang, Z., Bishai, D., & Harman, J. (2008). Convergence of body mass with aging: The longitudinal interrelationship of health, weight, and survival. *Economics & Human Biology, 6*, 469–481. doi:10.1016/j.ehb.2008.06.006.

Yates, F. A. (1966) *The art of memory.* Chicago: University of Chicago Press.

Ybarra, O., & Park, D. C. (2002). Disconfirmation of person expectations by older and younger adults: Implications for social vigilance. *Journals of Gerontology: Psychological Sciences, 57B*, P435–P443. doi:10.1093/geronb/57.5.P435.

Ybarra, O., Winkielman, P., Yeh, I., Burnstein, E., & Kavanagh, L. (2011). Friends (and sometimes enemies) with cognitive benefits: What types of social interactions boost executive functioning? *Social Psychological and Personality Science, 2*, 253–261. doi:10.1177/1948550610386808.

Yeatts, D. E., & Cready, C. M. (2008). Consequences of empowered CAN teams in nursing home settings: A longitudinal assessment. *The Gerontologist, 47*, 323–339. doi:10.1093/geront/47.3.323.

Yeh, M. A., Jewell, R. D., & Hu, M. Y. (2013). Stereotype processing's effect on the impact of the myth/fact message format and the role of personal relevance. *Psychology and Marketing, 30*, 36–45. doi:10.1002/mar.20587.

Yesavage, J. A., Brink, T. L., Rose, T. L., Lum, O., Huang, V., Adey, M., & Leirer, V. O. (1983). Development and validation of a geriatric depression screening scale: A preliminary report. *Journal of Psychiatric Research, 17*, 37–49. doi:10.1016/0022-3956(82)90033-4.

Yeung, S. M., Wong, F. K. Y., & Mok, E. (2011). Holistic concerns of Chinese stroke survivors during hospitalization and in transition to home. *Journal of Advanced Nursing, 67*, 2394–2405. doi:10.1111/j.1365-2648.2011.05673.x.

Yngvesson, B. (2010). *Belonging in an adopted world: Race, identity, and transnational adoption.* Chicago: University of Chicago Press.

Yoon, S. M. (2005). The characteristics and needs of Asian American grandparent caregivers: A study of Chinese-American and Korean-American grandparents in New York City. *Journal of Gerontological Social Work, 44*, 75–94. doi:10.1300/J083v44n03_06.

Yoon, S. S., Burt, V., Louis, T., & Carroll, M. D. (2012). Hypertension among adults in the United States, 2009–2010. *NCHS Data Brief, 2012(107)*, 1–8. Retrieved from http://www.cdc.gov/nchs/data/databriefs/db107.htm.

Yu, T., & Adler-Baeder, F. (2007). The intergenerational transmission of relationship quality: The effects of parental remarriage quality on young adults' relationships. *Journal of Divorce & Remarriage, 47*, 87–102. doi:10.1300/J087v47n03_05.

Zabriskie, R. B., & Kay, T. (2013). Positive leisure science: Leisure in family contexts. In T. Freire (Ed.), *Positive leisure science* (pp. 81–99). New York: Springer.

Zahariou, A. G., Karamouti, M. V., & Papaioannou, P. D. (2008). Pelvic floor muscle training improves sexual function of women with stress urinary incontinence. *International Urogynecology Journal, 19*, 401–406. doi:10.1007/s00192-007-0452-3.

Zahodne, L. B., Glymour, M. M., Sparks, C., Bontempo, D., Dixon, R. A., MacDonald, S. W. S., et al. (2011). Education does not slow cognitive decline with aging: 12-year evidence form the Victoria Longitudinal Study. *Journal of the International Neuropsychological Society, 17*, 1039–1046. doi:10.1017/S1355617711001044.

Zarit, S. H., & Reamy, A. M. (2013). Future directions in family and professional caregiving for the elderly. *Gerontology, 59*, 152–158. doi:10.1159/000342242.

Zarit, S. H., & Zarit, J. M. (2006). *Mental disorders in older adults* (2nd ed.). New York: Guilford.

Zarit, S. H., & Zarit, J. M. (2007). *Mental disorders in older adults: Fundamentals of assessment and treatment* (2nd ed.). New York: Guilford.

Zarit, S., & Femia, E. (2008). Behavioral and psychosocial interventions for family caregivers. *Journal of Social Work Education, 44*, 49–57. doi:10.5175/JSWE.2008.773247711.

Zatorre, R. J., Fields, R. D., & Johansen-Berg, H. (2012). Plasticity in gray and white matter: Neuroimaging changes in brain structure during learning. *Nature Neuroscience, 15*, 528–536. doi:10.1038/nn.3045.

Zelinski, E. M., & Kennison. R. F., Watts, A., & Lewis, K. L. (2009). Convergence between longitudinal and cross-sectional studies: Cohort matters. In C. Hertzog & H. Bosworth (Eds.), *Aging and cognition: Research methodologies and empirical advances* (pp. 101–118). Washington DC: American Psychological Association.

Zeng, Y., Gu, D., & George, L. K. (2011). Association of religious participation with mortality among Chinese old adults. *Research on Aging, 33*, 51–83. doi:10.1177/0164027510383584.

Zerr, I. (Ed.). (2013). *Understanding Alzheimer's disease.* Retrieved from http://www.intechopen.com/books/understanding-alzheimer-s-disease. doi:10.5772/46004.

Zhan, H. J. (2006). Joy and sorrow: Explaining Chinese caregivers' reward and stress. *Journal of Aging Studies, 20*, 27–38. doi:10.1016/j.aging.2005.01.002.

Zhang, H. (2012). *The effect of primary and secondary control on social anxiety in Latino and Asian American college students.* Senior Theses, Trinity College, Hartford, CT. Retrieved from http://digitalrepository.trincoll.edu/theses/251.

Zheng, Z., Shemmassian, S., Wijekoon, C., Kim, W., Bookheimer, S. Y., & Pouratian, N. (in press). DTI correlates of distinct cognitive impairments in Parkinson's disease. *Human Brain Mapping.* doi:10.1002/hbm.22256.

Zimdars, A., Nazroo, J., & Gjonça, E. (2012). The circumstances of older people in England with self-reported visual impairment: A secondary analysis of the English Longitudinal Study of Ageing (ELSA). *British Journal of Visual Impairment, 30*, 22–30. doi:10.1177/0264619611427374.

Zimprich, D., & Martin, M. (2002). Can longitudinal changes in processing speed explain longitudinal age change in fluid intelligence? *Psychology and Aging, 17*, 690–695. doi:10.1037/0882-7974.17.4.690.

Zimprich, D., & Martin, M. (2009). A multilevel factor analysis perspective on intellectual development in old age. In C. Hertzog & H. Bosworth (Eds.), *Aging and cognition: Research methodologies and empirical advances* (pp. 53–76). Washington DC: American Psychological Association.

Zippel, K. S. (2006). *The politics of sexual harassment: A comparative study of the United States, the European Union, and Germany.* New York: Cambridge University Press.

Zogg, J. B., Woods, S. P., Sauceda, J. A., Wiebe, J. S., & Simoni, J. M. (2012). The role of prospective memory in medication adherence: A review of an emerging literature. *Journal of Behavioral Medicine, 35*, 47–62. doi:10.1007/s10865-011-9341-9.

Zurlo, K. A., & Beach, C. M. (2013). Racial disparities in depression care among older adults: Can the perspectives of clinicians and patients be reconciled? *Current Translational Geriatrics and Experimental Gerontology Reports, 2*, 24–30. doi:10.1007/s13670-012-0036-z.

NAME INDEX

involved in holding information in mind and simultaneously using that information,
sometimes in conjunction
with incoming information
to solve a problem, make
a decision, or learn new
information., 163–164, **184**

Zone of maximum comfort In
    competence-environmental
    press theory, area in
    which slight decreases in
    environmental press occur.,
    130, **156**
Zone of maximum performance
    potential In competence-
    environmental press theory,
    area in which increases
    in press tend to improve
    performance., 130, **156**